EAST ASIA
AND THE
UNITED STATES

EAST ASIA
AND THE
UNITED STATES

An Encyclopedia of Relations Since 1784

N–Z

Edited by James I. Matray

GREENWOOD PRESS
Westport, Connecticut • London

Library of Congress Cataloging-in-Publication Data

East Asia and the United States: an encyclopedia of relations since 1784 / edited by James I. Matray.
p. cm.
Includes bibliographical references and index.
ISBN 0–313–30557–9 (alk. paper : set).—ISBN 0–313–32446–8 (alk. paper : A-M).—ISBN 0–313–32447–6 (alk. paper : N-Z).
1. East Asia—Relations—United States—Encyclopedias. 2. United States—Relations—East Asia—Encyclopedias. I. Matray, James Irving, 1948–
DS518.8.E53 2002
303.48'25073'03—dc21 2002019542

British Library Cataloguing in Publication Data is available.

Library of Congress Catalog Card Number: 2002019542
ISBN: 0–313–30557–9 (set)
0–313–32446–8 (A-M)
0–313–32447–6 (N-Z)

First published in 2002

Greenwood Press, 88 Post Road West, Westport, CT 06881
An imprint of Greenwood Publishing Group, Inc.
www.greenwood.com

Printed in the United States of America

The paper used in this book complies with the Permanent Paper Standard issued by the National Information Standards Organization (Z39.48–1984).

10 9 8 7 6 5 4 3 2 1

To the Memory of My Parents,
Theodore John Matray
and
Caroline Kathryn Werstler Matray

Contents

Maps follow page xxix.

Preface

In 1941, publisher Henry R. Luce told his readers in *Life* magazine that they were living in the "American Century," and subsequent events provided substantial support for the accuracy of his assessment. By 2000, the United States not only was the most economically and militarily powerful nation in human history, but its politics, society, and culture were worldwide sources of admiration, envy, and emulation. On 11 September 2001, however, the terrorist attack on the Pentagon in Washington D.C. and destruction of the World Trade Center in New York City demonstrated that a segment of the world's population considered U.S. dominance of the international system intolerably oppressive. Prior examples of hostility toward perceived American hegemony, although far less repugnant, provided further evidence that the U.S. record in foreign affairs has been mixed. American intervention made the difference in achieving victory over the Central Powers in World War I and the Axis in World War II. The United States also won the Cold War, resulting in the demise of the Soviet Union and the disappearance of Communist regimes across the globe. But U.S. policies in East Asia led to frustration in Korea and failure in Vietnam, as well as hostile relationships with revolutionary nationalist movements throughout the area. This helped explain why the only nations other than Cuba still under Communist rule after the Cold War ended were China, North Korea, Vietnam, and Laos. Despite a global focus early in the new century on waging a "war against terrorism," the future of these countries may well dictate the ultimate course of world affairs. In fact, some East Asia experts have predicted that the next 100 years will be "China's century."

American fascination with East Asia began at least as early as 1784 with the voyage of the *Empress of China* to Guangzhou in China. U.S. Secretaries of State John Quincy Adams, Daniel Webster, and William H. Seward all had visions of creating an American empire in the Pacific. In April 1870, Rear Admiral Robert W. Shufeldt, who later negotiated the first treaty between Korea and a Western power, spoke for them when he declared that "the Pacific Ocean is to be hereafter the field of our commercial triumphs. . . . [It] is and *must* be essentially *American*. Through it and by us, China and Japan must acquire a new civilization and adopt a new creed, for it is in this sense that 'Westward still, the Star of Empire takes its way.' " Students, scholars, and those with a casual interest in U.S.–East Asian relations will find this historical encyclopedia a useful guide for understanding the origins and impact of this American missionary quest to transform East Asia. Its primary emphasis is on diplomatic, economic, and political developments, with a secondary focus on military affairs and cultural interaction.

This encyclopedia contains descriptive essays covering all the significant people, controversies, treaties, agreements, and alliances affecting U.S.–East Asian relations over the past two centuries. In certain areas, entries appear in groups, such as battles, military operations, and treaties. There is an individual entry on almost every nation in East Asia, but in place of concise summaries, readers will need to consult entries about more narrowly defined issues, individuals, policies, and events related to Japan, China, Vietnam, and Korea. There also are an ample number of in-depth entries on specific topics that relate to Burma, Cambodia, Indonesia, Laos, Malaysia, Micronesia, the Philippines, Thailand, and Taiwan. References at the end of each entry provide guidance to sources for readers desiring more information. Entries appear in alphabetical order, with cross-references in the text of each, designated with an asterisk, assisting users interested in learning about related items. A chronology will help the student and layperson put the events in the entries into historical context. This book also contains a list of acronyms, a selection of maps, and a selected bibliography. Reprints of primary source documents on U.S.–East Asian relations from the 1850s through the 1960s are easily accessible in the Department of State's *Foreign Relations of the United States*. Organized by region, country, and event, individual series volumes are not listed in the bibliography to conserve space.

Completion of this valuable research tool would not have been possible without the participation of an outstanding group of contributors from nine different countries. Although most are established scholars in the field, many writers are graduate students just beginning their academic careers. Following each entry is the name of its author, and biographical summaries of all contributors appear in the section called "About the Editor and Contributors." This encyclopedia uses the current spelling of Korean names and places, and the pinyin rather than Wade-Giles spelling for Chinese, along with selective cross-references. I thank my colleague Kenneth J. Hammond for his help on the latter, as well as his insightful advice in ensuring analytical accuracy. As important, he prepared without complaint several entries at the end of the project that other contributors had abandoned.

Cynthia Harris of Greenwood Press deserves credit for providing outstanding advice and, for a second time, showing extraordinary patience. All authors should be so lucky to have an editor with her personal and professional skills. Most important, Juanita Stern devoted many hours to the encyclopedia, quietly and competently making seemingly endless editorial changes in the text. As always, my wife, Karin, provided unconditional affection and constant encouragement in my completion of this project, and my children, Benjamin and Amanda, were regular but welcome distractions. Finally, I dedicate this encyclopedia to the memory of my parents, who had unqualified faith in the power of education to improve the lives of their children. Both children of immigrants, they worked at difficult jobs to provide us with the opportunity to enjoy prosperous, productive, and happy lives. Thanks to them, my brother Paul and I are living their American dream.

Chronology

1784 *Empress of China* arrives in Guangzhou harbor

1791 John Kendrick's *Lady Washington* becomes the first American ship to arrive in Japan

1808 John Jacob Astor establishes American Fur Company

1811 Formation of the Pacific Fur Company

Founding of Astoria on the Pacific coast of the Oregon Territory

1822 Bryant and Sturgis begin to buy hides on the California coast for export and sale in China

1833 Roberts Mission achieves commercial treaties with Siam and Muscat

1840 First Opium War begins between Britain and China

1841 Britain gains control over Hong Kong

1842 U.S. naval squadron under the command of Commodore Stephen Kearney arrives at Guangzhou in China

Signing of the Treaty of Nanjing, the first unequal treaty with China

President John Tyler announces the existence of a special relationship between the United States and Hawaii

1844 Caleb Cushing negotiates the Treaty of Wangxia between the United States and China

1845 Commodore James Biddle exchanges ratifications of the Treaty of Wangxia at Guangzhou

1846 Dr. Peter Parker becomes U.S. Commissioner to China

1851 Outbreak of the Taiping Rebellion in China

First two Chinese community associations in the United States, the Syi Huiguan and the Sanyi Huiguan, formed in San Francisco

Secretary of State Daniel Webster writes instructions for Commodore John Aulick to open negotiations with the government of Japan for a commercial treaty

1852 American Board of Commissioners for Foreign Missions established

1853 Commodore Matthew C. Perry embarks on his mission to East Asia

1854 Perry negotiates the Treaty of Kanagawa between the United States and Japan, the first between Japan and a Western nation

United States signs Treaty of Naha with Okinawa

1856 Townsend Harris arrives in Japan as the first U.S. ambassador

Outbreak of the Second Opium War in China

Peter Parker recommends U.S. seizure of Taiwan

1857 Townsend Harris negotiates Convention of Shimoda with Japan

1858 The United States signs the Harris Treaty with Japan

Treaty of Tianjin signed between Western powers and China

1860 Beginning of the "Expel the Barbarian" Movement in Japan

1861 Japanese extremists assassinate Henry Heuksen, translator for U.S. Ambassador to Japan Townsend Harris

Convention of Beijing in 1860 forces China to establish the Zongli Yamen

Anson Burlingame named first U.S. minister in Beijing

1862 Frederick T. Ward forms the Ever-victorious Army to fight the Taiping rebels

Russell and Company founds the Shanghai Steamship Navigation Company

Zongli Yamen creates a foreign languages academy named the Tongwen Guan

1866 Koreans attack U.S. ship *General Sherman*, killing all its crewmen

1867 United States purchases Alaska from Russia

Midway Island claimed as U.S. territory

Charles LeGrande stages punitive attack on Taiwan

1868 Meiji Restoration in Japan ends the Tokugawa shōgunate

United States signs the Burlingame-Seward Treaty with China

1869 Frederick F. Low appointed U.S. minister to China

1870 Young Men's Christian Association begins operations in China

1871 Low leads punitive expedition against Korea

Iwakura Mission leaves Japan on an inspection tour of Western nations

1872 U.S. Senate rejects a treaty negotiated with a Samoan chieftain

First Chinese students arrive for study in the United States

1873 Qing Dynasty agrees to end the requirement for Western diplomats to perform the kowtow during audiences with the emperor

Meiji government lifts the ban on practicing Christianity in Japan

1875 United States negotiates a reciprocity treaty with Hawaii

1876 Chefoo Convention signed between Britian and China

1877 First General Convention of Protestant Missionaries convenes

1878 United States signs a convention with Japan granting it conditional tariff autonomy

Commodore Robert W. Shufeldt begins around-the-world cruise

U.S. ratifies treaty with Samoa ceding the harbor at Pago Pago to the United States

1879 Japan and China clash over control of the Ryūkyū Islands

1880 United States signs Angell Treaty with China

1881 China's Zongli Yamen withdraws Chinese Educational Mission from the United States

1882 U.S. Congress passes the Chinese Exclusion Act

Chinese Consolidated Benevolent Association established

Shufeldt Treaty negotiated between the United States and Korea

1883 Lucius H. Foote arrives in Korea as the first U.S. ambassador

Kim Ok-kyun leads rebellion against the monarchy in Korea

1885 China recognizes France's colonial rule over French Indochina

Rock Springs Massacre of Chinese laborers in Wyoming

1887 U.S. missionaries involved in Pohnpei crisis

White planters stage uprising in Hawaii against the monarchy

Hawaiian King Kalakaua accepts new constitution, reducing his powers

United States renews treaty with Hawaii, adding a provision for an exclusive naval base at Pearl Harbor

1889 Young Men's Christian Association begins operations in Japan

Britain, Germany, and the United States agree to a tripartite condominium over the Samoan Islands

1890 General Conference of Protestant Missionaries convenes

Young Women's Christian Association begins operations in China

Publication of Alfred Thayer Mahan's *The Influence of Sea Power upon History, 1660–1783*

1891 United States and Britain sign an agreement to limit seal hunting

1893 Fur seal hunting arbitration decision issued

Hawaiian rebellion ousts Queen Lili'uokalani, ending the monarchy

James H. Blount begins investigation of Hawaiian Revolution

President Grover Cleveland withdraws Hawaiian annexation treaty from U.S. Senate consideration

1894 Signing of the American-Japanese Treaty

Renewal of Angell Treaty between United States and China

Outbreak of the Sino-Japanese War

Republic of Hawaii established

1895 Japan and China sign Treaty of Shimonoseki

Taiwan becomes part of the Japanese Empire

Triple Intervention forces Japan to return the Liaodong Peninsula to China

1896 Philippine Revolution begins against Spanish colonial rule

1897 Germany seizes Jiaozhou, Qingdao, and Yantai on Shandong Peninsula

Japanese warship arrives off the coast of Hawaii

U.S. Senate defeats a treaty to annex Hawaiian Islands

1898 Beginning of public references to the Ōkuma Doctrine

Formation of the American Asiatic Association

Outbreak of the Spanish-American War

Commodore George Dewey commands destruction of Spain's Pacific fleet at the Battle of Manila Bay

United States annexes Hawaii

Senator Albert J. Beveridge delivers "The March of the Flag" speech

Formation of the Anti-Imperialist League

1899 Treaty of Paris transfers the Philippines, Guam, and Puerto Rico from Spain to the United States

Outbreak of the Philippine-American War

Agreement signed between the United States and Germany to partition the Samoan Islands

U.S. Secretary of State John Hay issues first Open Door note

1900 Congress passes legislation establishing the Territory of Hawaii

Boxer Uprising begins in China

Multinational China Relief Expedition liberates foreign embassies in Beijing

Hay issues second Open Door note

1901 Balangiga Massacre occurs in the Philippines

Supreme Court issues rulings in Insular Cases

Chinese government accepts the Boxer Protocol

1902 Britain and Japan form the Anglo-Japanese Alliance

Philippine-American War ends

1903 Young Women's Christian Association begins operations in Japan

1904 Outbreak of the Russo-Japanese War

1905 Britain acknowledges Japanese control over Korea

George Kennan meets with President Theodore Roosevelt to promote an accord with Japan

Taft-Katsura Agreement signed

Formal enunciation of the Ōkuma Doctrine

Roosevelt mediates the Treaty of Portsmouth, ending the Russo-Japanese War

Establishment of Japanese-Korean Exclusion League in San Francisco

Homer B. Hulbert meets with Secretary of State Elihu Root in a failed effort to obtain U.S. support for ending Japanese rule in Korea

1906 Shanghai Drug Conference convenes

1907 Hulbert joins Korean leaders in delivering petitions to the Second Hague Peace Conference protesting Japanese colonial rule

Japan and Russia sign agreement recognizing each other's sphere of influence in Manchuria

U.S. Great White Fleet begins around-the-world cruise

1908 President Roosevelt finalizes Gentlemen's Agreement with Japan

United States remits Boxer Indemnity to China

Puyi becomes last emperor of China

Root-Takahira Agreement provides for the United States to respect Japan's control over Korea and Japan to respect U.S. control in the Philippines

1909 Japanese businessman Shibusawa Eiichi visits the United States

Knox Neutralization Scheme initiates Dollar Diplomacy in Manchuria

1910 Entente between Japan and Russia divides Manchuria into spheres of influence

Japanese annexation of Korea

1911 Chinese Revolution to establish a republic begins

First of three Hague Opium Conferences convenes

Signing of the American-Japanese Treaty

Renewal of Anglo-Japanese Alliance

Treaty to ban the hunting of pelagic seals signed

Beginning of Korean Conspiracy Case

1912 Sun Zhongshan becomes president of the Republic of China

Puyi abdicates as emperor, ending the Qing Dynasty

Yuan Shikai replaces Sun Zhongshan as president of the Chinese Republic

Six Power Consortium arranged

1913 United States recognizes Republic of China

California passes Land Law discriminating against Asian-Americans

Woodrow Wilson announces U.S. withdrawal from Six Power Consortium

1914 Outbreak of World War I

Japan declares war on Germany and seizes Qingdao on Shandong Peninsula and all German islands north of the equator

1915 Japan conveys its Twenty-One Demands to China

Secretary of State William Jennings Bryan announces nonrecognition of forcible changes in status quo in China that violate U.S. treaty rights

1916 Japan-American Relations Committee established

Beginning of the Warlord Era in China, lasting until 1928

1917 Negotiation of the Lansing-Ishii Agreement

Immigration Act extends the Chinese Exclusion Act to other Asians

1918 United States joins Japan in launching the Siberian intervention

1919 March First Movement in Korea protests Japanese colonial rule

Korean Provisional Government created in Shanghai

Outbreak of the May Fourth Movement in China

Peking Union Medical College opens with Rockefeller Foundation funding

Versailles Peace Treaty signed, establishing the League of Nations and the Mandate System, but rejecting inclusion of a racial equality clause in the League Covenant

Japanese retention of Shandong contributes to the decision of the U.S. Senate to reject ratification of the Versailles Peace Treaty

1920 Soviet Union creates the Far Eastern Republic, a puppet regime in Siberia

1921 Sun Zhongshan reestablishes the Republic of China at Guangzhou

Founding of the Chinese Communist Party in Shanghai

Washington Conference convenes

Four Power Pact signed to preserve the status quo in the Pacific

1922 Nine Power Pact affirms the Open Door Policy in China

Signing of the Five Power Pact to limit naval armaments

United States and Japan resolve the Yap controversy

Japan agrees to restore Chinese control over the Shandong Peninsula

Katayama Sen helps found Japan Communist Party

1923 United Front formed between the Guomindang and the Communist Party

Formal abrogation of the Anglo-Japanese Alliance

Abrogation of Lansing-Ishii Agreement announced

1924 First of four Geneva Conferences on the drug trade convenes

U.S. military leaders adopt War Plan ORANGE

Congress restricts immigration with a racial quota system with passage of the National Origins Act

California's legislature passes law barring Asian immigration

1925 Formation of the Institute of Pacific Relations

Creation of the Korean Communist Party

May Thirtieth Movement begins in China to protest unequal treaties

Socialist reformer and journalist Anna Louise Strong makes her first trip to China

1926 Jiang Jieshi, new Guomindang leader in China, begins the Northern Expedition to unify China and end Warlord Era

Hirohito becomes emperor of Japan

1927 Geneva Naval Conference convenes

Guomindang forces massacre Communist Party members at Shanghai, ending first United Front

1928 United States signs treaty with China restoring tariff autonomy

Signing of the Kellogg-Briand Peace Pact to outlaw war

Formation of the Taiwanese Communist Party

Socialist reformer and journalist Agnes Smedley first travels to China

Japanese military extremists assassinate Chinese warlord Zhang Zoulin

1929 Stock market crash in the United States ignites global depression

1930 London Naval Conference results in the adoption of new limits on naval armaments covering all classes of military vessels

Ho Chi Minh and others establish the Vietnamese Communist Party

1931 Japanese extremists assassinate Prime Minister Hamaguchi Yūkō

Mukden Incident initiates Manchurian Crisis

1932 U.S. Secretary of State Henry L. Stimson sends identical messages to Japan and China, refusing to recognize forcible changes in the status quo

Lytton Commission begins League of Nations investigation of the Manchurian Crisis

Kim Gu kills the head of the Japanese Residents Association and maims Japanese Ambassador Shigemitsu Mamoru in Shanghai

Japanese military and naval forces attack Shanghai

Japan's government accepts the creation of the puppet government in Manchukuo

Japanese Prime Minister Inukai Tsuyoshi assassinated in abortive military coup

1933 Japan withdraws from the League of Nations

1934 Japan enunciates the Amō Doctrine

Manchukuo's President Puyi made emperor

Tydings-McDuffie Act provides a timetable for the independence of the Philippines

Members of the Chinese Communist Party begin the Long March

1936 Young militant Japanese military officers assassinate government officials

London Naval Conference convenes

United States signs Silver Agreement with Republic of China

Japan and Germany join in forming the Anti-Comintern Pact

Xian Incident results in the Guomindang and the Chinese Communist Party forming a United Front to fight the Japanese

1937 Marco Polo Bridge Incident in China ignites World War II in Asia

General Claire L. Chennault begins to work for China's Jiang Jieshi

President Franklin D. Roosevelt delivers Quarantine Speech

Brussels Conference convenes

Release of the movie *The Good Earth*

Rape of Nanjing by Japanese military forces

Italy joins Ant-Comintern Pact

Japanese pilot sinks USS *Panay* on Yangze River in China

1938 Terms of the Lansing-Ishii Agreement made public

Publication of Edgar Snow's *Red Star Over China*

1939 Formation of the Hukbalahap in the Philippines

U.S. military leaders begin to develop War Plan RAINBOW

United States announces six-month notice of the termination of commercial treaties with Japan

U.S. Pacific Fleet transferred from San Diego to Pearl Harbor

Ida Pruitt begins work to create Chinese Industrial Cooperatives in China

Outbreak of World War II in Europe

Soviet Army defeats the Japanese at the Battle of Nomonhan

1940 China's government at Nanjing under Wang Jingwei signs treaty with Japan

American cryptologists first break Japanese code with *Magic*

French colonial officials sign the Hanoi Convention, allowing Japan to deploy military forces in northern French Indochina

United States embargoes scrap iron, steel, iron ore, copper, and brass to Japan

Tripartite Pact signed between Japan, Germany, and Italy

1941 U.S. Congress passes Lend Lease Act

Conversations between Secretary of State Cordell Hull and Japanese Ambassador Nomura Kichisaburō attempt to resolve U.S.-Japan differences

Ho Chi Minh organizes Vietminh to oust both the French and the Japanese

Japanese military forces occupy southern French Indochina

U.S. government freezes Japanese assets in the United States

United States rejects Japanese proposal for a meeting between President Roosevelt and Prime Minister Konoe Fumimaro

Japanese combat aircraft stage attack on Pearl Harbor

U.S. declares war on Japan

Japanese forces attack British Malaya, the Dutch East Indies, and the Philippines

1942 U.S. aid to China through "over the Hump" flights from India begin

Jimmy Doolittle leads air raid on Japan

Fall of Corregidor in the Philippines to Japanese forces

Bataan Death March

Battle of Coral Sea between U.S. and Japanese air and naval forces

Battle of Midway Island between U.S. and Japanese air and naval forces

United States signs Lend Lease agreement with the Republic of China

Song Meiling, wife of Jiang Jieshi, arrives in the United States to begin eight months of lobbying for U.S. support for the Republic of China

1943 Casablanca Conference issues unconditional surrender doctrine

Chindits launch invasion of Burma

U.S. Congress repeals Chinese Exclusion Acts

U.S. military begins island-hopping strategy against Japan in the Pacific war

Cairo Conference convenes, resulting in the issuance of the Cairo Declaration promising independence "in due course" to Korea and the return of land captured by Japan to China

1944 Merrill's Marauders begin military operations in Burma

Dixie Mission sent to Communist headquarters at Yan'an in China

U.S. Navy captures Tinian, Guam, and Saipan in the Pacific war

Japanese launch Ichigo Offensive against Guomindang forces in China

Battle of the Philippine Sea

Great Marianas Turkey Shoot

Battle of Leyte Gulf leads to U.S. recapture of the Philippines

President Roosevelt replaces Lieutenant General Joseph W. Stilwell with Lieutenant General Albert C. Wedemeyer as military adviser to Jiang Jieshi in China

1945 President Franklin D. Roosevelt, British Prime Minister Winston Churchill, and Soviet Premier Joseph Stalin meet at the Yalta Conference

Deer Mission arrives in French Indochina to assist the Vietminh in operations against the Japanese

Battle of Iwo Jima

Battle of Okinawa

Death of President Franklin D. Roosevelt

Operation OLYMPIC outlines plan for the occupation of Kyūshū

Massive Allied firebombing of Japanese cities

Germany surrenders, ending World War II in Europe

Potsdam Declaration issued

United States drops atomic bombs on Hiroshima and Nagasaki

United States and Soviet Union agree to divide Korea into military zones of occupation

President Harry S. Truman issues General Order Number 1

Formation of the Committee for a Democratic Far Eastern Policy

Ho Chi Minh proclaims the establishment of the Democratic Republic of Vietnam

Sukarno and Mohammed Hatta declare the independence of Indonesia

Japan formally surrenders, ending World War II in Asia

Chinese Civil War begins

U.S. occupation of Japan begins

U.S. occupation of southern Korea begins

Claire L. Chennault establishes Civil Air Transport in China

U.S. Ambassador Patrick J. Hurley escorts Mao Zedong to Chongqing for a meeting with Jiang Jieshi

France invites Bao Dai to establish the State of Vietnam

General George C. Marshall travels to China on a mission to end the fighting between the Communists and the Guomindang and secures a cease-fire

Moscow Agreement provides a plan to reunite Korea

1946 Outbreak of First Indochina War between France and Vietminh

Tōkyō War Crimes Trials begin

Chinese Civil War resumes

George F. Kennan outlines the containment policy in the "Long Telegram"

Joint Soviet-American Commission convenes in Seoul to implement Moscow Agreement to reunite Korea

Philippines gains independence from United States

Publication of Theodore H. White's *Thunder Out of China*

U.S. Congress passes the Fulbright Act

1947 Assassination of Aung San in Burma

Guomindang forces massacre Taiwanese in the February 28 Incident

President Harry S. Truman requests military and economic aid for Greece and Turkey in the Truman Doctrine speech to Congress

Creation of General Agreement on Tariffs and Trade

Promulgation of the new Japanese constitution

National Security Act establishes the Central Intelligence Agency, Joint Chiefs of Staff, Department of Defense, and National Security Council

U.S. administration begins over the Trust Territory of the Pacific Islands, which includes all the Marshalls, Marianas, and Carolines

General Wedemeyer conducts fact-finding mission to China and southern Korea

Autumn Harvest Uprising occurs in southern Korea

Chinese Communist forces cross the Yellow River

United States refers the issue of Korea to the United Nations

Beginning of the "reverse course" in U.S. occupation policy in Japan

1948 Britain grants independence to Burma

Formation of the Federation of Malaya

Congress passes China Assistance Act

Establishment of Joint Commission on Rural Reconstruction in China

Open Payments Agreement signed

Beginning of the "Malay Emergency"

Establishment of the Republic of Korea ends the U.S. occupation of Korea

Establishment of the Democratic People's Republic of Korea

Soviet troops withdraw from North Korea

Execution of Tōjō Hideki, Hirōta Koki, and five other war criminals

1949 Japanese government establishes the Ministry of International Trade and Industry

Elysee Accords between France and Democratic Republic of Vietnam

Implementation of the Dodge Plan in Japan

Chinese Communist forces cross the Yangze River

U.S. forces withdraw from South Korea

Major military border clashes begin at the thirty-eighth parallel in Korea

State Department releases the China White Paper

Soviet Union explodes its first atomic device

Mao Zedong proclaims establishment of the People's Republic of China

China's government orders the imprisonment of U.S. diplomat Angus Ward

Retreating Guomindang forces begin military operations in Burma

Jiang Jieshi and his Guomindang government flee to Taiwan

Netherlands grants independence to Indonesia

Sun Liren conspires to stage a coup to oust Jiang Jieshi from power on Taiwan

1950 President Truman announces the end of U.S. involvement in China's civil war

Soviet Union begins boycott of the United Nations to protest the refusal to seat the People's Republic of China in place of the Republic of China

Secretary of State Dean G. Acheson delivers National Press Club speech

Senator Joseph R. McCarthy delivers speech in Wheeling, West Virginia, charging that 205 Communists worked in the State Department

Sino-Soviet Treaty of Friendship and Alliance signed

Tibet made an autonomous region in the People's Republic of China

Soviet Union and the People's Republic of China recognize the Democratic Republic of Vietnam

U.S. Congress approves the Korean Aid Act after almost two years of debate

United States recognizes Bao Dai's State of Vietnam

United States recognizes Norodom Sihanouk's government in Cambodia

Laotian Communist leader Souphanouvong founds Pathet Lao

President Truman names John Foster Dulles to negotiate a Japanese peace treaty

National Security Council Paper 68 proposes a huge increase in defense spending

U.S. State Department official John F. Melby leads mission to East Asia to Indochina, the Philippines, Malaya, Thailand, and Indonesia for recommendations on providing U.S. economic and military aid

Outbreak of the Korean War

UN Security Council passes two resolutions calling for international action for the defense of South Korea

Truman sends the U.S. Seventh Fleet into the Taiwan Strait

MacArthur named commander of the United Nations Command

UN forces halt North Korean offensive at the Pusan Perimeter

Philippine Defense Minister Ramon Magsaysay crushes Hukbalahap rebellion

Inch'ŏn Landing results in the liberation of South Korea

Adoption of the Colombo Plan

Chinese military intervention in the Korean War begins

At Wake Island, MacArthur predicts to Truman that China will not intervene in Korea

MacArthur launches Home by Christmas Offensive in the Korean War

Massive Chinese counterattack forces UN troops to evacuate North Korea

John S. Service dismissed from the State Department as security risk

1951 United Nations condemns China for aggression in Korean War

Counterattacks of UN forces restore battlelines in Korea at the thirty-eighth parallel

Sterling Payments Agreement signed

State Department dismisses O. Edmund Clubb as security risk

United States, Australia, and New Zealand sign ANZUS Treaty

United Nations approves moratorium resolution on discussing Chinese representation for the first time

Truman recalls General MacArthur

Lieutenant General Matthew B. Ridgway becomes commander in Korea and head of the U.S. occupation of Japan

Establishment of the Military Assistance Advisory Group, Taiwan

U.S. Congress holds hearings on recall of MacArthur

Military stalemate emerges in the Korean War

Opening of Korean War armistice negotiations at Kaesŏng

U.S.-Philippines Mutual Defense Pact signed

Signing of the Japanese Peace Treaty in San Francisco

U.S.-Japan Security Treaty signed

Korean War armistice negotiations resume at P'anmunjŏm

Japanese Prime Minister Yoshida Shigeru says in a letter to Dulles that Japan will recognize the Republic of China

1952 Chinese and North Koreans officially accuse United States of practicing germ warfare in Korean War

Establishment of the China Committee (CHINCOM) to restrict trade to the People's Republic of China

Japan regains its sovereignty and the U.S. occupation ends

Deadlock over prisoner of war repatriation begins at P'anmunjŏm

U.S. Army creates Special Forces unit known as the Green Berets

Sino-Japanese Peace Treaty signed

People's Republic of China expels missionaries

U.S. Congress passes McCarran Immigration Act

Committee for a Democratic Far Eastern Policy dissolved

1953 Burma Conference convenes

Zhou Enlai enunciates Five Principles of Peaceful Coexistence

U.S.-Japan Treaty of Friendship, Commerce, and Navigation signed

Korean Armistice Agreement signed

Navarre Plan implemented in French Indochina

1954 U.S.-Japan Mutual Defense Assistance Agreement signed

United States stages nuclear test at Bikini Atoll

	Japanese ship *Lucky Dragon* showered with nuclear fallout
	Opening of Geneva Conference on Korea and Indochina
	Eisenhower refers to domino theory during press conference
	Secretary of State Dulles fails to organize United Action for multinational military action in French Indochina
	Fall of the French stronghold at Dien Bien Phu
	Geneva Accords achieves cease-fire, ending the First Indochina War
	United States helps with the creation of a special forces unit in Thailand
	Formation of the Southeast Asia Treaty Organization
	State Department terminates the employment of John Paton Davies
	Start of the first Taiwan Strait Crisis
	U.S.-China Mutual Defense Treaty signed as part of Operation ORACLE
	United States ratifies Mutual Defense Treaty with the Republic of Korea
	General J. Lawton Collins begins mission to South Vietnam
1955	Congress passes Formosa Resolution
	American Friends of Vietnam formed
	Bandung Conference of nonaligned nations convenes in Indonesia
	Ngo Dinh Diem defeats Bao Dai in an election for president in South Vietnam
	Establishment of the Republic of Vietnam
	Michigan State University Group begins its training and advisory program in the Republic of Vietnam
	Beginning in Geneva of ambassadorial talks between the United States and the People's Republic of China
	Publication of Graham Greene's *The Quiet American*
1956	Souvanna Phouma leads coalition government in Laos
	Kim Il Sung orders the execution of rival Pak Hŏn-yŏng in North Korea
	South Vietnam's President Ngo Dinh Diem rejects nationwide elections
	PRRI-Permesta rebellion begins in Indonesia
1957	Anti-American revolt occurs in Taibei, Taiwan
	Britain grants independence to Malaysia
	Last meeting of the Institute of Pacific Relations
	United States agrees to revise U.S.-Japan Security Treaty of 1951
1958	Sukarno's military forces crush PRRI-Permesta Rebellion
	Second Taiwan Strait Crisis occurs
	Sino-American ambassadorial talks move from Geneva to Warsaw, Poland
	U Nu tranfers authority in Burma to Ne Win
1959	Air America formed from Civil Air Transport
	North Vietnamese leaders develop plan to expand and improve Ho Chi Minh Trail
	Lee Kuan Yew becomes prime minister of Singapore
1960	Ouster of Syngman Rhee in South Korea
	Jang Myŏn elected prime minister in the Republic of Korea
	Anpo crisis in Japan protests renewal of U.S.-Japan Security Treaty
	U.S.-Japan Mutual Cooperation and Security Treaty signed
	Kong Le stages coup in Laos
	Vice President Richard M. Nixon and Senator John F. Kennedy debate protection of Jinmen and Mazu in U.S. presidential campaign
	Creation of the National Liberation Front in Vietnam
1961	Congress passes Fulbright-Hayes Act

Implementation of Strategic Hamlets Program in Vietnam

Opening of Geneva Conference on the Laotian Crisis

Pak Chŏng-hŭi stages coup and establishes military junta in South Korea

Establishment of the Peace Corps

Soviet leader Nikita Khrushchev tells President Kennedy in Vienna that his nation will support "wars of national liberation" against colonialism

Ikeda Hayato meets with Kennedy in Washington

President Kennedy meets with Chen Cheng of the Republic of China

Walt W. Rostow and Maxwell D. Taylor conduct mission to the Republic of Vietnam

Kennedy meets with Pak Chŏng-hŭi in Washington

1962 United States begins Operation RANCH HAND to defoliate South Vietnam

Ne Win stages coup and seizes power in Burma

Establishment of the Military Assistance Command, Vietnam (MACV)

Geneva Accords provide for the neutralization of Laos

United States begins secret air war in Laos against Communist forces

U.S. pressure persuades the Dutch to transfer West Irian to Indonesia

Indonesia begins clash with Malaysia

1963 Buddhist uprising against the Diem government

Battle of Ap Bac in Vietnam

Ferdinand Marcos elected president of the Philippines

Pak Chŏng-hŭi elected president of the Republic of Korea

Norodom Sihanouk of Cambodia ends U.S. military and economic aid programs

Ouster and assassination of Ngo Dinh Diem

Assassination of President John F. Kennedy

1964 President Lyndon B. Johnson approves OPLAN 34A

Nguyen Khanh seizes control of Saigon government

General William C. Westmoreland assumes command of MACV

DeSoto Patrols by U.S. military vessels begin off the coast of North Vietnam

Summer Olympic Games held in Tōkyō

North Vietnamese torpedo boats attack U.S. destroyer in Tonkin of Gulf

Congress passes Tonkin Gulf Resolution

1965 Nguyen Van Thieu and Nguyen Cao Ky take power in South Vietnam

Viet Cong attack U.S. Special Forces base at Pleiku in Vietnam

Operation ROLLING THUNDER begins systematic U.S. bombing of North Vietnam

First U.S. combat troops land at Danang in the Republic of Vietnam

Meeting between President Lyndon B. Johnson and Pak Chŏng-hŭi

Japan-Korea Treaty on Basic Relations signed

Singapore ends brief union with Malaysia and asserts independence

Norodom Sihanouk breaks relations between Cambodia and the United States

Suharto crushes Communist Party in Indonesia

Republic of China signs Status of Forces Agreement with United States

U.S. Congress passes Immigration Act, ending quota system

1966 Battle of the Ia Drang Valley

Johnson meets South Vietnam leaders Thieu and Ky in Hawaii

President Johnson confers with Pak Chŏng-hŭi in Seoul

Ouster of Sukarno in Indonesia

Republic of Korea signs Status of Forces Agreement with United States

Operation MARIGOLD attempts at peace in Vietnam initiated

Publication of J. William Fulbright's *Arrogance of Power*

1967 Operation CEDAR FALLS levels village of Ben Suc in Vietnam

Operation JUNCTION CITY staged in South Vietnam

Great Proletarian Cultural Revolution begins in China

Creation of Association of Southeast Asian Nations

Lyndon B. Johnson outlines San Antonio Formula for peace in Vietnam

Lin Biao's *Long Live the Victory of People's War* published

Thieu elected president and Ky vice president of the Republic of Vietnam

Implementation of the Phoenix Program begins in Vietnam

Japanese Prime Minister Satō Eisaku first outlines the Three Non-Nuclear Principles

1968 Winter Olympic Games held in Sapporo, Japan

North Korea seizes USS *Pueblo*, a U.S. surveillance ship

North Vietnam and Viet Cong launch Tet Offensive

Seige at Khe Sanh in South Vietnam

My Lai Massacre occurs in South Vietnam

Pak Chŏng-hŭi resists sending more South Korean troops to Vietnam in meeting with Johnson at Honolulu, Hawaii

Johnson announces partial halt in the bombing of North Vietnam

United States returns Bonin Islands to Japan

Start of Paris Peace Talks to end Second Indochina War

United States ends Operation ROLLING THUNDER

Committee of Concerned Asian Scholars splits from the Association for Asian Studies

1969 Death of Ho Chi Minh

Operation MENU begins secret bombing in Cambodia

Retina, later Team Spirit, military exercises begin in South Korea

Implementation of Vietnamization begins

President Richard M. Nixon announces Nixon Doctrine on Guam

Withdrawal of first U.S. combat troops from Vietnam

Provisional Revolutionary Government replaces National Liberation Front

Nixon-Sato Communiqué released, pledging U.S. return of Okinawa to Japan

1970 Henry A. Kissinger and Le Duc Tho begin secret talks to end Vietnam War

Formation of National League of Families of Americans Missing in Southeast Asia

Lon Nol stages coup and replaces Norodom Sihanouk in Cambodia

U.S. and South Vietnamese forces launch Cambodian incursion

Four students killed by Ohio National Guardsmen at Kent State University

1971 Lam Son 712 invasion by South Vietnamese forces into Laos

Ping-Pong Diplomacy begins rapprochement between the United States and the People's Republic of China

State Department official Marshall Green reportedly coins the term "Golden Triangle"

Korean Central Intelligence Agency fails in attempt to assassinate dissident Kim Dae-jung

Publication in the *New York Times* and other newspapers of the Pentagon Papers

Announcement that Nixon will travel to China early in 1972

Nixon Shocks damage U.S.-Japan relations

Prime Minister Tanaka Kakuei's concessions settle U.S.-Japan textile dispute

United States advocates UN representation for both Chinas

United Nations votes to expel Republic of China and seat People's Republic of China

1972 President Nixon visits China

Issuance of the Shanghai Communiqué

North Vietnam launches Easter Offensive in South Vietnam

Operation LINEBACKER 1 begins massive U.S. bombing of North Vietnam

Japan regains control over Okinawa

National Security Adviser Kissinger announces that "peace is at hand"

Operation LINEBACKER 2 stages "Christmas Bombings" of North Vietnam

1973 Paris Peace Accords end Vietnam War

Operation HOMECOMING brings U.S. prisoners of war back from Vietnam

United States and the People's Republic of China open liaison offices in each other's capital

Jiang Jingguo initiates "total diplomacy" to reestablish ties with nations that had broken relations with the Republic of China

Opening of the Tōkyō Round trade negotiations

Korean Central Intelligency Agency kidnaps dissident Kim Dae-jung in Tōkyō

1975 Vang Pao and his Hmong army flee into Thailand

Communist forces seize control of South Vietnam, Cambodia, and Laos

Establishment of the People's Republic of Kampuchea

Souphanouvong becomes president of the People's Republic of Laos

Indonesian troops invade East Timor

Death of Jiang Jieshi

President Gerald R. Ford orders raid to liberate the crew of U.S. ship *Mayaguez* in Cambodia

Lockheed Scandal

1976 Mao Zedong dies

Establishment of the Socialist Republic of Vietnam

Ax murders at the demilitarized zone in Korea

Koreagate Scandal

1977 President Jimmy Carter announces plans to withdraw U.S. troops from South Korea

U.S. Congress votes to deny any rehabilitation aid to Vietnam

Termination of the SEATO alliance

Fukuda Doctrine signals Japanese commitment to economic development of Southeast Asia

Mass exodus of boat people from Southeast Asia begins

Vietnam invades Cambodia

1978 Implementation of the Four Modernizations begins in China

Japan normalizes relations with the People's Republic of China

1979 United States formally recognizes the People's Republic of China

Congress passes the Taiwan Relations Act

United States announces that it will accept 15,000 boat people

Sino-Soviet Treaty of Friendship and Alliance expires

Assassination of Pak Chŏng-hŭi

Chŏn Du-hwan seizes power in South Korea

1980 People's Republic of China formally creates four Special Economic Zones

Kwangju Incident occurs in South Korea

1981 Chŏn Du-hwan the first foreign leader to meet with Ronald Reagan

Mohamad Mahathir becomes prime minister of Malaysia

Prime Minister Suzuki Zenkō pledges to expand Japan's role in regional defense

1983 First meeting between Reagan and Prime Minister Nakasone Yasuhiro

Soviet plane shoots down Korean Airlines Flight 007

Former Japanese Prime Minister Tanaka Kakuei sentenced to four years in prison

1984 Guomindang operatives assassinate Henry Liu in the United States

Brunei gains independence from Britain

1985 Compact of Free Association for Micronesia signed

1986 Ouster of Ferdinand Marcos in the Philippines

Corazon Aquino assumes power in the Philippines

Dangwai becomes the Democratic Progressive Party on Taiwan

1987 Protests in South Korea against military rule reach a crescendo

Issuance of South Korea's Democracy Declaration

1988 South Korean President No Tae-u announces "Nordpolitik" policy

Summer Olympic Games held in Seoul, Korea

Li Dengwei elected president of the Republic of China on Taiwan

1989 Establishment of Asia-Pacific Economic Cooperation forum

United States imposes trade sanctions against Myanmar

Tiananman Square Massacre in China

Chinese dissident Fang Lizhi takes refuge in U.S. embassy

U.S. government support helps block coup against Aquino government in the Philippines

1990 First meeting between No Tae-u and Soviet leader Mikhail Gorbachev

Burma's Khun Sa indicted for drug trafficking

Mohamad Mahathir proposes creation of an East Asian Economic Caucus

1991 Japan deploys minesweepers in the Persian Gulf

Tōkyō accepts a cost-sharing arrangement to fund U.S. military bases in Japan

Gorbachev and No meet on Cheju Island in South Korea

United States and Japan agree to the Structural Impediments Initiative

CBS televises documentary of convict labor in China videotaped by Wu Hongda

United Nations arranges elections in Cambodia

Both Koreas admitted to the United Nations

Beginning of North Korean Nuclear Controversy

1992 Kim Young-sam becomes first civilian president of South Korea since 1961

U.S. naval forces leave Subic Naval Base in the Philippines

1993 Japan's Liberal Democratic Party loses power for the first time since 1955

President Bill Clinton proposes creation of a "New Pacific Community"

1994 World Trade Organization replaces the General Agreement on Tariffs and Trade

Agreed Framework temporarily ends the North Korean nuclear dispute

Death of Kim Il Sung

1995 United States establishes formal relations with the Socialist Republic of Vietnam

Chinese dissident Wu Hongda expelled from the People's Republic of China

1996 People's Republic of China conducts military exercises in the Taiwan Strait and fires missiles at Taiwan

South China Sea Islands dispute focuses on Spratly Islands

1997 Beginning of the East Asian Financial Crisis

Thailand receives loan from the International Monetary Fund

Republic of Korea requests a loan from the International Monetary Fund

President Jiang Zemin visits the United States

Release of Chinese dissident Wei Jingsheng from prison

1998 President Clinton visits China

Japanese government implements economic stimulus package

Fall of the Suharto regime in Indonesia

2000 South Korean President Kim Daejung visits North Korea

President Clinton visits Socialist Republic of Vietnam

New Status of Forces Agreement provides greater jurisdiction to South Korea

2001 U.S. surveillance plane lands on Hainan Island after collision with a Chinese warplane

Acronyms

AAA	American Asiatic Association
ABCFM	American Board of Commissioners for Foreign Missions
AFV	American Friends of Vietnam
AIT	American Institute in Taiwan
AMG	American Military Government (in Korea)
ANZUS	Australian-New Zealand-United States (Security Treaty)
APEC	Asia-Pacific Economic Cooperation (forum)
ARF	ASEAN Regional Forum
ARVN	Army of the Republic of Vietnam
ASEAN	Association of Southeast Asian Nations
CAT	Civil Air Transport
CBI	China-Burma-India (Theater)
CBS	Columbia Broadcasting System
CCBA	Chinese Consolidated Benevolent Association
CCP	Chinese Communist Party
CDFEP	Committee for a Democratic Far Eastern Policy
CER	Chinese Eastern Railway
CFC	Combined Forces Command
CHINCOM	China Committee
CIA	Central Intelligence Agency
CIC	Chinese Industrial Cooperatives
CIG	Central Intelligence Group
CIDG	Civilian Irregular Defense Group
CMB	China Medical Board
CMC	Central Military Commission
CMSNC	China Merchant Steamship Navigation Company
COCOM	Coordinating Committee (on East-West Trade Policy)
COI	Coordinator of Information
COSVN	Central Office for South Vietnam
CPSU	Communist Party of the Soviet Union
CPUSA	Communist Party of the United States of America
CPV	Chinese People's Volunteers
DCI	Director of Central Intelligence
DJP	Democratic Justice Party
DLP	Democratic Liberal Party
DMZ	demilitarized zone
DOD	Department of Defense
DPP	Democratic Progressive Party
DRP	Democratic Republican Party
DPRK	Democratic People's Republic of Korea
DRV	Democratic Republic of Vietnam
ECA	Economic Cooperation Administration
EUSAK	Eighth U.S. Army in Korea
FBI	Federal Bureau of Investigation

FEC	Far Eastern Commission
FEC	French Expeditionary Corps
FER	Far Eastern Republic
FSO	Foreign Service Officer
GATT	General Agreement on Tariffs and Trade
GDP	gross domestic product
GMD	Guomindang
GNP	gross national product
IAEA	International Atomic Energy Agency
ICP	Indochinese Communist Party
ICSC	International Commission for Supervision and Control
IMF	International Monetary Fund
IMTFE	International Military Tribunal for the Far East
IRC	International Rescue Committee
IPR	Institute of Pacific Relations
ITO	International Trade Organization
IWA	International Wheat Agreement
IWC	International Wheat Council
JCP	Japan Communist Party
JCRR	Joint Commission on Rural Reconstruction
JCS	Joint Chiefs of Staff
JSP	Japan Socialist Party
KAL	Korean Air Lines
KCIA	Korean Central Intelligence Agency
KMA	Korean Military Academy
KPA	Korean People's Army
KPG	Korean Provisional Government
KPR	Korean People's Republic
KWP	Korean Workers' Party
LDP	Liberal Democratic Party
MAAG	Military Assistance and Advisory Group
MACV	Military Assistance Command, Vietnam
MFN	most-favored-nation
MIA	missing in action
MITI	Ministry of International Trade and Industry
MPR	Mongolian People's Republic
MSA	Mutual Security Act
MSU	Michigan State University
MSUG	Michigan State University Group
NATO	North Atlantic Treaty Organization
NDC	National Defense Commission
NDP	New Democratic Party
NGO	nongovernmental organization
NKDP	New Korea Democratic Party
NLF	National Liberation Front
NPT	(Nuclear) Non-Proliferation Treaty
NNRC	Neutral Nations Repatriation Commission
NPA	New People's Party
NSA	National Security Agency
NSC	National Security Council
NSP	National Security Planning (Agency)
NTB	non-tariff barriers
NVA	North Vietnamese Army
OPA	Open Payments Agreement
OSS	Office of Strategic Services
OWI	Office of War Information
PAVN	People's Army of Vietnam
PEC	President's Export Council
PI	Partai Indonesia
PKI	Indonesian Communist Party
PKO	Peace Keeping Operations
PKP	Partido Komunista ng Pilipinas (Philippine Communist Party)
PLA	People's Liberation Army
POL	petroleum, oil, and lubricant
POW	prisoner of war
PPS	Policy Planning Staff
PRC	People's Republic of China
PRG	Provisional Revolutionary Government
PRRI	Pemerintah Revolusioner Republik Indonesia
PRK	People's Republic of Kampuchea
PRU	Provincial Reconnaissance Units
PUMC	Peking Union Medical College

ROC	Republic of China
ROK	Republic of Korea
RSFSR	Russian Socialist Federated Soviet Republic
RVN	Republic of Vietnam
RVNAF	Republic of Vietnam Air Force
SCAP	Supreme Commander for the Allied Powers
SCNR	Supreme Council for National Reconstruction
SEATO	Southeast Asia Treaty Organization
SEANWFZ	Southeast Asia Nuclear Weapon-Free Zone
SEZ	Special Economic Zones
SFRC	Senate Foreign Relations Committee
SISS	Senate Internal Security Subcommittee
SKWP	South Korean Workers' Party
SMR	South Manchurian Railway
SOFA	Status of Forces Agreement
SOG	Special Operations Group
SPA	Sterling Payments Agreement
SRV	Socialist Republic of Vietnam
SSNC	Shanghai Steamship Navigation Company
SVN	State of Vietnam
TAC	Treaty of Amity and Cooperation (in Southeast Asia)
TCP	Taiwanese Communist Party
TEA	Trade Expansion Act
TRA	Taiwan Relations Act
TTPI	Trust Territory of the Pacific Islands
UCR	United China Relief
UK	United Kingdom
UMNO	United Malays National Organization
UN	United Nations
UNC	United Nations Command
USAAF	U.S. Army Air Force
USAFIK	U.S. Armed Forces in Korea
USAMGIK	U.S. Army Military Government in Korea
USC	United Service to China
USIS	United States Information Service
VIVA	Victory in Vietnam Association
VNA	Vietnamese National Army
VOC	Vereenigte Oost-Indische Compagnie
WTC	Wheat Trade Convention
WTO	World Trade Organization
YMCA	Young Men's Christian Association
YWCA	Young Women's Christian Association
ZOPFAN	Zone of Peace, Freedom, and Neutrality

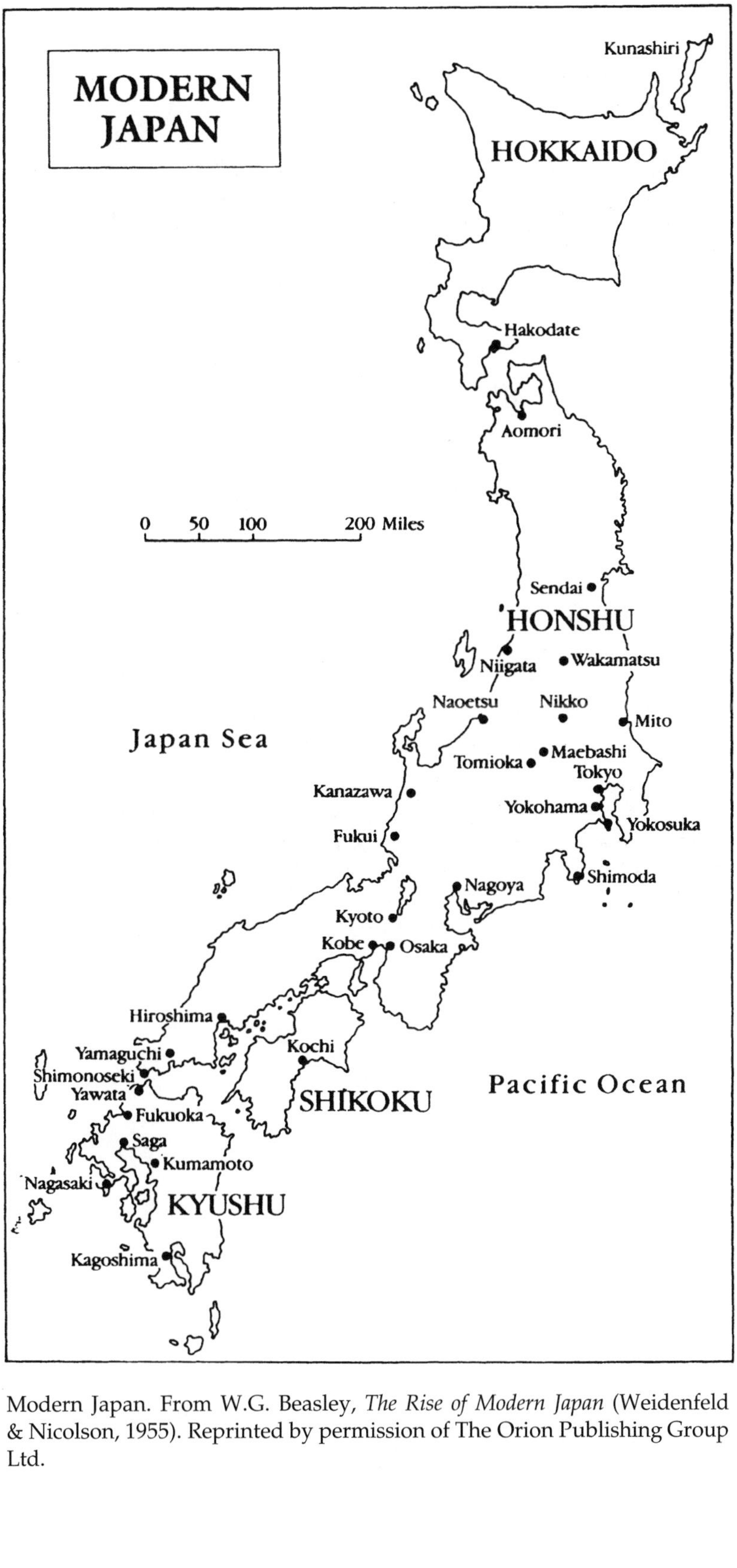

Modern Japan. From W.G. Beasley, *The Rise of Modern Japan* (Weidenfeld & Nicolson, 1955). Reprinted by permission of The Orion Publishing Group Ltd.

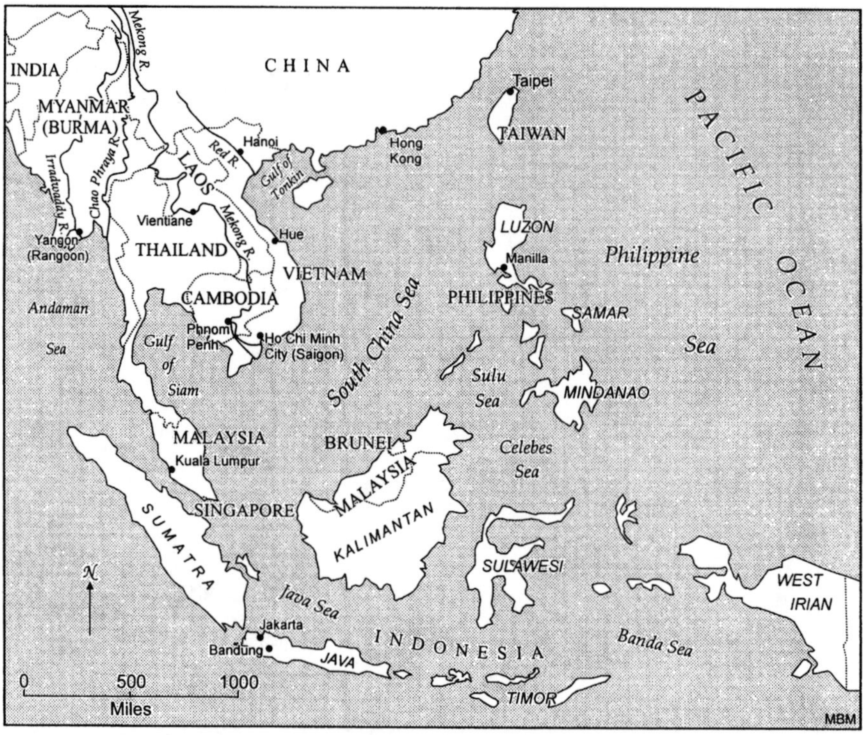

Above: Contemporary Southeast Asia. From *The Limits of Empire: The United States and Southeast Asia Since World War II* by Robert J. Mcmahon. © Columbia University Press, 1999. Reprinted with the permission of the publisher.
On opposite page: The Ryukyu Islands. From Gregory Smits, *Visions of Ryuku: Identity and Ideology in Early-Modern Thought and Politics* (Honolulu: University of Hawai'i Press, 1999). © 1999 University of Hawai'i Press. Reprinted with the permission of the publisher.

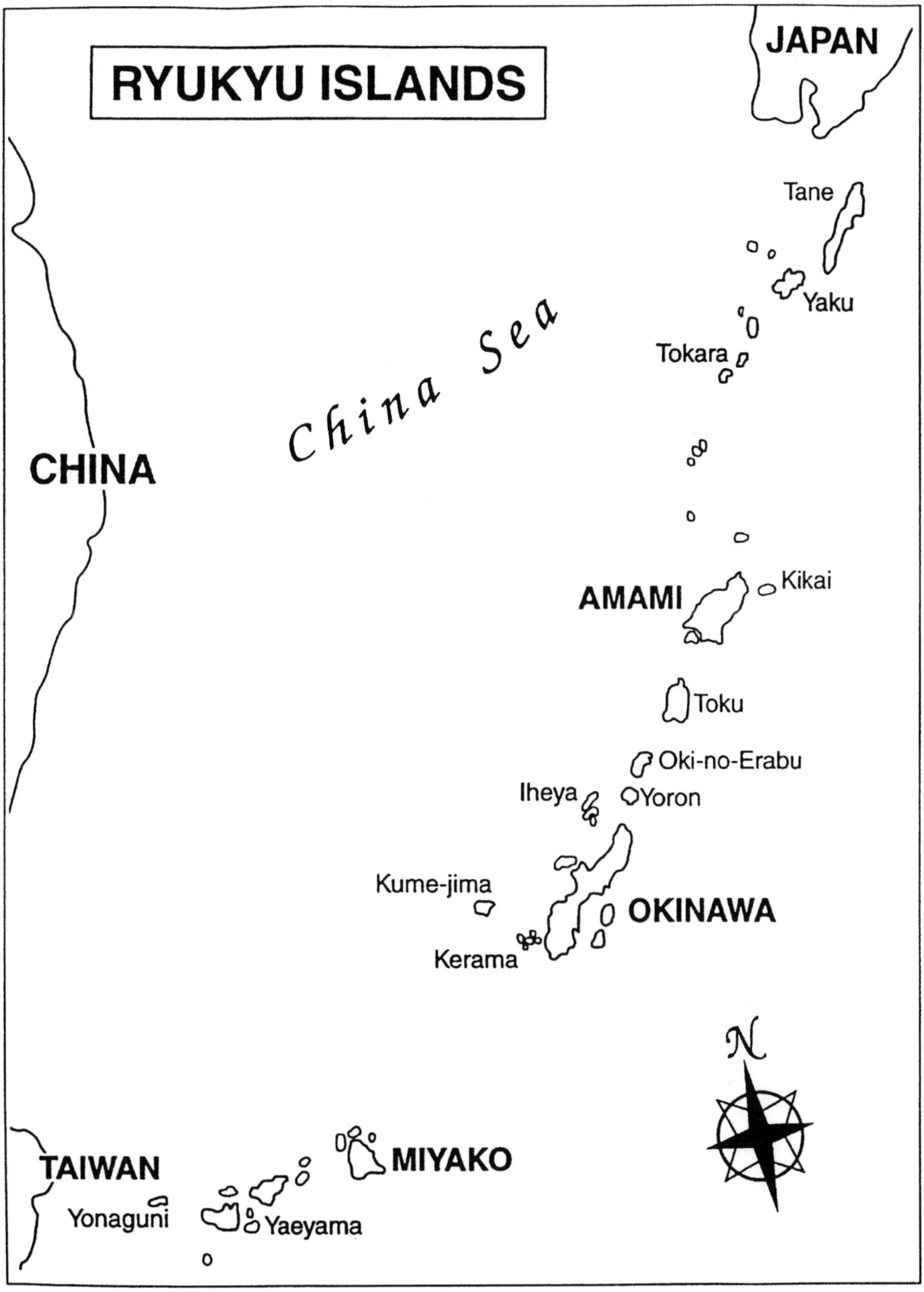
RYUKYU ISLANDS
JAPAN
Tane
Yaku
China Sea
Tokara
CHINA
AMAMI
Kikai
Toku
Oki-no-Erabu
Iheya
Yoron
Kume-jima
OKINAWA
Kerama
N
TAIWAN
MIYAKO
Yonaguni
Yaeyama

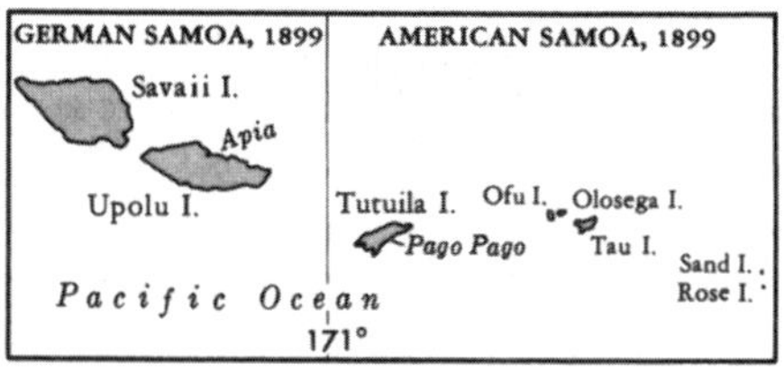
GERMAN SAMOA, 1899
AMERICAN SAMOA, 1899
Savaii I.
Apia
Upolu I.
Tutuila I.
Ofu I.
Olosega I.
Pago Pago
Tau I.
Sand I.
Rose I.
Pacific Ocean
171°

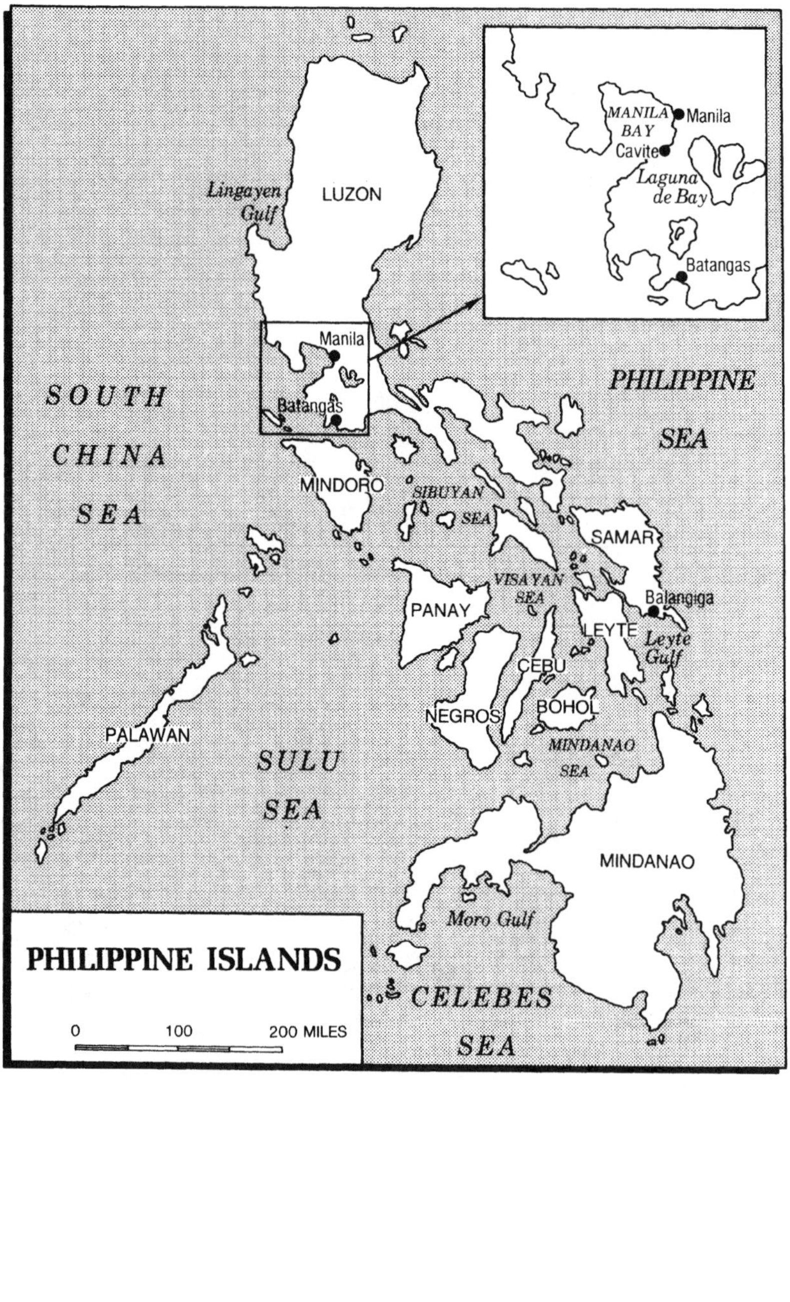
PHILIPPINE ISLANDS
0
100
200 MILES
LUZON
Lingayen Gulf
Manila
Batangas
MANILA BAY
Cavite
Laguna de Bay
SOUTH CHINA SEA
PHILIPPINE SEA
MINDORO
SIBUYAN SEA
SAMAR
PANAY
VISAYAN SEA
Balangiga
LEYTE
Leyte Gulf
CEBU
BOHOL
NEGROS
PALAWAN
SULU SEA
MINDANAO SEA
MINDANAO
Moro Gulf
CELEBES SEA

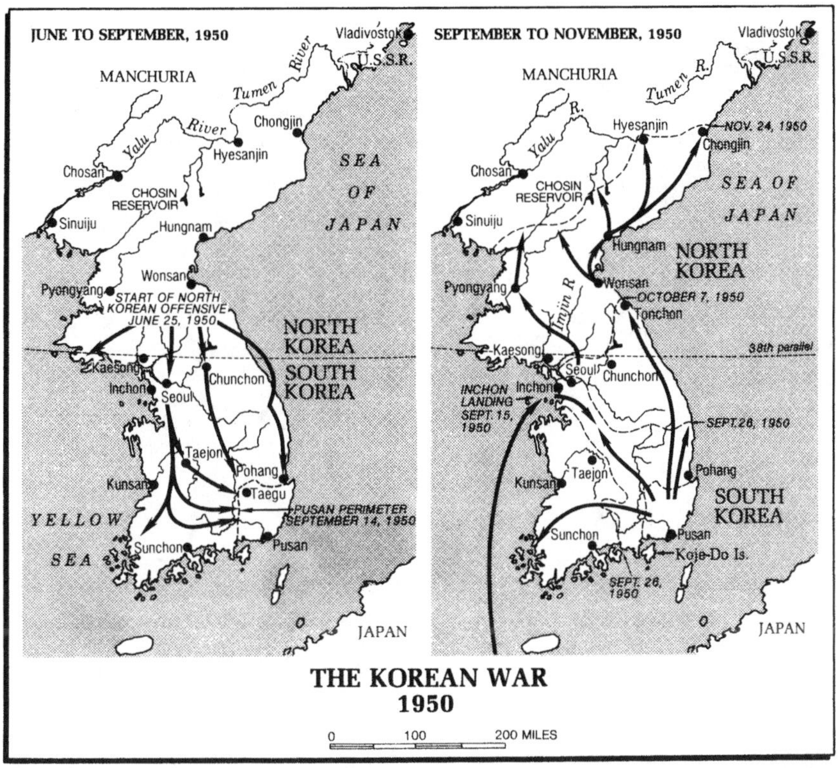

Opposite page, top: The Partition of Samoa, 1899. From *A History of American Foreign Policy*, 2nd ed., by Alexander DeConde (New York: Scribner's, 1971). Copyright © 1971 Charles Scribner's Sons. Reprinted with the permission of The Gale Group.

Opposite page, bottom: The Philippine Islands. Reprinted with the permission of The Free Press, a Division of Simon & Schuster, Inc., from *For the Common Defense: A Military History of the United States of America*, Revised & Expanded Edition by Allan R. Millet and Peter Maslowski. Copyright © 1984, 1994 by The Free Press.

Above: The Korean War, 1950. Reprinted with the permission of The Free Press, a Division of Simon & Schuster, Inc., from *For the Common Defense: A Military History of the United States of America*, Revised & Expanded Edition by Allan R. Millett and Peter Maslowski. Copyright © 1984, 1994 by The Free Press.

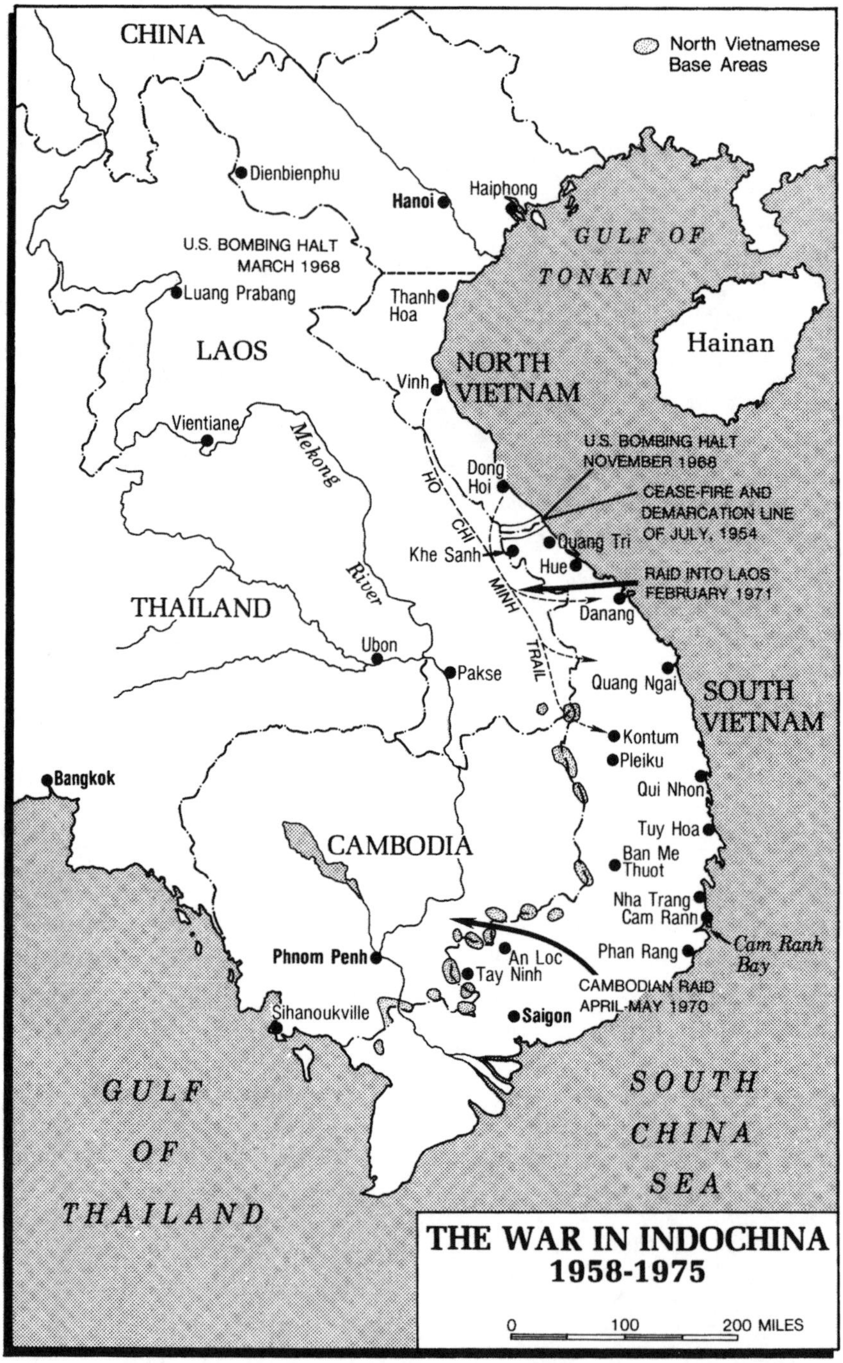

The War in Indochina, 1958–1975. Reprinted with the permission of The Free Press, a Division of Simon & Schuster, Inc., from *For the Common Defense: A Military History of the United States of America,* Revised & Expanded Edition by Allan R. Millett and Peter Maslowski. Copyright © 1984, 1994 by The Free Press.

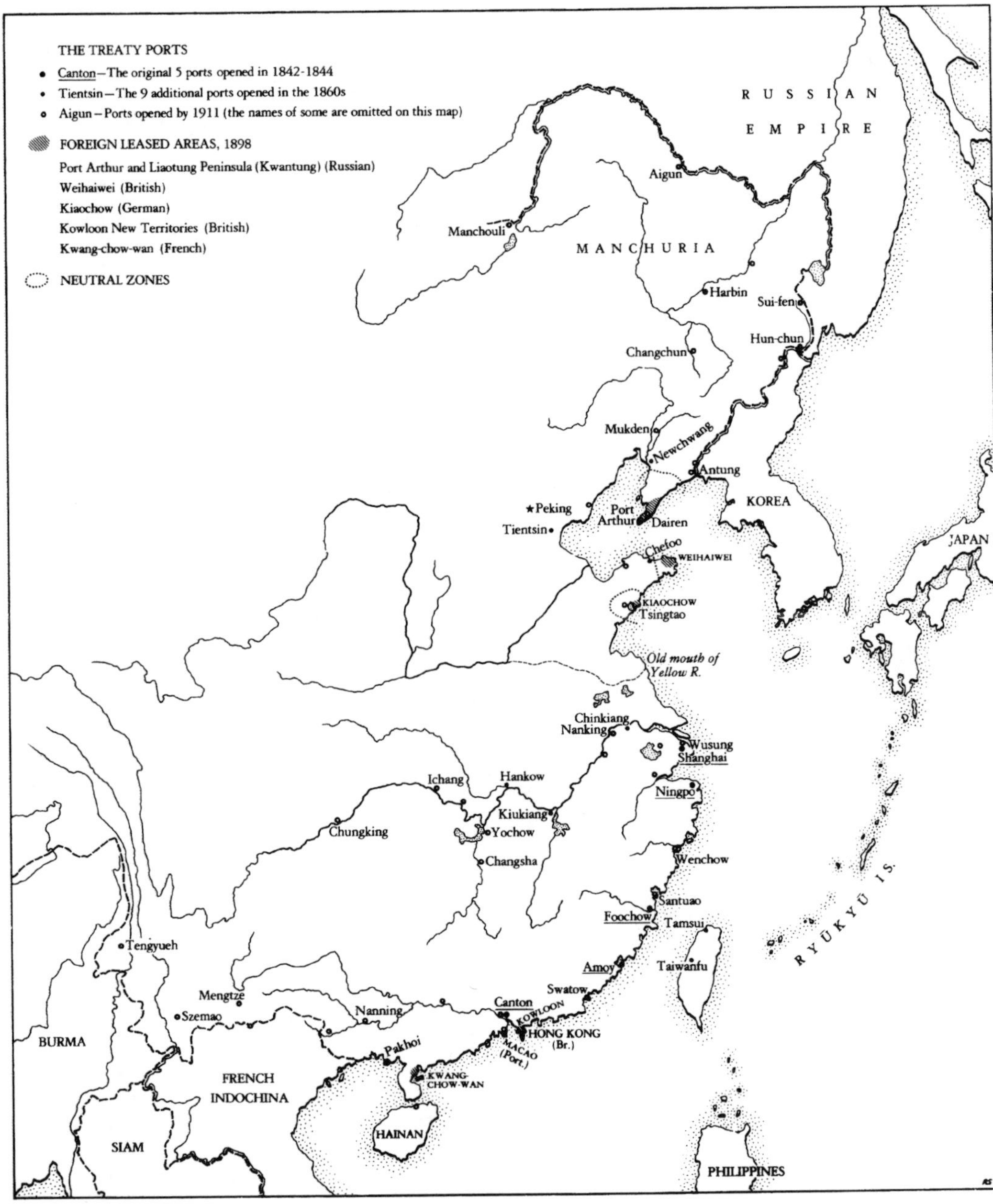

Foreign Encroachment on China. From Fairbank, John K., Edwin O. Reischauer, and Albert M. Craig, *East Asia: Tradition and Transformation*, Revised Edition. Copyright © 1989 by Houghton Mifflin Company. Used with permission.

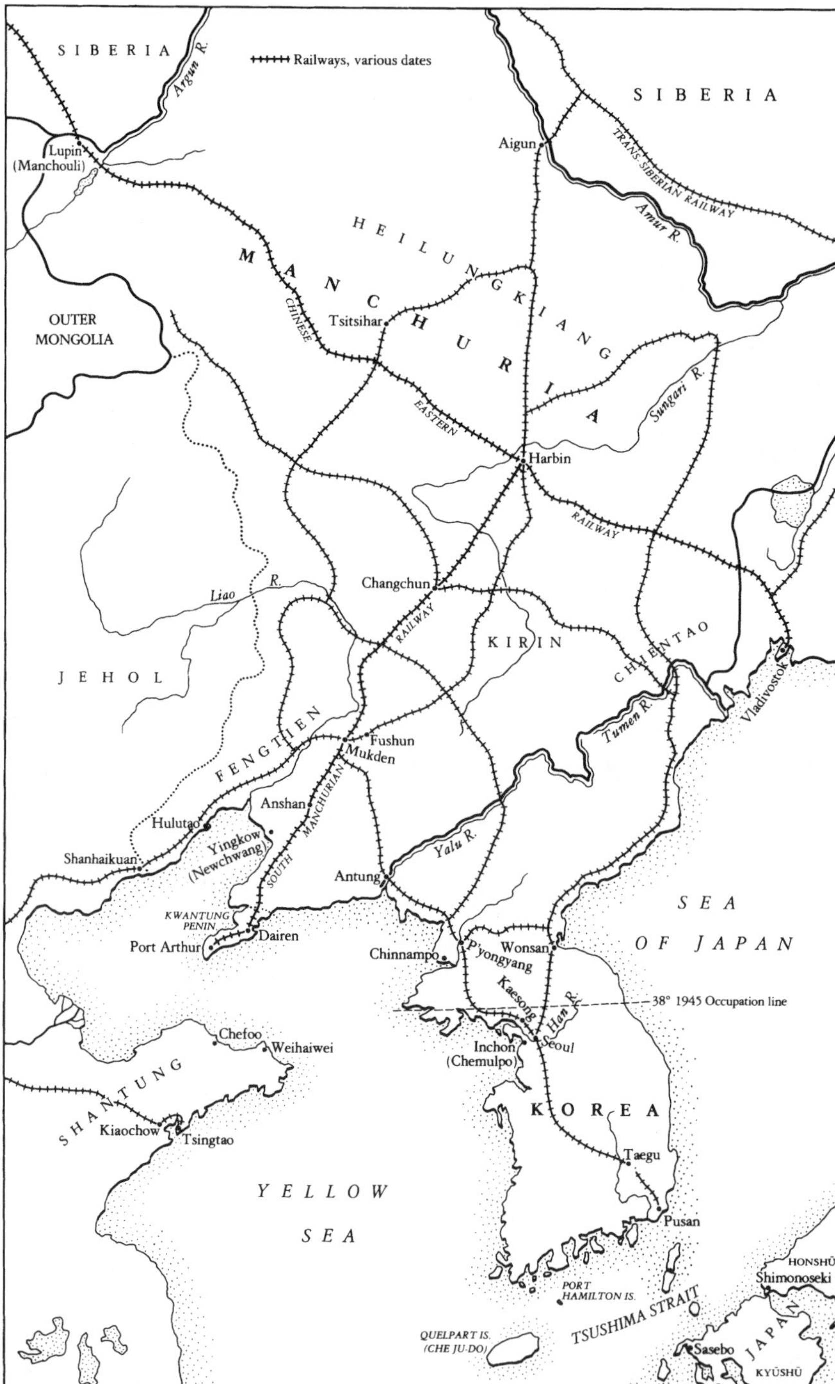

International Rivalry in Korea and Manchuria. From Fairbank, John K., Edwin O. Reischauer, and Albert M. Craig, *East Asia: Tradition and Transformation*, Revised Edition. Copyright © 1989 by Houghton Mifflin Company. Used with permission.

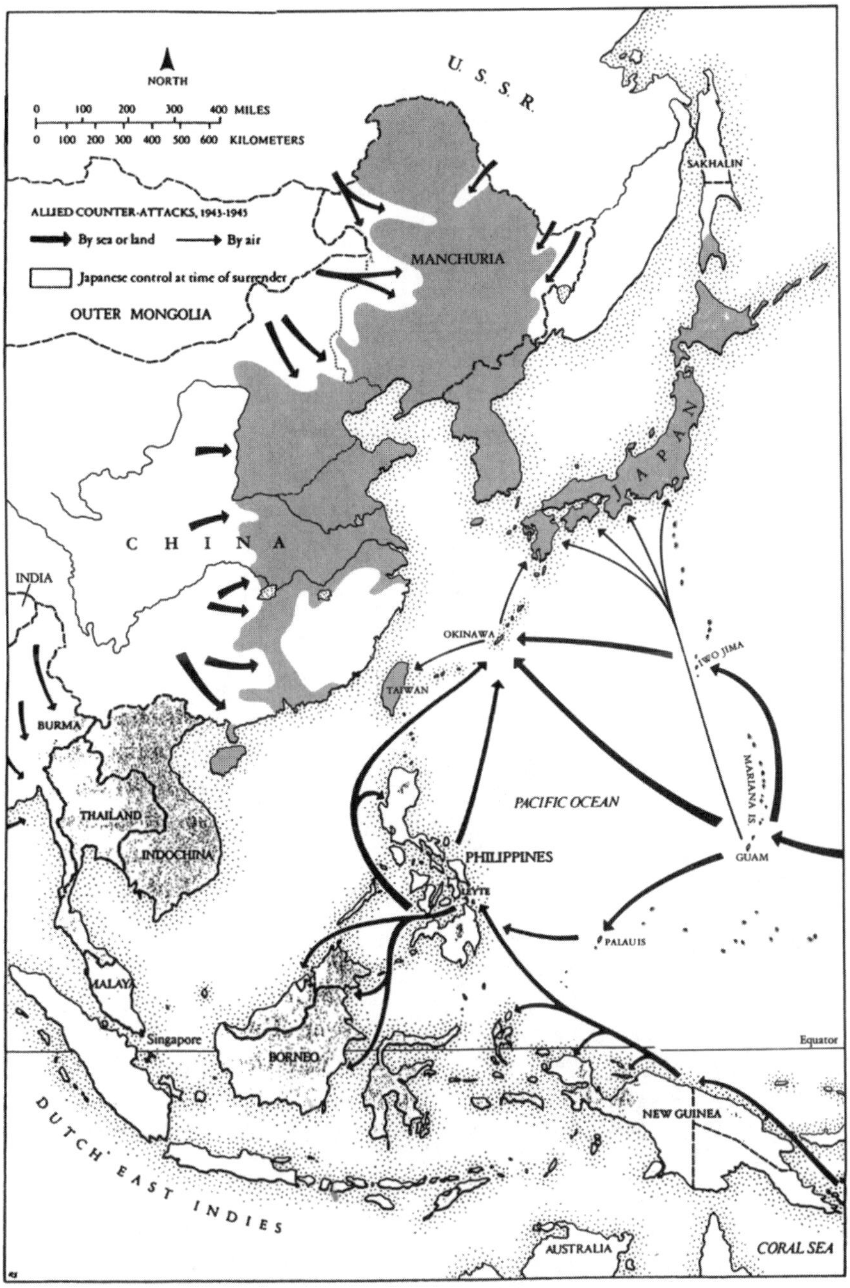

World War II in Greater East Asia. From Fairbank, John K., Edwin O. Reischauer, and Albert M. Craig, *East Asia: Tradition and Transformation,* Revised Edition. Copyright © 1989 by Houghton Mifflin Company. Used with permission.

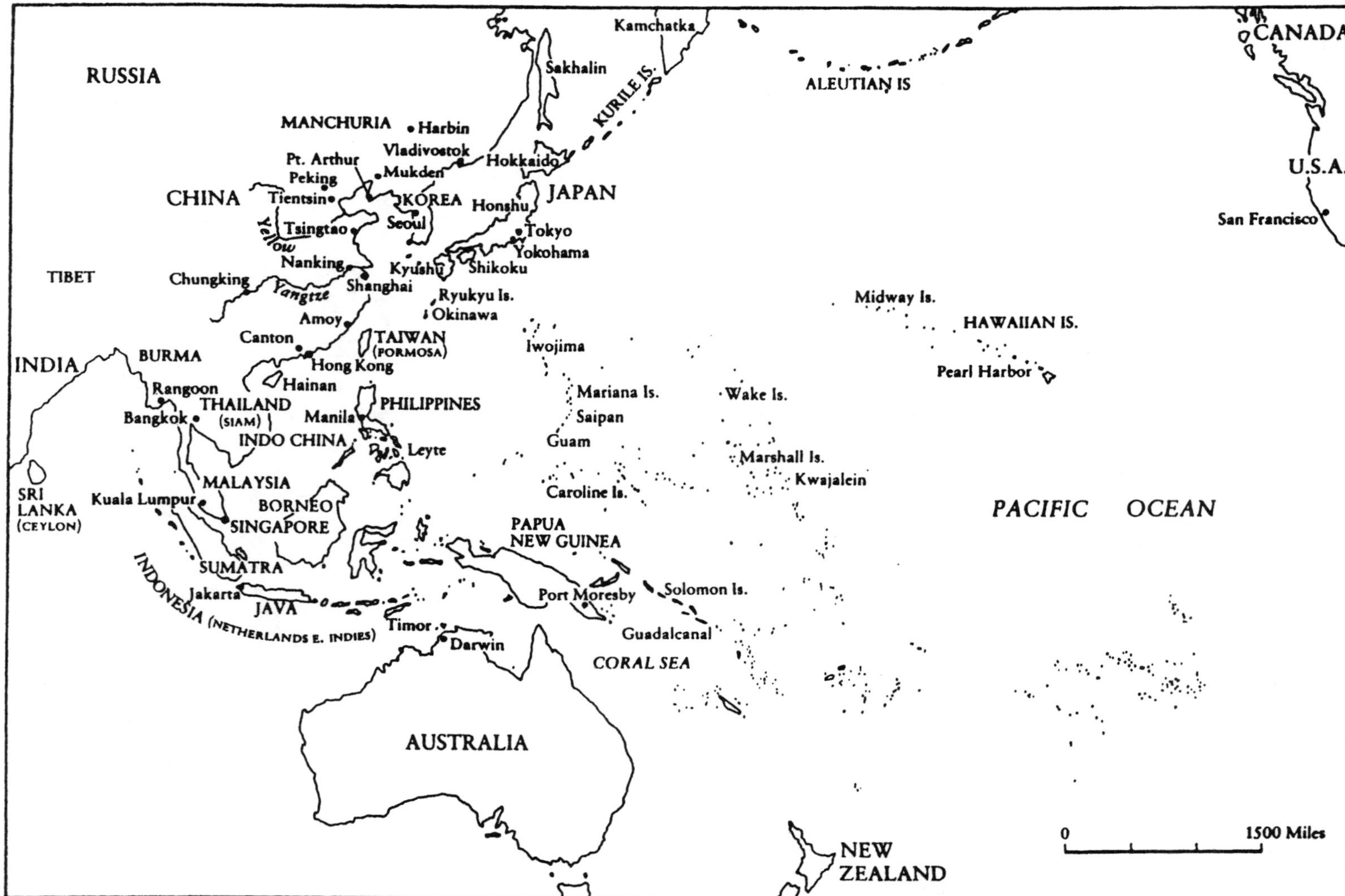

The Asia-Pacific Context. From Sydney Giffard, *Japan among the Powers, 1890–1990* (New Haven, CT: Yale University Press, 1997). Copyright © 1994 by Sydney Giffard. Reprinted with the permission of the publisher.

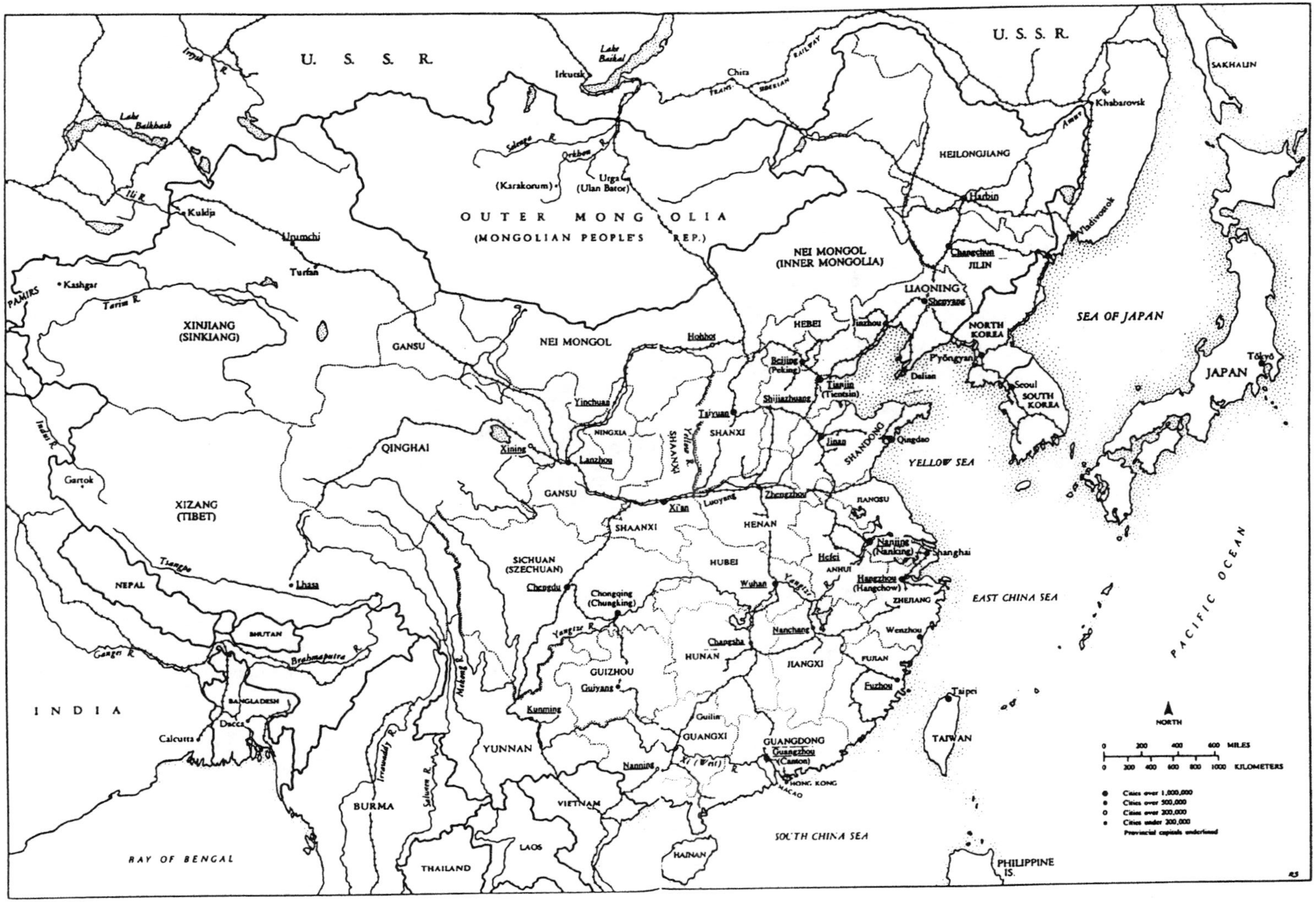

China: The People's Republic. From Fairbank, John K., Edwin O. Reischauer, and Albert M. Craig, *East Asia: Tradition and Transformation*, Revised Edition. Copyright © 1989 by Houghton Mifflin Company. Used with permission.

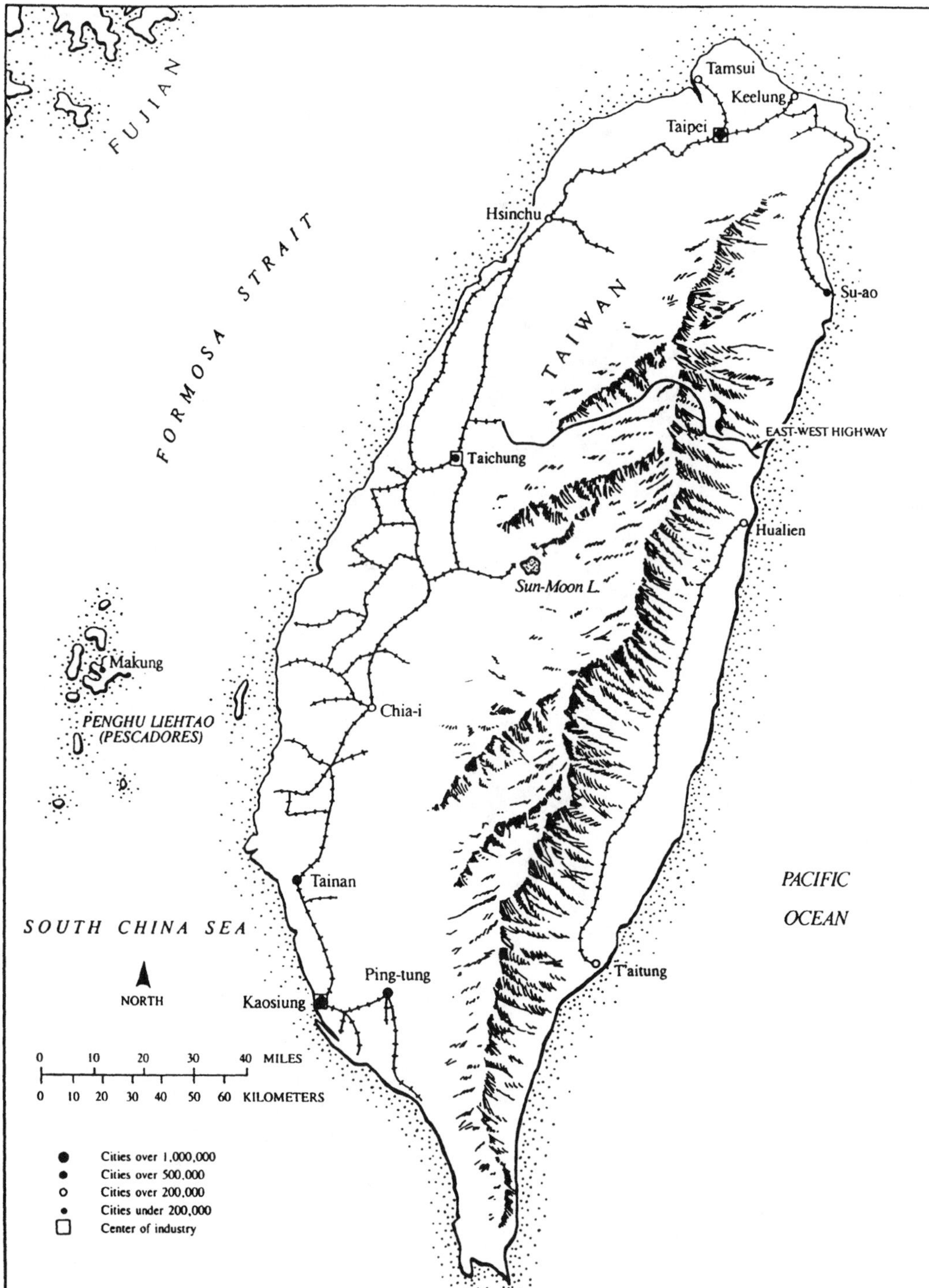

Taiwan. From Fairbank, John K., Edwin O. Reischauer, and Albert M. Craig, *East Asia: Tradition and Transformation*, Revised Edition. Copyright © 1989 by Houghton Mifflin Company. Used with permission.

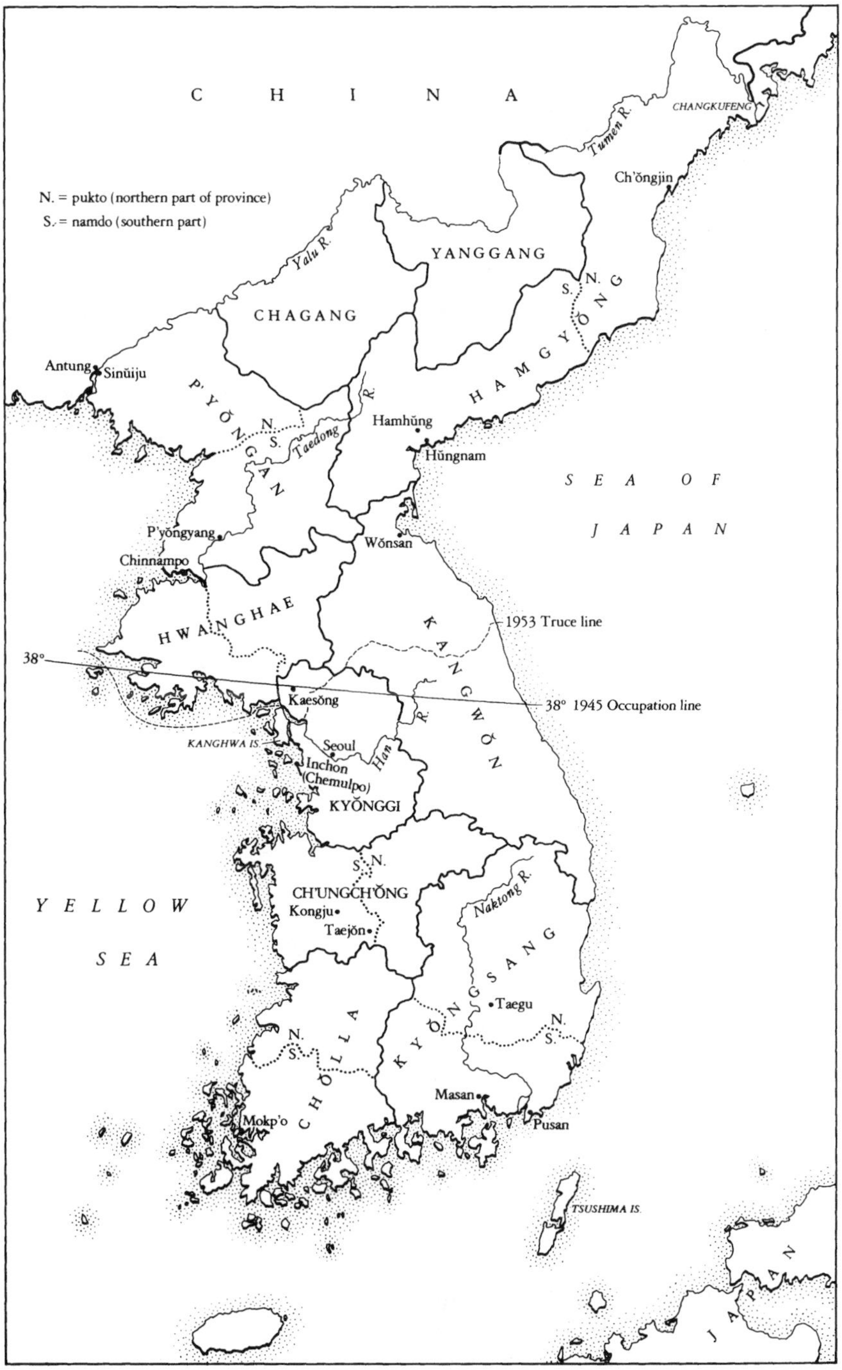

Korea in Recent Times. From Fairbank, John K., Edwin O. Reischauer, and Albert M. Craig, *East Asia: Tradition and Transformation*, Revised Edition. Copyright © 1989 by Houghton Mifflin Company. Used with permission.

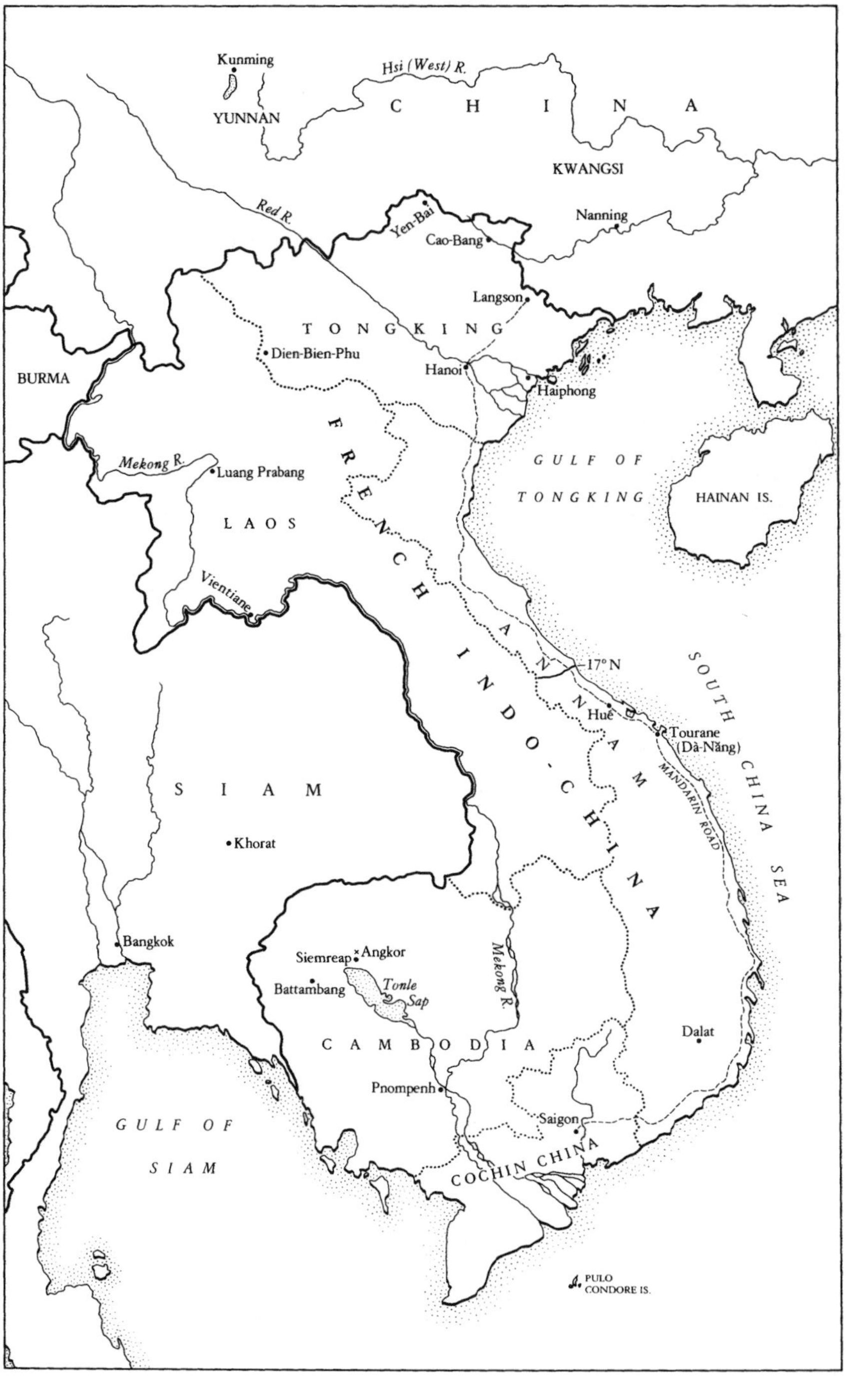

Above: French Indo-China. From Fairbank, John K., Edwin O. Reischauer, and Albert M. Craig, *East Asia: Tradition and Transformation,* Revised Edition. Copyright © 1989 by Houghton Mifflin Company. Used with permission.
Opposite page, top: Singapore. From Fairbank, John K., Edwin O. Reischauer, and Albert M. Craig, *East Asia: Tradition and Transformation,* Revised Edition. Copyright © 1989 by Houghton Mifflin Company. Used with permission.
Opposite page, bottom: Hong Kong. From Fairbank, John K., Edwin O. Reischauer, and Albert M. Craig, *East Asia: Tradition and Transformation,* Revised Edition. Copyright © 1989 by Houghton Mifflin Company. Used with permission.

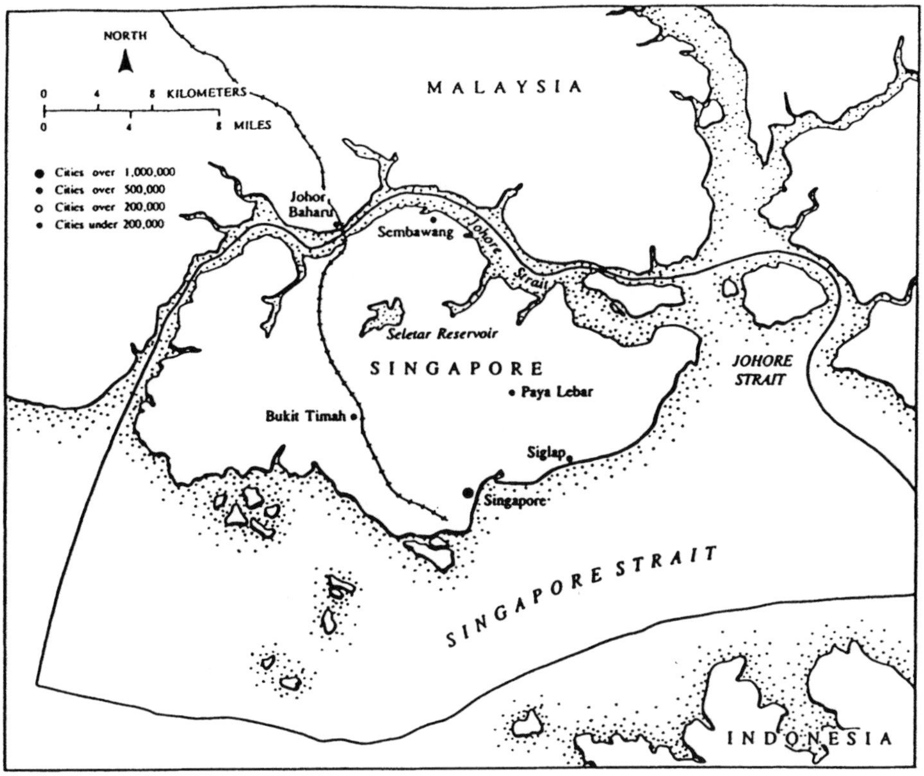
NORTH
0 4 8 KILOMETERS
0 4 8 MILES
Cities over 1,000,000
Cities over 500,000
Cities over 200,000
Cities under 200,000
MALAYSIA
Johor Baharu
Sembawang
Johore Strait
Seletar Reservoir
SINGAPORE
Paya Lebar
Bukit Timah
Siglap
Singapore
JOHORE STRAIT
SINGAPORE STRAIT
INDONESIA

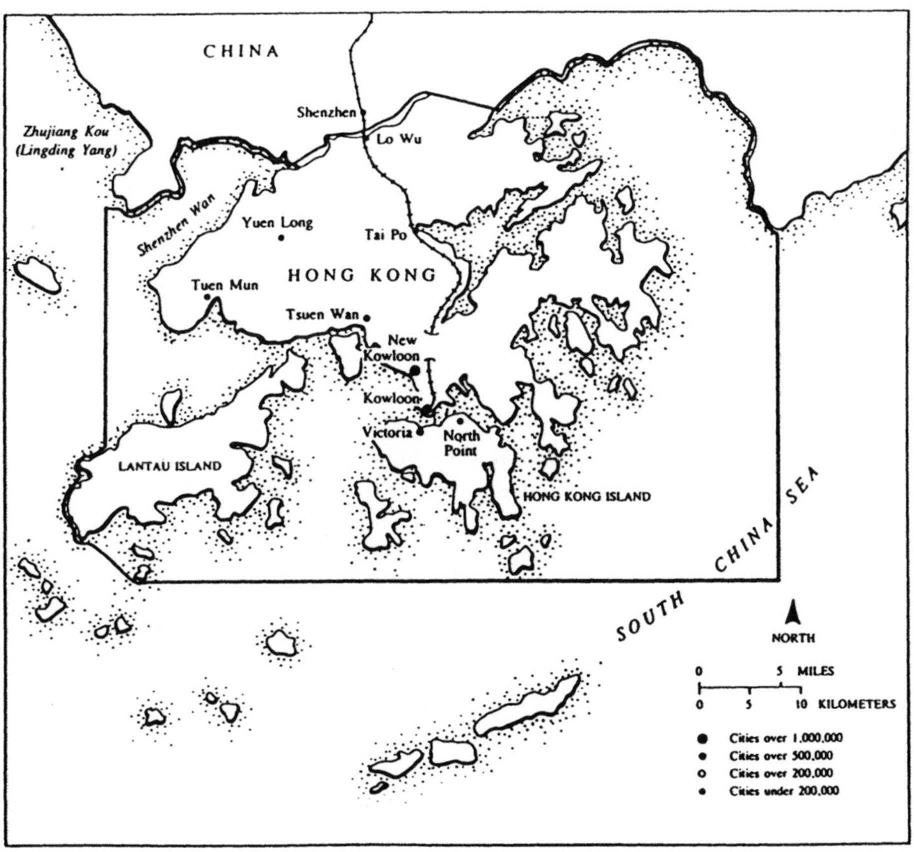
CHINA
Shenzhen
Lo Wu
Zhujiang Kou (Lingding Yang)
Shenzhen Wan
Yuen Long
Tai Po
HONG KONG
Tuen Mun
Tsuen Wan
New Kowloon
Kowloon
Victoria
North Point
LANTAU ISLAND
HONG KONG ISLAND
SOUTH CHINA SEA
NORTH
0 5 MILES
0 5 10 KILOMETERS
Cities over 1,000,000
Cities over 500,000
Cities over 200,000
Cities under 200,000

N

NAKASONE YASUHIRO (1918–)

Nakasone Yasuhiro was prime minister of Japan from 1982 to 1987, far longer than any of his peers and second only to Satō Eisaku* and Yoshida Shigeru* in the postwar era. After graduating from Tōkyō University, he entered the Ministry of the Interior in 1941. During World War II, he enlisted in the Imperial Navy. Soon after the war, he entered politics and was elected to the lower house of the Diet in 1947. As a young politician during the U.S. Occupation of Japan*, he became known for his effective criticism of the Yoshida administration for its subservience to SCAP* and General Douglas MacArthur*. He also advocated revising the Japanese Constitution of 1947* and rearmament. After participating in the establishment of the Liberal Democratic Party* (LDP) in 1955, he remained estranged from the party's mainstream because the political heirs of Yoshida, such as Ikeda Hayato* and Satō, dominated it. Even though he became minister of transportation in 1967, director general of the Defense Agency in 1970, and head of the Ministry of International Trade and Industry* (MITI) in 1972, he had to wait to become the prime minister.

On taking office, Nakasone's slogan was to "supervise the end of the postwar era." His administration also searched for a more active international role for an emergent economic superpower. Nakasone's dynamic leadership style, which was often dubbed "presidential," was rather unusual in Japanese politics, with its emphasis on top-down decision making and heavy reliance on media publicity and public opinion. Initially, as leader of a relatively small faction, Nakasone had to depend heavily on the support of Tanaka Kakuei* and his powerful LDP faction to maintain power, but he gradually broadened his political base as his popularity rose and particularly after Tanaka suffered a stroke in 1985. For Nakasone, by far the greatest domestic policy agenda was administrative reform, particularly the privatization of national railroads, telephone, and tobacco state monopolies, which were privatized successfully. His domestic initiatives coincided with contemporary neoconservative trends in Western democracies, especially those of President Ronald Reagan* in the United States and Prime Minister Margaret Thatcher in Britain. In fact, Nakasone and Reagan formed a close partnership because of their personal and ideological affinity, as well as their strong anti-Sovietism and emphasis on greater military strength. Their frequent meetings prompted references to the "Ron and Yasu Show."

Nakasone took pains to align Japan's defense posture more closely with that of the United States. In his first meeting with Reagan in early 1983, he unabashedly called the Japan-U.S. security relationship a military alliance, referred to Japan as "an unsinkable aircraft carrier" for the West, and signed a Japan-U.S. Defense Technology Exchange Agreement, a significant exception to the traditional policy of prohibiting arms exports. He also sought to respond to U.S. requests for greater defense spending by lifting briefly the ceiling that limited defense spending to less than 1 percent of Japan's gross national product. Disputes over U.S.-Japan Postwar Trade Relations* escalated in his years, which forced Nakasone to publish the Maekwa Report, proposing a comprehensive opening of the Japanese market to foreign goods and services. His rather hawkish defense posture often alarmed both Japanese citizens as well as Asian neighbors. Nakasone also was criticized severely in the United States for his September 1986 racial comments about American minorities, for which he later formally apologized. After Nakasone stepped aside as prime minister in November 1987, he maintained political influence within the LDP.

K. Hayano, *The Japanese Prime Minister and Public Policy* (Pittsburgh, PA, 1993); Nakasone Yasuhiro, *Seiji to jinsei: Nakasone Yasuhiro kaikoroku* [Politics and Life: Memoirs of Nakasone Yasuhiro] (Tōkyō, 1992); Watanabe Akio (ed.), *Sengo Nihon no saishō tachi* [Postwar Japanese Prime Ministers] (Tōkyō, 1995).

Kamimura Naoki

NASUTION, ABDUL HARIS (1918–2000)

General Abdul Haris Nasution was one of the most influential Indonesian military figures of the twentieth century. A skilled military and political leader, as well as a devout nationalist and Muslim, the firmly anti-Communist Nasution decisively shaped Indonesian military doctrine and ideology for much of the postwar period. Born in Kotanopan, North Sumatra, he graduated from the Bandung Military Academy in 1942 and became a division chief in the Indonesian People's Military. He was chief of Division 1 in the Siliwangi Military Command from 1946 to 1948 and then armed forces chief of staff from 1949 to 1952 and again from 1955 to 1962. In 1962, Sukarno* named General Achmed Yani as chief of staff and "promoted" Nasution to the nominally more powerful, but functionally symbolic post of defense minister, a position he held until the spring of 1966, when Sukarno attempted to dismiss him.

Nasution played a major role in the development not only of Indonesian military doctrine, but also the military's role in the Indonesian polity and economy. He was largely responsible for the concept of territorial warfare, under which regions of the country would be organized independently to defend against external attack, a notion that also provided the basis for the doctrine of Civic Mission, a homegrown version of the U.S. Army's Civic Action Program. Perhaps most important, the Indonesian takeover of Dutch enterprises in 1957 provided the basis of Nasution's argument that the military must perform a "dual function" (*dwi-fungsi*) as both defenders of the Indonesian Revolution and guardians of the nation's political and economic stability. Nasution's success in defeating the PRRI-Permesta Rebellion* and U.S. fears about increased Soviet influence in Indonesia* led to a shame-faced reversal of administration policy under President Dwight D. Eisenhower*. When Nasution visited the United States in the summer of 1958, he found U.S. officials more receptive to his requests for military aid. He also became friends with General Maxwell D. Taylor*, then U.S. Army chief of staff, a crucial relationship that Nasution continued to cultivate even as U.S. economic and military assistance was withdrawn because of Indonesia's military confrontation with Malaysia* from late 1962 until 1966.

During the Indonesia Crisis of 1965*, Nasution escaped capture by Lieutenant Colonel Untung's forces. During the alleged coup of 30 September, Untung's soldiers, however, accidentally shot and killed his daughter, provoking much public outrage, especially when President Sukarno failed to attend her funeral. Nasution maintained close liaison contact with the U.S. embassy during the struggle with Sukarno and the Indonesian Communist Party massacres that followed. Many U.S. officials in fact expected Nasution, not General Suharto*, to take power. He was appointed speaker of the Provisional People's Consultative Assembly in 1966, but declined requests from military officers to replace Sukarno. Nasution emerged as a quiet but persistent critic of the New Order regime of Suharto. He already had earned Suharto's ire during the early 1960s when he investigated Suharto for smuggling in northern Sumatra and now opposed the government's blatant corruption. Furthermore, the military under Suharto distorted his concept of its "dual function" to achieve military dominance in the political and economic sphere. Nasution retired from the military in 1972, but remained active as an author on Indonesian politics and religion.

H. Feith, *The Decline of Constitutional Democracy in Indonesia* (Ithaca, NY, 1962); A. Kahin and G. McT. Kahin, *Subversion as Foreign Policy: Eisenhower, Dulles, and the Indonesian Debacle* (Ithaca, NY, 1994); G. McT. Kahin, *Nationalism and Revolution in Indonesia* (Ithaca, NY, 1952); C. L. M. Penders and U. Sundhaussen, *Abdul Haris Nasution: A Political Biography* (Queensland, 1985).

Bradley R. Simpson

NATION-BUILDING STRATEGY

The nation-building strategy was the U.S. Cold War policy of promoting U.S. influence and defeating Communist revolutionaries in newly independent Third World countries. The formulation of this strategy was partly influenced by the success of American postwar economic and military assistance programs in Europe and Japan. It also was shaped by official acceptance of development and modernization theories put forth by American social scientists who argued that industrial nations such as the United States could play a major role in modernizing Third World societies. This could be done, they claimed, by U.S. help in creating constitutional governments, efficient bureaucratic institutions, prosperous economies based on access to Western technology and markets, and a sense of nationhood transcending parochial regional and political loyalties. These scholars urged the United States to develop training, technical assistance, and land reform programs to meet these goals and often worked with U.S. officials in devising these programs.

The effort to carry out the nation-building strategy reached its height in the 1960s, when modernization theorists such as Walt W. Rostow* held senior positions in the Kennedy and Johnson administrations and when the United States promoted nation-building programs in the Republic of Vietnam*, Thailand*, and the Philippines*. Efforts to implement the strategy, however, frequently were thwarted by the recipient governments, especially in South Vietnam, who showed an interest only in programs that helped them consolidate their political power while ignoring or rejecting projects that threatened this power. The strategy also was attacked by Americans who opposed the escalating U.S. involvement in the Second Indochina War*, especially academic critics who questioned its assumptions. Opponents of the strategy asserted that it was based on assumptions that overestimated the U.S. ability to influence Third World nations and condescendingly regarded these countries as "underdeveloped" nations in need of improvement. Moreover, they charged that the strategy was used to strengthen unjust and authoritarian anti-Communist governments in the Third World. Because of its close association with the war in Vietnam, the term "nation building" fell out of use by the 1970s, but some of the ideas of development theories that shaped the strategy still exercise an influence in formulating U.S. policies toward the Third World. *See also* Wesley R. Fishel; Strategic Hamlets Program.

J. K. Black, *Development in Theory and Practice: Bridging the Gap* (Boulder, CO, 1991); N. Cullather, "Development? Its History," *Diplomatic History* (Fall 2000); I. L. Gendzier, "Play It Again, Sam: The Practice and Apology of Development," in Christopher Simpson (ed.), *Universities and Empire: Money and Politics in Social Sciences During the Cold War* (New York, 1998); M. H. Hunt, *Ideology and U.S. Foreign Policy* (New Haven, CT, 1987); R. A. Packenham, *Liberal America and the Third World: Political Development Ideas in Foreign Aid and Social Science* (Princeton, NJ, 1973).

Joseph G. Morgan

NATIONAL LEAGUE OF FAMILIES OF AMERICANS MISSING IN SOUTHEAST ASIA

Established in 1970, the National League of Families of Americans Missing in Southeast Asia was dedicated to obtaining information about U.S. soldiers missing in the Second Indochina War*. Initially working with the U.S. government to discredit the Democratic Republic of Vietnam* for its unwillingness to release U.S. prisoners of war (POWs) or even information about them, it parted company with President Richard M. Nixon* in the spring of 1973—during Operation HOMECOMING—when the president insisted that all living American soldiers had returned to the United States after the Paris Peace Accords*. For the next twenty-two years, the league sought to create a political and popular climate of suspicion about North Vietnam, the Socialist Republic of Vietnam* after 1975. Although its initial goal had been to gain knowledge about the fates of its members' loved ones, many of whose planes (most of the soldiers were pilots) crashed in remote areas, it began working with another organization, the Victory in Vietnam Association, to prevent reconstruction assistance from going to Vietnam. It also sought to avert the reclassification of soldiers from missing in action (MIA) to a presumed finding of death.

President Ronald Reagan* offered a more sympathetic ear to the league and its cause. Hence, the issue of POWs/MIAs in Vietnam received far greater public and political attention and figured more prominently in talks with the Vietnamese over normalizing relations. In addition to the ubiquitous bracelets, flags, and ceremonies, all designed to sustain public remembrance of those supposedly left behind, as well as keeping diplomatic pressure on the Vietnamese, the league's actions helped foster the culture of novels and films depicting heroic Vietnam veterans returning to Southeast Asia to rescue their forgotten comrades. No American soldiers were ever found to have been left behind, and the United States and Vietnam resumed full diplomatic relations in 1995 under President Bill Clinton*.

H. B. Franklin, *M.I.A. or Mythmaking in America: How and Why Belief in Live POWs Has Possessed a Nation* (Brooklyn, 1992); T. C. Jespersen, "The Bitter End and the Lost Chance in Vietnam: Congress, the Ford Administration, and the Battle Over Vietnam, 1975–1976," *Diplomatic History* (Spring 2000); M. Jensen-Stevenson and W. Stevenson, *Kiss the Boys Goodbye: How the United States Betrayed Its Own POWs in Vietnam* (New York, 1990).

T. Christopher Jespersen

NATIONAL LIBERATION FRONT

The National Front for the Liberation of South Vietnam (Mat tran dan toc giai phong Mien nam Viet nam), commonly called the NLF, was founded on 20 December 1960 as the official leadership organization for the guerrilla war then already under way in the Republic of Vietnam*. It presented itself as a coalition of South Vietnamese Communists and non-Communists, controlled by neither the Democratic Republic of Vietnam* nor its Communist members. Its president, Nguyen Huu Tho, was a Saigon attorney without a known record of membership in the Vietnamese Communist Party. In 1969, the NLF was superceded by the Provisional Revolutionary Government of the Republic of South Vietnam (PRG), which maintained the same theory that it was independent of Hanoi.

During the Second Indochina War*, those in the United States and other Western countries who sympathized with the guerrillas in South Vietnam usually called them the NLF. Many of these people accepted in whole or in part the claims the NLF made that it was an independent organization not dominated by Communists. Supporters of the U.S. war effort against the guerrillas usually thought of the NLF as a sham, a puppet controlled by North Vietnam, and called the guerrillas the Viet Cong*. They later often said that the true situation was revealed at the end of the war, when Vietnam was united under Communist rule and its leaders were all North Vietnamese, adding that none of the leaders of the NLF had any important role in the postwar Socialist Republic of Vietnam*.

Each viewpoint was mistaken in important respects. It is plain in retrospect that Nguyen Huu Tho had been largely a figurehead. The people in the NLF who had real power were the Communists. Furthermore, the nominal independence of the NLF from Hanoi's control also had been a public relations ploy. The real Communist power structure behind the mask of the NLF (and later the PRG), however, had not been made up simply of North Vietnamese. South Vietnamese Communists—some of them in the NLF structure in South Vietnam, and some in Hanoi—had a great deal of real power. The commonly heard statement that none of the South Vietnamese who had been listed as official leaders in the NLF emerged in leading postwar positions is simply false. Le Duan, head of the Communist Party in Hanoi from 1969 until he died in 1986, had been born in South Vietnam. He brought other southerners, notably the NLF leaders Ung Van Khiem and Vo Van Kiet, into the highest leadership of the Communist government after the war ended and Vietnam was reunified. Vo Van Kiet in fact became prime minister in 1991.

J. Race, *War Comes to Long An: Revolutionary Conflict in a Vietnamese Province* (Berkeley, CA, 1972); Truong Nhu Tang, *A Viet Cong Memoir* (New York, 1985).

Edwin E. Moise

NATIONAL ORIGINS ACT (26 May 1924)

On 26 May 1924, President Calvin Coolidge signed into law the most restrictive immigration legislation in U.S. history. When the law was put into effect on 1 July, the Tōkyō press declared it a day of national mourning. The Immigration Act of 1924 (also known as the Quota Immigration Law, National Origins Act, and the Japanese Exclusion Act) effectively ended all Asian immigration to the United States. Its key provisions were quota restrictions based on national origins derived from the census of 1890 rather than 1910, quota admitted for any one year reduced from 3 to 2 percent, and aliens barred from entering the United States who were ineligible for citizenship. The 1924 law built on the Immigration Act of 1917, which established a Pacific Barred Zone by extending the Chinese Exclusion Acts* to other Asians. The zone covered South Asia from Arabia to French Indochina*, including India, Burma*, Thailand*, Malaya*, Dutch East Indies, Polynesia, and parts of Arabia and Afghanistan. In 1922 and 1923, two key U.S. Supreme Court decisions, *U.S. v. Ozawa* and *U.S. v. Thind*, had ruled that the naturalization right did not apply to Asians.

On 10 April 1924, while the National Origins Act was still pending in the U.S. Senate, Japanese Ambassador Hanihara

Masanao wrote a letter to Secretary of State Charles Evans Hughes* expressing his reservation about the bill and warning that "grave consequences" might result between the two nations if it passed. Hoping that these words might persuade Congress to eliminate the Japanese exclusion provision in the bill "in the interest of our international relations," Hughes transmitted the letter to the Senate. But this effort backfired, as Senator Henry Cabot Lodge* and supporters of the bill described Hanihara's words as a "veiled threat." Subsequent passage of the 1924 Immigration Act was a major factor in the worsening of Japanese-American relations during the interwar period. Along with Hughes, John V. A. MacMurray*, chief of the Far Eastern Division of the State Department, had urged Hanihara to use tough language because they worried at the time that such exclusionist legislation would weaken the "conciliatory party" in Japan. Five days after passage of the bill, in a letter to Senator Lodge, MacMurray wrote, "I fear that our labors to create a better feeling in the East, . . . are largely undone." In fact, many Japanese began attacking U.S. "white imperialism." Burgeoning right-wing organizations in Japan exploited discrimination against the Japanese in the United States to promote mass agitation that not only discredited a policy of international cooperation, but also threatened the survival of Japanese civilian leadership. *See also* U.S. Immigration Act of 1965.

R. Daniels, *The Politics of Prejudice: The Anti-Japanese Movement in California, and the Struggle for Japanese Exclusion* (Berkeley, CA, 1977); B. O. Hing, *Making and Remaking of Asian America Through Immigration Policy, 1850–1990* (Stanford, CA, 1993); J. Vialet, *A Brief History of U.S. Immigration Policy* (Washington, DC, 1980).

Roger Y. M. Chan

NAVARRE PLAN

The Navarre Plan, named after French General Henri Navarre, proposed a slow buildup of French and Vietnamese military strength sufficient for large-scale action against Ho Chi Minh* and his Vietminh* during the campaign season of 1954 and 1955. Considered a brilliant strategist, Navarre was appointed commander of France's forces in Indochina on 8 May 1953, although he had little knowledge of the situation there. French Prime Minister René Mayer urged him to find an honorable way out of the First Indochina War* (1946–1954), while keeping French casualties to a minimum. Navarre developed the plan after three weeks in French Indochina*, providing for the French to use cautious restraint, and reconstituting the French Expeditionary Corps (FEC). The FEC would maintain a defensive position north of the eighteenth parallel, using mobile units for short engagements and avoiding a general battle. In the south, the FEC would launch an offensive aimed at eliminating the Vietminh, then taking the offensive to the north. Navarre's aim was to create a military situation leading to a political solution to the conflict. Needing reinforcements from France, he admitted that the best he could accomplish would be a military stalemate.

The French government approved the Navarre Plan, although it did not reach a decision on what to do about the defense of northern Laos*. In the spring of 1953, the Vietminh commander, General Vo Nguyen Giap*, had sent troops into Laos from the remote village of Dien Bien Phu*, in mountainous northwestern Vietnam, just a few miles from the Laotian border. Giap then withdrew, but the French expected that the Vietminh would attack again in 1954. For the French command, the taking of Dien Bien Phu became a critical objective to prevent another attack on Laos and create a mooring point from which an offensive could be launched to destroy a major part of the Vietminh army. Navarre decided to draw the Vietminh into battle where superior firepower and control of the skies would ensure success. He took the calculated risk of garrisoning Dien Bien Phu with the best units and reserves from the Tonkin delta. According to Navarre, Giap lacked the logistic capacity to concentrate enough troops to overwhelm the garrison. The French artillery and air power would pulverize any artillery the Vietminh attempted to emplace on the heights overlooking the valley. Two airfields in the valley would supply and reinforce the garrison.

Dien Bien Phu, according to Navarre, would inflict a stunning defeat on the Vietminh and was the final element in the Navarre Plan. The United States agreed to support his plan in 1953 with nearly $400 million in assistance, indicating American approval of what was considered a more aggressive campaign in Indochina. But some of his subordinates, including Major General René Cogny, commander of the Tonkin theater, were unconvinced that Navarre's strategy was sound. The battle at Dien Bien Phu began on 13 March 1954, and soon it became apparent that Navarre totally had miscalculated Giap's intentions and capabilities. The Vietminh had superior numbers, guns, and strategy. After being bombarded for almost two months, the French finally were forced to surrender on 7 May. The Navarre Plan represented the last French effort to take the offensive in the First Indochina War. Even though Dien Bien Phu was not a significant victory for the Vietminh militarily, the war-weary French became determined to end the war at the Geneva Conference of 1954*. The failure of the Navarre Plan convinced the Eisenhower administration that the United States would have to halt the Communist advance in Indochina on its own.

J. Dalloz, *The War in Indochina 1945–1954* (Dublin, 1990); W. Duiker, *U.S. Containment Policy and the Conflict in Indochina* (Stanford, CA, 1994); P. Ely, *Mémoires: L'Indochine dans La Tourmente* (Paris, 1964); H. Navarre, *Agonie de l'Indochine, 1953–1954* (Paris, 1956); J. Roy, *The Battle of Dien Bien Phu* (New York, 1965).

Kathryn C. Statler

NE WIN (1911–)

From 1962 to 1988, Ne Win served as political leader of Burma*, although with a variety of titles. Born Shu Maung, he attended Rangoon University, but left without a degree. After his university experience, he joined the nationalist movement and was, along with Aung San*, one of the "Thirty Comrades" trained in Japan during World War II. It was at this time that he took the name Ne Win. Ne Win stayed in the military after independence, serving as commander in chief of the armed forces from 1949 to 1971. He was not active in politics in the 1950s until asked by Prime Minister U Nu* to head a caretaker government, lasting from 1958 to 1960. During that time, he was occupied primarily with domestic political issues.

After retaking power in a coup in March 1962, Ne Win instituted a military government, which he headed until 1988. He was distrustful of foreign powers, and the first few years of his rule saw a pulling back from the world. One component was his autarkic economic program, the Burmese Way to Socialism. Interestingly, however, Burma continued to purchase arms and military equipment from the United States from 1958 to 1970. By the mid-1960s, Ne Win began an effort to balance his contacts with the People's Republic of China* (PRC) and the Soviet Union by reaching out again to the United States and visiting Washington in 1966. Until the United States formally recognized the PRC under President Jimmy Carter*, he paid more attention to relations with the neighborhood superpower, China, than with the distant superpower, the United States. He visited the PRC three times from 1975 to 1977, but made no repeat visit to the United States.

After joining the Asian Development Bank in 1973, Ne Win worked assiduously during the late 1970s to cultivate regional and economic relations. He extended the effort to the United States in the 1980s; Burma resumed economic cooperation with the United States in 1980, and military aid from Washington began again in 1981. But Ne Win continued to emphasize Burma's neutralism by cultivating relations with a wide range of countries and international institutions. Burma's 1987 appeal to the United Nations for least-developed-nation status did result in some increased economic aid from both the United Nations and the United States, but also was perceived as an admission that Ne Win's Burmese Way to Socialism had failed. It also made it easier for people to express their growing disenchantment with the government; one result was widespread support for the initially student-led democracy protests of 1988. Ne Win responded to the 1988 democracy protests by resigning on 23 July from his post as chairman of the ruling Burma Socialist Programme Party. Thereafter, however, he was widely rumored to be maintaining preponderant control from behind the scenes.

C. Liang, *Burma's Foreign Relations: Neutralism in Theory and Practice* (New York, 1990); R. H. Taylor, *The State in Burma* (Honolulu, HI, 1987).

Anne L. Foster

NEUTRALIZATION OF TAIWAN

President Harry S. Truman* announced on 27 June 1950 that he had ordered the U.S. Seventh Fleet to protect Taiwan* against invasion from the People's Republic of China* (PRC) and to prevent Guomindang* (Nationalist) attacks against the mainland. Coming two days after the start of the Korean War*, this "neutralization" of Taiwan extended U.S. protection to the Republic of China* under Jiang Jieshi*, reversing the policy Truman had declared less than six months earlier. His action infuriated leaders of the Chinese Communist Party* in Beijing, for whom the Nationalist government on Taiwan was the last remaining obstacle to the conclusion of the Chinese Civil War* and China's reunification. Although Truman wanted to avoid tying the United States to Jiang's regime, U.S. protection for Taiwan became a long-term commitment, formalized in the U.S.-China Mutual Defense Treaty of 1954*, and for many years was the major obstacle to reconciliation between the United States and the PRC.

On 6 January 1950, Truman had declared that the United States would not intervene to prevent the fall of Taiwan and would not provide military aid to the Nationalists, a statement that anticipated Taiwan's fall to the PRC within the next year. Few believed that Nationalist forces, after collapsing on the mainland, could defend the island effectively in the face of a determined Communist attack. The Joint Chiefs of Staff did not want the island to fall into Communist hands because of its strategic position, but they also did not want to commit U.S. forces to direct support of Taiwan. Instead, they recommended a military survey, which would lead to renewed U.S. military aid. Secretary of State Dean G. Acheson* opposed this, arguing that further U.S. involvement in the Chinese Civil War would force the Chinese into the arms of the Soviets. As the debate continued in the early months of 1950, Pentagon supporters of aid to Taiwan included General Douglas MacArthur* and Secretary of Defense Louis Johnson, whereas John Foster Dulles*, special consultant, and Dean Rusk*, assistant secretary of state for Far Eastern Affairs, proposed neutralizing Taiwan. By early June, even Acheson was considering a policy reversal if Jiang Jieshi could be removed from power on Taiwan, an outcome that Washington encouraged.

Korea provided the impetus for action. When Truman and his advisers met at Blair House on 25 June, Acheson proposed that Truman order the Seventh Fleet to neutralize Taiwan. He still wanted to avoid alignment with Jiang and suggested that the future status of Taiwan might be determined by the United Nations. At the Blair House meeting the next evening, Truman approved Acheson's recommendation. In his 27 June statement, the president announced that he had ordered the Seventh Fleet "to prevent any attack on Formosa" and that, as a corollary, he was calling on the Nationalists to cease all air and sea operations against the mainland and on the Seventh Fleet to "see that this is done." Determination of the future status of Taiwan, he said, would have to await the restoration of peace in the Pacific, a peace settlement with Japan, or consideration by the United Nations.

There was virtually no discussion of the Taiwan decision at the Blair House meetings, the groundwork for the decision already having been laid. The attack on the Republic of Korea* put a premium on military and strategic considerations, but it also gave force to the argument for action to demonstrate U.S. resolve. It also raised the importance of domestic political considerations, since both Truman and Acheson needed to protect their political flank as they acted to intervene in Korea. The president's decision was popular in the United States initially, but after Chinese Intervention in the Korean War*, his order that the Seventh Fleet should prevent Nationalist attacks against the mainland came increasingly under fire. When Dwight D. Eisenhower* became president in January 1953, one of his first acts was to declare a reversal of that policy. Before long, however, he obtained a secret promise from Jiang to consult with Washington before undertaking any offensive operations against the mainland on a larger scale than the small-scale raids Truman had allowed. *See also* China Assistance Act of 1948.

R. D. Accinelli, *Crisis and Commitment: United States Policy Toward Taiwan, 1950–1955* (Chapel Hill, NC, 1996); T. J. Christensen, *Useful Adversaries: Grand Strategy, Domestic Mobilization, and Sino-American Conflict, 1947–1958* (Princeton, NJ, 1996); B. Cumings, *The Origins of the Korean War*, Vol. 2: *The Roaring of the Cataract, 1947–1950* (Princeton, NJ, 1990).

Harriet Dashiell Schwar

NGO DINH DIEM (1901–1963)

President of the Republic of Vietnam* from June 1954 to November 1963, Ngo Dinh Diem was initially the focus of U.S. support in its Nation-Building Strategy* in Vietnam. He was the third of six sons born to a prominent Catholic clan near Hue, and his father served as counselor to Emperor Thanh Thai. After studying for the civil service at the French-run School of Law and Public Administration in Hanoi, he rose to minister of the interior in 1933. Diem resigned when France proved itself unwilling to grant the states of French Indochina* greater autonomy and then shunned public life for the next two decades. In 1945, Ho Chi Minh* asked him to join the government of the Democratic Republic of Vietnam* because of his ardent nationalism. Diem, who was a strident anti-Communist, refused the offer and then traveled through Vietnam, Europe, and the United States, seeking political support. During this time, he made important contacts with Vietnamese exiles in Paris, as well as Americans such as Cardinal Spellman and Senators John F. Kennedy* and Mike Mansfield*. Emperor Bao Dai*, believing the United States backed Diem and seeing the Vietminh* as a threat to his political future, appointed Diem prime minister. Two weeks after he took office, the French signed a cease-fire agreement at the Geneva Conference of 1954*.

A Catholic in a predominantly Buddhist nation and a recluse for twenty years, Diem was not well known in Vietnam and relied almost exclusively on his family. He concentrated authority in his own hands and those of his brothers, and failed to enact reform programs or build a broad-based popular government. Nevertheless, Diem initially succeeded at staving off challenges to his authority. He stalled the reunification elections called for in the Geneva Accords of 1954* and held a fraudulent election for the presidency of South Vietnam in 1955, defeating Bao Dai with 98.2 percent of the vote. Diem also defeated the Cao Dai*, Binh Xuyen*, and Hoa Hao sects, and survived a coup attempt in 1960. Meanwhile, he sought and received massive assistance from Washington, exceeding $2 billion in the 1950s. After recognizing Diem's regime, President Dwight D. Eisenhower* dispatched Colonel Edward G. Lansdale* to counsel him in anti-Communist counterinsurgency. His proponent Wesley R. Fishel* was another key adviser. Diem spent eight of every ten U.S. aid dollars for internal security, but Communist guerrilla activities resumed in the late 1950s. In response, he and his brother Ngo Dinh Nhu* conducted policies of repression, launching raids and frequently arresting and torturing relatives of Communist Party members. The Saigon government also failed to build support from the peasantry, reimposing old taxes and exactions and returning land to the landlords.

When Kennedy became president, he demanded that Diem institute domestic reforms, but believed there was no other viable alternative. During the Kennedy administration, the size of the Army of the Republic of Vietnam* increased by 100,000 men, and U.S. forces in Vietnam rose to more than 16,000. Simultaneously, Diem intensified his oppression of the Buddhist majority and his political opponents, eliciting hostility toward the regime and support for the National Liberation Front* from most segments of the South Vietnamese population. Nhu set up the totalitarian Personalist Labor Party and was a leading spokesman for the Strategic Hamlets Program*. In the summer of 1963, Buddhist demonstrations and rallies occurred with increasing frequency. In June, an elderly Buddhist monk, Thich Quang Duc, publicly burned himself alive in protest of the Saigon regime. Six more monks followed his example over the next months. Many South Vietnamese and Americans realized that Diem's regime was on its last legs, including Undersecretary of State W. Averell Harriman*, Assistant Secretary of State Roger Hilsman*, and new U.S. Ambassador Henry Cabot Lodge Jr.* As anti-Diem attitudes intensified on both sides of the Pacific, U.S. officials indicated to disgruntled generals, led by Duong Van Minh*, that they "would not thwart" their planned coup, resulting in Diem's Assassination* on 1 November 1963. Later, as the United States withdrew from Vietnam and the Saigon regime crumbled in the 1970s, Diem's reputation was rehabilitated to a certain extent. Many South Vietnamese began to perceive him as a courageous nationalist whom the United States had victimized.

E. J. Hammer, *A Death in November: America in Vietnam, 1963* (New York, 1987); S. Karnow, *Vietnam: A History* (New York, 1983); M. B. Young, *The Vietnam Wars, 1945–1990* (New York, 1991).

Robert K. Brigham

NGO DINH NHU (1910–1963)

Younger brother of President Ngo Dinh Diem* of the Republic of Vietnam*, Ngo Dinh Nhu was a principal reason for the failure of the U.S. Nation-Building Strategy* in Vietnam. Born into a prominent Catholic family near Hue, he graduated from the elite École Nationale des Chartres in Paris and worked in the French colonial bureaucracy, but was removed as punishment for nationalist activities. In September 1953, Nhu organized a demonstration in Saigon to advocate a third force alternative to French Colonialism* and Ho Chi Minh*. Thereafter, he became interested in the French theory of personalism, a blend of Christianity and Marxism. Nhu founded the Personalist Labor Party, which in later years functioned as an intelligence source for himself and his brother.

Nhu wielded enormous influence and power with Diem, who appointed him minister of the interior in his government after winning the 1955 election. He also became head of the secret police and the Vietnamese Special Forces, which effectively served as his personal army. Using these resources, Nhu struck at his brother's enemies, terrorizing and torturing suspected Communists and other opponents of the Diem regime. A skilled organizer, he also set up a web of secret societies and spies designed to preserve Diem's power. In addition, Nhu supported and oversaw the Strategic Hamlets Program*. Ignoring the needs of the peasantry, he built too many hamlets too quickly, and corruption ran rampant. Broken promises allowed the National Liberation Front* to subvert many hamlets, and others disintegrated.

For years, U.S. officials advised Diem that Nhu and his equally abrasive wife were destroying the Saigon government's image and that he should send them away. But Diem was too dependent on Nhu and refused to do so. In August 1963, Nhu attacked Buddhist pagodas in an effort to put down their increasingly frequent demonstrations against the government. This action further alienated the South Vietnamese people and helped convince U.S. policy makers, such as Assistant Secretary of State Roger Hilsman*, that Nhu had to be removed from power. Once again, Diem refused. New U.S. Ambassador Henry Cabot Lodge Jr.*, acting on instructions, then told a group of South Vietnamese generals, led by Duong Van Minh*, that a new government would receive U.S. support, resulting in the ouster and assassination of Diem and Nhu on 1 November 1963. Madame Nhu, who was out of the country at the time, survived. *See also* Diem's Assassination.

E. J. Hammer, *A Death in November: America in Vietnam, 1963* (New York, 1987); S. Karnow, *Vietnam: A History* (New York, 1983); M. B. Young, *The Vietnam Wars, 1945–1990* (New York, 1991).

Robert K. Brigham

NGUYEN CAO KY (1930–)

Nguyen Cao Ky served in the Republic of Vietnam* as air force vice marshal, premier (1965–1967), and vice president (1967–1971) during the Second Indochina War*. Born in the northern province of Son Tay, he was trained by the French as a pilot in Morocco, France, and Algeria. He returned to French Inchochina* in 1954, just as the First Indochina War* ended, and settled in South Vietnam. Ky quickly rose through the ranks of the new Republic of Vietnam Air Force (RVNAF), and by 1960, he became commander of the Tan Son Nhut air base outside of Saigon. He also began working with the Central Intelligence Agency*, flying agents into the Democratic Republic of Vietnam*. Ky was involved in the November 1963 coup against President Ngo Dinh Diem*, and shortly thereafter was named commander of the RVNAF.

Ky made his first major appearance on the public stage in September 1964 during a short-lived attempted coup against the government of Nguyen Khanh*. Two disgruntled generals sent their troops into Saigon, and Ky dispatched his aircraft to hover threateningly over their headquarters until they surrendered. Khanh promoted Ky to major general and made him RVNAF vice marshal. In December 1964, a group of younger military officers headed by Ky and General Nguyen Van Thieu* launched a purge that amounted to a coup of the Military Revolutionary Council that ignited a series of confusing coups and countercoups resulting in the emergence of a weak civilian government. In June 1965, Ky and Thieu, known as the Young Turks, seized power for themselves, with Ky as prime minister and Thieu as commander in chief. The fifth government since Diem's Assassination*, it was the longest lasting.

U.S. officials regarded Ky as flashy and ostentatious and did not take him seriously. After he survived his first six months in office, however, President Lyndon B. Johnson* publicly embraced him, literally and figuratively, at a summit in Hawaii in early 1966. Johnson obtained Ky's agreement to a broad program of reform and pledged in return a renewed commitment to the Saigon government. The Honolulu meeting signaled to the Buddhists that Ky would attempt to maintain absolute power, sparking protests, which rapidly spread to include students, labor, Catholics, and some military elements. The demonstrations, anti-American in tone, demanding free elections for a civilian government, quashed U.S. hopes of a viable Saigon regime and exposed the weakness of the American position in Vietnam. Ky suppressed the crisis by sending 1,000 South Vietnamese marines to Danang.

As a result of the Honolulu communiqué, the Saigon government drafted a new constitution and held national elections. But Ky demanded a strong executive and clauses to permit the president to assume almost dictatorial powers during an emergency. He also insisted upon disqualification of Communists and "neutralist sympathizers" from holding office. Succumbing to U.S. pressure, Ky reluctantly ran for vice president, with Thieu heading the successful ticket, in the September 1967 elections. Thereafter, the rivalry between Thieu and Ky intensified, dividing and weakening the government. Meanwhile, Ky headed South Vietnam's delegation to the Paris Peace Talks*, which opened in November 1968. Ky and General Duong Van Minh* tried to run against Thieu in the 1971 elections, but Thieu forced their removal from the ballot. Ky fled to the United States in 1975 and settled in California.

G. C. Herring, *America's Longest War: The United States and Vietnam, 1950–1975* (New York, 1996); S. Karnow, *Vietnam: A History* (New York, 1983); Nguyen Cao Ky, *Twenty Years and Twenty Days* (New York, 1976).

Robert K. Brigham

NGUYEN KHANH (1927–)

Nguyen Khanh was general in the Army of the Republic of Vietnam* (ARVN), prime minister (1964), and premier (1964–1965) of the Republic of Vietnam* during the Second Indochina War*. Born in 1927 in northern Vietnam, he was raised in the south by his father and stepmother, a popular actress and singer. In 1943, Khanh quit school to join the Vietminh* in its struggle against the Japanese and French Colonialism*, but soon he was expelled. He then joined the French, who provided his military training. Khanh supported President Ngo Dinh Diem* in 1954 and was appointed deputy chief of staff. He began to oppose Diem in 1960, and as commander of the Second Corps, his support was important to the November 1963 coup that resulted in Diem's Assassination*. In late January 1964, Khanh led a bloodless coup that ousted the new government led by General Duong Van Minh*, making himself prime minister. The U.S. role in Khanh's coup remains somewhat unclear. At the very least, U.S. officials knew about the plot and did not prevent it. U.S. policy makers regarded Khanh as shrewd, but inept, incompetent, and lacking in the skills required to govern effectively. Both President Lyndon B. Johnson* and U.S. Ambassador to South Vietnam Henry Cabot Lodge Jr.*, however, approved of Khanh's fierce anti-Communist stance and his opposition to a neutralist solution.

The Khanh era was characterized by chronic instability. Soon after he took power, his regime descended into upheaval and chaos, as many South Vietnamese feared he simply would reinstate the people and policies of the old Diem regime. Many also resented him because he had ousted the popular "Big Minh." Khanh's government faced massive problems, including chaos in the cities and a total lack of authority in the countryside. Military operations and the Strategic Hamlet Program* had come to a standstill. In March 1964, Washington reevaluated its policy. Although alarmed by the weakness of Khanh's regime, the Johnson administration granted the Saigon government additional aid, including military equipment, deciding that U.S. global credibility rested on preventing a Communist victory in South Vietnam. But Khanh did little to assuage American fears. Preoccupied with thwarting his internal rivals, he dismissed some key officers in the ARVN, shattering the army's morale. He also replaced the province and district chiefs who had been appointed by the Minh government, further contributing to upheaval in the rural administrative structure. Training programs, army pay, rural subsidies, and the conscription program all were neglected. Although Khanh devised ambitious plans to expand government control in the spring of 1964, he never implemented them successfully. Amid rapidly rising desertion rates in the ARVN and the growing rate of infiltration of men and supplies from the north, students, Catholics, and Buddhists fought with one another and against the government. A coup plot in July 1964 failed only because of U.S. opposition.

After the Gulf of Tonkin Incidents* in August, Khanh assumed near-dictatorial powers and severely curtailed civil liberties. His actions sparked immediate and angry public protests, forcing him to resign. The internal upheaval in South Vietnam persuaded Johnson to delay escalation of the war. He was unwilling even to respond to National Liberation Front* attacks while the political base in the south remained so unstable. Despite his resignation as head of state, Khanh retained a position in the temporary governing triumvirate, with Generals Minh and Tran Thien Khiem. Khanh also retained major authority as commander in chief of the armed forces and resumed his position as president for a brief stretch, later creating a civilian government called the High National Council. It was short-lived, however, and alienated Catholics and Buddhists. In February 1965, Generals Nguyen Cao Ky* and Nguyen Van Thieu* took power in Saigon. Khanh finally withdrew from politics and accepted a position as a roving ambassador. He was exiled to the United States and settled in Florida.

F. FitzGerald, *Fire in the Lake: The Vietnamese and the Americans in Vietnam* (Boston, 1972); G. C. Herring, *America's Longest War: The United States and Vietnam 1950–1975* (New York, 1996); S. Karnow, *Vietnam: A History* (New York, 1983).

Robert K. Brigham

NGUYEN THI BINH (?–)

Nguyen thi Binh, the daughter of a middle-class Saigon revolutionary family, was descended from revolutionary Pham van Trinh, according to popular belief. Her first involvement in the struggle against French Colonialism* and the United States came in the mid-1950s, when she participated in a demonstration against American ships that had entered the Saigon River to support the returning French. She was jailed, as were most other leaders of the action. She next appeared in U.S. files as a member of the National Liberation Front* (NLF), founded in 1960, and according to Dr. Quynh Hoa, was one of the three most important women revolutionaries during the Second Indochina War*, the others being Hoa herself and Nguyen thi Dinh*. The three played differing roles: Hoa, a physician, was the NLF minister of health, and Dinh, a warrior, led the People's Revolutionary Army, second in command in the Viet Cong*. Binh, who was legally trained, became minister of justice in the NLF. After Binh became openly identified with the NLF, she kept her personal life and activities secret from the Central Intelligence Agency*, which was able to report in a file on her only that she was married and had a child.

Binh was clearly among the top leaders of the NLF. In 1970 or 1971, she went to Paris to work with Le Duc Tho* in the Paris Peace Talks*. Binh authored a seven-point proposal that was at variance with the one that Tho and Henry A. Kissinger*, national security adviser under President Richard M. Nixon*, were formulating, more in the interests of the South Vietnamese than that of the Hanoi-based Tho. Kissinger, in his memoirs, castigated her as a stupid woman, hoping she would soon drop from sight. Although Tho and the Democratic Republic of Vietnam* ultimately prevailed over the wishes of the Provisional Revolutionary Government, the political arm of the NLF, Binh did not disappear. She moved to Hanoi and next became minister of education in the new government of the Socialist Republic of Vietnam* (SRV). Although her friend Dinh may have had more real power as head of the Women's Union, Binh had greater international visibility, since she traveled abroad frequently, speaking as the representative of the peace-loving Vietnamese against the warmongering Americans. She was particularly visible in the Third World. After some years as a goodwill ambassador, Binh traveled to the United States, visiting New York and Salt Lake City in 1991. She was not able to make her presence known publicly however, because the Vietnamese refugee community recognized her as a member of the NLF. Whether or not she was a Vietnamese Communist Party member is still unknown. In 1992, Binh became vice president of the SRV, serving until her retirement from public service.

H. A. Kissinger, *Years of Upheaval* (Boston, 1982); S. C. Taylor, *Vietnamese Women at War: Fighting for Ho Chi Minh* (Lawrence, KS, 1999); M. A. Tetrault, "Vietnam" in M. A. Tetrault (ed.), *Women Revolutionaries of Africa, Asia, and Latin America* (Columbia, SC, 1997).

Sandra C. Taylor

NGUYEN THI DINH (?–1985)

Madame Nguyen thi Dinh, or "Mrs. Dinh," as those Americans who knew of her existence called her, was a peasant who grew up in the Mekong Delta. Her family was revolutionary at least as early as the 1920s, and she married an elder brother's friend. It was a love match, and when her husband was captured and jailed at the infamous Con Dao prison (the former French penal colony of Poulo Condore), Dinh took up arms in his place. When he died there, she gave her infant son to her parents to raise and went to join the revolutionaries herself. It was, as she later said, no real choice. Dinh had "No Other Road to Take," a title she gave her memoirs some thirty years later. She soon became skilled at fighting, and traveled to Hanoi to urge Ho Chi Minh* himself to give the people of Ben Tre weapons so that they could fight back. In 1960, the uprising in Ben Tre, which she led, succeeded in fooling the Saigon soldiers who surrounded her women, armed as they were with sticks, noisemaking devices, firecrackers, and wooden guns. The soldiers dropped their weapons and fled. This marked the beginning of outright revolution.

Later in 1960, Dinh was a founding member of the National Liberation Front*. She soon became famous among her own people, as a sharpshooter and skilled killer. Although they did not always admire her tactics, which were decidedly untraditional for a woman, people knew who she was. It amused her no end that later the famous John Paul Vann, who fought against her (although he did not know he was fighting a woman) was the subject of a biography Neil Sheehan wrote in which she never was mentioned. That was all right, Dinh told biographer Christine Pelzer White, since her own people did not even honor her, although there was a tradition of valiant women warriors in Vietnam. This dated to the legendary Trung sisters, who defeated the Chinese in 40 A.D. Ultimately routed, the two women killed themselves rather than be taken captive. Dinh survived the Second Indochina War* and devoted herself to women's causes, becoming head of the Vietnamese Women's Union in the 1960s. She provided advice to the Public Broadcasting Service for its television series on the Vietnam War that it produced in 1983. Dinh died in Saigon.

Nguyen thi Dinh, M. V. Elliott (trans.), *No Other Road to Take* (Ithaca, NY, 1976); S. C. Taylor, *Vietnamese Women at War: Fighting for Ho Chi Minh* (Lawrence, KS, 1999); Truong Nhu Tang, *A Viet Cong Memoir* (New York, 1986).

Sandra C. Taylor

NGUYEN VAN THIEU (1923–2001)

A general in the Army of the Republic of Vietnam* (ARVN) during the Second Indochina War*, Nguyen Van Thieu also served as chief of state from 1965 to 1967 and president from 1967 to 1975 of the Republic of Vietnam*. Born near Phan Rang in the central coastal region of Vietnam, he joined the Vietminh* in 1945, but quickly grew disillusioned with their tactics and turned to the French. After graduating from the National Military Academy in 1949, Thieu continued his military training in Vietnam, France, and the United States. Under President Ngo Dinh Diem*, he commanded the Military Academy in Da Lat and later an ARVN infantry division. In the 1963 Diem coup, Thieu led a brigade against the presidential guard and after Diem's Assassination*, his influence grew. He and Air Force Vice Marshal Nguyen Cao Ky* were known as the Young Turks, and led a coup against Nguyen Khanh* in February 1965. A civilian government replaced Khanh's regime, with Thieu serving as its deputy premier and defense minister before the Young Turks dissolved the government and assumed power themselves in June 1965. In contrast to the derision U.S. officials expressed for Ky, Washington initially regarded Thieu, who became commander in chief, as an effective military leader who possessed good judgment. Thieu then outmaneuvered his political rival Ky to head the national ticket in the 1967 elections, with Ky in the second position. Thieu and Ky won, but received only 34.8 percent of the vote.

In the spring of 1968, the Thieu government was able to regain some of the initiative it had lost during the Tet Offensive* and extend its influence into a few new areas. It also adopted a new economic program to combat rampant inflation, but serious problems remained, including reform and refugees, and intensified after Tet. Thieu promised to increase civilian influence in his government, but withdrew into himself instead, making most decisions on his own. The rivalry between Thieu and Ky intensified, factionalizing the government. Moreover, when the Paris Peace Talks* opened in May 1968, Thieu, wary of his U.S. allies, claimed that he was railroaded into negotiations. He refused to engage in any talks that included the National Liberation Front* (NLF), while demanding that the Democratic Republic of Vietnam* negotiate directly with his Saigon regime. Thieu calculated that he would fare better with the Republicans than the Democrats and hoped to delay the issue until after the U.S. elections in November. Some American officials advocated negotiating without Saigon, but President Lyndon B. Johnson* was reluctant to do so.

After Richard M. Nixon* won the presidency, serious negotiations began at Paris. When Henry A. Kissinger* and Hanoi's chief negotiator Le Duc Tho* started secret talks in 1970, Tho demanded the removal of Thieu from office as a necessary precondition for any peace agreement. Sensing his own vulnerability, Thieu had Ky removed from the ballot and ran unopposed in the 1971 elections, this time winning with a doctored 94.3 percent of the vote. Exasperated U.S. officials in Saigon urged Washington to disassociate itself from Thieu, but Kissinger and Nixon were unwilling to abandon him. Kissinger and Tho reached an agreement in October 1972, but Thieu blocked it with demands for many concessions, hoping to drive a wedge between Hanoi and Washington and force a continuation of the war. He knew that his regime would not long survive U.S. withdrawal. This strategy succeeded in the short term. Nixon, over Kissinger's objections, supported Thieu's position until his own reelection. Eventually, with $1 billion of military hardware, secret promises of additional aid, and threats that further resistance would mean a separate peace, Nixon persuaded Thieu to accept the Paris Peace Accords* in January 1973.

After the cease-fire, Thieu launched military offensives to reclaim territory he had lost to the NLF. In late 1973, he proclaimed the Third Indochina War and stepped up military attacks on the Provisional Revolutionary Government, the NLF's government-in-waiting. Despite initial successes, the ARVN soon was sustaining losses of 500 men per week. U.S. withdrawal resulted in a severe economic crisis in South Vietnam, which was compounded by political agitation. U.S. aid cutbacks in 1974 exacerbated Thieu's woes, and in 1975, the North Vietnamese launched their final offensive, the Ho Chi Minh* campaign. Thieu finally resigned on 21 April 1975, ten days before General Duong Van Minh* surrendered unconditionally to the People's Army of Vietnam. He left Vietnam, settling in Britain and later the United States.

G. C. Herring, *America's Longest War: The United States and Vietnam 1950–1975* (New York, 1996); S. Karnow, *Vietnam: A History* (New York, 1983); G. T. H. Nguyen and J. L. Schecter, *The Palace File* (New York, 1986); M. B. Young, *The Vietnam Wars, 1945–1990* (New York, 1991).

Robert K. Brigham

NINE POWER PACT (6 February 1922)

The Nine Power Pact was part of an interlocked series of treaties concluded at the Washington Conference* designed to regulate international relations and reduce the dangers of friction in the Western Pacific. The parties to the pact—Belgium, the British Empire, China, France, Italy, Japan, the Netherlands, Portugal, and the United States—included all those powers with significant interests in the region, except the Soviet Union, which had not been invited to Washington and denounced the outcome. The nine signatories agreed to respect "the sovereignty, the independence, and the territorial and administrative integrity of China" and to refrain from taking advantage of conditions in China to establish special rights or privileges. The principle of "equal opportunity for the commerce and industry of all nations throughout the territory of China" was affirmed. Based on resolutions that the U.S. delegation put to the conference, these provisions reflected more a desire to stabilize competition between the powers in China than sympathy for China's aspirations. The Nine Power Pact, in essence internationalizing the U.S. Open Door Policy*, was regarded by the Western powers, especially the United States and Britain, as a means of curbing Japan's drive for hegemony in China. Agreement was assisted by Japan's conciliatory mood, for it did not want to jeopardize other treaties already negotiated at the conference.

China signed the Nine Power Treaty, but its delegation remained disappointed by the outcome. Existing territorial and other concessions held by the outside powers were not affected, although Japan agreed during the conference to relinquish some of its holdings in the Shandong Agreement*, as did the British. On other issues, such as extraterritoriality, China Tariff Autonomy*, and foreign forces stationed in China, the Chinese gained little satisfaction, even if the outcome did give the internally troubled nation a breathing space. In the short term, the Western powers achieved a diplomatic success with the Nine Power Pact, which seemed to be buttressed by the Four Power Pact*. Nevertheless, the Washington settlement overall, by ensuring Japan's naval dominance in the western Pacific, had left the Nine Power Pact hostage to Japan's goodwill. When that power violated its provisions by staging the Mukden Incident* in September 1931, the inherent weakness of the pact was brutally revealed. With the United States and Britain unable to agree even on a suitable diplomatic response to Japan's challenge, its relevance steadily lessened as the Washington settlement collapsed. *See also* Five Power Pact; Manchukuo; May Fourth Movement.

T. H. Buckley, *The United States and the Washington Conference, 1921–1922* (Knoxville, TN, 1970); W. R. Louis, *British Strategy in the Far East 1919–1939* (Oxford, UK, 1971).

Ian McGibbon

NIXON DOCTRINE

Long before U.S. foreign policy in Southeast Asia collapsed with the end of the Second Indochina War* in April 1975, the lessons of Vietnam were being translated into politics at the highest levels. In July 1969, President Richard M. Nixon* at a news conference on Guam* first explained what the press would call the Nixon Doctrine, the logical corollary to Vietnamization*. In a subsequent report to Congress, Nixon spelled out his administration's intentions in terms the war-weary American public could well comprehend: there were "lessons to be learned from our Vietnamese experience—about unconventional warfare and the role of outside countries, the nature of commitments [and] the need for public understanding and support." In the case of nonnuclear aggression, Nixon went on record that the United States would "furnish military and economic assistance when requested in accordance with our treaty requirements." Manpower, however, would come from the nation under threat. Some argued that such a policy in fact raised the nuclear threshold, but none could doubt that Nixon's words accurately reflected the mood of the nation.

R. H. Ferrell, *American Diplomacy* (New York, 1975); J. W. Pratt, V. P. De Santis, and J. M. Siracusa, *A History of United States Foreign Policy* (Englewood Cliffs, NJ, 1980); E. C. Ravenal, "The Nixon Doctrine and Other Asian Commitments," *Foreign Affairs* (January 1971).

Joseph M. Siracusa

NIXON, RICHARD M. (1913–1994)

President of the United States from 1969 to 1974, Richard M. Nixon ended the Second Indochina War* and established the first diplomatic contact with the People's Republic of China* (PRC). Born and raised in Southern California, family financial troubles forced him to turn down a scholarship he had earned to Harvard University and attend Whittier College. After graduating from law school at Duke University, Nixon returned to California and started a small-town legal practice. During World War II, he joined the U.S. Navy as a supply officer. After the war, Nixon entered politics and won a seat in the U.S. House of Representatives in 1946, where he made a national name for himself as a member of the House Un-American Affairs Committee when Whittaker Chambers, an editor for *Time-Life*, accused former State Department official Alger Hiss of being a Communist spy. In 1950, he was elected to the U.S. Senate and two years later, Dwight D. Eisenhower*, the Republican presidential nominee, chose him as his running mate. After victory, Nixon served as vice president of the United States for the next eight years. When Eisenhower wanted an administration official to make a partisan speech or an international goodwill trip, he normally gave the assignment to Nixon, who developed a reputation as both an expert in foreign affairs and an unscrupulous politician. In 1960, he lost the presidential election to John F. Kennedy* in a tight race. After defeat in the 1962 election for California governor, he practiced corporate law in New York and built the political support required for his nomination and election as president in 1968 over Vice President Hubert H. Humphrey.

Almost all of Nixon's major foreign policy initiatives in East Asia came in his first term. To end the Vietnam War, he initially offered to negotiate a settlement with the Democratic Republic of Vietnam* based on withdrawal of all foreign troops. When Hanoi rejected this proposal, Nixon, as he had warned, retaliated in force. First, he approved Operation MENU* for secret bombing of Vietnamese Communist bases in Cambodia*. He also prepared to order heavy attacks on the north, which might have included the tactical use of nuclear weapons, but backed off when his advisers warned him that the proposed offensive, code-named DUCK HOOK, might not work, but would galvanize domestic opposition. To reduce political pressure related to the war, Nixon phased out the draft and created a volunteer military. He also adopted a policy of Vietnamization* that promptly withdrew 170,000 Americans from Vietnam. Then, in April 1970, Nixon ordered the Cambodian Incursion*, which ignited a series of angry domestic protests that climaxed in the killing of four students at Kent State University. In the summer of 1971, sensing the need for a peace settlement to win reelection, Nixon sent National Security Adviser Henry A. Kissinger* to negotiate in secret at the Paris Peace Talks* with Hanoi's representative Le Duc Tho*. In March 1972, North Vietnam staged the Easter Offensive* against the Republic of Vietnam*, threatening to topple the government of President Nguyen Van Thieu*. In response, Nixon launched the first of the intense LINEBACKER Bombings*, breaking up enemy supply lines and ending the assault. A second barrage of air attacks against Hanoi in December 1972, he believed, caused North Vietnam to sign the Paris Peace Accords.*

Although ending the war helped him win reelection, Nixon's Visit to China* also received strong popular support. Since the mid-1960s, Nixon had hinted that the time had come for the United States to reconsider its policies toward China. Washington and Beijing had exchanged signals for two years, notably with Ping-Pong Diplomacy* and policy changes on Chinese Representation in the United Nations*. In January 1971, Chinese Foreign Minister Zhou Enlai* sent a note to Nixon, saying that the only issue dividing the two countries was U.S. troops in Taiwan*, adding that Nixon would be welcome to visit China. In June, after agreeing that Kissinger would go to Beijing to arrange Nixon's trip, Washington ended the trade embargo against the PRC. From 21 to 28 February 1972, Nixon was mainly a tourist in China, but did meet with Mao Zedong* for an hour and released the Shanghai Communiqué*, in which the two sides agreed to disagree on a number of issues. Although playing the "China card" provided leverage with the Soviet Union, the decision to move toward U.S.-PRC Normalization of Relations* caused turbulence in U.S. relations with Japan. In 1969, Nixon met with Japanese Prime Minister Satō Eisaku* and resolved the Okinawa Controversy* in the Nixon-Sato Communiqué*. But in the summer of 1971, three U.S. moves became known in Japan as the Nixon Shocks*. First, Nixon did not tell Japan about his China trip, Satō learning of the dramatic change in U.S. policy three minutes before Nixon went public with the news. Second, Nixon announced a month later that the United States was taking the dollar off the gold standard, making Japanese exports more expensive. Third, in September, Washington warned Japan that it would impose import quotas on textile goods in the absence of voluntary restraints by October 15.

Nixon left a contradictory legacy in U.S.–East Asian relations. His efforts to suppress the Pentagon Papers* and approval of the Phoenix Program* were targets of criticism. But in July 1969, on Guam* while returning from a visit with the troops in Vietnam, he casually explained that the obligation of halting Communist advances in East Asia was with the people under direct threat, although the United States would support their resistance with both military and financial support. This was not a new approach, but the press reported the Nixon Doctrine* as a major policy initiative. Yet Nixon seemed unwilling to reduce the U.S. military involvement in Southeast Asia during his second term, resulting in Congress in 1973 prohibiting bombing of Cambodia, repealing the Tonkin Gulf Resolution, and passing the War Powers Act to limit the president's power to send U.S. troops abroad. Nixon's relations with Congress worsened during investigation of the Watergate political scandal that made him in August 1974 the first U.S president to resign from office. He spent the next twenty years rebuilding his reputation in an effort that emphasized his skill and expertise in world affairs. Nixon wrote several books defending his foreign policy, repeating the argument that he had achieved "peace with honor" in Vietnam, but that Congress was responsible for the fall of South Vietnam because it withheld aid. The accolades after his death that highlighted his accomplishments in world affairs caught many observers off guard, indicating that Nixon enjoyed a good deal of success in his effort to rehabilitate his reputation.

W. P. Bundy, *Tangled Web: The Making of Nixon's Foreign Policy, 1968–1974* (New York, 1998); H. A. Kissinger, *White House Years* (Boston, 1979); H. A. Kissinger, *Years of Upheaval* (Boston, 1982); R. M. Nixon, *RN: The Memoirs of Richard Nixon* (New York, 1978).

Nicholas Evan Sarantakes

NIXON-SATŌ COMMUNIQUÉ

U.S. President Richard M. Nixon* and Japan Prime Minister Satō Eisaku* met in Washington in November 1969 at a critical moment in world affairs, summarizing in this statement the results of their discussions. The United States had decided to reduce not only its military role in the Second Indochina War* through Vietnamization*, but also its security commitments in East Asia with announcement of the Nixon Doctrine*. Moreover, the U.S. economy was starting to experience declining productivity and rising inflation, focusing criticism on the flood of Japanese imports that contributed to a growing adverse trade balance. Satō was a strong supporter of the Japanese alliance with the United States and the U.S. war in Vietnam, sources for him of harsh criticism and political opposition. He also was facing growing pressure in Japan to gain early reversion in the Okinawa Controversy*. The communiqué addressed these sources of tension in what had become a more equal U.S.-Japan partnership.

In the first of fifteen points, Nixon gave assurances that the United States would continue to work for peace and security in East Asia through honoring its defense treaty obligations. Satō, stressing the importance of U.S. troops in the area, said that the security of the Republic of Korea* and the Republic of China* on Taiwan* were essential to Japan's own security. Both leaders then "expressed the strong hope that the war in Viet-Nam would be concluded before return of the administrative rights over Okinawa to Japan," but that their goal was "accomplishing the reversion during 1972." They also affirmed the support of the two governments for firmly maintaining the U.S.-Japan Mutual Cooperation and Security Treaty*. Both were committed to strengthening the world trade and monetary system. Nixon stated his determination to control inflation in the United States, and Satō declared his intention to accelerate rapidly the reduction of Japan's trade and capital restrictions and remove residual import quota restrictions. The prime minister agreed to expand Japanese aid programs in Asia in support of U.S. efforts to promote regional economic development. After endorsing expanded cooperation in space exploration and scientific projects, Nixon explained U.S. initiatives for strategic arms limitations with the Soviet Union and Satō reiterated Japan's support for complete disarmament under international supervision.

Satō's visit to Washington had ignited the biggest demonstrations in Japan against the Vietnam War to that point, leading to 1,700 arrests and countless injuries. But after issuance of the Nixon-Satō Communiqué on 21 November, U.S. de-escalation of its involvement in that conflict caused criticism in Japan of government support for U.S. Vietnam policy to diminish and then disappear. More important, the Okinawa reversion treaty, signed on 17 June 1971, had a positive effect on U.S.-Japan relations. But that summer the Nixon Shocks* destroyed whatever degree of goodwill Satō had built with the communiqué he had signed just eighteen months earlier. Nixon's decisions, without consulting Japan, to reconcile with the People's Republic of China* and let the dollar float on world currency markets did permanent damage to the U.S.-Japan partnership and forced Satō to resign as prime minister. *See also* U.S.-Japan Postwar Trade relations.

W. LaFeber, *The Clash: A History of U.S.-Japan Relations* (New York, 1997); J. I. Matray, *Japan's Emergence as a Global Power* (Westport, CT, 2000); M. Schaller, *Altered States: The United States and Japan Since the Occupation* (New York, 1997).

James I. Matray

NIXON SHOCKS

During the summer of 1971, President Richard M. Nixon* implemented three dramatic changes in U.S. foreign policy that rocked the U.S. relationship with Japan. These "Nixon Shocks" were the announcements that the United States would begin the process of normalizing relations with the People's Republic of China* (PRC), allow the dollar to float on world currency markets, and impose import quotas on Japanese textiles. Each policy shift constituted a reversal of a key ingredient in the U.S.-Japan partnership that Prime Minister Yoshida Shigeru* had helped to build from the end of World War II until his resignation in December 1954. By then, a consensus was firmly in place in Japan supporting what observers labeled the Yoshida Doctrine of relying on U.S. protection and following Washington's lead in foreign policy. This included Japan recognizing the Republic of China* on Taiwan*, rather than the PRC, despite the objections of those Japanese who wanted to resume what had been a close traditional economic relationship with China. The Japanese government, under the control of the Liberal Democratic Party*, followed a course consistent with U.S. China policy in part because the United States maintained policies on trade and finance favoring Japan. These included unfettered access to the U.S. market and an exchange rate of 360 yen to the dollar, contributing to Japan's emergence as an economic power.

In July 1971, Washington announced that Nixon's Visit to China* would occur early in 1972. Washington hoped to gain Beijing's cooperation with Vietnamization* in achieving an orderly U.S. withdrawal from Vietnam and to exploit the Sino-Soviet split for its advantage. This embarrassed Japan because the Nixon administration had provided just a few minutes' notice of its plans to pursue a reconciliation. However, Tōkyō should not have been surprised, because Washington had been moving toward relaxing relations, abandoning references to "Red China" and promoting a Two China Policy* at the United Nations. The second Nixon Shock came in August when the Nixon administration, responding to declining exports during a prolonged economic recession, announced that it would allow the dollar's value to float on world currency markets, making U.S. goods more competitive in world trade. Finally, Washington imposed a 10 percent surcharge on Japanese imports. Prime Minister Satō Eisaku* immediately traveled to Washington for consultations, complaining to Nixon that Japan had not received the kind of treatment a "partner" deserved. One meeting could not repair the damage, although the Nixon administration eased tensions a bit by setting a specific date for U.S. withdrawal from Okinawa as no later than May 1972, confirming the pledge made in the Nixon-Sato Communiqué* of 1969.

There was a permanent shift in U.S. relations with Japan as a result of the Nixon Shocks. Washington lifted the surcharge, but only after Tokyo revalued the yen upward nearly 17 percent and agreed to accept a voluntary reduction of 9.2 percent on Japanese synthetic textile and apparel exports to the United States. Even though Satō signed an agreement in February 1972 promising greater access for U.S. imports to Japan, discord continued to dominate future U.S.-Japan Postwar Trade Relations*. Meanwhile, Japanese business interests were pressing for Japan to normalize relations with Beijing as well. In September 1972, new Prime Minister Tanaka Kakuei* made a historic five-day visit to China, signing a communiqué establishing formal diplomatic ties with the PRC. Japan then approved export-import bank loans and an oil import agreement with the PRC, causing Sino-Japanese trade to expand 83 percent in value to more than $2 billion in 1973, an amount greater than that with Taiwan. Bilateral trade and Japanese investment in China increased further after Tōkyō and Beijing finally signed a Treaty of Peace and Friendship in 1978. Exposing the effect of the Nixon Shocks, a key provision of the accord, clearly referring to Soviet regional ambitions, said that both nations opposed attempts for hegemony in Asia. Japan seemed willing to work in tandem with the PRC, not just the United States, to advance its interests in Asia.

W. LaFeber, *The Clash: A History of U.S.-Japan Relations* (New York, 1997); J. I. Matray, *Japan's Emergence as a Global Power* (Westport, CT, 2000); M. Schaller, *Altered States: The United States and Japan Since the Occupation* (New York, 1997).

James I. Matray

NIXON'S VISIT TO CHINA

When President Richard M. Nixon* went to China in February 1972, it signaled a rapprochement between the United States and the People's Republic of China (PRC), ending more than two decades of hostility between the two countries. Arrangements for the trip were made during a secret visit to Beijing in July 1971 by National Security Adviser Henry A. Kissinger*. Nixon's surprise announcement on 15 July 1971, that he had accepted the invitation of Premier Zhou Enlai* to visit China, marked a stunning policy reversal. Since the Chinese Civil War* had ended, the United States had continued to recognize the Republic of China* (ROC) on Taiwan* and had signed the U.S.-China Mutual Defense Treaty of 1954* with the Guomindang* (Nationalist) government under Jiang Jieshi*. Washington also supported the ROC in the dispute over Chinese Representation in the United Nations*. Finally, U.S. troops still were fighting in the Second Indochina War* and the rhetoric of the Chinese Cultural Revolution* poured out of Beijing. Nonetheless, the strategic interests of both nations dictated reconciliation. After years of escalating rhetorical confrontation between the two leading Communist powers, Soviet-Chinese relations had reached their nadir with fighting on the Sino-Soviet border during 1969, giving Beijing a powerful reason to break out of its isolation, and Nixon wanted to strengthen his hand as he pursued détente with Moscow and sought to implement Vietnamization*. The announcement shocked world leaders, jarring U.S.-Japan relations as one of the Nixon Shocks* and setting the stage for the UN General Assembly to oust the Chinese Nationalists and seat the PRC in October 1971.

Nixon met with Communist Party Chairman Mao Zedong* at the outset of his visit and spent more than fifteen hours in wide-ranging talks with Premier Zhou. Qiao Guanhua*, the PRC vice foreign minister, and Kissinger negotiated the Shanghai Communiqué*, which set forth the differing views of both governments on Taiwan and other major issues. Secretary of State William P. Rogers held extended meetings with Foreign Minister Ji Pengfei. The visit began the process of U.S.-PRC Normalization of Relations*, which ended with establishing formal diplomatic relations in January 1979 under President Jimmy Carter*. Although it had been predicted that a U.S. policy shift toward China would ignite bitter controversy and exact a high political price, the controversy failed to materialize. Critics of U.S. Vietnam policy welcomed the move, and the surprise announcement preempted any congressional opposition that might have come from Republican supporters of the Nationalists. The drama and pageantry of the visit from 21 to 28 February, covered in detail by the press and extensively televised, captured popular imagination. Americans watched with great interest as Nixon and his wife,

Pat, visited the Great Wall and other historic and scenic places in Beijing, Shanghai, and Hangzhou, were feted at banquets, and attended a ballet on a revolutionary theme staged by Mao's wife, Jiang Qing. *See also* Ping-Pong Diplomacy.

H. Harding, *A Fragile Relationship: The United States and China Since 1972* (Washington, DC, 1992); J. Holdridge, *Crossing the Divide: An Insider's Account of the Normalization of U.S. China Relations* (Lanham, MD, 1997); H. A. Kissinger, *White House Years* (Boston, 1979); R. M. Nixon, *RN: The Memoirs of Richard Nixon* (New York, 1978); P. Tyler, *A Great Wall: Six Presidents and China: An Investigative History* (New York, 1999)

Harriet Dashiell Schwar

NO TAE-U (1932–)

Born in North Kyŏngsang Province, No Tae-u was president of the Republic of Korea* (ROK) from 1988 to 1993. In 1951, he entered the Korean Military Academy (KMA) in its first class, which included Chŏn Du-hwan* and other future political and military leaders. Graduating in 1955, No and fellow KMA graduates organized the secret *Hanahoe* club, a group that supported Pak Chŏng-hŭi* within the ROK military. After studying at U.S. military schools, he fought in the Second Indochina War* in the late 1960s. In 1978, No was promoted to major general and became the assistant director of operations for the presidential security force. His fortunes changed suddenly after Pak Chŏng-hŭi's Assassination* in October 1979. When Chŏn initiated a military facedown with his rivals in December, No brought troops from his division to Seoul, earning appointment as commander of the Capital Guard Command. He participated in the May 1980 decision to declare martial law, and when Chŏn became president in August, he replaced him as commander of the Military Security Command. Retiring as general, he was political affairs and home affairs minister before his election to the National Assembly in 1985, representing the ruling Democratic Justice Party (DJP).

Political opposition to Chŏn's dictatorship grew after No entered the assembly. Under the joint leadership of Kim Young-sam* and Kim Dae-jung*, the opposition demanded constitutional revision to provide for popular election of the president. In 1986, No, in consultation with Chŏn, proposed a parliamentary cabinet system, but opposition forces did not retreat. After Chŏn declared in April 1987 his intention to "protect the constitution" and the DJP nominated No as its presidential candidate that June, even average citizens joined antigovernment demonstrations. On 29 June, No dramatically announced South Korea's Democracy Declaration*, providing for direct presidential election, amnesty for Kim Dae-jung, local government autonomy, and freedom of the press. Ending the political crisis, it led to passage of a new constitution that allowed the people to choose the president. With the slogan "Opening of the era of an ordinary man," No won the December election against a divided opposition

No had trouble governing after taking office in February 1988 because his DJP failed to secure a majority in the assembly. This led in January 1990 to the merger of the DJP with the parties of Kim Young-sam and Kim Jong-p'il* to form the Democratic Liberal Party (DLP). Although No was judged a "weak" president, partially because of his bland personality, he was relatively successful in foreign affairs. In September 1988, he opened the Summer Olympics in Seoul. No vigorously pursued a "Nordpolitik" that called for rapprochement with the Democratic People's Republic of Korea*, the Soviet Union, and the People's Republic of China* (PRC). This led to the normalization of relations with the Soviet Union in 1990, with all East European countries and the PRC following suit by 1992. Meanwhile, for the first time, the prime ministers of the two Koreas met, resulting in their signing in December 1991 of the Basic Agreement on North-South

Reconciliation, Nonaggression, Exchange, and Cooperation and the Agreement on the Nonnuclearization of the Korean Peninsula. Earlier that year, the two Koreas were admitted simultaneously into the United Nations. No received support from U.S. President George H. W. Bush*, with whom he maintained cooperative relations through frequent mutual visits.

In domestic affairs, local elections occurred in 1988, the first since 1961, when the military junta abolished local autonomy. During No's tenure, more than 2 million houses were built. Just prior to the presidential election in December 1992, he left the DLP and formed a "neutral cabinet" with nonpartisan dignitaries. Kim Young-sam was elected president and then gained passage of a special law to punish those held responsible for military rule that resulted in the arrest of No and Chŏn in 1995. After conviction, South Korea's Supreme Court sentenced him to seventeen years in jail for the 1979 military mutiny, treason in 1980, and corruption while in office. He was released in December 1997 after a special amnesty agreement reached between president Kim Young-sam and president-elect Kim Dae-jung. No Tae-u was calculating and cautious, but also surprisingly artistic, being interested in music, poetry, and novels. *See also* Gorbachev-No Summits.

The Korea Times, 23 December 1997; D. S. Macdonald, *The Koreans: Contemporary Politics and Society* (Boulder, CO, 1990); D. Oberdorfer, *The Two Koreas: A Contemporary History* (Reading, PA, 1997).

Kim Hakjoon

NOMONHAN, BATTLE OF

See BATTLE OF NOMONHAN

NOMURA KICHISABURŌ (1877–1964)

Nomura Kichisaburō was Japan's ambassador to the United States during the year before the Pearl Harbor Attack*. Graduating from the Imperial Naval Academy in 1898, Nomura served in the Russo-Japanese War* (1904–1905) and was stationed in Germany and Austria between 1908 and 1911. From 1914 to 1919, he was a naval attaché at the Japanese embassy in Washington, where he became acquainted with Franklin D. Roosevelt*. Nomura attended the Paris Peace Conference in 1918 and the Washington Conference* of 1921 and 1922. After serving as deputy chief of the naval general staff and commander in chief of the naval stations of Kure and Yokosuka, he participated in the Japanese assault on Shanghai in 1932 following the Mukden Incident* the prior September, where he lost the sight of one eye. Nomura became an admiral in 1933 and retired from active duty in 1937.

In 1939, Nomura was appointed as foreign minister in the Abe cabinet, but his policies were blocked by some rebellious officers in the Foreign Office. Because of his reputation as a pro-Anglo-American admiral and a personal friend of now President Roosevelt, he was asked to go to Washington as ambassador in 1940. After arriving in February 1941, Nomura worked to prevent war between the United States and Japan, embracing the belief that any compromise was preferable to conflict. His failure to transmit to Tōkyō vital information from discussions with Secretary of State Cordell Hull* caused a misunderstanding between the two governments. His efforts for peace in vain, he was forced to submit the declaration of war after Japan attacked Pearl Harbor. Between 1944 and 1946, Nomura served as adviser to the Privy Council and was elected to the Diet's upper house in 1954. *See also* Nomura-Hull Conversations.

H. Conroy, "Nomura Kichisaburo: The Diplomacy of Drama and Desperation," in R. D. Burns and E. M. Bennett (eds.), *Diplomats in Crisis: United States-Chinese-Japanese Relations, 1919–1941* (Santa Barbara, CA, 1974); Hirosuke Kiba (ed.), *Nomura Kichisaburō* (Tōkyō, 1961); Nomura Kichisaburō, *Beikoku ni tsukaishite* [Mission to the United States] (Tōkyō, 1946).

Hirobe Izumi

NOMURA-HULL CONVERSATIONS

Concerned about deteriorating American-Japanese relations in 1940, the Japanese government appointed Nomura Kichisaburō*, known as a pro-American admiral and a friend of President Franklin D. Roosevelt*, as ambassador to the United States. Arriving in Washington in February 1941, he and Secretary of State Cordell Hull* conferred many times, but could not reach an agreement to prevent war before the Pearl Harbor Attack*. The Nomura-Hull conversations focused initially on the so-called Draft Understanding, which had been prepared by a group of private citizens that included Father James M. Drought, Bishop James E. Walsh, and Ikawa Tadaō, an adviser to Prime Minister Konoe Fumimaro*. It endorsed the Open Door Policy* and the independence of China, but also a few points favoring Japan, such as recognition of Manchukuo*. Hull, who received the Draft Understanding on 9 April, was disappointed greatly by its contents, but willing to continue conversations with Nomura to keep open every channel for diplomatic contact with Japan.

Hull and Nomura began talks about the Draft Understanding on 14 April. Two days later, Hull laid out for Nomura the famous "four principles" without which the United States would not make any agreements with Japan:

> (1) respect for the territorial integrity and the sovereignty of each and all nations; (2) support for the principle of non-interference in the internal affairs of other countries; (3) support for the principle of equality, including equality of commercial opportunity; (4) non-disturbance of the status quo in the Pacific except as the status quo may be altered by peaceful means.

Hull then suggested that Nomura ask Tōkyō to examine the Draft Understanding, which he had emphasized was informal and noncommittal, to decide whether Japan wanted to propose it to the United States as the basis for starting conversations. But Nomura simply cabled it to his Foreign Office in Tōkyō, recommending its approval, and did not send the four principles until May. It was only in September that Japan's government recognized the great importance of Hull's principles as the basis of U.S. policy. Tōkyō mistakenly thought that the Draft Understanding was the official U.S. proposal. At a liaison conference on 18 April, the cabinet and the Supreme Command were generally in favor of accepting it, but Foreign Minister Matsuoka Yōsuke* was abroad at the time and after his return, voiced his displeasure with the Draft Understanding being discussed in his absence. Shortly thereafter, in a conversation with U.S. Ambassador Joseph C. Grew*, he bitterly attacked American attitudes toward Japan.

On 21 June, Hull outlined U.S. policy for Nomura in an "oral statement" that was critical of Japan's ties to Nazi Germany. In response, Matsuoka was so infuriated that he insisted on terminating negotiations with the United States. Konoe instead reformed his cabinet, expelling Matsuoka. However, many in the Japanese military, surprised by the stiffness of Hull's oral statement, now leaned more toward initiating war with the United States. Although Nomura did his best to reach an agreement, Hull was inflexible because he knew that Japan had decided to occupy all of French Indochina* as a result of *Magic** breaking the Japanese communications code. During July, Japan moved into southern Indochina, and the U.S. government froze all Japanese assets in the United States and imposed an oil embargo on 1 August. Hoping to avoid war, Konoe proposed a meeting between himself and Roosevelt, based on what he assumed was U.S. support for the Draft Understanding. Since the State Department did not favor it and

Hull did not expect the meeting to succeed, Washington rejected the proposal on 2 October. Konoe, who had demanded continuation of negotiations over the objections of the military, now resigned. Tōjō Hideki* formed a new cabinet on 18 October and sent Kurusu Saburō*, an experienced diplomat, to Washington to help Nomura conduct the final talks with Hull. On 26 November, Hull presented the two Japanese diplomats with his famous note calling on Japan to retreat from China and return to the situation before the Mukden Incident* of September 1931. Tokyo construed this as an ultimatum and decided on war against the United States.

R. J. C. Butow, "The Hull-Nomura Conversations: A Fundamental Misconception," *American Historical Review* (July 1960); H. Conroy, "Nomura Kichisaburo: The Diplomacy of Drama and Desperation," in R. D. Burns and E. M. Bennett (eds.), *Diplomats in Crisis: United States-Chinese-Japanese Relations, 1919–1941* (Santa Barbara, CA, 1974); C. Hull, *Memoirs*, 2 vols. (New York, 1948); J. G. Utley, *Going to War with Japan, 1937–1941* (Knoxville, TN, 1985); U.S. Department of State, *Foreign Relations of the United States, 1931–1941*, Vol. 2: *Japan* (Washington, DC, 1943).

Hirobe Izumi

NORTH KOREA

See DEMOCRATIC PEOPLE'S REPUBLIC OF KOREA

NORTH KOREAN NUCLEAR CONTROVERSY

The North Korean nuclear controversy began in April 1991 when U.S. satellite reconnaissance photographs revealed that the Democratic People's Republic of Korea* (DPRK) was building a heavily guarded nuclear installation at Yongbyŏn, fifty-five miles north of its capital at P'yŏngyang. North Korea claimed it was an electricity plant, but there were no generators outside the facility. In June, after the defense minister of the Republic of Korea* (ROK) warned that South Korea might have to stage a commando raid to destory the nuclear plant in self-defense, the DPRK indicated its willingness to allow the International Atomic Energy Agency (IAEA) to conduct inspections. North Korea had signed the Nuclear Non-Proliferation Treaty (NPT) in 1985, but had refused to allow the IAEA to conduct inspections until the United States withdrew its nuclear weapons from South Korea. When progress on an inspections agreement stalled that fall, Japan suspended talks for recognition and economic aid until the DPRK allowed inspections and the Soviet Union ended North Korea's access to nuclear technology, and the United States bolstered the ROK's defensive capabilities. In December, the DPRK signed with the ROK an expression of principles pledging not to "test, receive, possess, store, deploy or use nuclear weapons." As such, instead of the IAEA, a Joint Nuclear Control Commission would inspect any nuclear installations suspected of being used for anything other than peaceful purposes. However, by February 1992, the DPRK again had declared that it would not permit access to North Korea.

International concern about North Korea's nuclear program escalated in the summer of 1992 when the IAEA determined that the DPRK had extracted plutonium from its nuclear energy facility three times between 1998 and 1992. On 25 February 1993, the IAEA board of governors adopted a resolution urging the DPRK to accept a special inspection. On 12 March, the DPRK announced its withdrawal from the NPT. In response, the United States referred the issue to the United Nations and threatened sanctions. It also agreed to hold high-level talks with North Korea that the People's Republic of China* (PRC) arranged. At the first round on 2 June 1993 held in New York City, the United States called on North Korea to return to the NPT, allow IAEA inspections, and execute a Joint Declaration of the Denuclearization of the Korean Peninsula. The DPRK demanded that the United States stop the Team Spirit Military Exercises*, renounce nuclear threats against North Korea, allow mutual inspections that included U.S. military bases in the Republic of Korea* (ROK), and recognize the DPRK. In the second round of talks in Geneva on 14 July, North Korea added the demands that the United States drop the DPRK from its list of terrorist nations, support a peace treaty to replace the Korean Armistice Agreement*, and endorse the North Korean unification plan based on a "democratic federation" system. Washington responded with its own demand for a substantial advance in North Korean talks with both South Korea and the IAEA on inspections as a precondition to holding the third meeting. It would take about one year to schedule the third round of high-level talks in Geneva, which originally were to be held within two months after this second round ended.

During the ensuing year, the United States, the DPRK, the ROK, Japan, and the IAEA became embroiled in a series of diplomatic maneuvers. To maintain leverage, North Korea was not entirely cooperative with the IAEA on the terms of inspection after it had allowed the installation of inspection equipment at the Yongbyŏn nuclear facility. Although the IAEA was asking for routine inspections of seven declared sites, the DPRK wanted to allow only regular maintenance of inspection equipment. President Bill Clinton* considered imposing sanctions against North Korea if the IAEA declared an interruption in the continuity of safeguards. Not wanting to precipitate a crisis and in accordance with the desires of South Korea, Washington urged compromise. Then, on 3 December, the DPRK proposed routine inspections of five sites, in return for the end of Team Spirit Military Exercises and adding to the agenda for the third round of talks the establishment of diplomatic relations. To force acceptance of its package deal and divert attention from a radiochemical laboratory that the IAEA wanted to inspect, the DPRK launched a discharge operation at a nuclear reactor on 12 May 1994 to make fuel measurements impossible. After the IAEA adopted a resolution calling for sanctions against the DPRK on 10 June, the DPRK declared its withdrawal from the IAEA. Clinton was prepared to order U.S. military action to destroy North Korea's nuclear facilities, but allowed former President Jimmy Carter* to attempt to mediate an agreement. His personal visit to P'yŏngyang resulted in North Korea agreeing to halt its nuclear program and resume negotiations regarding inspections.

In October 1994, the DPRK agreed at the third round of meetings to consult with the IAEA on inspections and resume inter-Korean dialogue as soon as possible, and the United States pledged to help North Korea replace its graphite-moderated reactors with light water-moderated reactors. The DPRK also issued a statement after the talks that it had "decided unilaterally to suspend . . . the effectuation of its withdrawal from the NPT." Even though this "Agreed Framework" was supposed to settle the North Korean nuclear controversy, it was not completely over. The United States, Japan, and the ROK could not reach agreement on how to fund the new energy facilities in North Korea, causing an impatient DPRK to resume its nuclear program. Already, the North Koreans had practiced brinkmanship during the talks when it launched the Nodong-1 missile and ordered all foreigners except diplomats to leave the country. During 1998, North Korea sent another missile into Japanese airspace, and refused to answer U.S. questions about the purpose of an underground exhaust facility of a nuclear plant at Gumchangri. In March 1999, the DPRK finally accepted visits from U.S. inspectors to the site in return for 600,000 tons of food aid. Shortly after the first visit in May to Gumchangri, however, a former high-ranking officer in the DPRK's missile unit fled to the PRC, where, before being deported, he issued a statement claiming that concealed nuclear weapons facilities existed at a site thirty kilometers from Gumchangri. His statement was not released, however, until the summer of 2001. The controversy therefore remained unresolved, as the United States continued trying not only to determine the DPRK's nuclear capabilities, but also halt any future development of the North Korean nuclear program.

Chŏng Ok-im, *Pukhaek Mŭnje ŭi Obaek-p'alsip-p'al il* [588 Days of the North Korean Nuclear Issue] (Seoul, 1995); M. Heo, "The Characteristics of North Korean Negotiating Behavior: A Theoretical Deviation or Pseudo-Negotiation?," *Korea and World Affairs* (Fall 1998); J. I. Matray, "Korea's Quest for Disarmament and Reunification," in C. Kim and J. I. Matray (eds.), *Korea and the Cold War: Division, Destruction, and Disarmament* (Claremont, CA, 1993); Nam Chan-sun, *P'yŏngyang ŭi haek miso* [Nuclear Smile of P'yŏngyang] (Seoul, 1995); Tokbyul Ch'uijeban [Special Report Group], "Talbuk Inmin'gun Changsŏng ŭi Ch'unggyŭk Chŏngŭn" [A Shocking Witness of a Fled General from the People's Army], *Shindonga* (August 2001).

Heo Man-ho

O

ŌHIRA MASAYOSHI (1910–1980)

Ōhira Masayoshi became prime minister of Japan in December 1978 after he defeated incumbent Prime Minister Fukuda Takeo* in the first presidential primary of the Liberal Democratic Party* (LDP), with the strong backing of Tanaka Kakuei*. His administration, however, suffered from a continuing political struggle with Fukuda, as well as challenges from opposition parties exploiting the LDP's slim majority in the Diet. Born in Kagawa Prefecture, Ōhira graduated from Hitotsubashi University and entered the Ministry of Finance. After World War II, he entered politics, becoming a protégé of Ikeda Hayato* and developing a close alliance with Tanaka. He served as foreign minister under both men. When Ōhira became the prime minister, restoring fiscal balance was a top priority. He proposed introduction of a general consumption tax in the summer of 1979, which contributed to the LDP's failure to gain a majority in the Diet's lower house in the October 1979 elections. This election "defeat" triggered a notorious Forty-Day Conflict between the mainstream Ōhira-Tanaka factions and the Fukuda-Nakasone Yasuhiro*-Miki Takeo* factions within the LDP, in which these opposition factions sought to snatch the premiership and other government posts.

In the international and security realm, the Ōhira administration sought to redirect the orientation of Japanese foreign policy away from an emphasis on independence and a reduced reliance on the United States, which the previous Tanaka and Fukuda administrations had pursued, toward reaffirming the Japan-U.S. security relationship and solidarity within the Western Alliance. In response to the Soviet invasion of Afghanistan late in 1979 and the renewed U.S.-Soviet tension, as well as the Iranian hostage crisis, which he saw as revealing the weaknesses of a troubled and inward-looking superpower, Ōhira sought to demonstrate his strong support for President Jimmy Carter*. He quickly supported the boycott of the Moscow Olympic Games in 1980 over widespread opposition in Japan. Ōhira also searched for an appropriate international role for an emerging Japanese economic superpower and advanced the concept of "comprehensive security" as part of his efforts. He was host of the 1979 economic summit of industrialized nations in Tōkyō and sought to coordinate oil policy among the participating powers in the wake of the second major jump in world oil prices after the revolution in Iran. Ōhira died a sudden death in the midst of general election campaigns and helped bring about a dramatic LDP victory.

K. Hayao, *The Japanese Prime Minister and Public Policy* (Pittsburgh, PA, 1993); Ōhira Masayoshi, *Ōhira Masayoshi kaikoroku* [Memoirs of Ōhira Masayoshi] (Tōkyō, 1983); Watanabe Akio (ed.), *Sengo Nihon no saishō tachi* [Postwar Japanese Prime Ministers] (Tōkyō, 1995).

Kamimura Naoki

ŌKAWA SHŪMEI (1886–1957)

A leading ultranationalist intellectual and advocate of pan-Asianism in Japan before 1945, Ōkawa Shūmei gained notoriety for committing one of the most bizarre courtroom acts in recent history. During the Tōkyō War Crimes Trials*, he suddenly reached forward and slapped the bald head of General Tōjō Hideki*, who was sitting in front of him. After graduating from Tōkyō Imperial University in 1911, Ōkawa had short stints as a teacher, writer, and translator before deserting an earlier interest in Christianity to focus his studies on Asian philosophy and Japanese traditional culture. Encounters with several Indian nationalists solidified his Pan-Asianism. In 1918, he went to work for the South Manchuria Railway Company, rising to the directorship of the Research Bureau in 1929. Meanwhile, Ōkawa helped found the Yūzonsha in 1919, a right-wing nationalist organization, but left it in 1923 after an internal dispute. He then created his own organizations, which by the 1930s, were financed mainly by industrialist Ishihara Hiroichirō. Arrested and sentenced to a five-year prison term for his untranationalist activities, Ōkawa after his release in 1937 rejoined the South Manchuria Railway as a senior adviser, holding after 1939 a joint appointment as head of the Continental Studies Department at Hōsei University in Tōkyō.

Prior to war with the United States, Ōkawa advocated a plan that called for the withdrawal of Japanese troops from China in 1940, and the establishment of a joint U.S.-Japan firm to export raw silk from Japan and tungsten from China to the United States while importing American oil and steel in exchange. This project, he surmised, would encourage Britain to pressure Jiang Jieshi* to negotiate a peace settlement with Japan, and thereby avert a potential U.S.-Japan war over China. It also was consistent with Ōkawa's predictions that in the near future, the world would be divided into an American block and an Euro-African block, requiring Japan to create an Asian block by pursuing an active policy of southward expansion and nonaggressive defense in China. The Dutch East Indies were a crucial source of oil and rubber, so if Tōkyō controlled the flow of commodities that the United States required, Ōkawa reasoned, a compromise arrangement could be negotiated without war. Despite his numerous political connections, Prime Minister Konoe Fumimaro*, as well as his successor Tōjō Hideki, remained unconvinced of the utility of Ōkawa's project.

After Japan's Pearl Harbor Attack*, Ōkawa became a leading propagandist for achieving the Greater East Asia Co-Prosperity Sphere* in the war against the Anglo-Saxon world order. His stance on Pan-Asianism and the Shōwa Restoration resulted in him being labeled the main theoretical leader of the ultranationalists at the war crimes trials. Ōkawa was arrested as a war criminal and was the only civilian not to have occupied a government post among the twenty-eight Class-A defendants. Ōkawa's long sessions of ranting and raving in various languages in his jail cell, and the infamous slap on Tōjō's head, sparked an investigation into his fitness to stand trial. Two Tōkyō University psychiatric medicine professors made a diagnosis of syphilis of the brain. After a second examination in February 1947, they concluded that Ōkawa was unfit to stand trial. Suspecting that he was feigning insanity to escape sentencing, SCAP* psychiatrists observed Ōkawa for three weeks and judged him fit to stand trial. But the court exempted him, although Ōkawa himself asserted his fitness. Released in 1948, and still suffering from occasional hallucinations and delusions, Ōkawa continued to write on Islam and Asia, as well as translating the Koran from Chinese, French, and German versions to Japanese. He judged postwar Japan a psychological slave of the United States after three years of brainwashing about war guilt and the new Japanese Constitution of 1947*. Ōkawa's position served as one of the intellectual foundations for subsequent attempts to revise the "MacArthur Constitution."

T. Ōtsuka, *Ōkawa Shūmei to kindai Nihon* [Ōkawa Shūmei and Modern Japan] (Tōkyō, 1990); R. Storry, *The Double Patriots* (London, 1957); C. Szpilman, "The Dream of One Asia-Pan-Asianism: The Case of Ōkawa Shūmei," in H. Feuss (ed.), *The Japanese Empire and Its Legacies* (Bonn, 1998).

Hyung Gu Lynn

OKINAWA, BATTLE OF

See BATTLE OF OKINAWA

OKINAWA CONTROVERSY

The Okinawa controversy involved the postwar demand of Japan for the United States to restore Japanese control over this island, which the Americans had governed as a colony in everything but name since the Battle of Okinawa* in April 1945. During early U.S. Occupation of Japan*, the United States showed little interest in Okinawa, but in 1950, an agreement between the military and the State Department that allowed progress to begin with Japan on a peace treaty included a decision to retain exclusive control over both the Bonin and Ryūkyū Islands. Facing increasing political pressure for the return of both sets of islands, Japan's Prime Minister Yoshida Shigeru* resisted surrendering formal claim to them in the Japanese Peace Treaty*. U.S. representative in Tōkyō John Foster Dulles*, who was sympathetic and concerned, then devised the legal concept of "residual sovereignty," whereby the inhabitants of the islands would keep their Japanese citizenship and the territory eventually would revert to Japanese administration at some future date. During the Korean War* and afterward, however, the United States built a number of bases on the island, turning Okinawa into the centerpiece of its base system in the Pacific. Bombers based there could strike targets anywhere in China, as well as a good portion of Asian territory in the Soviet Union. Moreover, since the United States administered the territory, Americans never had to get prior approval from another nation to use the bases in this territory. Despite the importance of Okinawa, the Japanese constantly voiced the desire for its return.

During his 1954 State of the Union address, President Dwight D. Eisenhower* said the United States intended to maintain a long-term presence on Okinawa. The president hoped this statement would end Japanese agitation on the issue, but he also came close to returning the island. In 1957, U.S. Ambassador Douglas MacArthur II* warned Washington that the U.S.-Japan Security Treaty of 1951* needed revision and in September, now Secretary of State Dulles authorized him to negotiate a new treaty. While waiting on Japanese politics, MacArthur visited Okinawa. Military officials shocked him with their arrogant attitudes toward native islanders and their neocolonial attitudes toward Okinawa. After returning to Tōkyō, he wrote Dulles that Americans could not continue to rule the island as a colony, and should set the groundwork for reversion. Dulles and Eisenhower agreed and talked between themselves about returning the island immediately under some agreement that treated the bases there as enclaves, separate from the authority of the new treaty. Prime Minister Kishi Nobusuke* did not take advantage of this thinking. Unable to forge a consensus for a larger area, Kishi decided to limit the treaty revision only to the home islands. Since the Okinawa prefecture was heavily laced with U.S. bases and Japanese administration would raise the troublesome issue of being drawn into an American war, he decided to make no effort at regaining this territory in 1960.

In the mid-1960s, Okinawa dominated U.S.-Japanese relations. Prime Minister Satō Eisaku* raised the issue when he visited Washington early in 1965, suggesting to Secretary of State Dean Rusk* that the United States return all the Ryūkyūs other than Okinawa. The American made no response to this proposal. In August, when Satō visited the occupied prefecture, he declared that the postwar period would not come to an end until Okinawa was once again Japanese. Thereafter, Japanese economic aid to the prefecture skyrocketed, eroding American influence there. Most U.S. officials realized that returning Okinawa was only a matter of time, but made clear to Japan that reversion would have to wait at least until the end of the Second Indochina War*. U.S. Ambassador U. Alexis Johnson*, with the approval of Rusk and President Lyndon B. Johnson*, pushed a number of reforms that were designed to alleviate pressure and buy time, including allowing the flying of the Japanese flag on Okinawan fishing boats, more travel between Okinawa and the rest of Japan, and direct election of the governor. As important, in June 1968, Johnson used an executive order to return the Bonin Islands* to Japanese administration. By then, Okinawa had become a hotly debated issue in Japanese politics. Leftist political activists used the prolonged U.S. occupation of the prefecture as an issue to develop nationalist sentiment against the treaty with the United States. Satō worked to limit the agitation, preserving both the American alliance and the effectiveness of the bases for U.S. use in the Vietnam War.

In 1968, Okinawan voters forced more action out of Satō when they elected a chief executive who had campaigned on a platform of immediate reversion. The next year, the new administration of Richard M. Nixon* accepted that it was no longer a question of if, but how the islands should be returned. The major stumbling block was the question of storing nuclear weapons after reversion. In March, Satō told the Diet that, in accordance with his Three Non-Nuclear Principles*, he would not allow nuclear weapons on Okinawa following reversion. Given Japanese sensitivities about nuclear weapons, this requirement easily could have scuttled an agreement. Although Nixon and National Security Adviser Henry A. Kissinger* were sympathetic, the Joint Chiefs of Staff were adamantly opposed. Ambassador Johnson developed a proposal that resolved the matter: the United States would remove all nuclear weapons from Okinawa, and the Japanese would agree to allow emergency consultations. Satō made another visit to Washington in November and, in the Nixon-Satō Communiqué*, the United States agreed to return the Ryūkyūs to Japanese administrative control. After two-and-a-half years of complicated negotiations, Okinawa became Japanese again on 15 May 1972. The American bases and alliance with Japan remained as strong as ever.

W. LaFeber, *The Clash: A History of U.S.-Japan Relations* (New York, 1997); J. I. Matray, *Japan's Emergence as a Global Power* (Westport, CT, 2000); N. E. Sarantakes, *Keystone: The American Occupation of Okinawa and U.S.-Japanese Relations, 1945–1972* (College Station, TX, 2000).

Nicholas Evan Sarantakes

ŌKUMA DOCTRINE

Throughout his political career, Ōkuma Shigenobu* was a vocal proponent of an active Japanese policy in Asia, especially in China. His Pan-Asianist views on foreign policy came to be known as the Ōkuma Doctrine by 1898, when he became prime minister for the first time. This label originated in part from his actions as foreign minister, when he dispatched a warship to

Hawaii in May 1897 at a time when tensions over Japanese emigration were at a peak. Undoubtedly influenced by advice from his good friend Fukuzawa Yukichi* that Japan should become the "leader of Asia," Ōkuma's "doctrine" held that instability in China would encourage further intrusions by Western powers and deprive Japan of markets unless Japan guided China toward modernization and enlightenment while restraining the Western imperialists. This role as intermediary, according to Ōkuma, would allow Japan to repay her ancient cultural debts to China.

For all his saber-rattling speeches, Ōkuma was cautious in actually acting on his doctrine. As early as 1895, Philippine independence activist José Ramos visited Japan, looking to acquire weapons for the independence movement. But Foreign Minister Ōkuma declined to offer support, noting that because no Japanese immigrant community existed in Manila, the issue of independence for the Philippines* was not a concern of the Japanese government. When the Spanish-American War* began in August 1898, Prime Minister Itō Hirobumi* and Foreign Minister Ōkuma maintained neutrality. After the Ōkuma cabinet was formed that June, Philippine independence leaders anticipated support from the advocate of modern Pan-Asianism, but Ōkuma staunchly turned a deaf ear to requests for help. Further, Ōkuma quickly welcomed American achievement of Philippine Annexation*, after suggesting that if U.S. control was not possible, perhaps the Philippines could be placed under a joint Japan-U.S. trusteeship.

After the Russo-Japanese War*, as an opposition leader, Ōkuma criticized the Treaty of Portsmouth* for failing to provide reparations and reflecting American fears of the "yellow peril," arguing that Japan should have continued to fight. After the Japanese government formally enunciated the Ōkuma Doctrine in 1905, it remained fundamentally unchanged for a decade. In his second cabinet from 1914 to 1916, Ōkuma supported Foreign Minister Katō Kōmei* in declaring war against Germany and imposing the Twenty-One Demands* on China. During an exchange in 1915, President Charles Eliot of Harvard University warned Ōkuma of adverse U.S. public opinion regarding Japanese policy toward China. Ōkuma replied that Japan wanted to secure with the Twenty-One Demands the stability and peace of East Asia through preventing the division and collapse of China. Although not as U.S.-oriented as the views of Hara Kei* or Shibusawa Eiichi*, the Ōkuma Doctrine was also different from the Pan-Asianist attitudes of Uchida Ryōhei, Tōyama Mitsuru, or Ōkawa Shūmei*, in that Ōkuma did not see conflict between East and West as inevitable. He claimed Japan's mission was to synthesize the East and West and contribute to the progress of human civilization. The Ōkuma Doctrine was the predecessor to the "consortium imperialism" in China many so-called liberals advocated in prewar Japan. *See also* Amō Doctrine; Greater East Asia Co-Prosperity Sphere.

Sadao Asada, *Ryōtaisenkan no Nichibei kankei-Kaigun to seisaku kettei katei* [Interwar Japan-U.S. Relations: The Navy and the Policymaking Process] (Tōkyō, 1993); M. Hatano, *Kindai Higashi Ajia no seiji hendo to Nihon no gaikō* [Political Change in Modern Asia and Japanese Diplomacy] (Tōkyō, 1995); J. Lebra-Chapman, *Okuma Shigenobu: Statesman of Meiji Japan* (Canberra, 1977).

Hyung Gu Lynn

ŌKUMA SHIGENOBU (1838–1922)

One of the leading Japanese politicians of the Meiji and Taishō eras, Ōkuma Shigenobu twice served as prime minister, and held ministerial posts in numerous other cabinets. He learned Dutch and English, as well as finance and commerce, from foreign merchants in Nagasaki. In 1868, Ōkuma entered the new Meiji government's Finance Ministry. Soon after his patron Ōkubo Toshimichi was assassinated, Ōkuma, in 1881, publicly advocated a

British-style parliamentary government, whereas other leaders favored a Prussian model. That year, his actions in a land deal alienated many of his colleagues, resulting in his ouster by consensus. In 1888, Itō Hirobumi* offered Ōkuma the post of foreign minister to dampen opposition to the government. His primary assignment was the abolition of unequal treaties. Unlike his predecessors, he chose to negotiate with the powers separately, rather than at a joint conference. After pushing through an equal treaty with Mexico in 1888 to set a precedent, a deep split emerged among government officials over the proposed terms. A new U.S.-Japan Treaty was signed in 1889, but when the terms published in the *London Times* were relayed to Japan, a domestic protest movement blocked ratification. Later the same year, Ōkuma survived an assassination attempt, but lost his right leg in the bomb explosion. He was forced to resign to recuperate, and all further negotiations ceased.

In 1897, Ōkuma was once again appointed foreign minister, this time in the Matsukata cabinet. The next year, he formed the first party coalition cabinet with Itagaki Taisuke, but the cabinet fell apart after four months because of conflicts between the two parties. By this time, Ōkuma was known for his outspoken views on relations with China, notably the Ōkuma Doctrine*, in which Japan was to lead China to the path of modernity. After years in opposition, Ōkuma was enticed out of retirement in 1914 with an offer to become prime minister. During his tenure, Japan declared war against Germany, and delivered the Twenty-One Demands* against China. Angered that Foreign Minister Katō Kōmei* had not consulted them before declaring war against Germany, genrō (elder statesmen) Yamagata Aritomo and Inoue Kaoru called Ōkuma to a meeting, where it was agreed that they would be consulted before action on all major diplomatic issues. However, Katō was staunchly opposed to genrō interference in foreign policy, and again took independent action in putting forth the Twenty-One Demands. Ōkuma protected Katō from the criticism, but unsuccessfully attempted to have him appointed as his successor when he resigned in 1916.

Ōkuma and Katō had personal ties through Fukuzawa Yukichi*. However, rather than related personal histories, it was more likely similar outlooks on foreign policy that made Ōkuma so supportive of Katō. Both favored an aggressive China policy and the commercial expansion in Asia advocated by various Japanese industry and trade associations. Whereas Seiyūkai leaders Hara Kei* and Takahashi Korekiyo opposed Japanese entry into World War I because of the anticipated negative impact on relations with the United States, Ōkuma believed that expansion in Asia could be attained without alienating either the United States or Britain. Resigning without ensuring Katō as his replacement, the failure of the foreign policy Ōkuma and Katō advocated conversely improved the credibility of the Hara and Seiyūkai policy aimed at greater cooperation with the United States. Once Hara became prime minister in 1918, this led to the Four Power Pact* of 1921 and the Five Power Pact* of 1922 at the Washington Conference*. Ōkuma himself spent the last few years of his life studying Greek and Chinese philosophy, and writing occasionally on political issues.

F. Dickinson, *War and National Reinvention: Japan and the Great War, 1914–1919* (Cambridge, MA, 1999); J. Lebra-Chapman, *Okuma Shigenobu: Statesman of Meiji Japan* (Canberra, 1977); S. Okuma (ed.), *Fifty Years of New Japan*, 2 vols. (London, 1909).

Hyung Gu Lynn

OPEN DOOR POLICY

The Open Door policy represented the guiding principle behind U.S. China policy at the end of the nineteenth century and continued to influence Sino-American relations in the twentieth century. Its two central ideas were protection of China's territorial integrity and equal access to China's markets or, as Secretary of State John Hay* put it, "a fair field and no favor." The policy grew out of what historian Michael Hunt has termed the Open Door ideology, a broad conviction based on the first two assumptions plus the idea that Chinese reform was essential to the process of resisting partition. This ideology was promulgated by a troika that Hunt labels the Open Door constituency: missionaries, business representatives, and diplomats. Taking a slightly different tack, other historians describe the Open Door as a specific diplomatic episode, a larger doctrine, a tactic for maximizing commercial and religious access to China, and a historical interpretation explaining U.S. expansion, especially in Asia.

The concept of the Open Door grew out of a series of nineteenth-century treaties compelling China to open its gates to foreign commerce and influence and through which China sought to play the powers against each other. American economic interest in China rested in part on fears of overproduction at home. Although the China market generally failed to fulfill American dreams, its allure persisted. In 1895, the British, French, Germans, Russians, and Japanese began cordoning off spheres of influence in China, thus jeopardizing the Open Door, which the British formerly had championed. The United States sought to thwart this partition of China, which the weakened Qing Dynasty appeared unable to prevent. Prominent theorists, including Brooks Adams and Alfred Thayer Mahan*, regarded access to China as vital to U.S. prosperity and security. The Philippines*, acquired after the Spanish-American War*, were to be a steppingstone to an informal empire of economic expansion in Asia.

In 1899, influenced by W. W. Rockhill* and Englishman Alfred E. Hippisley, Secretary of State Hay issued the first of his famous circular Open Door notes, calling on the powers to allow free access to trade in China. Significantly, he did not bother to consult the Chinese. Although none of the imperial powers embraced his ideas, they were not willing to reject them openly, so each evasively endorsed Hay's circular. The first note, was a moderate success, given the lack of U.S. leverage in the region, but ultimately it prevented neither further foreign encroachment nor Chinese unrest. Then, in 1900, the Boxer Uprising* broke out, putting Hay's policy to the test. Anxious that the China Relief Expedition* to rescue foreign nationals might serve as a pretext for more land grabs, Hay dispatched his second Open Door note, reiterating that it was U.S. policy to respect the Chinese "territorial and administrative entity," to regard cooperative local authorities as China's legitimate representatives, and "to safeguard the principle" of equal trade. These efforts did little to strengthen Sino-U.S. relations, since they were made as the United States was closing its own doors to Chinese immigrants through Exclusion Acts* and since the policy offered no revision of the unequal treaties. Thereafter, the goals behind the Open Door continued to shape U.S. policy. The provisions of the Open Door were adopted in several treaties, including the Nine Power Pact* of 1922, and strains of the ideology persisted for decades.

W. I. Cohen, *America's Response to China: A History of Sino-American Relations* (New York, 1990); M. H. Hunt, *The Making of a Special Relationship: The United States and China to 1914* (New York, 1983); T. J. McCormick, *China Market: America's Quest for Informal Empire, 1893–1901* (Chicago, 1967); J. C. Thomson Jr., P. W. Stanley, and J. C. Perry, *Sentimental Imperialists: The American Experience in East Asia* (New York, 1985).

Shannon Smith

OPEN PAYMENTS AGREEMENT (31 May 1948)

The Open Payments Agreement (OPA) was a government-operated trade arrangement between the sterling area countries and Japan. The agreement was signed by the Supreme Commander for the Allied Powers (SCAP*) and Britain on 31 May 1948. It opened Japan's trade relations with Britain and its colonies, as well as India, New Zealand, South Africa, Ceylon, Pakistan and Burma*. The OPA was a short-lived agreement, but it paved the way for Japan's postwar trade relations with its sterling neighbors in Asia and the Pacific.

Britain and the United States, which signed the agreement, had respective motives behind the opening of Japan's trade relations with the sterling area. The U.S. objectives in signing the agreement were threefold. First, the United States wanted to promote Japanese economic recovery. Second, the agreement was expected to ease the burden of the U.S. Occupation of Japan* on the American taxpayer. Third, Washington wanted to build Japan into a bulwark against Communism* in East Asia in accordance with the Truman administration's Reverse Course*. Britain's primary aim was to facilitate the return of British and Commonwealth commercial interests in Japan.

Trade between Japan and the signatories of the OPA remained limited because of the clause in the agreement that permitted the SCAP to convert sterling balances into dollars at six-month intervals. Britain, therefore, set limitations on trade to prevent a dollar drain from the central reserves in London. Trade limitations, however, led to dissatisfaction among the sterling member countries, and as a result, Britain superceded it with the Sterling Payments Agreement* in 1951.

W. S. Borden, *The Pacific Alliance: United States Foreign Economic Policy and Japanese Trade Recovery, 1947–1955* (Madison, WI, 1984); R. Buckley, *Occupation Diplomacy: Britain, the United States and Japan 1945–1952* (Cambridge, UK, 1982); A. Rix, *Coming to Terms: The Politics of Australia's Trade with Japan 1945–57* (Sydney, 1986).

Yokoi Noriko

OPERATION CEDAR FALLS

Operation CEDAR FALLS was a major search-and-destroy operation launched in January 1967 by the United States against North Vietnamese–Viet Cong* bases during the Second Indochina War*. The objective was the elimination of the so-called Iron Triangle, northwest of Saigon, as a major Communist base and staging area, which was to be accomplished by obliterating a region of 60,000 square miles. The operation began with the forced evacuation and total destruction of the village of Ben Suc. This was followed by more intensive bombing and artillery fire and the bulldozing of jungle. Engineers detonated explosives into the Viet Cong's extensive tunnel system. CEDAR FALLS lasted nineteen days, and the commanding U.S. general predicted that after the leveling of this area, the Communists never would recover. In fact, although the Viet Cong lost nearly 800 soldiers in CEDAR FALLS, many escaped and, with the support of the returning inhabitants, they soon reestablished their Iron Triangle base. It was a major staging area for the Tet Offensive* a year later.

B. W. Rogers, *Cedar Falls–Junction City: A Turning Point* (Washington, DC, 1974); J. Schell, *The Village of Ben Suc* (New York, 1967).

Gary R. Hess

OPERATION JUNCTION CITY

Operation JUNCTION CITY was the largest U.S. military operation of the Second Indochina War*, involving twenty-two American infantry, four artillery, and four Army of the Republic of Vietnam* (ARVN) battalions. It was a massive search-and-destroy mission on the Cambodian border northwest of Saigon in February 1967, a month after Operation CEDAR FALLS* in the Iron Triangle. The objectives of the operation were to decimate a Viet Cong* division and a North Vietnamese Army regiment, to discover and destroy the

COSVN (Central Office for South Vietnam) headquarters, and to establish airfields and Special Forces camps to deny the enemy reaccess to the area. The plan was to surround the area using air mobile assaults and the only airborne assault of the war by the 173d Airborne, trapping and then killing enemy forces. These forces met little resistance and fought only three pitched battles in the nearly three-month campaign, all of them initiated by the enemy. The official body count was 2,728, compared with U.S./ARVN losses of 282, but the majority of these were killed by air and artillery. Also, U.S. Army figures showed only twenty-one armored personnel carriers, three tanks, and five artillery pieces lost in the battle.

General William C. Westmoreland*, head of Military Assistance Command, Vietnam* (MACV), used these figures to justify his strategy of attrition, and as an example of North Vietnamese propaganda when they claimed a victory with 13,500 killed and the destruction of 800 armored vehicles and 119 artillery pieces. But even though the Ninth Viet Cong Division was battered, most of these forces were able to escape to Cambodia*, where they relocated their training facilities and rebuilt their force in sanctuary. The COSVN also was able to move to Cambodia, but large quantities of food and supplies were left behind to be destroyed. A bridge was built to facilitate return to the area and three C-130-capable airfields and a Special Forces base camp were created, but other operations precluded assigning regular forces to control the area. The operation was thus a mixed success. No serious efforts were made to pacify local villages, and the enemy still was able to stage troops in the area. Both sides learned the importance of the Cambodian sanctuary when Washington denied Westmoreland permission to pursue the enemy across the border.

W. Morrison, *The Elephant and the Tiger* (New York, 1990); G. Moss, *Vietnam: An American Ordeal* (Upper Saddle River, NJ, 1998); W. C. Westmoreland, *A Soldier Reports* (Garden City, NY, 1972).

Larry R. Beck

OPERATION MENU

Operation MENU was the secret bombing of Cambodia* during the Second Indochina War*. This was part of the strategy that President Richard M. Nixon* implemented of combining troop withdrawals and Vietnamization* with the use of U.S. air power in ways that President Lyndon B. Johnson* had not permitted. Within two months of taking office, Nixon, in March 1969, authorized a top-secret B-52 bombing campaign directed against North Vietnamese and Viet Cong* sanctuaries in Cambodia. Military leaders had long sought such authorization, only to be denied by Johnson. Over a fourteen month period, Operation MENU resulted in 3,600 bombing missions—code-named Breakfast, Lunch, Snack, and Supper—that dropped more than 100,000 tons of bombs on mostly sparsely populated areas just inside Cambodia, which had long harbored Viet Cong-North Vietnamese bases and supply lines and the supposed COSVN (Central Office for South Vietnam) headquarters. To assure the secrecy that he later claimed was necessary to protect Cambodia's Prince Norodom Sihanouk*, who allegedly had approved the operation, Nixon went to extraordinary lengths, including falsification of military records and concealment from high-ranking officials. When U.S. and Army of the Republic of Vietnam* ground forces attacked the sanctuaries in the Cambodian Incursion* of May 1970, the secrecy of the bombing ended. The secret bombing of Cambodia later became the basis for one of the proposed articles of impeachment against Nixon.

A. Isaacs, *Without Honor: Defeat in Vietnam and Cambodia* (Baltimore, MD, 1983); W. Shawcross, *Sideshow: Kissinger, Nixon and the Destruction of Cambodia* (New York, 1979).

Gary R. Hess

OPERATION OLYMPIC

U.S. war plans in the Pacific war called for the eventual physical subjugation of the Japanese home islands. If sustained air and naval operations could not do the job, a massive ground invasion would be launched. The overall plan was called Operation DOWNFALL. General Douglas MacArthur* would command all ground and air forces. Admiral Chester W. Nimitz would control all the naval forces. Phase 1 of DOWNFALL, the lodgement in southern Kyūshū in the autumn of 1945, was named OLYMPIC. Phase 2, directed against Tōkyō and the Kantō Plain in the spring of 1946, was Operation CORONET. To be committed in OLYMPIC would be the U.S. Army's Sixth Army, encompassing the U.S. Marines' Fifth Corps (three divisions) plus the U.S. Army's Eleventh Corps (two infantry and one calvary division) and First Corps (three divisions). The Ninth Corps (two divisions) could conduct a feint off Shikoku Island. Follow-up sources numbered one airborne and one infantry division. These forces were to land at four sites in the areas of Miyazaki, Ariake Bay, and Kagoshima, to isolate Kyūshū and destroy enemy forces deployed there. Three infantry and one airborne division were held in reserve.

U.S. planners had hoped to enjoy a decisive three-to-one margin of numerical superiority over the defenders. Rapid Japanese reinforcement of Kyūshū quickly offset these optimistic plans, bringing the opposing ratios closer to one to one. Initial American estimates of Japanese defense strength approximated 230,000 troops as of late April 1945. The two identified combat divisions were expected to be built up slowly to six (or ten at most) divisions in due course. New estimates prepared just before the end of the war boosted Japanese manpower totals to 680,000. After the defeat of Japan, fuller information revealed a total of 735,000 men on Kyūshū. An ominous U.S. intelligence amendment was issued on 29 July, casting a pall over prospects for the success of OLYMPIC.

The tactical and strategic situation had changed drastically by the summer of 1945. With the vicious recent Battle of Okinawa* very much in mind, President Harry S. Truman* and his senior advisers dreaded "another Okinawa" on the Japanese home islands, costing perhaps a million U.S. casualties. This concern contributed to Truman's decision to launch Atomic Attacks* against Japan. Nevertheless, in recent years, American revisionist historians, relying preponderantly on U.S. sources, have questioned the reliability of the figures on anticipated U.S. casualties, preferring numbers at the lowest range of the spectrum. Japanese materials produce more sobering estimates, closer to Truman's worst fears. Indeed, Japanese sources reveal that the Japanese Army prayed for an enemy invasion in order to inflict a level of losses (caused largely by kamikaze attacks and ground forces plus civilian resistance) that would give pause to Allied hopes of crushing Japanese resistance swiftly and at a manageable cost. In any case, the dropping of the atomic bombs on Hiroshima and Nagasaki in August 1945, and Soviet Russia's hurried but belated entry into the Pacific war, mercifully obviated the need to implement Operation OLYMPIC, thus saving many thousands of lives on both sides. *See also* Battle of Iwo Jima.

T. Allen and N. Polmar, *Code-Named Downfall: The Secret Plan to Invade Japan—and Why Truman Dropped the Bomb* (New York, 1995); A. D. Coox, *Japan: The Final Agony* (New York, 1970); H. Saburo in collaboration with A. D. Coox, *Kogun: The Japanese Army in the Pacific War* (Quantico, VA, 1959); J. R. Skates, *The Invasion of Japan: Alternative to the Bomb* (Columbia, SC, 1994).

Alvin D. Coox

OPERATION ORACLE

This is the code name for a failed plan that proposed to use a UN Security Council cease-fire resolution to end the first of the

Taiwan Straits Crises*. It was the brainchild of Secretary of State John Foster Dulles* as part of his strategy to solve the "horrible dilemma" facing the United States of either abandoning the offshore islands or fighting to deny them to the People's Republic of China* (PRC) after the crisis had started on 3 September 1954. Washington started negotiating with Britain and New Zealand on how and when to take action soon after the crisis began. Various factors resulted in the proposal of Operation ORACLE being delayed until 28 January 1955. First, the three major players had different goals in mind. Washington wanted only to maintain the status quo, whereas Britain and New Zealand hoped action would result in turning over the offshore islands of Jinmen and Mazu to the PRC, thereby accepting a two-China answer to the "Taiwan* problem." It took a great deal of personal effort for Dulles to gain an agreement confining the scope of ORACLE to a simple cease-fire. Second, there was a strong objection from Jiang Jieshi*, who categorically objected to any step that might hint at the acceptance of two Chinas. To mollify him, Washington offered to sign the U.S.-China Mutual Defense Treaty of 1954* with Taibei that the Republic of China* (ROC) had long sought. Then, Beijing, after charging the United States with aggression against Taiwan, convicted eleven U.S. pilots and two civilians (who in fact worked for the Central Intelligence Agency*) for espionage.

Taiwan was placed on the UN Security Council agenda on 31 January 1955, along with a decision to invite the PRC to be present at the discussion of the item. Two days later, Beijing rejected the invitation. But the three sponsoring nations could not agree on how to proceed. London not only changed the direction of ORACLE, but practically killed the operation by objecting to discussing the resolution after Beijing had turned down the invitation. Never tabled was the New Zealand cease-fire resolution, which called on the PRC and the ROC to terminate their conflict immediately and find a peaceful solution. The Taiwan Strait Crisis subsided in late April 1955, after Premier Zhou Enlai* expressed at the Bandung Conference* the PRC's willingness to negotiate with the United States to relax tension in East Asia. Washington decided not to pursue the issue further. When the second Taiwan Strait Crisis started in August 1958, Dulles briefly considered reviving ORACLE, but he soon decided against it because it suggested a two-China solution. Taiwan, therefore, remained on the UN Security Council agenda indefinitely.

There are a few significant points derived from this aborted operation. First, Washington for the first time indirectly accepted a two-China formula for resolving the Taiwan question. As the crisis evolved, Dulles developed a "two-pronged approach" of preventing the Communists from taking the offshore islands through ORACLE while safeguarding Taiwan with a security pact. Second, although President Dwight D. Eisenhower* and his key advisers, and even those members of Congress most friendly to Jiang accepted this strategy, London, Wellington, Taibei, and Beijing would not cooperate. Britain blocked ORACLE after the PRC rejected the UN Security Council's invitation. The Guomindang* (Nationalist) government gained the mutual defense treaty without complying with Washington's desires. Without the cooperation of both his allies and the enemy, Dulles's "perfect design" achieved nothing positive despite his enormous efforts.

Chang Su-Ya, " 'Anlihui tinghuo an': Meiguo yinfu diyici taihai weiji celue zhi yi" ["Operation Oracle": John Foster Dulles and the First Taiwan Strait Crisis], *Bulletin of the Institute of Modern History* (June 1993); R. Foot, "The Search for a Modus Vivendi: Anglo-American Relations and China Policy in the Eisenhower Era," in Warren I. Cohen and Akira Iriye (eds.), *The Great Powers in East Asia, 1953–1960* (New York, 1990); T. L. Steele, "Anglo-American Tensions over the Chinese Offshore Islands, 1954–58," Ph.D. dissertation, University of London, 1992.

Chang Su-Ya

OPERATION RANCH HAND

Military strategists long held the belief that chemical defoliation would play a useful role in waging the Second Indochina War*. In 1961, President Ngo Dinh Diem* of the Republic of Vietnam* requested that the U.S. government begin aerial spraying of herbicides to assist in military operations against the Communist insurgency. In August, the South Vietnamese began preliminary herbicide operations with American help. By November, President John F. Kennedy* approved the U.S. Air Force's use of herbicides in Southeast Asia. In January 1962, the program known as Operation RANCH HAND began and continued thereafter to be a joint effort of the U.S. and South Vietnamese governments. The chemical applications were particularly effective against the mangrove forests and (somewhat less so) toward the jungle scrub that provided the enemy with cover and concealment. Another use of the herbicides was to destroy crops, a measure that sought to deprive the Viet Cong* of needed foodstuffs. The use of herbicides peaked in 1967, with 1,687,758 acres sprayed, 85 percent of which was for defoliation and 15 percent of which was for crop destruction.

Herbicide operations were originated by a request from ground commanders or a province chief. Following approval at the highest levels of the U.S. Military Assistance Command, Vietnam,* survey flights began over the intended target area. Typically, RANCH HAND pilots flew 18–27 missions daily from air bases at Danang and Bien Hoa. These missions usually occurred when the temperature was below eighty-five degrees and winds were less than ten knots. Spraying usually lasted only four minutes, the time in which the capacity of the herbicide tanks could be deposited at the optimum rate of three gallons per acre. One UC-123 plane could spray an area eighty meters wide and sixteen kilometers long at 2,500 feet in altitude. Numerous agents were used in Vietnam, all in use in U.S. agriculture for decades, designated by colors based on the varying herbicide, defoliant, and desiccant mixtures of which they were composed. The three in greatest use were Agent Orange, the leading all-purpose jungle herbicide; Agent Blue, targeted mainly at woody plants; and Agent White, which had the same impact as Orange but acted much more slowly. In addition to operations over South Vietnam, the RANCH HAND sprayings also occurred over Laos* from 1965 to 1969, where they mainly concentrated on the areas traversed by the Ho Chi Minh Trail*. Some defoliation missions also took place in the Democratic Republic of Vietnam* over the northern portion of the demilitarized zone.

By 1970, the U.S. government banned the use of Agent Orange and terminated the employment of fixed-wing aircraft in spraying. In December 1970, Secretary of Defense Melvin Laird announced the phase-out of the use of all remaining herbicides, although he reserved the right to restart the program if American lives became jeopardized. In January 1971, a Defense Department directive immediately ended crop destruction operations over South Vietnam. Over a nine-year span, RANCH HAND operations used 18 million gallons of chemicals and destroyed 20 percent of Vietnamese jungle forests. However, doubts lingered as to whether the effect of denying the enemy the use of defoliated areas was worth the adverse impact upon the civilian population of South Vietnam. In addition to creating a flood of refugees that became a nightmare for the Saigon government, the destruction RANCH HAND wreaked served to drive many peasants into active support of the National Liberation Front*. After the war, the ecological devastation in Southeast Asia was considerable, and significant incidences of birth defects were found among the Vietnamese population in sprayed areas. Similar occurrences among the offspring of the 1,200 American servicemen involved in the program have led to partially successful litigation against the federal government.

W. A. Buckingham Jr., *Operation Ranch Hand: The Air Force and Herbicides in Southeast Asia, 1961–1971* (Washington, DC, 1982); P. F. Cecil, *Herbicidal Warfare: The Ranch Hand Project in Vietnam* (New York, 1996); F. Wilcox, *Waiting for an Army to Die: The Tragedy of Agent Orange* (New York, 1983).

Kent G. Sieg

OPERATION ROLLING THUNDER

Following attacks on the U.S. advisory effort in the Republic of Vietnam* at the Pleiku Incident*, President Lyndon B. Johnson* on 13 February 1965 authorized the implementation of Operation ROLLING THUNDER, the systematic bombing of North Vietnam. In conjunction with the much larger-scale bombing of Communist-held areas in South Vietnam (Operation ARC LIGHT) and aerial defoliation (Operation RANCH HAND*), ROLLING THUNDER marked the most intensive use of air power in world history. The main aim of the bombing of North Vietnam was to cause the Democratic Republic of Vietnam* (DRV) to reach a crossover point, where its support of the Viet Cong* insurgency in the south would become too costly for it to continue. Another goal of the bombing program was to bolster the Saigon regime, then under the leadership of Nguyen Van Thieu* and Nguyen Cao Ky*. It also would preserve U.S. credibility as a world power by punishing the Vietnamese Communists.

Initially, the bombing was restricted, but gradually the target list expanded. During its first phase, infiltration routes below the twentieth parallel were attacked. By mid-1965, the target scope was expanded to include static military targets far northward, but this failed to bring about any desire from Hanoi to begin peace talks. U.S. planes began to bomb petroleum, oil, and lubricant (POL) targets in mid-1966, eliminating 75 percent of North Vietnamese capacity within three months. Yet an examination commissioned by Secretary of Defense Robert S. McNamara*, the study was code-named JASON, revealed that the bombings were a strategic failure, since North Vietnam was able to retain adequate reserves in decentralized locales. In light of the ineffectiveness of the POL campaigns, McNamara began an effort to hold the line on the number of ROLLING THUNDER operations, as well as on additional troop augmentations, and instead advocated the establishment of an electronic barrier across the demilitarized zone and into Laos*. After another bombing halt ending in early 1967 failed to initiate peace talks, the third phase of ROLLING THUNDER began, which involved air attacks on major industrial targets and infrastructure in North Vietnam, including targets in the buffer zone near China and in the previously restricted areas around Hanoi and Haiphong.

ROLLING THUNDER failed to achieve any of its stated aims and proved to be an ineffectual lever for compelling the Hanoi leadership to begin peace negotiations. Infiltration only increased in correlation to the bombing; air interdiction never could restrict the southward flow of supplies to the point where inadequate supplies reached the Viet Cong, and the bombing provoked the introduction of regular North Vietnamese Army units to the south. Furthermore, the bombing served to harden the resolve of the DRV leadership, which refused even to entertain the idea of negotiations, based for example on the San Antonio Formula*, with the Americans while bombs fell on their territory. In addition, the bombing failed to stabilize the political situation in the south as a revolving door of governments came and went during the height of the war. In a 31 March 1968 speech after the Tet Offensive*, Johnson set the stage for the opening of the Paris Peace Talks* by declaring a partial halt to the bombing of North Vietnam. ROLLING THUNDER ended on 31 October 1968, when negotiators in Paris worked out an understanding that provided reciprocal guarantees. By then, the costs for both sides of the bombing effort were high. Several more times bombs (a total of 643,000 tons) were dropped on North Vietnam than on the Axis powers during all of World War II, inflicting $600 million in damage and 50,000 casualties. For the United States, 650 planes were lost at a price of $6 billion, captured U.S. pilots became a key bargaining chip for the Hanoi leadership at Paris, and the attacks generated domestic and international public protest of immense proportions, all of which only made successful prosecution of the war even more elusive for the U.S. government.

M. Clodfelter, *The Limits of Air Power: The American Bombing of North Vietnam* (New York, 1989); R. Littauer and N. Uphoff (eds.), *The Air War in Indochina* (Boston, 1972).

Kent G. Sieg

OPLAN 34A

In the early 1960s, the Central Intelligence Agency* (CIA) organized several programs for covert paramilitary harassment of the Democratic Republic of Vietnam*. Some teams were dropped into North Vietnam by air; others raided the coast in small boats. The personnel who went on the missions were Vietnamese, other Asians, and a few Europeans—not Americans—but the United States controlled the operations. By 1963, the CIA was thinking of cutting back on these operations because too many men were being lost for too little result. But the U.S. military decided to take them over and expand them. Operations Plan (OPLAN) 34A was drawn up in December 1963, a graduated plan of covert military pressures against North Vietnam, building up from very minor covert raids to fairly serious bombing. The program then was trimmed down to eliminate the riskier elements, and the version President Lyndon B. Johnson* actually approved on 16 January 1964, although bigger than the CIA's program, was too small to have more than symbolic significance. A military organization, the Special Operations Group (SOG), was formed to take over the operations from the CIA, later renamed the Studies and Observations Group to make its nature less obvious.

In its first months, the SOG, like the CIA, used primarily Vietnamese personnel, not Americans, for operations against North Vietnam. Between January and July 1964, more than sixty men were air-dropped into North Vietnam; they were promptly captured and accomplished nothing. For maritime operations, the SOG brought in larger, faster boats than the CIA had used, so that a heavily armed party of twenty or even thirty men could be landed on the North Vietnamese coast to blow up a bridge or some other facility. Coastal raiding parties suffered some losses, but most of the men were able to return safely, and they did often succeed in destroying their targets. But the only important result of OPLAN 34A was to arouse the North Vietnamese. On 2 August 1964, a few miles from an island that had recently been hit by an OPLAN 34A raid, North Vietnamese naval vessels attacked a U.S. Navy destroyer in the first of the Tonkin Gulf Incidents*. *See also* Second Indochina War.

E. E. Moise, *Tonkin Gulf and the Escalation of the Vietnam War* (Chapel Hill, NC, 1996); S. D. Tourison, *Secret Army, Secret War* (Annapolis, MD, 1995).

Edwin E. Moise

"OVER THE HUMP" FLIGHTS

During the Pacific war, Rangoon, Burma*, was threatened seriously when the Japanese took Moulmin on 30 January 1942. The Chinese foresaw the fall of Rangoon and worried about the isolation they again would confront unless another supply route could be found as an alternative. U.S. President Franklin D. Roosevelt* had the same worry and, at a cabinet meeting on 30 January, proposed an air freight route with a land route as a supplement. Chinese Foreign Minister Song Ziwen* proposed an air route that covered only 700 miles of "flying over comparatively level stretches" between Sadiya in northeast India and Kunming in China. But he did not mention that between the two points rose the Himalayas, providing over this "Hump" the most hazardous flight route in the world. After Japanese forces occupied Rangoon on 8 March, the Burma Road* to China was cut off and the air route came into operation. General Joseph W. Stilwell*, commander of U.S. Army forces in the China-Burma-India Theater* and the supervisor of the Lend Lease* to China, was designated to manage flights "over the Hump."

Flights over the Hump endured endless hardships and dangers. By April, owing to interruptions by the monsoon and by airdrops to the refugees, each transport had managed to make an average of only two round-trips a month, resulting in delivery to the Republic of China* a monthly average of less than 100 tons. Extremely unsatisfied, Guomindang* (Nationalist) government leader Jiang Jieshi* presented three demands to Stilwell at the end of June, one of which was to deliver 5,000 tons a month over the Hump, beginning in August. Jiang's government wanted Washington to concentrate on increasing the capacity of air transportation over the Hump to keep war material coming for its own use and to fuel and maintain the Flying Tigers of General Claire L. Chennault*. But the prevailing "Europe first" strategy of the United States and the terrible flying conditions made increasing tonnage impossible. Roosevelt, however, decided to try to meet China's demands, cabling in October that in 1943, 100 transport planes would be assigned to deliver 5,000 tons a month over the Hump. Tonnage, he promised, would rise from 3,000 in May to 5,500 in July to 8,000 in September.

The Trident Conference on 11 May 1943 was a turning point. There, the United States turned to the policy of attaching the same importance to Asia as Europe and made the promise to raise Hump deliveries to 10,000 tons a month. Despite all the promises, crews and equipment were inadequate, maintenance poor, the airfield in Assam shoddy and inadequate, and the weather treacherous. Natural obstacles of terrain and climate were extreme, and the monsoon of the summer months thickened the misery. To raise Hump deliveries to 10,000 tons a month as Trident prescribed was a difficult struggle. An Office of Strategic Services unit rescued 125 U.S. crewmen in 1943, but this represented less than a third of all who went down, with the rest lost to death or capture. Nevertheless, with reinforcements and new commitment after the Trident Conference, morale and flying conditions improved. After the rains ended, Hump delivery was raised to a remarkable 13,000 tons in November. Tonnage in 1944 continued to rise, finally reaching the unprecedented total of 46,000 early in 1945. The Hump flights made an important contribution to defeating Japan in World War II.

B. W. Tuchman, *Stilwell and the American Experience in China* (New York, 1972); T. H. White and A. A. Jacoby, *Thunder Out of China* (New York, 1946).

Xiang E

P

PAK CHŎNG-HŬI (1917–1979)

In May 1961, Pak Chŏng-hŭi seized power in a military coup in the Republic of Korea* (ROK), ruling thereafter as chairman of the National Reconstruction Council until 1963 and then as president from 1963 to 1979. Born in Kumi near Taegu, he was the last son of a poor rural family. Pak taught at a primary school for three years until April 1940, when he entered the Military Officer Training Academy of the Manchurian Imperial Army in Changchun, China, and then attended the Japanese Military Academy in 1942. In 1944, Pak became a sublieutenant in Japan's Kwangtung Army, serving until the end of World War II. Returning to southern Korea in May 1946, he became an officer in the Constabulary Army during the U.S. Occupation of Korea*. In October 1946, while suppressing an insurrection at Taegu, South Korean police under the direction of the U.S. military government killed his closest brother, a regional leader in the South Korean Workers' Party (SKWP), thereby causing Pak to join the SKWP, then under Communist leadership, in an act of anti-Americanism. The new ROK government arrested him in November 1948, but he escaped execution with the help of his army colleagues and after actively assisting in the arrest of other SKWP members. Removed from the military, he was sentenced to ten years in prison.

Pak returned to service in the Korean War* and then received artillery training in the United States in 1954. During the late 1950s, he gained the loyality of a group of young officers, including Chŏn Du-hwan* and Kim Jong-p'il*, who helped him seize political power on 16 May 1961. Pak had criticized the previous government of Jang Myŏn*, who had become prime minister after the Syngman Rhee's Ouster* in April 1960, for inefficiency and established dictatorial power. Before the end of 1961, he had dissolved all political and social organizations and arrested more than 3,000 leftists and more than 4,000 suspected criminals. Meanwhile, Pak also nullified farming and fishing debts and investigated high-level business corruption, while implementing such social reforms as family planning, reduction of illiteracy, simplification of family rituals, and closure of dance halls. Surprisingly, Pak's ideological background caused Kim Il Sung*, leader of the Democratic People's Republic of Korea* (DPRK), to propose secret talks for national reunification, but the meeting of a North Korean envoy with Pak's junta created friction with Washington. More troublesome, however, was domestic political opposition, led by dissidents Kim Dae-jung* and Kim Young-sam*, and U.S. pressure on Pak to fulfill his original pledge to quickly restore civilian rule. Despite public criticism for scandals linked to funding of his Democratic Republic Party, Pak won the presidential election in 1963 by a narrow margin.

Pak's focus on economic development contributed to his pursuit of Japan-Korea Normalization*, resulting in a treaty in 1965 that boosted bilateral trade and Japanese investment. The United States also strongly supported the reconciliation. To further mitigate U.S. criticism of political repression in South Korea, he offered troops to fight in the Second Indochina War* during the Kennedy-Pak Conference* in November 1961. This strategy was effective with President Lyndon B. Johnson*, who accepted an increasing number of South Korean troops to serve Vietnam during the Johnson-Pak Conferences*. In return, Pak gained funds and advice to modernize the ROK army, economic aid, cooperation for scientific and technological development, and access to world trade markets. By the late 1960s, South Korea was experiencing rapid economic growth, winning public support for Pak. Reelected in 1967 and again in 1969, he gained revision of the Korean constitution to allow himself a third successive term in 1971. Pak altered the constitution again in 1972, giving himself almost unlimited powers, leading to rising censorship, political repression, and torture of political prisoners.

Economic success in South Korea allowed Pak to implement a positive policy toward the DPRK. In the 1970s, his overtures led to a series of bilateral contacts: the North-South Red Cross Talks, the 4 July North-South Joint Communiqué, and the North-South Coordinating Committee. Yet when these exchanges failed to produce any substantive results, Pak, in an official declaration on 23 June 1973, recognized the existence of "two Koreas." Meanwhile, the gross national product continued to rise at about 10 percent annually. Pak's political leverage with the United States, however, had evaporated after 1969 with changes in U.S. East Asia policy under President Richard M. Nixon*. The Nixon Doctrine* and Vietnamization* resulted in U.S. withdrawal from Southeast Asia. Meanwhile, Pak made every effort to stress the critical necessity of maintaining a U.S. presence in South Korea. After the ROK's efforts to maintain support in Congress led to the Koreagate* scandal in October 1976, new President Jimmy Carter* not only criticized Pak for violating human rights, but reiterated campaign plans to withdraw U.S. troops from the ROK. An increasing sense of vulnerability already had caused Pak to begin developing nuclear weapons. Then, in 1979, as public resistance against his regime peaked in Pusan and Masan, Pak was assassinated by his old friend Kim Jae-kyu, who was the director of the Korean Central Intelligence Agency. *See also* Pak Chŏng-hŭi's Assassination.

Cho Kap-jae, *Nae Mudŏm-e Ch'im-ŭl Paet-ŏra!: Kŭndaehwa Hyŏgmyŏngga Pak Chŏng-hŭi ŭi Pijang-han Saeng-ae* [Spit on My Grave!: The Tragic Life of Park Chung-hee, the Modern Revolutionist], 4 vols. (Seoul, 1999); K. Hong, "Unequal Partners: ROK-U.S. Relations During the Vietnam War," Ph.D. dissertation, University of South Carolina, 1991; Yi Dŏ-sung, *Silrok Pak Chŏng-hŭi wa Hanil-hoedam* [An Authentic Record: Park Chung-hee and Korea-Japan Talks] (Seoul, 1995).

Heo Man-ho

PAK CHŎNG-HŬI'S ASSASSINATION

Pak Chŏng-hŭi*, president of the Republic of Korea*, was killed by Kim Jae-kyu, director of the Korea Central Intelligence Agency (KCIA), about 7:40 P.M. on 26 October 1979. On that evening, there was an informal dinner at a secure residence in Seoul attended by Pak, Kim Jae-kyu, Kim Kye-wŏn (chief presidential secretary), and Ch'a Chi-ch'ŏl (chief of presidential security service). Kim Jae-kyu left the dinner at

6:40 P.M. after a disagreement over current political issues (insurrections in Pusan and Masan, and the divestiture of the deputy of the opposition leader Kim Young-sam*). He apparently then armed himself with a pistol, and ordered his subordinates Pak Sŏn-ho and Pak Hŭng-ju to prepare the assassination. Returning to the dinner, Kim fired the first bullet at Ch'a and the second at Pak. At the same time, Kim's men shot the presidential bodyguards. A few minutes later, Kim shot once more at Ch'a and Pak, using Pak Sŏn-ho's pistol because his pistol had jammed, and killed President Pak and the chief of presidential security. Perhaps if Ch'a had been armed, he could have saved the president.

Despite the seemingly spontaneous nature of Pak Chŏng-hŭi's assassination, the surrounding sociopolitical background explains the outcome. Pak's economic policy had confronted a series of difficulties toward the end of the 1970s, including a decline in exports resulting in a trade deficit, the increase of foreign debts, insufficient consumer goods, and severe inflation. Pak's retrenchment policy to cope with this situation sparked a series of the labor disputes in 1977 that reached their peak on 11 August when a young girl was killed as police repressed a sit-in strike staged by the workers of a textile export company in the main building of the opposition New Democratic Party (NDP). This incident triggered the rise of radical opposition movements against the Pak regime as labor unions, students organizations, and dissident intellectuals united with the opposition party.

Meanwhile, under pressure from the U.S. administration of Jimmy Carter*, the Pak government was forced to release opposition leader Kim Dae-jung* from house arrest in December 1978. Also, Kim Young-sam, having been reinstated as president of the NDP in May 1978, criticized the government's economic policy and demanded Pak's resignation. In response, Pak placed Kim Dae-jung under house arrest again, and mobilized disabled veterans to attack Kim Young-sam in the main building of the NDP. This political repression strengthened unrest among the South Korean people. On 16 October 1979, local citizens joined student demonstrations in Pusan that spread to Masan and Ch'ang-wŏn and eventually turned into a series of riots. The situation became so serious that the government finally declared martial law on 17 October.

The ensuing assassination of Pak Chŏng-hŭi was the result of a confrontation within his inner circle over the measures required to cope with this civil unrest. Kim Jae-kyu finally determined to kill Pak and Ch'a Chi-ch'ŏl because of a combination of Pak's favoritism for Ch'a, the blunt arrogance of Ch'a toward Kim, and Kim's anxiety that he would be eliminated because he favored a soft approach toward dissent. Some analysts have alleged that the Carter administration encouraged Pak's assassination because it strongly opposed his nuclear weapons development project, self-defense policy, and violation of human rights. But evidence of any direct U.S. involvement remains unsubstantiated. Kim Jae-kyu was known to meet frequently in 1979 with U.S. Ambassador William H. Glysteen Jr. and Robert Brewster, the department head of the Central Intelligence Agency * in Seoul. Yet if there had been an actual plan supported by U.S. intelligence agencies, the process of the assassination and its aftermath would have been different. The assassination of Pak resulted in the military coup led by Chŏn Du-hwan* on 12 December 1979, to be followed by the Kwangju Incident* on 17 May 1980. The ensuing political turmoil engendered strong South Korean Anti-Americanism*.

Cho Kap-jae, *Nae Mudŏm-e Ch'im-ŭl Paet-ŏra!* [Spit on My Grave!]: *Kŭndaehwa Hyŏgmyŏngga Pak Chŏng-hŭi ŭi Pijang-han Saeng-ae* [The Tragic Life of Pak Chŏng-hŭi, the Modern Revolutionist], vol. 1 (Seoul, 1999); *Joong-ang Ilbo*, 27 October 1997; U.S. House of Representatives, Subcommittee on International Organization, Committee on International Relations, *Investi-*

gation of Korean-American Relations (Washington, DC, 1978).

Heo Man-ho

PAK HŎN-YŎNG (1901–1956)

Pak Hŏn-yŏng was the leader of the Communist underground in Korea during World War II and later foreign minister of the Democratic People's Republic of Korea* (DPRK). Born in South Ch'ungch'ŏng Province, he was educated at the elite Kyŏnggi High School in Seoul. After studying English for a brief time at the Seoul YMCA, Pak left in 1920 for Tōkyō, where he was influenced by socialists such as Sakai Toshihiko. Lacking funds, he went to Shanghai in 1921. His interest in Communism* began there, and in 1922, he was one of fifty-seven Korean delegates to attend the First Congress of the Toilers of the Far East in Moscow. He reentered Korea that year as an agent of the Chinese Communist Party* and was arrested immediately by the Japanese colonial authorities. After serving an eighteen-month prison sentence, Pak worked as a reporter with the *Dong-a Ilbo* newspaper. Late in 1923, he helped create the Communist Tuesday Association in Seoul, and in 1925 he played a major role in the establishment of the Korean Communist Party. Following another jail term, Pak fled to Soviet East Asia and returned to Shanghai for one year before going back to Korea in 1933. He promptly served another six-year prison term. Upon his release in 1939, Pak went underground and began to reorganize the Korean Communist Party.

During the Pacific war, he reportedly worked as a bricklayer in Kwangju. In the early liberation period, Pak became leader of a rehabilitated Korean Communist Party in Seoul. In 1946, U.S. occupation authorities announced policies designed to cripple the power of the party. In September, they issued a warrant for Pak's arrest. They also believed that Pak and other Communists were responsible for a series of strikes and peasant protests across southern Korea in the fall of 1946. William R. Langdon, U.S. political adviser in Korea, later wrote to Secretary of State George C. Marshall* that there was "ample evidence" that Pak, with support from the northern Communists, was exploiting existing discontent among laborers and farmers. In his reexamination of the U.S. Occupation of Korea*, historian Bruce Cumings shows, however, that the autumn uprisings were in fact a classic case of peasant rebellion, fomented not by northerners, but by southern leaders of local people's committees driven by long-standing and deep social, economic, and political grievances.

After becoming head of the new South Korean Workers' Party in October 1946, Pak escaped to Soviet-occupied territory in the north. In 1948, he was appointed vice premier and foreign minister in the first cabinet organized by North Korean leader Kim Il Sung*. Pak was more of a genuine Communist internationalist than was Kim Il Sung, and better versed in Marxism-Leninism. The two competed for power and influence, but Pak was too influential at this stage to be purged or dismissed by Kim. He played a key role in persuading Joseph Stalin to approve a North Korean invasion of South Korea, arguing erroneously that a quick victory was certain because of an anticipated large guerrilla uprising and overwhelming popular support for liberation. During the Korean War*, as DPRK foreign minister, Pak claimed that the United States used Germ Warfare* against North Korea. His political career effectively ended as the result of a purge in 1953, which Kim directed against his allies in the government. On 1 April 1955, Kim Il Sung accused him of being a "hireling of U.S. imperialism." Pak became the scapegoat for Kim's failure to unify the country and was executed the next year.

B. Cumings, *The Origins of the Korean War*, Vol. 1: *Liberation and the Emergence of Separate Regimes, 1945–1947* (Princeton, NJ, 1981); Dae-Sook Suh (ed.), *Documents of Korean Communism*

1918–1948 (Princeton, NJ, 1970); R. Scalapino and C. Lee (eds.), *Communism in Korea: The Movement* (Berkeley, CA, 1972); U.S. Department of State, *Foreign Relations of the United States*, 1946, Vol. 8: *The Far East* (Washington, DC, 1971).

Steven Hugh Lee

PANAY INCIDENT

This Japanese air attack on this U.S. ship in December 1937 increased tensions between the United States and Japan five months after the Sino-Japanese War broke out on 7 July 1937 following the Marco Polo Bridge Incident*. Sino-Japanese fighting already had spread from north to south. By September, the Japanese had launched a full-scale assault on Nanjing, the capital of the Guomindang* (Nationalist) government, forcing Jiang Jieshi* to evacuate Nanjing and move to Hankou. In the meantime, some of the staff of the embassies and consulates also were evacuating Nanjing. Some took refuge in the gunboats moored in the Yangze River. On 12 December, a group of Japanese warplanes bombed and machine-gunned and sank a U.S. gunboat named the *Panay* on the river. Many were wounded and two people later died. Standard Oil tankers also were attacked and destroyed, with the captain of one tanker killed. On the same day, HMS *Ladybird* also was fired upon by the Japanese, and one seaman was killed and several wounded.

Several factors justified an immediate protest against these attacks. Every time the *Panay* changed its location, the U.S. consulate notified Japanese authorities. The gunboat also was flying a U.S. flag. It was reported that the weather had been clear. These incidents coincided with the Rape of Nanjing*, when Japanese soldiers indiscriminately killed countless Chinese civilians. The British government proposed economic sanctions (and some kind of possible military action) against Japan to the U.S. government. In Washington, anti-Japanese economic measures under the Trading with the Enemy Act were discussed, but President Franklin D. Roosevelt* was reluctant to act. Neither Britain nor the United States were prepared or willing to go to war with Japan at that time. The Japanese government insisted that the incident was "entirely due to a mistake." The United States accepted as satisfactory Tōkyō's prompt and sincere apology, and its promise to pay indemnities. The formal Japanese note arrived in Washington on Christmas Eve, formally settling the *Panay* incident between the two countries.

D. Borg, *The United States and the Far Eastern Crisis of 1933–1938* (New Haven, CT, 1964).

Ishii Osamu

P'ANMUNJŎM TRUCE TALKS

During the Korean War*, representatives from the People's Republic of China* (PRC), Democratic People's Republic of Korea* (DPRK), and United Nations Command (UNC) held armistice negotiations at P'anmunjŏm, Korea, from 25 October 1951 to 27 July 1953. The P'anmunjŏm truce talks led to the conclusion of the Korean Armistice Agreement*, which ended the fighting. Once the war reached a stalemate just north of the thirty-eighth parallel in late May 1951, U.S. officials once again sought a cease-fire, after General Douglas MacArthur* had scuttled a planned peace initiative in March. On 31 May, George F. Kennan* paid a personal visit to the Soviet delegate to the United Nations, Jacob A. Malik, and signaled Washington's willingness for truce talks. Kim Il Sung* visited Mao Zedong* on 3 June in Beijing, and although they decided not to refuse peace negotiations, they agreed that the more UNC troops Communist forces could eliminate on the battlefield, the more favorable terms they would gain at the negotiating table. On 23 June, Malik publicly proposed talks to achieve a cease-fire. After preparatory talks, the UNC and PRC-DPRK delegations began formal armistice negotiations at Kaesŏng on July 10 while the fighting continued. During August, the Communist delegation adjourned the talks in response to fabricated evidence of UNC violations of the Kaesŏng security zone. Lieutenant General Matthew B. Ridgway*, the UNC commander, agreed to resume negotiations only after the meeting place was changed to P'anmunjŏm, a small village east of Kaesŏng at the thirty-eighth parallel.

Negotiations at Kaesŏng had deadlocked on the first of four substantive agenda items, which called for the determination of a military demarcation line to establish a demilitarized zone (DMZ). A pattern had emerged with both sides waging a tit-for-tat diplomatic struggle that considered the talks a "political battle" and extension of the battlefield. For example, the UNC, contradicting public policy statements before the talks, demanded a demarcation line deep in North Korea. The Communist delegation angrily insisted on a line along the thirty-eighth parallel. After the talks resumed on 25 October at P'anmunjŏm, the negotiators agreed on the line of battle as the basis for a DMZ. The two sides then moved deliberately toward resolving the second agenda item, agreeing on terms for supervising the cease-fire. Whereas the UNC believed that if tougher provisions were approved, peace would last longer in Korea, the Communist side viewed the military cease-fire as merely a short transition period before peaceful reunification, and strict inspection terms an interference in the DPRK's internal affairs. By April 1952, negotiators had settled a third issue, providing for a postwar political meeting on Korea that would eventuate in the Geneva Conference of 1954*, but talks then deadlocked on the remaining agenda item regarding return of prisoners of war (POWs). While the UNC escalated its air war against North Korea to force acceptance of voluntary repatriation, the Communist delegation charged the UNC with waging Germ Warfare* to embarrass its adversary into approving the return of all prisoners. Neither tactic resolved a Korean War POW Controversy* that lasted more than a year.

Military operations continued during the P'anmunjŏm truce talks, as both sides paid more attention to the negotiations if fighting did not show progress at the front. They launched new offensive campaigns if the talks were not moving in the direction desired. On 8 October 1952, the negotiations adjourned, moving the political struggle to the United Nations in New York City. After intense diplomatic efforts under the leadership of India, a framework emerged to resolve the POW dispute. In late March 1953, Beijing and P'yŏngyang altered their tone in the P'anmunjŏm negotiations after Moscow began to pursue "peaceful coexistence" following Joseph Stalin's death on 5 March. Kim and Peng Dehuai*, the commander of Chinese forces, wrote to General Mark W. Clark*, the UNC commander, on 28 March, agreeing to exchange wounded and sick prisoners on the basis of voluntary repatriation. Two days later, Premier Zhou Enlai* of the PRC suggested immediate resumption of the talks, resulting in the delegations reconvening officially at P'anmunjŏm on 26 April. Both sides reached an agreement on 6 June providing for those prisoners who were unwilling to return to their own countries to be placed in the custody of a neutral commission for a period of ninety days after the truce became effective, during which each side could persuade its nationals to return home. After 575 meetings over more than two years, at 10:00 A.M. on 27 July 1953, the P'anmunjŏm truce talks concluded when Major General William K. Harrison Jr. and North Korean General Nam Il signed the armistice agreement.

R. Foot, *Substitute for Victory: The Politics of Peacemaking at the Korean Armistice Talks* (Ithaca, NY, 1990); A. E. Goodman (ed.), *Negotiating While Fighting: The Diary of Admiral C. Turner Joy at the Korean Armistice Conference* (Stanford, CA, 1978); J. Goulden, *Korea: The Untold Story of the War* (New York, 1982); S. G. Zhang, *Mao's Mil-*

itary Romanticism: China and the Korean War, 1950–53 (Lawrence, KS, 1995).

Li Xiaobing

PARIS PEACE ACCORDS (27 January 1973)

Representatives of the United States, the Republic of Vietnam*, the Democratic Republic of Vietnam* (DRV), and the Provisional Revolutionary Government (PRG) formally signed The Agreement on Ending the War and Restoring Peace in Vietnam at Paris on 27 January 1973. The Paris Accords marked the culmination of nearly five years of negotiations and, in the view of President Richard M. Nixon*, finally fulfilled his pledge of "peace with honor." The agreement consisted of nine chapters and four attached protocols. The first chapter reconfirmed the Geneva Accords of 1954* and the temporary division of Vietnam. The second part dealt with military provisions. It directed a cease-fire beginning on 27 January at 7:00 P.M. Washington time and listed the actions permitted by all sides during this period. It also specified the withdrawal of all U.S. and allied forces, exclusive of a small advisory force, from South Vietnam within sixty days. Furthermore, it prohibited the introduction of any outside forces into the territory of South Vietnam and limited replacement of the military forces already there to a one-to-one basis. Part three said that within the same sixty days, all American prisoners of war were to be released. However, the exchange of Vietnamese civilians was left to be worked out in future discussions.

As for Vietnam's political future, chapter four contained a joint U.S.–North Vietnamese statement that spelled out the South Vietnamese people's guaranteed right to determine their own future without outside interference. Elections would be organized by a National Council for National Reconciliation and Concord that would consist of members from all South Vietnamese parties. The next part acknowledged formally the continued existence of the South Vietnamese state by recognizing the demarcation line between it and North Vietnam, while at the same time providing for unification through future negotiations. The sixth chapter discussed the international machinery to supervise the boundary between the two Vietnamese states. Chapter seven dealt with Laos* and Cambodia* and reconfirmed the applicable provisions of the 1954 Geneva settlement and the Geneva Accords of 1962*. The next chapter expressed the commitment of both the United States and North Vietnam to seeking normalization, conciliation, and cooperation. The last chapter was procedural. The four protocols outlined the measures necessary for implementation of the agreement. These related to the return of the prisoners of war, creation of an International Control Commission to oversee the cease-fire, establishment of a Joint Military Commission setting up a temporary four-party group to be superseded by a two-party commission after U.S. withdrawal, and measures by which to conduct mine-clearing operations.

Almost immediately, the integrity of the Paris Accords came under assault. Within a week, DRV/PRG forces in the south had launched a land-grabbing effort. In response, President Nguyen Van Thieu* ordered counterattacks by the Army of the Republic of Vietnam* and simultaneously began his own aggrandizement program. Additionally, both North and South Vietnamese governments held back the release of large numbers of the other side's prisoners. During the balance of 1973, National Security Adviser Henry A. Kissinger* visited Hanoi and made several trips to Paris to negotiate full implementation of the rather ambiguously worded agreement with the result that numerous provisions were reworked. However, with the 1975 takeover of South Vietnam by northern forces, the Paris Accords became inoperative. Yet certain provisions of the agreement, such as those on accounting for missing personnel and promised development aid to Vietnam, remained basic issues in U.S. relations with the Socialist Republic of Vietnam* in ensuing years. *See also* Paris Peace Talks.

A. R. Isaacs, *Without Honor: Defeat in Vietnam and Cambodia* (Baltimore, MD, 1983); T. H. Nguyen and J. L. Schecter, *The Palace File* (New York, 1986); G. Porter, *A Peace Denied: The United States, Vietnam and the Paris Agreement* (Bloomington, IN, 1975).

Kent S. Sieg

PARIS PEACE TALKS

On 10 May 1968, these negotiations began to end the Second Indochina War*. At first termed "official conversations," the initial period of talks engaged only the representatives of the Democratic Republic of Vietnam* (DRV) and the United States and dwelt primarily on arranging for a complete cessation of Operation ROLLING THUNDER*, the bombing of North Vietnam. Leading the U.S. delegation was W. Averell Harriman*, a venerable statesman, and Cyrus Vance, a trusted troubleshooter of President Lyndon B. Johnson*; their counterparts for the DRV were Xuan Thuy*, Ha Van Lau, and, on an intermittent basis, Hanoi Politburo member Le Duc Tho*. These discussions, taking place at the Hotel Majestic, deadlocked early on the issues of reciprocal guarantees and the nature of representation for both the National Liberation Front* (NLF) and the Republic of Vietnam* (RVN). Unofficial "tea break" contacts between the delegations and behind-the-scenes Soviet involvement, however, engineered a breakthrough. By the end of October, the U.S. and DRV delegations had reached an unwritten "understanding" that ended in its entirety aerial bombardment of the north, allowed representatives from both the NLF and the RVN to sit with the DRV and U.S. delegations through an "our side–your side" formula, and provided for certain military guarantees, such as proscriptions against attacks on southern cities, limitations on infiltration, and full reestablishment of the demilitarized zone. The notorious disagreement over the shape of the conference table, along with a dispute over procedural matters, delayed the convening of the first working session of the four-party meetings until 18 January 1969.

The talks in Paris continued over the next four years along two distinct lines. At the Majestic, the plenary sessions began on 25 January 1969 and continued on a regular basis thereafter. Successive leaders of the U.S. delegation in these "formal" talks included the prominent diplomats Henry Cabot Lodge Jr.*, David K. E. Bruce*, and William Porter. However, these sessions soon devolved into unproductive accusatory rhetorical diatribe on all sides. There was another, more successful, track. U.S. National Security Adviser Henry A. Kissinger* began secret contacts with the North Vietnamese even before President Richard M. Nixon* had assumed office. He subsequently met with DRV representatives on a number of occasions during 1969 and encouraged the president to undertake an exchange of letters with Ho Chi Minh*. In conjunction with this secret diplomacy, the Nixon administration pursued stiffened military action while implementing Vietnamization*. In 1970, Kissinger began to engage in secret discussions with Tho; these ultimately led to the end of U.S. participation in the war. The April Cambodian Incursion* derailed momentum, however, and it was not until 31 May 1971, when Kissinger assured Tho that he would set a concrete deadline for the withdrawal of U.S. forces from South Vietnam and dropped insistence upon the mutual withdrawal of North Vietnamese forces, that movement forward began. Yet with characteristic obstinacy, on 26 June, Tho responded with a plan that called for the installation of a coalition regime in Saigon, a point Kissinger and Nixon found unacceptable. Impasse again arose.

Talks became more fruitful during 1972. In an effort to gain forward movement, on 25 January, Nixon publicly revealed Kissinger's secret talks with Tho. Nixon's dramatic opening to the People's Republic of China* soon followed, as did the scheduling of a summit in Moscow to discuss strategic arms limitation. Disturbed by the evolving détente between the United States and Hanoi's major allies, the North Vietnamese launched the Easter Offensive* at the end of March. Nixon's resumption of the bombing against the DRV and apparent Soviet preference to continue with the summit brought about a more conciliatory attitude in Hanoi. Beginning meetings with Kissinger in mid-July, Tho gradually conceded on a number of preconditions that the DRV had adhered to rigidly, such as insistence on unilateral withdrawal of all U.S. forces and the jettisoning of Nguyen Van Thieu* as RVN president. In October, on the eve of the U.S. presidential election, Kissinger announced that "peace is at hand," but the statement was premature, because the RVN produced sixty-nine modifications. Hanoi, likely seeing an opportunity to drive a wedge between the United States and the RVN, subsequently refused to make even minor concessions. In December, talks broke off. To assuage Thieu and compel Hanoi, Nixon ordered the second of the LINEBACKER Bombings* during the ensuing holiday season. The "Christmas Bombings" were the war's most concentrated bombardment and brought the DRV back to the table on 2 January 1973. Within a week, Kissinger and Tho worked out an agreement virtually identical to the one of October. Nixon's pledge of substantial and continuing military support gained Thieu's acceptance of the Paris Peace Accords*, initialed by Kissinger and Tho on 23 January and officially signed four days later.

W. Bundy, *A Tangled Web: The Making of Foreign Policy in the Nixon Presidency* (New York, 1998); A. E. Goodman, *Lost Peace: The Search for a Negotiated Settlement of the Vietnam War* (Berkeley, CA, 1986); W. Isaacson, *Kissinger: A Biography* (New York, 1992); R.D. Schulzinger, *Henry Kissinger: Doctor of Diplomacy* (New York, 1989).

Kent S. Sieg

PARKER, PETER (1804–1888)

As a medical missionary, and to a lesser degree as a diplomat, Peter Parker was a major figure in Sino-American relations during the nineteenth century. A devout Presbyterian, he took seriously the mandate of Matthew 28:16 to go and "teach all nations." In 1834, after earning a bachelor of arts and a medical degree from Yale University, Parker was sent to China by the American Board of Commissioners for Foreign Missions* as a medical missionary. An ophthalmic infirmary that Parker established in 1835 rapidly grew into the Guangzhou Hospital. By 1855, when Parker turned the hospital over to Dr. John Kerr, the institution had treated more than 50,000 patients. Not only did Parker's medical practice open many new relationships with the Chinese people, but he became the first foreign physician to train Chinese medical students in Western techniques relating to ophthalmology, tumor surgery, lithotomy, and anesthesiology. By the 1840s, Parker had gained an international reputation as the pioneer of the new profession of medical missionary, and his hospital had become the forerunner for similar institutions in China and elsewhere throughout the world.

Parker's greatest influence on U.S.–East Asian relations came as a pioneering medical missionary, but he also had some impact on the history of U.S. foreign policy. During a leave of absence in 1841 and 1842, he lobbied many influential Americans, such as President John Tyler and Secretary of State Daniel Webster,* to undertake a diplomatic mission to China. From 1834 to 1844, along with Elijah Bridgman and Samuel Wells Williams, Parker served as an adviser, interpreter, and translator for Caleb Cushing* in the negotiations for the Treaty of Wangxia*. The stipulations permitting Americans to build hospitals and churches in the treaty ports and to employ Chinese nationals as teachers can be attributed directly to Parker and to the gratitude of the Chinese commissioners for his skillful medical services.

In his subsequent career both as chargé (1846–1848 and 1850–1852) and U.S. commissioner to China (1855–1857), Parker accomplished little. Combative and tactless, he seemed unsuited for the practice of diplomacy during the turbulent years of the Taiping Rebellion*. He often quarreled with U.S. consuls and Chinese officials over such matters as claims cases and the Coolie Trade*, which Parker emphatically denounced as an "immoral traffic" in human beings. As commissioner, his main agenda involved revision of the Treaty of Wangxia. Secretary of State William L. Marcy instructed Parker to persuade the Chinese to extend the right to trade beyond the treaty ports and to obtain permission to establish a U.S. legation in Beijing. With high-ranking Chinese officials refusing to even meet with him, Parker accomplished nothing. By 1856, Parker had become so frustrated at Chinese intransigence that he recommended that the United States temporarily seize Taiwan* and hold it hostage to successful negotiations. He also recommended that the United States collaborate with Britain and France in using military force to compel the Chinese to be more flexible. Both the Pierce and the Buchanan administrations rejected these proposals, because neither wanted to take any steps that might involve the United States in a war with China. Ineffective as a commissioner, Parker was recalled in 1857. Thereafter, Parker withdrew from public affairs and lived a quiet life in Washington, D.C.

E. V. Gulick, *Peter Parker and the Opening of China* (Cambridge, MA, 1983); G. B. Stevens and W. F. Markwick (eds.), *The Life, Letters, and Journals of the Rev. and Hon. Peter Parker, M.D.* (Boston, 1896); T. Tong, *United States Diplomacy in China, 1844–60* (Seattle, WA, 1964).

Kenneth E. Shewmaker

PATHET LAO

The Pathet Lao (Lao Nation or Land of the Lao) was a popular front organization founded by Prince Souphanouvong* in 1950, that became synonymous with the Lao Communist movement. From its inception, the Pathet Lao had close ties to the Vietnamese Lao Dong Party. Pathet Lao troops fought as junior partners with the Vietminh* against French Colonialism* in the First Indochina War*. When the Vietminh wrestled control of most of Sam Neua and portions of Phong Saly, Luang Prabang, and Xieng Khounag provinces (all adjacent to the Democratic Republic of Vietnam*) from France in 1953, the Pathet Lao obtained key territorial bases, from which it waged war for the next twenty years against the Royal Lao government. During the Geneva Conference of 1954*, the United States successfully opposed Hanoi's and Beijing's efforts to win official recognition for the Pathet Lao or an autonomous zone of control for it in the northern provinces of Laos. The best the Communist side could obtain was Pathet Lao regrouping in Sam Neua and Phong Saly, where it was granted temporary administrative authority pending Royal Lao reestablishment of control and integration of the Pathet Lao into the government. The Pathet Lao had no intention of allowing the Royalists to regain control of its areas.

The Eisenhower administration advised anti-Communist and neutralist Lao leaders not to reintegrate the Pathet Lao, citing Czechoslovakia in the late 1940s as the inevitable fate of coalition governments with Communists. Neutralist leader Prince Souvanna Phouma* ignored U.S. warnings. From 1957 to 1958, the Pathet Lao joined a coalition government under his leadership. In May 1958, the Pathet Lao successfully contested supplemental legislative elections for the Lao National Assembly. This electoral success set off alarm bells in Washington. The Central Intelligence Agency* began a program to create a viable "Young Turk" non-Communist opposition to the Pathet Lao. Later in 1958, a pro-U.S. government replaced the coalition and harassed members of the Pathet Lao, imprisoning its leaders and eventually driving its forces back to their northern home bases. The civil war resumed, leading to the Laotian Crisis of 1961*. Although the Pathet Lao again joined a Souvanna coalition after the Geneva Accords of 1962*, North Vietnam did not abide by its provisions for withdrawal of troops and the United States soon countered with a program of covert support for its Lao allies. Thus, Laos was not neutralized, but rather underwent a de facto partition with seasonal ebb and flow warfare on the partition line.

After 1962, Souvanna increasingly allowed the United States to wage a proxy war in Laos against the Pathet Lao and North Vietnamese, climaxing in the Secret U.S. Air War in Laos*. The Pathet Lao grew in size and competency as a military force, but North Vietnamese troops assumed the brunt of the fighting and provided the military muscle. In the field of economic and social development, the Pathet Lao made strong gains in the areas it controlled. One year after the Paris Peace Accords* of January 1973 that ended the Second Indochina War*, the Pathet Lao again formed a coalition with Souvanna and joined the Royal Lao government as equals. The U.S. withdrawal from Southeast Asia after 1973 would determine the outcome in Laos. The Pathet Lao and North Vietnamese crushed the remnants of the formerly U.S.-supported Hmong* and increasingly dominated Lao civilian administration. With the collapse of Saigon and Phnom Penh in April 1975, the Pathet Lao seized power in Vientiane and forced its conservative coalition partners into exile in Thailand* and beyond. In December, the Lao People's Democratic Republic replaced the 600-year-old Lao monarchy.

M. Brown and J. J. Zasloff, *Apprentice Revolutionaries: The Communist Movement in Laos, 1930–1985* (Stanford, CA, 1986); M. S. Fox, *A History of Laos* (Cambridge, MA, 1997); P. F. Langer and J. J. Zasloff, *North Vietnam and the Pathet Lao: Partners in the Struggle for Laos* (Cambridge, MA, 1970); J. J. Zasloff, *The Pathet Lao: Leadership and Organization* (Lexington, MA, 1973).

Edward C. Keefer

PEACE CORPS

The Peace Corps, established in 1961 by President John F. Kennedy*, was inspired by fears current in the 1950s that United States officials were overly remote from the day-to-day concerns and life of ordinary people in developing countries. Alarmed that emphasis on military, rather than economic, aid and American support for elites risked the United States losing Cold War support in the Third World, Kennedy in his presidential campaign called on Americans, especially but not exclusively the young, to spend two years working in education, community development, or technological assistance programs in such countries, receiving relatively low salaries and sharing their hosts' living and working conditions. Headed for its first five years by R. Sargent Shriver, Kennedy's brother-in-law, the Peace Corps rapidly sent thousands of volunteers each year to what eventually was more than sixty countries throughout Asia, Africa, and Latin America. The majority of volunteers provided educational services, but agriculture, food production, health, environmental, conservation, and community development services also were well represented. Under the Peace Corps Act of 1961, the agency initially was independent, but in 1971, it was placed under the umbrella federal agency ACTION, established to coordinate both domestic and overseas volunteer programs, before regaining its independence in 1981. Winning over initially skeptical congressmen, the Peace Corps quickly succeeded in garnering strong bipartisan support for its relatively modest and unassuming programs and appropriations, which continued into the twenty-first century.

Although the Peace Corps's inception owed much to Cold War preoccupations, and both American radicals and host countries on occasion characterized it as an agent of U.S. cultural imperialism, the agency made strenuous efforts to remain apolitical. Volunteers, the majority recent college graduates, were sent only to countries that specifically requested their services, and were strictly forbidden to become involved in local politics or to have any contact with the Central Intelligence Agency*. Instead, the emphasis was on people-to-people contact; volunteers did not bring expensive equipment with them, but only their skills and abilities. Nevertheless, complicated political conditions significantly limited Peace Corps activities in East Asia. Peace Corps volunteers initially went to Malaysia*, the Philippines*, and Indonesia*. The extensive program in the Philippines in its early years won the Ramón Magsaysay* Prize, but others were less successful. In 1965, President Sukarno* of Indonesia ended all Peace Corps programs as a nationalist act of protest against U.S. neoimperialism, a move imitated in 1983 by Malaysia. A deliberate policy of refusing to send volunteers to any country where U.S. troops were engaged in combat precluded their service in the Republic of Vietnam*, Laos*, or Cambodia* during the Second Indochina War*, despite pressure from U.S. officials, and in later years those countries did not welcome the corps. Japan declined to use Peace Corps volunteers in English literacy programs, and the People's Republic of China* did not accept volunteers until 1995, when they began to train Chinese English-language teachers.

F. Fischer, *Making Them Like Us: Peace Corps Volunteers in the 1960s* (Washington, DC, 1998); D. Hapgood and M. Bennett, *Agents of Change: A Close Look at the Peace Corps* (Boston, 1968); E. C. Hoffman, *All You Need Is Love: The Peace Corps and the Spirit of the 1960s* (Cambridge, MA, 1998); G. T. Rice, *The Bold Experiment: JFK's Peace Corps* (South Bend, IN, 1985); M. Windmiller, *The Peace Corps and Pax Americana* (Washington, DC, 1970).

Priscilla Roberts

PEARL HARBOR ATTACK

The surprise attack by the Japanese Navy on the U.S. Pacific Fleet at Pearl Harbor, Hawaii, on 7 December 1941 was caused by Japanese fear of U.S. threats to Japan's position in East Asia. The attack was a temporary disaster for the U.S. Navy, but proved to be an even greater disaster for Japan. It also brought the United States fully into World War II, ensuring total defeat of the Axis powers. In the years prior to 1941, the United States reacted strongly to the expansionist policies of Japan in East Asia because of their negative effect upon the Open Door Policy*. After the Japanese invasion of China following the Marco Polo Bridge Incident* in July 1937, the U.S. government became more fearful regarding Japanese pursuit of the Greater East Asia Co-Prosperity Sphere* and also Tōkyō's drawing closer to Nazi Germany under the Anti-Comintern Pact*. The situation became particularly serious once war broke out in Europe in 1939 and Japan signed the Tripartite Pact* in 1940. The Americans could no longer rely on Britain, or any other European power, to help restrain Japan. With the collapse of France in 1940, Japan took advantage of French weakness to receive in July the right in the Hanoi Convention* to station troops and warships in northern French Indochina*, forcing France a year later to give them base rights in southern Indochina as well. This latter Japanese move posed an immediate threat to the British and Dutch colonies in Southeast Asia.

The U.S. government responded to the threat with tough talk, as Secretary of State Cordell Hull* demanded in April 1941 that Japan halt its aggressive behavior in East Asia in discussions with Ambassador Nomura Kichisaburō*. Washington also developed a program of economic pressure against Japan, restricting the export of vital raw materials. By July 1941, the Japanese could not obtain either scrap metal or petroleum products from the United States, and American agreements concluded with the Dutch and British ended their oil exports to Japan also. These restrictions at the least would choke off support of the military operations in China. At worst, they could bring economic disaster. The Japanese government believed it could not ignore the challenge. President Franklin D. Roosevelt* hoped the economic pressure would persuade the Japanese to negotiate to end its campaign in China, although he refused to meet with Prime Minister Konoe Fumimaro* in August 1941. New Prime Minister Tōjō Hideki* gained approval for a decision to strike out into Southeast Asia to seize the vital oil, rubber, and other materials needed to continue Japan's war in China.

The Pearl Harbor attack was but a part of an ambitious military program planned by the Japanese to conquer British Malaya* and the Dutch East Indies and to seize the Philippines*. Only the United States had significant military strength in the Pacific in the form of the Pacific Fleet based at Pearl Harbor, and it would have to be crippled to give the Japanese forces free rein in the western Pacific. The raid on Pearl Harbor was the most ambitious gamble in the entire plan. Admiral Yamamoto Isoroku*, whose plan it was, knew the element of surprise was vital, for unless the Pacific Fleet could be caught at anchor in Pearl Harbor, the attack would not be the crushing success needed to cripple the United States. A task force made up of the six largest aircraft carriers in the Japanese fleet, with escorting vessels, would cross the northern Pacific and then turn south to approach Hawaii from the north. This course was chosen deliberately because the task force was not likely to encounter any merchant ships in this remote area, although it was not the most direct approach and would require refueling at sea.

An American decoding project named *Magic** had been successful in breaking the Japanese diplomatic code, and it provided valuable information leading to the conclusion that after the end of November, the Japanese might well launch military operations in Southeast Asia. Indeed, after the Nomura-Hull Conversations* failed in November 1941, the Roosevelt administration knew an attack was imminent. But it was uncertain about target and timing. Because the Japanese kept strict radio silence during both their concentration in northern Japanese waters and their voyage across the northern Pacific to Pearl Harbor, U.S. naval intelligence was not able to monitor the movements of the attack force. Admiral Husband Kimmel, the commander of the U.S. Pacific Fleet, and General Walter Short, his counterpart in charge of U.S. Army forces in the islands, did not carry out thorough patrols in the Hawaiian area, even though they had been warned by Washington in late November of the possibility of Japanese military action. The Japanese were not credited with their ability to launch an attack upon a place so far from their home bases.

As a result, the attack on Sunday morning, 7 December, caught the American military forces in Hawaii completely by surprise. In two strikes about fifteen minutes apart, nearly 400 aircraft smashed the U.S. Army and U.S. Navy airfields around Pearl Harbor, crippling American naval power for the next several months. The battleships of the fleet were the main target. Two, the *Arizona* and *Oklahoma*, were never to sail again; of the other six, all but one were damaged so severely that none returned to service for a year or more. Aircraft losses were also severe. Out of about 480 army, navy and marine aircraft, only around 140 had not been destroyed or badly damaged. Japanese losses were twenty-nine aircraft and four midget submarines lost while trying to get into Pearl Harbor. U.S. casualties were nearly 2,330 military personnel killed. It was the most terrible battle loss for the U.S. Navy in its entire history. The day was not a total loss, however. The submarine base and the oil tanks standing in the open nearby were not touched, and most important, the three carriers of the U.S. Pacific Fleet were not at Pearl Harbor that day. For Japan, the attack was only temporarily successful, for in the long run a huge U.S. naval power built over the next three years played a key role in the defeat and destruction of the Japanese Empire.

H. Feis, *The Road to Pearl Harbor: The Coming of the War Between the United States and Japan* (Princeton, NJ, 1950); W. Lord, *Day of Infamy* (New York, 1957); G. W. Prange, *At Dawn We Slept: The Untold Story of Pearl Harbor* (New York, 1981); R. Wohlstetter, *Pearl Harbor: Warning and Decision* (Stanford, CA, 1962).

Ernest Andrade Jr.

PEKING UNION MEDICAL COLLEGE

The Peking Union Medical College (PUMC) was witness to the emergence of a secular, as distinct from a religious, motivation for U.S. cultural involvement with China in the first half of the twentieth century. Americans of this period expected that by exporting science and American higher education to China, Chinese culture would be transformed. Before the Chinese Communist Party* took power in 1949, PUMC was the Rockefeller Foundation's principal vehicle not only for introducing Western medical science to China, but also for implanting an inductive scientific spirit there.

In 1915, the China Medical Board (CMB) of the Rockefeller Foundation bought the land and the buildings of the Union Medical College in Beijing from the London Missionary Society to create a first-rate medical school. Here, CMB expanded and built 59 buildings—including a hospital with 225 teaching beds—on 25 acres at a cost of more than $8 million. The school opened in 1919 while construction was still under way. It began with a student enrollment of 140, and the faculty, recruited largely from the United States, numbered more than 60. The formal dedication of the PUMC was held in September 1921.

The goal of the PUMC was to train medical leaders in China, such as teachers, experts, and public health administrators. Its curriculum was patterned after those of major U.S. medical schools, especially that of Johns Hopkins University. The college set a high academic requirement for student admission. Its faculty was required to conduct scientific research. English was the medium of instruction. The PUMC also organized intensive courses for doctors to pursue advanced studies, often with CMB fellowships. In these courses, distinguished U.S. and European visiting professors brought the latest advances in Western medical research to China.

Despite the interruption caused by World War II, the PUMC had become one of the leading medical training centers in the world and the outpost of medical research in East Asia by 1949. The high percentage of PUMC graduates working in the teaching profession and in the public health field indicated that its programs had succeeded in training medical leaders in China. However, its commitment to the education of a small group of medical elite, its preference for medical research over a more populist approach to health care, and its promotion of quality over quantity was too costly, and it did not solve China's immediate health care problems. Not only did this situation alienate the school from the underdeveloped Chinese society, but viewed against the ideological goal of the founders, the PUMC failed to disseminate the scientific ethos to the tradition-bound masses and thus to transform Chinese culture.

The Rockefeller Foundation's involvement in the PUMC ended with the outbreak of the Korean War*. In 1951, the People's Republic of China* took over the school and renamed it the Zhongguo Xiehe Yixueyuan (China Union Medical College). Six years later, it became a division of the Chinese Academy of Medical Sciences. In 1959, a new school named the Zhongguo Yike Daxue (China Medical College) with an eight-year medical program was constituted on the old campus of the PUMC. The school became a frequent target of anti-imperialists during the Chinese Cultural Revolution* because of its previous American involvement and was closed in 1970. Nine years later, the school reopened with the name of Zhongguo Shoudu Yike Daxue (China Capital Medical College). Its official English name, however, remained the Peking Union Medical College. It continued to be the leading medical school in China. *See also* Ida Pruitt.

J. Z. Bowers, *Western Medicine in a Chinese Palace* (New York, 1971); M. B. Bullock, *An American Transplant: The Rockefeller Foundation and Peking Union Medical College* (Berkeley, CA, 1980); K. Chen, "Quality Versus Quantity: The Rockefeller Foundation and Nurses' Training in China," *Journal of American–East Asian Relations* (Spring 1996); R. B. Fosdick, *The Story of the Rockefeller Foundation* (New York, 1952); F. Ninkovich, "The Rockefeller Foundation, China, and Cultural Change," *Journal of American History* (March 1984).

Ena Chao

PENG DEHUAI (1898–1974)

Peng Dehuai, Chinese Communist Party* (CCP) leader and top military commander in the People's Liberation Army (PLA), was commander in chief of the Chinese People's Volunteers (CPV) in the Korean War* from 1950 to 1953. He was a former Guomindang* (Nationalist) army officer who led his regiment in insurrection and defection to the CCP in 1928. Peng became commander of the Thirteenth Division of the Red Army that year, Third Army Group in 1930, vice chairman of the Central Military Commission in 1932, and commander of the Shan-Gan Army Group, while Mao Zedong* was his political commissar, during the Long March from 1934 to 1935. As the CCP established the United Front* with the Jiang Jieshi* against the Japanese after the Marco Polo Bridge Incident* in July 1937 and reorganized its Red Army into the Nationalist Eighth Route Army, Peng was its deputy commander. He was one of the thirteen elected CCP Politburo members in 1945. After the CCP coalition with the Guomindang collapsed and the Eighth Route Army became the PLA, Peng served as the PLA's chief of the general staff, commander and political commissar of the Northwest Field Army Group, and commander of the First Field Army Group during the Chinese Civil War*. When the People's Republic of China* (PRC) was founded in 1949, he was appointed vice chairman of the Revolutionary Military Committee, chairman of the Northwest Military and Political Committee, commander of the Northwestern Military District, and deputy commander in chief of the PLA.

As forces under the United Nations Command (UNC) crossed the thirty-eighth parallel and moved toward China's border in October 1950, Peng was one of two members in the Politburo to support Mao's decision for Chinese Intervention in the Korean War*. He was appointed commander and political commissar of both the CPV forces and the Chinese–North Korean allied forces. From 1950 to 1953, he commanded 3 million Chinese troops in "the War to Resist U.S. Aggression and Aid Korea," as it was called in China. He planned and conducted all major operations against the UNC forces and made most of the important decisions at the Korean front, communicating with Mao in Beijing intensively every day, working closely with Kim Il Sung* and other North Korean leaders and commanders, and visiting Joseph Stalin in Moscow to discuss the Korean situation. Though there were differing opinions over military strategy and tactics, Peng loyally followed Mao's decisions and faithfully carried out his plans. He at times was frustrated about the CPV suffering very heavy casualties and the UN forces not being driven out of Korea, as well as Mao's son being killed in an air raid. Peng represented China and the Democratic People's Republic of Korea* (DPRK) during the P'anmunjŏm Truce Talks* and signed the Korean Armistice Agreement* in July 1953. He believed that the PRC had achieved a victory because it had saved the Communist regime in North Korea, prevented a possible U.S. invasion of China, received more military and economic aid from Moscow, and reestablished China as a world power.

After returning to China, Peng served as the defense minister and deputy premier. In 1955, he became a PLA marshal, one of the most powerful and revered military leaders of the Chinese Communist revolution. Outspoken and critical of Mao's radical domestic programs, especially the Great Leap Forward in 1958, Peng was accused by Mao in 1959 of forming a "right opportunist clique" and conducting "unprincipled factional activity" and was removed from all his posts. He lived thereafter under virtual house arrest. Peng wrote many long, personal letters to Mao and the Central Committee, appealing for suspension of his disgrace. These letters brought him more critiques and troubles in the early 1960s. In 1965, he had a chance to prove his innocence and loyalty by serving as the deputy director of the Remote Regional Reconstruction program in Sichuan Province. But he could not survive the Chinese Cultural Revolution*. He was arrested again in 1966 and sent back to Beijing, where he was criticized, denounced, and tortured through the 1960s. Peng died in jail. After Mao's death in 1976, the Central Committee announced Peng's rehabilitation in 1978, and his funeral was held in Beijing later that year.

J. Chen, *China's Road to the Korean War: The Making of the Sino-American Confrontation* (New York, 1994); J. Domes, *Peng Te-Huai: The Man and the Image* (Stanford, CA, 1985); X. Li and H. Li (eds.), *China and the United States: A New Cold War History* (Lanham, MD, 1998); D. Peng, *Autobiography of Peng Dehuai* (Beijing, 1984).

Li Xiaobing

PENTAGON PAPERS

The Pentagon Papers was the popular name for the classified Department of Defense (DOD) analysis of U.S. involvement in Vietnam, whose publication in 1971 touched off a political and constitutional controversy and led to a major U.S. Supreme Court ruling on freedom of the press. In 1967, Secretary of Defense Robert S. McNamara* initiated the forty-seven-volume study, which comprised two parts: first, an extensive narrative of U.S. policy making in Vietnam; and second, a collection of relevant documents. Daniel Ellsberg, a DOD employee, leaked the study to the *New York Times* and other newspapers. On 13 June 1971, the *Times* began publishing articles based on the study, including citations from documents. Claiming national security considerations, the Nixon administration requested that the *Times* not publish any more articles. When the *Times* refused, the government gained an injunction from the U.S. Second Court of Appeals. The *Times* appealed on grounds of freedom of the press.

New York Times v. United States went quickly before the Supreme Court, which, in a six-to-three decision, overturned the restraining order and ruled on behalf of the newspaper. The *Times* and other newspapers continued publication of articles based on the Pentagon Papers and, within a few months, several versions of major parts of the study were published in book form as well. The complete study was published by a congressional committee. Besides the controversy stirred by its very publication, the common interpretation of the Pentagon Papers added to long-standing criticisms of U.S. policy during the Second Indochina War*. In particular, the documents seemed to show that American officials acted duplicitously and concealed important information from the public. The adverse reaction to the study added to the pressures on President Richard M. Nixon* to end U.S. military involvement in Southeast Asia.

M. Shapiro (ed.), *The Pentagon Papers and the Courts: A Study in Foreign Policy Making and Freedom of the Press* (San Francisco, 1972); N. Sheehan et al., *The Pentagon Papers* (New York, 1971); S. Ungar, *The Papers and the Papers: An Account of the Legal and Political Battle Over the Pentagon Papers* (New York, 1972).

Gary R. Hess

PEOPLE'S REPUBLIC OF CHINA

Covering 3.7 million square miles, the People's Republic of China (PRC) is the world's third-largest nation, and by the end of the twentieth century, had the largest population at roughly 1.3 billion people. In October 1949, the Chinese Communist Party* (CCP) defeated the Guomindang* (Nationalist) Party under Jiang Jieshi* in the Chinese Civil War*. Mao Zedong*, founder and first president of the PRC, declared the new government's "lean-to-one-side" policy of favoring the Soviet Union in the Cold War. In December, he traveled to Moscow and in February 1950, signed the Sino-Soviet Treaty of Friendship and Alliance*. The United States delayed recognizing the PRC and maintained diplomatic relations with Jiang's Republic of China* (ROC) that had fled to Taiwan*. The outbreak of the Korean War* and the decision of President Harry S. Truman* to order Neutralization of Taiwan* prevented early reconciliation, and Mao's decision for Chinese Intervention in the Korean War* opened the most mutually hostile period in U.S.-PRC relations. China suffered more than a million casualties and spent $3.3 billion before signing the Korean Armistice Agreement*. The PRC's intervention in Korea provoked deep antagonism to Communism* and profound fear in the United States, especially for the China Lobby*.

After the Korean War, the PRC continued to offer military and economic aid to Communist movements in the world, especially in French Indochina*. It provided weapons and training to antigovernment guerrillas in Southeast Asia, and supported Third World nations in their struggles against the United States and other Western powers. The People's Liberation Army (PLA) attacked the ROC-held offshore islands in the Taiwan Strait Crises* of 1954 and 1958, escalating international tensions. Although the Eisenhower administration strengthened U.S. commitments to protect Taiwan, it also participated in the U.S.-PRC Warsaw Talks*. Presidents John F. Kennedy* and Lyndon B. Johnson* continued the CHINCOM* trade embargo against China and opposed granting to the PRC Chinese Representation in the United Nations* and most international organizations. In response, Mao mobilized the Chinese masses to carry on his revolution at home, launching the radical political campaigns of the Great Leap Forward in 1958 and the Chinese Cultural Revolution* in 1966. After the emergence of the Sino-Soviet split and the Chinese-Russian border military conflicts late in the 1960s, Beijing came to consider the "hegemonic" Soviet Union as more dangerous and provocative to China than the United States. The PRC's leaders acted to form a world alliance to stop "Soviet military expansion" through improving its relations with the major Western powers, including the United States and Japan. The PRC became a UN member and resumed its seat on the UN Security Council during 1971.

President Richard M. Nixon* welcomed the PRC's desire to reenter the world community, practicing Ping-Pong Diplomacy* and ending the trade embargo against the PRC in 1971. Nixon's Visit to China* and issuance of the Shanghai Communiqué* during 1972 were critical steps on the road to U.S.-PRC Normalization of Relations*. When President Gerald R. Ford traveled to Beijing in 1975, he agreed to terminate the U.S.-China Mutual Defense Treaty of 1954* with the ROC and withdraw U.S. military forces from Taiwan. The PRC-U.S. relationship improved further after Mao's death in 1976, when Deng Xiaoping* implemented the Four Modernizations*. To achieve economic growth and establish a market economy, Deng emphasized world peace and cooperation, resulting in closer ties with the United States and reestablishing formal relations on 1 January 1979. That year, he was the first top PRC leader to make a state visit to Washington and signed protocols with President Jimmy Carter* on trade, education, technology, and cultural exchanges. Later, Deng met Presidents Ronald Reagan* and George H. W. Bush* in Beijing during their visits to China. In the 1980s, Beijing conducted successful negotiations to resume sovereignty over Hong Kong* and Macau, regaining control over the two in 1997 and 1999 respectively. Meanwhile, there was a rapid rise of trade, visits, and exchanges between the PRC and the ROC.

Beijing was unable, however, to resolve the problems resulting from domestic economic and social change, especially rising demands for political reform. The PRC leaders in the summer of 1989 faced student demonstrations for political freedom and protesting corruption and abuse of power. On 4 June, Deng ordered the PLA's troops and tanks to open fire on the protesting students, resulting in the Tiananmen Square Massacre*. In response, Western countries vigorously protested Beijing's suppression of political freedom. The American people supported the Bush administration's policies suspending official bilateral exchanges with the PRC and joining industrial countries in imposing economic sanctions. The PRC-U.S. relations worsened during 1995 when ROC President Li Denghui* visited the United States and talked about an independent Taiwan. Beijing warned that if Taibei announced independence, the PRC would react with nonpeaceful means. In 1996, the PRC fired missiles into the Taiwan Strait, which fell only eight miles off Taiwan's shore. President Bill Clinton*, who had followed a policy of Constructive Engagement* toward Beijing, sent two U.S. aircraft carriers to the area. Sino-American relations improved when President Jiang Zemin* traveled to Washington in 1997 and Clinton visited Beijing in 1998. But Beijing's hard line against human rights, and its inflexible position on such issues as Taiwan, Tibet*, imbalanced trade, and nuclear technology remained major sources of tension. *See also* Special Economic Zones; Wu Hongda.

D. Goodman and G. Segal (eds.), *China in the Nineties* (New York, 1991); S. Kim (ed.), *China and the World* (Boulder, CO, 1998); X. Li and H. Li (eds.), *China and the United States: A New Cold War History* (New York, 1997); M. Meisner, *Mao's China: A History of the People's Republic* (New York, 1990); J. Spence, *The Search for Modern China* (New York, 1999).

Li Xiaobing

PERRY, MATTHEW C. (1794–1858)

Commodore Matthew Calbraith Perry's impact on U.S.–East Asian relations is embodied in the Perry Mission* to Japan and the Treaty of Kanagawa*. During the nineteenth century, because of a capacity to combine persuasion and force, U.S. naval officers often were authorized to conclude international agreements with groups and nations not considered to be civilized by Western standards. Perry's background as a career officer in the U.S. Navy equipped him well for the practice of what was called gunboat diplomacy. Following in the footsteps of his father and older brother Oliver Hazard Perry, Perry enlisted in the U.S. Navy as a midshipman in 1809 at age fifteen, serving with distinction in both the War of 1812 and the Mexican War. Perry attained the rank of captain in 1837 and received the title of commodore in 1841. Two years later, he assumed command of the newly created U.S. African Squadron.

By the 1830s, Perry had gained a reputation as a skillful naval diplomatist. In 1832, he cooperated with Chargé John Nelson in obtaining a claims settlement with Naples. In the 1840s, in response to the plunder of American merchant vessels, such as the *Mary Carver*, he destroyed several villages along the Ivory Coast and then forced the offending African chiefs to sign agreements promising to respect the lives and property of American citizens. In 1852, Perry ably defused a potentially dangerous dispute over fishing rights in Canadian waters through negotiating a compact with British Naval Commander Sir George Seymour to restrain the irate nationals of both countries. Although he never had served in the East India Squadron, his record as an effective naval commander and negotiator made him a logical choice to head the mission to Japan. *See also* James Biddle; John Kendrick; Robert W. Shufeldt.

S. E. Morison, *"Old Bruin": Commodore Matthew C. Perry, 1794–1858* (Boston and Toronto, 1967).

Kenneth E. Shewmaker

PERRY MISSION

The China market, rather than Japan itself, lay at the center of the mission to what Commodore Matthew C. Perry* called "the hermetic" empire of Japan. Except for a strictly controlled trade with the Dutch at the tiny island of Deshima in Nagasaki harbor and a few contacts with Chinese and Korean merchants, Japan deliberately had sealed itself from the outside world since 1638. By the 1840s, however, the opening of China to Western commerce, the increasing involvement of American whaling vessels in the rich fishery off Japan's east coast, and the technology of maritime steam navigation rendered Japanese isolationism untenable. Japan offered a conveniently located way station on the co-called Great Circle Route* between San Francisco and Shanghai, and the overriding objective was to obtain coaling stations on the Japanese islands. As an early proponent of steam-powered warships, Perry had a strong personal interest in acquiring coaling depots for the U.S. Navy in Japan.

The instructions for the mission to Japan, originally written by Secretary of State Daniel Webster* on 10 June 1851, set forth three major goals. In order of priority, the United States sought access to coal, what Webster called "that great necessary of commerce"; the humane treatment of American seamen wrecked upon Japan's shores; and the right of Americans to trade at one or more Japanese ports. As revised by Perry himself on 5 November 1852, the instructions allowed him wide latitude to use military force if the "semibarbarous" Japanese did not accede to American demands. Determined not to suffer the same fate as Commodore James Biddle*, who had been insulted and mistreated by the Japanese in 1846 and told never to return, Perry sailed into Edo (Tōkyō) Bay on 8 July with his fearsome squadron of warships belching a thick black smoke that both awed and alarmed the Japanese. When it became clear that Perry was unwilling to accept no for an answer and was willing to use military force, the Japanese agreed to receive President Millard Fillmore's letter. On 14 July, with considerable pomp and ceremony, Perry, accompanied by 250 armed sailors, delivered the letter and promised to return in the spring to receive an official answer to American demands. In February 1854, Perry returned with an even larger fleet and entered into the negotiations, which concluded with the signing of the Treaty of Kanagawa* on 31 March 1854. Although the treaty did not establish a formal trade relationship between the two countries, the Japanese agreed to open the ports of Shimoda and Hakodate to shipwrecked American seamen and U.S. vessels and to allow a U.S. consul to reside in Shimoda.

In terms of historical significance, through a combination of deft diplomacy and threats to unleash the formidable naval power at his command, Perry achieved what he called "this great object of my life." Not only had he reopened Japan to Western influence after more than 200 years of exclusion, but he also had gained for the United States the national prestige of doing so before the British and the Russian fleets could reach Edo Bay and had obtained coaling stations for the growing China trade. Perry failed, however, in his larger strategic vision. The lukewarm administration of President Franklin Pierce approved the Treaty of Kanagawa and a similar agreement with Okinawa (Treaty of Naha of 11 July 1854), but rejected Perry's recommendation that the United States pursue an imperial strategy modeled after that of Britain by establishing a protectorate over Taiwan* and taking possession of the Bonin Islands*. For the Japanese, the Perry Mission helped erode the authority of the Tokugawa shōgunate and led to the adoption of a policy of reluctantly granting concessions to Western nations, while striving to gain the resources and technologies necessary to the creation of a modern nation-state capable of determining its own destiny. *See also* Ii Naosuke; "Expel the Barbarian" Movement; Harris Treaty.

W. LaFeber, *The Clash: A History of U.S.-Japan Relations* (New York, 1997); K. E. Shewmaker, "Forging the Great Chain: Daniel Webster and the Origins of American Foreign Policy Toward East Asia and the Pacific, 1841–1852," *Proceedings of the American Philosophical Society* (September 1985); P. B. Wiley and I. Korogi, *Yankees in the Land of the Gods: Commodore Perry and the Opening of Japan* (New York, 1990).

Kenneth E. Shewmaker

PHAM VAN DONG (1906–2000)

Pham Van Dong was a leading member of the Vietnamese Communist Party and the prime minister of the Democratic Republic of Vietnam* during the Second Indochina War*. Born into a mandarin family in north central Vietnam, he became a founding member in 1925 of the Vietnamese Revolutionary Youth League (Viet Nam Thanh Nien Kach Menh Hoi) under the leadership of Ho Chi Minh*, the precursor to the Vietnamese Communist Party. For much of the 1930s, French colonial authorities imprisoned him for his revolutionary activities in French Indochina*. During World War II, he worked closely with Ho Chi Minh and Vo Nguyen Giap* to develop the Vietminh*, the organizational vehicle through which the Vietnamese Communists sought to overthrow French Colonialism* and its rule. In this period, he oversaw the Vietminh's efforts to gain the support of U.S. diplomats and intelligence officers who were working in southern China as part of the Deer Mission*.

Pham Van Dong played a central role during the First Indochina War* against the French and headed the Vietnamese delegation to the Geneva Conference of 1954*. Although convinced that the Vietnamese victory against the French at the battle of Dien Bien Phu* entitled the Vietnamese to a more favorable settlement, he reluctantly acceded to the temporary division of Vietnam at the seventeenth parallel under strong pressure from the Zhou Enlai*, the leader of the Chinese delegation. Serving as North Vietnam's prime minister beginning in 1954 and, after Ho Chi Minh's death in 1969, as the regime's most public spokesperson, Pham Van Dong generally was considered to be neutral in the Sino-Soviet dispute. He also played a key role in the secret negotiations at the Paris Peace Talks* between U.S. National Security Adviser Henry A. Kissinger* and Le Duc Tho*; he was reportedly a strong opponent of a negotiated settlement to the war without cessation of Operation ROLLING THUNDER*, the U.S. bombing of North Vietnam, and provisions for a coalition government. After reunification in 1975, he served as prime minister of the Socialist Republic of Vietnam* until 1987.

M. P. Bradley, *Imagining Vietnam and America: The Making of Post Colonial Vietnam, 1919–1950* (Chapel Hill, NC, 2000); S. Karnow, *Vietnam: A History* (New York, 1991); H. K. Khanh, *Vietnamese Communism 1925–1945* (Ithaca, NY, 1982); Q. Zhai, *China and the Vietnam Wars, 1950–1975* (Chapel Hill, NC, 2000).

Mark P. Bradley

PHAN BOI CHAU (1867–1940)

Phan Boi Chau, a Vietnamese patriot who influenced nationalist resistance to French Colonialism* in the twentieth century, recognized the monarchy's inability to oppose the French occupation. The classically trained scholar, therefore, worked to organize other elements within Vietnamese society and advocated violent resistance to colonial rule in French Indochina*. He actively sought outside help to achieve his objective of independence. His significance for U.S.–East Asian relations was indirect from the legacy he bequeathed to later Vietnamese nationalists, principally Ho Chi Minh*. A friend of the family, Phan Boi Chau met a young Ho and impressed upon him the importance of resistance and struggle. Years later, Ho still could recite lines of poetry told to him by Phan Boi Chau. Like his contemporary Phan Chu Trinh*, Phan Boi Chau disparaged Vietnamese reformists and mandarins. Unlike him, Phan Boi Chau championed organized, armed resistance and sought weapons and money from sympathetic individuals throughout Asia. He was captured by the French secret police in Shanghai in 1925, but simply given house arrest in Hue until his death.

D. G. Marr, *Vietnamese Anticolonialism, 1885–1925* (Berkeley, CA, 1971).

T. Christopher Jespersen

PHAN CHU TRINH (1882–1926)

A Vietnamese intellectual who sought to improve the conditions his compatriots faced because of French Colonialism*, Phan Chu Trinh believed, at least initially, that the French were prepared to assist the Vietnamese in following their path to civilization. He was educated in classical Chinese texts, and his importance for Vietnamese nationalism came from his reading of eighteenth-century Enlightenment writers and the close attention he paid to what French officials espoused as part of its *mission civilisatrice*. Rejecting Vietnam's existing monarchy as corrupt and incompetent and fearful that violence would kill thousands of his countrymen without expelling the French, he argued that the best way for the Vietnamese to respond to colonialism was through persistent efforts to work with the French in bringing about the modernization of Vietnamese society. He rejected assistance from other countries, specifically Japan, for fear that this simply would replace one colonialist nation with another.

In spite of Phan Chu Trinh's nonviolent stance, French officials considered him dangerous because he espoused independence. As part of mass arrests after a failed attempt to poison French officers in 1908, he was jailed, tried, and convicted of treasonous activities. He was later released and moved to France, where he wrote about colonial oppression in French Indochina*. His significance for U.S. relations with East Asia came after World War I, when he, along with a young Ho Chi Minh*, then living under the name Nguyen Ai Quoc and also living in Paris, approached both the secretariat of the Versailles Peace Conference in 1919 and the U.S. delegation to enlist support for Vietnamese independence. The two were rebuffed, never getting an audience with President Woodrow Wilson*, whose calls for self-determination struck a powerful chord among oppressed peoples everywhere. Whatever the appeal of his rhetoric, however, Wilson was not prepared to challenge the existing international system on behalf of Asian nationalists. Hence, the next generation of leaders in the region, notably Mao Zedong*, looked elsewhere for intellectual inspiration. When Phan Chu Trinh died, his funeral was a national event.

D. G. Marr, *Vietnamese Anticolonialism, 1885–1925* (Berkeley, CA, 1971).

T. Christopher Jespersen

PHILIPPINE-AMERICAN WAR (1899–1902)

The Philippine-American War was the result of the Spanish-American War* of 1898 and the decision of President William McKinley* to seek Philippine Annexation*, defying a strong consensus among Filipino elites for independence and nationhood. On 1 May 1898, Commodore George Dewey destroyed Spain's eastern fleet in the Battle of Manila Bay*. McKinley then ordered the organization of a U.S. expeditionary force to occupy Manila and several other port cities. Concurrently, Emilio Aguinaldo, leader of the Philippine Revolution of 1896*, had formed a Republican government and his army had accepted the surrender of many small Spanish garrisons, but failed to take Manila. On 14 August, the Spanish in Manila surrendered to U.S. forces under terms excluding Filipinos from any role in the city's subsequent occupation. A tense truce between U.S. and Filipino forces rapidly deteriorated after the United States asserted sovereignty over the islands under the Treaty of Paris of 10 December 1898. On 4 February 1899, two days before the U.S. Senate ratified the treaty, fighting broke out in Manila and quickly spread throughout central Luzon. The U.S. commanders in the Philippines—U.S. Army Generals Elwell S. Otis from February 1899 to May 1900, Arthur MacArthur* from May 1900 to July 1901, and Adna R. Chaffee* from July 1901 to July 1902—worked at several different levels to defeat Filipino nationalism. They initiated "attractive" public health and education projects, granted political autonomy to "friendly" districts, supervised military efforts to capture or kill guerrilla bands, and approved coercive martial law measures to punish resisting Filipinos.

In the first of three distinct phases of the war, the U.S. Eighth Army Corps defeated the Philippine Republic's field army in a conventional maneuver campaign lasting from February to December 1899. Local Republicans then began to construct clandestine intelligence and supply networks to support a two-tiered guerrilla force. *Fusileros*, small groups of full-time, rifle-armed insurgents, operated from camps in remote areas to ambush small detachments of U.S. troops, cut telegraph lines, and occasionally mount deadly infiltration attacks against U.S. garrisons. The *boleros*, or village militias, stayed in their communities to gather intelligence about U.S. forces, grow and carry food to the *fusileros*, and punish villagers who cooperated with U.S. authorities. Facing strong guerrilla resistance, Generals Otis and MacArthur mounted a sustained pacification effort. During the second phase of the war, from January 1900 to mid-1901, U.S. troops forced most guerrilla bands to surrender under the dual pressure of increasingly effective offensive patrols and martial law coercion exerted through provost courts and military commissions. By the summer of 1901, most of the provinces in the Philippines were pacified and the war's final phase was restricted to three provinces in south central Luzon and the island of Samar. These were secured between September 1901 and April 1902 through extensive population concentration and widespread property destruction outside designated secure zones, resulting in the final captures of the most charismatic guerrilla leaders: Vicente Lukban on Samar and Miguel Malvar in Batangas. This enabled President Theodore Roosevelt* to announce an end to the "Philippine Insurrection" on 4 July 1902.

The first U.S. military expedition to the islands in June 1898 was composed mainly of federalized National Guard regiments from fifteen Western states because most Regular U.S. Army units were committed to the Cuban campaign. Since these soldiers were not required to serve after the Treaty of Paris and Congress was initially unwilling to expand the Regular Army, 35,000 "U.S. Volunteers" were recruited to serve until spring 1901. Congress finally raised the Regular Army to 100,000 men in 1901, which allowed a sufficient force to complete the pacification campaign. The Philippine-American War was costlier for the U.S. military than the war with Spain. Of the combined total of 122,401 regular and volunteer soldiers who served in the Philippines between 30 June 1898 and 4 July 1902, 4,234 died: 2,701 of disease; 966 in combat; and 567 of other causes. The war also caused great human suffering in many areas of the Philippines. Brutal interrogations (the "water cure"), prisoner executions, shoot-on-sight orders, and use of population concentration triggered a contemporary political controversy in the United States, and later condemnatory comparisons to the Second Indochina War*. Historians have estimated that between 130,000 and 600,000 Filipinos died during the war and the cholera epidemic of 1902 and 1903, often judged as a direct consequence of the pacification.

B. M. Linn, *The Philippine War, 1899–1902* (Lawrence, KS, 2000); G. A. May, *Battle for Batangas: A Philippine Province at War* (New Haven, CT, 1991); G. A. May, "Why the United States Won the Philippine-American War, 1899–1902," *Pacific Historical Review* (November 1982); J. S. Reed, "External Discipline During Counterinsurgency: A Philippine War Case Study, 1900–1901," *Journal of American–East Asian Relations* (Spring 1995); W. T. Sexton, *Soldiers in the Sun: An Adventure in Imperialism* (Harrisburg, PA, 1939).

John S. Reed

PHILIPPINE ANNEXATION

Americans began trading with the Philippines*, a Spanish colony, in the 1790s. Throughout the nineteenth century, U.S. entrepreneurs helped cultivate crops, such as sugar, that changed the economy of the 7,000-island nation and opened it to global markets. Filipinos under Emilio Aguinaldo staged the Philippine Revolution of 1896* to claim independence, but Spanish troops forced Aguinaldo to flee to Hong Kong*, where, coincidentally, the U.S. Pacific Fleet under Commodore George Dewey lay at anchor. President William McKinley* took the United States to war against Spain in April 1898, setting the stage for U.S. annexation of the islands. The immediate cause was Spain's inability to stop a revolution in its Cuban colony, but at least as early as September 1897, McKinley had linked the possibility that war could bring both Cuba and the Philippines under his control. He especially valued Manila, a port from which U.S. power could be projected to protect growing U.S. interests in Asia against the growing efforts of European imperialists to seize parts of China. In the first military engagement of the Spanish-American War*, Dewey, on McKinley's orders, destroyed Spain's fleet in the Battle of Manila Bay* on 1 May 1898. The president then ordered 12,000 troops to pacify Manila and its island of Luzon.

U.S. forces easily dispatched the Spanish, but then encountered Aguinaldo's troops, now 37,000 strong. U.S. officials on the scene told McKinley that Aguinaldo was bringing order to the islands, but the president intended to keep at least Manila. McKinley then decided that he had to keep Luzon to protect Manila. On the advice of military officials and scholars who knew the country, he finally decided in September 1898 that Luzon had to be protected by seizing all the islands; otherwise Germany or Japan might intervene. Moreover, he knew that wealthier Filipinos preferred U.S. protection over rule by Aguinaldo's revolutionary government. As American troops moved into areas controlled, or claimed, by Aguinaldo, conflicts grew. On 4 February 1899, a U.S. sentry killed a Filipino soldier outside Manila. War erupted.

McKinley was facing an uphill fight to win Senate approval for annexation. Because of racial and constitutional reasons, many Americans, especially women (who identified with Filipinos, who had few political and economic rights), formed an Anti-Imperialist League* to defeat the treaty. Steel magnate Andrew Carnegie funded the organization out of fear that the United States was following the British imperial path. The outbreak of fighting, however, forced wavering senators to back McKinley, although George F. Hoar* remained a vocal critic. The president already had exerted his great powers of patronage on various senators. At the last moment, moreover, the Democrat Party's national leader, William Jennings Bryan*, surprisingly reversed course and favored the treaty. On 6 February, the pact barely received the required two-thirds approval, 57–27. The brutal Philippine-American

War* raged on until 1903, although Aguinaldo was captured in 1901. Conflict continued on some islands until the 1930s. McKinley's policies of "benevolent assimilation" never Americanized Philippine society as he had hoped. By 1907, Theodore Roosevelt* realized the islands were militarily indefensible. With the 1916 Jones Act, the United States reluctantly put the Filipinos on the road to independence, which they finally achieved under the Tydings-McDuffie Act* of 1934 after World War II on 4 July 1946. *See also* Insular Cases.

H. W. Brands, *Bound to Empire: The United States and the Philippines* (New York, 1991); M. Leech, *In the Days of McKinley* (New York, 1959); W. L. Williams, "United States Indian Policy and the Debate over Philippine Annexation: Implications for the Origins of American Imperialism," *Journal of American History* (March 1980).

Walter LaFeber

PHILIPPINE REVOLUTION OF 1896

Often confused with Filipino resistance against American colonialism (the Philippine-American War*), academics and political activists consider the Philippine Revolution of 1896 to be the first nationalist revolution in Asia. The event actually was a series of small uprisings and pitched battles between Filipino revolutionaries organized under the secret association Katipunan and Spanish forces in Manila and adjoining provinces. Although the rebels fared poorly militarily, the Spanish could not contain the spread of the rebellion. An armistice was signed in 1897, wherein the rebel leadership under Emilio Aguinaldo accepted exile to Hong Kong* and payment of 800,000 pesos in exchange for the cessation of rebel attacks. Within a year, fighting had resumed, as Filipinos perceived the increasing weakness of Spanish rule. By early 1898, the Spanish were in retreat in the island of Luzon, and Filipino revolutionaries were unified and remobilized by returning leaders. A third actor, however, joined the struggle when the United States declared war on Spain in April 1898. The U.S. Asiatic squadron under Admiral George Dewey, after transporting the Aguinaldo leadership back to Manila, destroyed the Spanish fleet on 1 May at the Battle of Manila Bay*.

On 12 June 1898, Aguinaldo formally declared Philippine independence, and a revolutionary congress was convened three months later to draw up a constitution that was modeled on the French, Belgian, and Latin American constitutions. On 21 January 1899, the Philippine republic was inaugurated with Aguinaldo as its first president. The celebration did not last long. The Treaty of Paris, signed 10 December 1898, ended the Spanish-American War*. The Spanish agreed to cede the Philippines*, Guam*, and Puerto Rico to the United States in return for a $20 million "gift." The agreement enraged the Filipinos, who were not represented in the negotiations, and by the time news of the treaty reached the Philippines, tensions were rising between the two "allies." On 21 December 1898, U.S. President William McKinley* proclaimed the policy of "benevolent assimilation" of the Philippines. Aguinaldo responded with a proclamation condemning the United States for the "violent and aggressive seizure" of the country. Hostilities broke out on 4 February 1899, and what followed was a brutal war of resistance directly affecting U.S. domestic politics. The Anti-Imperialist League* argued that Philippine Annexation* endangered U.S. democratic principles, but the U.S. Senate ultimately ratified the Treaty of Paris by a one-vote margin.

By the end of 1899, U.S. combat forces had reached 55,000 and had driven the Filipino revolutionaries out of the provinces they controlled. Aguinaldo eventually was captured on 23 March 1901, and a year later, William Howard Taft*, the first U.S. governor-general of the Philippines, declared, "The insurrection is over." But the impact of the revolution of 1896 had become embedded in the political consciousness of Filipinos, and this had an effect on the nature of American colonial rule. Early on, the United States, in part recognizing the legacy of 1896 and in part seeking to differentiate its rule from the other colonial powers in Asia, promised the Filipinos independence at a future date and significant Filipino participation in government until then. This stance won the cooperation of the Filipino political elite, but they continued to invoke the discourse of independence as they expanded their role in the colonial state. Eventually independence came in 1946 under the Tydings-McDuffie Act* of 1934, but Filipino nationalists thereafter would insist that the spirit of 1896 was unfulfilled because "neocolonial" relations kept the Philippines under U.S. influence.

T. Agoncillo, *Malolos: The Crisis of the Republic* (Quezón City, 1960); J. Blount, *The American Occupation of the Philippines, 1898–1912* (New York, 1913); S. C. Miller, *"Benevolent Assimilation": The American Conquest of the Philippines* (New Haven, CT, 1982); P. Stanley, *A Nation in the Making: The Philippines and the United States, 1899–1921* (Cambridge, MA, 1974).

Patricio N. Abinales

PHILIPPINE SEA, BATTLE OF THE

See BATTLE OF THE PHILIPPINE SEA

PHILIPPINES

The Philippines is an archipelago off the coast of Southeast Asia. It consists of 7,100 islands; the three largest are Luzon, Mindanao, and Palawan. It has a population of almost 70 million, of whom more than 80 percent are Catholic, 9 percent other Christian denominations, and 5 percent Muslim. The country was colonized twice, first by the Spanish, who governed from 1565 to 1898, and then the Americans, from 1899 to 1946. Until the mid-nineteenth century, Las Islas Filipinas (the colony was named after King Philip II) was of little importance to the Spanish imperial state. It functioned mainly as a transshipment point for trade between China and Mexico. To Spanish religious orders, however, the colony was a vital base for their missions to China and Japan. The "galleon trade" and the religious missions were the main reasons why the Spanish did not abandon this colonial backwater. The Mexican revolution of the 1820s changed all this, as the Spanish sought to preserve what was left of their empire by transforming its remaining possessions into producers of raw materials for European and American industries and opening them to global trade. The Philippines, together with Cuba, found a niche in the new order as an exporter of sugar and tobacco. By the late 1890s, though, Spain was finished as a power in Asia, its control in the Philippines severely undermined by the Philippine Revolution of 1896* and ended by the Spanish-American War* in 1898.

Like the Spanish, the primary interest of the United States in the Philippines was its access to East and Southeast Asia. Control over the colony after the Philippine-American War* ended tremendously expanded the U.S. presence in a region where the United States previously had only port privileges in Japan and southern China. Only later did American interest in Philippine commodities such as sugar, hemp, and coconut develop as a consequence of the growing trade between the new colony and the Asian mainland. Even then, Philippine exports to the United States never were significant. Nevertheless, domestic U.S. competitors led a successful movement during the Great Depression to grant the Philippines its independence, but World War II delayed the implementation of the Tydings-McDuffie Act* until 1946. That year, a presidential form of government with a bicameral legislature patterned largely after the United States was put in place. The new Philippine Republic's foreign policy was strongly pro-American. It echoed the anti-Communist line the U.S. government advocated in the 1950s and supported U.S. initiatives in the Cold War, especially under President Ramón Magsaysay*. The Philippines sent troops to the Korean War*, opposed the admission of the People's Republic of China* to the United Nations, and became the prime mover in the formation of the Southeast Asia Treaty Organization*. Filipino professional groups, such as the Philippine Jaycees, worked closely with the Central Intelligence Agency* in projects such as Operation BROTHERHOOD, a medical support team sent to Vietnam to assist refugees from Communism*.

The value of the Philippines to U.S. strategic interests continued even after the granting of independence. Through a series of economic and military agreements, in particular the U.S.-Philippines Mutual Defense Pact*, the United States continued to use the Philippines as a base for projecting its power in postcolonial East and Southeast Asia. Two of the largest military bases outside the American mainland were in the Philippines. Both Clark Air Force Base and Subic Naval Base played key roles in the the Second Indochina War*. Although the Philippine government and the Filipino elite benefited immensely from these arrangements, not everyone saw this close affinity as positive for the former colony. The Philippines never was accepted as a full member of the nonaligned movement, and its participation in the Association of Southeast Asian Nations* often was perceived as a way for the United States to voice its interest in the regional alliance. The controversy over the Philippine-American relationship escalated during the dictatorship of Ferdinand E. Marcos* and climaxed under President Corazon Aquino*, when the Philippine Senate voted not to extend the lease for U.S. bases in the country. In a way, the decline of U.S. influence forced the Philippines to become more involved in regional politics. *See also* Manuel L. Quezón; Marcos's Ouster; Subic Naval Base Controversy; Leonard Wood.

B. Anderson, "Cacique Democracy in the Philippines: Origins and Dreams," *New Left Review* (May–June 1988); R. Bonner, *Waltzing with a Dictator: The Marcoses and the Making of American Policy* (New York, 1987); D. Steinberg, *The Philippines: A Singular and Plural Place* (Boulder, CO, 1994); D. Wurfel, *Filipino Politics: Development and Decay* (Ithaca, NY, 1988).

Patricio N. Abinales

PHILLIPS, WILLIAM (1878–1968)

As a young foreign service officer, William Phillips helped create the Far Eastern Division of the U.S. Department of State. He acted as the division's first chief, and played a significant role in several major diplomatic efforts to ensure China's territorial integrity. One effort resulted in a 1908 decision by the United States to oppose recognizing Russian sovereignty over the growing North Manchuria Railway center of Harbin. The area lay at the junction of the Russian-controlled Chinese Eastern Railway and the Japanese-controlled South Manchuria Railway. There, the predominantly Russian population wanted to establish a municipal government. As third assistant secretary of state, Phillips warned that acknowledging Russian control would set three dangerous precedents: forfeiting U.S. extraterritorial rights there, undermining Chinese sovereignty in the region, and providing a model for similar moves by Japan in areas along its South Manchuria Railway. These arguments persuaded Secretary of State Elihu Root* to oppose the Russians, though he backed away from this position in the subsequent Root-Takahira Agreement*.

Phillips gained another opportunity to oppose foreign encroachment in China after the election of William Howard Taft* and the installation of Philander C. Knox* as secretary of state. On 10 May 1909, Phillips wrote a memorandum outlining the policy of the new administration on the need to preserve the Open Door Policy* and maintain Chinese territorial integrity. Phillips's position reflected a long-standing premise among U.S. diplomats that American commercial interests in Asia ultimately would surpass those of Europe and U.S. diplomatic efforts should aim at preserving market access despite the lack of an immediate stake, anticipating the emergence of Dollar Diplomacy* and the Knox Neutralization Scheme*. Son of a prominent New England family and graduate of Harvard College, he was best known to diplomatic historians for his failed efforts as ambassador to Italy from 1936 to 1941 to prevent the nation from declaring war on the Allies. Shortly thereafter, Phillips retired, publishing lively memoirs in 1952.

A. W. Griswold, *Far Eastern Policy of the United States* (New Haven, CT, 1966); W. Phillips, *Ventures in Diplomacy* (Boston, 1952); P. Varg, *The Making of a Myth: The United States in China, 1897–1912*, (East Lansing, MI, 1968).

Karl Gerth

PHOENIX PROGRAM

During the Second Indochina War*, Communist power in South Vietnam was based not only on military forces, but on administrative organizations and networks of political cadres that the Americans called the Viet Cong* Infrastructure. Operating as arms of the National Liberation Front*, in many areas these organizations were the local government. The United States and the Republic of Vietnam* (RVN) had been trying to destroy the infrastructure since the mid-1950s. In 1967, the Phoenix (Phung Hoang) Program was set up to achieve better coordination among the many U.S. and RVN bodies working to destroy the infrastructure, including RVN police forces, RVN province chiefs and district chiefs and their troops, and the Provincial Reconnaissance Units (PRU), small teams of Vietnamese often trained and led by U.S. Navy SEALs, capable of raiding deep into Communist-ruled areas. Each province and district had an American Phoenix adviser and an interrogation center for questioning prisoners, which also served as a central repository for information about Communist organizations. The Central Intelligence Agency*, which had created the PRUs, was heavily involved in establishing and running the Phoenix Program.

Effective implementation of the concept was delayed by the Tet Offensive* early in 1968, but soon it was inflicting serious losses on Communist organizations, and it continued to do so until the program was crippled by the U.S. withdrawal from South Vietnam under Vietnamization* after 1969. The way it worked varied widely from area to area, but hardly anywhere did it work as intended, with all the relevant organizations working in concert. But if one or two of those organizations worked effectively, significant results were achieved. Stories that Phoenix was a program of assassination and torture began to cause scandal in the United States in the early 1970s. Assassinations had occurred, mostly carried out by the PRUs, but not in numbers as large as sometimes suggested. At first, large numbers of Communists killed had been a mark of success, rather than a political liability, and some officers exaggerated the number of kills to make the program look good. The number captured alive had been greater than the number killed. Some captives had been brutally tortured, but others were interrogated without torture, sometimes producing more reliable information. Some had not been interrogated at all. Corruption existed, as some jailers could be bribed to release Communist prisoners, and some people not even suspected of being Communists were arrested simply so their families would have to pay bribes to win their release. Diversity made valid generalizations about the program difficult.

M. Moyar, *Phoenix and the Birds of Prey* (Annapolis, MD, 1997).

Edwin E. Moise

PHOUMI NOSAVAN (1919–1986)

During the last years of the Eisenhower administration, Phoumi Nosavan was Washington's favorite anti-Communist military politician in Laos*. A member of the Voravong family from Savannakhet in southeastern Laos and a distant cousin to Thai strongman Sarit Thanarat, Phoumi began his career as a member of Lao Issara (Free Lao), which opposed French Colonialism* at the end of World War II. He broke with the Lao nationalists when France offered Laos qualified independence within the French Union of Associated States. Phoumi joined the military forces of the new Lao State created under the Geneva Accords of 1954* and became an up-and-coming officer. In 1958, Colonel Phoumi allied himself with a group of Young Turk military men and politicians who formed the anti-Communist group Committee for the Defense of National Interests. He came to the attention of representatives of the U.S. Central Intelligence Agency* and the Department of Defense, who feared the growing influence of the Communist-led Pathet Lao* after their success in the 1958 supplemental elections.

In 1959, Phoumi joined a Royal Lao government, which persecuted the Pathet Lao and barred them from contesting the April 1960 general elections. He rigged the 1960 voting so that his handpicked candidate was elected prime minister. As defense minister in the new government, General Phoumi held the real power. Lao political life became heavily polarized and official corruption became rife. Captain Kong Le* staged his coup in August 1960, in good part to reduce Phoumi's influence. With clandestine support from the United States and Thailand*, Phoumi's forces marched from his stronghold in Savannakhet and retook Vientiane from Kong Le neutralists. The Eisenhower administration recognized the Boum Oum government with Phoumi wielding the real power. Kong Le and the Pathet Lao counterattacked, igniting the Laotian Crisis of 1961*. John F. Kennedy*, the new U.S. president, decided to support neutralism in Laos, and U.S. relations with Phoumi deteriorated. Among Kennedy's advisers, Phoumi's reputation was not good because he was the classic "fat" general, corrupt and almost never on the battlefield, rather than a "thin" general, who was honest and fought with his troops. He also consolidated his control of Laos's gambling casinos, gold and liquor monopolies, and reportedly the major brothels.

Still, the Kennedy administration needed to support Phoumi and his forces if it had any hope of successfully negotiating a neutrality deal with the Pathet Lao and the Democratic Republic of Vietnam*. W. Averell Harriman*, Kennedy's lead negotiator and adviser on Laos, became increasingly disenchanted with Phoumi and infuriated by his opposition to a coalition government. Washington cajoled and finally coerced Phoumi to join the coalition provided for in the Geneva Accords of 1962*. That year, in the neutralist government of Souvanna Phouma*, Phoumi was vice prime minister and minister of finance, taking him out of the military chain of command, but leaving his hands firmly in Laos's meager financial pockets. He regained the defense ministry as Souvanna's relations with the Pathet Lao soured, but he never held the power that he previously enjoyed. Phoumi flirted with coup attempts against Souvanna in 1964 and 1965. After one abortive coup too many where his hand showed too clearly, he was forced into exile in Thailand in April 1965. He left in Savannakhet an extravagant unfinished casino, a fitting epithet to one of Laos's most notorious "fat" generals.

M. Brown and J. J. Zasloff, *Apprentice Revolutionaries: The Communist Movement in Laos, 1930–1985* (Stanford, CA, 1986); T. N. Castle, *At War in the Shadow of Vietnam: U.S. Military Aid to the Royal Lao Government, 1955–1975* (New York, 1993); A. J. Dommen, *Conflict in Laos: The Politics of Neutralization* (New York, 1971); C. A. Stevenson, *The End of Nowhere: American Policy Toward Laos Since 1954* (Boston, 1972); R. Warner, *Back Fire: Secret War in Laos and Its Link to the War in Vietnam* (New York, 1995).

Edward C. Keefer

PING-PONG DIPLOMACY

The visit of a U.S. Ping-Pong team to the People's Republic of China* (PRC) in April 1971 was part of a web of official and unofficial contacts that President Richard M. Nixon* initiated in his pursuit of U.S.-PRC Normalization of Relations*, climaxing with Nixon's Visit to China* in February 1972. Thereafter, the term "Ping-Pong diplomacy" became synonymous with unofficial contacts between countries without diplomatic relations aimed at the improvement of relations. The Chinese invitation to the U.S. Ping-Pong team to visit China, extended on 6 April 1971 at an international Ping-Pong tournament in Japan, astonished everyone concerned. The PRC was still in the throes of the Chinese Cultural Revolution*. Even the presence of the Chinese Ping-Pong team in Japan was the PRC's first participation in an international sports event in several years. Although the invitation appeared spontaneous, both Washington and Beijing had been exchanging cautious signals of interest in improved relations. The invitation was evidently a step in that elaborately choreographed dance. Graham B. Steenhoven, the president of the U.S. Table Tennis Association and manager of the American team, accepted the invitation after consulting the U.S. embassy in Tōkyō.

Upon arrival, the American team enjoyed an impressive reception in China. Premier Zhou Enlai* received its members in the Great Hall of the People on 14 April and told them they had "opened a new chapter in the relations of the American and Chinese people." The Americans responded by inviting the Chinese team to tour the United States, and the Chinese promptly accepted. That same day, Nixon announced reductions in U.S. travel and trade restrictions with the PRC. China's Ping-Pong diplomacy was, as National Security Adviser Henry A. Kissinger* observed, vintage Zhou Enlai. It sent an unmistakable signal of interest in improved relations without making any official move that could be rebuffed. It conveyed an image of friendliness and moderation that undercut the uncompromising tone of many Chinese public utterances at the time, and it prepared both Chinese cadres and the U.S. public for the announcement three months later of the invitation to Nixon to visit China. But the Chinese Ping-Pong team was not so hospitable, soundly thrashing the American team.

J. Holdridge, *Crossing the Divide: An Insider's Account of the Normalization of U.S. China Relations* (Lanham, MD, 1997); H. A. Kissinger, *White House Years* (Boston, 1979).

Harriet Dashiell Schwar

PLEIKU INCIDENT

The Pleiku Incident in February 1965 provided the pretext for implementing Operation ROLLING THUNDER, the U.S. retaliatory raids against the Democratic Republic of Vietnam* that marked the beginning of the enormous escalation of the American involvement in the Second Indochina War*. Pleiku is near the Cambodian border in the Central Highlands of Vietnam, roughly equidistant from Saigon and the seventeenth parallel. Its location made it an important economic and strategic center; not only was it a regional market for mountain tribes, but it was the headquarters of the Second Corps Tactical Zone and the site of a large U.S.–Army of the Republic of Vietnam* (ARVN) military complex. At 2:00 A.M. on the morning of 7 February 1965, a Viet Cong* force launched an artillery attack on Camp Holloway, a lightly guarded U.S. helicopter base and special forces barracks in Pleiku. Nine American advisers were killed and 128 wounded, and ten U.S. planes were destroyed and numerous others damaged. This was one of ten Viet Cong attacks launched that day after termination of a unilateral Viet Cong cease-fire during Tet, the Vietnamese New Year. Although not the largest of these attacks, it resulted in the highest number of American casualties in the conflict to date.

The Pleiku attack provided the Johnson administration with the justification to order the evacuation of American dependents and to strike directly at North Vietnam in a "tit-for-tat" reprisal attack similar to the one launched in the wake of the Gulf of Tonkin Incidents* early in August 1964. National Security Adviser McGeorge Bundy* insisted that the Pleiku assault constituted the type of clear-cut provocation that President Lyndon B. Johnson* had cited as a trigger for retaliatory strikes against the North Vietnamese. These retaliatory raids, code-named Operation FLAMING DART, were carried out by 132 carrier-based American jets against four different barracks complexes inside North Vietnam less than fourteen hours after the Pleiku incident. FLAMING DART was the precursor to Operation ROLLING THUNDER, the sustained bombing campaign against North Vietnam that lasted until 31 October 1968.

Scholars still debate why the Viet Cong chose to attack the U.S. Special Forces base at Pleiku and why the United States responded as it did. Some see it as the logical consequence of a guerrilla war, whereas others consider it an attempt by the National Liberation Front* to gain leverage with the Soviet Union. Bundy later described the incident as a "streetcar" in that you could expect one to come along at any time and should be ready to board it as soon as it did. Indeed, attacks similar to the one on Pleiku had been anticipated by U.S. officials, since the Viet Cong usually launched heavy attacks after Tet cease-fires ended, and the assets and mechanisms for reprisal already had been put in place by an administration that perhaps had been pushed too far. Regardless of the reasons for the attack and its consequences, the Pleiku incident helped to set a precedent for future Viet Cong attacks on American interests in the weeks to come.

L. C. Gardner, *Pay Any Price: Lyndon Johnson and the Wars for Vietnam* (Chicago, 1995); G. McT. Kahin, *Intervention: How America Became Involved in Vietnam* (New York, 1986); S. Karnow, *Vietnam: A History* (New York, 1983).

Andrew L. Johns

POL POT (1925–1998)

Born Saloth Sar, the former schoolteacher began calling himself Pol Pot, his revolutionary name, in 1976, a year after the Khmer Rouge* seized political power in Cambodia*. Along with other party leaders such as Ieng Sary and Khieu Samphan*, Pol Pot led an ideologically driven campaign to change the nature of Cambodian society and purge it of allegedly antirevolutionary elements. The result was that between 17 April 1975, when Khmer Rouge forces entered Phnom Penh, and Vietnam's invasion of Cambodia on 25 December 1978, which forced the Khmer Rouge to flee to isolated jungle locations along the western border with Thailand*, Pol Pot oversaw the deaths of an estimated 1.7 million Cambodians, half from execution and the other half from starvation and disease, in what Jean Lacouture termed autogenocide. His fanatical commitment to Communism*, abhorrence of foreigners, particularly the ethnic Vietnamese in Cambodia, and complete disregard for the suffering of the people led to the inflicting of a human catastrophe on Cambodia, one from which the country and its people have yet to recover fully. Pol Pot's importance for U.S. relations with East Asia comes principally from how he came to power.

When Richard M. Nixon* became president in 1969, he decided to deal with the North Vietnamese use of Cambodian territory as sanctuary locations from U.S. troops in the Republic of Vietnam* by initiating a bombing campaign code-named Operation MENU* beginning that spring. Nixon sought to destroy the Central Office for South Vietnam, (COSVN), the command center for Vietnamese Communist forces in the south, but he also wanted to keep it secret from Congress and the American public. MENU had two main effects. First, it caused Vietnamese troops to disperse westward, farther into Cambodia. Second, U.S. bombing forced many peasants to relocate, radicalizing some in the process and leading them either to join the Khmer Rouge or become more sympathetic to the party's cause. Cambodia's longtime leader Prince Norodom Sihanouk* decided to reestablish relations with the United States, which he had broken off earlier in the 1960s, but in the process he lost critical support in the National Assembly. When he departed Cambodia in January 1970 for his annual visit to France for recuperation, Prime Minister Lon Nol* accepted the National Assembly's vote to become chief of state. This decision did not sit well with many peasants, but he received immediate recognition from the United States. Lon Nol then made a series of bad decisions, such as sending Cambodia's small and ill-equipped military to attack the Vietnamese, that hastened his decline. Also, he acquiesced to the Nixon administration's decision to stage the Cambodian Incursion* on 30 April 1970 in an effort to destroy the COSVN. Pol Pot's forces intensified recruitment, increased in numbers, and gained territory in the early 1970s until they finally entered the capital city of Phnom Penh in April 1975, coinciding with the end of the Second Indochina War*.

Thereafter until Vietnam's invasion, Pol Pot, known as Brother Number One, presided over one of the most brutal regimes in world history. He especially became increasingly determined to eliminate Vietnam and the Vietnamese people, launching border assaults as well as fiery rhetoric broadcast on radio despite Cambodia's much smaller size and weaker military. After forces of the Socialist Republic of Vietnam* invaded in December 1978, the Khmer Rouge were forced to live in densely forested areas along the border with Thailand, where they engaged in the smuggling of timber and gems with the cooperation of the Thai military, all under the assumption that they would one day return to power. Even toward the end of his life, Pol Pot lived under the illusion that his Khmer Rouge enjoyed vast support from the Cambodian people. He insisted his conscience was clear on what had happened during his rule, but only his death prevented the government from arresting and punishing him.

N. Chanda, *Brother Enemy: The War After the War* (New York, 1986); D. Chandler, *Brother Number One: A Political Biography of Pol Pot* (Boulder, CO, 1999); B. Kiernan, *How Pol Pot Came to Power: A History of Communism in Kampuchea, 1930–1975* (London, 1985); B. Kiernan, *The Pol Pot Regime: Race, Power, and Genocide in Cambodia Under the Khmer Rouge, 1975–79* (New Haven, CT: 1996); W. Shawcross, *Sideshow: Kissinger, Nixon and the Destruction of Cambodia* (New York, 1987).

T. Christopher Jespersen

PORTSMOUTH CONFERENCE

The Portsmouth Conference ended the Russo-Japanese War* in 1905 and helped establish a new balance of power in Asia that included Japan as a major imperial force on the continent. Japan had attacked Russia in a clash over economic and military influence in Northeast China and Korea. In 1905, in an effort to bring the war to a close and responding to a Japanese initiative, President Theodore Roosevelt* invited the warring parties to Portsmouth, New Hampshire, in an attempt to reach a peace accord. Roosevelt had applauded Japan's apparent defense of the Open Door Policy* and its assault on Russian territorial aggrandizement in Northeast Asia, but then his enthusiasm faded as Japanese victories mounted. At Portsmouth, he sought most of all the restoration of a balance of power in Asia and order in Russia. Oddly, even though the Russo-Japanese War had been fought on Chinese and Korean soil, neither were invited to Portsmouth. The plenipotentiaries who did attend and who would decide China's and Korea's fates to no small degree were Komura Jutarō of Japan and Sergei Witte of Russia. Foreign Minister Komura had helped lead his nation to war. Witte, the tsar's minister of finance from 1892 to 1902 and the chief architect of Russia's East Asian policy during much of that time, had opposed the aggressive course that had led to conflict with Japan. Theodore Roosevelt did not attend the conference in Portsmouth, but orchestrated discussions from Oyster Bay, Long Island.

Japan had won a series of land and naval engagements decisively, but was overextended. Tsarist officials reasoned that with superior resources and a larger population, Russia could outlast her enemy if the war continued, albeit at a high cost. The peace conference thus required greater negotiation than battlefield results alone might have dictated. Debate focused on Korea, Manchuria, the island of Sakhalin, and the Japanese demand for a financial indemnity. Japanese forces had occupied most of the two former areas; Russia was in no position to oust them and acceded to Japanese dominance. Sakhalin and the indemnity were more contentious issues. Ultimately, the powers decided to partition the island and, with the negotiations on the verge of breaking up, Komura agreed to withdraw his demand for an indemnity. Roosevelt won the Nobel Peace Prize for his efforts in achieving the Treaty of Portsmouth*, a somewhat incongruous addition to his trophy case. The Portsmouth Conference thus demonstrated the expanding world role of the United States, as Roosevelt successfully brokered an agreement to end a war he no longer saw as advantageous to American national interests. The war itself probably already had restored the balance of power in Asia, but the conference had confirmed it. Its outcome clearly reflected the shifting geopolitical situation, especially the rise of Japan as a continental power.

R. A. Esthus, *Double Eagle and Rising Sun: The Russians and Japanese at Portsmouth in 1905* (Durham, NC, 1988); R. A. Esthus, *Theodore Roosevelt and the International Rivalries* (Waltham, MA, 1970); E. P. Trani, *The Treaty of Portsmouth: An Adventure in American Diplomacy* (Lexington, MA, 1969); J. A. White, *The Diplomacy of the Russo-Japanese War* (Princeton, NJ, 1964).

Shannon Smith

POTSDAM DECLARATION

The Allies issued the Potsdam Declaration on 20 July 1945. It was begun in May 1944 by Joseph C. Grew*, who had been ambassador to Japan from 1932 until the start of the war. Grew hoped to soften the American stance of "unconditional surrender" that President Franklin Roosevelt* announced at the Casablanca Conference early in 1943, in hopes of inducing Japan to surrender before a cataclysmic U.S. invasion of the home islands became necessary. Grew also hoped to foster the basis for a U.S.-Japan understanding once the already bitter Pacific war was over. But Grew's initiative encountered two considerable obstacles. The American public, still enraged over the Japanese Pearl Harbor Attack*, strongly supported unconditional surrender. Indeed, there were sentiments for obliterating the Japanese entirely. Within the government, the U.S. Army preferred a surrender engineered by its invasion of the home islands, rather than induced by aerial bombardment or a naval blockade, since either of these outcomes would strengthen postwar funding for an American air force or navy.

Against these wartime considerations, Grew marshaled postwar concerns. A continuation of the fighting against Japan to the bitter end would play into the hands of the Soviet Union, and Grew was one of the earlier U.S. policy makers to make this argument. It was even possible that Japan itself might be communized if its death throes were too prolonged. Grew saw the institution of the Japanese emperor as the key. He did not propose firm promises to keep the monarchy intact, but he did argue that the matter ought to be kept open. Grew's use of the Soviet angle was well placed, since the U.S. Army's own invasion plans of Japan depended upon a Soviet attack on Japanese holdings on the Asian mainland. By the spring of 1945, with Roosevelt's death and Harry S. Truman* as president, questions about future Soviet conduct and intentions seemed more pressing. Further complications were added by the imminent success of the American atomic bomb project, which might itself induce a Japanese surrender if, Grew argued, it were coupled with some assurances for the emperor, and word from Moscow in June that Joseph Stalin was certain to insist on a Soviet occupation zone in Japan at the upcoming Potsdam summit conference.

Nevertheless, Grew's proposal would have been stillborn but for support from Secretary of War Henry L. Stimson* once Truman finally approved the U.S. Army's plan, code-named Operation OLYMPIC*, for the invasion of Kyūshū, first of the home islands. Stimson, however, was much more interested in using such a statement, even with some words about the emperor, as an ultimatum to force a fast surrender, rather than as the basis for a postwar understanding. Accordingly, Stimson wanted to insert warnings about a terrible new weapon and imminent Soviet intervention: surrender or else. This stance was much more acceptable to Truman as well, concerned as he was about the sentiments of the American public. The resulting declaration, however, was crafted by Secretary of States James F. Byrnes. He removed both assurances about the emperor and references to Stimson's threats. Byrnes hoped to induce the Japanese to surrender before the Soviets intervened and without any U.S. commitments. Japan's refusal to surrender led to the Atomic Attacks* and Tōkyō's request for peace terms. The personal intervention of Emperor Hirohito* guaranteed that Japan accepted the Potsdam Declaration without amendment. But, immediately after surrendering, the Japanese government made clear that it interpreted the declaration to mean that the monarchy could be retained if, in the declaration's own terminology, this was the free wish of the Japanese people. To no small degree, the ensuing U.S. Occupation of Japan* would revolve around the differing interpretations of those stipulations.

K. Inoue, *MacArthur's Japanese Constitution: A Linguistic and Cultural Study of Its Making* (Chicago, 1991); L. V. Sigal, *Fighting to a Finish: The Politics of War Termination in the United States and Japan, 1945* (Ithaca, NY, 1988).

Michael A. Barnhart

PRRI-PERMESTA REBELLION

Between December 1956 and March 1957, local army officers in Sumatra and Sulawesi revolted against the central government of Indonesia*. The United States intervened decisively on the side of the rebels in what became known as the PRRI-Permesta Rebellion, waging one of the largest, costliest, and most disastrous covert operations of the Cold War. The revolts reflected long-standing regional resentment at the centralization of wealth and power in Java, highlighted by the resignation of Ali Sastroamidjojo's cabinet in March 1957, the collapse of parliamentary democracy, and the declaration by Sukarno* of "Guided Democracy." The rebels also opposed Sukarno's toleration of the Indonesian Communist Party (PKI) and what they saw as the government's excessive bureaucracy, corruption, and economic neglect of the outer islands. Although rebel demands varied according to local circumstances, they generally included a return to the dual rule under Sukarno and Mohammed Hatta* and the 1945 constitution, some measure of regional autonomy, and a more equitable distribution of national income. The rebel officers, backed by regional political parties and religious groupings such as the Masjumi, set up local revolutionary councils and, in February 1958, formed the Revolutionary Government of the Republic of Indonesia

(Pemerintah Revolusioner Republik Indonesia, or PRRI), igniting a brief but fierce civil war. In response to the revolts, Sukarno had proclaimed martial law in March 1957, with broad support from the military. By June 1958, Indonesian troops under the command of General Abdul Haris Nasution* and loyal to Sukarno, had effectively crushed the rebellion, although isolated rebel units continued to resist the central government in Jakarta for nearly two more years.

By the end of 1956, U.S. officials led by Secretary of State John Foster Dulles* and his brother, Allen Dulles, the director of the Central Intelligence Agency* (CIA), had become convinced that Indonesia's government and military were falling under the influence of the PKI. They looked with dismay at the PKI's success in the 1955 elections and Sukarno's militant brand of neutralism. In September 1957, officials in the Eisenhower administration, fueled by near-hysterical and generally inaccurate CIA intelligence reports, decided to exploit the growing regional discontent. They sought through a massive covert operation to reverse Indonesia's supposed leftward drift by weakening or overthrowing Sukarno, checking the power of Java-based units of the military and the PKI, and even using force to break up Indonesia to preserve Western access to resource-rich western Sumatra. During the last few months of 1957, the United States provided millions of dollars in covert funds and modern weapons to the dissident colonels leading the regional rebellions. In January 1958, Washington intervened massively and directly by providing air cover to rebel military units and positioning U.S. naval vessels for possible intervention in Sumatra. In addition, U.S. forces and PRRI rebels operated freely from the British base complex in Singapore* and trained at U.S. facilities throughout the region. Jakarta countered in April 1958 by announcing a major arms purchase from the Soviet bloc.

Throughout the period, Eisenhower administration officials publicly insisted that the PRRI rebels were operating on their own. But U.S. support could no longer be denied after CIA pilot Allen Pope was shot down and captured in April 1958, shortly after a bombing run in Ambon in which hundreds of civilians were killed. But by the summer, it was becoming clear that the U.S.-sponsored forces were heading toward disaster. The Eisenhower administration finally recognized what internal critics of its policy had argued all along—that the United States was fueling a civil war between two anti-Communist factions of the same military. Washington abruptly resumed military assistance to the government it had been seeking to overthrow, alarmed at the role Soviet weapons had played in the ignominious defeat of rebel forces. The failed rebellions seriously damaged U.S. credibility in Indonesia and bolstered the PKI. Furthermore, it split the nationalistic and anti-Communist Indonesian military, ensuring the dominance of its Java-based units, and fatally crippled moderate political groupings, such as the Masjumi. In the wake of the PRRI-Permesta Rebellion, the army, Sukarno, and the PKI each emerged stronger than before, further polarizing Indonesian society and creating the essential preconditions for the far bloodier Indonesia Crisis of 1965*.

H. Feith, *The Decline of Constitutional Democracy in Indonesia* (Ithaca, NY, 1962); A. Kahin, *Rebellion to Integration: West Sumatra and the Indonesian Polity* (Amsterdam, 1999); A. Kahin and G. McT. Kahin, *Subversion as Foreign Policy: Eisenhower, Dulles and the Indonesian Debacle* (Ithaca, NY, 1994); U.S. Department of State, *Foreign Relations of the United States, 1958–1960,* Vol. 17: *Indonesia* (Washington, DC, 1994).

Bradley R. Simpson

PRUITT, IDA (1888–1985)

As an American social worker born in China, Ida Pruitt developed an understanding and appreciation of Chinese culture and China's twentieth-century fight for national sovereignty that transformed her into an anti-imperialist critic of U.S. China policy after World War II. The daughter of Southern Baptist missionaries, she lived until age twelve at a rural mission outpost in Penglai, Shandong Province. After completing high school and college in the United States, Pruitt returned to China to teach at her parents' mission school from 1912 to 1918. Although she loved China, she did not love teaching at mission schools and consequently left China in 1918 to pursue a career as a social worker in the United States. When the opportunity arose to go to Beijing as a medical social worker at Peking Union Medical College* (PUMC) in 1919, she eagerly returned. As head of the Social Services Department for the PUMC until 1938, Pruitt unwillingly became part of Western missionary efforts to "reform" and "modernize" China according to Western models. But she remained an unusually culturally sensitive administrator of a program that she designed to fulfill the special needs of her economically and socially diverse Chinese patients.

Pruitt's most concerted effort to affect the course of U.S. relations with China occurred during the years she served as executive secretary of the International Committee (and later, the American Committee) to support the Chinese Industrial Cooperatives (CIC) from 1939 to 1952. The CIC, known in the United States by its cable address "Indusco," was founded in 1938 during the Sino-Japanese War to set up small-scale production cooperatives that would fulfill local consumer needs and supply the Chinese Guomindang* (GMD) (Nationalist) Army with war materials in areas of China that were not occupied by Japan. Indusco cooperatives contributed in significant ways to China's wartime needs. They provided work for displaced skilled and unskilled laborers who were forced by the Japanese invasion to relocate to China's western interior. They also operated vocational training centers, health clinics, printing and publishing houses, and literacy classes for CIC members and their families.

Pruitt raised funds and promoted the CIC mission in the United States and among the Western missionary and business communities in China. In addition, she mediated between the Chinese and Western government and nongovernment constituencies, who were involved in determining the CIC's future and suspicious of the political orientation of the participating laborers and founding organizers of the CIC. The progressive Westerners who founded Indusco intended the cooperatives to be entirely producer-owned and operated, with minimal interference from the GMD government bureaucracy. Although Song Meiling*, wife of President Jiang Jieshi* of the Republic of China*, supported the CIC, conservatives in the GMD government, such as Finance Minister Kung Xiangxi*, fought for more centralization and government control over CIC production units. Fear that a pro-Communist ideological orientation would spread throughout the independent producer-owned operations resulted in the GMD government's reluctance to support CIC growth and development. Anti-Communist anxieties in the United States also affected Western support for the CIC, especially after the Chinese Civil War* resumed in 1945. Yet Pruitt fought these fears vigorously over the thirteen years she promoted the CIC and became a fierce critic of the U.S. government's openly anti-Communist China policy.

After the Chinese Communist Party* triumphed in the civil war and came to power in 1949, American support for the CIC evaporated. As the People's Republic of China* initiated its own cooperative and collectivization efforts, the CIC dissolved in 1952. Pruitt, however, remained active in the United States in her efforts to alleviate fears of the Chinese Communists among the American public. Although her audiences were small, she continued to promote understanding of China's unique culture and history, and respect for China's national right of self-determination, among her fellow Americans throughout the

1960s. Pruitt's legacy includes her significant contribution to the anti-imperialist tradition in American social and political thought.

M. King, "Ida Pruitt, Heir and Critic of American Missionary Reform Efforts in China," in P. Neils (ed.), *United States Attitudes and Policies Toward China: The Impact of American Missionaries* (Armonk, NY, 1990); I. Pruitt, *A Daughter of Han: The Autobiography of a Chinese Working Woman* (Stanford, CA, 1967); I. Pruitt, *Old Madam Yin: A Memoir of Life in Peking, 1926–1938* (Stanford, CA, 1979); S. B. Thomas, *Season of High Adventure: Edgar Snow in China* (Berkeley, CA, 1996).

Karen Garner

PUEBLO INCIDENT

When the United States became deeply involved in the Second Indochina War*, Premier Kim Il Sung* of the Democratic People's Republic of Korea* apparently saw an opportunity to move toward his goal of unification by force, perhaps in part by stirring up in South Korea the kind of guerrilla warfare that gave the United States so much trouble in the Republic of Vietnam*. During the late 1960s, there was a sharp stepping up of infiltrations through the demilitarized zone (DMZ) and around it by water, culminating in a series of dramatic incidents in 1968 and 1969 that easily could have brought renewal of the Korean War*. On 21 January 1968, a suicide squad of thirty-nine DPRK terrorists penetrated the DMZ and reached Seoul with the acknowledged mission of assassinating President Pak Chŏng-hŭi*. Their leaders were captured less than a mile from the presidential palace.

In this atmosphere, two days later, the DPRK attacked and captured the U.S. naval intelligence ship USS *Pueblo* with its officers and crew while in international waters in the Sea of Japan. P'yŏngyang's claim that the *Pueblo*, in reality a naval vessel disguised as a research ship, had entered its national waters (within the twelve-mile limit) was denied by the United States. After eleven months of difficult negotiations, the eighty-two officers and men of the *Pueblo* (and the body of one killed during the capture) were released to the United States. As a quid pro quo, the U.S. commander had agreed to sign a confession and an apology prepared by the North Koreans, but with their consent that he should repudiate the document before signing it. Given the demands of Vietnam, the Johnson administration chose to solve the problem diplomatically.

T. Armbrister, *A Matter of Accountability: The True Story of the* Pueblo *Affair* (New York, 1970); L. M. Bucher, *Bucher: My Story* (New York, 1970); E. R. Murphy Jr., *Second in Command: The Uncensored Account of the Capture of the Spy Ship* (New York, 1971).

Joseph M. Siracusa

PUSAN PERIMETER

During July 1950, military forces of the United States, the United Nations, and the Republic of Korea* (ROK) retreated during the Korean War* to the southeastern region of the Korean peninsula, holding a rectangular area north and west of the port city of Pusan on the southern coast. In this Pusan Perimeter, bloody battles were fought during the months of August and early September. More than two-thirds of South Korean territory fell into the hands of the Korean People's Army (KPA) after it invaded South Korea on 25 June 1950. In early August 1950, South Korean and U.S. troops barely managed to halt the Communist advance to the west of the Naktong River and at a line just above Taegu about eighty miles north of Pusan. Along a 140-mile arc north from Masan on the southern coast and then east to the East Sea, U.S. divisions occupied the western front, basing their position on the Naktong River. South Korean forces, reorganized by American military advisers into five divisions, defended the northern segment. The KPA made every effort to conquer South Korea before U.S reinforcements and additional equipment arrived, the Democratic People's Republic of Korea* (DPRK) committing thirteen infantry divisions and an armored division against the Pusan Perimeter. But by early September, the KPA, having spent too much time occupying South Chŏlla Province, was outmanned and outgunned. Moreover, United Nations Command (UNC) interior lines of communications and supply radiating from Pusan put the defenders in an advantageous position to move troops and supplies swiftly to meet each Communist military thrust.

During the last phase of defense of the Pusan Perimeter, the KPA's offensive nearly brought about the collapse of the defense line at the Naktong River, and Taegu became isolated at the beginning of September. At this juncture, the ROK government and its military headquarters, as well as that of the U.S. Eighth Army, moved to Pusan, as South Korean and U.S. troops took their last stand just south of what the Americans called the Davidson Line. Holding this line, the tide of battle changed and the Pusan Perimeter was secure. Despite heavy costs, defense of the Pusan Perimeter succeeded in buying time so that the United States could mount a full-scale intervention and launch the Inch'ŏn Landing* behind enemy lines on 15 September. South Korean and U.S. troops counterattacked and broke out of the Pusan Perimeter on 16 September, advancing slowly at first. But North Korean forces on 23 September began retreating rapidly, only to be met by UNC forces moving southward from Seoul. Under the command of Lieutenant General Walton H. Walker, the U.S. Eighth Army, by then organized as four corps, two U.S. and two ROK, rolled forward in pursuit, linking with the Tenth Corps on 26 September. About 30,000 North Korean troops escaped above the thirty-eighth parallel through the eastern mountains. By the end of September, the KPA ceased to exist as an organized force anywhere in South Korea.

R. E. Appleman, *South to the Naktong, North to the Yalu (June–November 1950)* (Washington, DC, 1992); C. Blair, *The Forgotten War: America in Korea, 1950–1953* (New York, 1987); S. Y. Paik, *From Pusan to Panmunjom* (New York, 1992); J. Toland, *In Mortal Combat: Korea 1950–53* (New York, 1991).

Han Kyu-sun

PUYI (1906–1967)

The last emperor of China, Puyi is more often remembered as the puppet ruler of the Japanese-dominated state Manchukuo* (formerly Manchuria) from 1932 to 1945. Nicknamed Henry by his English tutor, he ascended the throne in 1909. During the Chinese Revolution of 1911*, the emperor's mother negotiated frantically with Yuan Shikai* for a settlement that would guarantee their lives and financial security. Ignoring the claims to the presidency of Sun Zhongshan*, Puyi abdicated in favor of Yuan, who was authorized to form a provisional republic and establish national unity by embracing all anti-imperial forces. Briefly restored in 1917 by the intrigues of the Warlord Era*, he was again deposed and finally sought refuge in the Japanese concession in Tianjin by 1924. During July 1931, his brother visited Japan and met with various rightist politicians. Shortly after the Mukden Incident* in September 1931, representatives of the Kwantung Army visited Puyi to discuss Manchuria's future, assuring him that they merely were interested in helping the Manchurians establish an independent nation. They were vague about whether the new state would be a monarchy or a republic.

Negotiations continued through the fall and winter of 1931 and 1932 until Puyi agreed to be smuggled to Manchuria by sea and to accept the title "chief executive" of the State of Manchukuo. Tokyo belatedly recognized its creation in August 1932. Two years later, the Kwantung Army allowed Puyi to mount the throne as the Emperor of Manchoutikuo (Manchu

Empire), in imperial dragon robes sent from the museum in Beijing. As "Emperor," he served the Greater East Asia Co-Prosperity Sphere* loyally until 1945, including a state visit to Tōkyō. But in August 1945, when the Soviet Union invaded Manchukuo, he was dethroned and imprisoned. Released to the People's Republic of China* in 1950, he was again imprisoned and subjected to reeducation programs until his rehabilitation in 1959. His final years were spent as a gardener in Beijing's botanical gardens until his death from cancer.

D. Bergamini, *Japan's Imperial Conspiracy* (New York, 1971); H. Pu-Yi, *From Emperor to Citizen: The Autobiography of Aisin-Gioro Pu Yi* (Oxford, UK, 1987); J. Spence, *The Search for Modern China* (New York, 1990).

Errol M. Clauss

Q

QIAO GUANHUA (1913–1983)

Qiao Guanhua was an outstanding diplomat of the People's Republic of China* (PRC) who was influential in determining Beijing's policy in response to the decision of President Richard M. Nixon* to pursue U.S.-PRC Normalization of Relations*. Born to a gentry family in a southern Chinese town, Qiao was well educated in traditional classics in his early age. At age sixteen, he became a student at the well-known Qinghua University and majored in philosophy, but explored a wide variety of other subjects and learned English, Japanese, and German. After graduating, Qiao went to Japan for graduate school, where he gained exposure to leftist thoughts. In 1935, he transferred to Germany to complete his education. During that time, Qiao systematically studied Marxism and Leninism. In 1938, as the war between Japan and China intensified, he returned to China, hoping to contribute to the Chinese cause. In the next decade, Qiao worked as a writer and an editor for newspapers in Hong Kong* and in China. His writing was logical and persuasive, commanding a large number of readers. After he read one of his articles, Mao Zedong* said that it was "as powerful as two armored divisions." During this time, Qiao joined the Chinese Communist Party*.

Qiao's rich international exposure, his rigorous training, and his quick wit all prepared him to be a diplomat, often displaying brilliance, particularly in dealing with the Americans. In 1951, Qiao was included in the Chinese delegation at what became the P'anmunjŏm Truce Talks* in the Korean War*. Although not a negotiator, he was responsible for communicating with Beijing and proposing specific plans for discussion. The second milestone in Qiao's career as a diplomat was between 1971 and 1972, when the Sino-American rapprochement took place. In October 1971, the United Nations passed a resolution to replace Taibei with Beijing to resolve the dispute over Chinese Representation in the United Nations* and as a member of the UN Security Council. In November, Qiao was appointed as the chief of the Chinese delegation to the United Nations. Once again, he deeply impressed the Western journalists with his diplomatic brilliance. Upon returning from the United Nations, Qiao immediately was involved in preparations for President Nixon's Visit to China*. In fact, National Security Adviser Henry A. Kissinger* and Qiao Guanhua, then China's vice minister of foreign affairs, undertook most of the substantial negotiating between the PRC and the United States. While others were going sightseeing and attending banquets, Qiao and Kissinger were struggling to find appropriate words so that both sides would find it acceptable. After many sleepless nights, they worked out the draft of an agreement, which became the Shanghai Communiqúe*. Thereafter until the death of Mao in 1976 marked the peak of Qiao's career as a diplomat, serving as minister of foreign affairs and Beijing's UN ambassador. His influence waned, however, as the political climate shifted unexpectedly in China after 1978 under the leadership of Deng Xiaoping*.

H. C. Hinton, *Communist China in World Politics* (Boston, 1966); Wu Miaofa, *Waijiao caizi Qiao Guanhua* [Qiao Guanhua: The Talented Diplomat] (Shenzhen, 1998).

Li Yi

QUARANTINE SPEECH

This noted address, delivered at a public rally in Chicago on 5 October 1937, was fundamentally a response to Japan's undeclared war against China that followed the Marco Polo Bridge Incident* of July 1937. Heavy fighting broke out in Shanghai during August, as invading Japanese forces moved inland toward the Chinese capital of Nanjing. Confronted by the force of American isolationism, President Franklin D. Roosevelt*, like the leaders of Western Europe, responded to the unfolding events in East Asia with verbal condemnation, but little else. Yet Roosevelt feared that U.S. inaction, following the signing of the Anti-Comintern Pact* of 1936, would encourage Japanese expansionism, as well as the continuing German and Italian defiance of the territorial and military provisions of the Versailles Peace Treaty*.

At Chicago, Roosevelt, without confronting the isolationists directly, suggested that the challenge of international lawlessness demanded some form of U.S. response. He therefore proposed that the peace-loving nations "quarantine" the aggressors who were spreading the "epidemic of world lawlessness." He reminded Americans that just 10 percent of the world's population threatened the peace, freedom, and security of the remaining 90 percent, who, he urged, "must find some way to make their will prevail. . . . There must be positive endeavors to preserve peace." That Roosevelt seemed to advocate the support of collective security produced a vociferous outcry, demanding that he avoid involving the country in conflicts that did not concern it directly. Although leading newspapers appeared to favor some U.S. action, Roosevelt concluded that the American people were not prepared to accept greater overseas responsibilities. He thus refrained from following his "Quarantine" speech with any advocacy of forceful measures, even economic sanctions, against Japanese aggression.

R. A. Dallek, *Franklin D. Roosevelt and American Foreign Policy, 1932–1945* (New York, 1979); W. L. Langer and S. E. Gleason, *The Challenge to Isolation, 1937–1940* (New York, 1952).

Norman A. Graebner

QUEZÓN, MANUEL L. (1878–1944)

Manuel Luis Quezón was the first president of the Commonwealth of the Philippines*, the transitional body established by the United States on 15 November 1935 to prepare its Philippine colony for independence. Creating the Commonwealth distinguished the United States from other colonial powers in East and Southeast Asia. Whereas the Dutch, British, French, and Japanese regarded their colonies—the Netherlands East Indies, Malaya*, French Indochina*, and the Taiwan*-Korea-Manchuria grid, respectively—as permanent possessions, the Americans promised early on to grant their "Philippine possessions" independence. Cognizant of the popularity of the independence issue after the Philippine Revolution of 1896*, Quezón tapped popular sentiment to launch a political career that was Janus-faced in character. Publicly, he stood for independence and declared a preference for a government "run like hell by Filipinos" to one "run like heaven by Americans." But privately, Quezón assured the Americans that he preferred they stay.

Quezón rose to power and influence by developing elaborate patronage ties with U.S. officials in his home province and in Manila, the colonial capital. He owed his position as governor to Colonel Harry Bandholtz, the U.S. commandant of the Philippine Constabulary in his province. When he was elected to the first Philippine National Assembly in 1907, he became one of the leading lights of the body, thanks largely to the assistance of Bandholtz and other colonial officials. Quezón controlled the Naciónalista Party as well, which dominated colonial politics until World War II. With his position in the legislature and party secure, Quezón was well placed to benefit from increased Filipino participation in colonial governance. From 1913 to 1921, U.S. policy shifted firmly toward self-rule and "Filipinization" of the colonial state during the term of Governor-General Francis Burton Harrison. Overseeing this transformation were Quezón and his allies in the Naciónalista Party and the legislative assembly. The attempt by Harrison's successor, General Leonard Wood*, to reassert U.S. control four years later did little to erode the power of Quezón and the Filipinos. Within a few years, Quezón was elected president of the Philippine Commonwealth.

Quezón was a unique personality among the different nationalists emerging in Southeast Asia. Unlike many of his counterparts who revolted or protested against colonial rule, Quezón's "nationalism" helped stabilize the colonial order and brought him political gain. He also mastered American politics, pioneering an emerging Philippine political style heavily influenced by the U.S. politics of the period. At the height of his power, Quezón was a Filipino counterpart to the patronage politicians of party machines in New York, Chicago, and San Francisco. But he also showed that he could transcend the narrow bounds of patronage politics. When he became president of the Commonwealth, Quezón took steps to centralize political power by shifting the balance from a legislature and party system based on provincial and local elites to the office of the executive. He then tried to replicate his domestic successes in regional politics in the 1930s. Aware of growing tensions between Japan and the Western powers, Quezón sought to prepare the Philippines for war by asking his close friend General Douglas MacArthur* to oversee formation of a national army. But he assured Tōkyō of Philippine intentions not to be involved in any war. This "double-dealing" failed because far larger processes imposed themselves on colonial politics. Japan and the United States went to war, and Quezón, forced into exile in the United States, saw his dreams of a neutral Philippines with a strong central state evaporate.

A. Gopinath, *Manuel L. Quezón: The Tutelary Democrat* (Quezón City, 1987); A. McCoy, "Quezón's Commonwealth: The Emergence of Philippine Authoritarianism," in R. Paredes (ed.), *Philippine Colonial Democracy* (Quezón City, 1989); M. Quezón, *The Good Fight* (New York, 1946); P. Stanley, *A Nation in the Making: The Philippines and the United States, 1899–1921* (Cambridge, MA, 1974).

Patricio N. Abinales

R

RADFORD, ARTHUR W. (1896–1971)

Admiral Arthur W. Radford was a distinguished U.S. naval officer whose career spanned more than four decades, climaxing with service as chairman of the Joint Chiefs of Staff (JCS). By the early 1950s, he had acquired a reputation as an "Asia First" admiral who thought U.S. foreign policy and military strategy underestimated the importance of Asia. Born in Chicago and raised in Iowa, he graduated in 1916 from the U.S. Naval Academy and served on a battleship in the Atlantic during World War I. Completing flight training as a naval aviator after the war, he remained for the rest of his career an avid apostle of naval air power. It was during World War II that Radford's military duties first directly involved him in Asia. He was a carrier division commander in the Pacific in 1943 and chief of staff to the aircraft commander of the U.S. Pacific Fleet in 1944. After a stint in Washington as assistant to the deputy chief of naval operations, he returned to the Pacific in October 1944 to command a fast carrier task force in combat operations in the South China Sea and against Okinawa and Japan. After the war, Radford continued to rise in the naval hierarchy and was a conspicuous figure in the widely publicized "Revolt of the Admirals" against cuts in naval spending in 1949. That April, Radford became commander of the U.S. Pacific Fleet. During the Korean War*, the U.S. Seventh Fleet was transferred from Radford, with the result that he had no direct involvement in Korean military operations for the duration of the conflict. But at the same time, his responsibilities were extended to include the Mariana and Bonin Islands*, as well as the Ryūkyūs, Taiwan*, and the Philippines*.

In August 1953, Radford became JCS chairman, a choice that pleased the Republican right wing, which had lambasted President Harry S. Truman* for overstressing Europe at the expense of East Asia. Self-assured and outspoken, Radford's views on national security policy harmonized with the Eisenhower administration's New Look, with its emphasis on nuclear retaliation. During his four years as chairman, he was a dominant figure in Eisenhower's foreign policy councils and a proponent of a muscular posture in the Pacific that embraced a ready willingness to employ military force, including nuclear weapons. His combativeness toward Asian Communism* manifested itself most vividly during the Dien Bien Phu* crisis and the first of the Taiwan Strait Crises*, both in 1954. As the Vietminh* siege of Dien Bien Phu tightened, Radford advocated a plan for a massive U.S. air strike, code-named Operation VULTURE, to save the French garrision. He feared that loss of this key strong point would lead to abandonment of Indochina by France and undermine the U.S. strategic position throughout the region. According to General Paul Ely*, chairman of the French chiefs of staff, Radford intimated that he had support for VULTURE from President Dwight D. Eisenhower*, but in fact, neither the president nor the JCS endorsed the plan. Radford then lined up behind a scheme for United Action* in French Indochina* that included the possible option of joint military intervention with close allies, but this ultimately proved unfeasible.

During the eight-month crisis over the Nationalist-held offshore islands that began in September 1954, Radford again took a militant stance. Along with a majority of the JCS, he favored a U.S. guarantee to protect the most important of these islands, not because they were essential to the defense of Taiwan, but because their loss would impair Guomindang* (Nationalist) morale as well as U.S. prestige in Asia. The JCS chairman backed the U.S.-China Mutual Defense Treaty of 1954* with the Republic of China* signed in December (although he worried that a defensive alliance might thwart Nationalist hopes of returning to the mainland) and the Formosa Resolution* that Congress overwhelmingly approved in January 1955. He supported Eisenhower's decision in the crisis to extend a secret protective guarantee to Jinmen and Mazu, and he had no compunctions about supporting the use of atomic weapons to defend these tiny Nationalist outposts. In April 1955, the president dispatched Radford and Walter S. Robertson*, assistant secretary of state for the Far East, to Taiwan to inform Jiang Jieshi* of the withdrawal of the protective guarantee from the offshore islands and to propose a plan for their evacuation, which Jiang rejected. In August 1957, Radford resigned his post and retired from the U.S. Navy a few months after Eisenhower had reprimanded him openly for airing publicly his pessimism about the prospects for disarmanent. In the 1960 presidential campaign, Radford, as adviser to Republican candidate Richard M. Nixon*, spoke out against Senator John F. Kennedy* for criticizing the Eisenhower administration's seeming readiness to risk war with China over the offshore islands.

R. D. Accinelli, *Crisis and Commitment: United States Policy Toward Taiwan, 1950–1955* (Chapel Hill, NC, 1996); M. Billings-Yun, *Decision Against War: Eisenhower and Dien Bien Phu, 1954* (New York, 1988); *New York Times*, 18 August 1973; A. W. Radford, *From Pearl Harbor to Vietnam: The Memoirs of Admiral Arthur W. Radford*, S. Jurika Jr. (ed.) (Stanford, CA, 1980); R. J. Watson, *The History of the Joint Chiefs of Staff*, Vol 5: *The JCS and National Policy, 1953–1954* (Washington, DC, 1986).

Robert D. Accinelli

RANKIN, KARL L. (1898–1991)

Trained as a civil engineer at Princeton University, Karl Lott Rankin entered the Foreign Service in 1927, serving thereafter mostly in Eastern and Central Europe. His longest and most significant postings were in Taiwan*, first as chargé (1950–1953) and then as ambassador (1953 to 1957) to the Republic of China* (ROC). He had neither the experience nor language proficiency regarding China before his initial assignment to Guangzhou and then Hong Kong* on the eve of the Communist victory in the Chinese Civil War*. But Rankin was an adamant anti-Communist, especially as a result of his experiences in the Caucasus from 1922 to 1925 and in Athens and Belgrade after World War II. When he arrived in Taibei after the Korean War* began, he saw Taiwan's military and political potential as useful for containing the Communists, but considered the Guomindang* (Nationalist) regime of Jiang Jieshi* as expendable. His sympathy for the Nationalist government increased as the heightening of Cold War reinforced his conviction that Communism* had to be contained.

Though Rankin had little direct effect on policy making, he was able to push a reluctant Washington into closer cooperation with and deeper commitment to Jiang's regime. His proposals often appeared overly aggressive and hence were not adopted, but some were incorporated gradually into U.S. policy when circumstances allowed. Rankin did not favor sponsoring an ROC attempt to "Return to the Mainland," but recommended allowing the Nationalists to use the slogan to maintain the morale of Jiang's forces and to counter Communist propaganda. He believed that political, economic, and international factors were as important as military power in the "liberation" process. But Rankin also thought that the United States should lose no further ground to the Communists, because this would foster aggression. Therefore, he insisted that the Nationalists hold all offshore islands during the first of the Taiwan Strait Crises*. He recommended against any action that might enhance the prestige of the People's Republic of China* (PRC), opposing Operation ORACLE* and its provision for a UN-sponsored cease-fire, as well as the diplomatic contacts in August 1955 at Geneva that became the Warsaw Talks*. He also became more and more outspoken against granting the PRC Chinese Representation in the United Nations*.

Rankin's most significant recommendation was for the United States to make Taiwan a "policy asset," rather than a "liability," a concept that was adopted gradually after Chinese Intervention in the Korean War* resulted in the military defeat and then retreat of U.S. forces and became the basis of U.S. policy for the next two decades. His efforts helped lead to the negotiation of the U.S.-China Mutual Defense Treaty of 1954* and minimized the negative impact of the Taibei Anti-U.S. Riot of 1957*. Rankin argued that Foreign Service officers were not merely messengers, but could exert significant influence through policy implementation. He proved the truth of this claim during his unusually long term in Taiwan and indeed played a crucial role in determining the fate of the island. Soon after his arrival in Taibei, he coordinated the efforts of all U.S. missions and earned great respect from the ROC government. Although he did not refrain from pressuring the Nationalists when necessary, Rankin kept in mind Chinese sensitivities about legitimacy and independence. He spoke frankly to Jiang and his associates in private, but usually avoided public criticism and rarely let the Nationalists accept sole blame for problems in U.S.-ROC relations. Critics claimed that Rankin seemed to side with Jiang on all points, but his actions coincided with the desires of the State Department under Secretary of State John Foster Dulles*. In 1957, he became ambassador to Yugoslavia, retiring in 1960 after one tour of duty.

Chang Su-Ya, "Lanqin dashi yu yijiuwulin niandai de Zhongmei guanxi" [Ambassador Karl L. Rankin and U.S. Policy Toward Taiwan in the 1950s], *EurAmerica* (March 1998); K. L. Rankin, *China Assignment* (Seattle, WA, 1964).

Chang Su-Ya

RAPE OF NANJING

This was probably the most infamous act of Japanese imperialist brutality during the years before Japan staged the Pearl Harbor Attack*. In November 1937, after the Marco Polo Bridge Incident*, the Japanese invading army assaulted the capital of the Republic of China* at Nanjing, forcing the Guomindang* (Nationalist) government of Jiang Jieshi* to relocate to Chongqing. Under the extremely confused situation, Hang Liwu, chairman of the directors' board of Nanjing University, and some foreigners in the city decided to create an international relief organization to aid refugees. Soon the International Committee for the Nanjing Safety Zone was established. Among the fifteen members of the committee, there were seven Americans: Professors L. C. Smythe, M. S. Bates, and C. H. Riggs from

Nanjing University, and J. G. Magee of the American Episcopal Mission, J. V. Pickering of Standard Oil Company, W. P. Mills of the Presbyterian Mission, and C. S. Trimmet of Gu Lou Hospital. Hang Liwu was elected secretary general of the committee, but later was replaced by Bates because Hang had to convoy cultural relics out of Nanjing. The Nanjing Red Cross, headed by Magee, cooperated closely with the committee. After it was founded, the committee negotiated with both belligerents, requesting that they recognize the neutral position of the safety zone and not station troops, set up military facilities, or bomb within the zone to provide a refuge for the many thousands of refugees. Chinese headquarters agreed and withdrew its troops from the zone. Japanese command in Shanghai also promised not to attack the refuge. On 9 December, refugees began to enter the zone.

On 12 December, an American gunboat, a small oil tanker of Standard Oil, and two yachts were bombed by Japanese planes and sank. The U.S. government quickly protested to the Japanese government regarding the killing and wounding of those Americans on board. On 14 December, the Japanese Army occupied the city and began to massacre Chinese residents, even in the safety zone. Many Chinese appealed to the Safety Zone Committee for help to find their families. Associate Secretary General G. A. Fitcher, Bates, Smythe, and two other Americans, reporter F. Tillman Durdin and cameraman Arthur Mencken, risked their lives making inquiries about the massacre and recorded their findings in detail. The reports revealed how horrifying the savage actions of the Japanese soldiers were, including murders, arson, robberies, and rapes. The committee addressed hundreds of serious protests to the Japanese embassy, as well as to the Japanese Command in Nanjing, demanding an end to Japanese soldiers committing savage acts on Chinese. Yet these protests had no effect. As the slaughter continued in December, the U.S. embassy was looted, U.S. flags were torn down and trampled underfoot, and houses of some American diplomats were robbed. U.S. diplomat John M. Allison*, when accompanying a priest to Japanese Command to demand an end to the soldiers' savagery, was slapped in the face. Meanwhile, Fitcher and Bates sent their records to friends in Shanghai, and Smythe printed his evidence in a book. Durdin, a witness to three slaughters in December, sent a series of reports to the *New York Times*, exposing Japanese outrages at Nanjing to the world. The deeds of these brave Americans in helping China deepened Sino-American friendship.

Gao Xinglie, *Riben qinhua zuixing lu—Nanjing da tusha* [The Outrages in the Japanese Aggression Against China—-the Nanjing Rape] (Shanghai, 1985); S. Hsu (ed.), *Documents of the Nanking Safety Zone* (Shanghai–Hong Kong–Singapore, 1939).

Xiang Liling

REAGAN, RONALD (1911–)

From 1981 to 1989, President Ronald Reagan saw East Asia issues and problems largely through the prism of the reenergized containment strategy that reflected his determination to check Soviet power through reinvigorating U.S. military strength. Born in Illinois, he graduated from Eureka College, worked as a radio sportscaster, and then gained modest popularity in the 1930s as a Hollywood actor. With his career in decline after World War II, he spoke out against alleged Communists in the movie industry as president of the Screen Actors Guild. He left the Democratic Party in 1952 and became a leading conservative spokesman in the Republican Party, implementing his ideology during two terms as governor of California from 1966 to 1974. After his bid to displace Gerald R. Ford* as the Republican presidential nominee in 1976 failed, Reagan prevailed in 1980 and won the election over incumbent Jimmy Carter*. His campaign stressed that the Soviet Union had seized the global initiative in the 1970s and that recent U.S. leaders had allowed the nation's power and influence decline.

From the outset, the People's Republic of China* (PRC) was central to the new president's anti-Soviet strategy. For all Reagan's personal misgivings about Beijing's political system and ideological proclivities, he viewed a friendly, cooperative China as an indispensable U.S. strategic asset. He was delighted to find among his Chinese counterparts a parallel concern about Soviet intentions and a common commitment to check Soviet expansion. Reagan even managed through adroit diplomacy to prevent the sensitive question of Taiwan*—a state whose cause he had once championed—from threatening improved Sino-American relations. During his April 1984 state visit to the PRC, he deepened the burgeoning U.S. strategic partnership with Beijing, developing a cordial relationship with Deng Xiaoping*. He signed a wide range of agreements with the Chinese governing trade, nuclear cooperation, and technical, scientific, and cultural exchanges. Bilateral Sino-American trade increased sharply, the U.S. technology transfer policy with the PRC was liberalized, and the United States even became a major arms supplier to its former adversary.

Reagan also vigorously pursued close political, economic, and security bonds with the Association of Southeast Asian Nations* (ASEAN) and with its individual member-states. He continued and intensified the common U.S.-PRC-ASEAN efforts to isolate and punish the Socialist Republic of Vietnam* for its 1978 invasion and then occupation of Cambodia*, supporting in July 1981 the ASEAN-initiated International Conference on Kampuchea held in New York. Before Reagan's second term ended, Hanoi declared that it would withdraw all its troops from Cambodia by the end of 1989. By then, U.S. support for ASEAN had become the pivot around which U.S. policy toward Southeast Asia revolved, reflected in a sharp rise in trade between the United States and the ASEAN states in the 1980s. Addressing the annual ASEAN ministerial meeting in Bali, a first for an American president, Reagan proclaimed that "support for and cooperation with ASEAN is a linchpin of American Pacific policy."

For Reagan and his senior foreign policy strategists, the human rights records of East Asian states remained a decidedly secondary concern. His administration saw few advantages, and substantial disadvantages, in raising sensitive issues with nations largely supportive of U.S. foreign policy objectives. During a visit to the Philippines* in 1981, Vice President George H. W. Bush* went so far as to toast President Ferdinand E. Marcos* for his "adherence to democratic processes." But Marcos then engaged in actions so dictatorial and destabilizing that even the forgiving Reagan reluctantly had to desert him. After blatant election fraud and corruption in the presidential election of 1986, Washington recognized the opposition government of Corazon Aquino* on 25 February, the same day Marcos fled to Hawaii. Meanwhile, Reagan continued to give unqualified support to other human rights violators in East Asia, including the equally repressive, venal, and authoritarian Suharto* regime in Indonesia*. He acted to strengthen ties with the Republic of Korea*, hosting dictator Chŏn Du-hwan* as his first foreign guest at the White House early in 1981.

U.S.-Japan relations experienced considerable tumult during the Reagan years. On the one hand, security ties between the two allies deepened, especially after 1982 when Nakasone Yasuhiro* became prime minister. The Japanese leader fostered close cooperation with the United States on defense planning, intelligence gathering, and naval maneuvers. Responding in part to Reagan's pressure, Nakasone also initiated a modest defense buildup in 1987. On the other hand, the trade gap between the United States and Japan widened appreciably as U.S.-Japan Postwar Trade Relations* became a lightning rod for political critics within the United States, with some characterizing Japan as an economically rapacious state determined to conquer American markets. The Plaza Accord of September 1985 only partially eased the problem by forcing an upward valuation of the yen. But trade issues, however important and delicate during the 1980s, played second fiddle to security issues in Reagan's East Asian policy. His revived containment strategy gave an overarching coherence and consistency to U.S. regional strategy throughout his presidency, producing mixed results.

R. Foot, *The Practice of Power: U.S. Relations with China Since 1945* (New York, 1995); R. J. McMahon, *The Limits of Power: The United States and Southeast Asia Since World War II* (New York, 1999); M. Schaller, *Altered States: The United States and Japan Since the Occupation* (New York, 1997); G. P. Shultz, *Turmoil and Triumph: My Years as Secretary of State* (New York, 1993).

Robert J. McMahon

REINSCH, PAUL S. (1869–1923)

Paul S. Reinsch was U.S. minister to China from 1913 to 1919. He was born in Milwaukee to German-speaking immigrants and was educated at the University of Wisconsin, where he earned his bachelor of arts degree, a law degree, and a doctorate. In 1899, Reinsch was appointed to the faculty at his alma mater, where he remained for the rest of his academic career. He quickly established a national and international reputation as a student of world politics and colonialism, with particular expertise on East Asia. But it was his personal and political contacts, more than his scholarly credentials, that persuaded President Woodrow Wilson* to name Reinsch to head the U.S. legation in Beijing. Reinsch saw himself engaged in a mission to translate the American Open Door Policy* and Wilsonian rhetorical support for the new Chinese Republic into reality. He believed that the United States needed the huge commercial markets and investment opportunities that a modernized Chinese economy promised and the friendship of the newly awakened and potentially powerful Chinese nation. To achieve these objectives, Reinsch launched a concerted effort to secure a variety of concessions for U.S. business, to protect China's integrity and independence from the foreign powers, especially Japan, and to assist China in modernizing its political, economic, and educational institutions. He frequently resorted to aggressive and unorthodox tactics that included extensive lobbying of American corporations, the employment of personal agents, involvement in Chinese political affairs, and a liberal interpretation of State Department instructions and guidance.

Reinsch played a role in revealing the extent and dangers of Japan's imperialist ambitions toward China in the Twenty-One Demands* and managed to persuade the Beijing government to declare war against Germany in 1917, but failed to achieve his basic objectives. The unwillingness of American business to enter the China market, the ability of Japan to manipulate the European war to its advantage, the collapse of China's central government, and the lukewarm support of the Wilson administration undermined his dynamic and tireless efforts. Wilson's decision at the Paris Peace Conference to award Japan Germany's rights forced an exhausted Reinsch to resign in protest. Historians have criticized Reinsch for being naive, idealistic, and irresponsible; they have faulted him for disregarding realities in East Asia and the limits on U.S. influence, misreading the capabilities of American businessmen, and holding out false hopes to the Chinese, who regarded him as a sincere friend. These charges, as well as his limited understanding of China, have some validity. On the other hand, he offered sound and logical prescriptions to fulfill American official Open Door policy. He sought leverage to force Japan and the other powers to reach compromises with the United States and give China time and some breathing room to organize itself for the modern era. And he preserved enough U.S. influence and goodwill among the Chinese for his successors to build a more viable Sino-American relationship. *See also* Shandong Agreement; Edward T. Williams.

R. W. Curry, *Woodrow Wilson and Far Eastern Policy, 1913–1921* (New York, 1957); N. H. Pugach, *Paul S. Reinsch: Open Diplomat in Action* (Millwood, NY, 1979); P. S. Reinsch, *An American Diplomat in China* (New York, 1922).

Noel H. Pugach

REISCHAUER, EDWIN O. (1910–1990)

Edwin O. Reischauer devoted his life to promoting mutual understanding and respect between the United States and Japan as a scholar, intelligence officer, diplomat, and public figure. Born to American missionaries in Tōkyō, he grew up in Japan before moving to the United States to study history at Oberlin College and Harvard University. Reischauer's subsequent experiences in Paris, China, and Japan launched his long professional involvement in U.S.–East Asian relations. He returned to Harvard in 1938, but the Pearl Harbor Attack* interrupted his academic career. A brief stint as a consultant for the State Department in the summer of 1941 brought Reischauer into contact with public policy. The U.S. Army Signal Corps hired him to assist in building its training program for translators and cryptanalysts, which produced a generation of highly capable young Americans trained in the Japanese language. Reischauer also worked as a U.S. Army officer on *Magic**, which deciphered the Japanese code. In 1945, he rejected an offer to be the historian of the U.S. Occupation of Japan* and instead worked as a Japan specialist in the State Department on the issues of planning Japan's future and dealing with the Thirty-Eighth Parallel Division* in Korea.

Reischauer rejoined the faculty at Harvard in 1946 and thereafter served with distinction as a pioneer in the field of East Asian studies. Numerous of his graduate students went on to become distinguished scholars in their own right, collectively building Asian studies programs at academic institutions around the world. Fittingly, Harvard's Institute of Japanese Studies bears Reischauer's name. Perhaps a reflection of his academic experiences, he placed great faith in the prospects for cooperation and partnership between the United States and Japan. He was convinced that international conflict flowed from misunderstanding and mutual ignorance and sincerely believed that his role in life was to promote cross-cultural understanding. Such views found expression in the histories Reischauer wrote that became standard surveys, including *Japan: Past and Present* (1946), *The United States and Japan* (1950), and *East Asia: The Modern Transformation* (with John K. Fairbank* and Albert M. Craig, 1965).

After the Anpo Crisis* in 1960, Reischauer penned an essay titled "The Broken Dialogue" for *Foreign Affairs* that voiced his alarm at the acrimonious divide in Japanese politics over relations with the United States. The publicity that he attracted contributed to John F. Kennedy* nominating him as ambassador to Japan. From 1961 to 1966, Reischauer worked indefatigably to build cultural bridges between the United States and Japan. He hosted visits by prominent Americans, recruited capable officials who spoke Japanese, promoted programs of educational exchange, and made regular appearances before Japanese groups throughout the country. Critics on the Japanese left lamented at the time that the "Reischauer line" was in essence successful advocacy for strengthening the existing bilateral alliance by broadening its base of support. He dealt effectively with a wide range of problems as ambassador in a way that reflected his understanding of Japanese frustration with treatment as a junior partner, including payment of occupation costs, the Okinawa Controversy*, Japan-Korea Normalization* of relations, trade negotiations, Japan's membership in the Organization for Economic Cooperation and Development, the United States–Japan Conference on Cultural and Educational Exchange, U.S. nuclear testing, entrance of nuclear weapons into Japan, the U.S. military presence in Japan, and the escalating Second Indochina War*.

After Kennedy's assassination late in 1963, lack of rapport between Reischauer and President Lyndon B. Johnson*, as well as an attempt on his life in 1964 that left him physically weakened, prompted his decision to resign in 1966. But he remained an influential figure after returning to Harvard as a result of his scholarly activities and public engagements involving Japan. As a symbol of the Cold War U.S.-Japan partnership, however, he became the target of younger scholars who did not share his view of Japanese "modernization" and his criticism of Communism*. By the 1980s, as U.S.-Japan Postwar Trade Relations* soured, journalists also assailed him, focusing on his tolerance of Japanese predatory economic behavior. Although often shrill and misplaced, such criticism nevertheless exposed Reischauer's greatest weakness, which was his constitutional aversion to conflict. He retired from Harvard in 1981.

Matsukata Haru, *Samurai and Silk: A Japanese and American Heritage* (New York, 1986); E. O. Reischauer, *My Life Between Japan and America* (New York, 1986); E. O. Reischauer Oral History, John F. Kennedy Presidential Library, Boston, MA; P. Smith, *Japan: A Reinterpretation* (New York, 1997).

Aaron Forsberg

REPUBLIC OF CHINA

In 1928, Jiang Jieshi* established this government at Nanjing after his Northern Expedition reunified China. But its origins date from the Chinese Revolution of 1911* that toppled the Qing Dynasty. In 1913, President Woodrow Wilson* recognized the Chinese Republic under Yuan Shikai*, who headed China's government amidst rising opposition until his sudden death in 1916. During the next decade, China endured the Warlord Era*, characterized by constant warfare between armies under local military leaders contesting for political power. Sun Zhongshan*, China's foremost advocate of republicanism, had fled to Shanghai in 1918, where he reorganized his Guomindang* (Nationalist) Party. Sun shared the anger and bitterness of the Chinese people toward the Versailles Peace Treaty* that climaxed in the May Fourth Movement* of 1919. Two years later, he proclaimed reestablishment of the Chinese Republic at Guangzhou and turned to the Soviet Union for military and economic assistance and advice, as well as forming a political alliance with the Chinese Communist Party* (CCP).

Sun died in 1925, and Jiang, commander of the Guomindang (GMD) military, consolidated political power. He never trusted the Soviet Union or the CCP and, after launching the Northern Expedition in July 1926, split with the Chinese Communists in May 1927. Nationalist forces entered Beijing in July 1928, and that October, the GMD adopted a provisional constitution as the basis for governing China during a period of tutelage that was to last six years. With its seat of government at Nanjing, the new Republic of China (ROC) gained recognition from Western powers, and the United States even granted China Tariff Autonomy*. But the Mukden Incident* in September 1931 then signaled the start of Japanese aggression in China. Rather than focusing on Japan, however, Jiang concentrated on destroying the CCP under Mao Zedong* until his capture in the Xian Incident* late in 1936 forced him to join a United Front* against Japan as the price of his release. The Marco Polo Bridge Incident* in July 1937 opened the Sino-Japanese War, which lasted until 1945. The ROC was compelled to relocate to Chongqing, where Jiang's government fought as a partner in the Grand Alliance in World War II, and Wang Jingwei* claimed leadership of the ROC at Nanjing.

In 1945, the Chinese Civil War* resumed, resulting in the Communist victory that forced the ROC to relocate on Taiwan* in 1949. At first, the United States accepted the inevitability that the People's Republic of China* (PRC) would eradicate Jiang's regime. But the Korean War* confirmed an emerging U.S. commitment to defend the ROC, as President Harry S. Truman* declared the Neutralization of Taiwan*. Despite U.S. pressure, most nations recognized the PRC, rather than the ROC, except for Japan, the Republic of Korea*, and a handful of others. As Taibei's lone defender, the United States signed a military agreement in 1951 and the U.S.-China Mutual Defense Treaty in 1954*, providing Jiang's government with $2.5 billion in military and $1.5 billion in economic aid from 1950 to 1965. In 1955, during the first of the Taiwan Strait Crises*, Congress passed the Formosa Resolution* authorizing the president to protect Taiwan and "related positions and territories." Washington also maintained support for Taibei Chinese Representation in the United Nations*. Although Taiwan's economic growth brought an end of U.S. aid in 1968, the U.S.-ROC relationship remained solid until the 1970s, when President Richard M. Nixon* first adopted a Two China Policy*. After the ROC was expelled from the World Bank in 1970 and lost its UN seat in 1971, Nixon's Visit to China* in February 1972 and issuance of the Shanghai Communiqué* sent U.S. relations with the ROC on a downward slide. U.S.-PRC Normalization of Relations* in January 1979 led to abrogation of U.S.-ROC defense treaties and withdrawal of U.S. military personnel. In April, Congress passed and President Jimmy Carter* signed the Taiwan Relations Act* (TRA) to repair the estrangement and build a new relationship.

Despite its flight from the mainland in 1949, the ROC maintained as official the myth that it was China's legal government. This rationale justified the minority of mainlanders dominating the Tawainese majority, as well as the political structure with a national party and government for all of China and a separate provincial party and government for Taiwan. Gradually, Taiwanese entered the GMD bureaucracy and were elected to the provincial assembly and as mayors, but the National Assembly remained composed of legislators elected in Nanjing in 1948. As these representatives aged and passed away, replacements were made by appointment. The assembly was a rubber stamp for the GMD dictatorship, which enforced its authority through various security forces. But economic development and rising social stability brought greater freedom and the release of some political prisioners. In 1969, elections filled vacancies in the assembly and a few Taiwanese won seats. Jiang Jingguo*, who became ROC president in 1978, opened the political process further. In 1986, parties other than the GMD, though still illegal, were able to run candidates. Forty years of martial law ended in 1987, and opposition parties, notably the Dangwai*, became legal. Upon the death of the now widely admired Jiang in 1988, Vice President Li Denghui* became president, promising more reform, but also restored control over the mainland.

In the 1980s, the ROC gradually improved its international standing, as Taiwan emerged as a fledgling democracy and moved from the ranks of developing countries to a newly industrialized nation. As Taiwan's exports boomed, countries set up trade offices in Taibei that functioned as unofficial consulates. The U.S.-ROC relationship also entered a new phase of greater equality. Although the ROC had always had considerable bipartisan support in Congress, the importance Washington placed on its relationship with Beijing placed limits on Taibei's efforts for greater international recognition. In 1994, a bipartisan congressional petition urged U.S. support of Taiwan's application to the United Nations and revision of sections of the TRA that prohibited U.S. officials from visiting Taiwan. In response, the administration of President Bill Clinton* created a

Taibei Economic and Cultural Representation Office and allowed high-level bilateral meetings and visits by U.S. officials to Taiwan although it was unwilling to support Taiwan's UN bid. After President Li Denghui's visit to Cornell University in June 1995, the PRC's launching of two ballistic missiles into the Taiwan Strait in March 1996 led to deployment of the U.S. Navy. These events demonstrated that although Washington would continue to provide for the ROC's security, Beijing would continue to threaten Taiwan. In 2000, despite PRC intimidation, Dangwai politician Chen Shuibian, who had spoken about independent status for Taiwan, won a closely fought race to become president of the ROC, ending the era of GMD dominance. *See also* Kennedy-Chen Conference; Taibei Anti-U.S. Riot of 1957; Taiwanese Communist Party.

R. N. Clough, *Cooperation or Conflict in the Taiwan Strait* (Lanham, MD, 1999); J. K. Fairbank and E. O. Reischauer, *China: Tradition and Transformation* (Boston, 1989); C. Hughes, *Taiwan and Chinese Nationalism: National Identity and Status in International Society* (London, 1997); M.A. Rubinstein (ed.), *Taiwan: A New History* (New York, 1999); N. B. Tucker, *Taiwan, Hong Kong, and the United States, 1945–1992* (New York, 1994).

Roger Y. M. Chan

REPUBLIC OF KOREA

The Republic of Korea (ROK) has been one of the world's most pro-American nations and faithfully supportive of close ROK-U.S. defense and economic relations. For many years after the U.S.-backed ROK was officially proclaimed in Seoul on 15 August 1948, the republic was dominated by strong rulers exercising virtually unchecked powers. Syngman Rhee*, the first president, became increasingly dictatorial and corrupt until a student-led revolt forced him to resign in April 1960. After a year, the moderate successor government of Jang Myŏn* was ousted by a military junta headed by Major General Pak Chŏng-hŭi*, whose iron-fisted rule ended abruptly with his assassination in October 1979. Pak's successor was General Chŏn Duhwan*, who created another authoritarian regime. Under Pak and Chŏn, the ROK experienced dramatic industrial development and became an economic powerhouse. But the discrepancy between economic prosperity and political backwardness created growing public discontent. Near the end of Chŏn's regime, South Koreans demanded an end to military rule. The "June Resistance" in mid-1987 resulting in issuance of South Korea's Democracy Declaration* was the turning point for the ROK in abandoning authoritarianism and embracing civil society and the rule of law. In the 1990s, under Presidents No Tae-u*, Kim Young-sam*, and Kim Dae-jung*, its developing democracy threw off all vestiges of military rule. But its once famed economy, the world's eleventh largest, collapsed, forcing Seoul to seek a bailout loan from the International Monetary Fund in response to the East Asian Financial Crisis* starting in 1997.

The ROK has maintained a close partnership with the United States since it became a sovereign state after U.S. Occupation of Korea* ended in 1948. Washington assisted it fully in providing protection under the U.S.-South Korea Mutual Security Treaty* after the Korean War* ended and rehabilitating its poverty-stricken economy. The relationship between the ROK and the United States was asymmetrical. The United States made decisions, and the ROK had to adhere to them on the level of military support and the content and magnitude of economic assistance. In fact, the United States was the "protector" and "big brother" of South Korea as it faced the persistent threat from the Democratic People's Republic of Korea* in the north. Since the late 1980s, however, the ROK's rise to prominence in the world community has brought about many changes in its relations with the United States. As South Koreans have become willing to translate their growing political and economic influence into actions, the ROK-U.S. relationship has grown more complex and strains have developed. This has been most apparent in the area of trade. U.S. pressure to open South Korea's markets to more American exports collided with industrial policies and domestic interests in the ROK and was resisted. During the 1990s, the ROK-U.S. discord derived from Seoul's conciliatory approaches to North Korea, indicating that the United States and South Korea have become allies out of necessity. The ROK, which had received unqualified U.S. support in its dealings with Kim Il Sung* in the past, often became disappointed with the altered U.S. posture as it sought to increase ties with Kim Jong Il*. *See also* Korean Aid Act; Gorbachev-No Summits; North Korean Nuclear Controversy; Rhee's Ouster; Pak Chŏng-hŭi's Assassination; South Korean Anti-Americanism; Thirty-Eighth Parallel Division.

B. Cumings, *Korea's Place in the Sun: A Modern History* (New York, 1997); J. Kim, "From Patron-Client to Partners: The Changing South Korean–American Relationship," *Journal of American–East Asian Relations* (Fall 1993); Kim Jinwung, *Han'gukin ŭi Panmi Kamjong* [The Anti-Americanism of the Korean People] (Seoul, 1992); D. S. Macdonald, *The Koreans: Contemporary Politics and Society* (Boulder, CO, 1988); D. Oberdorfer, *The Two Koreas: A Contemporary History* (Reading, PA, 1997).

Kim Jinwung

REPUBLIC OF VIETNAM

The Republic of Vietnam (RVN) was the successor government to the State of Vietnam (SVN), a regime established by the French and anti-Communist Vietnamese politicians to provide an alternative to the Communist-led Vietminh* during the First Indochina War*. The State of Vietnam was established in the spring of 1949, after an exchange of letters between French President Vincent Auriol and former Emperor Bao Dai* in which the French government promised to recognize Vietnam's independence and negotiate the transfer of powers to Vietnamese authority. Bao Dai would be the SVN's chief of state with the power to appoint a premier and cabinet, as well as regional governors. Bao Dai's efforts to form an effective government were circumscribed by continuing French controls over the SVN's finances, armed forces, and foreign policy, bitter infighting among Vietnamese officials and politicians, and widespread popular support for the Vietminh as the true champions of Vietnamese independence. Despite these difficulties, President Harry S. Truman* not only decided to recognize the SVN as Vietnam's legitimate government on 4 February 1950, but then approved an economic and military aid program to the SVN.

France slowly granted the SVN more power after protracted negotiations with Bao Dai early in the 1950s, but did not formally grant full independence until a month after the French defeat in May 1954 at Dien Bien Phu*. Bao Dai appointed Ngo Dinh Diem* as premier in an apparent bid to win continuing American support. Diem soon engaged in a bitter contest for power as he struggled against French officials and Vietnamese army officers who backed his regime and sect leaders from the Cao Dai*, Hoa Hao, and Binh Xuyen*, who challenged his authority. He also had to deal with an influx of refugees from the north after partition at the Geneva Conference of 1954*. Despite negative reports from the Collins Mission*, the Eisenhower administration sent increasing amounts of aid to the RVN, as well as a growing number of military and political advisers. But Washington, acting on the advice of Central Intelligence Agency* operative Edward G. Lansdale*, did not fully support Diem until he broke the power of the sects in the spring of 1955. It then approved a massive police and governmental training program under Michigan State University's Wesley R. Fishel*. Diem followed up his victory over the sects by organizing a plebiscite against Bao Dai in October 1955, and ousted Bao Dai as chief of state after winning 98.2 percent of the vote. He then declared the establishment of the Republic of Vietnam on 26 October.

Diem held elections for a constituent assembly on 4 March 1956, approving a final draft of the constitution in July that contained provisions for a strong presidency, a unicameral national assembly, and a constitutional court. This structure essentially was a facade for a dictatorship headed by Diem and his family, whose repression of dissent alienated most segments of Vietnamese society and sparked a Communist-led insurgency against the regime in the late 1950s. Presidents Dwight D. Eisenhower* and John F. Kennedy* both sent aid and more military advisers to assist Diem, but their advice that Diem make efforts to broaden the base of his support and reform his regime was ignored repeatedly. When Ngo Dinh Nhu*, Diem's brother, tried in 1963 to suppress demonstrations led by Buddhist dissidents, the Kennedy administration approved a military coup that led to Diem's Assassination* in early November. The new Military Revolutionary Committee headed by General Duong Van Minh* was overthrown by General Nguyen Khanh* on 30 January 1964, initiating a period of prolonged instability that witnessed eight changes of government. In June 1965, General Nguyen Van Thieu* and Air Vice Marshal Nguyen Cao Ky* took power and ruled the RVN for nearly two years, finally agreeing to hold elections for a new constitutional assembly after disgruntled military officers and Buddhist organizations staged a bloody series of protests in the spring of 1966.

A new constitution was completed at the end of 1966, providing for the popular election of a president and national legislature, as well as creation of an independent judiciary. On 3 September 1967, elections for the presidency and the legislature were held, with Thieu and Ky winning by a plurality of 34.8 percent. During the years that followed, Thieu steadily consolidated his control over the government, undercutting Ky, controlling the appointment and promotion of military officers, and winning the consistent support of Presidents Lyndon B. Johnson* and Richard M. Nixon*. He won a second term after running in an uncontested election in 1971 and fought to prevent the United States from making concessions to the Democratic Republic of Vietnam* in the Paris Peace Talks*. After reluctantly accepting the Paris Peace Accords* in January 1973, Thieu's power rapidly eroded as the United States withdrew its remaining military forces from South Vietnam. His government faced mounting difficulties thereafter as it tried unsuccessfully to deal with problems caused by rapid inflation, widespread corruption, growing war weariness, and reductions in U.S. aid appropriations. When the North Vietnamese army launched a series of offensives in the spring of 1975, the Army of the Republic of Vietnam* rapidly collapsed. Thieu resigned on 21 April. Vice President Tran Van Huong, his successor, resigned on 28 April. Two days later, his replacement, Duong Van Minh, surrendered to North Vietnamese troops. *See also* French Indochina; Nation-Building Strategy; Second Indochina War; Vietnamization.

J. Buttinger, *Vietnam: A Dragon Embattled* (New York, 1967); Bernard B. Fall, *The Two Vietnams: A Political and Military Analysis* (New York, 1967); A. E. Goodman, *Politics in War: The Bases of Political Community in South Vietnam* (Cambridge, MA, 1971); G. Kolko, *Anatomy of a War: Vietnam, the United States, and the Modern Historical Experience* (New York, 1985); R. Scigliano, *South Vietnam: Nation Under Stress* (Boston, 1964).

Joseph G. Morgan

REVERSE COURSE

During 1947 and 1948, the U.S. Occupation of Japan* underwent a major change in policy, with its emphasis shifting essentially from democratic and social reforms to programs for rapid economic recovery. Apart from the desire to make Japan less of a drain on American economic and financial resources, the world situation at the time dictated this shift. With the intensification of the Cold War in Europe and East Asia in 1947, the Truman administration and, gradually, General Douglas MacArthur*, the Supreme Commander for the Allied Powers (SCAP*) in Japan, decided to undertake a new "reverse course" in Japan.

The U.S. reversal of policy in Japan corresponded closely with the rapid decline of the Guomindang* (Nationalist) Party under Jiang Jieshi* in China and the rise of the Chinese Communist Party* under Mao Zedong*. Rocked by the Chinese Civil War*, the Republic of China* no longer appeared capable of serving as the bastion against Communism* in Asia. The wartime American image of postwar East Asia, where the United States and a pro-American China cooperated as partners to construct a new order, evaporated. Accordingly, Washington viewed a politically and economically stable Japan, the most modernized country in Asia, as a potential bulwark against Soviet expansion. In a speech titled "The Requirements of Reconstruction" delivered on 8 May 1947, Undersecretary of State Dean G. Acheson* called for the reconstructing of Japan as the anti-Communist "workshop" of Asia.

As the Cold War intensified, the image of Japan as a buffer came to dominate American thinking about Asia, and Japan's domestic developments began to assume particular significance largely for this reason. By early 1948, there appeared marked signs in U.S. occupation policy that Washington had come to view Japan in the general framework of containing Communism. Meanwhile, George F. Kennan*, the architect of the containment policy, maintained that "the United States should devise policies toward Japan which would assume the security of that country from Communist penetration and domination as well as from military attack by the Soviet Union and would permit Japan's economic potential to become once again an important force in the affairs of the area, conducive to peace and stability." By 1948, the Japanese press openly informed its readers of the U.S. intention to rehabilitate Japan as a "protective wall" against the Communist advance in Asia. By then, SCAP had halted the breakup of the *Zaibatsu**, released conservative Japanese politicians from prison, and purged leftists from politics and government. *See also* Joseph M. Dodge; Great Crescent; Yoshida Shigeru.

R. Buckley, *Occupation Diplomacy: Britain, the United States, and Japan, 1945–1952* (New York, 1982); A. Iriye, *The Cold War in Asia: A Historical Introduction* (Englewood Cliffs, NJ, 1974); M. Schaller, *The American Occupation of Japan: The Origins of the Cold War in Asia* (New York, 1985).

Zhang Hong

RHEE, SYNGMAN (1875–1965)

Syngman Rhee (Yi Sŭng-man), the first president of the Republic of Korea* (ROK), was born at P'yŏngsan, Hwanghae Province, now North Korea. After studying Chinese classics at home, he enrolled in an American Methodist school at Seoul in 1894. Influenced by his teacher, the famous reformer and independence fighter Sŏ Jaip'il, Rhee joined the All Peoples Congress and worked for antigovernment newspapers, leading in 1899 to arrest and a sentence of life imprisonment. After the Russo-Japanese War* resulted in Japan dominating Korea in 1905, however, King Kojong* sent him to see President Theodore Roosevelt* in a failed appeal for help under the 1882 Shufeldt Treaty*. Rhee then entered George Washington University, earning a bachelor of arts in 1907. Two years later, he received a master of arts degree from Harvard University and in 1911, a doctorate in government from Princeton University. By then, Japanese Annexation of Korea* had occurred. In 1912, with the help of American missionaries, Rhee, who had returned to Korea in 1910, fled to the United States. After the March First Movement* of 1919, the Korean Provisional Government (KPG) was formed at Shanghai and Rhee was elected its first president. He established the Korean Commission in Washington, D.C., to lobby on behalf of the KPG and Korean independence. Accusing him of misusing funds, the KPG impeached him, but undaunted, Rhee went to Geneva in 1932 to lobby the League of Nations for mandate status for Korea as an alternative to Japanese rule.

After the Pearl Harbor Attack*, Rhee delivered Voice of America broadcasts to Korea to incite an uprising against Japan. In February 1945, when the Allies approved the Yalta Agreement on the Far East*, he openly argued that the Soviet Union would try to expand its influence in Asia, and criticized its dominance over East Europe. With the Thirty-Eighth Parallel Division* of Korea in August, Rhee falsely said that at Yalta, President Franklin D. Roosevelt* had conceded to the Soviet demand for an ice-free port on the Korean peninsula. His intense hostility to Communism* delayed his return to Korea as a "private citizen" until October. However, Rhee's reputation was high among Koreans, and the Korean People's Republic, organized just before U.S. forces arrived at Seoul on 8 September 1945, elected him its president. Korean conservatives also wanted him to lead their party. But Rhee refused these offers and began organizing his own party. Then, in December 1945, he mobilized opposition to the Moscow Agreement on Korea* with Kim Gu* because it called for a trusteeship. A year later, he went to Washington to urge that the United States sponsor creation of a separate government in South Korea, arguing that the Soviet Union would not permit a free government for all Korea. Washington, for its own reasons, finally agreed and in the fall of 1947 persuaded the United Nations to observe tainted elections in May 1948. As a result, the ROK was established on 15 August 1948, with Rhee as president. Soon Rhee adopted a "march north" policy to reunify Korea, asking the United States for military aid that Washington refused to provide for fear of igniting a civil war.

Rhee faced not only a guerrilla insurgency in South Korea beginning in the fall of 1948, but rising opposition to his dictatorial rule and unhappiness with increasing economic deterioration. In May 1950, elections gave his critics a majority in the ROK legislature. North Korea's Kim Il Sung* ordered the invasion of the ROK in June 1950 in part because he believed South Koreans would greet his forces as liberators. Only the decision of President Harry S. Truman* to commit U.S. troops in the Korean War* under the United Nations saved Rhee's regime. But after General Douglas MacArthur* restored Rhee's control following his Inch'ŏn Landing* in September 1950 and UN forces invaded the Democratic People's Republic of Korea*, many world leaders strongly opposed recognizing Rhee's authority over all Korea after he visited P'yŏngyang during October. Chinese Intervention in the Korean War* removed this possibility, although Rhee pressed for continuation of hostilities to achieve reunification. He created a political crisis in the summer of 1952 when he imposed martial law to force a change in the constitution to permit his popular election as president. The United States considered sponsoring a coup to remove him then and later in June 1953, when Rhee released North Korean prisoners of war to scuttle the Korean Armistice Agreement*. Rhee bluffed that the ROK forces would fight against the Communists alone to compel the Eisenhower administration to agree to conclude later in 1954 the U.S.–South Korea Mutual Security Treaty*, in return for his promise not to obstruct the truce. Rhee's authoritarian rule intensified thereafter, as exemplified in the unlawful constitutional revision in 1955 to allow him unlimited terms. In 1956, he was elected president a third time. But when the notorious rigged presidential election in March 1960 triggered the student uprising of 19 April 1960, it led to the Rhee's Ouster*, forcing him to resign and flee to

Hawaii. *See also* Henry Chung; U.S. Occupation of Korea.

R. Allen, *Korea's Syngman Rhee: An Unauthorized Portrait* (Tōkyō, 1960); R. T. Oliver, *Syngman Rhee: The Man Behind the Myth* (New York, 1954).

Kim Hakjoon

RHEE'S OUSTER

Known as the April Revolution, this event temporarily ended dictatorial rule in the Republic of Korea* (ROK) in 1960. The origins of the fall of Syngman Rhee*, the ROK's first president, date from his declaration of martial law in May 1952 during the Korean War* to ensure his reelection. Thereafter, his popularity declined rapidly, but in 1954, he again by political manipulation amended the constitution so that it would permit an indefinite number of terms in office. In 1955, the embittered opposition countered by forming the new Democratic Party and the new reformist Progressive Party. In the presidential election of 1956, Rhee won a third term mainly because of his use of police-state methods and the death of the Democratic Party's candidate just ten days before the election. But Jang Myŏn*, Democratic Party candidate for vice president, defeated his running mate. In 1958, the opposition Democratic Party again scored remarkable gains in the National Assembly election, occupying at least one-third of the seats despite Rhee's suppression of opposition candidates and manipulation of the voters. Rhee then forced passage of a new national security law, providing for death sentences or heavy prison terms for vague crimes, such as "disseminating Communist propaganda." Cho Bong-am, who in the 1956 presidential election won 23.5 percent of the votes, was executed in 1959 after conviction as "a North Korean spy."

In the presidential election scheduled for 15 March 1960, the Liberal Party named Rhee and Yi Ki-bung, and the Democratic Party nominated Cho Pyŏng-ok and Jang Myŏn as presidential and vice presidential candidates respectively. Rhee already had formed the Anti-Communist Youth Corps to terrorize the opposition. His home minister, who controlled government officials and policemen, executed a detailed program to rig the whole election. Opposition campaign workers were arrested and beaten repeatedly. The death of Cho on 15 February only intensified the anger and frustration of the masses against Rhee. On 28 February, students at Taegu's Kyŏngbuk High School staged antigovernment demonstrations, later identified in South Korean history as "the first beacon of the April Revolution." On election day, in many rural areas and military camps, teams were formed, with the head of each ensuring that the other members voted for the Rhee ticket. At Masan that day, the first civilian protests against election fraud erupted. The next day, it was officially announced that Rhee's allies had won, but opposition leaders declared that "the illegal election was void." Antigovernment parades and demonstrations followed in major cities.

On 11 April, the corpse of a high school student who was killed by the police on 15 March at Masan was found. Shocked by the picture of the bullet having penetrated his face, the vast majority of citizens in the major cities rallied voluntarily in protest against the election. After Rhee said the students might have been manipulated by Communists, students of Korea University in Seoul staged demonstrations against him. On 19 April thousands of university, as well as high school students, marched on the presidential office. In an event later called Bloody Tuesday, police fired on them, killing at least 115 and injuring no fewer than 727. In response, the government declared martial law, but the United States issued a communiqué sympathizing with the demonstrators the next day. Demonstrations and riots occurred daily thereafter, but ROK Army troops remained uninvolved. On 21 April, Rhee's cabinet resigned, as did Jang Myŏn, the incumbent vice president, who urged Rhee to resign. Rhee's refusal infuriated demonstrators, who burned the houses of the leaders of the Liberal Party and the Anti-Communist Youth Corps. About 300 professors at Seoul then staged anti-Rhee demonstrations, demanding Rhee's outright resignation. On 26 April, Rhee finally stepped down, fleeing with his wife to exile in Hawaii. Elections under a new parliamentary system made Jang Myŏn prime minister later that year.

S. Han, *The Failure of Democracy in South Korea* (Berkeley, CA, 1974); Q. Kim, *The Fall of Syngman Rhee* (Berkeley, CA, 1983); H. Lee, *Korea: Time, Change, and Administration* (Honolulu, HI, 1968).

Kim Hakjoon

RHO TAE-WOO

See NO TAE-U

RIDGWAY, MATTHEW B. (1895–1993)

During the Korean War*, General Matthew Bunker Ridgway commanded the U.S. Eighth Army from December 1950 until April 1951 and then the United Nations Command (UNC) until May 1952. Born at Fort Monroe, Virginia, he graduated from the U.S. Military Academy in 1917. Thereafter, he rose through the ranks as an infantry officer. At the time of the Pearl Harbor Attack* in December 1941, Ridgway was serving under General George C. Marshall*, U.S. Army chief of staff. Ridgway commanded the Eighty-second Airborne in Europe during 1943 and 1944. In 1946, he represented General Dwight D. Eisenhower*, then chief of staff, on the military staff committee of the United Nations. In September 1949, General J. Lawton Collins*, the new chief of staff, named him his deputy.

With the death in December 1950 of Lieutenant General Walton H. Walker, Ridgway replaced him as commander. After examining UNC lines on 2 January 1951, he ordered a retreat to the Han River, leaving Seoul, the capital of the Republic of Korea* (ROK), in enemy hands. But within weeks, U.S. and ROK forces were prepared to counterattack, implementing thereafter Ridgway's "meat grinder" strategy. On 14 March, UNC forces reoccupied Seoul and moved north of the thirty-eighth parallel. Ridgway now prepared his forces to combat a Chinese counterattack. Meanwhile, he opposed a plan to escalate the war that General Douglas MacArthur* had proposed because he believed it risked a world war without offering any possibility of success. In April 1951, President Harry S. Truman* named Ridgway as UNC commander upon MacArthur's Recall*. During the fierce Chinese spring offensives in 1951, he ordered reinforcement of the battlefront, advising Lieutenant General James A. Van Fleet, his successor as commander of the U.S. Eighth Army, that any northward advance would create more casualties than the gains would justify.

In Tōkyō, Ridgway continued to advocate an armistice in Korea. He assumed responsibility for opening the negotiations at Kaesŏng with China and North Korea in July 1951 that would become the P'anmunjŏm Truce Talks*. Despite acrimonious exchanges over the next nine months, Ridgway saw the negotiations as a necessary alternative to an endless and costly struggle for power over Korea. Nevertheless, he showed a tendency to be impatient, inflexible, and dogmatic, even before the Korean War POW Controversy* stalled progress toward a Korean Armistice Agreement*. In 1952, Ridgway succeeded Eisenhower as supreme commander of the North Atlantic Treaty Organization in Europe. Then, during the Eisenhower administration, Ridgway, its U.S. Army chief of staff, voiced strong opposition to a U.S. military commitment to prevent a Vietminh* victory in French Indochina*. His experiences in Korea also caused him to advocate de-escalation of the Second Indochina War* in 1968 as one of the "Wise Men" during the presidency of Lyndon B. Johnson*.

C. Blair, *The Forgotten War: America in Korea, 1950–1953* (New York, 1987); M. B. Ridgway, *The Korean War* (Garden City, NY, 1967); M. B. Ridgway, *Soldier: The Memoirs of Matthew B. Ridgway* (New York, 1956).

Norman A. Graebner

ROBERTS MISSION

The Roberts Mission was the first official attempt of the United States to develop treaty relations with the Asian countries. Edmund Roberts was a merchant from New Hampshire who operated a business in the region of the Indian Ocean in the early nineteenth century. He also had served as a special agent in the consular service to conclude commercial treaties with a number of nations in Southeast Asia, including Siam, Muscat, and Cochin, China. With the rapid growth of American business in China after the virgin trip of the *Empress of China** to that country, Roberts also developed interest in that market. However, he and many other American merchants found the Co-hong system under which they, like all other Western merchants, traded with China to be increasingly restrictive. Consequently, there was a growing demand among the merchant community for the U.S. government to be more involved in the China trade. Washington, however, thought the country's primary interest was in its trans-Atlantic trade, whereas the interest in the trans-Pacific trade remained marginal, and it turned a deaf ear to the merchants' demand.

Roberts and his fellow merchants in the China trade continued to mount pressure on the White House. Finally, in 1832, President Andrew Jackson commissioned Roberts to represent the U.S. government on a trip to the western Pacific, with the mission of negotiating treaties with the countries there that would give privileges to American merchants to facilitate U.S. trade. In 1833, he successfully opened Siam and Muscat to American trade, and obtained for the Americans a number of privileges, including the most-favored-nation status and fixed tariff charges. But in other places, he was not as lucky. He was first turned down in Cochin, China. Worse, when he arrived at Guangzhou, the only trading port open to Westerners, the Chinese refused to recognize his official status. They ordered the U.S. warships that accompanied him to "unfurl their sails and return home; they will not be permitted to delay and loiter about, and the day of their departure must be made known. Hasten, hasten!" Not ready for any use of force, Roberts left empty-handed.

Originally, Roberts's plan included Korea and Japan as destinations, but failure in China convinced him that he was not prepared for successful negotiations with these two countries. So he returned to the United States with the two treaties he had concluded. In 1835, Jackson sent Roberts back to Asia to exchange ratification of the treaties with Siam and Muscat, and to proceed to negotiate a similar treaty with Japan. But on his way to Japan, Roberts died of the plague at Macau in June 1836. The two treaties that he negotiated became the first official treaties between the United States and Asian countries, and were the precedent for agreements with other states in the Pacific. However, the failures of his mission also demonstrated that in the early nineteenth century, the United States was not ready for a larger involvement in East Asia.

A. DeConde (ed.) *A History of American Foreign Policy* (New York, 1978); A. X. Jiang, *The United States and China* (Chicago, 1988).

Li Yi

ROBERTSON, WALTER S. (1893–1970)

As assistant secretary of state for Far Eastern affairs from 1953 to 1959, Walter S. Robertson played an influential role in formulating and implementing U.S. policy in Asia. When the United States entered World War II after the Pearl Harbor Attack*, he left a successful investment banking career in Virginia to serve in government. The State Department sent Robertson to the U.S. embassy in China in 1944. When General Patrick J. Hurley* resigned as ambassador in 1945, he took charge of the embassy until Ambassador J. Leighton Stuart* arrived several months later. During this interlude, Robertson assisted General George C. Marshall* on his unsuccessful mission to China. Negotiations during the Marshall Mission* with Mao Zedong* left him convinced that compromise between the Chinese Communist Party* (CCP) and the Guomindang* (Nationalists) was impossible. Nor did he see any prospect for normal relations with a CCP regime. A staunch defender of the Nationalists, Robertson believed that the United States, acting on the advice of the China Hands*, contributed to the defeat of Jiang Jieshi* in the Chinese Civil War* by withholding assistance.

Robertson, a Democrat, returned to private life in 1946, but he soon became swept up in the politics surrounding the "loss" of China to Communism*. When he voiced strident criticism of U.S. China policy in testimony before Congress in 1948, he attracted the notice of the Truman administration's conservative critics. After the Republican presidential victory of Dwight D. Eisenhower* in 1952, John Foster Dulles* asked Robertson to be assistant secretary of Far Eastern affairs to preempt right-wing attacks on the administration. Robertson worked closely with Dulles and maintained good relations with congressional leaders, such as Walter H. Judd*. Although few men in public life were as conservative or fervently anti-Communist as Robertson, his personal integrity and gracious manner set him apart from other like-minded leaders, such as Senator Joseph R. McCarthy*. Assistant Secretary Robertson dealt effectively with problems concerning relations with allies in East Asia. In difficult negotiations with President Syngman Rhee* of the Republic of Korea*, he won assent to the Korean Armistice Agreement* of 1953. He relied on such capable officials as John M. Allison* in handling Japanese affairs, particularly regarding trade, rearmament, and popular dissatisfaction with the U.S. military presence. Robertson was a vigorous advocate of the Republic of China* on Taiwan*, pressing hard for the negotiation and ratification of the U.S.-China Mutual Defense Treaty of 1954*.

Dulles was less enthusiastic about Jiang, but joined Robertson in shaping the U.S. policy of not recognizing the People's Republic of China* (PRC). During the 1954 crisis in French Indochina* at Dien Bien Phu* and the Taiwan Strait Crises*, Robertson urged a confrontational stance toward Beijing. Research on the first decade of the PRC suggests that his understanding of the Chinese Communist regime's brutality and hostility toward U.S. objectives was more shrewd than his numerous critics have allowed. But his tendency to identify any opposition to an anti-Communist stance as unwitting support for world Communism carried high risks, resulting in support for unwise policies, such as U.S. intervention in Indonesia* in the 1950s. By replacing independently minded diplomats critical of either the Guomindang or containing the PRC, he left a deep void of expertise in the State Department. He resigned for health reasons in 1959.

W. S. Robertson Oral History, Dwight D. Eisenhower Presidential Library, Abilene, KS; J. C. Thomson Jr., P. W. Stanley, and J. C. Perry, *Sentimental Imperialists: The American Experience in East Asia* (New York, 1981); N. B. Tucker, *Uncertain Friendships: Taiwan, Hong Kong, and the United States, 1945–1992* (New York, 1992); S. G. Zhang, *Deterrence and Strategic Culture: Chinese-American Confrontations, 1949–1958* (Ithaca, NY, 1992).

Aaron Forsberg

ROCK SPRINGS MASSACRE

The late-nineteenth-century American West was a hostile and violent region for

Chinese immigrants. The Rock Springs massacre of 2 September 1885 was one of the most brutal anti-Chinese incidents that occurred during this period. Vicious attacks against Asians had happened earlier in California, but the worst and most widespread anti-Chinese riots took place outside of California during the 1880s. The Rock Springs incident of racial violence between Chinese and white workers resulted from power struggles between organized labor and management. The Union Pacific Railroad first introduced 150 Chinese laborers to Rock Springs, Wyoming Territory, in 1875 to break a mining strike. In the fall of 1885, there were 331 Chinese and 150 whites employed by the company in the mine. When the Chinese workers refused to join the whites in a proposed strike, white hostility toward them increased. On 2 September 1885, an early morning dispute between Chinese and white coal miners at a company shaft triggered the bloody riot. In the afternoon, about 150 armed men began to attack the Chinese quarters of the town. By midnight, a mob had killed twenty-eight Chinese laborers, wounded fifteen, and caused several hundred others to flee. More than eighty cabins were burned to the ground. A week later, under the protection of federal troops, the surviving Chinese returned to work in Rock Springs. Meanwhile, Chinese diplomats sent a fact-finding team to investigate and demanded indemnity for losses and punishment of the guilty at Rock Springs. Many who were involved in the investigation belonged to the Knights of Labor, the major labor organization that had lobbied hard for passage of the first of the Chinese Exclusion Acts* in 1882.

U.S. Secretary of State Thomas F. Bayard insisted that the federal government was not liable for the massacre on the grounds that the riot had occurred in a territory and both the assailants as well as assailed were aliens. Nevertheless, "solely from a sentiment of generosity and pity," President Grover Cleveland asked Congress to indemnify for the Chinese losses. Finally, in February 1887, the U.S. government paid $147,748.74 to the Chinese government for the survivors who lost property. Not one of the people who murdered, burned, or robbed the Chinese was ever brought to justice. The Rock Springs massacre ignited anti-Chinese riots across the Western states. News of these instances of Chinese suffering sparked anti-American campaigns in Guangzhou and Chongqing in the spring of 1886. The anti-Chinese riots, and the U.S. government's response to them, placed China in an untenable position. The Qing Dynasty needed Washington's support in its disputes with Japan, and could not allow the immigration issue to disrupt relations. Chinese leaders wanted to adopt a policy of self-restriction of emigration of Chinese laborers in exchange for a U.S. promise to protect the Chinese already in the United States. However, the painful negotiating experience of the Rock Springs incident revealed the mounting exclusionist sentiment in the United States, causing Beijing's hopes to disappear. By 1895, China's government had rejected the option of retaliating against U.S. interests in China. *See also* Coolie Trade.

P. Crane and A. Larson, "The Chinese Massacre," *Annals of Wyoming* (1940); S. Chan, *Asian Americans: An Interpretive History* (Boston, 1991); M. H. Hunt, *The Making of a Special Relationship: The United States and China to 1914* (New York, 1983); C. Storti, *Incident at Bitter Creek* (Ames, IA, 1991); S. H. Tsai, *The Chinese Experience in America* (Bloomington, IN, 1986).

Ena Chao

ROCKHILL, W. W. (1854–1914)

William Woodville Rockhill was an American adventurer, journalist, historian, diplomat, and adviser. During 1884 and 1885, he was attached to the U.S. legation in China, and the next year was transferred to be the chargé at the U.S. legation in Seoul. The Korean capital had just been disturbed by a brief siege of the foreign compounds by traditionalists hoping to stem the tide of Japanese-sponsored modernization in the country. Rockhill, who sympathized with the Chinese position of retaining Korea's position as a tributary state of the Qing empire, began at this time an association with the Chinese minister to Korea, Yuan Shikai*, that would survive the length of their careers. From 1888 to 1893, he traveled to Tibet* and Mongolia, and from 1893 to 1913, fulfilled diplomatic duties in Greece, Rumania, Serbia, and Turkey. Rockhill, whose views of Asian affairs were trusted by Secretary of State John Hay*, was influential in the anouncement of the Open Door Policy* in 1899 that attempted to preserve China from outright colonization by a foreign power, particularly Japan. In 1901 Rockhill participated in the reparations conference at Beijing that followed suppression of the Boxer Uprising*. He cautioned against imposing too severe demands on the Chinese government, and particularly against territorial compensation. *See also* Boxer Protocol; Horace N. Allen; Lucius D. Foote; Kojong; Shufeldt Treaty.

W. W. Rockhill, *China's Intercourse with Korea from the XVth Century to 1895* (London, 1905); W. W. Rockhill, *Diary of a Journey Through Mongolia and Thibet in 1891 and 1892* (Washington, DC, 1894); W. W. Rockhill, *Diplomatic Audiences at the Court of China* (London, 1905); W. W. Rockhill, *The Land of the Lamas: Notes of a Journey Through China, Mongolia and Tibet* (New York, 1891); W. W. Rockhill, *The Life of the Buddha, and the Early History of His Order* (London, 1884); W. W. Rockhill, *Notes on the Ethnology of Tibet: Based on the Collections in the U.S. National Museum* (Washington, DC, 1895).

Pamela K. Crossley

ROMULO, CARLOS P. (1899–1985)

Filipino patriot, diplomat, author, educator, and first president of the UN General Assembly, Carlos Peña Romulo was born in Camiling, near Manila, in the Philippines*. His father was a guerrilla fighter during the Philippine-American War* from 1899 to 1904 who was an active member of the revolutionary government of Emilio Aguinaldo. Ironically, Romulo gained prominence in the United States as the most trusted Asian spokesman during his later life. By his own admission, he was filled with hatred toward Americans, and all things American, when he was growing up. On the other hand, probably because of his U.S. education, he gained some respect for American ways and ideals. Romulo received his bachelor of arts degree from the University of the Philippines, and a master of arts degree in English from Columbia University in 1921. Upon completion of his graduate studies, he returned to the University of the Philippines to work as an English professor, as well as chairman of the same department, a position he held from 1923 to 1928. In 1929, he was appointed a university regent. He was editor and publisher of a chain of Philippine newspapers, and served with the Philippine Independence Mission to the United States.

During World War II, Romulo joined the staff of General Douglas MacArthur* as secretary of press relations and was commissioned as a major in the U.S. Army. From 1943 to 1944, he served in Philippine war cabinets in exile in the United States. He was promoted to the rank of brigadier general in 1945 and accompanied MacArthur during the recapture of Manila. In the same year, Romulo served as a seasoned diplomat for his country in various negotiations with the United States, including amendments attached to the Philippine Rehabilitation Act of 1946. Thereafter, he became secretary of foreign affairs in 1950 and was ambassador to the United States from 1952 to 1953 and again from 1955 to 1961. In 1962, Romulo became the president of the University of the Philippines, and in 1965 the secretary of education. Reappointed secretary of foreign affairs in 1969, he served until 1984. During these years, he was also his country's UN delegate. Among the many honors he received during his long life, two accomplishments stand out. First, he was the first Asian chosen to be president of the UN General Assembly in 1949. Second, he was the only Filipino journalist awarded the prestigious Pulitzer Prize for a series of outstanding articles on the Southeast Asian political situation in the late 1930s and early 1940s.

M. W. Myer, *A Diplomatic History of the Philippine Republic* (Honolulu, HI, 1965); *New York Times*, 9 November 1986; G. E. Taylor, *The Philippines and the United States* (New York, 1964).

Dirk A. Ballendorf

RONG HONG (1828–1912)

Rong Hong, more commonly known as Yung Wing, was the first recorded Chinese to study in the United States. He was educated in an American missionary school at Macau, having been selected to study there by its founder Samuel Robbins Brown. In 1847, Brown returned home and took Rong, who received further schooling at Yale University from 1850 to 1854. He married an American and was naturalized as a U.S. citizen. Reflecting on China's fate, Rong concluded that if China's youth gained the same Western education he had, they would expose China to modern technology and China's future would be more auspicious. Accordingly, in 1854, he returned to China to promote its modernization. In 1863, Rong went to see Zeng Guofan, governor-general of Jiangsu and Jiangxi, who was planning to build Western factories to make weapons. He proposed constructing machine-building factories first, and then arms plants, shipyards, and farm-machinery factories. Zeng agreed and entrusted Rong with the purchase of machinery in the United States.

In October 1863, Rong traveled to the United States with an American engineer. One year later, he returned with a batch of machines, with which the Jiangnan Arsenal was constructed at Shanghai. This was the first munitions factory China built in its Westernization Movement. In 1868, Rong proposed that a school be attached to the factory, which received approval and was implemented. Soon, he proposed again that the Chinese government send thirty boys between twelve and fourteen years of age to the United States each year to study for fifteen years, learning knowledge and skills desperately needed for China's economic development. In the winter of 1870, after Zeng and Li Hongzhang* endorsed it, the Qing court adopted his plan. Two years later, the first group was selected and settled near the Connecticut River under Rong's supervision. While learning in American schools and living with American families, 120 boys from 1872 to 1875 inevitably were influenced by the American lifestyle. In the eyes of the conservative court officials, this was intolerable because it violated Chinese tradition. Under demand from these officials, the Qing government decided to withdraw all the boys in 1881. Upon hearing the news, Rong, who in 1875 had been appointed associate minister to the United States, contacted influential Americans in educational circles in an effort to stop the removal. The president of Yale University wrote a letter to the Chinese government in a failed attempt to reverse the decision.

During the Sino-Japanese War from 1894 to 1895, Rong acted as the financial agent in the United States for Zhang Zhidong, the Chinese commissioner of southern ports, and afterward returned to China to serve for a time in Zhang's secretariat. His attempts to gain Qing approval of a plan to suppress the opium trade and to negotiate a loan of $15 million for the purchase of warships to allow China to defend itself against Japan both failed. In 1896, he translated some provisions of American bank law and advanced to the court a proposal for establishing a Chinese national bank. The Ministry of Revenue approved his proposal and appointed him to travel to the United States on an investigative mission, but the factional tangle within the court prevented implementation of his plan. In 1897, he was charged to construct a railway from Tianjin to Zhengjiang. He planned to use American capital in the construction because, in his view, relations with the United States were uniquely uncomplicated and China could borrow American capital without political risk. "We will borrow their merchants' financial strength and we will control the authority," he told court officials. Yet this plan came to naught because of a German protest. In 1900, the court wanted to imprison Rong because he had participated in 1898 reform activities, but he escaped to the United States. He died shortly after receiving an invitation from Sun Zhongshan* to return to China after the Chinese Revolution of 1911*.

Cai Guanluo (ed.), *Qingdai qibai mingren zhuan* [Seven Hundred Biographies of Famous People of Qing Dynasty] (Beijing, 1984); W. Yung, *My Life in China and America* (New York, 1909); Zhao Erxun, *Qingshi gao* [Manuscript of Qing Dynasty History] (Beijing, 1977).

Cai Daiyun

ROOSEVELT, FRANKLIN D. (1882–1945)

As president of the United States from 1933 to 1945, Franklin Delano Roosevelt was responsible for formulating U.S. policy during the prolonged crisis with Japan that led to the Pearl Harbor Attack*, for determining U.S. strategy in the Pacific war that followed, and for establishing postwar U.S. goals in Asia. Born into a patrician family in New York, Roosevelt grew up in a world of privilege, marked by travel to Europe, education at the Groton School, Harvard College, and Columbia Law School. Politics was his only serious vocational interest, and he modeled his career on that of his illustrious cousin Theodore Roosevelt*. After serving as assistant secretary of the navy under Woodrow Wilson*, he was the Democratic nominee for vice president in 1920. The following year, Roosevelt was stricken with polio myelitis, which left him crippled for the remainder of his life. In a dramatic political and personal comeback, he was elected governor of New York in 1928 and, four years later, in the midst of the Great Depression, defeated incumbent Herbert Hoover* in the presidential election. Roosevelt won reelection an unprecedented three times, serving until his death.

Roosevelt concentrated on domestic problems in his first term, but also began a policy of trying to contain Japan's expansion. He continued the Stimson Doctrine* of nonrecognition of Manchukuo*, but established diplomatic relations with the Soviet Union in a policy reversal to foster strategic cooperation against Japan. When Japan renewed its warfare against China after the Marco Polo Bridge Incident* in July 1937, Roosevelt delivered in October his Quarantine Speech* in a failed effort to prepare the public for the necessity to take positive action to deter aggression. He did not apply the Neutrality Laws to warfare in China, thus permitting the United States to provide symbolic support to the Guomindang* (Nationalist) government of Jiang Jieshi* with war material. After 1938, Roosevelt wanted to avoid war with Japan so that the United States could concentrate on the more formidable threat posed by Nazi Germany. When Germany overran the Netherlands and France in the spring of 1940 and began bombing Britain, the United States became the sole restraint to Japan achieving its Greater East Asia Co-Prosperity Sphere*. Roosevelt reinforced the Philippines*, stationed the Pacific fleet at Pearl Harbor, imposed economic sanctions, and in 1941 refused to compromise on the Open Door Policy* during prolonged negotiations with Japan.

After Pearl Harbor, Roosevelt presided over development of global strategy to defeat the Axis in World War II, but was always conscious of the interrelationship of military developments with long-term political aims. American planning for postwar Asia always had to be integrated with the higher priority of defeating Germany. His vision for Asia also differed sharply from that of the British, French, and Dutch.

Like other American officials, Roosevelt anticipated that the war would end not only the Japanese Empire, but Western empires as well. He believed that the U.S. policy in the Philippines of moving toward self-government with the promise of independence at a specific date in accordance with the Tydings-McDuffie Act* provided a model for ending colonial rule in South and Southeast Asia. Roosevelt was convinced that the idealism of the Allied cause required the liberation of all subject peoples. Toward that end, he tried to persuade Prime Minister Winston Churchill to liberalize British policy during the 1942 crisis in India and worked to end France's empire in Indochina by proposing creation of an international trusteeship.

Closely related to his anticolonialism was Roosevelt's determination that China would become one of the "four policemen" (along with Britain, the Soviet Union, and the United States) responsible for preserving postwar international order. Cultivating China's international stature, he invited Jiang to meet him and Churchill at the Cairo Conference* in November 1943. He advocated ending extraterritoriality in China and the exclusion of Chinese immigrants from the United States. Roosevelt already had sent General Joseph W. Stilwell* to help build the Guomindang Army, but bitter friction with Jiang led the generalissimo to request his recall. Hoping to avert renewed civil war with the Chinese Communist Party*, he dispatched General Patrick J. Hurley* to China during late 1944 in a failed effort to create a coalition government. Thus, by the last months before his death, Roosevelt saw his Asian aspirations being challenged by Europeans who were determined to reassert the imperial order and by Jiang, who squandered U.S. aid and ignored American advice on military priorities. *See also* Cordell Hull.

R. A. Dallek, *Franklin D. Roosevelt and American Foreign Policy, 1932–1945* (New York, 1979); W. F. Kimball, *The Juggler: Franklin Roosevelt as Wartime Statesman* (New York, 1991); W. R. Louis, *Imperialism at Bay: The United States and the Decolonization of the British Empire* (New York, 1978); F. W. Marks III, *Wind Over Sand: The Diplomacy of Franklin Roosevelt* (Athens, GA, 1982); G. Smith, *American Diplomacy During the Second World War* (New York, 1985).

Gary R. Hess

ROOSEVELT, THEODORE (1858–1919)

Before becoming president in 1901, Theodore Roosevelt had been a Republican New York State legislator and had worked in various federal government capacities. His international experience came from trips abroad as a youth born into a wealthy family. In 1903, he declared that "the seat of power" had shifted from the Atlantic and Mediterranean and was inevitably about to shift "westward to the Pacific." "In the century that is opening," Roosevelt believed, "the commerce and the command of the Pacific will be factors of incalculable moment in the world's history." As assistant secretary of the navy in 1898, he quickened the shift during the Spanish-American War* by working with President William McKinley* to have the U.S. Asiatic Squadron attack Spain's colony of the Philippines* in the Battle of Manila Bay*. In 1899 and 1900, he successfully campaigned for Philippine Annexation* so Manila could be the U.S. naval base for Asian operations. Roosevelt believed that this power, plus cooperation with Britain and Japan, who seemed to agree with Washington's advocacy of an Open Door Policy* in all of China, best protected U.S. business and missionary interests. The enemy was Russia, as it tried to colonize parts of northern China while being led by a government Roosevelt damned as "utterly insincere and treacherous." When Japan attacked Russia in 1904, igniting the Russo-Japanese War*, he privately said, "the Japs have played our game because they have played the game of civilized mankind." Racist to the point that he called inefficient people "Chinese," Roosevelt admired Japan's military and industrial prowess.

By 1907, however, Japan had used its victory over Russia not to ensure the open door, but to occupy Korea and southern Manchuria. Roosevelt had agreed to the first takeover with the Taft-Katsura Agreement* during 1905 (so secret that an obviously embarrassed president managed to keep it hidden until five years after his death), and accepted the second with the 1908 Root-Takahira Agreement*. Japan in turn promised to respect U.S. control over the Philippines, but by 1907 Roosevelt knew he could not defend them. Tension between the two nations grew more dangerous as California harshly treated Japanese-Americans and Japanese citizens, treatment that Roosevelt condemned and attempted to ameliorate with the Gentlemen's Agreement*. In 1906 and 1907, both Japan and the United States secretly drew up plans for war against the other. His policies also were failing elsewhere. During 1904 and 1905, an effective Chinese boycott of U.S. goods to protest American treatment of Chinese in the United States stunned Roosevelt. When he asked American bankers to protect U.S. interests by taking over railway concessions in China, they refused. By 1908, he was calling the Philippines "our heel of Achilles," ordering the U.S. Pacific base to be moved from Manila to Hawaii, and concluding that Americans did not have the proper character for successful imperialism. Roosevelt chastized his successor William Howard Taft* for worsening the U.S. position in 1910 by challenging Japan and Russia in Manchuria. Having underestimated Asian nationalism, and overestimating U.S. power, Roosevelt spent the last ten years of his life largely ignoring Asia, running again for president on a new Progressive political agenda, and finally lusting for war in Europe. *See also* Philippine-American War; Portsmouth Conference; Treaty of Portsmouth.

H. K. Beale, *Theodore Roosevelt and the Rise of America to World Power* (Baltimore, MD, 1956); R. H. Collin, *Theodore Roosevelt, Culture, Diplomacy, and Expansion: A New View of American Imperialism* (Baton Rouge, LA, 1985); M. H. Hunt, *The Making of a Special Relationship: The U.S. and China to 1914* (New York, 1983); A. Iriye, *Pacific Estrangement: Japanese and American Expansion, 1887–1911* (Cambridge, MA, 1972); F. Marks III, *Velvet on Iron: The Diplomacy of Theodore Roosevelt* (Lincoln, NE, 1979).

Walter LaFeber

ROOT, ELIHU (1845–1937)

Elihu Root was a founding member of the U.S. foreign policy establishment, which took shape in the first decades of the twentieth century. Serving as secretary of state from 1905 to 1909, he displayed a sharp but deferential intelligence, which nicely complemented the more aggressive temperament and dominating desire of President Theodore Roosevelt* to grasp the reins of U.S. foreign policy. Together, Roosevelt and Root fashioned a more strategic approach to growing U.S. interests in East Asia, with a special focus on improving U.S.-Japanese relations and diverting the potential Japanese threat away from the Philippines* and the wider U.S. Pacific presence. Born in Clinton, New York, he gained admission to the New York bar in 1867 and followed the well-trodden, upwardly mobile path of corporate law before hitching his future to Roosevelt's rising political fortunes. Root's first exposure to nascent U.S. interests in East Asia came after President William McKinley* named him secretary of war in 1899. With the United States exerting military authority over the newly acquired Philippines, his responsibilities included developing civilian government in the islands in close cooperation with William Howard Taft*.

As secretary of state, Root looked favorably on Japan as an exemplar of Western-style development and order in East Asia and applauded Japan's initiative in the Russo-Japanese War*, but also feared the

Japanese as a "proud, sensitive, warlike people." He once wrote that the main object of diplomacy was to "keep the country out of trouble" and he helped do so in U.S.-Japanese relations, most notably through both the Gentlemen's Agreement* and the Root-Takahira Agreement* of 1908. After leaving the State Department, Root was elected senator from New York State. There, he worked with Senator Henry Cabot Lodge* to draft reservations as conditions for Senate ratification of the Versailles Peace Treaty*. With the return of a Republican to the White House in 1920—Root's preeminence as elder statesman on foreign affairs provided new opportunities to influence the direction of U.S.–East Asian relations, most notably at the Washington Conference* of 1921 and 1922, where he took a hand in the negotiations over the Nine Power Pact* concerning China. Root outlived all but a handful of his contemporaries, and died four years before the Pearl Harbor Attack* comprehensively unraveled his earlier endeavors to advance U.S.-Japanese amity.

P. Jessup, *Elihu Root, 1845–1937*, 2 vols. (New York, 1938); R. W. Leopold, *Elihu Root and the Conservative Tradition* (Boston, 1954); R. A. Esthus, *Theodore Roosevelt and Japan* (Seattle, WA, 1967); W. LaFeber, *The Clash: A History of U.S.-Japan Relations* (New York, 1997); C. Neu, *The Troubled Encounter: United States and Japan* (New York, 1979).

Roger K. Hodgkins

ROOT-TAKAHIRA AGREEMENT (30 November 1908)

The Root-Takahira Agreement consisted of the exchange of notes between U.S. Secretary of State Elihu Root* and Japanese Ambassador Takahira Kogoro designed to lesson tensions between the United States and Japan over issues related to China. As both the American and Japanese presence in East Asia and the Pacific had expanded over the preceding decade, the leaders of both nations came to realize that some form of accord was necessary to clarify conflicting interests. After the Japanese victory in the Russo-Japanese War* of 1904–1905, Korea had become a protectorate of Japan, and formal Japanese Annexation of Korea* came in 1910. In 1907, Japan and Russia in effect divided Manchuria, an act that violated the Open Door Policy* and threatened Chinese territorial integrity. Meanwhile, anti-Japanese riots erupted in California, where citizens were alarmed at the rising number of Japanese workers in their state. President Theodore Roosevelt*, who had sent his nation's Great White Fleet* to Japan a month earlier in a show of U.S. naval strength, was surprised by the virulence of the California race riots. He also became increasingly worried about the vulnerability of the Philippines* to attack by the Japanese, as well as the possibility that the United States could be shut out of the China market.

Prior to Root and Takahira meeting in Washington, preliminary talks in Japan were conducted by John C. O'Laughlin, a newspaper man with close ties to Roosevelt. O'Laughlin came to recognize the Japanese desire to preserve the status quo in Asia while maintaining friendly relations with the United States. Moreover, he saw Japanese expansion in southern Manchuria as an issue that could be set aside if that part of China were seen as outside China's territorial and administrative control. Meanwhile, Japan considered trade with the United States more important than the treatment of Japanese immigrants in California. The Japanese leaders also saw solidifying the hold on Korea and Manchuria as their main objective. In October, negotiations began in Washington on drafting a statement reaffirming friendship and cooperation. Although Japanese insistence on respecting China's "integrity," rather than "territorial integrity," created some friction, discussions between Root and Takahira proceeded harmoniously. The talks were held in private and the Chinese were not even informed of them until the finalized agreement was about to be made public.

In the notes exchanged between Root and Takahira on 30 November, the two governments agreed to respect each other's possessions in the Pacific region, maintain the status quo in East Asia, and affirm "the independence and integrity of China and the principle of equal opportunity for the commerce and industry of all nations in that Empire." The agreement confirmed U.S. recognition of Japan's possessions in Korea and Manchuria as previously accorded in the secret Taft-Katsura Agreement* of 1905. Meanwhile, Roosevelt had arranged a Gentlemen's Agreement* with Japan to protect Japanese in the United States in return for Japan's pledge to limit immigration. This constituted a major concession for Tōkyō, although some Japanese leaders already were considering measures to stem the dispersal of their citizens to non-Asian lands. The Root-Takahira Agreement did compromise the principle of the Open Door by recognizing Japan's foothold in Manchuria, but the Roosevelt administration was in no position to displace the Japanese, or the Russians either. Moreover, both Roosevelt and Root were impressed with the vigor and efficiency of the modernized Japan, and both viewed China as a backward and helpless nation that could only cling to what remained of its territorial integrity if the Western powers and Japan were restrained. Perhaps the principal outcome of the compromises in the Root-Takahira exchange was the placating of public opinion in both the United States and Japan. After the notes were exchanged, Root suggested that the agreement might be placed before the U.S. Senate, if not for ratification, then at least for comment. Roosevelt replied by asking Root, "Why invite the expression of views with which we may not agree?"

T. A. Bailey, "The Root-Takahira Agreement of 1908," *Pacific Historical Review* (March 1940); W. LaFeber, *The Clash: A History of U.S.-Japan Relations* (New York, 1997); C. E. Neu, *An Uncertain Friendship: Theodore Roosevelt and Japan, 1906–1909* (Cambridge, MA, 1967).

Michael J. Devine

ROSTOW, WALT W. (1916–)

Born in New York City, Walt Whitman Rostow was an economic historian who held top-level national security appointments in the administrations of Presidents John F. Kennedy* and Lyndon B. Johnson*. After earning his bachelor of arts degree at Yale University in 1936, he attended Oxford University for two years as a Rhodes scholar. He then returned to Yale and received his doctorate in 1940. During World War II, Rostow served with the Department of State and the Office of Strategic Services. After the war, he returned to academia and became a professor of economic history at the Massachusetts Institute of Technology in 1950. There, he concentrated his research on the modernization process in the developing world. With regard to Asia, Rostow argued that the United States had to redirect its foreign aid policy toward economic growth, rather than merely supporting military forces. This argument represented a long-term anti-Communist strategy using economic means that aimed to weaken the appeal of Communism* in the Third World through political and economic reforms. Although Rostow had been an occasional consultant to the administration of President Dwight D. Eisenhower*, he gained greater influence as one of the key idea men in the next two administrations. Joining Kennedy's White House in January 1961 as deputy to National Security Adviser McGeorge Bundy*, he advised on a wide range of policy issues related to the developing world and foreign aid programs. Rostow moved to the State Department in November as chairman of the Policy Planning Council, where he worked for long-term foreign policy guidelines. Then, in February 1966, he returned to the White House as President Johnson's national security adviser.

Rostow's role in making policy toward Asia was controversial, particularly in relation to the Second Indochina War*. Applying his theory of development to the Republic of Vietnam* under President Ngo Dinh Diem*, he advocated political and economic "modernization" as a long-term solution to the Communist challenge from the National Liberation Front*. In the short term, however, Rostow considered U.S. military actions as essential to prevent Communist infiltration from the Democratic Republic of Vietnam*. In October 1961, with General Maxwell D. Taylor*, he went on a mission to Vietnam, and recommended increased aid and sending of combat troops to fight the Viet Cong*. While in the State Department from late 1961 to 1966, Rostow was not directly involved in operational aspects of Vietnam policy. After returning to the White House as Johnson's national security adviser in 1966, however, he strenuously supported increasing use of military power to press North Vietnam to a decision to end the war, even opposing de-escalation after the Tet Offensive*. Rostow left public office in January 1969 and thereafter taught at the University of Texas. He wrote numerous books on economic development and foreign policy. But it was his book *The Stages of Economic Development: A Non-Communist Manifesto* (1960) that earned him a wide reputation as an authority on Third World economic development. *See also* Nation-Building Strategy; Strategic Hamlets Program.

Current Biography (1961); J. L. Gaddis, *Strategies of Containment: A Critical Appraisal of Postwar American National Security Policy* (New York, 1982); M. H. Hunt, *Lyndon Johnson's War: America's Cold War Crusade in Vietnam, 1945–1968* (New York, 1996); J. Lodewijks, "Rostow, Developing Economies, and National Security Policy," in C. D. Goodwin (ed.), *Economics and National Security: A History of Their Interaction* (Durham, NC, 1991).

Ma Sang-yoon

RUSK, DEAN (1909–1994)

David Dean Rusk was among the most influential shapers of U.S. policy toward East Asia after World War II, eventually serving as secretary of state under Presidents John F. Kennedy* and Lyndon B. Johnson*. His interest in East Asia developed during three years spent as a Rhodes scholar at Oxford University, where he prepared a study of the Mukden Incident*, which strongly criticized the failure of the League of Nations and the United States to take firm action against Japan. During the late 1930s, Rusk, as an academic at Mills College specializing in international affairs, supported firm U.S. action in support of China and the Allied powers in Europe. Called to active military service in 1940, he soon was assigned to the War Department's Military Intelligence section as a specialist on British Asia. In 1943, Rusk went to the China-Burma-India Theater* as chief of war plans for General Joseph W. Stilwell* and oversaw the building of the new Burma Road*, opened in 1945. As part of Stilwell's plans to combine the forces of the Chinese Communist Party* with those of the Guomindang* (Nationalist) Party under Jiang Jieshi*, he approved the dropping of small amounts of supplies to the Communists at Yan'an and Ho Chi Minh* in French Indochina*. Fully aware of the corruption and disorganization of the Republic of China*, Rusk still admired Jiang as a proud and dominating nationalist who had held China together for more than a decade.

In July 1945, Rusk joined the policy section of the War Department's Operations Division, where he was briefed on the effects of the Atomic Attacks*, a decision he always defended as saving more lives than it cost. Thereafter, he participated in drafting directives for the U.S. Occupation of Japan*, and was particularly eager to exclude the Soviet Union from any role in postwar Japan and to ensure that Pacific islands under United Nations trusteeship were turned over to U.S. guardianship. In August, Rusk proposed the Thirty-Eighth Parallel Division* of Korea into U.S. and Soviet occupation zones. In 1946, he joined the State Department as assistant chief of the Division of International Security Affairs, before returning to the Pentagon later that year as special assistant to Secretary of War Robert P. Patterson. In 1947, he rejoined the State Department, handling all matters relating to the United Nations. In the late 1940s, Rusk helped persuade the Dutch to grant independence to Indonesia.*

In 1949, Rusk became deputy undersecretary of state and then in 1950, assistant secretary of state for Far Eastern Affairs, positions that required him to deal with the Communist victory in the Chinese Civil War* and the Korean War*. He opposed U.S. military intervention in China on behalf of the Nationalists as pointless and helped John F. Melby* to draft the China White Paper* of 1949, which laid the blame for the Communist victory squarely upon Guomindang inefficiency and corruption. Rusk supported cessation of further U.S. military aid to Jiang's regime after it fled to Taiwan*, and anticipated that the Communists shortly would take over the island. When the Democratic People's Republic of Korea* invaded the Republic of Korea*, Rusk advocated immediate UN action in support of South Korea, together with increased aid to the embattled French in Indochina and the Neutralization of Taiwan*, using the U.S. Seventh Fleet to block a Communist invasion. Chinese Intervention in the Korean War* in late 1950 led Rusk to state publicly and without authorization that the United States should not recognize the People's Republic of China*, but help the Chinese people overthrow it.

After leaving office in 1953, Rusk was president of the Rockefeller Foundation. Under his leadership, the organization shifted its orientation and funded numerous agricultural, educational, and political enterprises in developing nations, including many in Asia. In the 1950s, his continuing interest in foreign affairs was demonstrated as well by his presidency of the influential Council on Foreign Relations. He returned to government service as secretary of state for Presidents Kennedy and Johnson. Rusk was firmly identified with the American escalation of the Second Indochina War*. He supported both Kennedy's initial decision to send U.S. advisers and increasing aid to the Republic of Vietnam* under Ngo Dinh Diem* and Johnson's steady escalations, defending these policies both publicly and in private. He disagreed with the decision in March 1968 after the Tet Offensive* not to increase U.S. forces, but instead to seek a negotiated peace settlement. After leaving office, Rusk defended U.S. policy toward Indochina as justified, although with hindsight he argued that Kennedy should have shown his resolve by making a massive initial commitment of 100,000 U.S. troops in 1961 or 1962. But he also defended limiting the war, arguing that China might have entered the war and pushed it to the nuclear level if the United States had used more force against North Vietnam. Until his death, Rusk continued to lay much of the blame for the U.S. defeat upon American protesters, public opinion, and the media.

W. I. Cohen, *Dean Rusk* (Totowa, NJ, 1980); D. Rusk, *The Winds of Freedom*, E. K. Lindley (ed.) (Boston, 1963); D. Rusk, *As I Saw It*, D. S. Papp (ed.) (New York, 1990); T. J. Schoenbaum, *Waging Peace and War: Dean Rusk in the Truman, Kennedy, and Johnson Years* (New York, 1988).

Priscilla Roberts

RUSSELL AND COMPANY

Russell and Company, founded by the Boston-based family among others, was one of the earliest American businesses that ventured into the East Asian trade after the successful voyage of the *Empress of China** in 1783. Building its fortune in the East Asian trade, it was also one of the American companies that, during the nineteenth century, played the role of "backseat driver" of the U.S. diplomacy in East Asia. After 1800, Russell and Company was among those American firms that pushed for a more active official role in expanding the China trade. After the 1844 Sino-American Treaty of Wangxia*, the firm grew rapidly and soon replaced Perkins and Company as the leading U.S. business in China, buying and selling a wide range of goods, including opium. When the Chinese market became more open to foreign trade during the following two decades, Russell and Company widened its investment in China. The company's greatest fortune in China came, however, after the Treaty of Tianjin* in 1858, which opened China's coastline, as well as the major interior waterways, to foreign businesses. In 1862, Russell and Company founded the Shanghai Steamship Navigation Company (SSNC) and started to penetrate the China market. The existing Chinese shipping business, conducted mainly by wooden boats that relied heavily on wind, tide, and manpower, quickly was squeezed out of the market. Virtually free from significant competition, the SSNC won a tremendous amount of profit for Russell and Company over the next decade.

The Chinese became increasingly concerned about the loss of profit as well as control over their national shipping market to foreigners, especially the SSNC. In 1872, the China Merchant Steamship Navigation Company (CMSNC), a private firm, but sponsored and supervised by Chinese officials, was founded to rival the SSNC's dominance of the Chinese shipping market. With substantial official support in the form of subsidies, tax breaks, and government contracts, the CMSN initiated several rounds of price wars with the American company. Britain had joined the competition, founding two steamship companies in 1874 to operate in Chinese water. This inflicted a serious blow on the SSNC and was to change the company's fortune. When its profit steadily diminished in the Chinese shipping market, Russell and Company decided to withdraw. A deal was negotiated with China's officials that stipulated the transfer of the entire SSNC assets to the CMSNC by 1877 at a price of 5,000,000 taels of silver. Although the Chinese considered this a nationalist triumph, it became more widely recognized that Russell and Company had the better of the deal. After the sale of the SSNC, Russell and Company gradually withdrew its capital from China, and its role in U.S. diplomacy in China diminished. *See also* Bryant and Sturgis.

A. Feuerwerker, *The Early Industrialization in China* (New York, 1958); Y. Li, "The Bureau that Invited Merchants," Ph.D. dissertation, University of Washington, 1993.

Li Yi

RUSSELL, MAUD M. (1893–1989)

Maud Muriel Russell spent a lifetime promoting social justice, women's rights, and cross-cultural understanding between the United States and China as a foreign secretary in China for the Young Women's Christian Association (YWCA) (1917–1943), executive director of the Committee for a Democratic Far Eastern Policy* (CDFEP), (1946–1952), and an independent U.S. China policy activist (1952–1989). Born into a white, middle-class, Protestant family in Hayward, California, her fascination with China and its struggles to modernize emerged at a very early age. While attending the University of California at Berkeley, she was inspired by the evangelical Student Volunteer Movement and by her involvement with the campus YWCA. In 1917, she became a YWCA foreign secretary to aid Chinese women in their liberation movement. Once in China, Russell quickly immersed herself in language study and in YWCA activities that encouraged women's involvement in community service and educational programs outside their traditional Confucian and patriarchal homes.

Russell's entry into China coincided with the development of a vibrant Chinese nationalist movement that protested Western and Japanese imperialism in China and rejected the traditional Confucian organization of society. After witnessing the May Fourth Movement* in 1919 and repeated instances of Western gunboat diplomacy in the 1920s, she observed the abysmal working conditions and economic exploitation that Chinese endured at foreign-owned factories. As Russell studied the evolution of the Chinese nationalist movement and Marxist theory, she concluded that the Chinese Communist Party* (CCP) could lead China to regain true national independence, to modernize, and to liberate oppressed Chinese women and workers. She also became convinced that the CCP's rival, the Guomindang* (Nationalists) was reactionary and fascist in nature. Russell's standards for judging the CCP's admirable qualities and the Guomindang's failings were grounded in her Christian Socialist and feminist beliefs, and her experiences in watching China fight Japanese Colonialism*. She admired the CCP's social justice programs under Mao Zedong* and the nationalist sympathies that it advocated in the Sino-Japanese War after the Marco Polo Bridge Incident* in 1937.

During the late 1930s, Russell began a crusade to educate the American people and U.S. government about the various political forces in China. She never wavered in her support for the CCP until Mao died in 1976, even though the People's Republic of China* (PRC) evolved into a brutal totalitarian regime and the U.S. government investigated and persecuted her as a Communist subversive for years after her return to the United States in 1943. Instead, Russell called on Americans to learn more about the social and economic improvements that the CCP brought to China and about the corruption and venality of the Guomindang regime that received U.S. support with millions of tax dollars. First as executive director of the CDFEP and then as an independent activist, she toured the United States each year until 1979, speaking to religious, social, political, and labor groups and urging U.S. recognition of the PRC.

Russell also publicly addressed other U.S. Asia policies. She criticized the U.S. Occupation of Japan* when strategists retreated from their early goals of promoting participatory democracy and social programs and implemented the Reverse Course* to transform Japan into a staunch Cold War ally. She denounced U.S. involvement in the Korean War* and U.S. aid to French Colonialism* in French Indochina* and, after 1954, direct U.S. "interference" in Vietnam's civil war. In addition to public speaking engagements, Russell published the *Far East Reporter* from 1952 to 1989, reprinting articles written by other Western and Asian journalists and adding her own left-wing analysis. Called before both the Senate Internal Security Subcommittee and House Un-American Activities Committee in the 1950s and 1960s, she was labeled a Communist and relegated to the radical margins of the American political spectrum. Although Russell's principled critiques of U.S. Cold War policy in Asia gained legitimacy in academic circles, her fierce allegiance to the CCP destroyed her political credibility. However, her long-running involvement in U.S. China policy activism was remarkable given the small number of women who historically have been able to influence the making of foreign policy worldwide. Moreover, Russell's attempts to disabuse Americans of their ethnocentric tendencies were laudable.

H. Deane, *Good Deeds and Gunboats: Two Centuries of American-Chinese Encounters* (San Francisco, 1990); K. Garner, "Challenging the Consensus: Maud Muriel Russell's Life and Political Activism," Ph.D. dissertation, University of Texas at Austin, 1995.

Karen Garner

RUSSO-JAPANESE WAR (1904–1905)

The Russo-Japanese War marked a significant turning point in world history for several reasons. First, Japan emerged as a major regional power. Second, an Asian country defeated a European enemy for the first time in the modern era. Third, Russia confronted losses on the battlefield and revolution at home. Fourth, the United States first welcomed and then became nervous about the shifting balance of power in East Asia. In 1895, Japan won the Sino-Japanese War decisively, but the Triple Intervention* of Russia, Germany, and France forced it to give up many of the spoils gained in the Treaty of Shimonoseki*. In 1896, Russia obtained a treaty with China to extend its Trans-Siberian Railway across China's Manchurian provinces. In 1900, in response to the Boxer Uprising*, the Russians occupied Manchuria and then refused to withdraw. In 1902, determined to prevent another European revision if it went to war again, Japan signed the pivotal Anglo-Japanese Alliance*. These events set the stage for the coming conflict between Russia and Japan, as each sought economic and military dominance in northeast China and Korea. For the United States, Russian railway development originally appeared likely to expand international trade. As the Russians moved instead to limit access to Manchuria, the United States looked to Japan to counterbalance Russian expansion and to protect its Open Door Policy*.

In 1904, Japan launched a surprise attack on Russian naval forces at Port Arthur, sinking most of Russia's Pacific fleet. In a series of land and naval engagements, the Japanese scored a string of victories, astonishing most of the Western world. From the sidelines, President Theodore Roosevelt* applauded, commenting privately that the Japanese "are playing our game." Frustrated with Russian territorial aggrandizement and duplicity, Roosevelt, and much of the U.S. press, proclaimed the Japanese the real Western and civilized power in this war. Both the president and the press labeled the Russians barbarous, decadent, and Asiatic. Many Jewish-American bankers, who were opposed to Russian anti-Semitism, went even further in their support, giving Japan attractive lending arrangements while cutting off the Tzar's access to funds.

In spite of their victories, the overextended Japanese were poorly positioned to carry out a lengthy war. For the Russians, military defeat abroad had contributed to the outbreak of the Revolution of 1905 at home, supplying a powerful incentive for peace. Roosevelt was eager to see a settlement. His initial enthusiasm for the conflict had faded as Japanese victories mounted; he did not want the Russians forced off the Pacific shelf, he warned, nor did he want that country plunged into chaos at home. Seeking to restore both peace and the balance of power in Asia, and responding to a Japanese initiative, Roosevelt offered to mediate negotiations and invited the parties to Portsmouth, New Hampshire. The resulting Treaty of Portsmouth* restored the balance of power in Asia. Roosevelt, as broker of the agreement, received the Nobel Peace Prize. But the president also recognized that Japan's emergence as a continental power carried significant implications for U.S. economic ambitions in Asia.

R. A. Esthus, *Double Eagle and Rising Sun: The Russians and Japan at Portsmouth in 1905* (Durham, NC, 1988); W. LaFeber, *The Clash: A History of U.S.-Japanese Relations* (New York, 1997); I. Nish, *The Origins of the Russo-Japanese War* (New York, 1985); J. A. White, *The Diplomacy of the Russo-Japanese War: An Adventure in American Diplomacy* (Princeton, NJ, 1964).

Shannon Smith

S

SAIONJI KINMOCHI (1849–1940)

Saionji Kinmochi, best known as the last genrō or senior statesman of the Meiji oligarchy, was one of the key advisers to Emperor Hirohito* in the 1920s and 1930s. He believed in maintaining peaceful relations with the United States and tried to curb the increasing influence of the military in the government. Born the second son in the aristocratic Tokudaiji family, he was adopted by another court family, the Saionji. In 1871, he went to France and studied European institutions and law until 1880. Upon returning to Japan, he served the government in the 1890s as a member of the Privy Council, vice president of the House of Peers, education minister, and acting foreign minister. Being sympathetic to political party movements, Saionji joined the Seiyūkai in 1900 and succeeded Itō Hirobumi* as its president in 1903. Between 1901 and 1913, Saionji and Katsura Tarō* alternated as premier, with Saionji forming his first cabinet in 1906. His government was not popular among the military and the bureaucracy because of his support for constitutionalism, party government, and nonintervention in the Chinese Revolution of 1911*. His second cabinet was brought down by the army in 1912 when it refused to fund two additional divisions, leading to the so-called Taishō political crisis, in which Katsura's cabinet also was forced to resign and Saionji, too, renounced the party presidency and retired from party politics.

When Hara Kei*, the next Seiyūkai president, became premier in 1918, he asked Saionji to head Japan's delegation at the Versailles Peace Conference in 1919 because of his known support for international cooperation, especially with the Anglo-Saxon powers. His contribution to the conference was in name only. Saionji's most trying years came after Yamagata Aritomo passed away, making Saionji the only surviving genrō in 1924. During the turbulent years of the 1930s, when Japan witnessed the rise of ultranationalism and militarism, the last genrō's influence over important national decisions declined. The only means he had to prevent the military from expanding its influence over the government was the power to nominate premiers. He privately criticized the military's aggressive policies, but the actions he took were ineffective.

When the Japanese Army officers assassinated Manchurian warlord Zhang Zuolin* in 1928, Saionji insisted that they should be punished to maintain control over the army and to preserve Japan's reputation abroad, but he failed to prevail. He then undermined the political parties by selecting a nonparty man to form a "neutral" cabinet after the military's coup attempt in 1932, which took the life of Premier Inukai Tsuyoshi*. Japan's withdrawal from the League of Nations in 1933 saddened him. As Japan's isolation abroad increased and the political crisis at home deepened, Saionji requested that he share the duty of recommending the premier with the lord keeper of the privy seal. Saionji's final and most disappointing choice for premier was Konoe Fumimaro*, whose first cabinet decided to expand the Marco Polo Bridge Incident* of July 1937 into an all-out war with China. Saionji firmly opposed appointing Konoe as lord keeper of the privy seal in 1938, fearing that he might allow the army to extend its power to the palace. Saionji's faith in Konoe was utterly betrayed when the second Konoe cabinet signed the Tripartite Pact*. In November 1940, on his deathbed, Saionji advocated naming Admiral Nomura Kichisaburō* as ambassador to the United States, hoping that he would relax the strained relations.

P. Duus, *Party Rivalry and Political Change in Taisho Japan* (Cambridge, MA, 1968); T. M. Oakes (ed.), *The Saionji-Harada Memoirs* (Detroit, 1968); Y. Oka, *Five Political Leaders of Modern Japan* (Tōkyō, 1986).

Kawamura Noriko

SAITŌ MAKOTO (1858–1936)

A Japanese Navy admiral and politician, Saitō Makoto served as navy minister, governor-general of Korea, and prime minister. In 1884, he went to the United States to study while being the first military attaché to the Japanese embassy. Upon his return to Japan in 1888, Saitō entered the General Headquarters of the Navy and filled a number of posts before becoming vice minister of Japan's navy in 1898. In 1906, Saitō became navy minister in the cabinet of Saionji Kinmochi*, and over the next nine years, retained the post in five successive cabinets. He resigned in 1914 and retired to the inactive roster. Appointed governor-general of Korea in 1919, Saitō occupied the post until 1927 and, after a stint as plenipotentiary to the Geneva Naval Conference, returned for a second term in Korea from 1929 to 1931. Saitō served as prime minister from May 1932 to July 1934, presiding over a "national unity cabinet" that oversaw the recognition of Manchukuo* and the decision to withdraw from the League of Nations. After the cabinet was forced to resign, Saitō was appointed lord keeper of the privy seal in 1935, but was assassinated in the 26 February Incident in 1936.

American and British diplomats perceived Saitō as representing the moderate faction of Japan's navy. He was aware of the importance of shaping American perceptions of Japan. For example, in 1908, while traveling in the United States, Saitō warned Saionji of the propensity of the U.S. Navy to consider Japan as the hypothetical enemy. He suggested that the Japanese government request that the Great White Fleet* make a friendly stop in Yokohama. Many American newspapers reported the welcoming of the fleet as a sign that Japan had been cowed into submission, but within Japan, Saitō's proposal was viewed as a success in smoothing relations. Later, as governor-general of Korea after the 1919 March First Movement*, Saitō implemented a concerted program to convince American, Canadian, and British missionaries of the benefits of Japanese Colonialism* in Korea. Persuaded by Prime Minister Wakatsuki Reijirō to be Japan's chief representative at the Geneva Naval Conference of 1927*, Saitō cooperated with Ishii Kikujirō* in devising a conciliatory arms reduction policy. Hard-liners in Japan's navy, such as Katō Hiroharu, suspected that Saitō would sacrifice military strategic considerations for political and diplomatic aims, but a full-fledged clash was averted temporarily when the negotiations broke down because of disagreements between the Americans and the British.

While Saitō was in his second term as governor-general of Korea, Saionji and Hamaguchi Yūkō* enlisted Saitō's aid in pushing through an agreement at the London Naval Conference of 1930*. As one of the leaders of the moderate faction favoring the London Naval Treaty in the Japanese Navy, Saitō, along with Okada Keisuke, Suzuki Kantarō*, and Takarabe Takeshi, was able to suppress the protests of Katō Hiroharu and the antitreaty faction. After the Mukden Incident* of September 1931 and the 15 May Incident of 1932 when military extremists assassinated Prime Minister Inukai Tsuyoshi*, Saitō was selected in May 1932 to form a new cabinet because he was close to Saionji and other court officials. Many foreign officials, including the authors of the Lytton Report*, welcomed the news, viewing Saitō and Navy Minister Okada as the moderates who would steer Japan to a more internationalist course. Contrary to these expectations, however, Foreign Minister Uchida Yasuya and Army Minister Araki Sadao were able to maintain a hard line, resulting in Japan's withdrawal from the League of Nations. After his resignation as prime minister, Saitō helped Saionji midwife the birth of the Okada cabinet in hopes that it could install a less confrontational foreign policy. Targeted for his high-profile moderate position, Saitō was murdered, dealing a severe blow to the advocates of a moderate foreign policy toward the United States.

Shishaku Saitō Makoto den [Biography of Viscount Saitō Makoto], 4 vols. (Tōkyō, 1942); Itō Takashi, *Shōwa shoki no seijishi kenkyū* [Political History of the Early Shōwa Period] (Tōkyō, 1969); D. Titus, *Palace and Politics in Prewar Japan* (New York, 1974).

Hyung Gu Lynn

SAKATANI YOSHIRŌ (1863–1941)

A career Finance Ministry bureaucrat and politician in Japan, Sakatani Yoshirō, along with his father-in-law Shibusawa Eiichi*, was a leading exponent of unofficial diplomacy between the United States and Japan in the interwar period. After graduating from Tōkyō Imperial University, he entered the Finance Ministry in 1884, rising to become vice minister. He was instrumental in raising foreign loans to finance the Russo-Japanese War* in 1904 and 1905, and in persuading Jacob Schiff of Kuhn Loeb to become a major subscriber to Japanese foreign bond issues. Sakatani became finance minister in the first cabinet of Saionji Kinmochi* in 1906, but resigned in 1908 after clashes over railways budget allotments with Communications Minister Yamagata Isaburō. He then embarked on an overseas tour, which took him through Europe and North America. Upon his return, he was mayor of Tōkyō (1912–1915) and then went on an around-the-world trip in 1916, this time as the chief delegate to the Paris Economic Conference. In 1919, Sakatani was appointed special financial adviser to the Chinese government. Apparently, Secretary of State Robert Lansing*, when he signed the Lansing-Ishii Agreement* of 1917, agreed that a Japanese financial adviser should be sent to supervise both the use of loans under the Six Power Consortium* and Chinese currency reform. However, in 1919, Lansing opposed sending Sakatani because it constituted political interference. U.S. opposition, combined with domestic political tensions, scuttled the appointment. Taking responsibility for the fiasco, Ishii Kikujirō* resigned his post as ambassador to the United States.

Sakatani's involvement with nongovernmental organizations (NGOs) began in January 1915, when the director of Japan's delegation to the Panama Pacific Exposition held in San Francisco wrote to him suggesting the establishment of a committee on U.S.-Japan relations. In February 1916, Sakatani and Shibusawa formed the Japanese-American Relations Committee. When the Institute of Pacific Relations* (IPR) was established in 1925, Shibusawa and Sakatani consulted closely in starting up the Japan Council of the IPR. As each council was to be self-financed, they raised funds from several *Zaibatsu** and the Foreign Ministry. Another NGO whose leadership was composed mainly of members from the Japanese-American Relations Committee was the League of Nations Association, with Shibusawa as president and Sakatani as vice president. Although Sakatani consistently disavowed any intention on Japan's part to annex Manchuria in the late 1920s and early 1930s, his words generally were met with skepticism by his American counterparts. After the Mukden Incident* in September 1931, however, Sakatani in his public addresses claimed that Japan was justified in establishing Manchukuo*. Moreover, his eldest son was one of the top civilian officials governing the puppet state in its formative stage. In February 1932, Sakatani even sent Ishii to the United States as the representative of the Japan League of Nations Association to defend Japanese actions in Manchuria.

This pattern of using international associations as vehicles for damage control when Japan encountered image problems in the United States was not new. After the 1919 March First Movement* in Korea, Sakatani asked the representative in Japan of the International Peace Association to go to Korea to collect all reports critical of Japanese rule by foreign missionaries. In addition, Sakatani and Shibusawa provided funds to several Japanese international relations organizations, which were undertaking a concerted public relations campaign to deflect American criticisms of Japanese Colonialism* in Korea. After Shibusawa's death in 1931, Sakatani took over the various presidencies his father-in-law had held in many of the NGOs. However, the fact that he was committed to more than 100 organizations as chairman or director, and also sought to justify expansion in Manchuria, meant that he had neither the time nor the persuasiveness to help improve deteriorating U.S.-Japan relations in the 1930s. To his death, Sakatani believed that Japanese exploitation of Manchuria and China in cooperation with the United States and Britain was a feasible policy, reflecting his unwavering view on the power of business diplomacy.

Y. Sakatani, *Why War Between Japan and the United States of America is Impossible* (Tōkyō, 1921); *Sakatani Yoshirō den* [Biography of Sakatani Yoshirō] (Tōkyō, 1961); Kawamura Naoki, *Nihon gaikōshi no shomondai* [Issues in Japanese Diplomatic History] (Tōkyō, 1986)

Hyung Gu Lynn

SAMOA PARTITION

The Convention of 1899 ended more than thirty years of an unusual U.S. entanglement in East Asia precipitated by American idealism and a friendship treaty between the United States and Samoa in 1878 that ceded the harbor at Pago Pago to the United States. The diplomatic treaty negotiated in 1899 by Britain, Germany, and the United States partitioned the Samoan Islands along the longitude 171 degrees West into German-controlled Western Samoa and the U.S. territory of American Samoa. Washington's desire to maintain control of Pago Pago conflicted with the tradition prevailing in U.S. foreign policy of noninterference with European powers.

Early U.S. diplomatic efforts to gain a foothold in Samoa had miscarried until 1878, when Secretary of State William M. Evarts* persuaded the U.S. Senate to ratify a limited agreement for trade privileges and a nonexclusive naval base at Pago Pago. Increasing international rivalries, exacerbated by a growing U.S. naval presence in the Pacific, expanding American consular mischief, and multiplying domestic issues at home, demanded a solution. Propounding an idealistic moral interest in Samoan independence and neutrality, Secretary of State Thomas F. Bayard refused to accept German dominance in the islands, especially after a German-instigated Samoan civil war. In March 1889, only a sudden hurricane interrupted a near naval clash between U.S. and German military vessels. This incident persuaded the contestants to seek a negotiated settlement at the Berlin Conference in April 1889. The General Act of Berlin, signed by Britain, Germany, and the United States, sought to create a stable government under a tripartite condominium with nominal powers allotted to the natives. Unfortunately, this agreement failed to resolve the competition.

Finally, in 1898, a violent internecine dispute over succession to the Samoan monarchy forced Germany to suggest partition. Pleased to escape from an entangling alliance while keeping the harbor at Pago Pago, the United States consented, although it meant abandoning the issue of indigenous rights. Britain surrendered its Samoan claims in exchange for German concessions in West Africa, Tonga, and the Solomons. Germany retained possession of Western Samoa until 1919, when New Zealand assumed administration under the Mandate System* of the League of Nations and later the United Nations. It finally was granted its independence in 1962. American Samoa became an unincorporated territory of the United States, maintaining that status into the twenty-first century.

The Samoan experience provided the neophyte American diplomats lessons in foreign policy decisions, though most went unheeded. In the twentieth century, this would have unfortunate consequences for U.S.–East Asian diplomacy. A deteriorating European balance of power placed restrictions on the ability of Germany and Britain to respond to new challenges to Pacific stability, enhancing the advantageous nature of the Samoan settlement for the Americans while illustrating the global implications of regional decisions. U.S. actions in Samoa effectively obliterated native independence and autonomy that the Americans claimed to champion through imposing Western solutions on an Asian society. The effects of domestic politics on foreign policy also surfaced as an enduring characteristic of U.S. diplomacy. *See also* Micronesia.

S. Anderson, " 'Pacific Destiny' and American Policy in Samoa, 1879–1899," *Hawaiian Journal of History* (1978); J. W. Ellison, "The Partition of Samoa: A Study in Imperialism and Diplomacy," *Pacific Historical Review* (September 1939); P. M. Kennedy, *The Samoan Tangle: A Study in Anglo-German-American Relations 1878–1900* (New York, 1974); G. H. Ryden, *The Foreign Policy of the United States in Relation to Samoa* (New Haven, CT, 1933).

Nancy Clopton

SAN ANTONIO FORMULA

As the Second Indochina War* escalated after 1965, the U.S. government sought to bring about negotiations with the Democratic Republic of Vietnam* through the use of a number of diplomatic overtures involving intermediaries. Perhaps the most successful effort occurred during the fall of 1967 during a peace initiative known as PENNSYLVANIA. On 29 September, President Lyndon B. Johnson* spoke before the National Legislative Conference in San Antonio, Texas. In a major policy statement, he put forth a new offer to the North Vietnamese, one based upon prior discussions conducted through Hanoi's representative in Paris, Mai Van Bo, and French colleagues of unofficial American envoy Henry A. Kissinger*. What became known as the San Antonio Formula was Johnson's attempt in his speech to extend an olive branch to Hanoi. "The United States is willing to stop all aerial and naval bombardment of North Vietnam when this will lead promptly to productive discussions," the president said. "We, of course, assume that while discussions proceed, North Vietnam would not take advantage of the bombing cessation or limitation." But despite simultaneous rescinding of authorization to bomb Phuc Yen airfield and a scaling back of the overall level of bombing, North Vietnam eschewed the chance to enter into negotiations.

In Paris the next day, Bo said that his government had refused him permission to enter into direct exchanges with Kissinger in light of continued bombings, which most oddly the U.S. government had not restricted to coordinate with the Paris peace effort. A 3 October article in North Vietnam's official newspaper *Nhan Dan*, reporting on the Hanoi politburo's rejection of Johnson's formula for peace, asserted that the U.S. president had no right to insist on military de-escalation from North Vietnam while he was ordering attacks by U.S. planes on its territory. In mid-October, the two French intermediaries received from Hanoi a final and categorical rejection of the San Antonio Formula. Soon thereafter, North Vietnam launched military operations on U.S. positions near the demilitarized zone. The United States resumed bombing of North Vietnam on 24 October with an attack on Phuc Yen.

Despite Hanoi's outright rejection of the San Antonio Formula, it nevertheless continued to be the Johnson administration's basis for opening peace negotiations. North Vietnamese recognition of Johnson's need for some form of quid pro quo was evident in a December statement by Foreign Minister Nguyen Duy Trinh in which he all but guaranteed that his government would engage in peace talks after the cessation of U.S. bombing of the north. In response, the Johnson administration in January 1968 accepted publicly that the North Vietnamese could continue to infiltrate "the normal amount of goods, munitions and men to South Vietnam." After the Tet Offensive* and based on indications of a favorable North Vietnamese response received through the governments of Romania, Norway, and Sweden, on 31 March, Johnson ordered a partial halt to the bombing, a move that led to the opening of peace negotiations. American negotiators at the Paris Peace Talks* continued to insist upon the broadly defined guarantees of the San Antonio Formula and were successful in obtaining North Vietnamese agreement to them that October.

A. E. Goodman, *Lost Peace: The Search for a Negotiated Settlement of the Vietnam War* (Berkeley, CA, 1986); G. C. Herring, *LBJ and Vietnam: A Different Kind of War* (Austin, TX, 1994); G. C. Herring, *The Secret Diplomacy of the Vietnam War: The Negotiating Volumes of the Pentagon Papers* (Austin, TX, 1983).

Kent G. Sieg

SATŌ EISAKU (1901–1975)

A career bureaucrat before entering politics, Satō Eisaku was prime minister of Japan from 1964 to 1972 and recipient of the 1974 Nobel Peace Prize. Brother of Prime Minister Kishi Nobusuke*, he graduated from Tōkyō Imperial University and joined the Ministry of Railways. His career moved forward slowly until the U.S. Occupation of Japan*, when Satō began a rapid rise through the civil service. As vice minister in 1947, Prime Minister Yoshida Shigeru* noticed him while recruiting promising young bureaucrats to enter politics as members of his Liberal Party. Elected to the Diet in 1949, Satō became head of the Ministry of Postal Services and Telecommunications in 1951. He suffered a serious setback when he was indicted for taking bribes from the shipping industry to increase government subsidies of ship construction. Charges were dropped in 1956 as part of a general amnesty, but his public image was stained for years to come. Satō became a major player in Japanese politics only after the fall of his mentor Yoshida. He held cabinet posts under his brother Kishi, and then Ikeda Hayato*, who was given a diagnosis of cancer and resigned in 1964. Satō replaced him and served longer than any other postwar Japanese prime minister.

Two major elements of Satō's foreign policy were an unwavering support of the United States and an intense determination to achieve the restoration of Japanese authority over the Ryūkyū Islands, which included Okinawa, home to important U.S. military bases. After preliminary discussions during 1965 and 1966 on the reversion issue, Satō secured an agreement in November 1967 with U.S. President Lyndon B. Johnson* for return of the Bonin Islands*. But resolving the Okinawa Controversy* was more difficult because it had become a major point of contention in Japanese politics. Political activists on the left were using the prolonged U.S. occupation of the prefecture as an issue to develop nationalist sentiment against the U.S.-Japan Mutual Cooperation and Security Treaty*. In 1968, Okinawan voters forced more action out of Satō when they elected a governor who had campaigned on a platform of immediate reversion. The new Nixon administration realized that Okinawa had moved to the forefront of U.S.-Japan relations and negotiated a compromise to resolve the issue of storing nuclear weapons on the island after reversion. In November 1969, President Richard M. Nixon*, following a meeting with Satō in Washington, announced in the Nixon-Satō Communiqué* that the United States would soon return the Ryūkyūs to Japanese administrative control. After technically difficult negotiations, the island reverted to Japan on 15 May 1972, with U.S. bases as strong as ever.

Satō also tried to improve Japan's reputation in Asia and the Pacific. In 1965, he achieved Japan-Korea Normalization* as Japan signed a treaty with the Republic of Korea* establishing formal diplomatic relations. In 1967, he went on an extended tour of Southeast Asia to stimulate trade, visiting Burma*, Malaysia*, Singapore*, Laos*, the Republic of Vietnam*, Thailand*, Indonesia*, the Philippines*, Australia, and New Zealand. Satō also promoted regional economic development, helping establish and fund the International Development Bank for Asia. Japan took a strong lead as well in the fight against nuclear proliferation. In January 1968, Satō announced that Japan's government formally had adopted the Three Non-Nuclear Principles*, renouncing the possession, production, and introduction of nuclear weapons as basic premises of its foreign policy. The antinuclear principles were part of a larger, four-point nuclear code that Japan would follow, calling for Tōkyō to work for nuclear disarmament, depend on the American umbrella for protection from hostile nuclear powers, and develop nuclear power sites solely for civilian purposes. In 1970, Japan signed the Nuclear Non-Proliferation Treaty. Two years after Satō resigned in 1972, he became the first Japanese citizen to win the Nobel Peace Prize. The committee cited his strong antinuclear stand and successful efforts to regain Okinawa through peaceful means. Satō died from a stroke he suffered in a Tōkyō restaurant.

T. R. H. Havens, *Fire Across the Sea: The Vietnam War and Japan, 1965–1975* (Princeton, NJ, 1987); Satō Eisaku, *Satō Eisaku nikki* [The Diary of Satō Eisaku], 6 vols. (Tōkyō, 1997–1999).

Nicholas Evan Sarantakes

SCAP

The Supreme Commander for the Allied Powers, better known as SCAP, was the authority for the U.S. Occupation of Japan*. At its surrender on 16 August 1945, Japan was a ruined nation on the verge of starvation and political chaos. Although officially working through a Far East Commission comprising of eleven Allied nations, General Douglas MacArthur* became the supreme commander of the occupation. He arrived in Japan in September, backed by a force of 400,000 U.S. troops. The Japanese expected retribution and harshness; they were surprised to find the Americans willing and able to rebuild their nation. Understanding the difficulties of administering a nation with an alien culture and language, the U.S. decision to retain Emperor Hirohito* allowed the Japanese people to accept reforms more easily. Furthermore, the United States did not impose direct military rule on Japan. In Tōkyō, MacArthur supervised a huge bureaucracy, but SCAP governed through the Japanese. Staff sections paralleled ministries in the emperor's government, with military government teams to monitor implementation of occupation policies. SCAP was divided between those officials wanting a harsh occupation and those who saw the need to rehabilitate Japan quickly before the specter of Communism* arose. Its initial emphasis was on reforming and demilitarizing the Japanese system. SCAP wrote the new Japanese Constitution of 1947*, which protected civil liberties and prohibited a capacity to make war. Sent to the Diet by the emperor, it was adopted as an amendment to the old Meiji document. In 1946, Yoshida Shigeru* became Japan's prime minister and the amicability between this retired diplomat and the haughty general set the tone for the occupation.

But inflation, a bankrupt economy with no savings or investment capital, the slow pace of rebuilding, the rise of leftist influence, and the specter of international Communism forced a change in SCAP's policies. Believing that organized labor had become dominated by leftists, MacArthur outlawed a general strike and excluded government employees from collective bargaining. SCAP began a program to rapidly raise industrial production. In March 1948, George F. Kennan*, the director of the State Department's Policy Planning Staff, went to Japan. He determined that the nation had to be rapidly rebuilt to develop into a self-sustaining bulwark against the Communist threat in Asia. Implementation of a Reverse Course* in occupation policy followed, with reparations cut to nothing. Leftists suffered a "Red purge," and former militarists were rehabilitated and reinstalled in prominent positions. Unions were hounded out of existence. Japan was now remilitarized and reindustrialized. In 1949, banker Joseph M. Dodge* developed a plan to jump-start the Japanese economy, although austerity measures to balance the budget caused great hardships. The SCAP strengthened the central government and gave it a major role in overseeing industrial development and establishing economic controls. A Police Reserve and a Maritime Safety Force were created. With Japan's security assured, John Foster Dulles* began to arrange terms for restoring Japan's sovereignty in 1950 and also negotiated the U.S.-Japan Security Treaty of 1951*. The Japanese Peace Treaty* was signed in September 1951 and came into effect the next year, marking the official end of the occupation.

T. Cohen, *Remaking Japan: The American Occupation as New Deal* (New York, 1987); R. B. Finn, *Winners in Peace: MacArthur, Yoshida, and Postwar Japan* (Berkeley, CA, 1992); J. C. Perry, *Beneath the Eagle's Wings: Americans in Occupied Japan* (New York, 1980); M. Schaller, *The American Occupation of Japan: The Origins of the Cold War in Asia* (New York, 1985).

Kent G. Sieg

SEBALD, WILLIAM J. (1901–1980)

During the U.S. Occupation of Japan*, William J. Sebald was the Department of State's political adviser to General Douglas MacArthur*. A graduate of the U.S. Naval Academy and a lawyer, his first major exposure to Japan was as a U.S. Navy language officer in Japan in the 1920s. After practicing law in Kōbe in the 1930s, Sebald served in World War II in the U.S. Navy's Combat Intelligence Division. After Japan's surrender, the State Department recruited him to act as a legal specialist working for the political adviser to the Supreme Commander for the Allied Powers (SCAP*). When George Atcheson, the first political adviser, unexpectedly died in August 1947, Sebald replaced him. As chief of the Diplomatic Section of SCAP, he was in effect de facto ambassador in Tōkyō during the occupation. Sebald also was deputy, and later acting chairman, of the Allied Council for Japan, an advisory board to MacArthur, composed of representatives from the British Commonwealth, China, the Soviet Union, and the United States. In this last capacity, he was influential in helping reinforce MacArthur's authority in resisting external interference in U.S. administration of the occupation from 1945 until the formal return of sovereignty to Japan in 1952.

Sebald describes his importance in U.S.–East Asian relations in *With MacArthur in Japan*, his memoir of his service in Tōkyō from 1945 to 1952. In addition to personal insights, it highlights vividly the difficulty of accommodating the sometimes-conflicting demands of serving an independently minded and occasionally obstructive MacArthur while remaining responsive and sensitive to the interests of the State Department. In many respects, Sebald was the consummate civil servant and diplomat, adept not only in interacting effectively with his Japanese counterparts, but in displaying equal agility in balancing the different agendas of Washington and SCAP general headquarters. His long exposure to Japan inclined Sebald to be sensitive to Japanese interests and, in keeping with the views of other Japan Hands, such as Max Bishop, Niles Bond, and C. Nelson Spinks, his reporting frequently stressed the importance of avoiding an overly hectoring or condescending U.S. approach toward postwar Japan. His predisposition to view events from a Japanese perspective, as well as close personal acquaintances with leading Japanese politicians such as Shidehara Kijūrō* and, most notably, Prime Minister Yoshida Shigeru* arguably ensured that Sebald would play a central role in facilitating cooperation between Washington and Tōkyō in the immediate aftermath of the war. Not only did his reports from Tōkyō influence State Department thinking in Washington, but he also periodically was important in providing advice to John Foster Dulles*, the special consultant on Japan, during Dulles's various visits to Tōkyō in 1950 and 1951 to negotiate the Japanese Peace Treaty*.

Sebald also played an important role in discussions about the postwar status of Emperor Hirohito*, relaying to MacArthur the results of conversations with former Prime Minister Ashida Hitoshi*. Both Sebald and MacArthur believed his resignation would cause domestic chaos and leave Japan exposed to Communism* and were quick to point out to the emperor the undesirability of abdication. Not surprisingly, given his close association with it, Sebald judged the American administration of Japan from 1945 to 1952 to have been, on balance, a favorable one. Although he noted that U.S. occupation was at times overly interventionist and inclined to tinker too deeply with the social and institutional features of Japan, he argued that it succeeded in realizing its three main goals of democratization and demilitarization, adoption of the U.S.-authored Japanese Constitution of 1947*, and keeping Japan free from Communist control and wedded to the alliance with the United States. After his time in Japan, Sebald was ambassador to Burma* from 1952 to 1954 and then ambassador to Australia from 1957 to 1961.

J. W. Dower, *Embracing Defeat: Japan in the Wake of World War II* (New York, 1999); H. B. Schonberger, *Aftermath of War: Americans and the Remaking of Japan, 1945–1952* (Kent, OH, 1989); W. J. Sebald, *With MacArthur in Japan* (London, 1965).

John Swenson-Wright

SECOND INDOCHINA WAR (1959–1975)

The First Indochina War* was ended by the Geneva Accords of 1954* that split Vietnam at the seventeenth parallel. The two halves were supposed to be reunited through elections under international supervision in 1956, but these elections did not occur. Until early 1959, Communist leaders of the Democratic Republic of Vietnam (DRV) in the north forbade their followers in the south to use large-scale armed violence. While this policy was in place, President Ngo Dinh Diem* of the Republic of Vietnam* (RVN) in the south was able to destroy most of the Communist organizations in South Vietnam. In the first half of 1959, however, the DRV authorized what was left of the Communist forces in the south to launch a guerrilla war, and began sending additional personnel down the Ho Chi Minh Trail* running from North Vietnam through Laos* to the south. In the early years of the war, the guerrillas, known as the Viet Cong*, were essentially all South Vietnamese, as were the officers leading them. A supreme command in North Vietnam was a mixed group of Communist leaders from north and south. On the other side, the Army of the Republic of Vietnam* (ARVN), its officers, and its supreme command were a mixture of northerners and southerners. The Viet Cong, in short, were far closer to being purely South Vietnamese than were the RVN forces.

President John F. Kennedy* sent the ARVN enough weapons to give it a great advantage in firepower over the guerrillas, and increasing numbers of U.S. personnel, including Green Berets*. Theoretically, the Americans were only advisers, but by early 1962, American pilots, both of helicopters and fixed-wing aircraft, were joining directly in the combat. The ARVN was handicapped by lack of popular support, and poor policies caused partly by distrust between senior ARVN officers and President Diem. The Viet Cong grew in strength. A political crisis in 1963 pitted the Catholic President Diem against the Buddhists, who made up a majority of the population. U.S. officials, notably Roger Hilsman*, who believed there was no possibility Diem could defeat the Viet Cong, and who hoped someone else would do better, encouraged the military coup that led to Diem's* Assassination in November 1963. A succession of military governments that followed did no better, and soon the Viet Cong were winning the war. By the fall of 1964, North Vietnamese troops of the People's Army of Vietnam (PAVN) were deploying in South Vietnam as well. The U.S. government, now under President Lyndon B. Johnson*, drew up plans for a major expansion of the U.S. role in the war, including bombing of North Vietnam, but delayed implementation because Johnson was running as the "peace candidate" in the election of 1964.

In 1965, President Johnson ordered massive U.S. bombing of Communist forces in South Vietnam, escalation of the Secret U.S. Air War in Laos*, and Operation ROLLING THUNDER* for somewhat more limited bombing of North Vietnam. U.S. bombing of Cambodia* (Operation MENU*) began under President Richard M. Nixon* in 1969. By the time the air war ended in 1973, U.S. bombers and fighter-bombers had expended more than 3,200,000 tons of aerial munitions in South Vietnam, 2,093,300 tons in Laos, 880,108 tons in North Vietnam, and 539,129 tons in Cambodia. Arguments that the air war was limited refer mostly to North Vietnam, especially the northern half of North Vietnam. Johnson feared triggering a war against the People's Republic of China* or the Soviet Union, initially refusing to order air strikes against Hanoi, Haiphong, and the area immediately adjoining the Chinese border, but later doing so, a few targets at a time. Johnson ordered a complete halt to bombing of North Vietnam in October 1968, and Nixon did little bombing there until 1972. More important, Johnson put U.S. ground troops into combat in Vietnam in 1965, and for the next three years the ground war grew in intensity. The period of the most bloody combat began in January 1968 when the Communists staged the Tet Offensive*, lasting through May of that year.

The American public, expecting a quick and not very expensive victory, had strongly supported the war when Johnson began putting large numbers of Americans into combat. As the costs increased without any victory in sight, increasing numbers of people, the Congress, and even the officials running the war lost faith in it. The number of American deaths was far smaller than those PAVN and Viet Cong troops killed, but a growing number of Americans thought the price being paid was more than the war was worth. Public support for the war had begun to fade after 1965, with rising numbers of protestors—almost all peaceful and orderly at first, but increasingly raucous and sometimes violent from

1968 onward—demonstrating against the war. In response, President Nixon decided in the summer of 1969 that the Communist forces had weakened enough for him to begin pulling U.S. forces out of South Vietnam. He also ordered the troops still there to be less aggressive in seeking combat with enemy troops, while Vietnamization* strengthened the ARVN so it could take over combat responsibilities from the Americans. During the withdrawal, morale and discipline among American forces in Vietnam declined severely. Drug use became widespread, and there were "fraggings"—armed attacks by U.S. soldiers against their superiors.

By 1972, there was war in most of South Vietnam, Laos, and Cambodia, but American participation was limited to aerial bombing and the provision of weapons and supplies to indigenous forces. Legislation passed late in 1970 forbade the use of U.S. ground troops in Cambodia or Laos, and Nixon's troop withdrawals had reduced U.S. ground combat to negligible levels even in South Vietnam during 1971. Finally, in January 1973, the Paris Peace Accords* provided for a cease-fire in South Vietnam, with the future of the country to be settled by vaguely defined political processes. All U.S. forces were to withdraw from South Vietnam; all foreign troops were to leave Cambodia and Laos. The cease-fire was violated by both sides. By this time the Communist troops in the south were overwhelmingly North Vietnamese; the South Vietnamese Viet Cong had been eroded by years of casualties. American air support for the ARVN ended completely in January 1973, and there were only a few air strikes in Laos after this point. Heavy U.S. bombing of Cambodia went on until halted by Congress in August 1973.

Once there were no more Americans in Vietnam, the U.S. Congress saw less reason to give generous support to U.S. allies in Indochina. Military aid, mostly to the ARVN, but smaller quantities going to the governments of Lon Nol* in Cambodia and Souvanna Phouma* in Laos, declined sharply in 1974. The ARVN was structured to fight with lavish supplies and plentiful air support, and when deprived of these things it proved very vulnerable. Cambodia's government teetered on the edge of extinction for months before falling to the Communist Khmer Rouge* in April 1975. But the fall of the Saigon government of Nguyen Van Thieu* was more sudden; a PAVN offensive that began in March 1975 took the whole country by the end of April. There was no serious resistance when Communist forces finished the conquest of Laos a few months later. *See also* Battle of Ap Bac; Battle of the Ia Drang Valley; Gulf of Tonkin Incidents; Khe Sanh; LINEBACKER Bombings; Military Assistance Command, Vietnam; Nation-Building Strategy; Operation CEDAR FALLS; Operation JUNCTION CITY; Operation RANCH HAND; Paris Peace Talks San Antonio Formula; William C. Westmoreland.

G. C. Herring, *America's Longest War: The United States and Vietnam, 1950–1975* (New York, 1986); A. Isaacs, *Without Honor: Defeat in Vietnam and Cambodia* (Baltimore, MD, 1983); S. Karnow, *Vietnam: A History* (New York, 1983); J. Race, *War Comes to Long An: Revolutionary Conflict in a Vietnamese Province* (Berkeley, CA, 1972); W. S. Turley, *The Second Indochina War* (Boulder, CO, 1986).

Edwin E. Moise

SECOND OPIUM WAR (1856–1859)

Chinese refusal to grant more economic concessions led to Britain instigating this war and imposing the Treaty of Tianjin* on China. When the Treaty of Nanjing* and the Treaty of Wangxia* were approaching their renewal date, Britain, France, and the United States attempted to revise these agreements. In December 1855, Peter Parker*, the U.S. commissioner to China, arrived in Guangzhou and put forward the request for the revision. Refused by Ye Mingchen, the governor-general of Guangdong and Guangxi, Parker wrote to the

British minister on 30 January 1856, suggesting joint action. Because Britain preferred resorting to force, whereas Washington disliked the idea, Parker went alone north to Shanghai to negotiate with the local administration, but achieved nothing. The Second Opium War between China and Britain broke out in October 1856. Parker wrote to the State Department three times, suggesting making use of the opportunity to occupy Taiwan*. Secretary of State William Marcy rejected the proposal. While the Anglo-French force was attacking Guangzhou in November, the U.S. government instructed Parker to protect the Americans in China and avoid the war so as not to hinder the Sino-American friendship.

James Buchanan, after becoming president in 1857, continued the policy of advancing U.S. commercial interests through treaty revision accomplished without coercion. When Britain asked the United States to join the war in March, Secretary of State Lewis Cass refused, explaining that there was not any incident to justify war between the United States and China. Washington preferred negotiation alone with the Chinese government, he said, rather than joining the action of Britain and France. On 18 April, William B. Reed was appointed U.S. minister to China with the mission of treaty revision. Cass gave Reed the instructions that the requests of Britain and France to grant foreign diplomats the right of residence in Beijing, to open the Yangze, and to promise protection of foreign missionaries and their converts were fair. It was hoped that he could achieve these objectives by advancing firm claims and thus persuading the Chinese to make the decisions themselves. Reed also was to tell the Chinese that the United States would not join the existing hostile action, interfere in China's internal affairs, or seize any piece of Chinese territory for itself. Finally, Cass told Reed to mediate an end to the war as early as possible.

After allied forces took Guangzhou in December 1857, and in February 1858, issued a demand for treaty revision, Reed asked the U.S. government to use force to compel the Chinese to negotiate with him. But Cass disagreed, instructing him only to tell the Chinese that the United States was willing to mediate. In April 1858, when allied forces arrived off the northern coast, China's government asked Reed to act as mediator to avert a clash. But Reed demurred. Military pressure thus forced China to negotiate. Guiliang and Qiying, the two Chinese officials at the talks, twice invoked U.S. aid to soften allied demands and both times were spurned. Under threat of force, the Chinese bowed to British and French demands. To maintain the goodwill of the American and Russian neutrals, the Chinese agreed to revise their treaties as well. On 18 June, the United States and China signed the revised treaty in Tianjin. In June 1859, a second allied expedition came north to exchange the new treaties, accompanied by John Ward, the new U.S. minister to China. Hengfu, the chief Chinese negotiator, again asked Ward for help, but Ward replied that he would speak to the British only after he had completed his own trip to Beijing. On 16 August, Ward exchanged the new treaty ratification of instruments with the Qing government.

Chouban yiwu shimo, Xianfeng [Complete Record of the Management of Barbarian Affairs in the Qing Dynasty, Xianfeng Period] (Beijing, 1930); M. H. Hunt, *The Making of a Special Relationship: The United States and China to 1914* (New York, 1983); Zhao Erxun, *Qingshi gao* [Manuscript of Qing Dynasty History] (Beijing, 1977).

Xiang Liling

SECRET U.S. AIR WAR IN LAOS

The United States waged a secret air war in Laos* beginning in the early 1960s to combat Communist infiltration down the Ho Chi Minh Trail* and to contest North Vietnamese and Pathet Lao* control over northeastern Laos. U.S. air operations were clandestine because they directly violated the Geneva Accords of 1962*—as did North Vietnamese ground operations there. At first, the U.S. government employed contract airlines, Air America* and Bird and Sons, to supply ethnic Lao irregulars fighting the North Vietnamese. Airplanes and helicopters ferried supplies, equipment, and troops to and from hundreds of grass runways in Laos mountains. In 1963, the United States established a small, secret air force operating out of Thailand* that flew single-engine aircraft in reconnaissance and combat missions over Laos. Concerned about a North Vietnamese offensive in the Plain of Jars and rising activity along the Ho Chi Minh Trail, the United States instituted a far more extensive reconnaissance program in June 1964, employing U.S. Air Force and U.S. Navy jets. U.S. contract pilots also joined Thai and Lao in flying combat missions in planes with Lao Air Force markings.

In June 1964, Pathet Lao anti-aircraft fire shot down two U.S. reconnaissance jet aircraft. In retaliation, the Johnson administration launched a one-shot air strike on the enemy anti-aircraft sites. The attack was only a qualified success, as half the planes hit the wrong target. This action, however, marked a turning point in the air war. By the end of 1965, the United States was engaged in two distinct and regular bombing campaigns in Laos: BARREL ROLL over northeastern Laos and STEEL TIGER over the Ho Chi Minh Trail in southeastern Laos. As the air war expanded, U.S. jets screamed over Laos, search-and-rescue helicopters plucked downed pilots from Lao mountains, tankers refueled jets in the sky, and airborne control planes circled over Laos twenty-four hours a day communicating with forward air controllers in single-engine planes, who then provided targeting assistance for U.S. sorties. The U.S. air attaché's office in Vientiane bulged with employees, including "civilians" in Hawaiian shirts, cowboy boots, and camouflage jackets. The secret air war grew each year in size and complexity.

In January 1970, facing a furious North Vietnamese counterattack on the Plain of Jars, the Nixon administration for the first time authorized deployment of B-52 bombers in Laos. The massive payloads of these bombers were called upon to save pro-American forces on the ground and to signal Hanoi. For public consumption, the B-52s were attacking the enemy positions on the South Vietnamese side of the border, but this extensive air campaign could not be kept secret indefinitely. During Senate hearings in 1969, the truth of the air war slowly unfolded, fueling antiwar sentiment. Over the next three years, U.S. air power and Hmong* and other ethnic irregulars on the ground battled North Vietnamese regulars in a seesaw battle. By the end of 1972, the North Vietnamese controlled virtually all of eastern Laos and pro-U.S. irregular forces were spent. In January 1973, the Paris Peace Accords* included Laos as part of the projected settlement. The United States dismantled its secret air war in a matter of weeks. Faced with escalating war, Prime Minister Souvanna Phouma* asked for and received two U.S. B-52 bombing runs in early 1973, but for all purposes the war was over. In May 1975, with the Lao government under Pathet Lao control and the North Vietnamese on the verge of eliminating the last guerrillas, the United States airlifted Hmong leader Vang Pao* and several thousand of his followers to exile in Thailand. *See also* Second Indochina War.

T. N. Castle, *At War in the Shadow of Vietnam: U.S. Military Aid to the Royal Lao Government, 1955–1975* (New York, 1993); K. Conboy and J. Morrison, *Shadow War: The CIA's Secret War in Laos* (Boulder, CO, 1995); J. Hamilton-Merritt, *Tragic Mountains: The Hmong, the Americans, and the Wars for Laos, 1942–1992* (Bloomington, IN, 1993); U.S. Department of State, *Foreign Relations of the United States, 1964–1968,* Vol. 18 *Laos* (Washington, DC, 1998); J. Van Staaveren, *Interdiction in Southern Laos, 1960–1968* (Washington, DC, 1973).

Edward C. Keefer

SERVICE, JOHN S. (1909–)

During World War II, Foreign Service officer John Stewart Service compiled political reports in China detailing the strengths and weaknesses of both the Chinese Communist Party (CCP) and Guomindang* (GMD) or Nationalist forces that inspired anti-Communists to attack his loyalty to the U.S. government in the early Cold War years. Born to YMCA missionary parents in Sichuan, China, he attended missionary schools in Chengdu and Shanghai and then worked briefly for an architectural firm in Shanghai before returning to the United States in 1927. After graduating from Oberlin College in 1932, he renewed his friendship with fellow China "mish-kid" John Paton Davies*, who worked for the U.S. State Department. Davies advised Service to take the Foreign Service exam and seek employment with the Division of Chinese Affairs. Hired in 1933 as a clerk at the U.S. Consulate in Kunming, he received a diplomatic posting in 1935, starting the State Department's Chinese language training course in Beijing. There, Service watched growing Japanese aggression culminating in the July 1937 Marco Polo Bridge Incident* that marked the official beginning of World War II in Asia. He also witnessed the formation of the United Front* of CCP and GMD forces to oppose the Japanese invasion of China*.

When the U.S. embassy relocated to Chongqing in 1941, Service accompanied the new ambassador, Clarence Gauss, who directed him to investigate and report on the political viability of the CCP and the GMD. After the U.S. declaration of war on Japan following the Pearl Harbor Attack*, his contacts with CCP liaisons and firsthand observations of the GMD persuaded him that the U.S. government needed to amend its policy of unconditional support for the corrupt and ineffective government of Jiang Jieshi* and to develop a relationship with the CCP leaders at the Communist headquarters in Yan'an. He soon was reassigned to work with General Joseph W. Stilwell*, commander of U.S. forces in China. After Washington approved his recommendation to send an observer mission to report firsthand information from Yan'an, Service accompanied the Dixie Mission* and interviewed top CCP leaders, including Mao Zedong*, from July to October 1944. Service reported favorably on the CCP's professed commitment to "democracy."

When Service returned to Chongqing, Stilwell had been recalled, Patrick J. Hurley* had arrived, and Gauss was preparing to resign. Hurley revived the policy of unconditional support for GMD and soon clashed with those who wanted to offer U.S. support to Jiang's government only if it showed progress in democratic reform and accepted a coalition with CCP representation. Now Ambassador Hurley accused these U.S. diplomats of harboring Communist sympathies that undermined official U.S. policy in China. Soon thereafter, Service's loyalty to the U.S. government was questioned when he became involved with Philip Jaffe, Communist sympathizer and publisher of *Amerasia*, who had printed in his journal sensitive, but unclassified, State Department reports Service provided. A Federal Bureau of Investigation probe of the *Amerasia* affair cleared Service of charges that he had violated the Espionage Act, but nevertheless, his career was tainted. When Hurley resigned in November 1945, he accused Service, and other China Hands*, of sabotaging U.S. China policy. The U.S. Senate investigated Service in December, and again he was cleared of all charges.

Suspicion regarding Service's loyalty to the U.S. government resurfaced several times early in the Cold War. A 1950 Senate investigation of charges Senator Joseph R. McCarthy* of Wisconsin made that Communists had infiltrated the State Department questioned Service and cleared him of any wrongdoing. A State Department Loyalty Security Board review subsequently found Service guilty of "willful disclosure of confidential information" and fired him in 1951. After several appeals of this decision, the Supreme Court ruled in Service's favor in 1958. The State Department reinstated Service and assigned him to the U.S. consulate in Liverpool, England. In 1962, he retired. Nearly ten years later, as the United States began negotiations with the People's Republic of China*, government officials and Cold War revisionist historians reevaluated Service's State Department record. His political analysis of the GMD was legitimized, and his foresight in advocating U.S. relations with the CCP leaders finally won praise.

J. W. Esherick (ed.), *Lost Chance in China: The World War II Despatches of John S. Service* (New York, 1974); E. J. Kahn, "Foresight, Nightmare, and Hindsight," *The New Yorker* (8 April 1972); J. S. Service, *The Amerasia Papers: Some Problems in the History of U.S.-China Relations* (Berkeley, CA, 1971); J. S. Service, "State Department Duty in China, the McCarthy Era, and After, 1933–1977," Oral History, The Bancroft Library, University of California at Berkeley, 1981.

Karen Garner

SEWARD, WILLIAM H. (1801–1872)

William Henry Seward was secretary of state under Abraham Lincoln and Andrew Johnson, working to expand U.S. interests in the Pacific and the Caribbean. As governor of New York from 1839 to 1843, he pushed for canals and railroads not only to tie the nation together, but to link East with West and ultimately with Asian markets, where he hoped as well to instill American values (including Christianity). A powerful Whig senator in 1853, Seward simultaneously opposed landed expansion southward for the slave states and pushed commercial expansion across the Pacific by proclaiming a "Seward Doctrine." "The empire of the seas alone is real empire," he proclaimed, and thus Asian markets would be "the prize," "the chief theatre of events in the world's great hereafter." Seward was the nineteenth-century prophet of U.S. power in East Asia. He was, however, a prophet without the necessary power during his lifetime. The slavery question paralyzed policy during the 1850s and took the nation into war. Seward and his new Republican Party nevertheless took advantage of the conflict to advance his vision. A transcontinental railway, a treaty to bring in Chinese laborers, tariffs to spur industry, homestead acts to settle the West—all were part of a plan that was later termed "continentalism," that is, developing the continent for both its wealth and so it could become a bridge to Asian markets.

After brilliantly serving Lincoln as wartime secretary of state until 1865, acting successfully to dissuade the European powers from intervening in the American Civil War, Seward hoped to realize his "doctrine." But President Andrew Johnson became a deadly enemy of congressional Republicans, and his plans were trapped in the political crossfire. He nevertheless set out to achieve a three-part policy. First, Seward sought naval bases in the Caribbean to control the eastern access to the long-dreamed-of gateway to the far Pacific, an isthmian canal. He also attempted to obtain sole U.S. rights to build a canal in Nicaragua. These moves fell victim to local or U.S. Senate opposition. Second, he tried to develop links across the Pacific. An attempt to tie Hawaii into the U.S. orbit with a reciprocity treaty failed (although a treaty in 1875 did exactly that). His strong support for the plan to lay telegraph cable through Alaska and Russia led to failure, but information gathered helped him achieve his greatest success, the purchase in 1867 of Alaska from a declining Russia for $7.2 million. As a friend observed, Alaska was a drawbridge to Asia. Third, Seward formulated tactics that shaped U.S. policies for the next half century: cooperation with European powers (instead of going it alone), and using force (instead of depending only on diplomacy or economic lures as Americans had in the 1840s.) He thus cooperated with European ships to blast open the Straits of Shimonoseki after Japan tried to close it in 1864. Historian Tyler Dennett claimed that after Seward, no basic principles were added to U.S. policy toward Asia.

T. Dennett, "Seward's Far Eastern Policy," *American Historical Review* (October 1922); E. N. Paolino, *The Foundations of American Empire: William Henry Seward and U.S. Foreign Policy* (Ithaca, NY, 1973); G. G. Van Deusen, *William Henry Seward* (New York, 1967); C. Vevier, "American Continentalism: An Idea of Expansionism, 1845–1910," *American Historical Review* (January 1960).

Walter LaFeber

SHANDONG AGREEMENT

The Shandong Agreement between China and Japan in February 1922, concluded outside but during the Washington Conference* of 1921 and 1922, resolved a long-standing and bitter dispute between the two nations. The American delegation, collaborating with its British counterpart, played a decisive role in brokering the deal, which removed the final roadblocks to the signing of the Nine Power Pact*, thereby ensuring the success of the conference and stabilizing international politics in East Asia. The dispute arose in 1914, when Japan entered World War I on the side of the Allies and seized the German sphere of influence in Shandong Province. In the Twenty-One Demands* of 1915, Tōkyō forced China to accept any settlement Japan made with Germany to dispose of German rights in Shandong. During 1917 and 1918, Japan extracted from China secret agreements confirming and expanding its rights in Shandong. Meanwhile, Japan secured pledges from Britain, France, and Russia in one of the Secret Treaties to support Japanese claims at the peace conference.

Japan therefore was in a strong position when the issue arose at the Versailles Peace Conference. Ignorant of the secret Sino-Japanese treaties, China's delegates argued for revocation of German rights. Japan's revelation of the agreements forced the dumbfounded and embarrassed Chinese delegation to turn to Woodrow Wilson* and the U.S. delegation to support the justice of its case. The U.S. delegation overwhelmingly backed the Chinese, and Wilson was sympathetic to China's plight. But convinced of the force of Japan's brief under international law and even more fearful that Japan would walk out and undermine the League of Nations, Wilson joined with Britain and France in agreeing to transfer Germany's rights to Shandong. The president did extract an oral Japanese pledge to return Chinese sovereignty to the province at some unspecified time. This promise was inadequate to satisfy rising nationalist sentiments in China, which burst forth in the May Fourth Movement*, and China's delegation refused to sign the peace treaty.

The Shandong decision also had severe repercussions in the United States. Public resentment against the decision fueled American opposition to the Versailles Peace Treaty* and contributed to its defeat in the Senate. In addition, Japan's pressure to force a weak China to accept its terms for return of the province increased tensions in the region. Finally, the failure to isolate the issue from the upcoming Washington Conference worried U.S. policy makers. Secretary of State Charles Evans Hughes* and British Foreign Secretary Arthur Balfour agreed to have their experts serve as friendly mediators and suggest compromises. Anglo-American intervention, combined with diplomatic pressure on Beijing and Tōkyō, resolved the central and thorny issue of the Shandong Railway, allowing Japan to retain a degree of control if the Chinese paid a Japanese loan and paved the way for return of the province to China.

R. Fifield, *Woodrow Wilson and the Far East: The Diplomacy of the Shantung Decision* (New York, 1952); A. W. Griswold, *The Far Eastern Policy of the United States* (New York, 1938); N. H. Pugach, "American Friendship for China and the Shantung Question at the Washington Conference," *Journal of American History* (June 1977).

Noel H. Pugach

SHANGHAI COMMUNIQUÉ

The Shanghai Communiqué, issued on 27 February 1972, symbolized the new rapprochement that President Richard M. Nixon* achieved between the United States and the People's Republic of China* (PRC) and laid the groundwork for U.S-PRC Normalization of Relations* in 1979 under President Jimmy Carter*. A striking aspect of the communiqué was that rather than omitting or glossing over contentious issues such as the Second Indochina War*, it acknowledged differences between Washington and Beijing and laid out the positions of both sides. This framework was agreed upon by Chinese Premier Zhou Enlai* and National Security Adviser Henry A. Kissinger* in Beijing in October 1971. Kissinger initially offered Zhou a conventional draft that papered over deep bilateral divisions, but Zhou rejected it out of hand and proposed a draft setting forth the PRC's positions on a number of issues with blank spaces for the U.S. positions. The approach became that of the communiqué, although many hours of negotiation were needed then before agreement on a mutually acceptable outline, and many more were required between Kissinger and Vice Minister Qiao Guanhua* during Nixon's Visit to China* before agreement was reached on the final document.

After setting forth divergent U.S. and Chinese positions on a number of issues, the communiqué stated the principles on which the United States and the PRC were in agreement. It declared that both nations were prepared to base their future relations on the principles of respect for sovereignty and territorial integrity, nonaggression, noninterference in the internal affairs of other states, equality and mutual benefit, and peaceful coexistence; that progress toward normalization of relations between China and the United States was in the interests of all countries, and that both sides would facilitate the development of people-to-people contacts and trade between the two nations. Although it did not mention the Soviet Union, it stressed the common strategic interests of the United States and China, declaring that both were opposed to efforts by any country or group of countries to establish hegemony in East Asia.

The most difficult issue was Taiwan*. After intense negotiations, the two sides agreed on a carefully crafted pair of statements. The Chinese statement reaffirmed the PRC's position that Taiwan was a province of China, that the liberation of Taiwan was an internal affair, and that all U.S. forces and military installations should be removed from Taiwan. The U.S. statement acknowledged that all Chinese on either side of the Taiwan Strait maintained that there was just one China and that Taiwan was a part of China. It declared that the U.S. government did not challenge that position. It reaffirmed U.S. interest in a peaceful settlement of the Taiwan question by the Chinese themselves and, "with this prospect in mind," affirmed the ultimate objective of the withdrawal of all U.S. forces and military installations from Taiwan. The United States, it declared, would reduce progressively its forces and installations on Taiwan as tension in the area diminished. The Shanghai Communiqué became the cornerstone of the future U.S.-PRC relationship. Its principles were reaffirmed in the Joint Communiqué of 15 December 1978, announcing the establishment of diplomatic relations between the two nations on 1 January 1979, in the Joint Communiqué of 17 August 1982 allowing for U.S. arms sales to Taiwan, and on numerous other occasions.

J. Holdridge, *Crossing the Divide: An Insider's Account of the Normalization of U.S. China Relations* (Lanham, MD, 1997); H. A. Kissinger, *White House Years* (Boston, 1979).

Harriet Dashiell Schwar

SHIBUSAWA EIICHI (1840–1931)

Widely regarded as the father of modern capitalism and entrepreneurism in Japan,

Shibusawa Eiichi was a leading proponent of reliance on the non-governmental organization (NGO) to improve U.S.-Japan relations before and after World War I. He was a staunchly antiforeign samurai in late Tokugawa, Japan before returning in 1868 from an inspection tour of Europe. Profoundly affected by his visit, he became a new convert to capitalism and commerce. The new Meiji government hired Shibusawa for his knowledge of Western commercial matters, and he entered the Finance Ministry in 1869, with Ōkuma Shigenobu* and Inoue Kaoru as his patrons in the government. In 1872, he became the vice minister of finance, but resigned in 1873, along with Minister Inoue, when the cabinet rejected their financial policies. Thereafter, Shibusawa started numerous joint stock companies, and promoted the establishment of chambers of commerce throughout the country. Upon his retirement in 1916 from active management of businesses, it was estimated that Shibusawa had started more than 500 companies. He also took a strong interest in establishing networks with his American and British counterparts. During his life, Shibusawa visited the United States and Europe four times, meeting with Presidents Theodore Roosevelt*, William Howard Taft*, and Woodrow Wilson*. He was the primary force behind various organizations designed to promote Japanese-American relations, including such NGOs as the Japanese-American Relations Committee, the Japan International Association, and the Japan Council of the Institute of Pacific Relations*, among others.

After his first trip to the United States in 1902, Shibusawa decided that an exchange of visits between chambers of commerce would be useful to ease growing tensions. The first American delegation visited Japan in 1908, and the return Japanese delegation went to the United States in 1909, with Shibusawa as head of the mission and most of the discussions centered on the immigration issue and tariff rates. The American-Japanese Treaty of 1911* can be attributed in part to Shibusawa's "business diplomacy." When California's legislature passed a law barring aliens from owning real estate for agricultural purposes in California in 1913, businessmen in Japan and the United States established the Japanese-American Emergency Society to mount an organized protest. Shibusawa was elected president of the NGO. After his third trip to the United States in 1915, he formed, in response to encouragement from various sources, including President Wilson, Theodore Roosevelt, and Frank Vanderlip, the permanent Japanese-American Relations Committee to promote cooperative business ventures in China. In 1921, a delegation of Japanese businessmen visited the United States and Britain. Shibusawa was initially appointed to head the mission, but his differences with the Foreign Ministry about the role of businessmen in diplomacy resulted in the head of the Mitsui *Zaibatsu** replacing him as chief representative.

Shibusawa believed that businessmen should be active in promoting amicable U.S.-Japan relations, especially supporting the League of Nations and arms reduction. In contrast, most of the younger generation of businessmen agreed with the Foreign Ministry position that businessmen should stick to specific economic issues, and leave general U.S.-Japan relations to the diplomats. Shibusawa stayed in New York during the Washington Conference* and received daily updates. But a generational change was under way in the 1920s among business leaders in Japan, as well as in the United States, as those who had helped Shibusawa form networks began to pass away. His declining political influence in Japan in the latter half of the 1920s, combined with his advanced age, meant that despite the strain in Japanese-American relations triggered by the anti-Japanese immigration law passed in California in 1924, Shibusawa spent less time on "business diplomacy" projects than on such undertakings as the exchange of dolls promoted by Sidney L. Gulick* and the Japan International Children's Friendship Society. He managed to convince himself that such exchanges would improve Japanese-American relations. Upon Shibusawa's death, Sakatani Yoshirō*, his son-in-law, and Ishii Kikujirō* took over as the leaders of the Japanese-American Relations Committee. His vision of U.S.-Japan relations based on networks of businessmen continued to exist after his death, but changes in the political context and the perceptions of younger industrialists guaranteed that his "business diplomacy" would not wield the same influence as it had in the 1920s.

J. Hirschmeier, "Shibusawa Eiichi: Industrial Pioneer," in W. W. Lockwood (ed.), *The State and Economic Enterprise in Japan* (Princeton, NJ, 1965); M. Kimura, *Shibusawa Eiichi-minkan keizai gaikō no sōshisha* [Shibusawa Eiichi—The Pioneer of Private Business Diplomacy] (Tōkyō, 1991); K. Obata, *An Interpretation of the Life of Viscount Shibusawa* (Tōkyō, 1937).

Hyung Gu Lynn

SHIDEHARA KIJŪRŌ (1872–1951)

As Japanese Foreign Minister from 1924 to 1927 and 1929 to 1931, Shidehara Kijūrō was most noted for his conciliatory foreign policy toward the West and China in the 1920s. A product of Japan's small core of career diplomats trained in the 1890s, he served as ambassador to the United States (1919–1922) as well as delegate to the Washington Conference* (1921–1922). Although a supporter of Japan's imperial position in Asia, he was despised by Japan's army and navy as the spokesman for the Europe-U.S. faction, as opposed to the Asia faction, in the Foreign Ministry. He was deemed naive and even traitorous for his support of the Washington treaties, his failure to protest Anglo-American racist immigration policies, his restraint in dealing with Jiang Jieshi* during his Northern Expedition, and, most notably, his approval of the treaty negotiated at the London Naval Conference of 1930*.

Shidehara often has been contrasted incorrectly with his rival Tanaka Giichi* regarding appropriate policies in dealing with the West and China (a matter of degree rather than substance). "Shidehara diplomacy" ultimately fell victim to conditions created by the Great Depression, army and navy attacks, mass politics, and the impact of the Mukden Incident* in September 1931. Efforts to conciliate China, the League of Nations, and the United States led to his fall that December. One of the great ironies of the ensuing Pacific war was the fact that the "New Order" of Tōjō Hideki*, based on the principle of "coexistence and coprosperity," borrowed its phraseology, but not its content, from Shidehara's diplomacy of the 1920s. In the wake of Japan's surrender in 1945, Shidehara was named prime minister during the U.S. Occupation of Japan* and served from October 1945 to April 1946. Thereafter, despite his vehement opposition, the "radical," in Shidehara's opinion, Japanese Constitution of 1947* became law. The real power in postwar Japan lay with Yoshida Shigeru*, although historian Peter Duus has labeled Yoshida foreign policy a "latter day variant of Shidehara diplomacy."

M. A. Barnhart, *Japan and the World Since 1868* (New York, 1995); P. Duus, *The Rise of Modern Japan* (New York, 1976); A. Iriye, *Power and Culture: The Japanese-American War, 1941–1945* (Cambridge, MA, 1981).

Errol M. Clauss

SHIGEMITSU MAMORU (1887–1957)

A high-ranking senior career diplomat before World War II and a prominent politician in the postwar period, Shigemitsu Mamoru served four times as Japan's foreign minister. He was generally viewed as a moderate, pragmatic member of the group in the Japanese foreign ministry favoring good relations with the United States and Britain after 1920. Following graduation from Tōkyō Imperial University, he entered the Foreign Ministry in 1911 and thereafter was posted to virtually all the major political capitals of the world. Shigemitsu quickly impressed his superiors with his intellectual skill and diplomatic acumen as part of the Japanese delegation at the Versailles Peace Conference in 1919. From 1925 to 1933, except for a year in Berlin, he was stationed in China. Shigemitsu then served as vice minister of foreign affairs, ambassador to the Soviet Union, and, replacing Yoshida Shigeru* ambassador to Britain. In December 1941, he became ambassador to the Guomindang* (Nationalist) government in China, but in April was recalled to Tōkyō to become foreign minister in the cabinets of Tōjō Hideki* and Koiso Kuniaki. After resigning in April 1945, Shigemitsu was recalled on 17 August to lead Japan's diplomatic establishment in the last wartime cabinet, in which capacity he presented the Japanese surrender on board the USS *Missouri* in Tōyō Bay. His selection for this task reflected his extensive contacts with British and U.S. diplomats, and also indirectly his well-known disagreements in the 1930s with Japan's militarists, as he favored a more liberal China policy, as well as a strategy of cooperation, rather than rivalry with London and Washington. Shigemitsu's loss of a leg in an abortive assassination attempt carried out by Korean exile leader Kim Gu* in Shanghai in 1932 to some extent had insulated him from military criticism and bolstered his popular reputation at home.

Despite his moderate reputation, Shigemitsu was a defendant at the Tōkyō War Crimes Trials* in 1946 and after conviction, sentenced to seven years' imprisonment as a Class-A war criminal. After U.S. adoption of the Reverse Course*, he was paroled in November 1950 and finally depurged in March 1952, just before the U.S. Occupation of Japan* ended. Shigemitsu then moved rather rapidly to rebuild his political influence through close association with conservative politicians and former bureaucrats, such as Kishi Nobusuke* and Nomura Kichisaburō* in the Japan Reconstruction League (Nihon Saiken Renmei), as well as his presidency of the Kaishintō (Progressive) Party. His policy preferences reflected the practical realism of a professional diplomat, in particular his support for Japan's rearmament in opposition to Liberal Party leader and Prime Minister Yoshida Shigeru. Arguably, Shigemitsu's forthright views facilitated the important 1953 compromise agreement with Yoshida, establishing the legitimacy of using Japan's defense forces to repel external aggression, a task that went beyond the then limited role of combating internal subversion. Later, in 1954, creation of the Self-Defense Forces provided a formal structure for Japan's defense establishment.

Shigemitsu's outspokenness on the rearmament issue reflected his tendency to minimize or at times overlook the public relations and personal dimension of day-to-day politics. This fact, perhaps more than any other, explained his failure to become prime minister. While leader of the Progressive Party, he was sharply criticized by younger Kaishintō members for ignoring the interests of the rank and file. Similarly, as foreign minister under Hatoyama Ichirō* from 1955 to 1956, he frequently found himself at odds both with colleagues and with the prime minister. In August 1955, for example, on a visit to Washington to persuade Secretary of State John Foster Dulles* to consider revising the U.S.-Japan Security Treaty of 1951*, Shigemitsu surprised his American negotiating partners by announcing that Japanese forces could be deployed abroad to assist U.S. forces in the event of a security crisis. This statement, in light of the prohibition in the Japanese Constitution of 1947* on the use of force for anything other than defensive purposes, not only ignited a storm of controversy among public and press opinion in Japan, but also drew private criticism from his senior colleagues. Kishi and Kōno Ichirō, for example, happily pointed out to the Americans during an August meeting that Shigemitsu's views were misguided and entirely out of line with cabinet thinking in Tōkyō. A similar pattern of isolation emerged during the Soviet-Japan normalization talks of 1955 and 1956. Such disagreements signaled not only his political marginalization, but also the tendency of Japanese decision making at this point to be shaped more by personal and factional rivalries, rather than national interests, which would be a source of irritation and frustration for the Eisenhower administration in dealing with Japan in the 1950s.

M. Shigemitsu, *Japan and Her Destiny* (London, 1958); M. Schaller, *Altered States: The United States and Japan Since the Occupation* (New York, 1997); J. Welfield, *An Empire in Eclipse: Japan in the Postwar American Alliance System* (Atlantic Highlands, NJ, 1988).

John Swenson-Wright

SHUFELDT, ROBERT W. (1822–1895)

Commodore Robert W. Shufeldt helped to propel the United States into East Asia in the 1880s through negotiating a treaty opening Korea, staging a world cruise, working for an isthmian canal and commercial development, and designing the new U.S. steel navy. Born in Red Hook, New York, he attended Middlebury College from 1837 to 1839, but entered the navy before graduating. Shufeldt served on a number of ships before resigning in 1854 to become a merchant steamship captain and working with several business visionaries trying to secure a transit road across the isthmus of Tehuantepec. When the Civil War was six months old, Secretary of State William H. Seward* appointed him consul general at Havana, where he reported on Confederate shipping and France's military intervention in Mexico. In 1863, Shufeldt resigned to rejoin the U.S. Navy, commanding the USS *Miantonomoh* and the USS *Proteus*. After the Civil War, he became captain of the USS *Wachusett* on the Yangze River, where he monitored American vessels dealing in opium and the Coolie Trade*. In 1867, while investigating the *General Sherman* Incident* on the west coast of Korea, he supported annexation of Korea's Nan Hoo islands. From 1870 to 1871, he led a U.S. Navy survey for an interoceanic canal across Tehuantepec, arguing that this would stimulate a U.S. presence in the Pacific. In 1875, Shufeldt became chief of the Bureau of Equipment and Recruiting, encouraging better pay and working conditions for sailors. He also urged the revival of U.S. commerce, especially exports, and preached that the U.S. Navy and merchant marine were "joint apostles" and "pioneers of commerce."

From 1878 to 1880, with the full backing of both Secretary of the Navy Richard W. Thompson and Secretary of State William M. Evarts*, Shufeldt took the powerful steam corvette USS *Ticonderoga* on a world cruise "with a view to the encouragement and extension of American Commerce." The circumnavigation covered 35,000 miles and anchored at forty-three ports in European colonial possessions on both African coasts, Zanzibar and Muscat, Aden, the Persian Gulf, India, and the Malay peninsula, ending in Japan, Korea, China, and Hawaii. He filed voluminous reports on the commercial opportunities of all ports visited, and called for a greatly expanded consulate service for Africa. He renewed existing treaties with Liberia, Muscat, and Zanzibar, and negotiated new treaties with two Madagascan chiefs and the sultan of the Comorro Islands. His most important task, however, was opening Korea to U.S. influence and trade. In spring 1880, Shufeldt gained letters of introduction to Korean authorities from Inoue Kaoru, Japanese minister for foreign affairs, who also provided charts of the Korean coasts. In Korea, he encountered an initial and natural assumption that war existed with the United States after the ill-fated expedition Frederick F. Low* initiated in 1871. Korea's minister of ceremony brusquely said that Koreans never would consent to a treaty with the country that had made war.

Undaunted, Shufeldt next visited Li Hongzhang*, the powerful viceroy of Zhili, with whom he consulted on Korean and naval matters before returning to the

United States in November 1880. When Secretary of State James G. Blaine authorized him to negotiate a Korean treaty, he returned to China and negotiated the Shufeldt Treaty* to open Korea from November 1881 to May 1882. Toward the end of the negotiations, he became impatient over delays, occasioned by Li's constant need to consult the large Korean mission and officials of the Zongli Yamen*. The commodore wrote a letter to Senator Aaron A. Sargent of California damning China as decadent, and the empress as "an ignorant, capricious and immoral woman." He argued that force was the only solution to use. Realizing its value in the politics of Chinese exclusion in California, Sargent published it in the San Francisco *Bulletin* in March 1882. The resultant storm of criticism in the United States almost terminated his career in the U.S. Navy, and damaged his health, but his treaty eventually was ratified on 9 January 1883. After the storm died down, Shufeldt was named president of the Second Naval Advisory Board. Here, he superintended designs and contracts for the U.S. Navy's first all-steel vessels, *Atlanta, Boston, Chicago*, and *Dolphin*. After retiring in 1884, Shufeldt lived in Nagasaki, Japan, where he preached a gospel of commercial expansion in Asia and Africa, and Hawaiian Annexation* once an isthmian canal was built. After the Republicans regained the presidency, he returned to the United States in 1889 and was offered the post of minister to China, but declined. He then lived in Arlington, Virginia. *See also* Angell Treaty.

F. C. Drake, *The Empire of the Seas: A Biography of Rear Admiral Robert Wilson Shufeldt, USN* (Honolulu, HI, 1984); K. J. Hagan, *American Gunboat Diplomacy and the Old Navy, 1877–1889* (Westport, CT, 1973); A. S. Hickey, "Rear Admiral Robert Wilson Shufeldt, United States Navy, Gentleman and Diplomat," *United States Naval Institute Proceedings* (1943); D. Long, *Gold Braid and Foreign Relations: Diplomatic Activities of U.S. Naval Officers 1798–1883* (Annapolis, MD, 1988); C. O. Paullin, "The Opening of Korea by Commodore Shufeldt," *Political Science Quarterly* (1910); R. W. Shufeldt, *The Relation of the Navy to the Commerce of the United States* (1878).

Frederick C. Drake

SHUFELDT TREATY (22 May 1882)

This agreement, the first between Korea and a Western nation, plunged the United States into the rivalry for control of that nation involving Russia, Japan, and China toward the end of the nineteenth century. Koreans also pointed to it later to justify charges of U.S. betrayal when Washington sanctioned Japanese Annexation of Korea* in the Taft-Katsura Agreement* and Root-Takahira Agreement*. Commodore Robert W. Shufeldt* set the stage for the treaty when he visited Japan and then China in the spring of 1880. He met with Li Hongzhang*, the powerful viceroy of Zhili, who, after Shufeldt returned to the United States, offered to make him a grand admiral in the Chinese Navy. Shufeldt returned to China, but also came authorized to negotiate a treaty to open Korea, an objective he had pursued since he investigated the *General Sherman* Incident* on Korea's west coast in 1867. Despite Li extending considerable social and military courtesies to Shufeldt, accompanying him on tours of inspection of forts and naval vessels, and lavishing attention on his adopted daughter (and niece) Molly Miller, who was Shufeldt's social hostess, the commodore was caught between the competing Chinese and Japanese efforts to control Korea, and the power struggle in the Korean court, which sometimes deadlocked decision making. Eventually, the intervention of King Kojong* in favor of negotiations would lead to a Korean envoy and a seventy-man trading mission proceeding to Tianjin to discuss the possibility of a treaty with the United States. Secretary of State James G. Blaine sent new instructions authorizing Shufeldt to negotiate, and Shufeldt worked with Li over the next six months to draft a treaty under the watchful eyes of the foreign legations at Tianjin.

Both Li Hongzhang and Yixin*, head of the Chinese Zongli Yamen*, wanted an article inserted into the U.S.-Korean treaty indicating that "Chosen" (Korea) was a dependency of China. When Shufeldt requested guidance from Blaine's successor, Secretary of State Frederick T. Frelinghuysen* remained silent, but Shufeldt continued negotiations. After completion at Tianjin, he took the treaty to Korea for signing on 22 May 1882, escorted by Chinese warships of Li's north naval squadron. The agreement omitted the "dependency clause," but was accompanied by an exchange of letters between Kojong and President Chester A. Arthur affirming it. It permitted U.S. citizens to trade and erect residences and warehouses in the open ports; set a tariff of 10 percent on necessities, 30 percent on luxuries and 5 percent on exports; guaranteed rights to victims of shipwrecks; provided for diplomatic and consular representatives; prohibited the opium trade; and granted the United States extraterritorial jurisdiction and most-favored-nation privileges. Most important, the United States promised to extend its "good offices" if Korea became involved in a dispute with another country. Thereafter, a succession of American diplomats, beginning with Lucius H. Foote* as the first U.S. ambassador, asserted that Korea was independent of China. This accorded with Japanese sentiments at the time in supporting elements of the Korean court resisting Chinese claims of suzerainty. It also led the United States and Japan to cooperate in resisting Li's doomed attempts to keep Korea within the Chinese orbit. *See also* Horace N. Allen; George C. Foulke.

H. G. Appenzeller, "The Opening of Korea: Admiral Shufeldt's Account of It," *Korean Repository* (1892); F. C. Drake, *The Empire of the Seas: A Biography of Rear Admiral Robert Wilson Shufeldt, USN* (Honolulu, HI, 1984); C. I. E. Kim and H. K. Kim, *Korea and the Politics of Imperialism, 1876–1910* (Berkeley, CA, 1967); Y. Lee, *Diplomatic Relations Between the United States and Korea, 1866–1887* (New York, 1970); D. Long, *Gold Braid and Foreign Relations: Diplomatic Activities of U.S. Naval Officers 1798–1883* (Annapolis, MD, 1988); M. F. Nelson, *Korea and the Old Orders in Eastern Asia* (Baton Rouge, LA, 1946).

Frederick C. Drake

SIAN INCIDENT

See XIAN INCIDENT

SIBERIAN INTERVENTION

The subject of continuing controversy among historians, this was the effort of British, American, French, and Japanese troops after World War I to halt the territorial gains of the new Bolshevik government in Russian East Asia and northern Manchuria. When the fledgling Soviet government withdrew from World War I and under the Treaty of Brest-Litovsk (March 1918) ceded sizeable amounts of territory to Germany, this prompted Allied and Japanese forces to deploy troops in Siberia in support of the anti-Bolshevik "Whites," who had promised to reopen the eastern front if victorious. President Woodrow Wilson* sent 5,000 American troops to Murmansk and 10,000 to Siberia, but only under great pressure from the Allies and out of fear of unilateral Japanese action. Wilson portrayed American involvement as a humanitarian effort to rescue about 70,000 Czechoslovak troops, who had fought with Russian troops during World War I and were now fleeing eastward toward the Pacific. European and U.S. troops withdrew in June 1920 after White Russian troops under Admiral Aleksander Vasilievich Kolchak were defeated by the Red Army. About 70,000 Japanese troops continued fighting against the Soviet-sponsored Far Eastern Republic*. They were withdrawn in response to rising domestic opposition to continuing losses and high costs, as well as Anglo-American pressure on Japan at the Washington Conference*.

L. C. Gardner, *Safe for Democracy: Anglo-American Response to Revolution, 1913–1923* (New York, 1984); G. F. Kennan, *Russia and the West Under Lenin and Stalin* (New York, 1961); B. M. Unterberger, *America's Siberian Expedition, 1918–1920: A Study of National Policy* (Durham, NC, 1956); J. A. White, *The Siberian Intervention* (New York, 1969); W. A. Williams, *America Confronts a Revolutionary World, 1776–1976* (New York, 1976).

Eileen Scully

SIHANOUK, NORODOM (1922–)

During the Second Indochina War*, Norodom Sihanouk struggled as the leader of Cambodia* to shield his country from full involvement in the fighting, until he was overthrown early in 1970. When King Monivong died on 23 April 1941, the French replaced him with Sihanouk, whose great-grandfather as king had grudgingly signed the documents in 1863 that made Cambodia a French protectorate. After World War II, he allowed a relatively democratic system to exist, but in 1952, he moved against his opponents and thereafter closely controlled Cambodia's political life. At the same time, Sihanouk began to oppose French Colonialism* and demand independence. U.S. officials feared his nationalistic tirades might increase Communist influence. But on 9 November 1953, Sihanouk signed an accord that gave Cambodia substantial independence. French influence further eroded after the Geneva Conference of 1954*. The United States, which had recognized Sihanouk's government in 1950, now sent an ambassador to Phnom Penh. In 1955, he resigned as king and for the next fifteen years, controlled Cambodian politics through the new Sangkum Reastre Niyum (Popular Socialist Community). In foreign policy, Prince Sihanouk pursued a nonaligned course, turning to France and the United States for military aid, but courting the Soviet Union and the People's Republic of China* (PRC) as well.

The United States disliked Sihanouk's contacts with Communist countries, but the prince had broad popular support and the absolute loyalty of the military. Seeing no alternatives, and pleased that he often suppressed leftists at home, U.S. diplomats recommended U.S. support for his government. The Central Intelligence Agency*, however, apparently assisted Cambodian dissidents. Relations between the United States and Sihanouk began deteriorating in 1962, just as the war in neighboring Vietnam was intensifying. In November 1963, Sihanouk stopped accepting American assistance. In 1964, he organized a violent demonstration at the U.S. embassy; the next year, a similar incident preceded a complete break in diplomatic relations that May. Sihanouk was especially angry at numerous attacks on Cambodian border villages by the Army of the Republic of Vietnam* and U.S. forces who were pursuing Viet Cong*. After the break in relations, he also accused the Americans and South Vietnamese of dropping poisonous chemicals on parts of Cambodia. At the same time, Sihanouk let it be known that he would not protest hot pursuit of the Viet Cong into Cambodia, provided only that the Republic of Vietnam* apologize and pay compensation for injuries. Whether he tacitly approved Operation MENU*, the secret bombing of Cambodian border regions beginning in 1969, remains a matter of bitter dispute.

By the end of 1968, Sihanouk's rule was increasingly fragile, even though he had restored relations with the United States. In March 1970, General Lon Nol* and Prince Sisowath Sirik Matak ousted him. U.S. intelligence services may have played some role in the overthrow. Deeply angered at the coup, Sihanouk joined forces with the Khmer Rouge*, his most bitter enemy, knowing, as he once put it, that he would be spit out like a cherry pit when he was no longer found useful. Sihanouk served as a figurehead and urged Cambodians to defect to the opposition. In April 1975, the Khmer Rouge, under Pol Pot*, gained power and began to turn Cambodia into a giant slave labor camp. Sihanouk returned to Phnom Penh in September, a virtual prisoner of the Khmer Rouge until the Vietnamese invaded early in 1979. Several members of Sihanouk's own family, including six of his children, died at the hands of the Khmer Rouge. But Sihanouk was part of the Khmer Rouge's delegation to the United Nations when he came to New York in January 1979 and sought and received the protection of the U.S. government. Not able to get satisfactory terms for asylum in either the United States or France, Sihanouk returned to China, where he remained until 1991.

Sihanouk deeply disliked the People's Republic of Kampuchea (PRK), under Hun Sen* and Heng Samrin*, which he considered to be a Vietnamese puppet state. Unwilling to support the remnants of the Khmer Rouge, he founded the National United Front for an Independent, Neutral, and Cooperative Cambodia. At the urging of the PRC, the Association of Southeast Asian Nations*, and the United States, Sihanouk's new resistance movement and other non-Communist groups joined the Khmer Rouge to form the Coalition Government of Democratic Kampuchea to counter the PRK in 1982. Complex negotiations involving the major world and regional powers finally resulted in a peace settlement in Cambodia in 1991, thanks in good part to Sihanouk's personal intervention. After elections in 1993, he engineered a new coalition government. On 21 September, the new National Assembly adopted a constitution that once again made him king, although without formal political power. In fragile health, Sihanouk retained influence, but spent much of his time in China.

D. Chandler, *The Tragedy of Cambodian History: Politics, War and Revolution Since 1945* (New Haven, CT, 1991); A. Issacs, *Without Honor: Defeat in Vietnam and Cambodia* (Baltimore, 1983); B. Kiernan, *How Pol Pot Came to Power* (London, 1985); M. Osborne, *Sihanouk: Prince of Light, Prince of Darkness* (Honolulu, HI, 1994); N. Sihanouk, as related to W. Burchett, *My War with the CIA: The Memoirs of Prince Norodom Sihanouk* (New York, 1972); W. Shawcross, *Sideshow: Kissinger, Nixon, and the Destruction of Cambodia* (New York, 1979).

Kenton J. Clymer

SINGAPORE

Located at the strategic tip of the Malay Peninsula at the entrance to the Malacca Strait, Singapore was once part of the sea-borne Srivijava Empire. Beginning in the tenth century, a commercial network slowly developed, linking the Chinese Empire on the Asian continent to Southeast Asia, a region subsequently known to the Chinese as Nanyang, or the Southern Sea. During the centuries that followed, many Chinese moved to that region and formed a number of enclaves where the Chinese populace outnumbered the natives. Singapore was one of these Chinese enclaves in Southeast Asia. Since the fifteenth century, the coming of the West has further added multicultural dimensions. A rivalry between the Netherlands and Britain ensued for control of the territory of what became Malaysia*, of which Singapore was a part. With the English prevailing, Malaysia became a British colony. After the two world wars, the British grip over its overseas colonies was significantly weakened and eventually challenged. In 1957, Malaysia won independence from British rule, but suffered from the problem of a multiethnic society after Britain's control was removed. Because the conflict between ethnic Chinese and Malays turned out to be irreconcilable, Singapore, the largest Chinese enclave, withdrew from Malaysia and became an independent city-state.

The majority of Singapore's 3 million people are ethnic Chinese. Many of these Chinese maintain close contact with their relatives or families elsewhere in the world, particularly the People's Republic of China* (PRC), Taiwan*, Hong Kong*, and the United States. On the other hand, the legacy of British Colonialism* well prepared the nation for full membership in the Western world. Culturally located between the Chinese and Western worlds, Singapore's foreign policy inevitably affected relations between the West and China, and especially U.S.-China relations. The role of Singapore in Sino-American relations became more important after it emerged as a newly industrialized nation with its per capita gross national product amounting to $14,210 in 1993, second only to Japan in East Asia. After independence, Singapore remained a major business partner of Taiwan and Hong Kong. After the PRC's Four Modernizations* started in late 1970s, Singapore became one of the major sources of foreign investment in China, and its economy became increasingly tied to China's market. Singapore thus occupied a key position to influence the course of the PRC's relations with the Western nations.

Singapore's influence is particularly sensible in the PRC-Taiwan–United States triangular relationship, a major problem area in Washington's relations with Beijing. Sharing the same cultural roots, but spared from political alignment between the two sides of the Taiwan Strait, Singapore served as the natural mediator in the incessant bickering between Beijing and Taibei. Lee Kuan Yew*, the long-term leader of Singapore, frequently flew back and forth between the mainland and Taiwan, talking the leaders of the two sides out of confrontation and into cooperation. Singapore thus achieved some goals of U.S. foreign policy that the Americans themselves failed to achieve. *See also* Association of Southeast Asian Nations.

C. Mackerras (ed.), *East and Southeast Asia* (Boulder, CO, 1995); M. Yahuda, *The International Politics of the Asia-Pacific, 1945–1995* (New York, 1996).

Li Yi

SINO-JAPANESE PEACE TREATY OF 1952

This treaty was signed on 28 April 1952 between the Republic of China (ROC) and Japan, and became effective on 5 August 1952. It fulfilled Tokyo's pledge in the Yoshida Letter* to the United States to recognize the government of Jiang Jieshi* on Taiwan*, rather than the People's Republic of China* (PRC). The Allies had not been able to conclude a peace treaty with Japan because of disagreements on terms among the occupation powers and inside the Truman administration. Before the start of the Korean War*, Japanese discontent with the prolonged U.S. Occupation of Japan* forced Washington to accelerate the peacemaking process to ensure that Japan would be its ally in the Cold War. In May 1950, President Harry S. Truman* appointed John Foster Dulles* as a special assistant to Secretary of State Dean G. Acheson* to undertake the task of negotiating an agreement, resulting in fifty-one nations signing the Japanese Peace Treaty* at San Francisco on 8 September 1951. China, despite being a member of the Grand Alliance and having fought the longest against Japan, was excluded because the United States and Britain disagreed about whether the Guomindang* (Nationalist) government of the ROC or the Communist government of the PRC should sign the treaty for China.

In June 1951, after prolonged debate, Dulles finally reached a compromise with British Foreign Minister Herbert S. Morrison on the China problem in making peace with Japan. The Dulles-Morrison agreement stipulated that Japan would renounce all title and claim to Taiwan, but without specifying to whom it was relinquishing these rights, thereby leaving open the question of the island's legal status. It also excluded both Chinas from the multilateral treaty and allowed Japan to conclude a bilateral peace agreement with the Chinese government it chose after regaining sovereignty. The ROC government was bitterly disappointed at this outcome because it had led the fight against Japan in China for eight years, and now its legitimacy was to be decided by its defeated enemy. It urged Washington to press Japan to conclude promptly a bilateral treaty with the ROC.

Dulles, however, seized this opportunity to push the ROC to devise a formula confining the scope of a bilateral treaty to territories under its actual control. Fearing that Japan might otherwise sign an accord with the PRC, Taibei hesitantly proposed that the treaty apply to "all territories which are now and may hereafter be under the actual control of either High Contracting Party." Dulles relied on this "self-restraining" clause to persuade a reluctant British government to acquiesce in Japan's signing a bilateral peace treaty with the ROC. He then pushed a similarly reluctant Japan to conclude a treaty of limited scope with Taibei.

Sino-Japanese peace treaty negotiations started on 20 February 1952 and lasted for more than two months, a very long time for a pact that in theory merely would parallel the San Francisco Peace Treaty. Tōkyō's efforts to avoid first the "name" then the "essence" of a "peace treaty" stalled and nearly wrecked the talks. Although Taibei repeatedly appealed for Washington's help, it was not until a few days before the San Francisco agreement came into force that the latter finally put pressure on Tōkyō to conclude a treaty with the ROC. Exploiting its leverage, Tōkyō still forced Taibei to make final concessions, most importantly that the treaty's scope would apply only to the ROC. Moreover, reparations were mentioned in the protocol alone, where the ROC waived all its claims on service reparations. On the surface, the Sino-Japanese Peace Treaty appeared to constitute a triumph of Cold War ideology over reality. But critics ignored the pragmatism of Dulles in restricting the ROC's jurisdiction and paving the way for a Two China Policy*. Indeed, the formula that defined the treaty's scope was the ROC government's first self-proclaimed legal restriction on its own jurisdiction. At the time when the two Chinese governments were contending for legitimacy of rule over "all China" through international recognition, this clause had great significance because it indicated not only Washington's, but also Taibei's pragmatism amidst the anti-Communist extremism that seemed to dictate the policies of both nations.

S. Chang, "The United States and the Long-Term Disposition of Taiwan in the Making of Peace with Japan, 1952–1952," *Asian Profile* (October 1988); S. Miyasato, "John Foster Dulles and the Peace Settlement with Japan," in Richard H. Immerman (ed.), *John Foster Dulles and the Diplomacy of the Cold War* (Princeton, NJ, 1990); H. B. Schonberger, "Peacemaking in Asia: The United States, Great Britain, and the Japanese Decision to Recognize Nationalist China, 1951–1952," *Diplomatic History* (Winter 1986).

Chang Su-Ya

SINO-SOVIET TREATY OF FRIENDSHIP AND ALLIANCE (15 February 1950)

The Sino-Soviet Pact of 15 February 1950 created a bilateral defense commitment, settled historic territorial issues between China and the Soviet Union, and initiated a modest program of Soviet aid to the People's Republic of China* (PRC). The treaty was to remain in force for thirty years. On 16 December 1949, Chinese Communist leader Mao Zedong* made his first trip abroad to Moscow. He stayed there for more than two months, during which he negotiated with Soviet leader Joseph Stalin on the terms of a Sino-Soviet treaty of friendship. In ideology, Mao already had joined the Soviet-led Communist bloc. But Stalin was suspicious of Mao, fearing that Mao would not submit to his dictation. His view did not change until the PRC sent troops to fight in the Korean War* in October 1950.

The major objective of the treaty was to establish a Sino-Soviet alliance to counterbalance the Japanese-American anti-Communist bloc in East Asia. Article 1 stipulated that the treaty was to prevent the rebirth of aggression and imperialism on the part of Japan "or any other state which would unite with Japan directly or any other form in acts of aggression." Despite Mao's weak negotiating position, some of the terms followed China's requests. Article 5 provided that Sino-Soviet economic and cultural cooperation should be developed in conformity with the "principles of equality, mutual interests, and also mutual respect for state sovereignty and territorial integrity and noninterference in the internal affairs of the other party." These were what Beijing later called the Five Principles of Peaceful Coexistence.

The Sino-Soviet treaty was short-lived. The first ideological conflict came in 1956 when new Soviet Communist leader Nikita Khrushchev issued the "secret report" to the Communist Party of the Soviet Union Congress, denouncing Stalin as a dictator. Other conflicts between the two Communist giants emerged on issues of foreign policy. In the early 1960s, Moscow withdrew its experts in China, unilaterally ended bilateral contracts, and canceled projects of scientific and technological cooperation. The Chinese openly criticized the Soviets of being anti-Marxist-Leninist revisionists. The denouement of the treaty came when armed conflicts between the two countries broke out in the border areas along the Ussuri River in 1969. On 3 April 1979, the PRC government declared that the treaty would expire without renewal.

H. L. Boorman et al., *Moscow-Peking Axis: Strength and Strains* (New York, 1957); O. Edmund Clubb, *China and Russia: The "Great Game"* (New York, 1971).

Song Yuwu

SIX POWER CONSORTIUM

The Six Power Consortium was an international banking agency, organized in 1912 and lasting in theory until 1920, to pool, float, and monopolize loans for Chinese economic modernization and development. It was designed to promote international financial cooperation in China after the Chinese Revolution of 1911* to minimize political-financial conflict among the great powers in East Asia and the growing tendency to harden and expand the spheres of influence. The powers also expected that their nationals would secure lucrative contracts to construct railroads, exploit mineral wealth, and create various enterprises. Meanwhile, the foreign powers would impose supervisory controls on the weak and vulnerable Chinese government to ensure effective expenditure of loan proceeds and the payment of interest and principal of the bonds issued by foreign banking groups.

In seeking entry into the consortium, the United States accepted the tenets of early twentieth-century finance capitalism. But in the eyes of U.S. leaders, Dollar Diplomacy* was also a device to preserve and strengthen the Open Door Policy* to advance legitimate commercial interests while upholding China's integrity and independence. Nevertheless, it was an admission by the administration of President William Howard Taft* that the United States lacked the strength and experience in China to act independently and, specifically, that its brash offensive against Japan and Russia under the guise of the Knox Neutralization Scheme* had failed miserably.

In effect, Washington returned to the cooperative approach that it had pursued when it demanded, and eventually gained, admission to the Anglo-French-German combination that had won the right to construct the Huguang Railways in central and South China. In 1911, the United States offered to broaden that banking combination by having the American Group (of four Wall Street banks) share its concession to issue a combined loan for national currency reform and Manchurian development. But U.S. leaders hoped to exclude Japan and Russia and, in fact, use the loan to penetrate their spheres in Manchuria.

The agreement was concluded in 1912, but the United States had to pay a heavy price. First, both Japan and Russia secured membership in the Six Power Consortium, because of the support of their British and French allies, which also were prepared to carry their share of any loans. Second, Manchuria was excluded from the purview of the consortium. Third, American bankers lost their bid to float a portion of their shares on European exchanges. Finally, the economic nature of a Chinese loan was abandoned as a consequence of the weakness of the Chinese Republic. Instead, the Reorganization Loan, issued in 1913 without U.S. participation, was frankly a political loan to maintain China's provisional president, Yuan Shikai*, in power.

These developments made the American bankers reluctant to continue in the consortium. The Wilson administration settled the matter when it refused to support the Reorganization Loan on the grounds that it encroached on China's administrative integrity and independence. But it was also disturbed that the United States had lost control over the consortium and, breaking from the cooperative approach, believed that Americans could do better by acting independently in China. That assumption proved to be erroneous. Instead, a chastened and much more powerful United States returned to the concept of international cooperative finance at the end of World War I, when it proposed the creation of a Second Chinese Consortium.

D. M. Crane and T. A. Breslin, *An Ordinary Relationship: American Opposition to Republican Revolution in China* (Miami, FL, 1986); F. V. Field, *American Participation in the China Consortiums* (Chicago, 1931); A. W. Griswold, *The Far Eastern Policy of the United States* (New Haven, CT, 1938).

Noel H. Pugach

SMEDLEY, AGNES (1892–1950)

As a socialist and journalist, Agnes Smedley used her considerable reportorial skills to build public support for social justice, participatory democracy, and women's rights. Because she believed that the Chinese Communist Party* (CCP) supported these causes as well, she became in the 1930s and 1940s a propagandist for the Chinese Communist revolution, and the U.S. government later persecuted her for it during the Cold War. Smedley grew up in a poverty-stricken family living on the farmlands in northern Missouri, and then in the mining towns of Colorado. At a very young age, she became acutely aware of unequal economic class relationships and of the ways that the wealthy, property-owning classes exploited and lived off the labor of the working classes. Smedley also observed the ways that working-class women became economically dependent on men through marriage and repeated pregnancies and childbirths. She vowed to get an education that would prepare her for a career so that she could remain independent and avoid a traditional marriage and motherhood. Smedley worked her way through several years of college, had two failed marriages and two abortions, became involved in Margaret Sanger's international movement to legalize birth control and the movement for India's independence from Britain, and, consequently, was persecuted and jailed by the U.S. government during World War I. But she never joined a Socialist or Communist party.

In Berlin in 1927, while working for India's independence movement, Smedley became interested in Chinese nationalism. As her political relationships with several Indian leaders deteriorated, and her common-law marriage to Indian nationalist Virendranath Chattopadhyaya ended, Smedley was determined to go to China in 1928 to aid the cause of the Chinese nationalist revolution. En route to China at a stopover in Moscow, Smedley met Song Qingling*, widow of Sun Zhongshan*, and learned about the ideas of the radical wing of China's Guomindang* (GMD) Party. In the 1930s, after Song Qingling returned to China, she and Smedley collaborated on various projects to publicize the cause of radical Chinese nationalism, and to criticize actions of the right wing of the GMD, led by Song Qingling's brother-in-law Jiang Jieshi*. During the 1930s, Smedley wrote and published stories praising what she saw as noble crusades to revolutionize social and economic relations in China and, ultimately, throughout the world. She worked closely with the radical GMD, leftist intelligentsia, and the CCP to relay carefully selected information to the outside world that would most benefit the Chinese revolution. She also cultivated friendships and shared her political views with American military and diplomatic personnel in China.

After 1937, Smedley went on speaking tours in the United States to influence U.S. policy making by generating American public support through her journalistic writing for her revolutionary causes and projects. During the 1940s, she wrote, spoke publicly, and testified before congressional committees about the dangers of U.S. interference in the Chinese Civil War*. Smedley condemned corruption within the GMD government and urged the U.S. government to end its economic and military support for an unpopular and undemocratic regime. By the late 1940s, her political position was attacked fiercely in the intensely anti-Communist climate of the Cold War. The right-wing American press printed U.S. government suspicions that she was a Soviet spy. The Federal Bureau of Investigation followed her constantly and kept records of her activities that Congress later used in its investigations of Communist subversion. By 1949, Smedley planned to return to China at the invitation of the newly established People's Republic of China*. In April 1950, while visiting a friend in London, she died after an operation to relieve a stomach ulcer. Although Smedley failed to influence U.S. China policy in the 1940s, she helped to build American sympathies for China in its war with Japan in the 1930s.

H. Deane, *Good Deeds and Gunboats: Two Centuries of American-Chinese Encounters* (San Francisco, CA, 1990); J. R. MacKinnon and S. R. MacKinnon, *Agnes Smedley: The Life and Times of an American Radical* (Berkeley, CA, 1988); A. Smedley, *Battle Hymn of China* (New York, 1943); A. Smedley, *China Fights Back: An American Woman with the Eighth Route Army* (New York, 1938); A. Smedley, *Chinese Destinies: Sketches of Present-Day China* (New York, 1933); A. Smedley, *Daughter of Earth* (New York, 1929); A. Smedley, *Portraits of Chinese Women in Revolution* (New York, 1976).

Karen Garner

SMITH, H. ALEXANDER (1880–1966)

H. Alexander Smith was U.S. senator from New Jersey from 1944 to 1959. As a prominent Republican on the Far Eastern subcommittee of the Senate Committee on Foreign Relations, he shaped U.S. foreign policy in East Asia in support of containing Communism*. His vigorous support for the Republic of China* (ROC) appropriately earned him the sobriquet Foremost Formosan. The major influence on his political outlook, Smith often recalled, was Woodrow Wilson*, who had been his professor at Princeton University. He supported an internationalism in foreign affairs throughout his life. Smith graduated in 1901 and pursued a varied career as a lawyer, professor, businessman, and administrator at Princeton. After World War I, he assisted Herbert Hoover* in carrying out relief activities in Belgium, an experience that influenced his drafting of the Smith-Mundt Act of 1948. That law made the Voice of America a permanent government agency and, together with the Fulbright Act*, established cultural exchange programs as an essential element of postwar U.S. foreign policy.

Despite the Democratic tide in the elections of 1944, Smith won a seat in the U.S. Senate. As a member of the small but powerful group of internationalist Republicans, he took great interest in East Asian affairs, especially after a trip to the region in 1949. Along with California Republican Senator William F. Knowland* and other members of the China Lobby* in Congress, Smith was convinced that Communism was gaining ground in East Asia because of the weakness of U.S. policy. He pressed for American support of the Guomindang* (Nationalists) in the Chinese Civil War* and then the government of Jiang Jieshi* after it fled to Taiwan* late in 1949. As Jiang's regime was collapsing and the Chinese Communist Party* consolidating its power in 1948 and 1949, the divided administration of President Harry S. Truman* attempted to distance itself from Jiang. In August 1949, Secretary of State Dean G. Acheson* released the China White Paper* to the press in an effort to place the blame on the Guomindang government. Public and congressional criticism of the State Department's China policy—to which Smith contributed—put the administration on the defensive. During the Korean War*, an enduring result of this pressure was U.S. support for the ROC on Taiwan.

Smith was a particularly effective advocate because he combined public exhortation and close cooperation with administrative officials in his approach to policy issues, such as implementation of the China Assistance Act of 1948* and the Japanese Peace Treaty* of 1951. The risk of Senate Republicans opposing a treaty with Japan negotiated by the Truman administration was high, given the partisan tension at the time. Smith consulted with John Foster Dulles* to ensure Senate support of the agreement before the signing ceremony, in which he took part. As the Yoshida Letter* demonstrated, the price of Senate approval was Japanese recognition of the ROC government (by means of the Sino-Japanese Peace Treaty of 1952*). He worked closely with the Republican administration of President Dwight D. Eisenhower* until he retired from the Senate in 1959. Smith then was a consultant to the State Department, attending the Colombo Conference in Indonesia* with the rank of ambassador.

R. L. McGlothlen, *Controlling the Waves: Dean Acheson and U.S. Foreign Policy in Asia* (New York, 1993); M. Guhin, *John Foster Dulles: A Statesman and His Times* (New York, 1972); *New York Times*, 28 October 1966; H. B. Schonberger, *Aftermath of War: Americans and the Remaking of Japan, 1945–1952* (Kent, OH, 1989).

Aaron Forsberg

SNOW, EDGAR (1905–1972)

As a liberal American journalist in China from 1928 to 1941, Edgar Snow became, during World War II, the preeminent foreign source for information on the Chinese Communist Party* (CCP) led by Mao Zedong* with the publication of *Red Star Over China* in 1938. With the reevaluation of U.S. Cold War–era foreign policy that began in the 1970s, diplomatic historians and U.S. policy makers came to appreciate his efforts to promote understanding and cooperation with the Communist world. Born into a middle-class family, Snow grew up in Kansas City, Missouri, yearning for fame, fortune, and adventure. Interested in journalistic writing from a very early age, Snow studied briefly at the University of Missouri's journalism school, but left and entered the business world in New York City in hopes of traveling around the world. In 1928, he embarked on his journey, stopping first in Shanghai. He planned to leave China in a few months, but career opportunities and personal circumstances keep him there for the next thirteen years. Through journalistic research and formal study with Chinese tutors, Snow learned the history of the Chinese Civil War* between the Guomindang* (GMD) and the CCP that began in 1927.

When Japan embarked on an aggressive campaign of economic and territorial expansion in China in 1931, Snow began to work with students and intellectuals in Shanghai and Beijing, whom he met through radical nationalist Song Qingling*, the widow of Sun Zhongshan*. His China reporting brought international attention to China's war against Japan. Snow also was critical of the undemocratic and corrupt nature of Jiang Jieshi* and his GMD government, which the United States recognized as China's legitimate government. He reported favorably on the honesty, selfless leadership, and democratic nature of the Chinese Communist movement that he had observed firsthand during a trip to the CCP stronghold at Yan'an. Snow's reports of the CCP were published in his journalistic masterpiece *Red Star over China* in 1938. Although the U.S. government never deviated from its wartime policy of full support to China through the GMD, Snow's reporting was partially responsible for discussion within the ranks of the U.S. State and War Departments about attaching conditions to U.S. aid to Jiang, and about establishing a formal relationship with the CCP. He spent the last years of the war in the Soviet Union, reporting on its struggle to defeat Nazi Germany. Although Snow observed great deficiencies in the Soviet system, he, like other American war correspondents, minimized his criticisms to build public support for the war effort. He also admired many aspects of the Soviet system.

After the war, Snow returned to the United States, where he lobbied for a more nuanced approach in Asia. His efforts, however, proved futile in a Cold War era when intense anti-Communism directed all U.S. policies, both foreign and domestic. After the triumph of the CCP over Jiang's GMD in 1949 and the start of the Korean War*, the United States severed all contacts with the People's Republic of China* (PRC). Because he had written sympathetically about the Communist movement in the Soviet Union and China, U.S. government investigative committees questioned Snow's loyalty to the United States. His steady reportorial relationship with the conservative *Saturday Evening Post* also ended. In the 1950s, Snow lived quietly in the United States, but in 1960, he moved to Switzerland. That year, he revisited China, at the PRC's invitation. As in 1938, his report, *The Other Side of the River: Red China Today*, brought new and unique information on Communist China to the West. Although he reported honestly on the progress and failings of the CCP government, the Western press dismissed his account as Red propaganda. After the Chinese Cultural Revolution* began in the mid-1960s, his contacts with high-ranking PRC officials dissolved. He continued to write about China thereafter as his health deteriorated, making his last visit to China, weakened by cancer, in 1970. When in 1971 President Richard M. Nixon* resumed contact with the PRC, Snow was too ill to travel and report on Nixon's Visit to China* firsthand.

J. M. Hamilton, *Edgar Snow: A Biography* (Bloomington, IN, 1988); E. Snow, *Journey to the Beginning* (New York, 1958); E. Snow, *The Other Side of the River: Red China Today* (New York, 1962); E. Snow, *Red Star over China* (New York, 1938); S. B. Thomas, *Season of High Adventure: Edgar Snow in China* (Berkeley, CA, 1996).

Karen Garner

SOCIALIST REPUBLIC OF VIETNAM

The Socialist Republic of Vietnam* (SRV) is the successor state to the Democratic Republic of Vietnam* (DRV), the Communist government Ho Chi Minh* formed in the aftermath of Japan's surrender in August 1945. In the months following victory in the Second Indochina War* in April 1975, the DRV's leaders decided to reunite the nation formally as soon as possible. This took place in July 1976 when the Socialist Republic of Vietnam was established with the national capital in Hanoi. Relations with the United States remained tense for several years after the war. There were attempts to normalize relations with the United States after Jimmy Carter* became president, but these efforts were thwarted by disagreements over the issues of U.S reparations to be paid to Vietnam and Vietnamese cooperation in finding U.S. servicemen missing in action (MIA), as well as the decision to give greater priority to the People's Republic of China* (PRC) and U.S.-PRC Normalization of Relations*.

Vietnamese-American relations became even more strained after the SRV invaded Cambodia* and overthrew the Pol Pot* regime in December 1978. In the years that followed, the administrations of Carter, Ronald Reagan*, and George H. W. Bush* maintained a policy of imposing economic sanctions against the SRV and supporting Cambodian guerrillas who attacked the Vietnamese army and the SRV's Cambodian allies.

Some improvement in Vietnamese-American relations, however, occurred in the 1980s. The SRV and the Reagan administration reached agreements for making arrangements to search for MIAs and organizing the orderly departure of Vietnamese who were permitted to emigrate to the United States. Further improvements occurred during the Bush administration, when the SRV withdrew its forces from Cambodia in 1989 and worked with Western, Chinese, and Russian diplomats in 1991 to broker an international settlement to the Cambodian conflict. In his last year as president, Bush permitted the sale of humanitarian supplies to the SRV and allowed U.S. companies to negotiate contracts for business ventures in Vietnam. The Clinton administration took the final steps in normalizing U.S. relations with the SRV by ending all economic sanctions in February 1994, opening American and Vietnamese liaison offices in May 1994, and then establishing full diplomatic relations in July 1995. Democrat Douglas "Pete" Peterson, a former Vietnam prisoner of war and Florida congressman, became the first U.S. ambassador to the SRV in 1977. Following a steady stream of Americans, President Bill Clinton* visited Vietnam in fall 2000, marking the climax of a decade of increasing bilateral trade and cooperative relations.

W. J. Duiker, *Vietnam: Nation in Revolution* (Boulder, CO, 1983); G. Kolko, *Vietnam: Anatomy of Peace* (New York, 1997); J. W. Morley and M. Nishihara (eds.), *Vietnam Joins the World* (Armonk, NY, 1997); G. Porter, *Vietnam: The Politics of Bureaucratic Socialism* (Ithaca, NY, 1993).

Joseph G. Morgan

SONG MEILING (1897–)

Song Meiling was the wife of Jiang Jieshi*, who later became the leader of the Republic of China* (ROC). Song became the "first lady" of China and had close ties with many politically influential Americans. She went to the United States in 1908 and soon became Americanized. In 1917, Song graduated from Wellesley College in Massachusetts and returned to China in August. Ten years later, she married Jiang. After the Marco Polo Bridge Incident* in 1937, Song helped China's government win American assistance. She invited Claire L. Chennault* to work for China after he organized the American Volunteer Air Force. After the Pearl Harbor Attack*, Song accelerated efforts to ally China with the United States. On her broadcasts and in articles, she described events in China and the sacrifices of the Chinese people. On 19 April 1942, Song published a letter in the *New York Times* appealing to the powers to abolish consular jurisdiction and other privileges they enjoyed in China, which provoked the attention of the U.S. government. In a June broadcast, she condemned the Japanese fomenting of disunity between the United States and China and expressed Chinese sincerity in cooperation with the Allies, which cleared away suspicion of the United States and had a positive impact on consolidating the partnership between the two countries.

Song's stay in the United States from November 1942 to July 1943 created a furor. On 7 February, she had a private talk with President Franklin D. Roosevelt* at the White House. Eleven days later, she made separate speeches in the House of Representatives and the Senate, in which she pointed out that the Allies should not forget Japan while concentrating on defeating Germany. Printed in full in almost all American newspapers, the speeches raised a "Song Wind." Then she spoke in New York, Boston, Chicago, San Francisco, and Los Angeles and met a broad assortment of people. Returning to Washington, Song again met with Roosevelt on the problem of a counterattack in Burma*. Under the influence of her visit, Congress passed a motion to abrogate the 1882 Chinese Exclusion Act in December 1943. When Sino-American negotiation for huge financial assistance reached an impasse, Song wrote a letter to Roosevelt on 27 February 1944, explaining the financial crisis in China and expressing hope for obtaining modern planes and other aid from the United States. Roosevelt replied on 3 March that he was willing to discuss the problem soon, but he died before seeing her. World War II ended a few months later, and the situation for the Chinese administration deteriorated. In December 1948, Song again went to the United States to seek aid, but President Harry S. Truman* rejected her request because he doubted the prospects for the ROC's survival. Madame Jiang continued to work for U.S. assistance and support for her husband's regime after it fled to Taiwan* late in 1949. After Jiang died, Song moved to New York City in 1975.

Hua Wen Publishers (ed.), *Song Meiling cexie* [Sidelight on Song Meiling] (Beijing, 1988); Wu Manzhen, *Kangzhan zhong de Songshi san jiemei* [Three Sisters of Song Family at Anti-Japanese War] (Beijing, 1995).

Xiang E

SONG QINGLING (1890–1981)

Song Qingling was the second wife of Chinese Guomindang* (Nationalist) Party leader Sun Zhongshan* and after 1949, a leading "democratic personage" in the People's Republic of China* (PRC). Born in Shanghai, she was the second daughter of the Chinese Christian Charles Jones Soong. Raised in the wealthy and Westernized circles of late imperial Shanghai, Song then was sent to the United States for higher education. In 1913, she graduated from Wesleyan College in Georgia. Returning to China, she married Sun in October 1914. Their marriage was part of a pattern of family linkages between the Songs and Sun's Nationalist movement. Her younger brother Song Ziwen* became the leading financial adviser to the Guomindang. Her older sister Ailing married Kung Xiangxi*, another Nationalist financial leader, and her younger sister Song Meiling* later married Jiang Jieshi*, Sun's successor as leader of the Guomindang.

In 1927, when the Nationalists under Jiang's leadership split with the Chinese Communist Party* (CCP), with whom they had been participating in a United Front* to fight Japan, Song Qingling remained loyal to the left wing of the Guomindang and its CCP allies. She fled for a while to Moscow, and also spent time in Berlin, later returning to China to join with other leftist, but non-Communist, leaders in forming the Chinese League for the Protection of Human Rights. In 1949, the Chinese Civil War* ended as the CCP drove the Nationalists to exile on Taiwan* and established the PRC. Song Qingling remained on the mainland and became a public supporter of the new regime, viewing the Communist revolution as the true embodiment of her husband Sun's vision of a modernizing China. She took part in political functions as chairwoman of the Guomindang Revolutionary Committee, one of the minor organizations invoking the idea of a revived United Front. From 1949, she also was one of the six, essentially honorific, vice chairmen of the PRC. She died in Beijing. Her former home has been preserved and opened to the public as a museum.

S. Seagrave, *The Soong Dynasty* (New York, 1985); J. D. Seymour, *China's Satellite Parties* (Armonk, NY, 1987); J. D. Spence, *The Search for Modern China* (New York, 1990); L. Van Slyke, *Enemies and Friends: The United Front in Chinese Communist History* (Stanford, CA, 1967).

Kenneth J. Hammond

SONG ZIWEN (1894–1971)

Song Ziwen, known as T. V. Soong in the West, was a prominent member of the government of the Republic of China* (ROC) who frequently represented President Jiang Jieshi* in his negotiations with the United States. A graduate of St. John's University in Shanghai, he went to the United States in 1912 to study economics at Harvard University and then at Columbia University, while working part time at the National City Bank. Song returned to China in 1917 and in January 1928, became the treasury minister of the Guomindang* (Nationalist) government. In July 1928, he negotiated a treaty with John V. A. MacMurray*, U.S. ambassador to China, in Beijing to achieve China Tariff Autonomy*. After the Mukden Incident* in September 1931 and Japan's subsequent attacks on China early the next year, Song made contacts with the U.S. diplomats in China, requesting that the United States take the initiative in forcing Japan to withdraw. He calculated that because the United States had important economic interests in the Yangze valley, it had to pay attention to Japanese aggression and would mediate. Soon, the United States presented notes to both China and Japan, demanding an end to the conflict.

Song went to Washington during April 1933 ostensibly to attend an economic symposium sponsored by President Franklin D. Roosevelt*, but actually on a mission to seek economic and political assistance. In his plan for "allying America and Europe against Japan," U.S. help was an important way to extricate China from its national crises. The first problem Song discussed with Roosevelt and Secretary of State Cordell Hull* was Japan's aggression, resulting in the issuance of a joint statement on 19 May, in which Song and Roosevelt said that the military conflict in Asia during the prior two years impaired world peace and that they urged an immediate end to the fighting. A second issue was Song's unsuccessful request for another deferred payment on the Boxer Indemnity. Finally, they discussed the problem of China's tariff and currency and determined the amount of U.S. aid China needed. Before leaving, Song signed the Cotton and Wheat Loan of $50 million from the Reconstruction Finance Corporation.

After the Marco Polo Bridge Incident* in July 1937, Song delivered a radio address on 22 October, urging the United States to take effective measures, including economic sanctions, to stop Japanese aggression. In June 1940, he went to the United States as Jiang's private representative to seek economic and military aid. He contracted the Tungsten Ore Loan of $25 million in October, a loan of $100 million in November, and the Metal Loan of $50 million in February 1941. In May 1941, President Roosevelt announced that Lend Lease* applied to China. After the Pearl Harbor Attack*, Song expressed Chinese indignation and China joined the United States in declaring war on Japan. On 21 December, Jiang appointed Song foreign minister, ordering him to stay in Washington to carry on negotiations. In March 1942, Song and U.S. Treasury Secretary Henry J. Morgenthau Jr. signed a joint statement confirming a loan of $500 million to China. In June, he and Hull signed a Lend Lease agreement, and American assistance to China grew sharply thereafter. In early October, Song submitted China's request for abrogation of their unequal treaty and the United States complied immediately. In January 1943, a new treaty provided the United States with the consular jurisdiction it previously had enjoyed. In December 1944, Song became the ROC's prime minister.

When the war ended in 1945, Jiang's government faced economic problems and resumption of the Chinese Civil War*. Song returned to the United States in August to ask for assistance. Washington promised financial aid to stabilize China's economy and military assistance to help transport Guomindang troops to northeast China. From late 1946 to early 1947, Song wrote to U.S. Ambassador J. Leighton Stuart* repeatedly, asking for huge financial assistance, but this time the United States refused. Song resigned in March 1947 and went back to China. He returned to the United States in May 1949, several months before Jiang and his government fled to Taiwan*, and settled there permanently.

Gu Weijun, *Gu Weijun huiyi lu* [Memoirs of Gu Weijun] (Beijing, 1983–88); Wang Song et al., *Song Ziwen zhuan* [Biography of Song Ziwen] (Wuhan, 1993); Wu Jingping, *Song Ziwen pingzhuan* [Critical Biography of Song Ziwen] (Fuzhou, 1992).

Xiang E

SOUPHANOUVONG (1909–)

Souphanouvong, the younger half-brother of Souvanna Phoma* and a minor prince in the Lao royal family, was a leader of the Pathet Lao*, a Communist front organization, and the most visible antagonist of the United States in Laos* during the Second Indochina War*. Known as the Red Prince, he was educated in France and Hanoi. He took a job as an engineer in central Vietnam in the employ of the French colonial Department of Public Works in 1938. In Vietnam, Souphanouvong married a Vietnamese wife and became an ardent anticolonialist. When Japan surrendered and before France could reestablish control in French Indochina*, Souphanouvong joined the anticolonialist Lao Issara (Free Laos), who declared Laos independent. Supported by the Vietminh*, he organized the only real military resistance—albeit unsuccessful—to French military forces returning to Laos. Souphanouvong narrowly escaped to Thailand*, where he continued to oppose French Colonialism* in a series of exile raids. In 1949, he broke with the dwindling Lao Issara and formed the Pathet Lao. With the Vietminh's successful 1953 campaign in eastern Laos and the partition of Vietnam at the Geneva Conference of 1954*, Souphanouvong and the Pathet Lao established themselves in Laos's two northern provinces contiguous to the Democratic Republic of Vietnam*. For the rest of the 1950s, the Eisenhower administration tried to keep him and the Pathet Lao out of Lao governments by all means possible. But in 1957, he joined a coalition government with Souvanna Phouma, and in 1958, the Pathet Lao successfully contested supplemental elections. A pro-American Lao government, which came to power in August 1958, imprisoned Souphanouvong, but he made a daring escape to the north.

After the Laotian Crisis of 1961* and the Geneva Accords of 1962*, Souphanouvong joined a coalition, but Laos became a divided country in practice. The Pathet Lao—considerably stiffened by 6,000 North Vietnamese troops—controlled most of the sparsely populated eastern half of the country, whereas the Royal Lao government, ostensibly neutral, but secretly supported by the United States and Thailand, held the western lowlands and the Mekong River towns. Throughout the 1960s and into the 1970s, fighting occurred on the dividing lines, especially the Plain of Jars, ebbing and flowing with the wet and dry seasons. Souphanouvong, the Pathet Lao, and growing numbers of North Vietnamese troops withstood the massive Secret U.S. Air War in Laos*, an Army of the Republic of Vietnam* incursion in 1971, and the U.S.-created Hmong* secret army. With the end of U.S. involvement in Indochina near in 1974, Souphanouvong declined an offer to join a new coalition government—although three Pathet Lao leaders took posts. He became instead the president of a National Political Consultative Council organized to remake Lao society after decades of war. His intelligence, organizational skills, and reputation, combined with the discipline of the Pathet Lao members of the council, ensured that the Pathet Lao dominated in the blueprint for a new Laos. When both Saigon and Phnom Penh fell in April 1975, the Pathet Lao was poised to seize the moment. It took control of the Mekong towns, ended the Lao monarchy, created the Lao People's Democratic Republic, and made Souphanouvong president of the new socialist state. With the Lao revolution accomplished, the secret Lao People's Revolutionary Party emerged, with its leader Kaysone Phomvihane exercising the real power. Souphanouvong played the role of figurehead, whose popularity helped to legitimize the Pathet Lao's cause.

M. Brown and J. J. Zasloff, *Apprentice Revolutionaries: The Communist Movement in Laos, 1930–1985* (Stanford, CA, 1986); P. F. Langer and J. J. Zasloff, *North Vietnam and the Pathet Lao: Partners in the Struggle for Laos* (Cambridge, MA, 1970); J. J. Zasloff, *The Pathet Lao: Leadership and Organization* (Lexington, MA, 1973).

Edward C. Keefer

SOUTH CHINA SEA DISPUTES

After World War II, the nations surrounding the South China Sea contested for ownership of the Paracel and Spratly Islands. The South China Sea is bordered by the People's Republic of China* (PRC) and Taiwan* to the north, Vietnam to the west, the Philippines* to the east, and Cambodia*, Thailand*, Malaysia*, Singapore*, Indonesia*, and Brunei* to the southwest and the south. The sea contains hundreds of scattered islets and coral reefs astride vital international shipping lanes. Rich in fishing resources, it is also believed to have vast deposits of petroleum. The Paracel Islands in the north, known as Xisha in Chinese and *Hoang Sa* in Vietnamese, have a land area of less than three square miles. The eastern part, the Amphitrite Group, has been in PRC hands since 1956. In 1974, the PRC ousted a Republic of Vietnam* garrison from the Cresent Group in the western part of the Paracels and gained control of the entire archipelago. Although the Paracels have been administered exclusively by the PRC since the Second Indochina War* ended, the Socialist Republic of Vietnam* (SRV) has continued to claim ownership of them.

The Spratly Islands in the south, with a total land area of probably less than two square miles, exceed the Paracels both in the total number of islets and reefs included and the area over which such features are scattered. There are six claimants to parts or the whole of the archipelago: the PRC, Taiwan, Vietnam, the Philippines, Malaysia, and Brunei. China—both the PRC and the Republic of China* (ROC)—and Vietnam lay claims to the whole archipelago on historical grounds. The Philippines claims an area slightly smaller than the full extent of the Spratlys on the grounds of geographical proximity, as well as their rights over 200-nautical-mile exclusive economic zones. Malaysia and Brunei each claim a southern part on the basis of rights over the adjacent continental shelf. The Spratlys are called Nansha by the Chinese, Truong Sa by the Vietnamese, and Kalayaan by the Filipinos, whereas the English names were given by the British Navy in the nineteenth century.

The Spratlys disputes have a long and complicated history. France occupied several major islands in 1932. Japan occupied the archipelago during World War II. After the war, Japan renounced the islands without assigning them specifically to any successor. China under the Guomindang* (Nationalist) government took over the archipelago after Japan left, and since 1956, the ROC has maintained a garrison on Itu Aba, the biggest island in the Spratlys. The Philippines staked a claim to an area called Kalayaan in 1956 and started to occupy islands in the early 1970s. In 1974, South Vietnam occupied five islands, which were inherited by the SRV in 1975. Malaysia occupied three reefs in the 1980s. In 1988, the PRC occupied six reefs, igniting a naval clash with Vietnam. In 1995, it took Mischief Reef, provoking a diplomatic crisis with the Philippines.

The official U.S. position on the South China Sea disputes was that the United States did not take sides regarding the territorial claims of any party and urged the parties concerned to solve the disputes peacefully. It has been in American strategic interest to see that regional stability not be disrupted and freedom of navigation in the area remained intact. Diplomatic efforts have been made by claimants to contain, if not resolve, the multilateral disputes over the Spratlys. But since the disputes have not only international, but also domestic political implications for those countries concerned, the prospects for a settlement seemed very slim as the twenty-first century began. Perhaps some arrangement of joint development or resource sharing may be worked out eventually, circumventing the thorny issue of sovereignty.

B. Catley and M. Keliat, *Spratlys: The Dispute in the South China Sea* (Aldershot, UK, 1997); C. Lo, *China's Policy Towards Territorial Disputes: The Case of the South China Sea Islands* (New York, 1989); M. S. Samuels, *Contest for the South China Sea* (New York, 1982); M. J. Valencia, *China and the South China Sea Disputers: Conflicting Claims and Potential Solutions in the South China Sea* (New York, 1996); M. J. Valencia, Jon M. Van Dyke, and N. A. Ludwig, *Sharing Resources of the South China Sea* (Honolulu, HI, 1999).

Chang Sheng-tai

SOUTH KOREA

See REPUBLIC OF KOREA

SOUTH KOREAN ANTI-AMERICANISM

After World War II, the Republic of Korea* (ROK) became one of the most pro-American nations in the world and faithfully supportive of the Korean-U.S. defense and economic alliance. As South Korean–American ties grew more complex during subsequent years, however, strains developed between the two Korean War* allies, and anti-Americanism escalated in South Korea. Not all South Koreans were anti-American or unappreciative of what Americans had done for their country, but a significant number of young Koreans were, especially those who were either college students or of college age. This strain of anti-Americanism seemed to permeate all aspects of South Korean society, including not only colleges and universities, but the Korean military, business, and government bureaucracy. Increasingly, more South Koreans periodically voiced criticisms of the United States over various aspects of South Korean–U.S. relations. This was probably most apparent in the area of trade. Also in South Korea, the question of how to build a new and more mature relationship between the ROK and the United States became an important issue that needed to be settled in South Korea's development toward full democracy.

Anti-Americanism has grown among Koreans basically because of the heavy and influential American presence in South Korea. Many problems have surrounded implementation of the U.S.–South Korea Status of Forces Agreement* of 9 July 1966. And violent demonstrations and, in particular, attacks on U.S. military installations have been triggered by the enhancement of national pride among the Korean people and their discontent with perceptions of the U.S. role in hampering the struggle for democracy in the ROK. In particular, the 1980 Kwangju Incident* inspired much of the anti-American rhetoric echoing throughout subsequent demonstrations across South Korea. Anti-Americanism worsened and became even more extensive because of the widening divergence of the two nations' interests represented by conflicts over trade. Anti-Americanism likely will persist as an undercurrent of South Korean society into the twenty-first century. But what matters more is that it also coexists with an admiration and respect for the United States and, paradoxically, a partiality among South Korea's youth for American values and popular culture. As a relatively new phenomenon, anti-Americanism plays an important role in relations between the ROK and the United States, and requires the attention of American and South Korean policy makers in addressing issues of mutual concern.

Kim Jinwung, *Han'gukin ŭi Panmi Kamjŏng* [The Anti-Americanism of the Korean People] (Seoul, 1992); J. Kim, "The Nature of South Korean

Anti-Americanism," *Korea Journal* (Spring 1994); J. Kim, "Recent Anti-Americanism in South Korea: The Causes," *Asian Survey* (August 1989).

Kim Jinwung

SOUTH KOREA'S DEMOCRACY DECLARATION

This declaration was the turning point in the political development of South Korea toward democracy. On 29 June 1987, No Tae-u*, then presidential candidate of the Democratic Justice Party, declared eight democratic reforms for achieving a peaceful end to political unrest in the Republic of Korea* (ROK). These included the promise of a constitutional amendment for direct presidential elections, the release of all political prisoners, a pardon for dissident Kim Dae-jung*, and the establishment of freedom of speech. President Chŏn Duhwan*, who had seized power in October 1979 after Pak Chŏng-hŭi's Assassination*, had retained authority through repression of political opposition, resulting in the Kwangju Incident* in May 1980. Late in 1983, however, he initiated a series of liberalization policies that allowed dismissed student dissidents and professors to return to campus, ended limits on political activities, and released political prisoners. His actions reflected confidence that he had consolidated power and won popular support with South Korea's spectacular economic growth. In addition, Chŏn recognized the necessity of creating a favorable political environment in preparation for the 1988 Seoul Olympic Games. Finally, he wanted to win the general election scheduled for February 1985 and thereby give his regime legitimacy.

Chŏn's liberalization policies reignited political dissent. In March 1984, the reinstated students began establishing Committees for the Promotion of Campus Autonomy and, during the fall semester, founded the National League of Students with forty-two participating universities, transforming the small student groups into a united national force. By April 1985, social groups were criticizing Chŏn's repressive regime, as the democracy movement, no longer comprising a few active dissidents, became organized and was gaining popular support. Meanwhile, political prisoners released the prior December had established in January 1985 the New Korea Democratic Party (NKDP). Thereafter, cooperation between the NKDP and the social groups to achieve democratization increased, although friction resulted from the fact that the former focused on procedural democracy, whereas the latter stressed genuine democracy. In the general elections in February, the NKDP won enough seats to act as a viable opposition party. But in August, Chŏn rejected the NKDP's proposal to create a special committee in the National Assembly to develop a compromise plan on constitutional amendments. In response, the NKDP in February 1986 organized a national signature campaign and mass protest meetings. On 30 April, Chŏn proposed discussions, if the NKDP stopped its insurgent activities outside the National Assembly, but when these talks occurred a year later, he declared his determination to preserve the existing constitution.

In May 1987, a new wave of resistance to Chŏn's regime began when the truth about the death of a Seoul National University student by water torture was revealed. Opposition leaders formed the Headquarters of the National Movement to Contend for a Democratic Constitution with the support of 2,196 politicians, intellectuals, and social and labor movement leaders representing twenty-five organizations to mobilize support to achieve constitutional amendments for direct presidential elections and dissolution of the military government. When Chŏn on 10 June named No Tae-u as his candidate for president, mass demonstrations immediately erupted nationwide, with more than 4 million citizens participating. Police efforts to suppress them were overwhelmed by the demonstrators in many cities. Fearing a popular revolution, Chŏn's advisers drafted South Korea's Declaration of Democracy, and it received final approval on 27 June. Chŏn later claimed that at least a year earlier he had considered accepting direct election of the president. In fact, he was planning to declare martial law or a state of emergency on 19 June 1987 to protect the existing indirect electoral system. Yet Chŏn concluded that popular resistance was so strong, No's election by the electoral college was in doubt, and even if No won, he would not be able to govern the nation effectively. Furthermore, more than thirty commanders of regions around Seoul opposed Chŏn's plan to mobilize the military.

U.S. intervention also played a decisive role in Chŏn's decision to approve No's issuance of South Korea's Declaration of Democracy on 29 June. Beginning early in 1987, Washington had pressed Chŏn's regime through various diplomatic channels to accept popular demands for democratization. In February 1987, Gaston J. Sigur Jr., assistant secretary of state for East Asian and Pacific affairs, traveled to South Korea and persuaded government leaders to break the political deadlock with talks aimed at free elections. In the middle of the June uprising, President Ronald Reagan* sent a letter to Chŏn urging a peaceful settlement. On 19 June, Michael H. Armacost*, undersecretary of state for political affairs, met with the ROK ambassador to emphasize that the U.S. government was urging Chŏn not to declare a state of national emergency, but rather to pursue real democratizing measures, such as the releasing and pardoning of political prisoners, the establishment of freedom of speech, and the amendment of the electoral law. On 21 June, Sigur said on a television talk show that the United States did not support military intervention to end the crisis in South Korea and repeated this position when he visited Seoul from 23 to 25 June. The Reagan administration's active involvement sought to avoid a second Kwangju incident that would worsen South Korean Anti-Americanism*. Rather than violent revolution, No's declaration led to constitutional revisions ending military rule, opening the way for election as South Korea's president of dissidents Kim Young-sam* and Kim Dae-jung.

Chosun Ilbo, January 1992; *Jungang Ilbo*, September 1999; Yŏ Hyŏn, "Sin'gunbu kwŏnwijuiuich'eje ŭi dŭngjang kwa Chŏngch'igaldŭng" [The Rise of the New Military Authoritarian System and Political Conflict], in Han Hungsoo, *Han'guk jŏngch'i dongtaeron* [Dynamism of Korean Politics] (Seoul, 1996).

Heo Man-ho

SOUTHEAST ASIA TREATY ORGANIZATION

A regional defense system for Southeast Asia paralleling the North Atlantic Treaty Organization (NATO), the Southeast Asia Treaty Organization (SEATO) was a largely ineffective alliance between Asian and Western powers designed to deter the expansion of Communism*. On 8 September 1954, following the Geneva Conference of 1954*, U.S. Secretary of State John Foster Dulles* negotiated the creation of SEATO as part of the 1954 Manila Pact. Included in the alliance were Australia, New Zealand, Pakistan, the Philippines*, and Thailand*, in addition to the Western powers France, Britain, and the United States. Taiwan* was excluded because the pact's definition of Southeast Asia did not include nations north of 21 degrees, 30 minutes north latitude. Despite lobbying from Dulles, the neutral countries of India, Burma*, and Indonesia* refused to join, preferring to remain nonaligned in the Cold War. In addition, because of restrictions imposed by the Geneva Accords of 1954*, Cambodia*, Laos*, and "the free territory under the jurisdiction of the State of Vietnam" could not participate officially in the pact. But a special protocol signed the same day extended the benefits of the treaty to those three countries as "protocol states."

Militarily, SEATO represented a device for putting on a more permanent basis the staff consultations that previously had been held by military officers of the treaty countries concerning security in Southeast Asia. Politically, it became the expression of a wider political alignment on the part of states concerned with Southeast Asia. The treaty created a council to provide for consultation among the signatories, but unlike NATO, did not include a unified military command or joint forces. The centerpiece of the treaty was Article 4, stating that in the event of "aggression by means of armed attack in the treaty area against any of the Parties or territory which the Parties by unanimous agreement may hereafter designate," the signatories would "act to meet the common danger." They also agreed that if "the integrity of the territory or the sovereignty or political independence of any Party . . . is threatened" by subversion, they would consult immediately "for the common defense." The U.S. Senate ratified the treaty overwhelmingly by a vote of 82–1. Dulles hoped that the mere existence of the alliance would discourage Communist aggression in Southeast Asia. The treaty arrangements alone, however, did not provide for increased security against internal subversive dangers to the stability of a member nation or a protocol state as intended. During the Laotian Crisis of 1961*, SEATO proved to be insufficiently flexible for dealing with emergencies of that nature, raising doubts about the reliability of the pledges of aid contained in the treaty and weakening the entire foundation of the alliance.

The SEATO treaty was useful, however, to the United States as an opaque aegis for military action in Southeast Asia. For example, in November 1961, President John F. Kennedy* considered sending U.S. combat troops to the Republic of Vietnam* to stabilize the situation there, but only if the force officially represented SEATO rather than the United States. In 1964, the pact provided President Lyndon B. Johnson* with justification for U.S. military retaliation against the Democratic Republic of Vietnam* after the Gulf of Tonkin Incidents*, although he never consulted with SEATO allies as the treaty stipulated. Eventually, even the United States abandoned SEATO to the vagaries of its own needs. In 1969, President Richard M. Nixon*, seeking to bring the war and domestic protest under control, initiated Vietnamization*. In his Nixon Doctrine*, he denied that membership in SEATO guaranteed a commitment of U.S. troops in Asian conflicts, seriously jeopardizing security provisions in the treaty. In the 1970s, profound differences appeared among the SEATO countries, especially as they questioned U.S. conduct in the Second Indochina War*. As Communist victories in Indochina mounted, these internal divisions eroded any lingering effectiveness of SEATO and led to the disbanding of the anachronistic alliance in 1977.

D. L. Anderson, *Trapped by Success: The Eisenhower Administration and Vietnam, 1953–1961* (New York, 1991); L. Buszynski, *SEATO: The Failure of an Alliance Strategy* (Singapore, 1983); G. Modelski (ed.), *SEATO: Six Studies* (Vancouver, BC, 1962).

Andrew L. Johns

SOUVANNA PHOUMA (1901–1984)

Souvanna Phouma, a prince of the Lao royal family, was prime minister of the kingdom of Laos* for much of the time from when it was under French rule during the early 1950s to the Pathet Lao* takeover in 1975. He sought to keep Laos neutral in the Cold War, walking a tight rope between the United States and the Democratic Republic of Vietnam*, but the balancing act ultimately proved impossible. Born in Vientiane, Souvanna was educated in Hanoi and then at the Universities of Grenoble and Paris, where he received degrees in engineering and architecture. He opposed French reoccupation of Laos in 1945, exiling himself to Bangkok, where he joined the anticolonial non-Communist Lao Issara (Free Laos) Movement. In 1951, the French persuaded Souvanna to be premier of Laos as an associated state within the French Union. After Dien Bien Phu* and the fall of French Indochina*, he served as head of a Lao coalition government from 1956 to 1958. The Eisenhower administration viewed Souvanna as a Communist sympathizer or, at best, a dupe of the Pathet Lao and North Vietnamese. U.S. ambassador J. Graham Parson and Walter S. Robertson*, assistant secretary of state for East Asia (whom Parsons succeeded in 1959), steadfastly opposed Souvanna and encouraged his conservative opponents in Lao politics.

During the Laotian Crisis of 1961*, President John F. Kennedy* decided Laos was not the place to make a stand in Southeast Asia. Souvanna's neutralism, not to mention his charm and sophistication, appealed to Kennedy's key adviser, W. Averell Harriman*, who championed his cause. Kennedy hoped that Souvanna would be the man to keep Laos from becoming entangled in the war in Vietnam. He therefore attempted to negotiate Laos's neutrality by international agreement. But soon after the Geneva Accords of 1962* were signed, it became clear that North Vietnam was not relinquishing of areas under its control, especially the Lao portions of the Ho Chi Minh Trail*. Washington secretly shored up the neutralist government forces, and Souvanna allowed the Secret U.S. Air War in Laos* against Communist forces. He accepted Central Intelligence Agency* support of a Hmong* secret army under Vang Pao*, which increasingly became the main opponents of the Pathet Lao and North Vietnamese in northeastern Laos.

In 1971, Souvanna opposed the invasion of Laos by U.S.-supported South Vietnamese forces, but his neutrality was only a veneer, as he secretly aligned his government with the United States. As a result, his uneasy relations with the Pathet Lao and its leader, his half brother Prince Souphanouvong*, became estranged. In 1974, he was chosen as prime minister of the coalition government with the Pathet Lao, but Hanoi's military triumph in the Second Indochina War* the following year meant that the Pathet Lao, by virtue of its alliance with Hanoi, would assume power soon in Laos. When the Pathet Lao and Souphanouvong took control of Laos in 1975 and the United States totally withdrew from Indochina, Souvanna's fortunes quickly waned. He was eased out of power, as the new Lao rulers transformed the kingdom into a socialist state firmly in the orbit of the Socialist Republic of Vietnam*. That year, Souphanouvong became president of the new People's Republic of Laos. Souvanna lingered on as an adviser whose views increasingly were ignored, but did not leave Laos for exile in France or Thailand*. He died of a heart attack.

T. N. Castle, *At War in the Shadow of Vietnam: U.S. Military Aid to the Royal Lao Government, 1955–1975* (New York, 1993); A. J. Dommen, *Conflict in Laos: The Politics of Neutralization* (New York, 1971); C. A. Stevenson, *The End of Nowhere: American Policy Toward Laos Since 1954* (Boston, 1972); P. Stieglitz, *In a Little Kingdom* (Armonk, NY, 1990); R. Warner, *Back Fire: Secret War in Laos and Its Link to the War in Vietnam* (New York, 1995).

Edward C. Keefer

SPANISH-AMERICAN WAR (April–July 1898)

In this conflict, the United States liberated Cuba and seized its first major base in the western Pacific (Manila), from which it could protect growing, and threatened, interests in East Asia. In turn, President William McKinley* paid the defeated Spanish $20 million in the peace treaty, a pact that also forced Spain to surrender Guam* (on the route to Manila), Cuba, and Puerto Rico. The two Caribbean islands gave the United States political control over strategic entries to a proposed isthmian canal that Americans had long hoped would make them more competitive in Asian markets. The conflict should thus be termed the Spanish-Cuban-Philippine-American War, since U.S. forces needed only three months to defeat Spain, but several years to set up controls over Cuba and at least four years to defeat Filipino nationalists who fought to drive out U.S. colonialism in the Philippine-American War* (1899–1902).

President McKinley, like most Americans, was appalled at the killing in the Philippines*, but he had determined to obtain at least Manila months before he took the country to war in April 1898. In late 1897, he and Assistant Secretary of the Navy Theodore Roosevelt* discussed the importance of the Philippines, an importance that grew as European powers moved to carve up China and thus threaten the U.S. Open Door Policy* of access to all of China. By 1897 as well, U.S. naval officials had drawn up detailed plans for taking the Philippines in case of war with Spain. While debate over declaring war raged in the United States, McKinley quietly reinforced the U.S. Pacific Fleet in April 1898. That force, under Commodore George Dewey, quickly destroyed Spanish ships at the Battle of Manila Bay*. McKinley then began sending thousands of troops to occupy Manila and Luzon, the first time a president had dispatched the U.S. Army to fight outside the Western Hemisphere. In June, he used the war's needs as the rationale to persuade Congress to approve Hawaiian Annexation*, after the Senate had blocked this action in 1897, and later negotiated the Samoa Partition* in 1899.

While 60,000 U.S. troops were fighting the Filipinos in 1900, McKinley ordered 5,000 of these soldiers to join the China Relief Expedition* to protect foreigners in Beijing against the Chinese in the Boxer Uprising* and the commercial open door against intervening European armies now in a position to further carve up China. The Philippines thus served McKinley's purpose for obtaining them, but by 1907 the islands were seen as indefensible against a rising Japan. President Theodore Roosevelt, an 1898 war hero who had ardently campaigned for annexing the Philippines, now called them "Our heel of Achilles," and pulled the major U.S. Pacific naval base from Manila to Pearl Harbor in Hawaii. The results of the 1898 war for U.S. interests and power in Asia, therefore, were dramatic but, as far as McKinley's costly Philippine policy was concerned, ephemeral.

J. C. Bradford (ed.), *Crucible of Empire: The Spanish-American War and Its Aftermath* (Annapolis, MD, 1993); M. Leech, *In the Days of McKinley* (New York, 1959). T. J. McCormick, *The China Market: America's Quest for Informal Empire, 1893–1901* (Chicago, 1967); D. F. Trask, *The War with Spain in 1898* (New York, 1981).

Walter LaFeber

SPECIAL ECONOMIC ZONES

The Special Economic Zones (SEZ) were an important part of economic reform in the People's Republic of China* (PRC) beginning in the late 1970s. In 1978, Deng Xiaoping* once again became the PRC's principal statesman and shifted the national goal toward rebuilding the country's sluggish economy under socialism. Creation of the SEZ was to designate special zones within China's territory where private and foreign investment in China would be possible. The presence of the foreign firms in these special zones presumably would develop into a gateway for the introduction of modern technology and capital. In 1980, the Chinese government officially approved the creating of four Special Economic Zones as part of the Four Modernizations*; they were Shenzhen, Zhuhai, Shantou, and Xiamen. All four had been small towns under jurisdiction of their host province, but as SEZs they came under the direct jurisdiction of Beijing. Two factors were common to all four zones. First, they all were along the southeastern coast, the most productive area of China, with three in Guangdong Province.

Second, the choice of all four zones followed the rule that geographically each had to be close or have easy access to the capitalist world overseas. Specifically, Shenzhen is close to Hong Kong*, Zhuhai to Macau, and Xiamen to Taiwan*, whereas Shantou is a well-known hometown for overseas Chinese.

In these four SEZs, the PRC first invested a large sum of funds to building up infrastructures, then provided privileges, such as tax breaks, for the foreign investors, particularly from overseas Chinese. The most successful of the initial SEZs was Shenzhen. A small town of several thousand people, it had been a border town next to Hong Kong known only for its busy customhouse. When it was chosen as one of the four SEZs, the Chinese government kept its eye on the rapidly rising wealth of the British colony across the border. Beijing pumped billions of dollars into this largely rural region, in which numerous skyscrapers and highway systems were erected and to which came thousands of well-trained Chinese. As a result, Shenzhen emerged as a major industrial city by 1988, with most of its businesses foreign-owned or joint ventures. The sudden prosperity of Shenzhen with capitalist input, however, became an ironic counter to the propaganda of "the advantages of socialism" and thus generated strenuous resistance from conservatives in the government. In 1992, the aged Deng took a trip to the south and paid a visit to Shenzhen, his brainchild. Satisfied with the achievement, he promised Shenzhen would be protected and encouraged his fellow countrymen to hasten the pace of reform, using Shenzhen as a model. Thereafter, Shenzhen became an icon for the success of Chinese economic reform.

J. K. Fairbank, *China: A New History* (Cambridge, MA, 1992); W. Rodzinski, *The People's Republic of China* (New York, 1988).

Li Yi

SPENDER, PERCY C. (1897–1985)

Percy Claude Spender, as Australia's minister for external affairs from 1949 to 1951, worked to create a strong partnership with the United States after World War II. Originally, he planned a career as a professional athlete, but he chose to practice law, where his treatment of hostile witnesses earned him the admiring, if unaffectionate, sobriquet of "the butcher bird." Spender believed that the British Commonwealth in itself was not an appropriate basis on which to erect a structure of collective security. Circumstances played favorably into his hands when the Korean War* began in June 1950. Squadron Seventy-seven of the Royal Australian Air Force was in fact already on standby in Japan, being under the operational control of the Fifth U.S. Air Force. On 29 June, these aircraft, along with the destroyer *Bataan* and the frigate *Shoalhaven*, were offered to the United States. Three days later, Mustangs of Squadron Seventy-seven were in action.

Spender had another chance to get the attention of Washington. On 30 June, President Harry S. Truman* committed U.S. ground troops in Korea. Australian Prime Minister Robert G. Menzies* decided to visit London to consult with the British government before deciding on Australian policy. He was told there that Britain was in accord with his own decision not to commit troops. With Menzies halfway across the Atlantic, Britain then decided to send a force of their own. Spender immediately proceeded to bully Acting Prime Minister Sir Arthur Fadden into issuing, without consulting either Menzies or other ministers, a statement Spender wrote to the effect that the Australian government had decided to offer ground troops for use in Korea in response to the appeal of the United Nations. Spender now wanted a Pacific Pact as a quid pro quo. He cleverly decided to try the candid approach when he met with Truman. A Pacific Pact, he explained, would be meaningless unless the

United States were a party to it. Truman agreed to discuss it with Secretary of State Dean G. Acheson*, who briefly told Spender that he could not conceive of Australia being subject to hostile attack, or of U.S. failure to provide aid.

Special Representative John Foster Dulles* was even more uncompromising when Spender met with him at Flushing Meadows, New York, to discuss the Japanese Peace Treaty*. There, Dulles confronted Spender with the most extreme and inflexible version of the American position, presenting him with a document that omitted any reference to limitations on Japanese freedom to rearm. Spender told Dulles that Australia never would accept such a treaty; the only solution was a Pacific Pact. The compromise agreed on after further discussions on 30 October among Spender, Dulles, and Assistant Secretary of State Dean Rusk* amounted virtually to the acceptance in principle of Australia's proposal. Spender's desires might have remained unfulfilled, however, except that the United States was in urgent need of a reliable ally following signs in late October of Chinese Intervention in the Korean War*. British Foreign Secretary Ernest Bevin said flatly that he could not endorse the U.S. suggestion that China's entry might make violation of the Manchurian border necessary. By contrast, Spender urged that it should be made clear in the UN Security Council that it would be disadvantageous for UN forces to continue to observe restraint indefinitely. These protestations of support caused the Joint Chiefs of Staff to press the State Department to explore at the earliest opportunity possibilities for a Pacific Pact with Australia.

However, it was becoming increasingly difficult for the United States to ignore Australian approaches. Spender was in full flight again. At the Security Council on 20 January 1951, a resolution to condemn China for engaging in aggression in Korea was drafted substantially on Spender's instructions, despite the fact that Menzies himself was counseling caution on directions from London. Dulles arrived in Canberra on 14 February for talks with the Australians and New Zealanders prepared to pretend that the issue of a Pacific Pact never had been raised in connection with that of the Japanese Peace Treaty. Spender promptly informed him that Australia never would accept the treaty Dulles was proposing without accompanying arrangements to ensure Australian security. Menzies himself urged Spender not to press too hard for a tripartite defense pact, for fear of jeopardizing at least a presidential pledge to protect Australia and New Zealand. But the butcher bird knew with whom he was dealing. Dulles admitted that he had intended to discuss a Pacific Pact all along. After three more days of vehement wrangling, the three delegations agreed on a draft security pact, which represented with marginal changes the text of the final (ANZUS) (Australian–New Zealand–United States) Treaty*.

G. Barclay and J. Siracusa (eds.), *Australian-American Relations Since 1945: A Documentary History* (Sydney, 1976); N. Harper, *A Great and Powerful Friend: A Study of Australian and American Relations Between 1900 and 1975* (St. Lucia, BWI, 1987); J. Siracusa and Y. Cheong, *America's Australia: Australia's America* (Claremont, CA, 1997); P. Spender, *Politics and a Man* (Sydney, 1972).

Joseph M. Siracusa

STATE OF VIETNAM

See REPUBLIC OF VIETNAM

STERLING PAYMENTS AGREEMENT (31 August 1951)

The Sterling Payments Agreement (SPA) between the sterling-area countries and Japan was signed on 31 August 1951 to expand trade relations. It replaced the Open Payments Agreement*, which governed sterling area–Japan trade relations from

1948 to 1951. During the U.S. Occupation of Japan*, Washington supported expansion of Japan's trade with non-Communist countries in the region, but it was doubtful about whether trade with the sterling area would benefit Japan. This was because the United States perceived Britain as drawing Japan into the agreement to control and limit Japan's trade with Britain's traditional trading areas. The politics of the Sterling Payments Agreement therefore highlighted the underlying tension in Anglo-Japanese trade and American perception of the agreement.

The Sterling Payments Agreement was a bilateral trade accord signed between sterling-area countries and their trading partners. It began with the Anglo-Argentine Agreement of September 1946, in preparation for sterling convertibility. With the failure of convertibility in July 1947, the Sterling Payments Agreement was extended indefinitely until sterling became convertible. Its main objective was to promote the conduct of orderly trade between the sterling area and its trading partners without a drain in Britain's dollar reserves through a division of trade accounts into American, transferable, and bilateral accounts. Each account had its own rules and regulations, with the American being the most flexible and the bilateral most limited.

When Japan signed the Sterling Payments Agreement in August 1951, it was included in the bilateral account. This meant that Japan could trade only with countries designated in the bilateral account, and sterling transfers were permissible only after they were approved by the Bank of England. Moreover, the dollar convertibility clause in the Open Payments Agreement was abolished, thereby preventing Japan from converting its sterling into dollars. When U.S. officials in Japan and Washington were informed of the conditions of Japan's new trade relations with the sterling area, they suspected Britain of attempting to safeguard its own trade in the area. Contrary to the American suspicions, however, the British plan sought to encourage an expansion of Japan's trade with the sterling area. It was hoped that sterling area–Japan trade would lead to a greater circulation of sterling in East Asia and to the eventual restoration of sterling as an international currency.

Despite British hopes for expanded trade, Japan did not look exclusively to the sterling area for raw materials. Therefore, trade levels did not increase significantly and the agreement was terminated in March 1957. Moreover, any attempt to restore sterling as the major currency in East Asia failed, as the eventual convertibility of sterling in 1958 led to the weakening of the currency. Although Britain was unable to fulfill its original objective, the Sterling Payments Agreement laid the foundation for expanding Japanese trade relations with such sterling countries in the Asia Pacific as Singapore*, Malaysia*, Australia, and New Zealand.

R. Buckley, *Occupation Diplomacy: Britain, the United States and Japan 1945–1952* (New York, 1982); A. Rix, *Coming to Terms: The Politics of Australia's Trade with Japan 1945–57* (Sydney, 1986); C. R. Schenk, *Britain and the Sterling Area: From Devaluation to Convertibility in the 1950s* (London, 1994).

Yokoi Noriko

STEVENS, JOHN L. (1820–1895)

John Leavitt Stevens was the U.S. ambassador to Hawaii in 1893, and according to the leader of the Hawaiian Revolution* against the monarchy that year, without his support "the overthrow would not only not have succeeded, but would never have been attempted." Born in Mount Vernon, Maine, he first attended Maine Wesleyan Seminary and then Waterville Liberal Institute, prior to his entering the Universalist ministry in 1845. A passionate abolitionist, he decided after ten years as a pastor that he could better attack slavery through journalism. With James G. Blaine, Stevens acquired the *Kennebec Journal* in

1855 and remained involved with the paper first as editor and thereafter sporadically between his diplomatic assignments, all of which resulted from his close association with Blaine and his Republican party loyalty. In 1870, he became minister to Paraguay and Uruguay, where he managed the U.S. legations to these two nations until 1874. During this time, Stevens negotiated a commercial treaty with Uruguay and mediated a dispute between Argentina and Uruguay. He was minister to Norway and Sweden from 1877 to 1883.

With the inauguration of Republican Benjamin Harrison in 1889, and Harrison's appointment of Blaine as secretary of state, Stevens easily secured another diplomatic assignment: minister to the Kingdom of Hawaii. The island nation long had been considered ripe for U.S. annexation, and Stevens was well aware of Blaine's interest in acquiring Hawaii. In Honolulu, Stevens quickly befriended members of the white, plantation-owning elite, many of whom were the children of American missionaries. Stevens's natural sympathies lay with the planters and merchants who chafed under the inefficient and corrupt administrations of King Kalakaua*, and his sister Lili'uokalani*, who assumed the throne in 1891. On 16 January 1893, with Harrison's administration about to leave office and Blaine now deceased, a group of Hawaiians planters led by Sanford B. Dole* staged a coup against the queen. Stevens responded with amazing speed and determination to assure the success of the revolution. After U.S. Marines landed, he declared a U.S. protectorate over the islands. On 1 February, Stevens then provided diplomatic recognition to the provisional government, clearly overstepping the bounds of his authority. Although he approved of his minister's recognition of Dole's provisional government, Secretary of State John W. Foster*, who supported annexation with a passion, was forced to deny that Ambassador Stevens had in fact established a protectorate.

The U.S. Senate failed to ratify the treaty of annexation that the Harrison administration drafted with the delegation the Hawaiian provisional government sent to Washington. The new administration of Grover Cleveland then withdrew the document because Secretary of State William Q. Gresham believed Stevens's actions were inappropriate. Based on the report James H. Blount* submitted after returning from Hawaii to investigate the rebellion, Cleveland and Gresham sought to bring about the restoration of Lili'uokalani. A new minister, Albert S. Willis, was sent to replace Stevens with instructions to ask the provisional government to relinquish its power. When officially called upon to step aside in December 1893, Dole politely refused. Six months later, Dole declared establishment of the Hawaiian Republic with himself as its president. Meanwhile, Stevens returned to Washington to face congressional hearings, and he remained adamant that he had no role in the coup. In sworn statements before a U.S. Senate committee investigating the Hawaiian affair, he repeatedly denied any complicity in plots to remove the queen. Following his return from Hawaii, Stevens lived in Augusta, Maine, and wrote *Picturesque Hawaii* (1894).

M. J. Devine, "John W. Foster and the Struggle for Annexation of Hawaii," *Pacific Historical Review* (February 1977); M. Tate, *The United States and the Hawaiian Kingdom: A Political History* (New Haven, CT, 1965); U.S. Department of State, *Foreign Relations of the United States, 1894*, Appendix 2 (Washington, DC, 1995); U.S. Senate Report 227, *The Hawaiian Islands: Report of the Committee on Foreign Relations*, 2 vols., 53d Cong., 2d Sess., 1894.

Michael J. Devine

STILWELL, JOSEPH W. (1883–1946)

U.S. General Joseph W. Stilwell was the commander of the China-Burma-India Theater* of operations during World War II from January 1942 until his recall to the United States in November 1944. A career military officer, he graduated from West Point in 1904. After learning Chinese, Stilwell became the U.S. Army's first language officer in China, serving there from 1920 to 1923. Thereafter, he was executive officer for the Fifteenth Infantry in Tianjin from 1926 to 1929, developing a deep knowledge of China's people and its politics. As U.S. military attaché from 1935 to 1939 with the Republic of China*, Stilwell watched Japanese aggression in China after the Marco Polo Bridge Incident* in July 1937. A hardworking and effective organizer of men, he understood what had to be done to defeat Japan. His grasp of the intricate political dynamics in China ultimately had a bearing on his ability to prosecute the war. In addition to fighting the Japanese, he also battled China's leader, Jiang Jieshi*, who wanted to protect his forces from casualties to spare them for the anticipated civil war against the Chinese Communist Party*. The two disagreed over strategy, specifically over the use of Chinese troops.

Stilwell also competed with other U.S. officers for the attention of Washington, most notably Major General Claire L. Chennault*, commander of the Fourteenth U.S. Air Force. He understood that ground troops were necessary to keep Japanese forces in check. But Chennault insisted that with enough strategic bombers, he could ruin Japan's war-making capacity. Stilwell's assessment proved correct when during 1944, Japanese troops overran the air bases used by Chennault's planes. Shortly afterward, and despite what appeared to be a political victory for Stilwell in his competition with Chiang, he was recalled by President Franklin D. Roosevelt*. Criticism from Jiang's supporters in Washington, coupled with a personal request from Jiang himself, led the president to replace Stilwell with Lieutenant General Albert C. Wedemeyer* during November 1944 to placate the Guomindang* (Nationalist) leader at a delicate time in U.S. relations with the Republic of China. Stilwell's significance for U.S. interests in Asia stemmed from his organizational effectiveness in training the Chinese troops placed under his command, his understanding of the Chinese Civil War*, and his insensitivity and arrogance toward Jiang, which ultimately contributed to his recall.

M. Schaller, *The U.S. Crusade in China, 1938–1945* (New York, 1979); B. W. Tuchman, *Stilwell and the American Experience in China, 1931–45* (New York, 1970); T. H. White (ed.), *The Stilwell Papers* (New York, 1948).

T. Christopher Jespersen

STIMSON DOCTRINE

The Stimson Doctrine of 3 January 1932 said that the United States would not recognize as legitimate any changes in the status quo in China resulting from the use of force. Although issued in response to the Japanese seizure of the Manchurian city of Jinzhao, it was the culmination of a long series of failed diplomatic initiatives to protect Chinese sovereignty after the Mukden Incident*. Japan had expanded its economic interests in Manchuria after the Russo-Japanese War* ended in 1905. By 1930, hundreds of Japanese businesses had operations there, promoting the immigration of more than 200,000 Japanese and controlling Manchuria's economic infrastructure. To protect these interests, Tōkyō deployed the Kwantung army to the area. China viewed Japanese dominance of Manchuria as a violation of its territorial sovereignty, but Japan pointed to the political chaos of the Warlord Era* to justify its claim that China's government was unable or unwilling to protect legitimate Japanese property rights in Manchuria. But after Jiang Jieshi* unified China in 1928, the new Nanjing government pressed Japan to evacuate Chinese territory.

In September 1931, after staging an explosion on the South Manchuria Railway, Japan's regional military commander ordered the redeployment of Japanese troops from Korea, allegedly to bolster efforts to curb banditry and lawlessness. The Council of the League of Nations met to discuss the crisis, but the Japanese delegate reassured them with a promise that Japanese troops would withdraw shortly. The U.S. government supported the policy of the League Council, as did the European democracies, to allow Japan time to initiate an honorable withdrawal. Secretary of State Henry L. Stimson* advocated coordination with League actions, fearing that a more assertive U.S. policy would undermine the efforts of Foreign Minister Shidehara Kijūrō* to reassert civilian control. But his confidence was misplaced. Facing a core of military commanders who had little respect for liberal civilian authority, as well as public enthusiasm for Japan's assertion of military power in Manchuria, Shidehara could not prevent continued advances by the Kwantung army in the winter of 1931.

Stimson understood that the United States had few options in responding to Japanese aggression. Budget cuts to combat the Great Depression meant that the U.S. Army and U.S. Navy were incapable of launching a campaign against the Japanese in Manchuria. The need to spur economic recovery also ruled out the alternative policies of trade sanctions or moral outrage because of the American dependence on the Japanese market. Moreover, any assertive U.S. policy would fall under the scrutiny of isolationists in the Senate, who would object to the United States assuming the role of international policeman. Finally, pacifist President Herbert Hoover* opposed any action against Japan that risked military conflict. But when the Kwantung army seized Jinzhao, Stimson realized that liberal elements in the Japanese government could not control military operations in Manchuria. Lacking options, he adopted the diplomatic strategy Secretary of State William Jennings Bryan* had used in response to the Twenty-One Demands* in 1915. In identical messages to Japan and China, he said the United States would refuse to recognize any actions that might "impair the treaty rights of the United States or its citizens in China."

Designed as a means of censuring Japan, the Stimson Doctrine was ineffective in curbing its aggression in China. The Kwantung army quickly asserted control over the economy of Manchuria and effectively removed non-Japanese foreign investment. Liberal opposition failed to restrain the Japanese Army's nationalistic expansionism. In 1932, the Japanese sponsored the creation of the state of Manchukuo*, effectively moving the sovereign control of Manchuria from China to Japan. In response to the Lytton Report* and the League Council condemnation of Japanese activity, Japan left the League of Nations in 1933. At the time of its implementation, the American public generally viewed the Stimson Doctrine as a constructive policy. The president even insisted that it be referred to as the Hoover-Stimson Doctrine. But subsequent Japanese aggression caused the policy to fall under opprobrium.

D. Borg and S. Okamoto (eds.), *Pearl Harbor as History: Japanese-American Relations, 1931–1941* (New York, 1973); J. D. Doenecke, *When the Wicked Rise: American Opinion-Makers and the Manchurian Crisis of 1931–1933* (Lewisburg, PA, 1984); A. Rappaport, *Henry L. Stimson and Japan, 1931–1933* (Chicago, 1963); C. Thorne, *The Limits of Foreign Policy: The West, the League of Nations and the Far Eastern Crisis of 1931–1933* (London, 1972).

Karen A. J. Miller

STIMSON, HENRY L. (1867–1950)

Henry Lewis Stimson served the federal government under seven presidents during the first half of the twentieth century in a broad range of capacities. A protégé of Elihu Root*, he had strong ties to the Republican Party leadership. Stimson was secretary of war under William Howard Taft*, reorganizing the War Department to make it more efficient and more capable of defending U.S. interests abroad. After U.S. entrance into World War I, he joined the U.S. Army and served briefly as an artillery officer. In 1928, he became governor-general of the Philippines*. Although he had little confidence in the Filipino people's capacity for independence, he did encourage the development of limited self-rule and envisioned a dominion status for the island. Stimson also defended free trade, vigorously opposing the efforts of American sugar producers to eliminate Philippine competition. Filipino nationalists accepted his paternalism largely because it was less offensive than that of his predecessor, Leonard Wood*. In 1929, Herbert Hoover* cut short Stimson's tenure when he appointed him secretary of state. In this capacity, Stimson continued to support a global U.S. military presence, but the Great Depression created complications in world affairs that forced him to moderate his position on a number of issues.

Stimson represented U.S. interests at the London Naval Conference of 1930*, where he sought an agreement to maintain the balance of naval power established by the Five Power Pact*. French insistence on the inclusion of provisions for mutual defense therefore blocked a sweeping naval arms treaty, and the limited agreement Stimson did achieve quickly unraveled. Relations between the United States and Japan began to deteriorate swiftly after the Mukden Incident* in September 1931. Although Stimson regarded the government of Jiang Jieshi* as inefficient and corrupt, he supported Chinese sovereignty over Manchuria and pressed for quick Japanese withdrawal from the region. After Japan ignored him, he issued early in 1932 the Stimson Doctrine* of nonrecognition. Stimson recognized that it was a rather modest policy, falling short of economic sanctions against the Japanese economy, but he lacked the support of President Hoover and the American people for a more assertive policy.

After the Republican defeat in the 1932 presidential election, Stimson left active government service. As a private citizen, he grew more strident in his calls for economic sanctions against Japan and promoted a response to its aggression based on principles of collective security. His support of an interventionist approach after the outbreak of World War II in Europe early in September 1939 explains the decision of President Franklin D. Roosevelt* to name him as secretary of war in the bipartisan cabinet he formed after his reelection in 1940. As secretary of war, Stimson was an ardent advocate of a trade embargo on Japan. Recognizing that diplomacy had failed to halt Tōkyō's military expansion, he urged the more aggressive step of embargoing the export of scrap iron and petroleum products to Japan. Stimson also prepared the U.S. Army for war, assuming that the first military operations against Japan would occur in Southeast Asia. After the Pearl Harbor Attack*, he worked for full conversion of the U.S. economy to war production. His fundamental distrust of the Japanese led him to support the internment of Japanese-Americans, regardless of their citizenship status. Stimson also advocated the policy of "unconditional surrender" to eliminate Japan and Germany as regional powers after the war.

By the summer of 1945, Stimson was able to accommodate his commitment to unconditional surrender with Japanese retention of a constitutional monarchy after a surrender. The prospect of a U.S. invasion of Japan, along with the possible necessity of support by Russian troops, caused him to conclude that this shift was essential to guarantee Japanese demilitarization. His concerns over the costs of an invasion of the Japanese home islands also led him to endorse the use of the atomic bomb. Stimson was the first to inform President Harry S. Truman* in April 1945 that the United States was developing the new weapon. Moreover, he identified key targets for the Atomic Attacks*, excluding Kyōto while selecting cities with both military installations and significant civilian populations. When the Japanese offered a conditional surrender after the bombing of Nagasaki, Stimson urged acceptance of the single condition of retaining the emperor. He resigned as secretary of war in September 1945, effectively removing himself from the postwar construction of U.S. foreign policy in the Pacific.

G. Alperovitz, *The Decision to Use the Atomic Bomb and the Architecture of an American Myth* (New York, 1995); R. N. Current, *Secretary Stimson: A Study in Statecraft* (New Brunswick, NJ, 1954); E. Larabee, *Commander in Chief: Franklin Delano Roosevelt, His Lieutenants, and Their War* (New York, 1987); H. L. Stimson, and M. Bundy, *On Active Service in Peace and War* (New York, 1947).

Karen A. J. Miller

STRAIGHT, WILLARD D. (1880–1918)

During a brief but active career as an imperialist promoter, Willard Dickerman Straight helped define the Open Door Policy* and Dollar Diplomacy* for the U.S. State Department and for American financial interests. Born in Oswego, New York, he was educated at Cornell University and then joined the Chinese Imperial Maritime Customs Service, where he became personal aide to its chief, Sir Robert Hart. In 1904, Straight left to report on the Russo-Japanese War* for Reuters, after which he secured an appointment as U.S. vice consul at Seoul. During his service in Korea, he witnessed firsthand the Japanese dissolution and absorption of its Korean protectorate, which persuaded him that the United States must oppose Japanese Colonialism* and expansionism in East Asia. After a short detour as vice consul in Havana, he returned to Asia in 1906 as consul general at Mukden, Manchuria. Mukden was a sensitive area, and Straight acquired his appointment not only through his considerable energy, charm, and ability, but also through his friendship with Alice Roosevelt Longworth and E. H. Harriman*.

Determined that the Americans must prevent the Russians and Japanese from taking more Asian territory, Straight built a network of contacts among the other young diplomats in the region. He went further, working closely with ambitious members of the Chinese government to create a public relations machine that would expose Japanese incursions on Chinese sovereignty. After an episode when Straight used an unloaded pistol to round up a group of Japanese soldiers, who had got into a brawl on the consulate grounds, the State Department recalled him to the United States, where he served briefly as chief of the Bureau of Far Eastern Affairs in 1908. Before leaving China, he negotiated a deal for an American-funded Chinese bank dedicated to the construction of Chinese-owned railroads. Straight believed the project would serve both U.S. and Chinese interests, shoring up China's ability to run its own affairs. The deal fell through when President Theodore Roosevelt* decided it was more important to reinforce an understanding with Japan in the Root-Takahira Agreement*. His negotiating effort qualified him for his next job representing the consortium of interests, known simply as the American Group, whose principal member was J. P. Morgan and Company.

Straight strove to ensure that the American Group would get a piece of whatever loans the other imperial powers might make to China, believing that the United States could both profit from the deals and ensure that China might someday follow in its steps as an independent republic. His sense of mission kept him active in the Chinese loan business long after bankers decided it was scarcely worth pursuing. After the Chinese Revolution of 1911* that overthrew the Qing Dynasty, Straight insisted the United States ought to deal with the military ruler Yuan Shikai*, and after Yuan, he insisted the United States ought to deal with the Chinese Republic. In 1915, National City Bank hired him to represent its American International Corporation in overseas lending. Meanwhile, he married Dorothy Whitney in 1911, and together they founded *The New Republic* and *Asia*, through which they promoted American interest in other cultures and an active foreign policy. Straight also created India House to ease Asian trade among New

York businessmen. In 1917, Straight resigned his job at the American International Corporation to join the American Expeditionary Force as a major. After organizing the War Risk Insurance Bureau, he transferred to the peace mission late in 1918 and soon after died of influenza. *See also* Tang Shaoyi.

H. D. Croly, *Willard Straight* (New York, 1924); M. H. Hunt, *Frontier Defense and the Open Door: Manchuria in Chinese-American Relations, 1895–1911* (New Haven, CT, 1973); A. Iriye, *Across the Pacific: An Inner History of American–East Asian Relations* (New York, 1967); W. LaFeber, *The Clash: A History of U.S.-Japan Relations* (New York, 1997); E. Rauchway, "Willard Straight and the Paradox of Liberal Imperialism," *Pacific Historical Review* (August 1997).

Eric Rauchway

STRATEGIC HAMLETS PROGRAM

Originally intended as a means for depriving the Viet Cong* "fish" of the peasant "sea" in the Republic of Vietnam*, the Strategic Hamlets Program, ironically, hastened the erosion of support for the regime of Ngo Dinh Diem* because of corruption and lack of effectiveness. South Vietnam's government launched this new version of the failed agrovilles in 1961. Designed by Sir Robert Thompson, head of the British team of advisers to Diem and the architect of similar counterinsurgency programs in Malaya* and the Philippines*, peasants from scattered villages would be relocated to hamlets surrounded by moats and fences and protected by well-trained military forces. In these fortified areas, they would be won over to the Saigon government with fair elections, land reform, good schools, and improved medical facilities. The Viet Cong guerrillas then would have no villages in which to hide, which would force them to come out into the open where the Army of the Republic of Vietnam* (ARVN) and American forces would be able to use their superior conventional firepower to destroy them. The villages were surrounded by barbed wire and other defenses, and the villagers were armed and trained in basic defense. Individually, the hamlets were to be antiguerrilla bastions; collectively, they were intended to confront the Viet Cong with a network of fortified hamlets organized into a crisscrossed line of defense.

Although the strategic hamlets received more government support than the agroville program—primarily because President Diem and his brother Ngo Dinh Nhu*, who was placed in charge of the program at its inception, expected it to give them more direct control over the villages—they remained unpopular with the peasants. By the end of 1962, 3,235 strategic hamlets had been built, leading South Vietnamese officials to claim that 34 percent of the populace lived under government control. In reality, these claims were guesswork. Further, despite U.S. and South Vietnamese efforts, the hamlets remained vulnerable to the Viet Cong both militarily and politically. The Viet Cong could concentrate their forces at will and destroy individual strategic hamlets with overwhelming force. One American study later showed that less than 10 percent of the hamlets possessed any military security. The most significant difference between the success the program enjoyed in Malaya and its failure in South Vietnam was that whereas the British had fortified Malay villages against Chinese insurgents, the Vietnamese had to fortify Vietnamese hamlets against other Vietnamese, who had grown up in those hamlets. Nevertheless, in areas where it was actually applied, the strategic hamlets program did give the Saigon government a short-term military advantage.

Politically, however, it proved a disaster. In the Mekong Delta, the program required massive relocation of peasants away from their ancestral homelands, which only further alienated them from South Vietnam's government. Diem never enacted the promised land reform, and large volumes of U.S. assistance money were diverted by corrupt government officials from hamlet medical, educational, and welfare programs into their own pockets. As a result, the peasants had no incentive to do anything to defend the villages against insurgents since they were not receiving any of the promised benefits. Indeed, the program was so unpopular that it may actually have increased Viet Cong appeal among the peasants. Its problems notwithstanding, the Strategic Hamlets Program continued for two years as the centerpiece of U.S. and South Vietnamese counterinsurgency efforts. After Diem's Assassination*, along with his brother Nhu's, in November 1963, the program was all but abandoned.

L. E. Cable, *Conflict of Myths: The Development of American Counterinsurgency Doctrine and the Vietnam War* (New York, 1986); F. FitzGerald, *Fire in the Lake: The Vietnamese and the Americans in Vietnam* (New York, 1972); R. Hilsman, *To Move a Nation: The Politics of the Foreign Policy in the Administration of John F. Kennedy* (New York, 1967).

Andrew L. Johns

STRONG, ANNA LOUISE (1885–1970)

As a radical journalist and advocate for socialist revolution in both the Soviet Union and China, Anna Louise Strong educated Americans about global struggles for social justice and acted as a liaison between the American Left and the worldwide socialist movement. Born in Friend, Nebraska, the daughter of a Congregational minister, she developed Christian Socialist sensibilities early in life. Strong attended Oberlin College, where she was encouraged to become a missionary. She pursued a secular career, but a missionarylike desire to "do good" never left her. Strong then earned a doctorate at the University of Chicago in 1908 in philosophy and religious studies. While there, she came into direct contact through Jane Addams and an internship at Hull House with the urban working class. Concerns about economic inequalities inherent in a capitalist system resulted in her decision to continue settlement-house work in New York. When she moved to Seattle, Strong's Progressive political orientation dictated her involvement with radical labor politics.

In 1921, Strong, disappointed with the failures of the radical American labor movement to transform exploitative working conditions, visited the new worker's state in the Soviet Union. Enamored with both the ideas and the individuals directing the socialist revolution in Russia, she dedicated herself to promoting the Bolshevik Party's accomplishments through her journalistic reports published in the United States. In 1925, Strong made her first visit to China. A second trip in 1927 inspired her lasting allegiance to China's revolutionary transformation. Although the right wing of the Guomindang* (GMD) Party led by Jiang Jieshi* launched an attack on all radical political forces in April that year, the Chinese effort to revolutionize society inspired Strong. She wrote about the noble causes of the Chinese revolutionaries, focusing especially on their objective of liberating Chinese women from all social and legal oppression. Through Song Qingling*, wife of Sun Zhongshan*, Strong maintained contact with Chinese radicals throughout the 1930s.

Strong spent the 1930s living in the Soviet Union with her Russian husband and propagandizing for the Communist Party of the Soviet Union (CPSU) as the leader of the international Communist movement. In 1938, she returned to China determined to build support for the revolutionaries. Visits to the Chinese Communist Party* (CCP) headquarters at Yan'an and contacts with GMD leaders who formed the United Front* confirmed Strong's commitment to working for the success of the Chinese revolution. After the outbreak of World War II, Strong joined progressive Americans working in China to funnel U.S. aid to the forces fighting Japan. Soon thereafter, she returned to the United States, where she stayed until 1944, writing and lecturing in support of the Allied effort and on the progress of the Chinese revolution. Strong's much-publicized radical sympathies drew attacks from anti-Communists inside and outside the U.S. government. Frustrated by an increasingly hostile U.S. political climate, she returned to China as the Chinese Civil War* resumed in 1945. Through her articles and lecture tours, Strong hoped to persuade American voters that the CCP had the visionary and democratic leadership that would best serve the Chinese people and was becoming a model for other non-Western peoples rejecting colonial rule.

After 1947, Strong's vigorous support for the CCP's leadership of postwar nationalist and revolutionary independence movements in the Third World alarmed the CPSU, which expelled her when she attempted to return to China by crossing through Soviet territory in 1949. The American Communist Party also ostracized her when she returned to the United States and publicly criticized the Soviet leadership. Isolated from the American Left, which had become her only constituency in the Cold War, Strong spent the 1950s defending her actions and promoting U.S. recognition of the People's Republic of China* through her monthly newsletter, *Today*. When she returned to China in 1958 at age seventy-three, Strong was eager for the recognition she felt was her due as a venerated friend of the Chinese revolution. She stayed in China for the rest of her life as a valued and privileged foreigner, and continued to promote the achievements of the CCP in her renamed newsletter, *Letter from China*. During the Chinese Cultural Revolution*, Strong escaped political attacks experienced by other foreigners. She was honored with a state funeral in Beijing.

H. Deane, *Good Deeds and Gunboats: Two Centuries of American-Chinese Encounters* (San Francisco, CA, 1990); L. Lubkeman, "Anna Louise Strong and the Stalinist Era," Ph.D. dissertation, University of Wisconsin, 1995; R. A. McCloy, *Revolution and Cosmopolitanism: Agnes Smedley, Anna Louise Strong and Pearl Buck Interpret China, 1920–1949* (Durham, NC, 1983); A. L. Strong, *I Change Worlds: The Remaking of an American* (New York, 1935); T. B. Strong and H. Keyssar, *Right in Her Soul: The Life of Anna Louise Strong* (New York, 1983).

Karen Garner

STUART, J. LEIGHTON (1876–1962)

John Leighton Stuart, a prominent missionary educator in China in the first part of the twentieth century, served as U.S. ambassador to China from July 1946 until August 1949. Born to missionary parents in Hangzhou, he was educated in the United States and returned to China in 1904 as a Presbyterian missionary. In 1919, he became president of the newly established Yenching University, a forerunner of Beijing University. His thirty years in this position gave him a wide range of connections among Chinese intellectuals and political leaders, leading in 1946 to his appointment as ambassador. He tried valiantly to support the mission of General George C. Marshall* to bring a peaceful end to the Chinese Civil War*, meeting with leaders ranging from Jiang Jieshi* to Zhou Enlai*. Although he was well aware of the defects of Jiang's government, Stuart thought the Guomindang* (Nationalists) held out more hope than the Chinese Communist Party* for a free and democratic China. After the Marshall Mission* failed, he urged strong U.S. support for Jiang's regime, but conditioned on reforms. He was dismayed when Washington did neither.

Stuart remained in Nanjing for three months after the city fell to Communist forces in April 1949. But his hopes for a mutually beneficial relationship between the United States and the new People's Republic of China* ran afoul of the deep hostility on both sides. In June, Huang Hua*, a former Yenching student who was in charge of the Alien Affairs Office in Nanjing, told Stuart he had received a message from Mao Zedong* and Zhou inviting Stuart to visit Beijing, but President Harry S. Truman* and Secretary of State Dean G. Acheson* ruled against such a trip. In a final effort, Stuart sent a message to Mao and Zhou through a member of an anti-Guomindang group allied with the Communists, saying that Americans believed states with different ideologies could live together peacefully and arguing that good relations with the United States would benefit China. The response brought back from Beijing renewed the suggestion of a Stuart visit but also declared that China did not need trade with the United States, and that the Soviets had supported China in more important ways than the Americans. Disappointed, Stuart left China three days before the publication of the China White Paper*. Soon afterward, in a stinging article titled "Farewell, Leighton Stuart," Mao called Stuart "a symbol of the complete defeat of the U.S. policy of aggression in China." Stuart suffered a stroke soon after returning to the United States and never regained his health. He resigned as ambassador at the end of 1952. *See also* Zhou-Stuart Conversations.

Y. Shaw, *An American Missionary in China: John Leighton Stuart and Chinese-American Relations* (Cambridge, MA, 1992); J. L. Stuart, *Fifty Years in China: The Memoirs of John Leighton Stuart, Missionary and Ambassador* (New York, 1954); U.S. Department of State, *Foreign Relations of the United States, 1949*, Vol. 8: *The Far East: China* (Washington, 1978).

Harriet Dashiell Schwar

SUBIC NAVAL BASE CONTROVERSY

Subic Naval Base, in central Luzon, the Philippines*, was the largest docking and repair facility outside the American mainland. It was one of 200 bases the United States retained after Philippine independence under the 1947 Military Bases Agreement with the Philippines. The agreement allowed the United States use of twenty-three base sites for ninety-nine years, renewable after expiration, while also stipulating that through negotiations, the bases could be expanded or, if necessary, new areas be opened for additional bases. Together with Clark Air Force Base, Subic was regarded as a vital installation in projecting American power in South and East Asia and a crucial link in a network of U.S. military bases ranging from the Republic of Korea* and Japan to the Philippines, created to contain Soviet and Chinese Communism*. Both bases became staging points and supply conduits, as well as major rest and recreation ports, during the Korean War* and the Second Indochina War*.

Controversy hounded Subic and Clark from their founding. For one, Filipino nationalists criticized the military bases agreement and other related treaties as "war damage blackmail" accompanying the grant of independence. Disbursement of funds under the $120 million Philippine Rehabilitation Act was limited to $500 unless the Philippine government accepted the Bell Trade Act of October 1945. This act required duty-free trade between the two nations from 1945 to 1954 and gradual introduction of tariffs over the next twenty years. And it added another controversial provision: an amendment that gave U.S. corporations and individuals the same rights as Filipinos to acquire public lands for agricultural and mineral exploitation, gain access to fishing areas, and secure ownership and operation of public utilities. Nationalists criticized this "parity rights" provision as disadvantaging Filipino business at a time when the economy had yet to recover from World War II. Faced with little other choice, the Philippine senate approved the trade act, and U.S. war damage payments began. The military treaties then followed, and with their approval, nationalists declared that the shift from colonial to "neocolonial" status of the Philippines was complete.

This initial controversy was followed by a series of others. A provision of the bases agreement gave U.S. military authorities sole jurisdiction over crimes that were committed by American personnel inside and outside the bases while doing their official duties. In a number of incidents in the late 1950s and early 1960s, American sentries shot Filipinos suspected of breaking into the bases, setting off widespread protests, particularly among students leading a nationalist resurgence. The part the bases played in the Vietnam War further enflamed Filipino nationalist sentiment. The shift to authoritarian rule under President Ferdinand E. Marcos* in 1972 deepened the bases controversy. Marcos, aware of the popularity of the antibases opposition, used these nationalist sentiments to obtain more aid and support from the United States for his regime. Anti-Marcos groups, especially the radical left, concentrated their attacks on this relationship to highlight the dictatorship's "subservience" to U.S. interests with the bases its principal symbol. In response, Marcos called for a review of the bases agreement in 1975. Publicly, the regime made clear that the issue was the assertion of Philippine sovereignty. The real bone of contention, however, was how much the United States would pay as "rental" for the bases. On 7 January 1979, agreement was reached that the U.S. government would reduce the size of the Subic and Clark bases, redesignate all bases as "Philippine bases," and fly the Philippine flag alongside the American. Reacting to criticism over the shooting of Filipinos by sentries, perimeter security was passed on to Filipino troops. President Jimmy Carter* also made a commitment to try to obtain from Congress military aid of $500 million over a five-year period, as well as expanded economic assistance.

Although Marcos's Ouster* and the ascension to power of Corazon Aquino* generally was viewed as a democratization process, the nationalist criticism of the bases did not disappear. In 1996, the Aquino government began to negotiate the extension of the soon-to-expire Military Bases Agreement, sparking a new round of protests. The negotiations themselves became contentious, as the new Philippine constitution included a provision that required the United States to set aside its long-held policy of neither confirming nor denying the presence of nuclear weapons. This issue eventually was set aside in favor of one more critical to the nearly bankrupt Philippine government: rental for the bases. Both sides finally agreed to an extension of the bases agreement to another five years. The new treaty then had to be approved by the Philippine senate in accordance with the new constitution, where nationalist sentiments had grown far stronger and one-third of the senators opposed the bases. Senators who saw the rental as too low combined with nationalist senators to defeat the treaty, despite pressure from Aquino and her allies. In 1992, the last of the U.S Navy ships left Subic Naval Base for Guam*, Clark Air Force base was closed earlier by the eruption of the volcano Mt. Pinatubo. Thus ended one of the more powerful legacies of U.S. influence and control in the Philippines. Thereafter, the Subic base was transformed successfully into a regional transport hub and free trade zone, used by American carrier corporations serving Southeast and East Asia. Nationalist protests continued, this time over the alleged failure of the departing Americans to clean up the environmental damage wrought by the navy facilities.

W. Berry, *U.S. Bases in the Philippines: The Evolution of a Special Relationship* (Boulder, CO, 1989); E. Garcia and F. Nemenzo, *The Sovereign Quest: Freedom from Foreign Military Bases* (Manila, 1988); F. Greene (ed.), *The Philippine Bases: Negotiating for the Future American and Philippine Perspectives* (New York, 1988); A. J. Gregor, *The Philippine Bases: U.S. Security at Risk* (Washington, DC, 1987); E. Romualdez, *A Question of Sovereignty: The Military Bases and Philippine-American Relations, 1944–1979* (Manila, 1980).

Patricio N. Abinales

SUHARTO (1921–   )

Suharto ruled Indonesia* from 1966 to 1998. His supporters credited him with maintaining Indonesia's stability and setting it on the path to economic development. His later, more numerous critics condemned his long legacy of corruption, political stagnation, authoritarianism, and human rights abuses, from which Indonesia was still struggling to recover at the start of the twenty-first century. Suharto was born in central Java near Yogyakarta. With relatively little education, he joined the Royal Netherlands' Indies Army at the age of nineteen. From 1945 to 1949, he rose swiftly through the ranks during Indonesia's war for independence from the Dutch. In 1962, Sukarno* appointed Suharto to head the Mandala command for the liberation of West Irian and then, from 1963 to 1965, the Trikora command responsible for the military confrontation with Malaysia*. Although not an especially skilled military leader, Suharto used his commands to build patronage networks and secure the loyalty of his soldiers, links he later used to consolidate his own power. In 1964, Major-General Suharto was named commander of the Army's Strategic Reserve Command (Komando Strategis Angkatan Darat). In this position, he launched a countercoup against an alleged coup attempt in the Indonesia Crisis of 1965* and asserted control over the army.

From October 1965 until March 1966, Suharto oversaw the extermination of the Indonesian Communist Party (PKI), in which many thousands of alleged members were killed and hundreds of thousands more imprisoned. During this period, he also adroitly whittled away at Sukarno's power until Sukarno was forced to transfer authority to him on 11 March 1966. His initial task was salvaging Indonesia's shattered economy. Suharto lacked the policy experience to devise or implement a program to restore economic stability and the confidence of foreign investors. Instead, he turned the task over to a group of mostly U.S.-trained economic advisers, who formulated a foreign investment law welcoming Western capital back to Indonesia on enviable terms. For the next thirty years, Indonesia experienced steady absolute economic growth, fueled in part by increases in oil revenues. To mobilize political support, the regime, which lacked an independent mass base, adopted a political organization known as Golkar, which comprised "functional groups"—peasants, workers, business, the army, and others. In 1967, Suharto assumed the presidency and gained reelection in tightly scripted balloting in 1973, 1978, 1983, 1988, 1993, and 1998. His New Order could best be described as a military bureaucratic regime, with a military administration that ran parallel to the civilian administration down to the village level. Suharto's politico-military administration proved adept at maintaining order, often through the brutal repression of political dissent, especially in areas such as Aceh and Irian Jaya. Despite Suharto's deplorable human rights record, successive U.S. administrations provided extensive political, military, and economic support, considering Indonesia a valuable anti-Communist bastion of stability in a strategically vital and unstable region.

Evidence of Indonesian stability, however, was misleading, as was its economic development. Suharto's fabulously corrupt family and its allies, using a vast network of military- and government-controlled businesses and foundations, diverted much of the nation's growing wealth to themselves, accumulating billions in the process and making Suharto one of the world's richest men. This corruption and unaccountability extended to foreign policy. In December 1975, Suharto authorized the invasion of the former Portuguese colony of East Timor after covert operations aimed at destabilizing the territory failed. Nearly a third of East Timor's population died as a result of the invasion and occupation, during which Indonesia never was able fully to consolidate control. The territory eventually regained its freedom in a UN-sponsored referendum in August 1999 more than a year after Suharto's ouster, after which Indonesian troops burned East Timor to the ground and displaced virtually the entire population. By the late 1990s, rising social and economic inequality and brutal repression of dissent had fatally undermined Suharto's legitimacy, which was based on the promise of political order and economic growth. Corruption meant that currency stability and the expectations of foreign investors were built largely on fictional assumptions. As a result, the East Asian Financial Crisis* of 1997 hit Indonesia's economy especially hard and detonated the tinder of nascent opposition to Suharto's rule. A mass movement of students, street vendors, and the urban poor emerged and demanded Suharto's ouster. The withdrawal of U.S. support for Suharto and the splintering of the army in the face of widespread and growing protest forced his resignation from power in May 1998.

H. Crouch, *The Army and Politics in Indonesia* (Ithaca, NY, 1978); D. Kingsbury, *The Politics of Indonesia* (New York, 1998); A. Schwartz, *A Nation in Waiting: Indonesia in the 1990's* (Sydney, 1999); J. Winters, *Power in Motion: Capital Mobility and the Indonesian State* (Ithaca, NY, 1995).

Bradley R. Simpson

SUKARNO (1901–1970)

A fiery, charismatic, and ofttimes mercurial national leader, Sukarno led the Indonesian struggle for independence from Dutch colonial rule following World War II. When Indonesia* formally achieved statehood on 27 December 1949, the veteran nationalist became president and remained the dominant political figure within the country until his fall from power in 1966. He was born into the aristocratic Javanese *priyayi* class, and his father was a schoolteacher. Despite being raised in modest material circumstances, Sukarno's privileged social status enabled him to receive a Western education. He earned an engineering degree in 1926, but by then had launched another career: as a very effective nationalist spokesman and agitator. A founder, in 1927, of the Indonesian Nationalist Party, Sukarno was twice jailed by Dutch authorities wary of his mounting public acclaim.

In 1942, Japan, after commencing its occupation of the Neitherlands East Indies, freed him and other top nationalists whom the Dutch had jailed or exiled. The pragmatic Sukarno saw collaboration with Japan as a golden opportunity to further the cause of ending Dutch Colonialism* and gaining Indonesian independence. When the Pacific war ended, he masterfully filled the political vacuum that suddenly appeared in the archipelago. On 17 August 1945, Sukarno proclaimed an independent Republic of Indonesia and was unanimously named president of the fledgling state. Within weeks, he presided over the drafting and promulgation of a constitution, the development of a cabinet form of government, and the establishment of a viable structure of civil and police authority.

Sukarno immediately looked to the United States for moral, material, and political support. Keenly aware of U.S. wartime proclamations opposing colonialism and favoring self-determination proclamations, he requested American diplomatic backing. Washington, however, reacted warily to the new regime and its charismatic but unpredictable leader. Unwilling to offend a staunch ally such as the Netherlands, the Truman administration initially tried to maintain a hands-off policy. Only when the Dutch-Indonesian struggle for power turned violent and especially after the Dutch "police action" of December 1948 did it shift course. Convinced that the Dutch resort to force would merely further destabilize Indonesia, and satisfied that Sukarno and his principal associates had anti-Communist preferences, Washington pressed the Dutch to grant independence to the Indonesian republic. The Truman administration's actions, however belated, earned Sukarno's gratitude. But, the ensuing honeymoon proved short-lived, as both the Truman and Eisenhower administrations tried to enlist Indonesia into the anti-Communist camp. Sukarno insisted on pursuing a policy of strict nonalignment, much to Washington's consternation, and he rejected all entreaties to join any form of bilateral or regional security pact with the United States. The Indonesian leader also regularly agitated for formal transfer from the Netherlands of the disputed territory of West Irian (West New Guinea) to the new Indonesian state, an issue that drove a wedge between Jakarta and a Washington solicitous of its North Atlantic Treaty Organization ally's position.

Sukarno's leading role in the nonaligned movement, his periodic anti-Western outbursts, and especially his cooperation with the Indonesian Communist Party all added further strain to Indonesian-American relations. In 1957–1958, Washington covertly encouraged and supported a group of dissident regional army commanders in a bold effort to undercut Sukarno. But the Indonesian military quickly crushed the PRRI-Permesta Rebellion*. After that policy disaster, the Eisenhower and Kennedy administrations sought to repair the breach and to reach an accommodation with a now strengthened Sukarno. President John F. Kennedy* offered to mediate the West Irian dispute and then applied unrelenting pressure on the Dutch to accept an agreement in August 1962 transferring the territory to Indonesia. But brief hopes for amicable relations ended in 1963 when Sukarno attacked the Federation of Malaysia* as a British neocolonial scheme. For President Lyndon B. Johnson*, his provocative "crush Malaysia" campaign, rejection of American aid, and increasingly vituperative anti-American speeches were intolerable. He feared that the Sukarno regime might soon align itself openly with the Communist powers. Then a group of junior army officers ignited the Indonesia Crisis of 1965*, and although Sukarno's role during the so-called "Gestapu" remains shrouded in mystery, the failed coup spelled his political demise. General Suharto* moved rapidly and brutally to restore control throughout the country, establishing himself as Indonesia's new strongman. Suharto gradually eased the aging revolutionary out of power by March 1966, but Sukarno left a major imprint on, and complex legacy within, the country he had done so much to create.

H. W. Brands, "The Limits of Manipulation: How the United States Didn't Topple Sukarno," *Journal of American History* (September 1989); P. F. Gardner, *Shared Hopes, Separate Fears: Fifty Years of U.S.-Indonesia Relations* (New York, 1997); G. McT. Kahin and A. R. Kahin, *Subversion as Foreign Policy: The Secret Eisenhower and Dulles Debacle in Indonesia* (New York, 1995); J. D. Legge, *Sukarno: A Political Biography* (New York, 1972); R. J. McMahon, *Colonialism and Cold War: The United States and the Struggle for Indonesian Independence, 1945–49* (Ithaca, NY, 1981).

Robert J. McMahon

SUN LIREN (1900–)

In 1944 and 1945, Sun Liren, a Virginia Military Institute alumnus, led the crack Chinese thirty-eighth Division in the Burma* campaigns under General Joseph W. Stilwell* and befriended his Deputy Chief of Staff Dean Rusk*. During Stilwell's aborted plot to assassinate Jiang Jieshi*, Sun probably was among the likely replacements. His first army outperformed all others in the Chinese Civil War*, and he corresponded regularly with Secretary of State George C. Marshall*. Dean G. Acheson* replaced Marshall in early 1949 and found Guomindang* (Nationalist) forces retreating to Taiwan*. Citing the island's strategic and economic importance to Japan, the Joint Chiefs of Staff (JCS) decided that it should not be allowed to fall to the Communists. But lacking forces for its defense, the JCS asked Acheson to hold it with economic and diplomatic means. Since the Nationalists had a "surfeit" of arms but poor leadership, Acheson forged National Security Council statements 37/2 and 37/5 aimed at holding Taiwan and producing a new government. Jiang resigned in favor of Li Zongren, who then promised the United States that he would appoint Sun governor. The Economic Cooperation Administration, at Acheson's request, formulated a recovery program and kept it on hold. Jiang, however, blocked Li and forced Acheson to settle for the appointment of Sun to commanding general of the Taiwan Defense Forces, which proved an empty title.

Acheson then queried the JCS about committing U.S. forces and, after receiving a negative response, drafted a policy amendment on 6 October calling for recognition of Jiang's underlying authority and pressuring him for reform. Sun, however, had a different idea—a coup. Suspecting as much, Jiang had hastily transferred loyal forces from Hainan Island to Taiwan, and confronted Sun in January 1950 with reports of his conspiracy. Sun, thinking fast, convinced Jiang that the reports were a Communist plot to divide them. Jiang resumed the presidency on 1 March, and eight days later, Sun signaled new plans for a coup. Rusk, now Acheson's assistant secretary for Far Eastern Affairs, offered two options—forcing Jiang to resign or supporting Sun's coup—with the latter preferred and the U.S. Seventh Fleet protecting Taiwan in either case. In response and unbeknownst to Acheson, President Harry S. Truman* sent Ohio businessman Karl W. V. Nix to both Sun and Jiang. Through Nix, Jiang promised to "do anything the president asked," and even explicitly offered to resign. Sun, in a 23 May letter carried by Nix, urged Truman to take decisive action—meaning his coup. Truman debriefed Nix on 16 June.

Historian Bruce Cumings cites a 1989 letter from Robert Strong, former chargé at Taibei, to Kenneth Krentz, his former consul general, indicating that the United States was about to support Sun "to the hilt." Be this as it may, when the Korean War* began, Truman demonstrated a clear preference for Rusk's first option—not the coup. On 25 June, at the second Blair House meeting, Truman ordered U.S. naval defense of Taiwan. Then, he stunned Acheson by revealing Jiang's offer to resign and proposing to replace him with General Douglas MacArthur*. Acheson asked Truman to wait and warned that Jiang might refuse to resign at the last minute and "throw the ball game." The president demurred, saying only that Jiang's replacement should be the next step. However, the U.S. military Neutralization of Taiwan* soon rendered this unnecessary. Sun weathered a bloody, Nazi-style purge in July, but was imprisoned for yet another plot in 1955. But he emerged from prison in the late 1980s to find Jiang's despotic regime moving toward the kind of democracy for which he had sacrificed so much.

B. Cumings, *Origins of the Korean War*, Vol. 2: *The Roaring of the Cataract, 1947–1950* (Princeton, NJ, 1990); R. L. McGlothlen, *Controlling the Waves: Dean Acheson and U.S. Foreign Policy in Asia* (New York, 1993).

Ronald L. McGlothlen

SUN YAT-SEN

See SUN ZHONGSHAN

SUN ZHONGSHAN (1866–1925)

Sun Zhongshan is recognized on both sides of the Taiwan Strait as the founder of modern China. He was born in Cuiheng, about forty miles north of Macau. His family was poor, without enough land to support themselves, so his father worked a variety of odd jobs. Sun was strongly influenced by his elder brother, Sun Mei, who emigrated to Hawaii in 1871. In 1879, he and his mother went to Hawaii to visit Sun Mei. Sun Zhongshan stayed there and began to study in missionary schools. In 1883, he was baptized a Christian, which alienated his brother, though they later reconciled. After returning to China in 1886, Sun enrolled in medical school in the British colony at Hong Kong*, graduating in 1892 and setting up a practice in Guangzhou. He then became involved in reformist politics and, in 1894, journeyed to Tianjin to submit a petition to Qing political leader Li Hongzhang*. As China's situation deteriorated in the Sino-Japanese War (1894–1895), his views became more radical and he participated in an abortive revolt in 1895 against the Qing government in Guangzhou. Forced into exile, he first went to Japan, then to Hawaii, and finally to England. There, in 1896, he was briefly arrested as a fugitive from charges related to the 1895 revolt, and held in the Chinese legation. After being freed through diplomatic and media pressure, this incident added to Sun's developing heroic image.

Sun went back to Japan in 1898 and began to work closely with other radical reformers and revolutionaries. A series of abortive revolts were planned and carried out, such as the Huizhou uprising of October 1900, in eastern Guangdong. By 1905, the need for better organization and planning led to the founding of the Revolutionary Alliance in Japan, which was meant to be an umbrella organization to coordinate and enhance the operations of its component groups and individuals. From 1905 through 1911, Sun traveled widely in the West, raising money and carrying out propaganda for the Revolutionary Alliance. He also provided ideological content for the alliance in the Three People's Principles: People's Nationalism, directed against the Manchu Qing Dynasty; People's Democracy, mainly concerned with creating a republican form of government to enable China's modern development; and People's Livelihood, based largely on the agrarian socialist ideals of Henry George's 1879 *Progress and Poverty*. In 1907 and 1908, the Revolutionary Alliance continued to foment rebellions, some along the frontier with French Indochina*, and others in 1910 and early 1911 in Guangzhou, none of which were successful. During 1910 and 1911, Sun was in the United States and Canada, giving speeches and raising money. When the Wuchang military mutiny of 10 October broke out in Hubei, Sun was in Denver, Colorado, where he read about the Chinese Revolution of 1911* in a newspaper. But instead of returning to China, he went to London on a diplomatic campaign to generate support to the newly emerging Republic. Returning to Hong Kong on 21 December, he went to Shanghai and, after complex negotiations, became president of the Republic of China* on 1 January 1912.

In February 1912, Sun transferred the presidency to Yuan Shikai*, who had demanded the post as part of the bargain for securing the abdication of Puyi*, the last Chinese emperor. After Yuan shunted him aside, Sun reconstituted the Revolutionary Alliance as the Guomindang* (GMD) Party, and won a majority in the elections for the national assembly in 1913. Yuan, however, thwarted Sun when he had himself made president for life. The GMD attempted a "second revolution" but its failure sent Sun again into exile in Japan. Two years later, Sun married Song Qingling*, a member of the Song family that was a major financial backer of his political activities and stayed close to the GMD long after Sun's death. In 1917, Sun "retired" to Shanghai, but just at this time, the new socialist state in Russia began to send envoys and organizers to East Asia. Attracted to the successful revolutionary movement in China's large neighbor, Sun oversaw the reorganization of the GMD into a more effective political mechanism with the assistance of Soviet advisers. He accepted Russian aid in founding a military academy in Guangzhou to train leaders for a revolutionary army. In 1923, Sun also agreed to a United Front* with the Chinese Communist Party* in the hopes of finally having a revolutionary movement strong enough to unify China and build a modern, progressive republic. But two years later, during an unsuccessful political mission in Beijing, Sun died of liver cancer and did not live to see this dream realized. *See also* Homer Lea.

M. Bergere, *Sun Yat-sen* (Stanford, CA, 1998); C. Y. Cheng, *Sun Yat-sen's Doctrine in the Modern World* (Boulder, CO, 1989); C. M. Wilbur, *Sun Yat-sen: Frustrated Patriot* (New York, 1976); J. Wong, *The Origins of a Heroic Image: Sun Yat-sen in London, 1896–1897* (Hong Kong, 1986).

Kenneth J. Hammond

SUZUKI KANTARŌ (1867–1948)

Suzuki Kantarō was prime minister of Japan at the end of World War II, playing a central role in arranging for the acceptance of surrender on 14 August 1945. He was born in a low-ranking samurai family in Ōsaka. Following graduation from the Japanese Naval Academy, he climbed the career ladder from second sublieutenant to admiral. He fought both in the Sino-Japanese War (1894–1895) and the Russo-Japanese War* (1904–1905). Suzuki also reached the top of the navy bureaucracy by becoming vice minister in 1914. He served as commander in chief of the combined fleet and as chief of navy general staff. In 1929, Suzuki was appointed grand chamberlain and privy councillor to Emperor Hirohito*. A moderate internationalist, he endorsed the unpopular treaty negotiated at the London Naval Conference of 1930*, and probably for this reason suffered near-fatal injuries at the hands of army extremists in the coup attempt of 15 May 1932, in which several politicians were assassinated, including Inukai Tsuyoshi*. In August 1944, Suzuki was appointed president of the Privy Council.

On 7 April 1945, Suzuki assumed the premiership. The Imperial Household expected him to bring the war with the Allies to an end. Both in the Japanese Army and the Navy there were many who insisted on fighting to a finish. The United States, Britain, and China issued the Potsdam Declaration* demanding Japan's unconditional surrender on 26 July 1945. Two days later in Japan, one morning newspaper described the attitude of Japan's government toward the declaration as that of *mokusatsu*, which was translated into English in foreign newspapers as "ignore." Prime Minister Suzuki had kept silence while hearing opinions of the cabinet members. At a press conference that afternoon, he used the same word, "mokusatsu."

On 6 August 1945, the first of the Atomic Attacks* came at Hiroshima. Early on 8 August the Soviet Union, in violation of the Soviet-Japanese Neutrality Treaty of 1941, declared war on Japan and the Red Army invaded Manchuria. The next day, a second atomic bomb was dropped on Nagasaki. Within the Japanese government there was still division on whether to surrender under the terms of the Potsdam Declaration between the peace faction led by the foreign minister and the navy minister on the one hand, and the hardliners represented by the army and the navy chiefs of staff and the war minister. To break the deadlock, Suzuki arranged a meeting in the presence of the emperor on 14 August. At the last moment of the conference, Suzuki asked for Hirohito's opinion, who sided with the peace faction, silencing those wanting to continue the war. Suzuki resigned as prime minister on 15 August after the emperor's broadcast announcing acceptance of the Potsdam Declaration. After the end of the war, he again became president of the Privy Council.

R. J. C. Butow, *Japan's Decision to Surrender* (Stanford, CA, 1954); H. Feis, *The Atomic Bomb and the End of World War II* (Princeton, NJ, 1966); L. V. Sigal, *Fighting to a Finish: The Politics of War Termination in the United States and Japan, 1945* (Ithaca, NY, 1988).

Ishii Osamu

SUZUKI ZENKŌ (1911–)

Raised in a subsistence fishing village in northern Japan, Suzuki Zenkō served as Japan's prime minister during the presidency of Ronald Reagan* from 1980 to 1982. During the 1930s, he worked in various local, regional, and national organizations connected to fisheries administration. Although first elected to the Diet in 1947 on the Socialist ticket, Suzuki established himself as a stalwart in the conservative Liberal Democratic Party* (LDP) after its creation in 1955. He was a consummate insider who successfully navigated the LDP's byzantine factional politics for decades. In June 1980, Suzuki was catapulted to Japan's top political position after the sudden death of Prime Minister Ōhira Masayoshi*. Although he had well-tested skills in mediating intraparty strife, his premiership was distinguished by a lack of a coherent policy vision or any strategy for leading the nation. Except for marginal involvement in international fisheries negotiations, Suzuki had scant experience in foreign affairs.

In May 1981, Suzuki visited the United States to discuss not only problems in U.S.-Japan Postwar Trade Relations*, but also cooperation in the area of military security. The joint communiqué he issued with President Reagan was notable for its forthright acknowledgment of the U.S.-Japan alliance and the support given it by increased Japanese defense efforts. The statement reflected the upward trajectory of Japan's defense posture since the late 1970s, as demonstrated by participation in joint air/sea military exercises earlier in the year. During his visit, Suzuki also publicly identified the defense of so-called sea lanes as part of Japan's responsibility. The undefined nature of Japanese sea lanes defense bred different interpretations about Japan's share in the common defense of the western Pacific and became a source of friction in U.S.-Japan relations. Suzuki later contradicted himself when he said that the U.S.-Japanese alliance did not have a military component and that his opposition to a hasty defense buildup had not been expressed adequately in the Reagan-Suzuki communiqué. This diplomatic faux pas led to a Washington-Tōkyō communication crisis that lasted until the avowedly pro-American Nakasone Yasuhiro* replaced Suzuki in November 1982 and endorsed U.S.-Japanese defense cooperation.

Kamiya Fuji, *Sengoshino nakano nichibei kankei* [U.S.-Japanese Relations in Postwar History] (Tōkyō, 1989); T. Maga, *Hands Across the Seas?: U.S.-Japan Relations, 1961–1981* (Athens, OH, 1997).

Shimizu Sayuri

T

TAFT, WILLIAM HOWARD (1857–1930)

William Howard Taft was president of the United States from 1909 to 1913. He had a wider interest and involvement in U.S.–East Asian issues, and could boast more experience of East Asia before his election, than all his presidential predecessors and many of his successors. Born into a prominent Ohio family, he secured appointment to the Ohio Supreme Court before the age of thirty. Thereafter, Taft become solicitor general of the United States and a federal circuit court judge in 1900. He agreed at the urging of President William McKinley* to become chairman of the Second Philippine Commission. Then Taft was the first U.S. civil governor of the Philippines*, emerging from his four years there with a national reputation, a paternalistic enthusiasm for the U.S. civilizing mission on behalf of what he termed the "little brown brothers," and a growing appreciation of China's significance to U.S. interests. After President Theodore Roosevelt* named him secretary of war in 1904, Taft undertook a mission to East Asia in 1905, which produced the secret Taft-Katsura Agreement*, an informal understanding for respect of mutual interests that included Japan's recognition of the U.S. hold on the Philippines, and U.S. recognition of Japan's control over Korea. Two years later, Taft visited Tōkyō again to manage U.S. tensions with Japan resulting from California's provocative reaction to Japanese immigrants.

As president, Taft did not allow the imposing Rooseveltian legacy to dictate his East Asian policies. With Secretary of State Philander C. Knox*, he immediately signaled his intention to focus on expanding U.S. commercial interests in China, as part of a wider effort to place U.S. diplomacy more effectively in the service of U.S. trade and investment. In practice, though, his Dollar Diplomacy* in East Asia achieved decidedly mixed results. Knox's bold plan for internationalization of Manchurian railroads to outmaneuver Japan fell apart ignominiously, and the Knox Neutralization Scheme* brought Japanese and Russian interests there into closer alignment. Taft played a more successful role in securing U.S. admittance to the Six Power Consortium* of European bankers that had negotiated an agreement to lend money for railroad systems in south China. Ironically, his attempts to encourage American private investment in China tended to be hampered by a chronic lack of interest among U.S. bankers in lending funds to China, especially as events there moved into a more anti-Western phase and the

Qing Dynasty began to disintegrate, climaxing in the Chinese Revolution of 1911*.

Most historians agree that Taft's determination to expand the U.S. commercial stake in China was inseparable from his growing apprehension at Japan's ambitions in East Asia in the aftermath of the Russo-Japanese War*. But Taft also seemed willing on occasions to embrace elements of a broader, more conciliatory strategy designed to encourage U.S. cooperation with Japan and other foreign powers in China, with the aim of advancing U.S. interests and standing with China's long-term modernization. The thrust of Taft's policies in East Asia prefigured the approach that several of his successors in the White House would follow. The basic problem of how to maintain the Open Door Policy* in China, protect the Philippines, and manage Japan's ambitions in Asia—without committing the United States to an unwanted war—would remain as vexatious as it had during the Taft-Knox years. After leaving the White House, Taft taught law at Yale University and then was chief justice of the U.S. Supreme Court from 1921 to 1930.

M. H. Hunt, *The Making of a Special Relationship: The United States and China to 1914* (New York, 1983); R. E. Minger, *William Howard Taft and United States Foreign Policy: The Apprenticeship Years, 1900–1908* (Urbana, IL, 1975); F. Ninkovich, *Modernity and Power: A History of the Domino Theory in the Twentieth Century* (Chicago, 1994); W. V. and M. V. Scholes, *The Foreign Policies of the Taft Administration* (Columbia, MO, 1970).

Roger K. Hodgkins

TAFT-KATSURA AGREEMENT (29 July 1905)

The Taft-Katsura Agreement was a secret executive memorandum negotiated in July 1905 by U.S. Secretary of War William Howard Taft* and Japanese Prime Minister Katsura Tarō*. It provided that the United States recognized the protectorate Japan established over Korea in November 1905, and Japan acknowledged U.S. control over the Philippines*, acquired after the Spanish-American War* in 1898. Japan's victory in the Sino-Japanese War and the Treaty of Shimonoseki* of 1895 had ended Chinese suzerainty over Korea, but Chinese influence in the court of Kojong*, the Korean king, had been replaced by the Russians. Defeat in the Russo-Japanese War* (1904–1905) demolished Russia's attempt to gain dominance on the Korean peninsula, and Japan quickly capitalized on its military victory. Japanese soldiers poured into the Korean peninsula. In February 1904, just weeks after Japan's decisive victory over the Russian naval forces at Port Arthur on China's Liaodong Peninsula, the Japanese government notified the administration of U.S. President Theodore Roosevelt* of a new relationship between Tōkyō and Seoul. Under the terms of this "alliance," as Japan referred to it, Kojong henceforth would be required to accept advice on administrative matters from the Japanese government, accept occupancy of Korean territories considered by Japan as important, and secure Japan's consent prior to making agreements with other nations.

Koreans immediately understood that the new alliance would lead to the end of their independence. Kojong looked to the United States for help to restrain Japan because Horace N. Allen*, the U.S. minister to Seoul, had assured him of American support, pointing to the 1882 Shufeldt Treaty*, which referred to the use of "good offices" to mediate disputes. Fearful of the wrath of the Japanese forces occupying his capital, the king sent his urgent back channel appeals to Washington. However, the secret negotiations between Taft and Katsura already had sealed Korea's fate. Taft was headed for a tour of the Philippines when he detoured to Japan, where he met quietly with Katsura. He was pleased that Katsura expressed "in strongest terms" Japan's position that the Philippines were in better hands with the United States than with another foreign power. When Katsura expressed a need for something similar in

Korea, lest that backward nation fall into "her former condition," Taft was quick to agree, suggesting that Japan establish a "suzerainty" over Korea. A memorandum was drafted on 29 July, and Roosevelt approved the secret agreement on 2 August. This unprecedented executive agreement remained secret for twenty years, until historian Tyler Dennett discovered Taft's memorandum in the Roosevelt papers.

The consequences of the Taft-Katsura Agreement were immediate. At Katsura's request, the United States, which had been the first nation to formally recognize Korea in 1882, withdrew its diplomats from Seoul. Left without foreign assistance, Korea was helpless. On 17 November 1905, Kojong was forced, virtually at gunpoint, to accept a Japanese protectorate over his nation. In 1910, formal Japanese Annexation of Korea* ended that nation's independent existence. The Taft-Katsura Agreement caused lasting resentment among Koreans who believed that the United States, for reasons of expediency, had abandoned their nation in time of need. Roosevelt made no move to use his good offices when informed of the plight of the Korean government because he viewed Japan as a modern, progressive state that could check Russian expansion in East Asia and thereby serve American interests. When Roosevelt, Secretary of State John Hay*, and Hay's successor Elihu Root* did receive petitions on behalf of the Korean government requesting U.S. good offices from Syngman Rhee* and Homer B. Hulbert*, the administration refused to act, stating lamely that the petition had not arrived through official channels. By the summer of 1905, Roosevelt was hoping the negotiation of the Treaty of Portsmouth* would achieve a balance of power in Asia, and preserve the Open Door Policy* in China. He was not prepared to upset the peace talks by raising questions about Korea's status. The Taft-Katsura Agreement became the basis for the Root-Takahira Agreement* of 1908, which reaffirmed U.S. and Japanese commitments to respect each other's possessions in East Asia.

C. I. Eugene Kim and H. Kim, *Korea and the Politics of Imperialism, 1876–1910* (Berkeley, CA, 1967); W. LaFeber, *The Clash: A History of U.S.-Japan Relations* (New York, 1997); Y. Lee "Korean American Diplomatic Relations, 1882–1905" and F. H. Harrington, "An American View of Korean American Relations, 1882–1905," in Y. Lee and W. Patterson (eds.), *One Hundred Year of Korean-American Relations* (Tuscaloosa, AL, 1986); J. E. Wilz, "Did the United States Betray Korea in 1905?," *Pacific Historical Review* (August 1985).

Michael J. Devine

TAIBEI ANTI-U.S. RIOT OF 1957

U.S.-Taiwan relations were not amicable in the 1950s, in spite of the fact that the Republic of China* (ROC) relied on Washington for support after it fled to the island from the mainland in 1949 after the Chinese Civil War*. This riot provided evidence both of the frustration the Guomindang* (Nationalist) government felt in response to U.S. policy toward Taiwan* and popular antipathy toward the existence of a large isolated American colony on the island. On 24 May 1957, an angry crowd broke into and ransacked the U.S. embassy and the U.S. Information Service Center in Taibei in protest over the acquittal of Robert G. Reynolds by a U.S. court-martial. Reynolds, a U.S. Army sergeant attached to the U.S. Military Assistance Advisory Group, Taiwan*, was accused of manslaughter in the death of an ROC citizen, who allegedly had intruded into the soldier's house. The siege of the embassy lasted six hours and ended only after a declaration of martial law. No Americans were seriously injured. The ROC government immediately offered full compensation and an apology.

Although Chinese officials denied that there was any anti-American feeling on the island, the presence of a large official U.S. delegation that was relatively highly paid and privileged was indeed a source of friction with the native population. Of the 10,000 Americans on the island, approximately 8,500 were U.S. government personnel and their dependents, most related to the military. Their much higher living standard made it difficult for the American community to mingle socially with Taiwan's local populace. Furthermore, U.S. military personnel and their dependents had diplomatic privileges and immunity from Chinese law, a reminder of extraterritoriality. In the Reynolds case, the prosecution appeared perfunctory, and when the court announced its verdict, the applause from the American audience in the courtroom rankled Chinese national pride.

Nationalist leaders also were unhappy with the United States. When Dwight D. Eisenhower* assumed the presidency in 1953, they had hoped that Washington would be sympathetic to their goal to reconquer the mainland. The Nationalists soon found out that the new administration was interested in protecting Taiwan from Communist control, but not in endorsing an attempt to return to the mainland. The Nationalists especially resented the U.S. Two China Policy* and thus were suspicious of the U.S.-PRC ambassadorial Warsaw Talks*, lest their fate be decided behind their backs. For some observers, there was good reason to believe that high-level Chinese officials had instigated the riot to vent Nationalist frustration with Washington.

Nevertheless, the ROC officials were eager to resolve problems regarding the legal status of American military personnel on the island. More than a year before the riot, Taibei and Washington had begun to negotiate, but they had been deadlocked for months on the question of criminal jurisdiction over military personnel while off duty and away from U.S. installations. The State Department was under pressure not to allow more American soldiers to be subject to the jurisdiction of foreign courts. But the ROC was unwilling to accept anything less than what the United States had given other nations. Although the Reynolds case stimulated the reopening of negotiations, it was not until 31 August 1965 that Taibei concluded a status-of-forces agreement with Washington. According to the arrangement, the Nationalist government could recall its waiver of jurisdiction and prosecute an American offender if he was accused of committing any of the following six crimes: homicide, rape, robbery, narcotics possession, arson, and security offenses against the ROC. The Nationalist government claimed it was satisfied with the agreement, but critics complained that this agreement "allocated jurisdictional territory according to the political map."

Chang Su-Ya, "Lanqin dashi yu yijiuwuling niandai de Zhongmei guanxi" [Ambassador Karl L. Rankin and U.S. Policy Toward Taiwan in the 1950s], *EurAmerica* (March 1998); K. L. Rankin, *China Assignment* (Seattle, WA, 1964); L. Tao, "The Sino-American Status of Forces Agreement: Criminal Jurisdiction over American Soldiers on Nationalist Chinese Territory," *Boston University Law Review* (1971); N. B. Tucker, *Uncertain Friendships: Taiwan, Hong Kong, and the United States, 1945–1992* (New York, 1994); U.S. Department of State, *Foreign Relations of the United States, 1955–57*, Vol. 3: *China* (Washington, DC, 1986).

Ena Chao

TAIPING REBELLION

A powerful reflection of rising antiforeign feeling in China, the Taiping Rebellion broke out in January 1851 under the banner of "Heavenly Kingdom of Great Peace" and with the intention of toppling the Qing Dynasty established by the Manchus. When the Taiping Army was attacking Nanjing in 1853, the Qing government's chief officer in Shanghai, Wu Jianzhang, addressed a request to the consuls of Britain, France, and the United States to send their warships into the Yangze River to assist the Qing Army in the defense of Nanjing. The U.S. government at that time adopted a neutral policy with both sides in the war and refused Wu's request. Moreover, it instructed its representative to China not to interfere in the affairs of the two sides.

In March 1853, the Taiping Army took Nanjing, changing its name to Tianjing (Heavenly Capital). The U.S. government gave directions to its new representative to China, Robert McLane, that he could recognize the Taiping government on a suitable occasion. To find the right moment, McLane paid Tianjing a visit by warship in May 1854. He did not land, and negotiations were conducted through exchanging notes. McLane's main point in his note was that anything occurring between the two sides should be settled in accordance with the treaties previously signed by the two nations. And the Taipings signaled that they would not interfere in trade. After returning to Shanghai, McLane added the demand for "enlarging the rights the treaty had granted to the United States and opening the hinterlands of China to the United States."

After the Anglo-French allied armies entered Beijing, treaties were concluded and the Qing court accepted all the demands of Britain and France in 1860. The United States, like other powers, then began to change its attitude from neutrality to support for the Qing government. In November 1861, the U.S. representative to China, Anson Burlingame*, arrived in Guangzhou with instructions to cooperate with Britain and France, who already had begun to assist the Qing government. In November 1862, Secretary of State William H. Seward* instructed Burlingame not to do anything that might weaken the confidence of the Qing court and not to give any material assistance or moral encouragement to the Taipings. But since the United States was at this time in the Civil War, it was unable to give support in substance to the Qing government.

Since 1859, Frederick T. Ward*, an American of Chinese nationality, had been commander of the "Ever-Victorious Army," which was trained in Western military techniques and use of Western arms. This force assisted the Qing Army in the defense of Shanghai first and later helped it defeat the Taiping Army. The U.S. government opposed Ward's operations while maintaining neutrality, but then extended approval. Burlingame directed in his instructions to the U.S. consul in Shanghai that this army should remain under the authority of China's government, but that foreigners should train the Chinese soldiers. When the Taiping government was to remit 500,000 taels of silver to the United States to buy ships in 1862, Burlingame instructed U.S. officials at Shanghai to help Qing administrators block the purchase. In November of that year, when a ship owned by the National City Bank entered the area under Taiping jurisdiction, again Burlingame helped the Qing government block the transaction.

Chouban yiwu shimo, Xianfeng chao, Tongzhi chao [Complete Record of the Management of Barbarian Affairs in the Qing Dynasty, Xianfeng and Tongzhi Periods] (Beijing, 1930); T. Tong, *United States Diplomacy in China 1844–60* (Seattle, WA, 1964).

Xiang Liling

TAIWAN

Located 100 miles off the southeast coast of China, Taiwan is a mountainous island 250 miles long and 60 to 80 miles wide. In 1949, Jiang Jieshi* reestablished his Guomindang* (Nationalist) government there after Communist forces expelled him from the mainland in the Chinese Civil War*. Taiwan, what Portugal called Formosa ("The Beautiful"), was colonized from Fujian. Traders and pirates visited the island before the Dutch East Indian Company established several posts there after 1624. In 1661, Koxinga, a Chinese regional leader who had controlled the Fujian coast for forty years, expelled the Dutch from Taiwan with a flotilla of 900 ships after the Qing Dynasty forced him off the mainland. The Chinese then tried to cut off Koxinga and his son's regime from access to mainland sources of manpower, food, and trading silk, but finally occupied the island in 1863. Taiwan was separated from Fujian and made a province in 1885. Over the next six years, the first governor, a lieutenant of Li Hongzhang*, built an arsenal at Taibei and based a naval force on the Penghus, instituted tax reform based on a land survey and population registration, and provided modern services. In 1895, Taiwan became part of the Japanese empire at the end of the Sino-Japanese War under the Treaty of Shimonoseki*. At that time, the island had about 3 million Chinese peasants engaged in subsistence farming and 120,000 aborigines of Malay origin, who submitted to Japanese rule because the Qing Dynasty had governed from a distance.

After Japan's surrender in August 1945, Taiwan was retroceded to China under terms agreed to at the Cairo Conference* in 1943 and in accordance with the Potsdam Declaration* of 1945. Rejoicing at their liberation from Japanese Colonialism*, the Taiwanese initially welcomed officials that the Republic of China* (ROC) sent from the mainland. But the Guomindang (GMD) government treated the island as almost conquered territory, exploiting both its people and resources. Deteriorating relations between the ruling mainlander minority and the native majority led to the February 28 Incident of 1947* that resulted in the systematic killing of thousands of Taiwanese leaders. In 1949, 2 million fleeing Nationalist soldiers and civilians arrived. Jiang Jingguo*, Jiang's son and chief of the provincial GMD, ruthlessly crushed all political opposition, imposing a rule more harsh, dictatorial, and exploitive than in colonial times. While mainlanders soon became dependent on modest government stipends, natives gradually began to participate more directly in the island's economic growth. Mainlanders dominated the national government, but Taiwanese became the majority among students in higher education and held most offices in local government.

Late in the 1960s, Taiwan's society began to change. Mainlanders and natives attended nine years of compulsory schooling together and intermarried. Assimilation accelerated further a decade later as a result of expanding education, urbanization, and affluence. U.S. military and economic aid after the Korean War* started had initiated economic growth. The Sino-American Joint Commission on Rural Reconstruction* boosted agricultural production and developed policies to resolve the historic conflict between landlords and tenants. Eventually, the ROC government leaders, who had no vested interest in the land, acted to end farm tenancy to achieve the goal of creating a stable and conservative rural society. But early reliance on sugar and rice production soon gave way to industrialization, a process the government dominated through its control over industrial monopolies. From flour milling and textiles in the late 1950s, Taiwan shifted to export industries in the 1960s, especially steel and petrochemicals. After U.S. aid ended in 1968, increasing American and Japanese investment fueled the island's industrialization and its economy boomed as it helped meet U.S. needs during the Second Indochina War*. As Taiwanese gained access to new skills and technology, industry moved into electronics in the 1970s and then into computers, automobiles, and military equipment in the 1980s. By 1990, Taiwan's per capita gross national product (GNP) was ten times higher than that of mainland China.

By the 1990s, Taiwan was an urban and industrial island with a population of more than 20 million. Taibei, its capital, was a bustling world-class city. Taiwan's GNP had increased from $8.1 billion in 1960 to $72.6 billion in 1986, competing as an Asian "tiger" economy with the Republic of Korea* for the world's fastest growth rate. But still unresolved was the claim of the People's Republic of China* (PRC) to sovereignty over Taiwan. After the death of Mao Zedong* in 1976, Beijing changed its policy from seeking liberation of Taiwan to calling for voluntary reunification. The PRC offered Taiwan the autonomy to maintain its own government, military forces, and economic system within the framework of one China. The ROC rejected the offer and remained committed under Presidents Jiang Jingguo (1978–1988) and Li Denghui* (1988–2000) to regaining power on the mainland. Meanwhile, unofficial trade between Taiwan and the mainland through Hong Kong* grew steadily. In 1987, the ROC ended the ban on travel to the PRC. Taibei's willingness to expand contacts with the mainland reflected confidence that progress toward democratization and socioeconomic opportunity, as well as broader material comfort and a thriving cultural life on Taiwan, had won the loyalty and support of the citizenry. The GMD hoped Taiwanese would convey to mainland relatives their belief in the superiority of the ROC's system. But these same factors caused other politicians to argue for Taiwan's status as an independent nation. *See also* Dangwai; Taibei Anti-U.S. Riot of 1957; Taiwanese Communist Party.

R. N. Clough, *Cooperation or Conflict in the Taiwan Strait* (Lanham, MD, 1999); J. K. Fairbank and E. O. Reischauer, *China: Tradition and Transformation* (Boston, 1989); I. C. Y. Hsu, *The Rise of Modern China* (New York, 1983); C. Hughes, *Taiwan and Chinese Nationalism* (London, 1997); M. A. Rubinstein (ed.), *Taiwan: A New History* (New York, 1999); N. B. Tucker, *Uncertain Friendships: Taiwan, Hong Kong, and the United States, 1945–1992* (New York, 1994).

James I. Matray

TAIWAN RELATIONS ACT (10 April 1979)

On 10 April 1979, this act authorized the continuation of U.S. relations with Taiwan* on an unofficial basis after the United States established diplomatic relations with the People's Republic of China* (PRC) and ended formal relations with the Republic of China* (ROC). It codified the arrangements for future U.S. interaction with Taiwan that Washington and Beijing had agreed on in the negotiations resulting in U.S.-PRC Normalization of Relations*, but with some modifications, especially a more explicit commitment to Taiwan's security. The draft Taiwan Enabling Act that President Jimmy Carter* sent to Congress early in 1979, reflecting the arrangements agreed upon with Beijing, provided for the continuation of U.S. commercial, cultural, trade, and other relations with Taiwan through nongovernmental means. It said that the United States continued to have an interest in a peaceful resolution of the Taiwan issue and expected it would be resolved peacefully, but it said nothing further about Taiwan's security, and it made no provision for continuing arms sales to the ROC. Congressional critics of normalization, angered by Carter's failure to consult Congress before formally recognizing the PRC and dissatisfied with the terms he had accepted, seized the opportunity to revise the terms of normalization by passing the Taiwan Relations Act (TRA). The administration successfully resisted proposals to give an official quality to the U.S. relationship with Taiwan, such as a proposal to create an official liaison office in Taibei, but accepted a number of amendments, especially the incorporation of new provisions concerning Taiwan's security.

The TRA declared that the U.S. decision to establish diplomatic relations with the PRC rested upon the expectation that the future of Taiwan would be determined by peaceful means and that any effort to resolve this question by other than peaceful means, including by boycotts or embargoes, would be a threat to the peace and security of the western Pacific area and of grave concern to the United States. It also declared that the United States would make arms available to the ROC in sufficient quantity to enable Taiwan to maintain a self-defense capability. The TRA established an American Institute in Taiwan (AIT) staffed by U.S. officials who were separated temporarily from government service, which would provide consular services to U.S. citizens and manage any U.S. programs in Taiwan. It contained provisions protecting Nationalist government assets in the United States from Communist takeover while ensuring that the absence of recognition would place no constraints on commercial relations. It provided that the AIT's counterpart (the Coordination Council for North American Affairs) could have as many offices as Taiwan previously had consulates. Congress approved the TRA by 339–50 in the House and 85–4 in the Senate. Some of Carter's advisers wanted him to veto it, but a veto could have been easily overridden. Instead, the president signed the act, assuring Beijing that he had substantial discretion in implementing the TRA and would do so in ways consistent with the understandings on normalization. The PRC denounced the act, but acquiesced.

H. Harding, *A Fragile Relationship: The United States and China Since 1972* (Washington, DC, 1992); N. B. Tucker, *Uncertain Friendships: Taiwan, Hong Kong and the United States, 1945–1992* (New York, 1994).

Harriet Dashiell Schwar

TAIWAN STRAIT CRISES

The Taiwan Strait Crises of 1954–1955 and 1958 threatened war between the United States and the People's Republic of China* (PRC) with the possible U.S. use of nuclear weapons, but neither nation wanted war and both crises eventually subsided. Hostilities in each case were confined to islands near the mainland coast, especially Jinmen, near Xianmen. President Dwight D. Eisenhower* and Secretary of State John Foster Dulles* would have been happy to see Jiang Jieshi* abandon the offshore islands, but he insisted on holding them, since they were symbols of his hope for the Guomindang* (Nationalists) to return to the mainland. Chinese sources now indicate that Beijing began shelling Jinmen in September 1954 as a warning against a U.S.-China defense treaty with the Republic of China* (ROC). At the time, however, Eisenhower and his advisers saw this as the opening gun of a military campaign aimed at seizing Taiwan* and agreed on a strategy of ambiguity: no public commitment to support Nationalist defense of the offshore islands, but no public statement to the contrary. Eisenhower wanted to avoid direct U.S. involvement in the defense of the islands, especially since the Joint Chiefs of Staff (JCS) advised that holding them against a full-scale PRC attack would require using nuclear weapons. He approved an effort by Dulles to persuade New Zealand to take the issue to the United Nations (Operation ORACLE*) and along with Dulles, decided to sign the U.S.-China Mutual Defense Treaty of 1954*. When Beijing captured a small island 200 miles north of Taiwan early in 1955, Eisenhower and Dulles pressed Jiang to order evacuation of the nearby Dachen Islands. In return, they promised U.S. protection for Jinmen and Mazu.

On 29 January 1955, Congress approved the Formosa Resolution*, authorizing U.S. military action to protect Taiwan and such related positions and territories as the president deemed necessary. But Eisenhower refused to issue a public commitment of U.S. support for defense of Jinmen and Mazu and gave Jiang only a secret pledge of U.S. assistance in case of an attack "at this time." Jiang was furious, but he reluctantly evacuated the Dachens with U.S. naval support. When Chinese Premier Zhou Enlai* rejected a UN invitation to join in discussions on Taiwan, Eisenhower and Dulles concluded that the PRC was bent on war. Thereafter, U.S. statements hinting at the use of tactical nuclear weapons in case of war in the Taiwan Strait raised tensions still further. Concerned at the apparent drift toward war, however, Eisenhower refused Jiang's request for U.S. acquiescence in Nationalist attacks on mainland air bases. In April, he sent, Admiral Arthur W. Radford*, JCS chairman, and Walter S.

Robertson*, assistant secretary of state for Far Eastern Affairs, to tell Jiang the United States would not defend Jinmen and Mazu and attempt to persuade him to reduce his forces on the offshore islands. In response to their offer of U.S. support for a blockade of the sea lanes along the China coast, Jiang angrily declared that he would defend the islands with or without U.S. support. Then, on 23 April, at the Bandung Conference*, Zhou declared that China was willing to enter into discussions with the United States and the first crisis eased. In August, Beijing and Washington began ambassadorial talks.

The 1958 crisis was briefer, but more dangerous. Beginning on 23 August 1958, a massive artillery bombardment threatened to cut off 100,000 Nationalist troops on Jinmen. Dulles argued that the increased number of Guomindang troops there and on Mazu meant that they now were integrated closely into the defense of Taiwan and had to be defended. Although Eisenhower reluctantly approved escort of ROC supply ships as far as the three-mile limit off Jinmen, he refused to pledge U.S. protection for the islands, which the Pentagon insisted would require use of tactical nuclear weapons. Then, on 6 September, Zhou declared Beijing's willingness to resume the Warsaw Talks*, then in abeyance. The next day, Soviet Premier Nikita Khrushchev wrote to Eisenhower, warning against an attack on the PRC, but behind the scenes, the crisis was straining the Sino-Soviet alliance. By the end of the month, the ROC's resupply of Jinmen had become increasingly effective, and both sides took steps to defuse the crisis. While Dulles publicly hinted at the possible withdrawal of Nationalist forces, on 6 October, PRC Defense Minister Peng Dehuai* announced that bombardment would be suspended for seven days, provided there was no U.S. naval escort. Washington promptly stopped the convoys. Two weeks later, Dulles visited Taiwan and extracted from Jiang a joint communiqué declaring that the Nationalists would rely primarily on peaceful means to achieve their mission of returning to the mainland. Peng announced the next day that PRC forces would not shell the offshore islands on even-numbered days, if there was no U.S. escort, and the crisis ended.

Eisenhower and Dulles later claimed they had deterred Chinese aggression in 1954–1955 and 1958, but historians are dubious. Eisenhower revisionists have praised the president's efforts to avoid war and restrain the hawks in the Pentagon during the 1955 crisis, but others have noted that U.S. nuclear threats increased tensions and that the Robertson-Radford offer of support for a blockade was very risky. More recently, Chinese historians, drawing on Chinese sources, have pointed out that Mao Zedong* pursued limited goals and specifically ruled out actions that would lead to a direct U.S.-China confrontation. According to Gordon H. Chang and He Di, the absence of war was due more to luck than to effective deterrence on either side. *See also* Ye Gongchao.

R. D. Accinelli, *Crisis and Commitment: United States Policy Toward Taiwan, 1950–1955* (Chapel Hill, NC, 1996); G. H. Chang and He Di, "The Absence of War in the U.S.-China Confrontation over Quemoy and Matsu in 1954–1955: Contingency, Luck, Deterrence?," *American Historical Review* (December 1993); T. J. Christensen, *Useful Adversaries: Grand Strategy, Domestic Mobilization, and Sino-American Conflict, 1947–1958* (Princeton, NJ, 1996); Q. Zhai, *The Dragon, the Lion, and the Eagle: Chinese, British, American Relations, 1949–1958* (Kent, OH, 1994); S. G. Zhang, *Deterrence and Strategic Culture: Chinese American Confrontations, 1949–1958* (Ithaca, NY, 1992).

Harriet Dashiell Schwar

TAIWANESE COMMUNIST PARTY

The Taiwanese Communist Party (TCP) stands out as the least successful Communist party in East Asia, and one of the few presenting no conceivable threat to U.S. interests. The party's inability to gain support removed one potential adversary to the Guomindang* (Nationalist) government under Jiang Jieshi*, which controlled the island after 1945. The lack of an effective Communist party also eased the implementation of U.S.-backed policies that later were hailed as vital to the island's economic development. Ironically, Taiwan became part of the Cold War without any indigenous Communist threat.

Japanese colonial rule of Taiwan from 1895 to 1945 provided the context for Communism* on the island. Organized in Shanghai in 1928, the TCP soon became a branch of the Japan Communist Party (JCP), and sought guidance from the Chinese Communist Party* (CCP). On the island, Taiwanese struggled to expand and to influence the small worker and peasant movements. The TCP suffered from disputes over national identity and affiliation with the international Communist movement, as the party's members were divided between CCP, JCP, and Taiwanese factions. Some islanders drifted away from the party, because of conflicts over their primary objective—a broad-based, anticolonial struggle as part of China, a Taiwanese nationalist movement, or a class-based conflict against Japanese and Taiwanese capitalists. Japan's brutal repression, coupled with its ability to provide the colony some measure of material progress and stability, thus limiting support for radical change, further weakened the party. The TCP had almost completely disappeared by 1937. Although the United States forged a cooperative, albeit cautious, relationship with Communist parties throughout the region in their shared struggle against Japanese Colonialism*, the Taiwanese Communists never were seen as important enough to contact.

After World War II the island was returned to China, then under Jiang's Nationalist government. The TCP, although by then a branch of the CCP, remained divided between factions of Taiwanese and Communists sent from the mainland. Lacking internal unity and broad support, the party was further devastated by the crackdown after the February 28 Incident of 1947*, then the White Terror beginning in the late 1940s. Those who survived fled to Hong Kong*, then the mainland. Most of these aging Communists suffered horribly during the political upheavals of the People's Republic of China*, especially the Hundred Flowers Campaign and the Chinese Cultural Revolution*. Although the Guomindang made anti-Communism a key facet of its rule on Taiwan, there existed none of the organized, armed resistance that had plagued the regime on the mainland. The failure of the TCP, then the CCP, to build a strong presence on Taiwan eased implementation of policies later seen as part of the island's economic miracle, such as land reform and import substitution. Moreover, it ensured that the Republic of China* did not need to devote resources to fighting guerrillas. This facilitated American efforts to build Free China and contain Communist China. Opposition to the Nationalists on Taiwan, especially from the Dangwai*, took a form more palatable to the United States, that of a moderate, reform-oriented movement.

Chen Fangming, *Xie Xuehong pingzhuan* [A Critical Biography of Xie Xuehong] (Taibei, 1991); F. Hsiao and L. Sullivan, "The Chinese Communist Party and the Status of Taiwan, 1928–1943," *Pacific Affairs* (Fall 1979); F. Hsiao and L. Sullivan, "A Political History of the Taiwanese Communist Party, 1928–1931," *Journal of Asian Studies* (March 1983); Lu Xiuyi, *Riju shidai Taiwan Gongchandang shi, 1928–1932* [A History of the Taiwan Communist Party During the Japanese Occupation Era, 1928–1932] (Taibei, 1989).

Steven E. Phillips

TAKESHITA NOBORU (1924–2000)

Takeshita Noboru became prime minister of Japan in 1987, replacing Nakasone Yasuhiro* after almost three decades of brokering political deals as a leader in the Liberal Democratic Party* (LDP). A mediocre student, he had to apply twice before gaining admission to Waseda University in

Tōkyō. He was drafted in 1944 and trained as a kamakiaze pilot, but Japan's defeat in 1945 allowed him to resume his studies and graduate in 1947. Takeshita taught English for four years before winning a local assembly seat. In 1958, he was elected to the first of eleven consecutive terms in the Diet, working thereafter in the Ministry of International Trade and Industry* and for Prime Ministers Ikeda Hayato* and Satō Eisakuo*. In 1972, Takeshita became construction minister under Prime Minister Tanaka Kakuei*, who had built a powerful coalition of support among rural voters, construction companies, and LDP government officials with a massive plan to build roads, tunnels, railways, and bridges. He used these same tactics to strengthen his political base. Tainted by the Lockheed Scandal* that discredited Tanaka, he returned to government in 1979 as minister of finance under Prime Minister Ōhira Masayoshi*, serving in this same post under Nakasone from 1982 to 1986. A fiscal conservative, Takeshita gained prominence as a key spokesman for Tōkyō in clashes with the United States over Japan's huge trade surplus.

Takeshita assumed leadership of Tanaka's faction in 1985 after his mentor's stroke, but was unable to secure a majority in the contest for LDP president in October 1987. Fearing an embarrassing deadlock, party leaders agreed that Nakasone would select his successor. Owing his own selection as prime minister to the Tanaka faction, he chose Takeshita. His unassuming manner and preference for compromise did not seem suited to Japan's need for vision as it pursued an expanded world role. He certainly lacked Nakasone's skill as a statesman. When U.S. President Ronald Reagan* called to congratulate him on becoming prime minister and asked, "Mind if I call you Noboru? Just call me Ron," Takeshita politely declined the offer. His willingness to assume a larger share of the defense burden, however, won praise in Washington, even though it revived fears of some Asian nations about Japanese militarism. During numerous foreign trips, he consistently tried to foster Japan's image as a contributor to global economic prosperity and political stability. While increasing Japanese investment in underdeveloped countries and financial support for the United Nations, Takeshita sent his foreign minister to monitor activities such as elections, troop withdrawals, and cease-fires in hot-spots around the globe.

Takeshita's domestic challenges were more difficult, including tax reform, soaring Tōkyō-area land prices, and raising domestic consumption. Moreover, Nakasone had failed to cut government spending, contributing to a $1 trillion national debt. Takeshita's answer was a 3 percent sales tax on goods and services to offset a $45 billion tax cut, measures that the Diet had passed by late 1988. He then braved certain opposition from his traditional constituency when he ended import quotas on beef and citrus products in an effort to improve U.S.-Japan Postwar Trade Relations*. To placate farmers, he formulated a program for rural improvement aimed at raising the standard of living and creating more jobs. Disclosure of an insider stock-trading scandal fatally wounded his administration, compelling a string of government leaders to resign. After Takeshita admitted receiving $1 million and his aide of thirty years committed suicide, he had no choice but to resign in May 1989. A quiet and dogged leader with infinite energy and an encyclopedic memory, his main strength was persuading people to set aside grievances and compromise.

Current Biography (1987); W. LaFeber, *The Clash: A History of U.S.-Japan Relations* (New York, 1997); J. I. Matray, *Japan's Emergence as a Global Power* (Westport, CT, 2000).

James I. Matray

TANAKA GIICHI (1864–1929)

As prime minister of Japan from 1927 to 1928, Tanaka Giichii followed a policy that most historians have judged "aggressive" toward China, setting the stage for the Mukden Incident* in September 1931. From his birth to a father who was a Chōshū foot soldier, his life was inseparably intertwined with the fate of the Japanese Imperial Army, which guided his actions later as a government leader. In 1892, Tanaka graduated from the Army War College. Command experiences in the Sino-Japanese War (1894–1895) and the Russo-Japanese War* (1904–1905) reinforced by studies in Europe, molded him into a leading organizational reformer within the service. The army's failed force buildup of 1911 convinced Tanaka of the imperative for a tactical alliance with emerging forces of party politics. His cultivation of major players in the Seiyūkai Party was an act of self-reinvention that yielded the desired political dividends when, after retiring from active service, he formed his own cabinet as Seiyūkai president in 1927. Meanwhile, World War I had opened his eyes to the concept of "total war" as the winning doctrine of modern warfare. This conviction explained his determination to effect the social regimentation essential for effective war mobilization and to pursue foreign and defense policies designed to achieve resource self-sufficiency.

Tanaka's policy in China must be understood in light of his military doctrine. He believed Manchuria's economic resources and military security were both vital to Japan in an age of total war planning. Accordingly, he sent three armed expeditions to Shandong between 1927 and 1929 in the name of protecting Japanese nationals from the fallout of the Northern Expedition. Acting simultaneously as foreign minister, Tanaka convened the so-called Eastern Conference in 1927 and established the basic tenets of his cabinet's China policy: (1) indirect control of Manchuria through local warlord Zhang Zuolin*; (2) pacification of China proper by a cooperative Jiang Jieshi*; (3) elimination of Soviet threats in north Manchuria and Inner Mongolia. Tanaka's attempt to negotiate the construction of five new rail lines into northern Manchuria was aimed at protecting Japan's tenuous grip on the Sino-Soviet border. But Zhang Zuolin's growing independence led to his murder at the hands of runaway elements in the Japanese Army in 1928, toppling the Tanaka cabinet and eliminating any hopes of maintaining a friendly but "independent" regime in Manchuria. In December 1928, the slain warlord's son and successor Zhang Xueliang* formally extended allegiance to Jiang's Guomindang* (Nationalists) and allowed the Nanjing government to unify China.

Tanaka sought to build a national security state capable of prosecuting total war within the bounds of parliamentary rule. Overseas, he intended to establish a post–World War I regional order in East Asia that was within the parameters of the treaty system fashioned at the Washington Conference* (1921–1922) and predicated on cooperation with the United States and Britain. Regardless of Tanaka's fundamentally restrained vision, the assertive middle echelon his China policy had helped to create in the army, rising Chinese nationalism, and the consolidating Soviet presence in East Asia undermined the very premises of his master plan and opened the way for the catastrophes that followed during the 1930s.

N. Bamba, *Japanese Diplomacy in a Dilemma* (Vancouver, BC, Canada, 1972); W. Morton, *Tanaka Giichi and Japan's China Policy* (Folkestone, UK, 1980); S. Ogata, *Defiance in Manchuria: The Making of Japanese Foreign Policy, 1931–1932* (Berkeley, CA, 1964).

Shimizu Sayuri

TANAKA KAKUEI (1918–1993)

Tanaka Kakuei was among the most powerful political leaders in postwar Japan, serving as prime minister from 1972 until scandal forced him from office in 1974. Born in 1918 to a poor farmer in a northern prefecture of Niigata, he became a self-made millionaire without a college education. Tanaka epitomized a breed of party politicians distinct from ex-bureaucrats, who dominated Japanese politics after World War II. After serving successfully in a series of important cabinet posts during Japan's high-growth period, he moved from the head of the Ministry of International Trade and Industry* (MITI) in the cabinet of Satō Eisaku*, his rival, to the premiership in July 1972. His main task was to recalibrate Tōkyō's relations with the United States and the People's Republic of China* (PRC) to suit the emerging multipolar world, in addition to the policy of détente that U.S. President Richard M. Nixon* was pursuing toward the Soviet Union. The growing U.S. trade deficit with Japan and Tanaka's long-established pro-PRC beliefs combined with the Nixon Shocks* dealt to Japanese officialdom over the previous summer to make this task all the more pressing.

The first shock was Washington's announcement in July 1971 of Nixon's Visit to China*, scheduled for early 1972. In September 1972, Tanaka traveled to Beijing and normalized relations with the PRC, despite opposition from a faction within his own party that supported the Republic of China* on Taiwan*. This historic step served to stabilize Japan's long-term relations with one of its powerful Communist neighbors. Nixon had consented to the Japanese approach to Beijing in August during his first summit meeting with Tanaka in Honolulu, but he had not sanctioned Tanaka's intent to declare the Japanese peace treaty with Taiwan null and void. Nixon's second shock was his decision in August 1971 to suspend dollar-gold convertibility and impose a 10 percent surcharge on imports. This increased the bilateral economic differences that Tanaka faced first as MITI minister. In October, he calmed the long U.S.-Japan textile dispute by acquiescing to most of the demands of the Nixon administration. Making the breakthrough possible was a 200-million-yen relief package that Tanaka put together for the overproducing Japanese textile industry. During the Honolulu summit, Tanaka pledged to take steps to reduce Japan's $3.5 billion trade surplus with the United States, including emergency U.S. imports. At a second summit with Nixon two years later, he renewed Japan's commitment to Japanese market liberalization.

The oil crunch triggered by the war in the Middle East in the fall of 1973 also generated U.S.-Japanese discord. The Tanaka cabinet's initial equivocation toward the U.S. initiative for concerted action by oil-importing nations accentuated Tōkyō's growing tendency to pursue an autonomous foreign policy. The combined effects of the runaway oil and consumer price inflation, Nixon's new dollar defense policy, and Tanaka's failed industrial relocation program caused serious economic dislocation in Japan and weakened his popular support. In November 1974, Tanaka resigned amid charges of financial misconduct. A year later the Lockheed Scandal* shook Japan, and Tanaka was arrested in July 1976. As the Lockheed trial dragged on, he retained his parliamentary seat and continued to exert behind-the-scenes influence in the factional alignments of the Liberal Democratic Party* and Japanese politics. *See also* U.S.-Japan Postwar Trade Relations.

I. M. Destler et al., *The Textile Wrangle: Conflict in Japanese-American Relations, 1969–1971* (Ithaca, NY, 1979); C. Johnson, *MITI and the Japanese Miracle: The Growth of Industrial Policy, 1925–1975* (Stanford, CA, 1982); W. LaFeber, *The Clash: A History of U.S.-Japan Relations* (New York, 1997); S. Ogata, *Normalization with China: A Comparative Study of U.S. and Japanese Processes* (Berkeley, CA, 1988).

Shimizu Sayuri

TANG SHAOYI (1860–1938)

Tang Shaoyi was a member of the third group of the Rong Hong* educational mission and went to the United States in 1874. After studying at Columbia and New York University, he returned to China in 1881. In 1907, Tang became the governor of

Liaoning Province. He believed that only the United States, which "continues to have in the Far East a national policy independent of all foreign alliances," held a position to join with China in defense of China's integrity. Together with U.S. Consul General Willard D. Straight*, Tang planned to use American capital to construct a railroad from Xinmin to Fakumen. U.S. money and diplomatic support, he hoped, would halt the economic expansion of Japan and Russia in that region. The economic crisis in the United States in 1907, as well as Japanese opposition, frustrated this scheme. Another plan Tang devised was to create a development bank in Manchuria to preserve the Open Door Policy*. The bank would be financed through a bank loan of roughly $13 million in the United States and repaid from the provinces' revenue and the uncollected part of the U.S. indemnity from the Boxer Uprising*. In August 1908, Tang negotiated with Straight a draft memorandum as a basis for further talks and in September had a contract to construct the Jinchao-Taonan railroad.

As the U.S. Congress decided to remit the American Boxer indemnity, the Chinese administration appointed Tang as special minister to travel to the United States. On 30 November 1908, he reached Washington with instructions to give thanks publicly for the remission and secretly to achieve two objectives: to negotiate a triple alliance of China, the United States, and Germany and to negotiate the bank loan. Although having the assistance of Straight, as well as other Americans, Tang found it difficult to make progress with the State Department. President Theodore Roosevelt* was not ready to challenge Japan in northeast China and was suspicious of the Chinese plans. Furthermore, the Root-Takahira Agreement* was concluded between the United States and Japan just at the time Tang was in Washington, reaffirming the U.S. commitment to the status quo in the Pacific and to amicable relations with Japan. Another obstacle to Tang's success was the removal of Yuan Shikai* as prime minister of China, who had authorized Tang to pursue the objectives of his mission. Desperately frustrated, Tang had to halt negotiations in the United States and left for Europe.

Feng Ziyou, *Geming yishi* [Revolutionary Historic Anecdote], Vol. 2 (Beijing, 1981); M. H. Hunt, *Frontier Defense and the Open Door: Manchuria in Chinese-American Relations, 1895–1911* (New Haven, CT, 1973); Li Xin (ed.), *Zhonghua Minguo renwu zhuan* [Who's Who of the Republic of China], Vol. 1 (Beijing, 1978); *Qingdai renwu zhuan* [Biography of Qing Dynasty] (Shenyang, 1992).

Cai Daiyun

TANG-WAI

See DANGWAI

TAO XINGZHI (1891–1946)

Tao Xingzhi, a protégé of American educator John Dewey, was an activist in China for opposition to Japanese aggression and the promotion of mass education. He was from Anhui and after graduation from Nanjing University, went to the United States to pursue his studies in politics. In 1914, Tao entered Illinois State University, where he earned a master of arts in politics in only one year. Then he studied for two years at the Normal School of Columbia University after receiving tuition from John Dewey, accepting the famous educator's theories. Tao attracted the attention of Guo Bingwen, acting president of Nanjing Normal Institute, who had been to the United States repeatedly to recruit qualified scholars from 1915 to 1916 and recruited him to return to China in August 1917 to join China's educational cause. Tao advanced many proposals to reform China's educational system, including "marrying off science" to spread scientific knowledge among the people and the experiment of "education from life" to merge China's education into the world education as an organic whole.

At the 1936 International New Education Conference in London, the National Anti-Japan and Saving-China Union authorized Tao to visit different countries as the national diplomatic representative. After Tao arrived in New York in November, he soon learned that seven famous scholars had been arrested in China after urging resistance against Japan. Tao immediately contacted Chinese leaders in the United States and an open letter signed by more than 300 people was issued to all overseas Chinese, calling for support of the seven scholars. Through Tao's solicitation, Dewey and fifteen other famous American scholars sent a telegram to China's government expressing concern over the incident. After the Marco Polo Bridge Incident* in 1937, Tao intensified his anti-Japanese activism among overseas Chinese and the American people through interviews with journalists, delivering speeches, and visiting groups that represented education, religion, medicine, culture, science, labor, women, and youth.

On 6 December 1937, Tao drafted for Dewey a statement supporting Chinese resistance against Japan and appealing for a boycott against Japanese goods. With Dewey's consent, he sent it to Romain Rolland, Bertrand Russell, Albert Einstein, and Mohandas Gandhi, who approved issuing the statement in December under their names. Tao also drafted a personal letter appealing for a boycott against Japanese goods and then sought to rally American popular support for it. He advocated that the United States should support Chinese resistance against Japan by "fixing the time for breaking off the relations with Japan." In addition, Tao investigated the amount of military supplies the United States and Britain exported to Japan and publicized the data at a mass rally in Los Angeles, which was then printed in newspapers and in a U.S. Senate report. In 1938, Tao returned to China to continue his anti-Japanese propaganda and support for mass education.

Zhou Hongyu (ed.), *Haiwai Tao Xingzhi yanjiu* [The Research on Tao Xingzhi Overseas] (Beijing, 1991); *Tao Xingzhi wen ji* [Collected Works of Tao Xingzhi] (Nanjing, 1981); Zhang Kaiyuan and Tang Wenquan, *Pinfan de rensheng* [Tao Xingzhi: A Confucius After Confucius] (Changsha, 1992).

Xiang E

TAYLOR, MAXWELL D. (1901–1987)

Maxwell D. Taylor was a professional soldier who, after his first retirement in 1959, returned to serve in the Kennedy and Johnson administrations with a reputation as a "political general." An able linguist, in the 1930s, he spent four years in Japan as an observer with the Imperial Guards Artillery Regiment before moving temporarily in 1937 to China for intelligence duties when the Sino-Japanese war began. In 1953, Taylor took command of the Eighth Army in the Korean War* at a time when the Korean Armistice Agreement* was imminent, a position he held until February 1955, when he was offered and accepted the post of chief of staff of the U.S. Army. Although Taylor served out his four-year term and did not resign in protest, as often alleged, he differed with President Dwight D. Eisenhower* over army policy. He wanted to build up conventional forces to allow the United States to fight limited wars, whereas the budget-conscious president preferred to rely on massive but probably unusable nuclear retaliation. In his 1959 book *The Uncertain Trumpet*, Taylor publicly aired his views, winning the attention and approval of Eisenhower's successor, John F. Kennedy*.

Kennedy initially brought in Taylor as a military adviser to investigate the 1961 Bay of Pigs fiasco, but he quickly assumed other responsibilities. Later that year, Taylor and Walt W. Rostow*, Kennedy's deputy national security adviser, headed a mission to the Republic of Vietnam*. Their report recommended the introduction of 6,000–8,000 American troops in the guise of a flood-relief force, a suggestion the president rejected, but was successful in advocating a major expansion in the numbers of U.S. military "advisers" and of military and economic aid, together with an increase in U.S. responsibilities for Vietnam. From 1962 to 1964, Taylor was chairman of the Joint Chiefs of Staff, in which capacity he opposed the commitment of further U.S. troops to the Second Indochina War*, but supported escalation through U.S. air strikes within Vietnam and bombing raids on the Democratic Republic of Vietnam*.

During a one-year term as U.S. ambassador to South Vietnam, which began in August 1964, Taylor continued to oppose the commitment of American ground forces, advice that President Lyndon B. Johnson* ignored. On his return, he served three years as a special consultant to Johnson, during which he frequently defended U.S. policies in Vietnam publicly. In March 1968, Taylor was one of only three so-called "Wise Men" to dissent from the view that the United States should seek to withdraw from the war by negotiating a peace settlement. In 1972, he advised National Security Adviser Henry A. Kissinger* that a resolution of the issue of North Vietnamese troops remaining in the south and several other contentious matters was necessary before reaching a peace agreement, but Kissinger largely ignored him. Thereafter, Taylor continued to defend U.S. Vietnam policies and to blame the defeat on criticism by the media and public opinion, which in his view had sapped the nation's resolve to win.

R. Buzzanco, *Masters of War: Military Dissent and Politics in the Vietnam Era* (Cambridge, MA, 1996); D. Kinnard, *The Certain Trumpet: Maxwell Taylor and the American Experience in Vietnam* (Washington, DC, 1991); J. M. Taylor, *General Maxwell Taylor: The Sword and the Pen* (New York, 1989); M. D. Taylor, *Swords and Plowshares* (New York, 1972); M. D. Taylor, *The Uncertain Trumpet* (New York, 1959).

Priscilla Roberts

TEAM SPIRIT MILITARY EXERCISES

The Team Spirit exercise, the annual combined South Korean–U.S. military maneuver, demonstrated close military cooperation between the two nations, as the words themselves imply. The annual field exercise, based on the U.S.–South Korea Mutual Security Treaty*, was designed to prepare for emergencies on the Korean peninsula, in particular an unprovoked attack by the Democratic People's Republic of Korea* (DPRK) against the Republic of Korea* (ROK). Its planners had hoped from the start that the landing of large numbers of heavily armed ROK and U.S. ground troops would make a powerful impression on the DPRK to the north. The combined military maneuver began in 1969, then called the Focus Retina, and was renamed the Freedom Bolt in 1971. In 1976, the name Team Spirit was adopted. The Team Spirit maneuver has been known as the largest in the world, often including 200,000 troops, about 70,000 of whom were Americans—those already in Korea and others flown in for the exercises.

North Korea, regarding Team Spirit as a grave threat to its national security, denounced the exercise as a dangerous war game intentionally designed to further poison North-South Korean relations. P'yŏngyang therefore demanded that the joint mobilization exercise be stopped. In particular, North Korean leader Kim Il Sung* called it "a dress rehearsal for an invasion" in 1993. Because the military exercise always brought a fierce reaction from the DPRK, both the ROK and the United States made use of it as an important bargaining chip for concessions from the north in the 1990s. For example, under the bilateral arrangement, South Korea agreed to cancel the 1992 Team Spirit exercise in return for North Korea's willingness to permit international inspection of its controversial nuclear facilities. In 1993, it was downsized to include 70,000 South Korean troops and 50,000 American troops, including the landing of 19,000 Americans from outside the country. During the 1990s, the Team Spirit exercise has been conducted with flexibility in accordance with progress toward permanent stability on the Korean peninsula. *See also* North Korean Nuclear Controversy.

B. Cumings, *Korea's Place in the Sun: A Modern History* (New York, 1997); Kim Jinwung, *Han'gukin ŭi Panmi Kamjŏng* [The Anti-Americanism of the Korean People] (Seoul, 1992); D. Oberdorfer, *The Two Koreas: A Contemporary History* (Reading, PA, 1997).

Kim Jinwung

TET OFFENSIVE (30 January 1968)

On 30 January 1968, the National Liberation Front* (NLF) and the People's Army of Vietnam (PAVN) initiated this military engagement, which was the decisive turning point in the Second Indochina War*. In mid-1967, Defense Minister General Vo Nguyen Giap* of the Democratic Republic of Vietnam* (DRV) proposed ending the war speedily and successfully in one master stroke. Giap, the hero of Dien Bien Phu* in the spring of 1954, formulated a plan based on three key assumptions. First, it assumed that the Army of the Republic of Vietnam* (ARVN), weak and demoralized, would collapse completely under the weight of the General Offensive. Second, Giap expected the people of South Vietnam would rally to the Communist cause and overthrow the government of the Republic of Vietnam* under Nguyen Van Thieu* in the General Uprising. Third, the resulting shock would sap the American will to continue U.S. intervention in Vietnam.

Giap scheduled the General Offensive for Tet 1968, the beginning of the lunar new year and the most important holiday in Vietnamese culture. Throughout the fall of 1967, NLF and PAVN forces staged diversionary raids in the Central Highlands and northern border regions, including a months-long siege of U.S. Marines at Khe Sanh*. These battles drew U.S. combat units away from urban areas and gave Communist forces valuable experience in large-scale conventional military operations. The NLF and PAVN then used the Christmas cease-fire to move their troops into position, and the Communists then called for a cease-fire during the Tet holiday. By January, they had moved 100,000 soldiers undetected into the cities. Only one U.S. commander, Lieutenant General Frederick Weyand, was not thrown off by these border raids. He did not like the emerging operational patterns, noticing that although his units on the Cambodian border were making few contacts, Communist radio traffic in the Saigon region was increasing. He persuaded General William C. Westmoreland*, commander of the Military Assistance Command, Vietnam*, to pull more troops back toward Saigon.

Communist forces launched the attacks on 30 January 1968, including an assault on the U.S. embassy in Saigon. Because of the intense secrecy in the planning and buildup, however, they failed to coordinate their efforts. The offensive was supposed to begin the next day, but the NLF commanders in Region 5 staged attacks on Danang, Nha Trang, and ten other cities twenty-four hours too early. The Tet Offensive later was regarded widely as a tactical defeat for the NLF and the North Vietnamese, but a strategic and political defeat for the United States. Giap failed to accomplish any of his military objectives, and two of his key assumptions had been wrong. The ARVN had held steady, and U.S. troops quickly regained control in the critical areas, with the exception of Hue, where the fighting lasted several weeks. The South Vietnamese population had not risen up in mass to overthrow their governing regime and welcome their Communist "liberators." Finally, both the NLF and PAVN had sustained major casualties, including as many as 50,000 battlefield deaths, compared with 3,895 for the United States and 4,954 for the ARVN. In fact, the NLF was so devastated that it took nearly two years to rebuild its cadre base to pre-Tet levels. But the Tet Offensive struck a demoralizing blow to American public support of the war in Vietnam. Both the timing and the intensity of the Communist offensive took the Americans by surprise, exposing the determination and continued vitality of the NLF and the North Vietnamese. That the NLF could infiltrate the American embassy compound in Saigon was stunning to most Americans who watched events unfold on television. As a result of the Tet Offensive, President Lyndon B. Johnson* withdrew from the presidential race in March 1968. American policy in Vietnam was now more about extricating itself "honorably" from Vietnam than about winning the war.

M. Gilbert and W. Head (eds.), *The Tet Offensive* (Westport, CT, 1996); G. C. Herring, *America's Longest War: The United States and Vietnam, 1950–1975* (New York, 1996); S. Karnow, *Vietnam: A History* (New York, 1983); M. B. Young, *The Vietnam Wars, 1945–1990* (New York, 1991).

Robert K. Brigham

THAILAND

Prathet Thai, or Thailand, was the name adopted for the former Kingdom of Siam in 1939, asserting the nationalist consciousness of the Thai regime in the late colonial period in Southeast Asia. By the year 2000, it was a nation of 61 million people, sharing borders with Cambodia* to the east, Laos* to the north, Myanmar (Burma*) to the west, and Malaysia* to the south. The Thai people originated in what is now southern China and, through a series of population movements, spread over the highlands of interior Southeast Asia and into the valley of the Chao Phraya River and the Khorat Plateau. The Chakri Dynasty established its rule at Bangkok in 1782. Thereafter, Siam was unique among the countries of Southeast Asia in that during the great colonial era of the nineteenth century, it did not fall under the direct rule of a foreign power. Its location between the colonial spheres of Britain and France meant that as rivalry between these powers intensified, Thailand's nominal independence became a goal for each of them, to deny supremacy to the other. This process reached its culmination from 1893 to 1903, when the territory of Siam was delineated by agreement between Britain and France, with significant tracts separated from the kingdom and given to French Indochina* and to the British Straits Settlements on the Malay Peninsula. An independent Siam was preserved as a buffer, but was strongly influenced by Britain, spurring the Thais to embark on a program of political reform and institutional modernization. By the middle decades of the nineteenth century, under King Mongkut, Western-style reforms were begun, and this process was deepened and expanded under King Chulalongkorn from 1868 to 1910.

American relations with Thailand date from 1833, when a commercial treaty was first signed. In the nineteenth century, as Britain and France dominated affairs in Siam and adjacent areas of Southeast Asia, the United States had a fairly low profile in the region. Colonial conquest of the Philippines* after the Spanish-American War* in 1898 caused American interests in Southeast Asia to expand. Following World War I, the United States supported Siam's efforts to improve its position in relation to the colonial powers at the Versailles Peace Conference. In a series of treaties from 1920 to 1926, first with the United States and then other Western powers, Thailand regained tariff autonomy and ended extraterritorial rights. Thai forces of modernization were advanced greatly by a coup against the monarchy in 1932. A coalition of civilian and military figures forced King Prajadipok to accept a constitution significantly limiting his powers and creating new institutions of government. The military soon emerged as the dominant force in Thai politics. By the end of the 1930s, a military strongman, Field Marshal Phibulsongkhram, was prime minister and the leader of a quasi-fascist movement sympathetic to the anti-Western rhetoric of the Japanese. When Japanese forces occupied Thailand during World War II, local government collaborated with the occupation forces. Thailand officially declared war on the Allies in 1942, though the Thai ambassador to the United States, Seni Pramoj, refused to deliver the message. Seni and a small group of Thai guerrillas worked together with resistance forces in Thailand led by Pridi Banomyong to launch the Free Thai Movement*.

After the defeat of Japan in August 1945, the United States replaced the British and French as the major power in Southeast Asia. Pridi was elected the first postwar prime minister, and Thai-U.S. relations grew increasingly close. The United States supported the Thai military with training and materials, as well as assisting the Thai government in suppressing a Communist insurgency in northeastern and southern Thailand. In 1954, Thailand became part of the U.S.-sponsored Southeast Asia Treaty Organization*. As U.S. involvement in the Second Indochina War* increased, Thailand became an important base for the air war, and an equally important venue of rest and recuperation for U.S. troops. U.S. military and civilian aid poured into Thailand, and Thai troops took part in combat in Vietnam. When the Paris Peace Accords* brought U.S. withdrawal, Thailand was left in a somewhat uncomfortable position. Through participation in the Association of Southeast Asian Nations* and a sometimes painful process of political reform and democratization, Thailand was able to reposition itself as a leading player in recent Southeast Asian political and economic life. Thailand's engagement with the world economy and its role as one of the "tiger" economies of the early 1990s led to its less desirable role as the starting point, in July 1997, for the East Asian Financial Crisis* and collapse of its speculative economic bubble. *See also* U.S. Recruitment of Foreign Troops to Fight in Vietnam.

N. Tarling (ed.), *The Cambridge History of Southeast Asia* (Cambridge, MA, 1992); T. Winichakul, *Siam Mapped: A History of the Geo-Body of a Nation* (Honolulu, HI, 1994); D. K. Wyatt, *Thailand: A Short History* (New Haven, CT, 1984).

Kenneth J. Hammond

THIRTY-EIGHTH PARALLEL DIVISION

This line divided Korea at the end of World War II into Soviet and U.S. zones of military occupation, creating the circumstances that would lead to the outbreak of the Korean War*. At the Potsdam Conference, held between 16 July and 2 August 1945, President Harry S. Truman* and Secretary of State James F. Byrnes hoped that U.S. possession of the atomic bomb would result in Japan's swift surrender and a unilateral U.S. Occupation of Korea*. Suspicious of Soviet activities in Eastern Europe, Truman wanted to limit the Soviet sphere of influence in Asia. U.S. officials did not expect an early entry into the Pacific war by the Soviet Union, and the decision to divide Korea into American and Soviet occupation zones was taken only after the Soviet Union declared war on Japan on 8 August.

On the evening of 10 August, Assistant Secretary of War John J. McCloy ordered two colonels, Dean Rusk* and Charles H. Bonesteel III, to determine a dividing line across Korea that would incorporate as much of Korea into an American occupation zone as possible, taking into consideration the location of U.S. troops in the Pacific. They recommended that Korea be divided along the thirty-eighth parallel, with U.S. soldiers occupying southern Korea and Soviet soldiers stationed north of that line. Seoul, the capital city, was included in the American zone. The choice of the dividing line was arbitrary, and it was decided in about thirty minutes. No thought was given to discussing the decision with Koreans, who were treated as pawns of great power politics. The decision was incorporated into a draft of the surrender order for Japan, known as General Order Number 1*.

Soviet armies entered Korea on 12 August, the same day that the State-War-Navy Coordinating Committee discussed the recommendations to divide Korea at the thirty-eighth parallel. At the meeting, Rear-Admiral M. B. Gardner suggested that the thirty-ninth parallel be proposed to the Soviets as the dividing line (on 26 July, the Soviet Union and the United States had agreed to divide Korea at the forty-first parallel for future air and naval operations), but the consensus was that the Soviets would not accept a line that far north. The United States submitted its proposal to Joseph Stalin on 15 August and he accepted it the same day, much to the surprise of some American officials, including Dean Rusk. If Stalin had refused, the Joint Chiefs of Staff were ready to order immediate occupation of the southeastern port city of Pusan. But Stalin still hoped to have a say in the occupation of Japan, and he was unwilling to risk Allied enmity over Korea. The division led to the creation of two mutually antagonistic states: the Republic of Korea* and the Democratic People's Republic of Korea*. The thirty-eighth parallel cut across two important strategic regions, the Ongjin Peninsula, a territory inaccessible to South Korea except by sea, and Kaesŏng. Serious cross-border fighting erupted in these places in the spring and summer of 1949, more than a year prior to North Korea's attack on South Korea. *See also* Moscow Agreement on Korea.

Bruce Cumings, *The Origins of the Korean War*, Vol. 1: *Liberation and the Emergence of Separate Regimes, 1945–1947* (Princeton, NJ, 1981); J. L. Gaddis, *The United States and the Origins of the Cold War, 1941–1947* (New York, 1972); J. I. Matray, "Captive of the Cold War: The Decision to Divide Korea at the 38th Parallel," *Pacific Historical Review* (Spring 1981); U.S. Department of State, *Foreign Relations of the United States, 1945*, Vol. 6: *The British Commonweath, The Far East* (Washington, DC, 1969).

Steven Hugh Lee

THREE NON-NUCLEAR PRINCIPLES

In December 1967, Japan's Prime Minister Satō Eisaku* announced in the Diet the introduction of the three non-nuclear principles, under which Japan's government officially committed itself to a policy of prohibiting manufacture, possession, or transit through Japan of nuclear weapons. Formally underlined with a cabinet directive, his announcement of this government policy both expressed and reinforced the widespread Japanese popular aversion to nuclear weapons that had existed since the end of World War II. As the only nation to have experienced the trauma of Atomic Attacks* (at Hiroshima and Nagasaki), postwar Japan had a readily understandable "nuclear allergy" that had featured prominently in the country's foreign and security policies during and after the U.S. Occupation of Japan*. Indeed, despite periodic private efforts by top conservative politicians and defense officials to consider developing an independent nuclear capability, the nuclear taboo remained as a major constraint, at least publicly, preventing Japan from pursuing a more conventional defense policy. By contrast, progressive voices in postwar Japan, particularly within the Japan Socialist Party, initially viewed the three non-nuclear principles as the basis for a new, distinctive diplomatic style, in which Japan would act as a positive example of the merits of an intentionally nonconfrontational foreign policy.

The three non-nuclear principles, alongside other distinctive expressions of Japan's reluctance to become embroiled in armed conflict, such as Article 9, the well-known antiwar clause of the Japanese Constitution of 1947*, became associated with a diplomatic stance—variously characterized as "one-country pacifism" and a "low-profile" foreign policy—that arguably would help insulate Japan from regional and global conflict. Despite Japan's public commitment to a non-nuclear position, however, recent archival revelations and the testimony of leading officials in both Japan and the United States have suggested that this was more a rhetorical than a substantive undertaking. In 1981, Edwin O. Reischauer*, a former U.S. ambassador to Japan, revealed in an interview that Japan's government privately and implicitly had recognized the right of U.S. ships carrying nuclear weapons to enter Japanese waters. Far more dramatic in 1994, Wakaizumi Kei, who acted as Satō's private emissary in negotiations with the United States over the Okinawa Controversy*, revealed in a published memoir that Satō and President Richard M. Nixon* in November 1969 signed a secret understanding allowing the United States to reintroduce nuclear weapons into Japanese territory during a security crisis in East Asia.

Japan's commitment to the three nonnuclear principles resurfaced as a political issue in April 2000, when the leader of the Japan Communist Party publicized in the Diet declassified U.S. government documents indicating that Prime Minister Kishi Nobusuke* in 1960 had accepted that the United States might introduce nuclear weapons into Japan. These revelations pointed to the disturbing gap between the public and private position of Japan's leaders. This inconsistency has troubled Japan's neighbors, some of whom, especially the People's Republic of China*, claimed in the 1990s that Tōkyō was able and willing to develop an independent nuclear deterrent capacity. Other observers highlighted Japan's advanced nuclear energy program, pointing out that the country's cutting-edge, fast-breeder reactors provided sufficient fissionable material to manufacture one or more nuclear devices. But not only was there no direct evidence of a government commitment to a conversion program, but public opinion in Japan remained resolutely opposed to the nuclear option. Although a 1970 Japanese White Paper declared that nuclear weapons were constitutional if used purely for defensive purposes, Japan was a signatory of the Nuclear Non-Proliferation Treaty and therefore not in a position to acquire nuclear weapons without violating its existing treaty obligations.

M. J. Green and P. M. Cronin (eds.), *The U.S.-Japan Alliance: Past, Present, and Future* (New York, 1999); J. I. Matray, *Japan's Emergence as a Global Power* (Westport, CT, 2000); E. O. Reischauer, *My Life Between Japan and America* (New York, 1986); Wakaizumi Kei, *Tasaku nakarishi o shinzemu to hossu* [The Best Course Available] (Tōkyō, 1994).

John Swenson-Wright

TIANANMEN SQUARE MASSACRE

The Tiananmen Square Massacre in 1989 was the result of the profound changes occurring in China's social and cultural life after the death of Mao Zedong*. Starting in 1978 when Deng Xiaoping* was restored to power in the People's Republic of China* (PRC), he set in motion a reform program aimed at moving the economy away from the rigid control of the Chinese Communist Party* and in a more market-oriented direction. The reform program, known as the Four Modernizations*, had a twofold outcome. On the one hand, it released the social dynamics and ushered China's economy into a new era of fast growth. On the other hand, social problems began to arise as a result of the loosening social and political control. It was the latter that planted seeds for the outbreak of the anger a decade later. Of all social problems accompanying the reforms, official corruption was most prominent. Deeper historical, institutional, and ideological roots aside, the direct precursor for corruption was the power that, during Mao's revolutionary era, had been concentrated in the hand of the party leaders. Therefore, despite the initial success of economic reform, social discontent grew throughout the 1980s and was particularly strong among the college students, whose anxiety and anger had sparked incessant campus protests.

The Tiananmen Massacre was triggered by the death in early spring 1989 of Hu Yaobang*, former party general secretary and a victim of antireform forces. In April, college students in Beijing gathered in Tiananmen Square to honor China's deceased leader. This spontaneous mourning movement quickly provided an opportunity to channel deep social discontent. The students first urged the government to eliminate corrupt officials and, when the government ignored these demands, further called for Premier Li Peng* to resign. The government responded by denouncing the protesters for creating turmoil, which further angered the students. On 4 May, a historic day for China when mass protests occurred against the continuation of imperialist exploitation of China was confirmed under the Versailles Peace Treaty*, more than 1 million students took to the streets, recalling the events of 1919, and many Beijing residents joined in their ranks. They then erected tents in Tiananmen Square, swearing not to withdraw without receiving a satisfactory response from the government. As the situation gradually escalated out of control, the government decided to crack down on the movement. Troops were brought into the capital, and fired the first shot on 4 June. The soldiers quickly overran the unarmed students and citizens. The exact death toll never was revealed, but it certainly far exceeded the number of twenty-three given by government officials.

The Tiananmen Square Massacre shocked and angered many people around the world, among them Americans. In response, they urged their governments to impose sanctions on China. President George H. W. Bush* suspended a number of scheduled exchanges between the two countries, and the United States offered a haven for many Chinese student leaders and others who fled repression at home, notably Fang Lizhi*. There also were demands for the release of dissident Wei Jingsheng*. For many Americans who witnessed the massacre on television, the military assault on unarmed students who called for democracy stigmatized the Chinese regime. U.S. relations with China thus entered a period of acrimony, the first since the presidency of Richard M. Nixon* and his famous Visit to China* in February 1972. *See also* May Fourth Movement.

J. K. Fairbank, *China: A New History* (Cambridge, MA, 1992); *New York Times*, June–July 1989; Television Documentary, *We Will Never Forget* (Taibei, 1993).

Li Yi

TIBET

Since 1950, Tibet has been one of the five autonomous regions of the People's Republic of China* (PRC). Its international status, however, had been questioned for almost a century. Historically, the imperial regimes in China maintained a tributary relationship with the government in Tibet, as it did with many other countries, such as Vietnam and Korea. During the second half of the nineteenth century, European imperialism challenged and subsequently eroded this tributary system in the East Asian. Largely because of its geographic isolation, Tibet had not become a target of the imperialism until the twentieth century began. With competition for overseas territory intensifying, Britain moved northward from its colony in India across the Himalayas, and entered Tibet. After some insignificant resistance, the Tibetans signed the Treaty of Lhasa in 1904, renouncing its tributary relation with the Chinese regime and opening a few towns as trading posts for Britain. The Qing Dynasty of China, although unable to stop the British advance, never granted Tibet's independence, and the international status of Tibet therefore remained in doubt.

The period that followed World War I was particularly crucial to the further complication of the Tibetan issue. On the one hand, the British soon found that their interest in Tibet was hardly worth the cost paid, and thus slowed their adventure. Moreover, as its power quickly diminished as a result of the two world wars, Britain relinquished its status as a world power. On the other hand, the rise of Chinese nationalism in the mid-1920s and China's wartime alliance with Britain and the United States further strengthened its position to reclaim Tibet. This tip in the balance of power therefore prevented Tibet from becoming another Korea or Vietnam, and its independence never was finalized. Upon coming to power in 1949, the Chinese Communist Party* (CCP) inherited the nationalist legacy from its predecessor and reasserted the invalidity of the 1904 Treaty of Lhasa. Meanwhile, it engaged the Tibetan authorities in negotiations to reincorporate the region into the new PRC. Unprepared and unassisted, Tibet accepted the inevitable. In 1950, the PRC army entered Tibet and made it an autonomous region.

Historical tensions between the Tibetans and their rulers in Beijing, however, remained, particularly when Chinese-imposed reform was to change the tradition that the former had clung to for centuries. In 1959, a revolt against the Chinese broke out, and as the Chinese Army closed in on Lhasa, Dalai Lama XIV fled to India and began his independent movement in exile. During the height of the Cold War, the Tibetan issue essentially was ignored, but the fall of the Soviet Union in 1991 and the rise of China's prominence in Asia once again put Tibet under the spotlight. Since the 1980s, the Tibetans have made a few attempts to break from the PRC's control, but have been met with Chinese military crackdowns. The world community, headed by the United States, has expressed increasing concern over the human rights violations in Tibet under Chinese rule. In 1995, Dalai XIV won the Nobel Peace Prize for his persistent nonviolent campaign for Tibetan independence. Although the governments of most countries in the world accept China's claim over Tibet, support from the people for Tibetan independence movement remained strong as the new century began.

J. K. Fairbank, *China, A New History* (Cambridge, MA, 1992); L. Wang, *Sky Burial: The Fate of Tibet* (Hong Kong, 1998).

Li Yi

TŌJŌ HIDEKI (1884–1948)

General Tōjō Hideki was Japan's prime minister at the time of the Pearl Harbor Attack* that ignited war with the United States. Nicknamed the Razor because of his decisiveness, intelligence, and impatience, he was reared to be an army officer by his father, an ex-samurai who had risen to become a lieutenant general in the Imperial Army. Tōjō graduated from the army's prestigious War College in 1915 and was posted to Germany four years later. Upon his return, he received swift promotions and positions giving him access to political chiefs in the army and other ministries. In 1935, Tōjō became chief of the military police in Japan's puppet state of Manchukuo* and then chief of staff of Japan's forces stationed there. During this time, he gained experience in creating a highly centralized political and economic state that, he hoped, could be copied in Japan itself. From Manchukuo, Tōjō vigorously supported using the Marco Polo Bridge Incident* of July 1937 as a vehicle for eliminating the Chinese Guomindang* (Nationalist) regime of Jiang Jieshi*, as well as a way to secure laws that would reorder Japanese politics and society so as to prepare it for "total war." He returned to Japan in 1938 to become army vice minister, a post he used to attempt to forward direct army control of Japan's munitions and related industries.

In 1940, Tōjō became army minister in the newly formed second cabinet of Konoe Fumimaro*. By that time, it had become clear that Jiang was not going to be eliminated easily. Tōjō worked to secure an end to the fighting in China—albeit on terms that would see Japanese forces occupy much of that country's north—so as to prepare the army for the Soviet Union, its real foe. To pressure Jiang, Japan occupied the northern half of French Indochina* during July. In September, Japan's navy finally acquiesced to an alliance with Nazi Germany, resulting in the signing of the Tripartite Pact*. But the Imperial Army and Navy could not agree at that time whether to move farther south, as the army desired, to take advantage of German victories in Europe. This disagreement deepened during the spring of 1941 with reports of an impending German attack on the Soviet Union. Tōjō strongly favored a major buildup of forces in Manchuria to prepare for a strike against the Soviets. But the navy favored a move south against Britain and the United States. Although Tōjō got his buildup, the U.S. oil embargo of August compelled even him to abandon thoughts of a Soviet attack and instead proceed southward to capture the oil-rich Dutch East Indies.

Thus, in this rather backhanded way, the army accepted war with the United States, which unnerved Prime Minister Konoe, who resigned in October after Tōjō insisted that a firm decision for war was necessary. Under these circumstances, it fell to him to assume responsibility by becoming prime minister himself. Commanded by Emperor Hirohito* to undertake a sweeping reassessment of Japan's situation, Tōjō reported that war was the best course. Although somewhat speculative, he apparently hoped that the war would be over quickly, sealed by German victory over the Soviet Union and the need for China to seek terms, as Japan created a ring of island fortresses that would be too costly for the Americans to breach. In the meantime, Tōjō meant to use the war fever to secure at last the fundamental domestic reorderings that he had favored since his days in Manchukuo. He personally assumed the Home Ministry and other portfolios and oversaw creation of the Greater East Asia Co-Prosperity Sphere* Ministry that usurped much of the authority of the Foreign Ministry. But his plans for fundamental reforms were blocked repeatedly in the Diet. Worse, the U.S. conquest of the Mariana Islands, especially Saipan, forced him to resign in July 1944. Ironically, Tōjō's attempts at centralization branded him as a dictator to the victorious Allies, who swiftly moved to arrest him as a war criminal. Tōjō attempted suicide, but was saved by the speedy intervention of a U.S. medical team. He underwent extensive questioning during the Tōkyō War Crimes Trials*, accepted responsibility for his government's actions during the war, and was hanged in December 1948.

R. J. C. Butow, *Tōjō and the Coming of the War* (Stanford, CA, 1961).

Michael A. Barnhart

TŌKYŌ ROUND

Tōkyō Round, the seventh major negotiating session of the General Agreement on Tariffs and Trade* (GATT), reformed the international trade system in response, in part, to the newly competitive Japan. Ninety-nine countries sought to continue the historic process of trade liberalization that had come under stress because of American protectionism and the collapse of the postwar monetary regime. In September 1973, participants initialed the Tōkyō Declaration, which called for the traditional GATT objectives of large-scale tariff reductions, non-tariff barriers (NTB), special assistance for less-developed nations, and stabilization of exchange rates. Trade negotiations did not begin until 1975 with dialogue centered on the "Big Four" of the United States, Canada, the European Community, and Japan over agricultural and industrial trade barriers. A code prescribed "fair-trade" conduct in general categories (government procurement, subsidies, customs valuation, standards, antidumping, and import licensing) covering more than 800 NTBs. In addition, staged tariffs cuts dropped average industrial duty rates from 7 to 4.7 percent. The Tōkyō Round also established procedures for resolving disputes among the GATT members. The less-developed nations exited the talks critical of the lack of assistance given to the world's poor.

Important bilateral discussions occurred between the United States and Japan. One issue regarded a code for limiting discrimination in government procurement, an NTB that nations used to give domestic producers preferential treatment. Upon determining that Japanese concessions were inadequate, particularly on opening its telecommunications market, the United States refused to apply the code to Japan. This episode reflected the power of Japanese bureaucracies, a fact that had become apparent to the Americans. For diplomatic reasons, Japan's Ministry of Foreign Affairs pushed for free-trade policies, which would encourage good alliance relations, whereas the Ministry of International Trade and Industry* straddled both a liberal bent and protection of client industries. But both the Finance and Agriculture and Forestry ministries toed a protectionist line, the former to guard Japan's monetary reserves and the latter to defend, rigidly, the nation's vulnerable farmers. This power structure limited concessions, although politicians, particularly Ushiba Nobuhiko*, minister of external economic affairs, tried to avoid confrontation with the United States.

Meanwhile, Washington had engaged Tōkyō in numerous discussions to open up Japanese markets, although American protectionists hoped to stem the tide of imports of Japanese automobiles, electronics, and textiles. Robert Strauss, U.S. special trade representative, actively sought market access for American goods while urging Japan to restrict its exports of televisions and steel. But bilateral talks collapsed on the latter in March 1979, when the Japanese persisted in protecting Nippon Telephone and Telegraph Company from American telecommunications competition. Strauss spoke of retaliating by closing off American markets, Congress threatened a 15 percent import surcharge, and Europeans joined in complaining about inadequate Japanese concessions at the Tōkyō Round. Eventually, a deal ensued with Japanese promises to crack its markets and amend its trade balance. At the Tōkyō Round, Japan also offered concessions on agriculture amounting to $215 million; Washington responded by lowering barriers on nonfarm products from Japan. Although the Round did not alter greatly world agriculture protectionism, the NTB codes were heralded as an initial attempt to regulate these pernicious, widespread forms of protectionism.

Analysts have concluded that in economic terms, the Tōkyō Round reduced tariffs and NTBs and addressed key disputes in a difficult era when protectionism around the globe was ascendant. Of special import to U.S.-Japan Postwar Trade Relations* was the reemphasis on trade liberalism, however cautious. Free trade did not win out. Rather, "fair" or "managed" trade kept movement in a liberal direction. Politically, the Tōkyō Round enhanced cooperation. The GATT regime had been transformed by the collapse of the global monetary system, the strength of Japan, and the relative decline in hegemony of the United States. The Tōkyō Round brought new powers—namely the European Community and Japan—into the decision-making structure of the world economy. This provided for a truly multilateral trade order, a goal since World War II, and recognized Japan as a responsible global leader. In doing so, economic relations were not permitted to unsettle the Cold War alliance against Communism* or alienate Asia's rising nations with barriers to their trade.

S. Dryden, *Trade Warriors: USTR and the American Crusade for Free Trade* (New York, 1995); L. A. Glick, *Multilateral Trade Negotiations: World Trade After the Tokyo Round* (Totowa, NJ, 1984); T. R. Graham, "Results of the Tokyo Round," *The Georgia Journal of International and Comparative Law* (1979); G. R. Winham, *International Trade and the Tokyo Round Negotiation* (Princeton, NJ, 1986).

Thomas W. Zeiler

TŌKYŌ WAR CRIMES TRIALS

The Tōkyō War Crimes Trials was known officially as the International Military Tribunal for the Far East (IMTFE). Based on the Potsdam Declaration* and other Allied agreements, the Supreme Commander for the Allied Powers (SCAP*) created the IMTFE, with eleven judges representing the victorious nations involved in the Pacific war to try war criminals. The legal proceedings opened in Tōkyō on 3 May 1946, where twenty-eight top military and civilian Japanese leaders identified as Class-A war criminals were charged with crimes against peace and humanity in planning and waging an aggressive war. By the time the verdicts were handed down in November 1948, two defendants had died during the long proceedings, and one, Ōkawa Shūmei*, had been ruled mentally unfit for trial. The IMFE therefore dismissed the cases against these three men. Of the twenty-five charged, seven, including former Prime Ministers Tōjō Hideki* and Hirōta Koki*, were sentenced to death by hanging, which was carried out in December 1948. The remaining eighteen were condemned to prison sentences ranging from seven years to life in prison, but the sentences later were commuted.

The IMTFE was part of the Allied effort to dismantle the Japanese wartime machine in the plan during the U.S. Occupation of Japan* to demilitarize and democratize Japan. Angry about the Pearl Harbor Attack* and the three-and-a-half-year war that followed, countless Americans wanted to try, convict, and punish Emperor Hirohito*, but General Douglas MacArthur* and other U.S. leaders believed correctly that extracting revenge on the monarch would undermine popular support in Japan for the occupation. Besides the Tōkyō War Crimes Trials, a great number of lower-ranking Japanese military officers accused of specific cases of war crimes also were tried and either were executed or sentenced to various terms of imprisonment, both abroad and at home. The trials in Tōkyō, however, were the most conspicuous, as they involved the most notorious defendants. But the IMTFE later aroused much controversy. Subject to much debate has been the principle of holding an individual responsible for his government's policy and its ex post facto nature. Critics therefore have labeled the Tōkyō War Crimes Trials as victors' justice.

A. C. Brackman, *The Other Nuremburg: The Untold Story of the Tokyo War Crimes Trails* (New York, 1987); R. H. Minear, *Victors' Justice: The Tokyo War Crimes Trial* (Princeton, NJ, 1971).

Zhang Hong

TREATY OF KANAGAWA (31 March 1854)

Negotiated by Commodore Matthew C. Perry* and signed on 31 March 1854, the Treaty of Kanagawa was the first treaty between Japan and a Western nation, ending Japan's self-imposed seclusion policy that the Tokugawa government had initiated in 1639. Prior to 1853, the Russians, the British, and the Americans had made sporadic attempts to induce the Tokugawa shōgunate to end its policy of isolation. However, because of the prevailing view that Japan was poor and remote and did not promise substantial economic and political rewards, the Western powers considered it a relatively low priority, especially in comparison with the perceived alluring China market. Therefore, early efforts to open Japan were not supported with great military strength. It was the United States that forced open Japan's door to the outside world. With acquisition of Oregon in 1846 and California in 1848, it was developing into a Pacific power. Further, American ships, bound for the China trade, could use Japan as a way station, which gained added importance after shipwrecks left American sailors stranded in Japan. In July 1853, the Perry Mission* arrived at what is now Tōkyō Bay, comprising a squadron of four ships, including two steam-powered ones. Perry, a distinguished naval officer, was imbued with the sense of manifest destiny and was a strong advocate of expanding American naval interests in the Pacific. His instructions, originally written by Secretary of State Daniel Webster* in June 1851 and revised by Perry himself in November 1852, allowed wide latitude for the use of military force if the "semibarbarous" Japanese did not accede to American demands.

Anchoring off the coast, Perry presented to the Tokugawa authorities a letter from President Millard Fillmore requesting peace and friendship, the opening of trade relations, good treatment of American sailors and whalers shipwrecked by storms on Japanese coasts, and the right for American ships to use Japanese ports as coaling stations. After delivering the letter, Perry sailed away after declaring that he would return the next year with a larger force for a Japanese answer to the American requests. As promised, he returned in 1854 with more warships. Overwhelmed with this display of superior American military technology, top Japanese leaders, notably Ii Naosuke*, concluded that the Tokugawa government had no choice but to accede to the U.S. demand for a diplomatic agreement. Signed on 31 March 1854, the Treaty of Kanagawa was named after the small port town south of Tōkyō. Its main stipulations provided for the opening of the ports of Shimoda and Hakodate for American ships to purchase fuel, food, and other supplies and for limited trade. It also guaranteed better treatment of American shipwrecked sailors and whalers on the Japanese shores, the acceptance of a U.S. consul at Shimoda, and most-favored-nation privileges. In the next two years, the Tokugawa government was forced to sign similar treaties with other Western countries, including Britain, France, Holland, and Russia. The Treaty of Kanagawa not only broke down Japan's closed door, but initiated political change that led to the Meiji Restoration in 1868. *See also* "Expel the Barbarian" Movement.

W. G. Beasley, *Select Documents on Japanese Foreign Policy, 1853–1868* (Stanford, CA, 1955); W. LaFeber, *The Clash: A History of U.S.-Japan Relations* (New York, 1997); A. Walworth, *Black Ships off Japan* (New York, 1946); P. B. Wiley and I. Korogi, *Yankees in the Land of the Gods: Commodore Perry and the Opening of Japan* (New York, 1990).

Zhang Hong

TREATY OF NANJING (29 August 1842)

Signed aboard the *Cornwallis* moored in the Yangze River, the Treaty of Nanjing enabled Great Britain to extract harsh concessions from China after the First Opium War* (1839–1842). The main articles of the treaty agreed on by the two chief negotiators, Qiying and Henry Pottinger, dramatically altered China's conception of commerce and international relations. Since the instinct of the British treaty makers was to secure British trade in China, most of the provisions focused on the rights of merchants. They included (1) the abolition of the Guangzhou Cohong monopoly; (2) the opening of five treaty ports at Guangzhou, Fuzhou, Xiamen, Ningbo, and Shanghai; (3) the cession of Hong Kong*; (4) the guarantee of full security and protection for British citizens and property in China; (5) the establishment of a low tariff of import and export customs; (6) the recognition of extraterritorial rights of foreigners to be tried by their own consuls; and (7) the according of equal status to foreign officials and access to Chinese officials. The Supplementary Treaty at Bogue (Hu-men-zhai), signed 8 October 1843, added the most-favored-nation clause so that later treaties between China and other Western powers would benefit equally Great Britain. Ironically, in both treaties, the issue of opium, the drug that initiated the conflict, was left unmentioned.

Prior to the signing of the two treaties, American merchants were content to trade with China on an informal basis. Afterward, they worried that the British may have secured advantages in the China trade from the treaty. Despite assurances from China, the United States moved decisively to protect American commercial interests in China. In the summer of 1843, President John Tyler appointed Caleb Cushing* as the first commissioner to China. The Cushing mission set sail in July 1843 with instructions to secure for the United States the same commercial privileges that the British won through war. After five months of negotiation and Cushing's threat to journey north to see the emperor, Cushing secured his treaty. The Treaty of Wangxia*, the first Sino-American treaty, was signed on 4 July 1844. Although the treaty provisions acquired no territory for the United States, it secured the same terms as the Treaty of Nanjing, thus allowing the United States to expand its commercial privileges in China, establish consular posts, claim extraterritoriality and other rights, and determine tariff rates. Unanimously approved by the Senate, the Treaty of Wangxia regulated Sino-American relations until the Treaty of Tianjin* in 1858.

J. K. Fairbank, *Trade and Diplomacy on the China Coast* (Cambridge, MA, 1953); M. H. Hunt, *The Making of a Special Relationship: The United States and China to 1914* (New York, 1983); E. V. Gulick, *Peter Parker and the Opening of China* (Cambridge, MA, 1973).

Roger Y. M. Chan

TREATY OF PORTSMOUTH (5 September 1905)

This treaty was the peace settlement that ended the Russo-Japanese War* of 1904–1905. Mediated by President Theodore Roosevelt*, it was signed by Japan's Foreign Minister Komura Jutarō and Sergei Y. Witte, former Russian finance minister, at the Portsmouth Naval Base in New Hampshire on 5 September 1905. The Russians, whose Baltic fleet had been destroyed and fortress at Port Arthur conquered by Japan, recognized Japanese dominant status in Korea. Japan assumed control over Russia's leaseholds at Port Arthur, on the Liaodong Peninsula, and over the South Manchuria Railway. The negotiation almost broke down over Japan's demands that Russia pay indemnity and cede the island of Sakhalin. The Russian tzar was unwilling to pay an indemnity, apparently insisting that he would rather go to the front to fight the rebels in the Revolution of 1905 that had broken out during the war than pay a penny. On 26 August, Komura cabled Tōkyō that he intended to discontinue the negotiation because he thought Russia's agreement to pay the indemnity and cede Sakhalin were matters of national dignity. But when the Tōkyō government decided to withdraw these two demands, the tzar agreed to cede the southern half of Sakhalin. Negotiators finally reached a compromise at the final session on 29 August that Russia would not pay an indemnity, and Japan would receive southern Sakhalin. That the Russians paid no indemnity made the treaty highly unpopular in Japan and led to angry mass protests in Tōkyō. The treaty was unpopular in Russia as well, where critics ridiculed Witte as "Count Half-Sakhalin." But Roosevelt had succeeded in maintaining the balance of power in East Asia, reinforcing the Open Door Policy*. He received the Nobel Peace Prize for the mediation efforts in 1906. *See also* Japanese Annexation of Korea*.

T. Dennett, *Roosevelt and the Russo-Japanese War: A Critical Study of American Policy in Eastern Asia in 1902–1905* (Garden City, NY, 1925); Gaimushō, *Komura gaikōshi* [A History of Komura's Diplomacy] (Tōkyō, 1953); I. Nish, *The Origins of the Russo-Japanese War* (London, 1985); P. E. Randall, *There Are No Victors Here: A Local Perspective on the Treaty of Portsmouth* (Portsmouth, NH, 1985); E. P. Trani, *The Treaty of Portsmouth: An Adventure in American Diplomacy* (Lexington, KY, 1969).

Hirobe Izumi

TREATY OF SHIMONOSEKI (17 April 1895)

The Treaty of Shimonoseki concluded the Sino-Japanese War of 1894–1895. But because of the Triple Intervention* of Russia, Germany, and France, the terms of the treaty, all highly favorable to the victorious Japan, were not fully implemented. The peace negotiations at Shimonoseki, Japan, began on 20 March 1895, following the earlier rejection by the Japanese of a Chinese delegation headed by Zhang Yinhuan and Shao Youlian. Japanese Foreign Minister Mutsu Munemitsu, who conducted the peace negotiations for Japan, along with Prime Minister Itō Hirobumi*, considered Zhang and Shao of "minimal influence and reputation" within their own government and therefore unlikely to have the authority to negotiate and agree to terms they knew would be disastrous for China. After some procrastination, Viceroy Li Hongzhang*, the most prominent Chinese statesman of the nineteenth century, was appointed plenipotentiary, and Japan readily accepted his credentials. Li was assisted by John W. Foster*, a former U.S. secretary of state who had handled legal matters for the Chinese legation in Washington for more than a decade.

Despondent over his country's woeful predicament, the elderly Li, by then in his midseventies, attempted unsuccessfully to restrain the Japanese in their demands for territory, concessions, and an enormous indemnity, arguing for the necessity of Asian people to cooperate against Western imperialism. But the Japanese conceded nothing, not even a cease-fire. Then, on 24 March, as Li and his entourage were leaving after a negotiating session, a Japanese fanatic attempted to assassinate the Chinese viceroy. A pistol shot fired at close range left a bullet painfully lodged in Li's cheekbone. This incident shocked and embarrassed the Japanese government. "Throughout Japan," Mutsu noted, "there seemed to be less concern about the attack on Li than about the international criticism people feared it would occasion . . . a nation nearly driven to delirium by the joys of military triumph now suddenly presented itself as plunged into the depths of grief." Recognizing that the situation now required "great finesse," Mutsu feared negotiations might end with Li returning to China and Western public opinion turning against Japan. The Japanese immediately granted the truce Li had earlier proposed, and the emperor of Japan sent his personal physicians to treat the wounded Chinese diplomat.

Negotiations continued while Li and the Zongli Yamen* looked for signs of Western intervention to limit Japanese demands. At last, seeing no signs of foreign assistance, Li agreed to Japan's harsh demands and a treaty was signed at Shimonoseki on 17 April. The terms required China to recognize the independence of Korea, cede the Liaodong Peninsula, Taiwan*, and the Penghus, pay an indemnity of 200 million taels of silver, and sign a treaty of commerce opening Chinese ports to Japan on an equal basis with Western nations. Before the ink on the document could dry, Li's long-awaited European assistance came to the fore. But the Triple Intervention* of Russia, Germany, and France only denied the Japanese the Liaodong Peninsula. The war and the Treaty of Shimonoseki clearly established Japanese dominance in East Asia and set the stage for the Japanese Annexation of Korea* in 1910. Throughout the war and the peace negotiations, the United States maintained a strict neutrality, even though Secretary of State Walter Q. Gresham offered the good offices of the United States to both sides, and U.S. Minister Charles Denby* in Beijing and Edwin Dun in Tōkyō kept channels of communication open between the two warring nations. The Sino-Japanese War focused U.S. attention on East Asia and heightened its concerns that the European powers and Japan might carve up the disintegrating Chinese Empire. *See also* Japanese Colonialism.

J. M. Dorwart, *The Pigtail War: American Involvement in the Sino-Japanese War, 1894–1895* (Amherst, MA, 1975); J. W. Foster, *Diplomatic Memoirs*, 2 vols. (Boston, MA, 1909); M. Mutsu, *Kenkenroku: A Diplomatic Record of the Sino-*

Japanese War, 1894–1895, trans. by G. M. Berger (Princeton, NJ, 1982).

Michael J. Devine

TREATY OF TIANJIN (18 June 1858)

The Treaty of Tientsin ended the treaty-revision movement begun in 1854 by the United States, Britain, France, and Russia, and completely opened China to Western trade. Prior to the negotiations, President James Buchanan gave U.S. Commissioner William B. Reed detailed instructions restricting his discretionary powers. Buchanan, who had been secretary of state and was experienced in East Asian affairs, controlled U.S. policy toward China. Reed was to negotiate for claims and grievances against the Chinese government by U.S. citizens and for revising the Treaty of Wangxia* of 1844, which called for revision twelve years after its signing. The Chinese government agreed to negotiate with Reed during the Second Opium War* and after a combined British-French military campaign that culminated in the seizure of Tianjin in late May 1858.

Sino-American negotiations led to a treaty, signed on 18 June 1858, that granted the United States numerous concessions. These included the ability to correspond directly with the grand council at Beijing through sealed envelopes, an annual visit and sojourn to Beijing for the U.S. envoy, and the removal of legal obstacles that prevented U.S. citizens from obtaining leaseholds in Chinese trading ports. China agreed to lower tariffs, and granted the United States the use of two additional ports, in addition to the five original treaty ports granted in the Treaty of Wangxia. China also agreed to tolerate Protestantism and ensure the protection of Chinese converts.

Furthermore, the treaty guaranteed all of the old rights granted through the Treaty of Wangxia, including the most-favored-nation clause, which ensured for the United States all rights gained by other most-favored nations in their treaties with China. Thus, the United States gained permanent residence at Beijing and four more trading posts, including ports along the Yangze River, as a result of French and British treaties negotiated concurrently with China at Tianjin. An important aspect of the treaty was Reed's intentional omission of the word "opium" from its contents at the request of British Envoy Lord Elgin. The Treaty of Wangxia specifically had outlawed the opium trade, but Reed's exclusion of it from the Treaty of Tianjin gave the British an opportunity to advocate its legalization. Overall, the Treaty of Tianjin represented an example of U.S. efforts to advance its commercial interests in China. *See also* Treaty of Nanjing.

U.S. Senate, *Executive Documents* (Washington, DC, 1858); S. Teng, *The Taiping Rebellion and the Western Powers* (New York, 1971); T. Tong, *United States Diplomacy in China, 1844–60* (Seattle, WA, 1964).

William E. Emerson

TREATY OF WANGXIA (4 July 1844)

Caleb Cushing* negotiated this treaty, the first agreement between the United States and China. Prior to his departure on 31 July 1843, Cushing studied every book on China he could get his hands on and consulted with American merchants engaged in the China trade. Daniel Fletcher Webster, eldest son of Secretary of State Daniel Webster*, served as Cushing's secretary, and three missionaries familiar with the Chinese culture and language, Elijah Bridgman, Peter Parker*, and Samuel Wells Williams, were appointed as interpreters and translators. By the time the imposing squadron of four U.S. warships mounting more than 200 guns arrived at Macau on 24 February 1844, Cushing had fully prepared himself to attain U.S. goals.

The origins of the Cushing mission can be found in the Treaty of Nanjing*, which the British imposed on China in 1842 after their victory in the First Opium War*. Considered by the Chinese to be one of the greatest national humiliations in their history, it ceded Hong Kong*, opened five ports to British trade and residence, and granted extraterritorial privileges to British nationals accused of committing criminal offenses in China. Determined that the United States not be disadvantaged in its intense rivalry with Britain for the markets of East Asia, Cushing was told to seek concessions comparable to those granted in this treaty. Although the United States did not seek a territorial enclave like Hong Kong, Secretary of State Webster instructed Cushing on 8 May 1843 "to secure the entry of American ships and cargoes" into the treaty ports "on terms as favorable as those which are enjoyed by British merchants." The mission, Webster emphasized, "is entirely pacific" in its nature, and its objects were "only friendly and commercial."

The Treaty of Wangxia signed by Cushing and Imperial Commissioner Qiying on 4 July 1844 established formal diplomatic relations between the two countries, opened the five treaty ports to American trade, and included a most-favored-nation clause, which ensured that any subsequent concessions China granted to other nations automatically would accrue to the United States. Cushing's treaty even went beyond that of the Treaty of Nanjing by extending extraterritorial jurisdiction to Americans in civil as well as in criminal cases. On the recommendation of Cushing's missionary advisers, the treaty also granted Americans the right to establish churches, hospitals, and cemeteries in the treaty ports. Although the Chinese were predisposed to concede major concessions to the United States, Cushing proved to be an able negotiator. Not surprisingly, the accord won unanimous approval by the U.S. Senate in 1845.

This first Sino-American treaty had considerable historical significance. It contributed to an increase in trade between the two countries and to a growing American diplomatic and missionary presence in China, which, in turn, enlarged the Open Door constituency in the United States. The precedent-setting extraterritorial provisions, which the Chinese increasingly viewed as unequal and unfair, offered the protection of American law to U.S. citizens residing in China until 1943. Although Cushing's treaty has been criticized as a product of "hitchhiking imperialism," it also reflected China's strategy of "using barbarians to control barbarians" with such tactics as granting most-favored-nation status. Moreover, unlike the British diplomats that preceded him, Cushing did not explicitly threaten the use of military force. He also tactfully withdrew a demand to travel to the forbidden city of Beijing to deliver President John Tyler's letter when Qiying made it clear that he had no authority to negotiate if Cushing continued to demand an audience with the emperor.

W. J. Donahue, "The Caleb Cushing Mission," *Modern Asian Studies* (1982); C. M. Fuess, *The Life of Caleb Cushing*, 2 vols. (New York, 1923); M. H. Hunt, *The Making of a Special Relationship: The United States and China to 1914* (New York, 1983); K. E. Shewmaker, "Forging the Great Chain: Daniel Webster and the Origins of American Foreign Policy Toward East Asia and the Pacific, 1841–1852," *Proceedings of the American Philosophical Society* (September 1985); R. E. Welch Jr. "Caleb Cushing's Chinese Mission and the Treaty of Wanghia: A Review," *Oregon Historical Quarterly* (1957).

Kenneth E. Shewmaker

TRIANGULAR TRADE

"Triangular trade" was a term used to describe global trade flows between Europe, its Southeast Asian colonies, and the United States in the period before World War II. It was disrupted during the war, but the United States made a concerted effort to restore it in the postwar period. The reasons for this were to offset Communist uprisings in Southeast Asia, to enable European powers to bridge the dollar gap, and to maintain dollar circulation in international trade to protect American business interests. The system typically served colonial powers that exported their manufactured goods to their respective colonies in Southeast Asia, who usually were unable to pay for these imports through sales of raw materials. Therefore, they paid the outstanding balance using the dollars they had received from raw material exports to the United States. The triangular trading system, therefore, enabled colonial powers such as Britain to accumulate dollar reserves to offset their trade deficit with the United States.

During the war, the triangular trade system was disrupted because of the Japanese takeover of Southeast Asian territories, including Singapore*, Malaya*, and French Indochina*. With the end of World War II, the imperial powers returned to Southeast Asia to reclaim their colonial interests. President Franklin D. Roosevelt*, who wished to see an end to colonialism, initially opposed this. With the onset of the Cold War, however, the Truman administration saw the advantage of maintaining imperial rule because it would serve as a barrier to Communist infiltration. Imperial powers, for their part, sought to reestablish the triangular trading system to earn dollars through colonial sales of raw materials to the United States. Particular emphasis was placed on Malayan rubber and tin, which had been profitable in the prewar period. Washington supported this initiative because the lack of dollars in circulation in worldwide trade threatened to disrupt U.S. commercial interests. Moreover, promotion of trade with Southeast Asia was thought to improve living standards of the local populace, thereby reducing economic discontent and eliminating the breeding ground for Communist uprisings. The United States thus assigned more importance to Southeast Asia than it perhaps deserved, leading to its gradual involvement in the Second Indochina War*. *See also* British Colonialism; Dutch Colonialism; French Colonialism.

W. S. Borden, *The Pacific Alliance: United States Foreign Economic Policy and Japanese Trade Recovery, 1947–1955* (Madison, WI, 1984); J. Foreman-Peck, *A History of the World Economy: International Economic Relations Since 1850* (Hemel Hempstead, UK, 1995); A. J. Rotter, *The Path to Vietnam: Origins of the American Commitment to Southeast Asia* (Ithaca, NY, 1987); R. B. Smith and A. J. Stockwell (eds.) *British Policy and the Transfer of Power in Asia: Documentary Perspectives* (London, 1987); Watanabe Akio, "Sengo shoki no nichibei kankei to Tōnan Ajia: Senzen sankakubōeki kara sengo hangetsukō e" [U.S.-Japan Relations in Southeast Asia in the Early Postwar Period: From Prewar Triangular Trade to the Postwar Crescent], in C. Hosoya and T. Aruga (eds.), *Kokusai kankyō no henyō to nichibei kankei* [Transformation of the International Environment and U.S.-Japan Relations] (Tōkyō, 1987).

Yokoi Noriko

TRIPARTITE PACT (2 September 1940)

The Anti-Comintern Pact* signed by Germany and Japan in November 1936 was joined a year later by Italy, thus forming the Berlin-Rome-Tōkyō Axis. As a way of weakening Britain in East Asia and putting pressure on the Soviet Union, Adolf Hitler wanted to transform the Anti-Comintern Pact into a military alliance. Hitler's idea was expressed in a memorandum of January 1938, written by his trusted adviser and ambassador to Britain, Joachim von Ribbentrop, who sounded the opinion of Japanese military attaché in Berlin, Ōshima Hiroshi. Von Ribbentrop became foreign minister in February and his proposal was discussed in Tōkyō. The negotiations soon reached a stalemate. The German proposal was designed to form an alliance against not only the Soviet Union, but also Britain and France, whereas the Japanese wanted an alliance targeted only against the Soviet Union. Both expected the alliance to deter the United States from entering a future war in Europe and the ongoing one in China. Impatient, Germany concluded a military alliance with Italy in May 1939, and a nonaggression pact with the Soviet

Union that August. The Nazi-Soviet Non-Aggression Pact came as a great shock to the Japanese, and the cabinet of Hiranuma Kiichirō collapsed. A year of negotiations to conclude a military alliance came to a sudden end.

War broke out in Europe in September 1939, and German victories in Europe in the spring of 1940 encouraged the Japanese to resume negotiations. Japanese Foreign Minister Matsuoka Yōsuke* entertained a grand design. After concluding a tripartite military alliance, he wanted to induce the Soviet Union into an alliance, thus creating a four-power entente, which he thought would give Japan a position strong enough not only to deter the United States from entry into war either in Europe or Asia, but to enable Japan to ask it to mediate the ongoing conflict between Japan and China, and to achieve a modus vivendi between Japan and United States. He would fly with Jiang Jieshi* to Washington for talks with President Franklin D. Roosevelt*. Before Matsuoka could act on his grandiose plan, Heinrich Stahmer was dispatched from Berlin as a special envoy to Tōkyō for discussions. Eugene Ott, German ambassador to Japan, joined in the meetings. The Japanese Navy strongly opposed naming the United States, a hypothetical enemy, in a three-power alliance. Japan insisted that it would participate in the European war of its own volition. The treaty should not obligate Japan to enter automatically. There was also the matter of Germany's pre–World War I island possessions in the Pacific.

After Germany made some concessions, the Tripartite Pact was signed by Von Ribbentrop, Germany's foreign minister; Galeazzo Ciano, Italy's foreign minister; and Kurusu Saburō*, Japan's ambassador to Germany, on 2 September 1940. It provided that the three nations agreed to recognize one another's supremacy in their respective regions of the world. Under Article 3, "Germany, Italy, and Japan . . . undertake to assist one another with all political, economic, and military means, if one of the three Contracting Parties is attacked by a Power at present not involved in the European War or in the Chinese-Japanese conflict." The Soviet Union specifically was exempted under Article 5. The treaty would be effective for ten years. The signing of the treaty worsened U.S.-Japanese relations, contrary to Matsuoka's expectations. The United States decided to give economic aid to China and consulted with Britain about joint defense of Southeast Asia. When Matsuoka learned of the outbreak of war between Japan and the United States after the Pearl Harbor Attack*, he reportedly said in tears that "the conclusion of the Tripartite Pact was the biggest mistake in my whole life." On 11 December, German and Italy declared war on the United States in accordance with what they saw as their obligations under their alliance with Japan.

R. J. C. Butow, *Tōjō and the Coming of the War* (Princeton, NJ, 1961); P. W. Schroeder, *The Axis Alliance and Japanese–American Relations, 1941* (Ithaca, NY, 1958); H. L. Trefousse, "Germany and Pearl Harbor," *Far Eastern Quarterly* (November 1951).

Ishii Osamu

TRIPLE INTERVENTION

Japan defeated China under the Qing Dynasty in the Sino-Japanese War from 1894 to 1895, and in the Treaty of Shimonoseki* obtained several concessions from China. Among these, the Japanese were to gain the Liaodong Peninsula in southern Manchuria, including Port Arthur and Dairen, as well as Taiwan* and the Penghus. Japan had the intention of further exploiting China. But the Western powers saw a chance to divide a weakened China into colonial territories for themselves, but to the exclusion of Japan. Russia was disturbed by the proposed cession to Japan of Port Arthur, an ice-free harbor. Serge Witte, the Russian finance minister, invited France and Germany to join with Russia in demanding that Japan abandon its territorial acquisitions. France was interested in Taiwan, and Germany wanted to divert the attention of Russia from Western Europe to Asia. On 17 April 1895, the very day the peace treaty was signed, Russia formally proposed intervention to France and Germany. Six days later, the three ministers residing in Tōkyō visited the Japanese Foreign Ministry and suggested to Japan that it forsake the Liaodong Peninsula—with a veiled threat of a military intervention by the three powers if it refused.

In response, the Japanese government sought support from Britain, the United States, and Italy to counter this pressure. Only Italy responded favorably. On 4 May, the Japanese cabinet decided to return the Liaodong Peninsula. On 8 November, a treaty for that purpose was signed between Japan and China. On 27 December, Japan's forces evacuated the peninsula. Thereafter, in 1898, Germany secured railway and mining rights, as well as leasing a port, as part of a "sphere of influence" on the Shandong Peninsula. Russia gained the leased territory of Dairen and Port Arthur that same year, and extended its railway rights southward to these ports. France leased a port in southern China in 1899. In the meantime, Britain watched these moves, and responded by leasing a port on the Shandong Peninsula. Predictably, the Japanese deeply resented the actions of these Western powers, especially Russia, and built up military power in preparation for the Russo-Japanese War* of 1904 and 1905.

M. Edwardes, *The West in Asia, 1850–1914* (London, 1967); T. J. McCormick, *The China Market: America's Quest for Informal Empire, 1893–1901* (Chicago, 1967).

Ishii Osamu

TRUMAN, HARRY S. (1884–1972)

Harry S. Truman, president of the United States from 1945 to 1953, set the course of U.S. relations with the Guomindang* (Nationalist) regime in China and, after the end of the Chinese Civil War*, Taiwan*. He also decided to send American military forces to fight in the Korean War*. Born in Missouri, Truman had achieved little in his life before he served as a National Guard artillery officer in World War I. He returned to start a clothing business in Kansas City, winning election as a county judge because of his ties with the Pendergast machine. Truman then was elected to the U.S. Senate in 1934 and won reelection six years later, despite the lack of support from President Franklin D. Roosevelt*. He achieved national acclaim during World War II as chairman of a committee investigating the U.S. defense industry. Truman was the surprise choice to be the Democratic Party's vice presidential candidate in November 1944, succeeding to the presidency upon Roosevelt's death in April 1945. As was true of almost all American presidents until airplane travel made such trips easy, Truman never visited East Asia and hence depended on advisers to determine policy there.

Truman made a number of difficult and important decisions as president. Most important, in August 1945, after the Allies had issued and Tōkyō had rejected the Potsdam Declaration*, he ordered the Atomic Attacks* on Japan that ended World War II. He then named General Douglas MacArthur* to head the U.S. Occupation of Japan*, and after application of the Reverse Course*, this resulted in the former enemy becoming a close postwar partner of the United States in East Asia. But events did not develop as favorably in China, where the Guomindang of Jiang Jieshi* and the Chinese Communist Party* of Mao Zedong* confronted Truman with the Chinese Civil War. In December 1945, General George C. Marshall*, U.S. Army chief of staff, began an effort to arrange a ceasefire and a political settlement, but after brief success, fighting resumed and the Marshall Mission* was a failure. Disgusted by it, Marshall returned home to become secretary of state, advising the president to "let the dust settle" in China. Thereafter, during 1947, Truman implemented the containment policy against the Soviet Union that George F. Kennan* had recommended the prior year, resulting in application of the Truman Doctrine in the Mediterranean and the Marshall Plan in Western Europe. But regarding China, he only reluctantly dispatched Lieutenant General Albert C. Wedemeyer* on a fact-finding mission there and later approved the China Assistance Act of 1948*. Pressure, mostly from the Republican Party's adherents in Congress and the China Lobby*, continued to support the Nationalists, but Truman resisted it, leading to charges that he had "lost China" after the Communists prevailed during 1949 by allowing disloyal "China Hands*" to undermine Jiang's regime.

In Korea, Truman persuaded Soviet Premier Joseph Stalin to accept the Thirty-Eighth Parallel Division* of that country in August 1945, but the Cold War blocked reunification. In 1948, his administration applied a policy of qualified containment to provide the new Republic of Korea* in the south with the ability to defend itself. Then, in response to North Korea's attack on 25 June 1950, Truman referred the issue to the United Nations and, under its auspices, committed U.S. military power to defeat the aggressors. His principal consideration, shared by all major figures in his administration, was that without intervention, the U.S. position of opposing Communist expansion throughout the world would crumble. Truman believed that the Soviet Union ordered the North Koreans to attack and thus increased U.S. support for non-Communist regimes in East Asia, such as Bao Dai* in Vietnam, while ordering the Neutralization of Taiwan*. He did not ask Congress, however, for a declaration of war, fighting the Korean War* as a police action, manageable under his powers as president. Even before MacArthur, the UN commander, staged his Inch'ŏn Landing*, Truman had approved an offensive into North Korea, thereby inviting Chinese Intervention in the Korean War*. MacArthur's Recall* in April 1951 was in fair part a domestic decision, but what lay behind it was of high importance for East Asian relations, as he displayed moderation to the leaders and peoples of that region. Despite his efforts for peace at the P'anmunjŏm Truce Talks*, the Korean War POW Controversy* created a stalemate that lasted until Dwight D. Eisenhower* replaced Truman as president in January 1953.

R. H. Ferrell, *Harry S. Truman: A Biography* (Columbia, MO, 1994); A. Hamby, *Man of the People: A Life of Harry S. Truman* (New York, 1995); D. McCullough, *Truman* (New York, 1992); M. Schaller, *The American Occupation of Japan: Origins of the Cold War in Asia* (New York, 1985); W. W. Stueck Jr., *The Road to Confrontation: American Policy Toward China and Korea, 1947–1950* (Chapel Hill, NC, 1981).

Robert H. Ferrell

TSIANG TINGFU

See JIANG TINGFU

TWENTY-ONE DEMANDS

On 18 January 1915, Japan's attempt to expand its foothold in China through the aggressive diplomacy of the Twenty-One Demands altered its relations with not only China, but also the United States. Presented to the government of Yuan Shikai* in Beijing, the demands consisted of five groups with obvious emphasis attached to the first two. Group 1 concerned Germany's leased territory on the Shandong Peninsula that Japan had seized after declaring war on Germany after the start of World War I. Tōkyō demanded China's full consent for transfer of all the rights and concessions to Japan at the end of the war, but intended to use restoration of Shandong to China as a bargaining chip to secure its other demands. Group 2 addressed Japan's long-sought policy to dominate south Manchuria and eastern Inner Mongolia. It demanded the extension to ninety-nine years of leases on Port Arthur, Dairen, and the South Manchuria and Andong-

Mukden Railways, and privileges for Japanese nationals to own or lease land, to mine, and to reside in these areas. Group 3 was a proposal for Sino-Japanese joint ownership of the Hanyeping Company in central China. Group 4 demanded China's pledge not to cede or lease any port or island along its coast to any other nation except Japan. Group 5, which Japan's foreign minister characterized as "requests" at the start of negotiations, contained the most objectionable provisions for the United States and Britain as well as China. These called for employment of Japanese political, economic, and military advisers, joint policing in troubled areas, purchase of Japanese arms, and special economic and other privileges in certain parts of China, especially in Fujian.

The Chinese government resisted Tōkyō's diplomatic pressure and frustrated Japanese negotiators by procrastinating on discussion of major concessions. Despite Japan's efforts to keep the negotiations regarding the Twenty-One Demands strictly confidential, Yuan's government leaked information with the expectation of rallying anti-Japanese sentiments at home and encouraging the Western powers to intervene on China's behalf. Since the Allies could not afford to alienate Japan because of their need for its cooperation in the war against Germany, the United States was the only power who could stand firmly against Japan's encroachment on China. U.S. President Woodrow Wilson* became increasingly suspicious of Japanese motives, as alarming reports poured into the State Department from Paul S. Reinsch*, the U.S. minister in Beijing, who was sympathetic toward China's predicament. The contents of Group 5 and Tōkyō's failure to disclose them caused the U.S. government to send a diplomatic warning to Tōkyō on 13 March that the United States could not ignore Japan's attempt to establish political, military, and economic domination over China.

Apparently encouraged by Washington's attitude, China rejected Japan's revised version of the demand in late April. Japan responded by sending an ultimatum on 7 May, but, significantly, had eliminated Group 5 from its final desideratum. China and Japan signed a series of treaties on 25 May 1915, through which Japan secured its major objectives in south Manchuria and Shandong. However, Japan's gains came at a very high price. While Japan lost the trust of many Chinese who had looked to it as a leader of reform for modernization, the incident also greatly increased the suspicions of Western powers about Japanese intentions in China that seemed to be a potential threat to their respective spheres of influence there. Wilson emerged as a champion of the principles of the Open Door Policy* to preserve the territorial and administrative integrity of China against selfish Japan, who took advantage of the Western powers' preoccupation with their war in Europe. Moreover, the Japanese use of an ultimatum raised questions about the legality of the Sino-Japanese treaties of 1915. Secretary of State William Jennings Bryan* informed the Japanese government on 11 May 1915 that the United States would not recognize any Sino-Japanese agreement that might impair the U.S. treaty rights in China and violate the Open Door or China's territorial and political integrity. With Wilson's support, the Chinese delegates at the Paris Peace Conference in 1919 argued unsuccessfully that these treaties were signed under duress and thus should be abrogated. *See also* Dong Xianguang; Shandong Agreement; Versailles Peace Treaty.

W. G. Beasley, *Japanese Imperialism: 1894–1945* (New York, 1987); M. C. Chi, *China Diplomacy, 1914–1918* (Cambridge, MA, 1970); R. C. Curry, *Woodrow Wilson and Far Eastern Policy, 1913–1921* (New York, 1957); N. Kawamura, *Turbulence in the Pacific: Japanese-U.S. Relations During World War I* (Westport, CT, 2000); I. Nish, *Alliance in Decline: A Study in Anglo-Japanese Relations, 1908–23* (London, 1972).

Kawamura Noriko

TWO CHINA POLICY

The United States applied the Two China Policy toward China after 1970 to resolve the dilemma of how to maintain a relationship with the Chinese governments on the two sides of the Taiwan Strait. Unlike the division of Korea and of Germany, the division of China between the People's Republic of China* (PRC) on the mainland and the Republic of China* (ROC) on Taiwan* was the result of civil war. Therefore, after the Chinese Civil War*, both Beijing and Taibei claimed to have the only legitimate government representing all of China. Between the outbreak of the Korean War* and the election of Richard M. Nixon* as president, the United States recognized the Guomindang* (Nationalist) government on Taiwan as legitimate and refused to extend diplomatic recognition to the Communist PRC. Realizing the impossibility of the Nationalists regaining control of the mainland, however, the United States worked to create a separate nation on Taiwan, imitating the two-Koreas and two-Germanys model. But both Beijing and Taibei firmly insisted that there was only one China.

During Nixon's Visit to China* in 1972, the Two China Policy became the very focus of Sino-American negotiations. The PRC government insisted that the United States renounce its official relationship with the Guomindang government on Taiwan and recognize Taiwan as a province of China as a condition for rapprochement. On the other hand, the United States, although believing reconciliation with China was very important, had built and maintained strong political and economic ties with Taiwan over the previous two decades and resisted simply abandoning its long-term partner. Ultimately, Washington and Beijing agreed to issue the Shanghai Communiqúe* at the end of Nixon's visit, in which the United States acknowledged that there was but one China and that Taiwan was part of it. While the process of U.S.-PRC Normalization of Relations* continued, however, the Taiwan issue remained a major source of friction in bilateral relations, delying the formal U.S. recognition of the PRC until 1979.

After the official recognition between Washington and Beijing, the United States officially renounced the Two China Policy and terminated official relations with the ROC, maintaining exchanges only on nonpolitical levels. But Washington chose not to end the Two China Policy entirely. In April 1979, the U.S. Congress passed the Taiwan Relations Act*, which obliged the executive to regard any use of force against Taiwan as a threat to the security of the western Pacific and as of great concern to the United States. When President Ronald Reagan* was inaugurated in 1981, he reversed the policy of his predecessor Jimmy Carter* and reasserted positive U.S. responsibility for defense of Taiwan. In 1986, Reagan approved the sale of F-16 fighters to Taiwan to enhance the island's capacity for self-defense. The U.S. effort nevertheless remained halfhearted, for it did not want to destroy its relations with Beijing. During the 1990s, the U.S. government no longer openly campaigned for two Chinas, but reserved the right to prevent the PRC from using military force to threaten Taiwan.

M. Yahuda, *The International Politics of the Asia-Pacific, 1945–1995* (London, 1996); Song Qiang, *Zhongguo wei shenme shuo bu* [China Can Say No] (Beijing, 1996).

Li Yi

TYDINGS-MCDUFFIE ACT (24 March 1934)

The U.S. Congress passed the Philippine Commonwealth and Independence Act on 24 March 1934, known more commonly as the Tydings-McDuffie Act. On 1 May, this law then received approval from the Philippine National Assembly. It called for convening a convention to draft a republican constitution for the Commonwealth of the Philippine Islands, whose government would oversee a ten-year transition from an American colony to an independent country. There were two notable aspects of the Tydings-McDuffie Act. First, it was the result of an American promise to address the popular issue of Philippine independence and the efforts of Filipino political leaders, who styled themselves as nationalist spokesmen, to expand their role in U.S. colonial administration. This was an atypical relationship between colonizer and colonized in South and East Asia, where this interaction had become more belligerent by the 1930s. Second, the act set the Americans apart from their European and Japanese counterparts in South and East Asia. Whereas the British, Dutch, French, and Japanese regarded their colonial rule in the two regions as more or less permanent, the United States set out to do the opposite: grant its colony self-rule and foster relatively early independence.

Although unusual in its political generosity, the Tydings-McDuffie Act nevertheless was criticized by Filipino nationalists for the privileges the bill continued to confer on U.S. economic and military interests. Filipino historian Renato Constantino called it a "colonial document" that reflected the impact of "more than three decades of colonial education and cultural Americanization" of a Filipino "ruling elite that regarded the American concept of government and American political institutions as the highest development of democracy." U.S. Vice Governor of the Philippines* Joseph Ralston Hayden, however, offered a contrasting view:

> The instrument is colored by the ideas which have become current in the United States since 1933 as well as by our traditional political philosophy. It bears the imprint of the revolutionary changes which have swept over many parts of Europe and reversed the political trend in Japan during the twenty years. In form and substance it reveals the possession of a high degree of political capacity by those who drafted it. Although a product of the past, it is conspicuously an instrument of government for the troubled present and uncertain future. Above all, it is a Filipino and not a foreign instrument and provides the constitutional foundation for a genuinely Filipino government.

No study has addressed how other colonial states responded to this "uncolonial" conduct of the United States. Moreover, the question of whether the commonwealth government of the Philippines succeeded or not remains open to debate, partly because of the intervention of World War II.

R. Constantino, *The Philippines: A Past Revisited* (Manila, 1975); J. Hayden, *The Philippines: A Study in National Development* (New York, 1942).

Patricio N. Abinales

U

U NU (1907–1995)

U Nu was the first prime minister of Burma* (Myanmar since 1989) after it achieved independence in January 1948. He remained in that post until 1958, and served again from 1960 until 1962, when he was ousted in a coup led by General Ne Win*. As prime minister, U Nu forcefully promoted neutralism as Burma's best solution to its precarious geographical, strategic, and economic position. Under his leadership, Burma forged cordial ties with the United States and Britain. U Nu also, however, showed his foreign policy independence when Burma became the first Asian nation to formally recognize the People's Republic of China* (PRC) in 1949. But U Nu's foreign minister stressed that recognition did not mean approval, reflecting U Nu's judgment that Burma would receive little benefit from allying with Communist countries.

U Nu demonstrated the sincerity of his belief in having good relations with all sides in the Cold War with the March 1950 request for military and economic aid from the United States, which resulted in a September 1950 agreement. He decided in 1953 to request an end to this aid, as a result of problems arising from aid from the Guomindang* (GMD) and, indirectly, the United States to GMD troops on Burmese soil. Burma proposed a solution to this problem in the United Nations, and the United States partially supported the proposal. On U Nu's trip to the PRC in 1954, he publicly admonished the probably astonished Chinese leaders to make an effort to "coexist" with the United States. A few months later, when U Nu was in Washington, he similarly urged President Dwight D. Eisenhower* and Secretary of State John Foster Dulles* to improve relations with the PRC. U Nu took credit for having suggested to Dulles that the United States raise the level of U.S.-PRC Warsaw Talks* from the consul general to the ambassadorial level.

U Nu's promotion of good relations among all nations stemmed from his devout Buddhism, and prompted him to take an early and important role in the neutral, later nonaligned movement. Although mostly behind the scenes, he was a major player at the Bandung Conference* in 1955. By 1956, internal problems drew his attention back to Burma, and in 1958, he handed the government over to General Ne Win, for a limited time, so the country could prepare for elections. Those elections, held in 1960, saw victory for U Nu's party, but his rule was shaky until Ne Win led a coup, this time more permanent, in 1962. U Nu spent the years until 1980 primarily in prison or in exile (including one year in the United States). In the 1988 protests in Burma, he reentered the political scene, but no longer commanded much political support. He spent the period from December 1989 to April 1992 again under house arrest.

R. Butwell, *U Nu of Burma* (Stanford, CA, 1963); R. H. Taylor, *The State in Burma* (Honolulu, HI, 1987); U Nu, *Saturday's Son* (New Haven, CT, 1975).

Anne L. Foster

U THANT (1909–1974)

Secretary General of the United Nations from 1961 to 1971, U Thant was the first Asian to head this world organization. He attempted to mediate a peaceful settlement to the Second Indochina War*, but was unsuccessful because of the inflexibility of both President Lyndon B. Johnson* and the Communist leaders in the Democratic Republic of Vietnam*. Born at Pantanaw, Burma*, U Thant (U is an honorific title rather than a personal name) received his education at the University College in Rangoon. After the death of his father in 1928, he could not continue his studies, and returned to Pantanaw High School as senior master, becoming headmaster in 1931. His early career was in the Burmese educational service, including serving on the Council of National Education and the Executive Committee of the Heads of Schools Association. During Japanese occupation in World War II, U Thant was an educational official in the Burmese government. With independence in 1947, he became press director for the new government of Burma. In 1948, he was named director of broadcasting, and in 1949, secretary for the Ministry of Information. He moved to the prime minister's office as a projects secretary in 1953, assuming as well the duties of executive secretary of the Economic and Social Board in 1955.

U Thant's first encounter with the United Nations was serving as a member of the Burmese delegation in 1952 and 1953. In 1957, he became Burma's permanent representative. Soon after entering his career at the United Nations, U Thant emerged as a potential leader within the organization. During 1959, he was one of the vice presidents of the General Assembly, and in 1961 served as the chairman of the UN Congo Conciliation Commission and on the Committee on a UN Capital Development Fund. In September 1961, UN Secretary General Dag Hammarskjold was killed in a plane crash while on a mission to Congo. Washington and Moscow initially could not agree on an acceptable candidate to replace Hammarskjold, and U Thant was chosen as a compromise to be acting secretary general. In November 1962, he was elected to a regular term, and was reelected to another term in 1966. He stepped down in 1971 and lived in retirement until his death in New York City. His body was flown to Burma, where it became the focus of a bizarre incident involving antigovernment student protests. The military government had planned to bury U Thant in a relatively remote plot, but on 6 December 1974, students interrupted the funeral procession and carried off the body, interring it in a hastily built mausoleum at the University of Rangoon. Five days later, troops raided the campus and recovered U Thant's body, which was then placed in a grave at the Shwedagon Pagoda, one of Burma's most sacred sites.

J. Bingham, *U Thant: The Search for Peace* (New York, 1966); J. F. Cady, *The United States and Burma* (New York, 1976); U Thant, *View from the UN* (Garden City, NY, 1978).

Kenneth J. Hammond

UNIFICATION CHURCH

In 1954, the Reverend Sun Myung Moon founded the Holy Spirit Association for the Unification of World Christianity Unification in the Republic of Korea*. Known commonly as Unification Church, it is a messianic, millennial religion whose mission is to establish God's kingdom on earth by uniting all religions. Born in 1920, Moon was a Christian when he was a child. He spent two-and-a-half years in a Communist labor camp in the Democratic People's Republic of Korea* (DPRK) before forces of the United Nations liberated him during the Korean War*. Moon claimed that on Easter Sunday, Jesus appeared to him and asked him to take upon himself responsibility for the mission of establishing God's kingdom on earth. After founding Unification Church, he explained how he communicated with various other religious leaders (such as Moses and the Buddha) and with God himself. Moon's major works are the *Divine Principle* and *Outline of the Principle*.

In the late 1950s, Unification Church began to grow into a worldwide religious movement, sending missionaries to Japan and the West. By the early 1980s, it ranked third in adherents among new religions. That Unification Church emerged into such a large religious organization in just three decades resulted from effective marketing, the combining of its religious message with business, and the sacrificial devotion of the movement's members, who came to be known as Moonies. Unification Church excelled at publicizing itself to people, organizing large rallies, holding international conferences to which prominent academics were invited, and staging mass marriages. Businesses run directly by Moon's church or affiliated with the movement seemed to be profitable, and cultural activities, including the Little Angels Dance Troupe, the Go World Brass Band, and the New Hope Singers, prospered. Unification Church showed its keen interest in the print media business, running daily newspapers in Tōkyō, New York, and Washington.

Not only did established churches and U.S. government officials direct sharp criticism against Unification Church, but Moon served prison terms for tax evasion. Parents of Moonies paid investigators to kidnap and deprogram their children. Unification Church also distinguished itself from other religious associations through active involvement in politics. It presented itself as an enthusiastic advocate of a highly conservative and anti-Communist agenda. It mounted an active campaign against Communism* by organizing educational drives where its religious missions were based, advancing its anti-Communist program in South Korea, Japan, and North and South America. After the fall of Communism in Eastern Europe after 1989, Unification Church abandoned its hard-line policy against the DPRK and made continuous efforts to contact P'yŏngyang with offers of economic aid. In 1991, Moon visited North Korea and met Kim Il Sung*, the leader of the DPRK. Since then, Unification Church has been involved in various business projects and cultural exchange programs in North Korea.

J. Lofland, *Doomsday Cult: A Study of Conversion, Proselytization, and Maintenance of Faith* (New York, 1977); S. Matczak, *Unificationism: A New Philosophy and World View* (New York, 1982); F. Sontag, *Sun Myung Moon and the Unification Church* (Nashville, TN, 1977).

Han Kyu-sun

UNITED ACTION

In an attempt to stave off French defeat at Dien Bien Phu* in March 1954, President Dwight D. Eisenhower* and Secretary of State John Foster Dulles* devised a new American policy that contemplated American military intervention in French Indochina* under the mantle of United Action. On 29 March, Dulles, in a speech at the Overseas Press Club of America, announced the need for "united action" in Indochina. This was the Eisenhower administration's first public announcement of a U.S. plan for a coalition of Western powers and their Asian allies against any further Communist advance in Southeast Asia. Dulles intended his speech to be a warning to the Soviet Union, People's Republic of China* (PRC), and the Vietminh* of the possibility of some form of multilateral action in Indochina.

The Indochina issue dominated a National Security Council meeting on 25 March. The Vietminh siege of the French stronghold at Dien Bien Phu had reached a critical juncture, and the French now were requesting U.S. help to avert disaster. The Eisenhower administration had to consider the possibility of American intervention. Operation VULTURE, a U.S. air strike against Dien Bien Phu, was discussed, with both Dulles and Admiral Arthur W. Radford*, chairman of the Joint Chiefs of Staff, supporting the plan, but Eisenhower did not want to move forward without support from U.S. allies. Two objectives for the immediate future emerged: to create a framework for possible United Action to assist or possibly replace France in Indochina and to consider possible courses of action in case the French decided to withdraw from the area.

Throughout March and April, the concept of United Action slowly evolved from a straightforward attempt to arrange favorable conditions for an air strike to a more long-term effort to create a Southeast Asian alliance. Washington began to follow a two-track approach, enlisting support for intervention, to be followed by an alliance. The United States made it clear to the French that it would not intervene militarily in Indochina unless both France and Britain agreed to United Action. On 10 April, Dulles went to Europe to secure Western support. He had received some encouragement from Thailand*, the Philippines*, Australia, and New Zealand, but the French and British worried that United Action would torpedo the discussions on Indochina that were to begin on 8 May at the Geneva Conference of 1954*. The British in particular resisted being committed to a common defense of Southeast Asia that could drag them into the First Indochina War*. France believed that the Americans already had agreed to save Dien Bien Phu with Operation VULTURE and did not want to internationalize the conflict, fearing that Washington would gain control over the war effort.

United Action also faced problems at home because Congress was reluctant to move forward too quickly. Building on this reticence, Eisenhower set forth a number of conditions before he would approve United Action. First, there would have to be a coalition with active participation by Britain, Australia, and New Zealand, including, if possible, troops from Thailand, the Philippines, and other countries in the region. Second, France would have to agree to accelerate the independence of the Associated States and remain in the war until its conclusion. Third, use of U.S. troops would need advance approval of Congress. None of these conditions were met. Although United Action remained an option until Dien Bien Phu collapsed, it was a remote one, mostly used as a threat to try to gain more concessions from the Communists at Geneva. Historians disagree on whether Eisenhower deliberately set forth impossible conditions to keep the United States clear of the Indochina War.

M. Billings-Yun, *Decision Against War: Eisenhower and Dien Bien Phu, 1954* (New York, 1988); W. Duiker, *U.S. Containment Policy and the Conflict in Indochina* (Stanford, CA, 1994). L. Kaplan, D. Artaud, M. Rubin (eds.), *Dien Bien Phu and the Crisis of Franco-American Relations, 1954–1955* (Wilmington, DE, 1990); J. Prados, *The Sky Would Fall: Operation Vulture, the U.S. Bombing Mission in Indochina, 1954* (New York, 1983).

Kathryn C. Statler

UNITED CHINA RELIEF-UNITED SERVICE TO CHINA

United China Relief (UCR) was created during 1940 as part of an effort by disparate humanitarian, and largely religious, organizations engaged in aiding China in its struggle against Japanese aggression. It sought to coordinate and streamline fundraising activities. The UCR comprised eight agencies: the American Bureau for Medical

Aid to China, American Committee for Chinese War Orphans, American Committee in Aid of Chinese Industrial Cooperatives, American Friends Service Committee, Associated Boards for Christian Colleges in China, China Aid Council, China Emergency Relief Committee, and Church Committee for China Relief. Between 1941 and 1945, the UCR raised more than $37 million in aid for China and participated in the American celebration of its Asian ally's fight against the forces of fascism in the Pacific.

United China Relief changed its name to United Service to China (USC) in 1946 in an effort to separate its postwar activities from those it had conducted during the war. Despite its continuing commitment to aiding China's destitute, the USC found itself unable to raise money to the same extent. Caught in the middle of the greater concern Americans had for domestic matters and the alienation caused by the Chinese Civil War*, the USC suspended operations in mid-1951. At the height of its activities during World War II, the UCR aggressively promoted ideas of a China and Chinese population changing to become more like the United States and Americans. Though decidedly untrue, these ideas made enough of an impression on many Americans so that when revolution brought the Chinese Communist Party* to power under the leadership of Mao Zedong* in 1949, many people were genuinely shocked. This, in turn, helped fuel the notion Senator Joseph R. McCarthy* and others advanced that treasonous U.S. government officials had sold out China to Communism*.

T. C. Jespersen, *American Images of China, 1931–1949* (Stanford, CA, 1996).

T. Christopher Jespersen

UNITED FRONT

"United Front" was a policy that the Chinese Communist Party* (CCP) has followed of entering into a short-term alliance with one or more rivaling parties for the purpose of achieving long-term political goals. The United Front played a very important role in helping the CCP grow in its early years and gain power after the Chinese Civil War*. The Chinese Communists implemented United Front as a policy many times, but the following instances had the most success. First, the CCP, under encouragement from the Comintern based in Moscow, formed an alliance with Sun Zhongshan* and his political movement in 1923, and helped promote a new level of intense Chinese nationalism. This United Front aborted in 1927, when the Guomindang* (Nationalists), now under the leadership of Jiang Jieshi*, purged it from the Nationalist movement. The second United Front was formed in 1936 after the Xian Incident*, when Zhang Xueliang* arranged for the Communists and the Nationalists to stop their bloody civil war and join forces against Japan's invasion of China. The second United Front ended when the Japanese defeat approached and, in 1946, the civil war reignited. The CCP saw the United Front as one of the most important factors contributing to its victory, allowing it to identify its most important enemies and eliminate them one by one.

In 1978, after the Communist veteran Mao Zedong* died, the new Communist leaders in the People's Republic of China* recognized economic modernization as China's most urgent need. One of the strategies the PRC used to accomplish this aim was attracting foreign investment, so as to narrow the technological gap and meet the demand for capital. After Jiang's Republic of China* fled to the island in 1949, Taiwan*, which had built an industrialized economy under the three decades of Nationalist rule, emerged as a positive source of foreign investment. The CCP therefore modified its ideology and started to reemphasize Chinese nationalism. It extended gestures to Guomindang leaders on Taiwan, calling for a third United Front, and urged the Taiwanese people to return to the mainland in search for their ancestral roots. Meanwhile, the CCP opened its market in accordance with the Four Modernizations* for potential investors from Taiwan, hoping increased financial ties would first narrow the economic gap between the two Chinas and smooth the way toward its ultimate goal of reunification. While Beijing continued to campaign for a United Front in upgrading China's position in the world, Taibei searched for ways to respond effectively to the pressure.

M. J. Meisner, *Mao's China and After: A History of the People's Republic* (New York, 1986); S. Ogden, *China's Unresolved Issues: Politics, Development, and Culture* (Englewood Cliffs, NJ, 1989).

Li Yi

U.S.-CHINA MUTUAL DEFENSE TREATY OF 1954

This treaty between the United States and the Republic of China* (ROC) was signed on 2 December 1954, came into force on 3 March 1955, and was terminated on 16 December 1979 after the administration of President Jimmy Carter* recognized the People's Republic of China* (PRC). During the course of its existence, it was the basis of U.S. military, economic, and political support for "Free China" and a symbol of U.S. hostility against "Red China." Concluded at the height of the Cold War during the first of the Taiwan Straits Crises*, this treaty was one link in the U.S. global security system to contain Communist expansion. Indeed, the treaty's text followed closely the language of pacts between the United States and other Pacific nations. However, the negotiating process was anything but smooth, and some features in the Exchange of Notes suggested less than ideal relations between Washington and Taibei.

Taibei started pressing for a formal alliance with Washington after Dwight D. Eisenhower* became president in early 1953. The ROC sought either to participate in a U.S.-sponsored regional security pact or to negotiate a bilateral defense treaty. But Washington wanted to retain policy flexibility while making the most of the ROC's military potential to restrain the PRC, and was lukewarm about establishing a treaty relationship with Taiwan*. Unenthusiastic about Tabei's various ideas for regional alliances, the Eisenhower administration excluded the ROC from the Southeast Asia Treaty Organization*. It also continually postponed consideration of a draft bilateral pact that Taibei had handed to the State Department in late 1953. It was not until October 1954, in connection with a cease-fire maneuver at the United Nations in the first strait crisis, that Washington seriously considered concluding a defense treaty with the ROC. Secretary of State John Foster Dulles* devised Operation ORACLE*, which sought to prevent the Communists from seizing the offshore islands while safeguarding Taiwan with a security pact. Despite Dulles's emphatic denials, the treaty was, in fact, a "bribe" to pacify Jiang Jieshi*, who strongly objected to ORACLE.

Negotiations for the treaty were a tug-of-war over reciprocity and the degree of control the United States could have over Taibei's military disposition and operations. Jiang had agreed beforehand that not only would the treaty's scope be restricted to the territory then and thereafter under Guomindang* (Nationalist) control, but he would "seek prior agreement of the United States before undertaking any important military action." The Eisenhower administration wanted to include these understandings and a restriction on the ROC's military disposition in a treaty protocol. Taipei, however, fought against what it labeled an "American leash around the neck of Free China." In the end, Washington's position prevailed in the Exchange of Notes, and technically was an arrangement for implementation that did not require congressional approval. Taibei agreed that use and large-scale movement of its military forces, other than in self-defense, would be subject to joint agreement. Even though Washington made concessions on format, and Taibei yielded on substance, the ROC was gratified after conclusion of the mutual defense treaty. Jiang and his advisers used their bargaining power to maximize their chances for survival and placed the ROC on a par with other Pacific nations with respect to long-term U.S. support, which Washington heretofore had been unwilling to grant. Thereafter, the treaty was the basis of U.S. relations with the ROC until it was aborted and replaced by the Taiwan Relations Act* in 1979.

S. Chang, "Reluctant Alliance: John Foster Dulles and the Making of the United States-Republic of China Mutual Defense Treaty of 1954," in *Chinese Yearbook of International Law and Affairs*, Vol. 12 (Baltimore, 1992–1994); Ge Su, "Meitai gongtong fangyu tiaoyu de yunniang guocheng" [The Making of the U.S.-Taiwan Mutual Defense Treaty: 1948–1955], *Meiguo Yanjiu* [American Studies] (September 1990); Qingguo Jia, "Meitai gongtong fangyu tiaoyu de dijie jingguo" [The Conclusion of the U.S.-Taiwan Defense Treaty], *Meiguo Yanjiu* [American Studies] (January 1989).

Chang Su-Ya

U.S. IMMIGRATION ACT OF 1965

Historian John Hope Franklin has lamented that the United States was unable to win World War II "without the blatant racism that poisoned the entire effort." To counteract criticism of American racism and to build friendships in Asia, the United States supported establishment of the United Nations Commission on Human Rights that called for a commitment to end racial discrimination on a global basis. A direct result was the U.S. government's recognition of the need to reform its immigration policy. Cognizant of the new U.S. leadership role in the postwar world, Congress in 1952 passed the McCarran-Walter Immigration and Naturalization Act in an effort to achieve a balance between U.S. foreign policy objectives and the desire to prevent "opening the gates to a flood of Asiatics." Although this bill eliminated race as an obstacle to immigration and naturalization, it retained the principle of the National Origins Act*, the hallmark of U.S. immigration policy since 1924. In his veto, President Harry S. Truman* explained that although immigration policy was important domestically, it "is equally, if not more important, to the conduct of our foreign relations and to our responsibilities of moral leadership in the world."

It was not until 1965, however, that Congress passed an immigration act that repealed the national origins quota system and eliminated the Asia-Pacific Triangle provisions. Explaining this shift was a combination of new legislators sympathetic to change gaining office as a result of the landslide presidential victory of Lyndon B. Johnson*, minority lobbying from Asian-Americans, and intensification of the Cold War. The new system, effective 1 July 1968, provided 170,000 visas for people from the Eastern Hemisphere and 120,000 from the Western Hemisphere. Visas were issued on a first-come, first-served basis within seven preference categories. Immediate family members—spouses and minor children—were exempt from the quota.

The Cold War had a unique effect on race as a factor in U.S. foreign policy. First, among top U.S. government officials, there was growing realization that race discrimination in policy on immigration would hurt its struggle against Communism*. Thus, the passage of the 1965 Immigration Act removed one strategic propaganda issue from the Soviets because "American policy-makers no longer appeared hypocritical for opposing racial discrimination abroad while sanctioning it at home." Second, since the end of World War II, U.S. military involvement in the Korean War*, Taiwan*, and the Second Indochina War* had intensified disparagement of Asians in racial terms by U.S. service personnel. Sensitive to American ethnocentrism, many Asians and Asian-Americans perceived these conflicts as another manifestation of U.S. imperialism, a callous attitude toward Asian lives, and the lack of understanding of Asian culture. As Secretary of State Dean Rusk* told Congress in 1964, "what other people think about us plays an important role in the achievement of our foreign policies." Third, the sixth preference, permitting professionals and skilled workers to enter the United States, served the dual purpose of denying Communist nations in Asia skilled personnel by enticing professionals, engineers, and scientists to leave, while at the same time enhancing U.S. productivity with an infusion of talented immigrants.

B. O. Hing, *Making and Remaking Asian America Through Immigration Policy, 1850–1990* (Stanford, CA, 1993); M. C. LeMay, *From Open Door to Dutch Door: An Analysis of U.S. Immigration Policy Since 1820* (New York, 1987); D. M. Reimers, *Still the Golden Door: The Third World Comes to America* (New York, 1985); J. C. Vialet, *A Brief History of U.S. Immigration Policy* (Washington, DC, 1980).

Roger Y. M. Chan

U.S.-JAPAN MUTUAL DEFENSE ASSISTANCE AGREEMENT (8 March 1954)

Officially endorsed by the U.S. and Japanese governments on 8 March 1954, this key agreement established a foundation for U.S. military backing for Japan after it had regained its sovereignty in April 1952. The understanding was necessary under the terms of the Mutual Security Act (MSA), an extension of the Mutual Defense Assistance Act of 1949, that required separate bilateral agreements between the United States and its allies before formal provision of military equipment or related services. Attaining acceptance of the terms of the agreement was complicated by a variety of factors, both legal and political. Article 9 of the Japanese Constitution of 1947* prohibited Japan from participating in security arrangements that could be construed as anything other than purely defensive and was, therefore, at odds with the 1951 MSA, which required U.S. military allies to commit to the principle of collective security. Just as important, Japan's postwar leaders, especially Prime Minister Yoshida Shigeru*, citing economic difficulties and anxious to avoid anything that might encourage a reversion to prewar militarism, were reluctant to accept pressure from Washington, especially the Joint Chiefs of Staff (JCS), for a rapid expansion of Japan's armed forces.

In early 1953, the JCS, in considering the scale of military assistance to Japan, had proposed that Tōkyō aim at establishing a ground force complement of no fewer than 300,000 men. The Yoshida government balked at these figures, proposing in late 1953 in important discussions in Washington involving Ikeda Hayato* and Walter S. Robertson*, assistant secretary for Far Eastern Affairs, a more modest expansion to 180,000 men over three years. Ultimately, Washington recognized that it was futile and counterproductive to push Japan to commit to rapid rearmament, and Tōkyō took modest steps to enhance its military preparedness. In an exchange of official letters in early 1954, U.S. Ambassador to Japan John M. Allison* and Japanese Foreign Minister Okazaki Katsuo agreed that Japan would expand its overall defense strength by 41,000 men (10,000 of whom would be uniformed) and increase appropriations by 79 million yen for the National Security Agency (NSA), Japan's fledgling military forces. Although Japan was absolved from any obligation to commit to the concept of collective security, the understanding on mutual defense assistance helped pave the way for the introduction in 1954 of legislation converting the NSA into the Japanese Self-Defense Forces, as well as establishing a new Japan Defense Agency.

Under the terms of the Mutual Defense Assistance Agreement, a U.S. Military Advisory Group was to be activated in Japan, while Washington acknowledged its intention, but not a formal commitment, to fund $100 million in offshore procurement expenditures in Japan, as well as providing information and training for employees of

Japan's defense-related industries. In addition, the United States proposed, under the MSA, to sell some $50 million worth of surplus agricultural commodities to Japan, with the understanding that 20 percent of these sales would be used to support the development of Japan's defense sector. The March agreement did not eliminate bilateral disagreement over defense issues, and there was additional tension later in 1954 following Japanese requests for additional U.S. military aid and proposed cuts in Japan's defense budget. Nonetheless, the agreement was an important turning point in establishing a basis for active defense cooperation, as well as impressing on U.S. officials, especially in the embassy in Tōkyō, the importance of not overemphasizing the rearmament issue. By April 1955, Washington had accepted that the rearmament question should be downplayed. At the same time, the political leadership in Japan remained divided over defense issues, a division that was only partially resolved in 1956 with the formal establishment of Japan's National Defense Council.

M. Green, *Arming Japan: Defense Production, Alliance Politics, and the Postwar Search for Autonomy* (New York, 1995); M. Schaller, *Altered States: The United States and Japan Since the Occupation* (New York, 1997); J. Swenson-Wright, *Unequal Allies?: United States Security and Alliance Policy Toward Japan, 1945–1960* (Stanford, CA, 2001).

John Swenson-Wright

U.S.-JAPAN MUTUAL COOPERATION AND SECURITY TREATY (23 June 1960)

This agreement replaced the U.S.-Japan Security Treaty of 1951*, but opposition in Japan to its ratification during May and June 1960 ignited the worst political crisis in postwar Japanese history. In 1957, in the wake of a dispute about legal jurisdiction involving a U.S. soldier accused of shooting a Japanese woman, U.S. Ambassador to Japan Douglas MacArthur II* warned Secretary of State John Foster Dulles* that the time had come to revise the security agreement or risk losing the U.S. alliance with Japan. In response, Dulles agreed and gave MacArthur permission in early September to negotiate a new treaty. MacArthur and Foreign Minister Fujiyama Aiichirō drafted a new agreement that had a ten-year life span and required one year's notice prior to termination thereafter. The United States also made an explicit commitment to defend Japan in case of attack and surrendered its authority to intervene in Japanese domestic affairs. But domestic political developments forced Prime Minister Kishi Nobosuke* to insist on two changes in the draft. Many Japanese feared being dragged into a U.S. war, and compelled adoption of a revision limiting the defense obligations to Japan's home islands. The second issue was a U.S. pledge to consult the Japanese government prior to deployment of American troops or planes based in Japan. Realizing that this issue jeopardized the entire treaty, President Dwight D. Eisenhower* publicly stated that the United States would do nothing that ran counter to the wishes of the Japanese government, and new Secretary of State Christian Herter confirmed to the U.S. Senate Foreign Relations Committee that the Japanese had a veto. With these concessions, Kishi went to Washington to sign the treaty at the White House in January 1960.

Despite American acquiescence, the revised treaty was extremely controversial in Japan. Political activists on the left considered any agreement that allowed the continued presence of U.S. military bases in Japan, an acceptance of a de facto army of occupation and a violation of the provision in the Japanese Constitution of 1947* outlawing war as an instrument of foreign policy. But Kishi was determined to gain quick ratification and then use the new treaty to win new Diet elections. His heavy-handed, undemocratic actions to secure the Diet's approval sparked the Anpo Crisis*. The Diet ratified the treaty after a chaotic session early on the morning of 19

June. In Washington, the head of the Senate Foreign Relations Committee suggested delaying a vote on the treaty until the situation stabilized in Tōkyō. Senate Majority Leader Lyndon B. Johnson*, who was running for president and had benefited from bipartisan support of Eisenhower, ignored this advice, and on 22 June, the U.S. Senate approved the agreement by a vote of 90–2. Hours later, on what was 23 June in Tōkyō, MacArthur and Fujiyama exchanged instruments of ratification. Despite the uproar in Japan, the treaty proved quite durable. In 1970, under Prime Minister Satō Eisaku*, Japan agreed to automatic renewal of the treaty. Surviving a variety of U.S.-Japanese economic disputes and even the end of the Cold War, the treaty was the bedrock of U.S.-Japanese relations for decades thereafter into the twenty-first century.

J. I. Matray, *Japan's Emergence as a Global Power* (Westport, CT, 2000); G. Packard III, *Protest in Tokyo: The Security Treaty Crisis of 1960* (Princeton, NJ, 1966); M. Schaller, *Altered States: The United States and Japan Since the Occupation* (New York, 1997).

Nicholas Evan Sarantakes

U.S.-JAPAN POSTWAR TRADE RELATIONS

Bilateral trade was the central element in the American-Japanese relationship after 1945, bringing immeasurable benefits to both countries, but also provoking bitter rivalry. The initial postwar expansion of U.S.-Japan trade was inseparable from the Cold War. Cut off from the world in 1945, the Japanese were dependent upon aid during the U.S. Occupation of Japan*. Architects of the Reverse Course* in U.S. policy saw in expanded trade a means of strengthening Japan and cementing the U.S.-Japan alliance in the Cold War. Fortuitously, U.S. spending on the Korean War* created a market for Japanese manufacturers. The U.S.-imposed embargo under the CHINCOM* of Mainland China that accompanied the war, however, severely curtailed Sino-Japanese trade. Thereafter, American leaders exerted considerable pressure on Japan to limit trade with the People's Republic of China* (PRC) while expanding trade with the Western powers. Despite U.S. encouragement, Japan's trade with Southeast Asia did not expand as rapidly as Washington expected.

A reorientation of Japan's trade westward was the result. The United States and Japan concluded a Friendship, Commerce, and Navigation Treaty in April 1953. Japan became a member of the General Agreement on Tariffs and Trade* (GATT) with U.S. support in September 1955. Afterward, Japanese manufacturers exported a growing volume of consumer goods to the United States as Japan's economy surged forward during the "miracle" years. U.S. exports to Japan grew from $418 million in 1950 to $1.5 billion a decade later, whereas imports from Japan rose from a mere $182 million to $1.1 billion during the same period. Although the United States was becoming Japan's best export market, Japan's persistent deficit worried both countries. U.S. military spending in Japan covered the difference during the 1950s and continued through the Second Indochina War*. U.S. policy also tolerated Japanese imposition of restrictions on imports and investment for balance of payments reasons while encouraging the private transfer of industrial technology to Japan. But the flood of Japanese exports often prompted widespread calls for protection: on cotton textiles in the mid-1950s, synthetic textiles in the 1960s, then steel, and most dramatically, passenger cars in the 1980s. To resolve trade conflicts, the two countries frequently resorted to "voluntary export restraints" or "voluntary import expansion."

For both sides, trade has been bound up closely with national prestige. Success in the American market afforded the Japanese the opportunity to create a new identity symbolized by economic achievement and consumer society. If export gains in the 1970s and 1980s were a source of Japanese satisfaction, competition shook American confidence and prompted painful soul-searching. It led to legislation passed in 1974 providing for unilateral sanctions to be levied on nations whose "unfair" domestic practices blocked American exports. The Tōkyō Round* of GATT (1974–1979) partially addressed the problem of nontariff barriers to trade, but Japan's mounting surplus—$13 billion in a single year by the end of the 1970s—made trade a political issue, and both governments turned to more political solutions. Bilateral agreement in 1985 to revaluate the yen had little effect. Congress then extended the scope of its trade act in 1988, and the target was Japan. The Japanese understandably resented being criticized for selling high-quality consumer goods that Americans wished to buy. Since the U.S. government's inability to balance its own budget contributed to the trade gap, the Japanese often thought that they were blamed unfairly for American shortcomings.

Trade friction reached a peak just as the Cold War was ending during the presidency of George H. W. Bush*. In the 1980s, Japan's multinational companies invested heavily in the United States to surmount potential trade barriers. Although such investment was a vote of confidence in the U.S. economy, the immediate result was to inflame popular American opinion. Meanwhile, Japanese commentary on the United States was full of disdain, drawing attention especially to American social problems. Ambassadors Michael H. Armacost* and Walter Mondale attempted to manage day-to-day relations between the two nations during the period of greatest strain. If Japanese commentary on trade relations in the 1980s exhibited a triumphalist tone, the tables turned after the collapse of Japan's "bubble economy" in 1990. Having restructured to be competitive and developed new technologies, the U.S. economy rebounded in the 1990s. But owing to Japan's domestic economic weakness, the U.S. recovery did not bring an end to the trade deficit. Since Japanese firms had become major producers in the United States itself, bilateral trade friction in the 1990s increasingly became technical and not the same source of prior popular anxiety. After the East Asian Financial Crisis*, Washington's greater concern was Japanese economic weakness. Meanwhile, as interdependence among Pacific nations grew, U.S.-Japan trade issues became more important in a regional and global context. *See also* Ministry of International Trade and Industry; Triangular Trade.

M. H. Armacost, *Friends or Rivals?: The Insider's Account of U.S.-Japan Relations* (New York, 1996); A. E. Eckes Jr., *Opening America's Market: U.S. Foreign Trade Policy Since 1776* (Chapel Hill, NC, 1995); A. Forsberg, *America and the Japanese Miracle: The Cold War Context of Japan's Postwar Economic Revival, 1950–1960* (Chapel Hill, NC, 2000); T. K. McCraw (ed.), *America Versus Japan* (Cambridge, MA, 1985); S. Ostry, *The Post-Cold War Trading System: Who's on First* (Chicago, 1997).

Aaron Forsberg

U.S.-JAPAN SECURITY TREATY OF 1951

The U.S.-Japan Security Treaty, signed on 8 September 1951, established the defense provisions of the Japanese peace settlement, and complemented the ANZUS Treaty* and the U.S.-Philippines Mutual Defense Pact*. Although the treaty's terms did not spell out a formal guarantee of Japan's security, observers correctly regarded it as confirmation of a U.S.-Japanese "alliance" in the Cold War. Also, it stood at the center of political debate in Japan until it was replaced by the U.S.-Japan Mutual Cooperation and Security Treaty* of 1960. Approval came despite the fact that the Japanese Peace Treaty* negotiations between John Foster Dulles* and Prime Minister Yoshida Shigeru* revealed major differences between American and Japanese aims. Advisers to President Harry S. Truman* considered negotiating a multilateral Pacific defense pact. Since congressional authorization for offering any security guarantee depended upon the ally making an effort to defend itself, Dulles pressed Yoshida to rebuild Japan's military and issue the Yoshida Letter*, promising that Japan would recognize the Republic of China* despite its flight to Taiwan*.

Yoshida and most of the Japanese public, however, sought to concentrate the nation's resources on economic development. The prime minister recognized that as long as the United States maintained military bases on Japanese soil, Japan had a de facto guarantee of its security. He rebuffed Dulles, proposing instead the formation of a militarily insignificant force of 50,000 men, whereas the U.S. goal was between 300,000 and 350,000. Backing away from his initial demand for extensive rearmament, Dulles inserted Yoshida's pledge that "Japan will itself increasingly assume responsibility for the defense of its own homeland" into the preamble. The treaty authorized U.S. use of its forces based in Japan to defend Japan from armed attack, as well as to contribute to "peace and stability in the Far East." Dulles also pressed the Japanese to consent to permitting U.S. military forces to put down riots or other threats to Japan's internal security, if the Japanese government asked for help. The treaty prohibited Japan from granting bases or similar rights to any third power without prior American consent. Finally, the agreement contained no expiration date.

By allowing the United States to maintain its military bases in Japan and Okinawa, and to continue to use them in support of the Korean War* or other military operations overseas without Japanese consent, the security treaty essentially defined Japan as a military dependency of the United States. In 1954, the United States had about 210,000 troops stationed on its bases in Japan. That number dropped thereafter, reaching 58,000 in 1960. A separate Administrative Agreement, signed on 28 February 1952, set down the conditions governing the disposition of U.S. military forces. This unequal accord provided, for example, that the United States had complete criminal jurisdiction over American forces stationed in Japan. Consistent with his promise of limited Japanese rearmament, after the conclusion of the U.S.-Japan Mutual Defense Assistance Agreement*, Yoshida secured Diet legislation in 1954 that established the National Self-Defense Forces. It authorized a force numbering about 150,000.

The U.S.-Japan Security Treaty drew criticism from both sides of the political spectrum in Japan. Conservative nationalists such as Kishi Nobusuke*, who desired a more equitable partnership with the United States, called for revision of the treaty. Socialists, who opposed the alliance with the United States in principle, opposed such revision. Both sides used the unequal nature of the treaty and the unpopular aspects of the defense relationship with the United States for political advantage. This debate intertwined with disagreements over rearmament and the Japanese Constitution of 1947*, which renounced war. Disputes over these issues polarized politics during the 1950s, undercutting right-wing Socialists and liberal-minded political leaders such as Ishibashi Tanzan* and Ashida Hitoshi*, who might have formed the basis in Japanese politics for a center-left coalition. Instead, a majority joined the conservative Liberal Democratic Party* to keep the Socialists out of power. Thus, in combination with the constitution, the security treaty placed a severe strain on the Japanese political system. After the United States agreed to revise the treaty, public involvement in the debate grew, culminating in the Anpo Crisis* of 1960.

J. W. Dower, *Empire and Aftermath: Yoshida Shigeru and the Japanese Experience, 1878–1954* (Cambridge, MA, 1979); R. B. Finn, *Winners in Peace: MacArthur, Yoshida, and Postwar Japan* (Berkeley, CA, 1992); S. Miyasato, "John Foster Dulles and the Peace Settlement with Japan," in R. H. Immerman (ed.), *John Foster Dulles and the Diplomacy of the Cold War* (Princeton, NJ, 1990); H. B.

Schonberger, *Aftermath of War: Americans and the Remaking of Japan, 1945–1952* (Kent, OH, 1989); M. E. Weinstein, *Japan's Postwar Defense Policy, 1947–1968* (New York, 1971).

Aaron Forsberg

U.S. OCCUPATION OF JAPAN

On 2 September 1945, nervous Japanese representatives signed the instruments of unconditional surrender based on the Potsdam Declaration* and General Douglas MacArthur* took charge of the nation as Supreme Commander for the Allied Powers (SCAP*). The occupation that followed was an American show different from others, such as the U.S. Occupation of Korea*. Americans and Japanese both expected the worst, but each soon discovered that familiar stereotypes failed to describe the other. Neither sought to continue the war. U.S. distribution of more than $2 billion in food, fuel, and medicine prevented starvation and disease from ravaging Japan's populace. The Americans were struck by the Japanese cooperation with the unfamiliar foreigners as they rebuilt their nation, but there was an asymmetry in the relationship. Numerous incidents and rampant prostitution near military bases showed that not all Americans showed consideration for the Japanese. Some Japanese resented their nation's dependence on the United States. Observers likened General MacArthur to a Tokugawa-era shōgun, but Washington decided basic policies beforehand. During the initial phase, the Americans sought to demilitarize and democratize Japan to prevent a return to the militaristic imperialism that led to war. SCAP worked through existing parliamentary institutions and the bureaucracy. It preserved the imperial institution, but pressed Emperor Hirohito* to renounce his divinity. The prevailing mood reflected the Americans' missionary confidence and the willingness of the Japanese to follow their new guides.

MacArthur's General Order Number 1* assigned the task of demobilizing the Japanese armed forces to the Japanese themselves. It was completed within two months. Posing a much greater logistical challenge was repatriating the 6.6 million Japanese military and civilian personnel stationed overseas. As in Germany, the victorious Allies investigated war crimes. Critics, however, have pointed out that the Tōkyō War Crimes Trials* were "victors' justice." More significant than the trials of Tōjō Hideki*, Ōkawa Shūmei*, Hirōta Koki*, and other top figures was the purge of about 200,000 military, government, and business leaders for their activities in support of the war. Under pressure from SCAP, the Japanese government abolished the Ministries of War, Navy, and Home Affairs. In the Japanese Constitution of 1947*, Japan renounced war as an instrument of national policy and pledged not to maintain armed forces. It also provided a solid foundation for parliamentary democracy, but the style of governance that took shape was much more bureaucratic than either the Americans or Japanese liberals desired. The requirements of indirect rule and the New Deal liberalism that inspired many SCAP reformers caused them to leave most former imperial civil servants in place, except for those obviously connected to the war effort. SCAP bombarded the Japanese with propaganda, and U.S. officials censored criticism of the occupation—initially from the nationalistic right and later from the radical left.

SCAP attempted to democratize Japan's economy by making landholders out of tenant farmers, breaking up the *Zaibatsu**, and encouraging trade unionism. As long as approximately 70 percent of farmers were tenants there was little hope for democracy to take firm root. The Land Reform Law of 1946 banned absentee land ownership. Its provisions for purchase enabled 4.75 million tenants to buy about 5 million acres of land from 2.34 million landowners by 1950. The zaibatsu dissolution program forced the family holding companies to sell their stock to the general public. Under pressure from the SCAP, the Diet passed a number of laws to provide legal protection for labor unions and collective bargaining. These reforms did not replicate the New Deal in Japan as many SCAP reformers wanted. Although the land reform virtually eliminated tenancy—and with it the threat of rural radicalism—farmers quickly became the political foundation after 1955 of the conservative Liberal Democratic Party*. In return, agricultural producers of rice and other commodities enjoyed protection from foreign competition, which became a major source of friction in U.S.-Japan Postwar Trade Relations*. *Zaibatsu*-busting only partially addressed the problem of fostering a more competitive marketplace. Similarly, by late 1947, union members numbered more than 6 million, up from less than 1,000 in 1945. Japanese union leaders, however, preferred militant activism to collective bargaining.

Since Japanese schools had fostered militaristic nationalism and enforced ideological conformity before the war, SCAP sought to reform Japan's education system. Although the occupation did lead to greater tolerance of independent thought in Japanese schools, American reformers failed to engage a broad segment of Japanese educators and intellectuals. Throughout Japan, SCAP purged teachers, established coeducation in public schools, deleted courses on "moral education" (*shushin*) from the curriculum, and expanded the number of universities. Japanese educators after the occupation restored "moral education" in modified form under a new name. Efforts to reduce the authority of the Ministry of Education met with only partial success. The former imperial universities, most notably Tōkyō University, and leading private universities continued to dominate Japan's system of higher education. More broadly, the occupation aroused Japanese cultural nationalism. Writers, artists, and other intellectuals of both the left and the right were keenly aware of Japan's rich cultural heritage. They tended to be critical of American culture as unrefined and lacking philosophical depth. American ignorance of Japan and the ubiquitous presence of things American in Japan after the war reinforced such preconceptions.

In 1947 and 1948, U.S. policy shifted dramatically in what has become known as the Reverse Course* aimed at transforming Japan into a bulwark against Communist expansion in Asia. The economic stabilization mission of Joseph M. Dodge* in 1949 reflected the depth of Washington's concern about Japan's economic health. Although SCAP pressed the Diet to pass antimonopoly legislation in 1947, U.S. officials did not follow through with plans to break up the monopolistic companies and two years later ended the program of extracting reparations. The security partnership between the United States and Japan's conservative establishment took concrete form during the Korean War* with the conclusion of the Japanese Peace Treaty* and the U.S.-Japan Security Treaty of 1951*. Japan's "American interlude" concluded when the treaties entered into force in April 1952, but not before Japan, in the Yoshida Letter*, agreed to recognize the Republic of China*. Although U.S. policy shifted dramatically in seven years, the reforms enacted were not entirely reversed. They accelerated changes already set in motion by Japan's often-forgotten liberals, such as Ishibashi Tanzan*, and charted new directions for the nation. The occupation also laid a firm foundation for continued U.S.-Japan cooperation in the Cold War. *See also* Open Payments Agreement; William J. Sebald; Sterling Payments Agreement.

J. H. Boyle, *Modern Japan: The American Nexus* (Fort Worth, TX, 1993); T. Cohen, *Remaking Japan: The American Occupation as New Deal* (New York, 1987); R. B. Finn, *Winners in Peace: MacArthur, Yoshida, and Postwar Japan* (Berkeley, CA, 1992); H. B. Schonberger, *Aftermath of War: Americans and the Remaking of Japan, 1945–1952* (Kent, OH, 1989); SCAP, *Political Reorientation of Japan, September 1945–September 1948* (Washington, DC, 1949).

Aaron Forsberg

U.S. OCCUPATION OF KOREA

During the military occupation years from 1945 to 1948, the United States played a decisive role in the formation of an independent Republic of Korea* (ROK). In mid-August 1945, when the defeat of Japan was imminent, the United States and the Soviet Union hastily agreed to the Thirty-Eighth Parallel Division* of the Korean peninsula into two zones of occupation for the purpose of accepting the surrender of Japanese forces and maintaining security until Korea's future course could be settled. As the Cold War deepened, Korea became the site of two antagonistic regimes based on diametrically opposed principles and sponsors. In keeping with the agreement between the two powers under General Order Number 1*, U.S. forces commanded by Lieutenant General John R. Hodge* occupied the southern zone on 8 September and established the U.S. Army Military Government in Korea (USAMGIK). The USAMGIK was the only government in southern Korea. Hodge rejected the claims to legitimacy from both the Korean Provisional Government, in exile in Chongqing and receiving support from China's Jiang Jieshi* and his Guomindang* (Nationalist) government, and the Korean People's Republic, established in Korea just before U.S. occupation forces arrived.

The United States did not give serious wartime consideration to its postwar policy toward Korea. About 2,000 civil affairs officers had been trained for duty in the U.S. Occupation of Japan*, and elaborate plans had been drawn up for that nation, but no one had been trained and no plans had been made for Korea. Hodge faced profound instability immediately upon arrival, resulting from intense political factionalism and Korean demands for self-government after enduring forty years of suffering under Japanese Colonialism*. At the Cairo Conference* in 1943, the Allies had promised independence "in due course," but Koreans translated this to read "in a few days." Hodge's first of many mistakes was to retain, on orders from Washington, Japanese adminstrators. He then allowed Koreans who collaborated with Japan to gain positions in an interim government. The USAMGIK also delayed land reform. Meanwhile, the Soviets spurned requests for cooperation and coordination to prepare the way for rapid reunification. The Moscow Agreement on Korea* in December 1945 provided for creation of a Joint Soviet-American Commission to select members of a provisional government, but its provision for a trusteeship set off angry protests in the U.S. zone led by Kim Gu* and other anti-Soviet Koreans. The Joint Commission negotiations from March 1946 until July 1947 failed to reach an agreement because the Soviets demanded exclusion of right-wing leaders who opposed trusteeship, and the United States insisted on their participation to prevent leftists and Communists, such as Pak Hŏn-yŏng*, from dominating a united postwar government in Korea.

In September 1947, the United States referred the Korean impasse to the United Nations, acting on a plan devised by State Department official John M. Allison*. That same month, the Joint Chiefs of Staff endorsed rising pressure from the U.S. Army for prompt withdrawal when it advised that Korea had no strategic significance. But the Soviets would not allow implementation in the north of a UN resolution calling for supervised elections to achieve reunification. Elections were held only in the south in May 1948, despite strong opposition in the United Nations and from Korean leaders such as Kim Kyu-sik*, resulting in the creation of the ROK in August. The three-year U.S. military occupation, however, would determine the features of subsequent South Korean society and the repressive nature of the first government under President Syngman Rhee*. From 1945 to 1948, the United States focused mainly on keeping southern Korea non-Communist in response to the Soviet Union's establishment of the Democratic People's Republic of Korea* under Kim Il

Sung* in the north. Under American influence, the ROK became a bulwark against Communism*, but the United States lost an opportunity to achieve other high-minded goals and paid little attention to satisfying Korean needs and desires. *See also* Korean Aid Act; Korean War.

B. Cumings, *Korea's Place in the Sun: A Modern History* (New York, 1997); J. Kim, "From Patron-Client to Partners: The Changing South Korean-American Relationship," *Journal of American–East Asian Relations* (Fall 1993); J. I. Matray, *The Reluctant Crusade: American Foreign Policy in Korea, 1941–1950* (Honolulu, HI, 1985).

Kim Jinwung

U.S-PHILIPPINES MUTUAL DEFENSE PACT (30 August 1951)

The U.S.-Philippines Mutual Defense Pact of 30 August 1951 was one of three interlocking security agreements accompanying the conclusion of the Japanese Peace Treaty*. Together with the U.S.-Japan Security Treaty of 1951* and ANZUS Treaty*, the pact with the Philippines* provided for defense of the principal U.S. allies in the Pacific area. Later in 1954, the United States completed its postwar security system in Asia with the U.S.–South Korea Mutual Security Treaty*, U.S.-China Mutual Defense Treaty of 1954*, and the Southeast Asia Treaty Organization*. The treaty with the Philippines also shaped the contours of relations between the two nations during the Cold War era. Its origins date from the efforts of John Foster Dulles* to bring the Pacific allies together into a U.S.-led alliance while negotiating the Japanese Peace Treaty. The Philippines already had granted the United States extensive rights to naval, air, and army bases in the archipelago in 1947. Although President Elpidio Quirino had supported the Pacific Pact idea, opinion in the government and the public at large focused more on obtaining Japanese reparations or American economic aid. Public opinion in Australia and New Zealand was hostile to the prospect of military cooperation with their former enemy, Japan. Dulles thus negotiated three separate agreements. Unlike the North Atlantic Treaty Organization, there was no requirement in the ANZUS Treaty or the pact with the Philippines for an immediate American military response. Congressional approval was required for use of U.S. forces in connection with both agreements. As long as the U.S. military remained stationed in the Philippines, however, the nation was secure from external attack.

The defense pact made the United States and the Philippines close partners in the Cold War through the 1980s. Clark Air Base and Subic Bay Naval Base outside Manila played a vital role in the Korean War* and the Second Indochina War*, as well as the protection of oil lanes to the Middle East. The United States trained, financed, and advised the military forces of the Philippines, especially during the presidency of Ramón Magsaysay*. Edward G. Lansdale*, for example, assisted the government in putting down the Hukbalahap* Rebellion. U.S. aid and war-related spending funneled precious dollars into the Philippines as the U.S. military presence in Southeast Asia grew in the 1960s. Owing in large part to rampant corruption and mismanagement under President Ferdinand E. Marcos*, to the Philippine economy stagnated despite U.S. aid. The important place of the Philippines in U.S. Cold War strategy, however, led to American tolerance of the authoritarian and corrupt Marcos government. U.S. support for Marcos and long-standing American ties with Philippine military forces, which increasingly were out of control during the presidency of Corazon Aquino*, undercut Filipino support for continued military partnership with the United States. Filipinos called for less dependence upon the Americans toward the end of the Cold War. Following the destruction of Clark Air Base after the eruption of Mt. Pinatubo and the Subic Bay Naval Base Controversy* in 1991, the U.S. agreed to close its bases in the Philippines.

H. W. Brands Jr., *Bound to Empire: The United States and the Philippines* (New York, 1992); N. Cullather, *Illusions of Influence: The Political Economy of United States-Philippines Relations, 1942–1960* (Stanford, CA, 1994); H. B. Schonberger, *Aftermath of War: Americans and the Remaking of Japan, 1945–1952* (Kent, OH, 1989).

Aaron Forsberg

U.S.-PRC NORMALIZATION OF RELATIONS

Normalization of relations between the United States and the People's Republic of China* (PRC) after two decades of almost no direct contacts was a process that took several years, culminating in establishment of formal diplomatic relations between the two nations on 1 January 1979. The process began during the presidency of Richard M. Nixon*. After Nixon took steps to ease restrictions on trade and travel to the China mainland, Beijing responded with its Ping-Pong Diplomacy* initiative in 1971. During Nixon's Visit to China* in February 1972, the Shanghai Communiqué* declared the interest of both nations in normalizing relations and laid out the framework for a modus vivendi on Taiwan*. In February 1973, Premier Zhou Enlai* and National Security Adviser Henry A. Kissinger* agreed on an exchange of liaison offices, headed by veteran diplomats David K. E. Bruce* and Huang Zhen. Taiwan remained the major obstacle to full normalization because the PRC claimed it as part of China, whereas the United States had defended the Republic of China* (ROC) since it fled to the island in 1949. In mid-1975, Vice Premier Deng Xiaoping* set three conditions for the United States to meet prior to establishing diplomatic relations: break diplomatic relations with Taibei, abrogate the U.S.-China Mutual Defense Treaty of 1954*, and withdraw all troops from Taiwan.

Progress toward U.S.-PRC normalization was stalled until President Jimmy Carter* became president in 1977. Over the next year, Soviet pressure in Afghanistan and elsewhere persuaded Carter that the time had come to improve relations with China to counterbalance the Soviets. He thus was playing the "China card" when he sent National Security Adviser Zbigniew Brzezinski to China in May 1978. Brzezinski told Chinese leaders that the United States had "made up its mind" to accept Deng's three points and wanted to proceed with normalization. After six months of intensive negotiations, largely conducted in Beijing and kept secret to avoid arousing domestic opposition in the United States, the two sides reached an agreement. On 15 December 1978, a U.S.-China joint communiqúe announced that the two nations would establish diplomatic relations on 1 January 1979. It said that the United States recognized the PRC as the sole legal government of China and that the people of the United States would maintain only cultural, commercial, and other unofficial relations with the people of Taiwan. Both sides reaffirmed the Shanghai Communiqúe, and the United States, going slightly beyond the specific language of that document, acknowledged the PRC's position that there was but one China and that Taiwan was part of it.

Along with the joint communiqúe, Washington and Beijing issued unilateral statements in December 1978. The United States announced that it would terminate diplomatic relations with Taiwan as of 1 January, end its mutual defense treaty after the one-year notification the treaty required, remove remaining military personnel from Taiwan within four months, and maintain commercial, cultural, trade, and other relations with Taiwan through nongovernmental means. It declared that the United States continued to have an interest in a peaceful resolution of the Taiwan issue and expressed the expectation that the Taiwan issue would be resolved peacefully. Carter said a few days later that U.S. sales of defensive arms to the ROC would continue for another year. The PRC statement declared China's opposition to continued U.S. arms sales to Taiwan and reiterated that reunification was entirely an internal affair. But the Chinese did not contradict the U.S. statement expressing the expectation of a peaceful resolution of the Taiwan issue. In January 1979, a month after conclusion of the agreement, Deng Xiaoping became the first PRC leader to visit the United States. On 1 March 1979, one day after the closing of the U.S. embassy in Taibei, Washington and Beijing established embassies. Leonard Woodcock*, head of the U.S. liaison office, became the first U.S. ambassador to China since 1949. *See also* Taiwan Relations Act.

Z. Brzezinski, *Power and Principle: Memoirs of the National Security Adviser, 1977–1981* (New York, 1983); J. Carter, *Keeping Faith: Memoirs of a President* (New York, 1982); J. Holdridge, *Crossing the Divide: An Insider's Account of the Normalization of U.S. China Relations* (Lanham, MD, 1997); M. Oksenberg, "A Decade of Sino-American Relations," *Foreign Affairs* (Fall 1982); P. Tyler, *A Great Wall: Six Presidents and China: An Investigative History* (New York, 1999).

Harriet Dashiell Schwar

U.S. RECRUITMENT OF FOREIGN TROOPS TO FIGHT IN VIETNAM

Soldiers from the Republic of Korea* (ROK), the Philippines*, Thailand*, Australia, and New Zealand fought in South Vietnam as part of an American effort to validate the Second Indochina War*. The United States began soliciting the service of foreign combat units late in 1964 when the political and military situation in the Republic of Vietnam* (RVN) began deteriorating, doing so without consulting the Saigon regime. The United States was preparing to send its own combat troops, but hoped to reduce the burden. Despite U.S. solicitation of these soldiers and underwriting their costs, there was little coordination between the various countries fighting in South Vietnam. Each country retained its own chain of command and fought under its own flag. Language barriers and American military ethnocentrism prevented the development of a unified allied theater command. General William C. Westmoreland*, commander of Military Assistance Command, Vietnam* (MACV), was more than content to use American dominance as leverage to coordinate allied operations.

Australia and New Zealand were the first countries to send troops to Vietnam. The two nations believed their national security required a policy of forward defense, keeping any nation directly threatening them as far from their borders as possible. In 1962, Australia sent thirty army instructors to South Vietnam, a commitment that eventually blossomed into a regiment of 7,600 men. New Zealand had reservations about the conflict in Vietnam and made only a token contribution to honor its ANZUS Treaty*. Never exceeding 600 men, New Zealand at first sent an engineering unit, which it later replaced with an artillery battery and two infantry rifle companies. By contrast, the ROK sent the largest contingent of troops to fight in Vietnam, second only to the United States. South Korea made its first offer in 1953 shortly after the Korean War* ended, but the United States consistently rejected ROK troops. After President Lyndon B. Johnson* directed U.S. diplomats to obtain humanitarian aid early in 1965, Washington quickly accepted an offer from President Pak Chŏng-hŭi* to commit an engineer unit. The RVN then asked the ROK to send an infantry division despite U.S. objections. But by spring, the Americans had changed their position after Johnson had sent the first U.S. combat units. Foreign assistance now was more than welcome, since it would reduce the number of U.S. soldiers needed to fight in Vietnam. At the first of the Johnson-Pak Conferences* in May 1965, South Korea's president agreed to deploy one division. A marine brigade and a second army division followed in September 1966. U.S. and ROK leaders were interested in sending a third division late in 1967, but new North Korean commando raids into the south prevented approval.

Like Australia, New Zealand, and the ROK, the Philippines initially sent service and support units to Vietnam when the United States requested third-country aid, but never any combat units. The United States entered into negotiations with the Filipino government in late 1964 about a larger military commitment. An agreement on what were essentially Filipino terms for U.S. payment of its troops was reached in March 1965, but the November election of Ferdinand E. Marcos* reduced chances for the troop deployment, since Marcos had opposed the plan during his campaign. Johnson sent several high-level diplomatic missions to Manila to persuade Marcos to reverse his stand. The new president agreed to send service and support units, but the resulting Philippine contingent totaled only 2,060 men. As opposition to the deployment grew, Marcos reduced and then removed the bulk of the men in 1968. Despite his reluctance to commit his armed forces, he offered the United States indirect support, proposing that the U.S. Army organize an all-Filipino combat unit that would serve in Vietnam. Washington rejected this idea because it reeked of using mercenary forces.

Of those nations sending troops to fight in Vietnam, Thailand was the closest in geographic proximity. At its peak in 1969 and 1970, the Thai contingent was just more than 11,500 men, or 14 percent of the Thai military. Thailand had supported the American effort in Vietnam for several years with bases for conventional air missions and covert operations. U.S. diplomats did not push the Thais to commit troops until 1967. Negotiations started after the Clark Clifford-Maxwell D. Taylor* mission visit to secure larger commitments of foreign troops. Bangkok agreed later that year to send one division, if the United States agreed to pay the costs of deploying the troops and provide the equipment. The Thais also wanted U.S. anti-aircraft missiles for use in Thailand and larger appropriations through the Military Assistance Program. Most of the third-country contingents left South Vietnam before the United States, but ROK soldiers actually remained until just after the completion of U.S. withdrawal in 1973.

R. M. Blackburn, *Mercenaries and Lyndon Johnson's "More Flags": The Hiring of Korean, Filipino, and Thai Soldiers in the Vietnam War* (Jefferson, NC, 1994).

Nicholas Evan Sarantakes

U.S.–SOUTH KOREA MUTUAL SECURITY TREATY (17 November 1954)

Current U.S. security arrangements with South Korea are based formally upon the 1954 mutual defense treaty between the Republic of Korea* (ROK) and the United States. The pact was signed in Washington on 1 October 1953, and entered into force upon exchange or ratification on 17 November 1954. The bilateral treaty was created in response to the strong demands of ROK President Syngman Rhee* for an American commitment to South Korea's security after the Korean War*. Rhee was uneasy about the uncertain cessation of Korean hostilities. Thus, at the last moment of the war, he threatened to disrupt the Korean Armistice Agreement* unless the United States made a formal commitment to guarantee the ROK's future security. Eager to end the war as quickly as possible, the Eisenhower administration agreed reluctantly to meet Rhee's demand. In return, Rhee promised not to undermine the armistice agreement.

The U.S.–South Korea Mutual Security Treaty combined with the U.S.-Japan Security Treaty of 1951*, ANZUS Treaty*, U.S.-Philippines Mutual Defense Pact*, U.S.-China Mutual Defense Treaty of 1954*, and the Southeast Asia Treaty Organization* to form the postwar U.S. security system in Asia. Consisting of six articles, the bilateral pact between the United States and South Korea affirmed that each signatory would regard an armed attack on the other in the

Pacific area as "dangerous to its own peace and safety and declares that it would act to meet the common danger in accordance with its constitutional processes." With this defense treaty, the United States assumed responsibility for defending the ROK's security. Backed by the continued presence of U.S. forces in South Korea and the stark reality of life along the demilitarized zone, the wisdom of the treaty was not questioned in the ROK and the United States at first. Its form was not threatened, for example, when President Jimmy Carter* publicly talked about withdrawing U.S. ground forces in 1977 and 1978. He soon reversed his stand and joined every other U.S. president in reaffirming the treaty.

During the 1990s, the reference to "mutual" gained increasing substance. According to the treaty, South Korea pledged to join with the United States if it were attacked anywhere in the "Pacific area." Significantly, the ROK was the most supportive in responding to U.S. Recruitment of Foreign Troops to Fight in Vietnam*, a product of South Korea's intense hostility to Communism* and its desire to repay the debt of outside assistance during the Korean War. But with the size and strength of the military forces that the ROK developed thereafter, the treaty's language clearly meant more than it did when the pact was written. Many South Koreans criticized the treaty because it provided the legal foundation for U.S. bases and the stationing of its forces in the ROK. Leftist intellectuals, students, and academics attributed the failure to achieve Korea's reunification in the 1990s to the presence of 37,000 U.S. troops. Thus, the treaty also contributed to South Korean Anti-Americanism*. *See also* U.S.–South Korea Status of Forces Agreement.

Headquarters, U.S. Forces in Korea, *The United States of America and the Republic of Korea, Status of Forces Agreement with Related Documents* (Washington, DC, 1967); B. I. Kaufman, *The Korean War: Challenges in Crises, Credibility, and Command* (Philadelphia, 1986).

Kim Jinwung

U.S.–SOUTH KOREA STATUS OF FORCES AGREEMENT (9 July 1966)

Many South Koreans have regarded this controversial document, which outlines terms for treatment of U.S. servicemen in South Korea, as a typical symbol of unfairness in relations with the United States. It has become a rallying point for South Korean Anti-Americanism*. Since the signing of the U.S.–South Korea Status of Forces Agreement (SOFA) on 9 July 1966, the Republic of Korea* (ROK) as a sovereign nation has had control "with respect to such matters as facilities used by U.S. forces, entry and exit of U.S. personnel, custom/taxation, criminal jurisdiction, claims payments by the United States, [and U.S.] employment of Korean citizens." In particular, under Article 22, the ROK could have exclusive "jurisdiction over members of the United States armed forces or civilian component, and their dependents, with respect to [criminal] offenses, except during hostilities and martial law." This seemingly fair agreement, however, restricted South Korea's exercise of criminal jurisdiction because of the escape clauses. Of particular importance, it stipulated that the United States "shall have jurisdiction" unless the Korean side "determines in a specific case that it is of particular importance that jurisdiction be exercised therein" by the ROK.

U.S. military authorities emphasized that the SOFA with South Korea was basically the same as similar agreements the United States has had with Japan, the Philippines*, and all North Atlantic Treaty Organization (NATO) countries. But South Korean critics countered that the agreement with the ROK had far less favorable standards than those with Japan and NATO nations in terms of fairness. In particular, they asserted that their country should exercise "full" criminal jurisdiction over American servicemen and their dependents. To meet these criticisms, South Korea and the United States agreed in December 1990 to eliminate the so-called automatic renunciation clauses, permitting the ROK's full jurisdiction over crimes committed by off-duty U.S. servicemen and their dependents. In cases of crimes committed by on-duty U.S. servicemen over which U.S. military authorities had had jurisdiction, South Korea only could file a protest against the "on-duty certificate" of the offender. In addition, the ROK could restore the facilities and lands that U.S. forces in Korea had not used, and both countries agreed that the United States would return nine air base sites to South Korea.

Despite the 1990 revision, the ROK government still viewed the SOFA as not providing sufficient fairness. The South Koreans continued to call for amendment of some clauses that stipulated preferential treatment of U.S. servicemen. The attention focused on the ROK's right to take custody of U.S. troops charged with crimes against Koreans at the time of indictment, instead of at the time of conviction. Seoul also sought to revise the agreement to allow the ROK government to inspect U.S. military facilities for environmental contamination and order U.S. forces to decontaminate all polluted soil before the United States returned the property to South Korea. On 28 December 2000, the ROK and the United States initialed a new SOFA that provided greater criminal jurisdiction over accused U.S. soldiers to Korean authorities with a speedier transfer of the accused from "upon completion of all judicial proceedings" to "at the time of indictment." Also, Washington and Seoul agreed that twelve crimes, among them murder, rape, and drug trafficking, would be affected by the new accord. There also was agreement to include a provision on environmental protection in the Agreed Minutes, an appendix of the SOFA, saying that the U.S. military would respect South Korean environmental laws and regulations. Despite some criticisms, most South Koreans welcomed the revised SOFA as a more equitable agreement.

Headquarters, U.S. Forces in Korea, *The United States of America and the Republic of Korea, Status of Forces Agreement with Related Documents* (Washington, DC, 1967); J. Kim "From Patron-Client to Partners: The Changing South Korean–American Relationship," *The Journal of American–East Asian Relations* (Fall 1993); Kim Jinwung, *Han'gukin ŭi Panmi Kamjŏng* [The Anti-Americanism of the Korean People] (Seoul, 1992); U.S. Embassy, Seoul, "United States, Korea Complete Status of Forces Agreement Negotiations," 29 December 2000.

Kim Jinwung

USHIBA NOBUHIKO (1909–1984)

Ushiba Nobuhiko built his postwar career as a successful negotiator for Japan. He participated in many difficult treaty negotiations, including the talks leading to Japan-Korea Normalization* of relations in 1965 and was Japan's ambassador to the United States from 1969 to 1973 during one of the worst periods in American-Japanese relations. After Ushiba graduated from the Law Department at Tōkyō Imperial University, he entered the Foreign Ministry in 1932. He was one of the young radicals who identified with the right-wing views of the Renovationist faction of the Foreign Ministry. His first overseas assignment was in the Japanese embassy in Germany from 1933 to 1937, and he returned to Germany in 1941 to work there until November 1943. In 1946, Ushiba resigned from the Foreign Ministry and spent the next two years working as defense counsel for indicted war criminals during the Tōkyō War Crimes Trials*. In 1949, he began working for the Foreign Exchange Control Board set up by the Supreme Commander for the Allied Powers (SCAP*). In 1951, Ushiba became the director-general for the International Trade Bureau of the Ministry of International Trade and Industry*. During his three years there, he participated in various trade negotiations with Western nations, including the Sterling Payments Agreement*.

In 1954, Ushiba returned to the Foreign Ministry and his career as a negotiator blossomed. Between 1954 and 1960, he was involved in reparations talks with Burma* (1954) and negotiations for commercial treaties with Australia (1957) and India (1958). He also was involved in the Tōkyō Round* of the General Agreements on Tariffs and Trade* in 1959. Ushiba was Japan's ambassador to Canada between 1961 and 1964. He was promoted to the post of deputy minister for foreign affairs on his return and then became involved in the final round of talks toward normalization of relations with the Republic of Korea*. In 1967, Ushiba was promoted to vice minister for foreign affairs and was involved in the initial talks over the U.S. return of the Bonin Islands* and, during the presidency of Richard M. Nixon*, resolution of the Okinawa Controversy*. He was Japan's ambassador to the United States from 1969 and 1973, which was one of the most difficult periods of Japanese-American relations, coinciding with the textiles wrangle and the Nixon Shocks*. He traveled widely in the United States, giving lecture tours to improve grassroots relations, between the two nations. On his return to Japan, Ushiba was involved in preparatory meetings for the first G-7 summit. In 1977, he was named minister for external economic relations under Fukuda Takeo*, where he dealt with Japan's trade surplus and growing friction in U.S.-Japan Postwar Trade Relations*. He resigned from the post the next year, but continued to work toward betterment of U.S.-Japan economic relations.

W. LaFeber, *The Clash: A History of U.S.-Japan Relations* (New York, 1997); M. Schaller, *Altered States: The United States and Japan Since the Occupation* (New York, 1997); Ushiba Nobuhiko, *Gaikō no shunkan: Watakushi no rirekishō* [A Moment in Diplomacy: A Memoir] (Tōkyō, 1984); Ushiba Nobuhiko, *Keizai gaikō e no shōgen* [A Testimony to Economic Diplomacy] (Tōkyō, 1984); Ushiba Nobuhiko, *Nihon gaikōshi jiten* [A Historical Dictionary of Japanese Diplomacy] (Tōkyō, 1992).

Yokoi Noriko

V

VANG PAO (1931–)

A member of the highland Hmong* tribal minority of Laos*, Vang Pao rose from modest beginnings to become the leader of an army supported by the Central Intelligence Agency* (CIA) that fought North Vietnam and the Pathet Lao* for control of northern Laos. Although he became a general in the Royal Lao Army, he remained at heart a resourceful and charismatic guerrilla fighter and clan leader. Born to a peasant family near the border with North Vietnam, Vang Pao was ambitious and capable. He joined the national police in France's colonial administration and earned a reputation as a skillful and ruthless opponent of the Vietminh*. Rising to become a police officer, Vang Pao transferred to the army and in 1953, joined an antiguerrilla program organized by French intelligence in Indochina. France's defeat at Dien Bien Phu* in 1954 relegated Vang Pao to garrison duty, but in late 1960 he came to the CIA's attention. With Laos fighting against a Communist insurgency supported by the Democratic Republic of Vietnam*, the CIA approved a proposal to support 1,000 Hmong guerrillas under Vang Pao. The CIA airlifted these men and their families from eastern Xieng Khouang to the mountains south of the Plain of Jars. Vang Pao's covert army received the CIA's support for the next fourteen years.

During the 1960s, Vang Pao harassed and often defeated the North Vietnamese and Pathet Lao by organizing his 10,000 fighters into Special Guerrilla Units. Without formal military training, he fought intuitively, appreciating the value of technology while maintaining his aura as tribal leader. The Hmong relied on his leadership and fought tenaciously for him. Vang Pao could call on massive U.S. air support, had his own small air force, and had the support of Thai artillery and eventually Thai volunteers. The United States came to rely almost exclusively on Vang Pao's army to contest the North Vietnamese on the ground in northern Laos. With the rainy season, his troops were airlifted into areas under North Vietnamese control, usually forcing them to retreat. In 1968, Vang Pao visited Washington and met with CIA Director Richard Helms. Between 1969 and 1972, the Hmong fought a series of seesaw battles for control of the Plain of Jars. In March 1970, the North Vietnamese almost forced Vang Pao's army from its headquarters at Long Tieng. With massive U.S. air support, including B-52 strikes and Thai reinforcements, he halted the attack and even regained ground. In the 1971 dry season and again in 1972, Vang Pao's forces again were saved by massive U.S. air support, including all-weather jets.

Vang Pao was number one on the Pathet Lao's and North Vietnam's enemy list in Laos. With the Paris Peace Accords* in 1973 and the subsequent cease-fire in Laos, he was deprived of U.S. air support except on a few emergency occasions. Eventually, North Vietnamese forces surrounded Vang Pao at his redoubt at Long Tieng, and his CIA adviser flew one last mission to rescue him and his extended family, airlifting them to Thailand*. He ultimately resettled with many Hmong followers in the United States. Vang Pao's enemies accused him of being a warlord and a drug processor. The Hmong traditional cash crop was opium-producing poppies, and he was both a military commander and clan leader who controlled his region for many years. These charges, however, are exaggerated. *See also* Golden Triangle; Secret U.S. Air War in Laos.

T. N. Castle, *At War in the Shadow of Vietnam: U.S. Military Aid to the Royal Lao Government, 1955–1975* (New York, 1993); A. W. McCoy, *Politics of Heroin in Southeast Asia* (New York, 1972); J. Hamilton-Merritt, *Tragic Mountains: The Hmong, the Americans, and the Wars for Laos, 1942–1992* (Bloomington, IN, 1993); R. Warner, *Back Fire: Secret War in Laos and Its Link to the War in Vietnam* (New York, 1995).

Edward C. Keefer

VERSAILLES PEACE TREATY (28 June 1919)

The Treaty of Versailles signed in June 1919 between the Allied powers and Germany at the conclusion of the Paris Peace Conference after World War I failed to resolve the major controversies that arose in East Asia during the war. The thorniest issue was the Shandong question. At the conference, the Japanese delegation was determined to retain all German rights and concessions in Shandong Province in China, including the leasehold at the port of Qingdao, whereas the Chinese delegation demanded direct restoration to China. President Woodrow Wilson*, as the leading advocate of self-determination, supported China's claim in an effort to check Japan's imperialist aspirations on the Asian continent. However, he could not prevail over Japan for two reasons. First, Japan already had signed secret agreements with Britain, France, and Russia that supported Japanese territorial claims at Paris. Second, Tōkyō threatened not to sign the treaty should its claim to Shandong be denied. In the end, Japan secured the rights in the Shandong Agreement* and China refused to sign the treaty. Under the Mandate System*, Japan also gained control under the League of Nations of Germany's islands in the Pacific north of the equator, which included the Carolines, Marshalls, and Marianas.

The Treaty of Versailles had far-reaching consequences in U.S. relations with both Japan and China. Although Japan saved face by securing former German rights and concessions in Shandong, the experience at the Paris Peace Conference aroused nationalist and anti-Western sentiments among Japanese leaders and escalated Japan's rivalry with the United States in the Pacific. This was because not only did the Wilson administration oppose Japan's expansionist aspirations on the Asian continent, but the Western nations refused to accept Japan's proposal to insert a clause upholding the principle of racial equality into the League of Nations Covenant. In China, many who were encouraged by the Wilsonian ideal of self-determination and counted on support from the United States for full restoration of Shandong felt betrayed by Wilson and the Western powers. A mass student demonstration against the Versailles Treaty held in Beijing's Tiananmen Square triggered a nationwide movement known as the May Fourth Movement*. In the United States, Senate Republicans, both the reservationists led by Henry Cabot Lodge* and the Irreconcilables, pointed to Wilson's compromise on the Shandong question as a major reason to oppose the treaty. The

United States never joined the League of Nations and eventually signed a separate peace with Germany in 1921. *See also* March First Movement; Washington Conference.

L. E. Ambrosius, *Woodrow Wilson and the American Diplomatic Tradition: The Treaty Fight in Perspective* (Lincoln, NE, 1987); R. W. Curry, *Woodrow Wilson and the Far Eastern Policy, 1913–1921* (New York, 1957); R. H. Fifield, *Woodrow Wilson and the Far East: The Diplomacy of the Shantung Question* (New York, 1952); N. Kawamura, "Wilsonian Idealism and Japanese Claims at the Paris Peace Conference," *Pacific Historical Review* (November 1997).

Kawamura Noriko

VIET CONG

This term for the South Vietnamese component of the Communist forces in the Second Indochina War* is politically contested. The National Liberation Front* (NLF) claimed it was a coalition that included but was not dominated by Communists. The government against which the NLF was rebelling preferred to call the guerrillas Viet Cong, an abbreviation of Viet Nam Cong San, meaning Vietnamese Communist. In fact, although many of the members of the NLF were not Communists, the organization had been created by and was always controlled by the Vietnamese Communist Party. After the Geneva Accords of 1954*, which ended the First Indochina War* and split Vietnam at the seventeenth parallel, the new government of Ngo Dinh Diem* in the south, the Republic of Vietnam* (RVN), refused to permit elections to achieve reunification scheduled for 1956. Until 1959, the RVN hunted down and destroyed most of the Communist organizations in South Vietnam without much opposition, because the leaders of the Lao Dong Party (Workers' Party, the name used by the Vietnamese Communist Party from 1951 to 1976) in Hanoi ordered their followers in the south to rely primarily on peaceful political struggle against the Diem regime.

By May 1959, the Lao Dong Party finally decided to authorize a guerrilla war in the south, and fighting broke out on a significant scale early in 1960. For the first four years, Viet Cong guerrillas were essentially all southerners. Most never had been outside South Vietnam, but the minority who had gone to the Democratic Republic of Vietnam* in the north under the Geneva Accords and came back to the south along the Ho Chi Minh Trail* beginning in 1959 tended to be more highly trained and occupied many of the top posts. In these years, Viet Cong were South Vietnamese guerrillas, whereas the Army of the Republic of Vietnam* (ARVN) contained a large proportion of North Vietnamese at all levels from top to bottom. The United States provided the ARVN with armored personnel carriers and both fixed-wing bombers and helicopter gunships after 1962. The amount of heavy weaponry coming from North Vietnam to the Viet Cong was tiny by comparison. The ARVN could use its substantial firepower advantage, however, only when it could find the elusive guerrillas. Many areas that government forces held during the day, the Viet Cong controlled at night.

The Viet Cong had several advantages. One was considerable popular support; countless peasants disliked the RVN because so many of its officials were corrupt, had supported the French, or allied with landlords. Rents were lower or abolished totally in areas where the Viet Cong were powerful. Another advantage of the Viet Cong was that it was a more unified force, better able to count on the loyalty of its officers. Divisions within the leadership of the RVN reached their greatest extreme in the events leading to Diem's Assassination* in 1963. In 1963 and 1964, the Viet Cong formed larger units, better armed with machine guns, mortars, and recoilless rifles. By 1964, it was unmistakably winning the war. Aside from increasing weapons shipments to the south, the Lao Dong Party leadership in Hanoi now began to send significant numbers of North Vietnamese regular forces to join the fighting.

From this point onward, Communist armed forces in South Vietnam included both the predominantly South Vietnamese units of the Viet Cong (formally the People's Liberation Armed Forces) and the predominantly North Vietnamese units of the People's Army of Vietnam (PAVN), called the North Vietnamese Army by the Americans. Both forces were under the same command, with southerners in PAVN units, and some northerners assigned to Viet Cong units beginning in 1964. The Viet Cong Infrastructure, as the Americans called it, also played a key role in the Communist war effort. A wide variety of people fulfilled political and administrative tasks in areas under Communist influence or outright rule in South Vietnam, such as political organizers, tax collectors, local administrative personnel, and heavily armed police units.

From 1965 to 1968, the majority of the Communist forces in the south were Viet Cong. The PAVN tended to be larger and better-armed units deployed in northern South Vietnam, and in the hills far from the coast. The Viet Cong operated more in small guerrilla units, and in the coastal and southern areas having the largest population. The Tet Offensive* in early 1968 seriously weakened, but did not destroy, the Viet Cong. The PAVN assumed the biggest burden of combat, but the Viet Cong remained a significant participant in the war effort until victory in 1975.

J. Race, *War Comes to Long An: Revolutionary Conflict in a Vietnamese Province* (Berkeley, CA, 1972); C. A. Thayer, *War by Other Means* (Sydney, 1989); W. S. Turley, *The Second Indochina War: A Short Political and Military History, 1954–1975* (Boulder, CO, 1986).

Edwin E. Moise

VIETMINH

The Vietminh—full name Viet Nam Doc Lap Dong Minh, meaning League for the Independence of Vietnam—was a nationalist organization under Communist leadership. It conducted small-scale resistance against Japanese and French rule in Vietnam during World War II, and then led a large-scale war of independence against France from 1946 to 1954. Ho Chi Minh* and other top leaders of the Indochinese Communist Party made the decision to establish the Vietminh at a meeting in May 1941 at Pac Bo in extreme northern Vietnam. Thereafter, the Vietminh created a political network stretching through most of Vietnam, and a small military force that at first was limited to extreme northern Vietnam. In World War II, the Vietminh was eager to establish friendly relations with the United States, providing intelligence about the Japanese in French Indochina* and rescuing downed U.S. pilots. Toward the end of the war, the U.S. Office of Strategic Services through the Deer Mission* provided the Vietminh with a modest quantity of arms and some instruction in how to use them.

In 1945, when Japan surrendered, Ho proclaimed the Democratic Republic of Vietnam* an independent nation. In the opening paragraph of his declaration of independence, he quoted from the American Declaration of Independence; he was doing everything he could think of to strengthen his relations with the United States, to give him some leverage in the struggle he was anticipating to prevent the return of French Colonialism*. His efforts were in vain. Once the war against Japan was over, the United States saw no reason to support him, and his letters to President Harry S. Truman* simply went unanswered. Worse, the French were returning before the end of September 1945. Fighting between French and Vietminh forces broke out in some areas almost immediately, developing into the full-scale First Indochina War* after December 1946. A stalemate soon resulted; the French had much better weapons and soldiers, and could take any chosen target, but did not have the manpower to control the whole country. The

Vietminh had much more popular support, so they were able to retain control of large areas despite their inferiority in combat forces. The United States, looking at a struggle in which one side was under Communist leadership and the other was a colonial power trying to impose its rule against the wishes of most of the people, refused at first to support either side. But as concern over Communism* increased, the United States committed itself to supporting Bao Dai* and the French in 1950. *See also* Pham Van Dong, Vo Nguyen Biap.

B. B. Fall, *Street Without Joy: Indochina at War, 1946–54* (Harrisburg, PA, 1964); G. Lockhart, *Nation in Arms: The Origins of the People's Army of Vietnam* (Sydney, 1989).

Edwin E. Moise

VIETNAM

See DEMOCRATIC REPUBLIC OF VIETNAM; REPUBLIC OF VIETNAM; SOCIALIST REPUBLIC OF VIETNAM

VIETNAMIZATION

At its height, the United States employed roughly 60 percent of its total infantry and about half of its strategic bomber capacity in prosecuting the Second Indochina War*. In the aftermath of the Tet Offensive* of 1968, President Lyndon B. Johnson* decided upon a policy of "de-Americanizing" the war in Vietnam to limit the exposure of U.S. forces to casualties and reduce the costs of maintaining 540,000 troops there. After Richard M. Nixon* became president in 1969, this policy accelerated and Secretary of Defense Melvin Laird renamed it Vietnamization. At a conference on Midway Island in May 1969, Nixon told President Nguyen Van Thieu* of the Republic of Vietnam* that U.S. troops no longer would undertake the bulk of fighting in Vietnam and that withdrawals would follow. Nixon then traveled to Guam*, where he issued the Nixon Doctrine*, which proclaimed that future U.S. interventions would be limited because the nation directly threatened would have to assume the military posture necessary for its defense.

Some of the objectives underlying Vietnamization eventually were realized. U.S. troop casualties fell rapidly; within a year, the rate of 300 per week was reduced to 100 per week. In addition, the Army of the Republic of Vietnam* (ARVN) greatly expanded to well over a million men. However, Vietnamization ultimately failed for several reasons. The gradual withdrawal of U.S. forces, begun in earnest during 1969, had a deleterious impact on the fighting morale of the remaining American troops and the ARVN. The ARVN performed miserably in major engagements, such as the temporary Cambodia Incursion* in 1970, and had its worst showing in a 1971 invasion of Laos* known as Lam Son 719, in which it was forced to abandon its equipment and retreat in disgrace. The ARVN morale remained low, and many of the better-educated men from the cities found numerous ways to avoid serving in the military, which was regarded as corrupt, faction-ridden, and propped up solely by U.S. support. Further, the South Vietnamese people never had been wedded to the repressive Thieu regime and thus lacked a strong commitment to defend their nation that their counterparts in the north and in the Viet Cong* possessed. Also, the ARVN officers, especially senior soldiers trained under the French, simply could not carry on the complex logistical method of fighting in which they had been trained by the Americans. In addition, Congress became increasingly restrictive on the ability of the president to resupply the South Vietnamese or to offer them air cover. A changed political and economic climate during the 1970s in essence meant that South Vietnam was on its own, without a source of supply, while its enemy continued to receive massive amounts of aid.

During the Easter Offensive* of 1972, the North Vietnamese badly mauled the

ARVN and routed it from the northern provinces of South Vietnam. Extensive American LINEBACKER Bombings* of North Vietnamese positions salvaged the situation for South Vietnam, but no such support was available after the Paris Peace Accords* were signed in January 1973. Moreover, this agreement allowed hundreds of thousands of North Vietnamese forces to remain in place inside the territory of South Vietnam. While scattered ARVN units fought bravely against the onrushing final offensive launched by the North Vietnamese in 1975, most units simply fell apart in the face of the ultimate challenge. The fall of Saigon at the end of April only clarified to the world what had been apparent to observers for several years. Vietnamization had been a mere smokescreen for U.S. withdrawal from Vietnam, a near ruse that allowed the United States to maintain a semblance of credibility while providing South Vietnam with, at best, an extremely tenuous chance at survival.

A. Isaacs, *Without Honor: Defeat in Vietnam and Cambodia* (Baltimore, MD, 1983); G. Kolko, *Anatomy of a War: Vietnam, the United States, and the Modern Historical Experience* (New York, 1985); R. D. Schulzinger, *A Time for War: The United States and Vietnam, 1941–1975* (New York, 1997); F. Snepp, *A Decent Interval: An Insider's Account of Saigon's Indecent End* (New York, 1977).

Kent G. Sieg

VINCENT, JOHN CARTER (1900–1972)

A career U.S. Foreign Service officer, John Carter Vincent advised a policy of limited economic and military support for Jiang Jieshi* and his Guomindang* (GMD) government that made him the target of attacks from anti-Communists in the Cold War era. Born in Seneca, Kansas, he moved with his family to Macon, Georgia, in 1906 after his mother died. Raised by his stepmother, a devout Southern Baptist, Vincent considered becoming a missionary, but after his graduation from Mercer University, joined the U.S. Consular Service in 1924. His first posting was at Changsha, Hunan Province, China, a center of anti-Christian and antiforeign nationalism in the 1920s during the Warlord Era*. As he witnessed China's political chaos, he studied its history, politics, geography, commerce, and language while in Changsha, Hankou, Beijing, Tsinan, and Manchuria from 1925 to 1936. In 1936, Vincent was transferred to Washington, where he served on the China desk of the State Department's Far Eastern Division. He urged his superiors to resist continued Japanese expansion in China by imposing economic and diplomatic sanctions on Japan and extending limited aid to the Guomindang government, especially after the Marco Polo Bridge Incident* ignited the Sino-Japanese War in July 1937. Vincent returned to China in 1941 to help coordinate U.S. military and diplomatic efforts to aid China at Chongqing.

After U.S. entry into World War II, Vincent voiced concern in his dispatches to Washington about the GMD's reactionary and coercive nature, urging that the U.S. government press the Republic of China* to enact democratic reforms. At the time, his China expertise was respected, resulting in his transfer to Washington in 1944 to work at the Office of Far Eastern Affairs. As he oversaw office operations, he became increasingly wary of reports that presidential emissary Patrick J. Hurley* sent from China that the GMD and the Chinese Communist Party* (CCP) were cooperating and moving toward a coalition government. Contradictory information from Foreign Service Officers (FSOs) John S. Service* and John Paton Davies*, combined with his own understanding of the profound differences between these rival Chinese parties, provoked his skepticism. When in November 1945 Hurley resigned as ambassador to China and returned to Washington, he charged that FSOs who favored aid to the CCP had undermined U.S. policy. Vincent never recommended such aid, but continued to counsel caution in sending U.S. aid and troops to help Jiang after Japan surrendered. He did not think this would advance the U.S. goal of promoting the emergence of a liberal Chinese government. When George C. Marshall* became secretary of state in 1947, after the failure of the Marshall Mission*, Vincent served as his chief adviser on China, struggling with increasingly hostile anti-Communist policy makers, as he argued against U.S. military action to prevent the fall of Jiang's government.

Increasingly, anti-Communists, including the influential China Lobby*, accused Vincent and other China Hands* of promoting a Communist agenda. In 1947, this adversely affected his promotion to a ministerial post. Although the State Department supported his nomination, it fought a bitter struggle with Republicans on the Senate Foreign Relations Committee, who reluctantly approved Vincent's appointment as U.S. minister to Switzerland (1947–1951). Allegations of Communist subversion and disloyalty to the U.S. government continued to haunt Vincent during his appointment there and as U.S. minister to Tangiers from 1951 to 1953. Accusations that Vincent was among the cadre of State Department officers who were responsible for the "loss" of China to Communism* when the CCP triumphed in the Chinese Civil War* in 1949 led to Vincent's questioning in a Senate Internal Security Subcommittee (SISS) inquiry in 1952. After the SISS investigation, he was called before a State Department Loyalty Security Board, which cleared him of any wrongdoing. A subsequent hearing before the Civil Service Loyalty Board, however, found "reasonable doubt" about his allegiance to the United States. Rather than face dismissal, Vincent retired from the State Department in 1953. He moved to Cambridge and associated informally with the Harvard East Asian Research Center until his death.

J. P. Davies Jr., *Dragon by the Tail: American, British, Japanese, and Russian Encounters with China and One Another* (New York, 1972); R. Y. Koen, *The China Lobby in American Politics* (New York, 1974); G. May, *China Scapegoat: The Diplomatic Ordeal of John Carter Vincent* (Prospect Heights, IL, 1979); *New York Times*, 12 December 1972.

Karen Garner

VO NGUYEN GIAP (1911–)

Vo Nguyen Giap remains a senior general in the People's Army of Vietnam (PAVN), and led the Vietnamese to victory over the French in the First Indochina War*. Born to a scholar gentry family in north central Vietnam, he was active in radical student anticolonial politics in the 1920s and in 1930, joined the Vietnamese Communist Party. Arrested by French colonial authorities and imprisoned from 1930 to 1932, he then earned a law degree from the University of Hanoi and became a secondary-school history teacher in Hanoi. During the Popular Front period in the late 1930s, his attention shifted to military matters and he authored an important tract that introduced Maoist military thought into Vietnamese anticolonial discourse for the first time. In World War II, he worked with Ho Chi Minh* to develop a series of revolutionary base areas and local militias in northern Vietnam that were intended as staging grounds for a military campaign to end French Colonialism*. Later in the war, he worked closely with U.S. military and intelligence operatives who, as part of the Deer Mission*, were posted in French Indochina* during 1945 to oversee the Japanese surrender. At the Vietnamese independence day celebration on 2 September 1945, Giap joined Ho Chi Minh in calling for closer relations with the United States.

During the war against the French, Giap led the Vietnamese military effort. After the People's Republic of China* (PRC) recognized the Democratic Republic of Vietnam* (DRV) in 1950, he received strong military support from China, including advisers, technical assistance, and weapons.

His relations with the Chinese, however, were far from harmonious. Giap would culminate a series of increasingly successful campaigns against the French with a decisive victory at the battle of Dien Bien Phu* in 1954, which brought an end to the French war. He played a central role in developing Vietnamese military strategy during the Second Indochina War* against the United States, particularly in the Battle of the Ia Drang Valley* (1965), at Khe Sanh* (1968), and during the Easter Offensive* (1972). But he was often at odds with his colleagues over tactics and strategy. In the planning and execution of the Tet Offensive* early in 1968, to which he was opposed, General Nguyen Chi Thanh, whose more aggressive tactics were favored by a majority of the Communist leadership, eventually superceded him. Following the Easter Offensive, he remained minister of defense, but was relieved of his direct command of the Vietnamese army. In the aftermath of the Vietnam War, he has played a largely ceremonial role in the Socialist Republic of Vietnam*, serving as a vocal proponent of closer relations with the United States.

M. P. Bradley, *Imagining Vietnam and America: The Making of Post Colonial Vietnam, 1919–1950* (Chapel Hill, NC, 2000); C. B. Currey, *Victory at Any Cost: The Genius of Viet Nam's Gen. Vo Nguyen Giap* (Washington, DC, 1997); G. Lockhart, *Nation in Arms: The Origins of the People's Army of Vietnam* (Boston, 1989); Vo Nguyen Giap, *Con Duong Chinh: Van De Dan Toc Giai Phong o Dong Duong* [The Proper Path: The Question of National Liberation in Indochina] (Hanoi, 1939); Vo Nguyen Giap, *Unforgettable Days* (Hanoi, 1978).

Mark P. Bradley

W

WANG JINGWEI (1883–1944)

Best known as China's leading collaborator with the Japanese during World War II, Wang Jingwei was an ardent Chinese nationalist from his youth until his death as a Japanese puppet. Typical of many revolutionaries of the late Qing era, he studied law in Japan on a provincial scholarship. As a frustrated young rebel, Wang tried to assassinate the Manchu regent in the spring of 1910, for which he was sentenced to life imprisonment. Released in 1911, he served as intermediary between Yuan Shikai* and Sun Zhongshan* in the Chinese Revolution of 1911*. During the years after the May Fourth Movement* of 1919, Sun asked Hu Hanmin and Wang Jingwei, his two longtime supporters, to draft new principles for reform of the Guomindang* (GMD) Party. Wang shared Sun's commitment to political and social reform, as well as his Soviet initiative and preference after 1915 for cooperation with Japan, rather than the West for national development. Sun died of cancer in 1925, leaving a will with a brief, patriotic, and pro-Soviet message widely believed to have been drafted by Wang.

With the GMD gaining power after the Northern Expedition of 1926–1927, the left wing of the party under Wang, in alliance with the Chinese Communist Party* (CCP), advocated democratic policy alternatives to balance the rightist influences of Jiang Jieshi*, the Shanghai bankers, and the Western Hills faction. The Sun Zhongshan legacy, Wang believed, included greater democracy, land reform, and promotion of mass organizations. Jiang favored a hierarchy of the army, the government, and the party, prevailing over Wang, who remained the second most powerful GMD leader. After the Xian Incident* in 1936, Jiang was forced to enter into a United Front* with the CCP against Japan. As the war escalated after the Marco Polo Bridge Incident* in 1937, Japanese savagery in the Rape of Nanjing* and Jiang's "scorched earth" policy appalled many Chinese nationalists. Wang and others saw resistance as leading to national suicide and the spread of Communism*, whereas negotiations might secure a respectable Sino-Japanese accord. Monitoring these views, Japan expected a powerful Chinese warlord to rise on Wang's behalf if it publicly committed itself to troop withdrawal from China over two years. The plan required Wang, who was not involved directly in planning the conspiracy, to retire to French Indochina*, where he would issue a statement responding to Japan's "announcement" of liberal terms.

In 1938, Wang publicly called for a negotiated settlement after the fall of his native Guangzhou and the burning of Changsha by retreating GMD upset him deeply. Jiang did the same through secret channels to Tōkyō, but then, in response to public criticism, adopted a policy of national resistance. Japan now implemented a divisive policy of offering false concessions. In December 1938, Wang defected from Jiang's government, not as a traitor, but as a patriot and independent "third force" seeking an honorable end to the war. After Japan promised withdrawal and Chinese autonomy, he lent his name to "the peace conspiracy" that failed to halt the escalating conflict. In 1939, Wang survived a GMD assassination attempt, ending the peace movement and beginning his full collaboration with the Japanese. In June 1939, he traveled to Japan and gained some minor concessions, such as use of the GMD flag and a revised Three Principles of the People as his regime's official program. Late in 1940, the Treaty of Nanjing established formal relations between Japan and the Restored Government of China. As leader of a new China, Wang failed to rally much support. His Nanjing government remained a docile puppet that symbolized Japan's exploitation of China. Wang died in Japan of natural causes before his regime collapsed, avoiding later war crimes trials that destroyed his politically active wife and associates.

J. Boyle, *China and Japan at War, 1937–1945: The Politics of Collaboration* (Stanford, CA, 1972); G. Bunker, *The Peace Conspiracy: Wang Ching-wei and the China War, 1937–1941* (Cambridge, MA, 1972); H. Ch'i, *Nationalist China at War, 1937–1945* (Ann Arbor, MI, 1992); J. Hsiung and S. Levine (eds.), *China's Bitter Victory* (Armonk, NY, 1992).

Errol M. Clauss

WAR PLAN ORANGE

ORANGE was the U.S. plan for war with Japan from 1924 until the Pearl Harbor Attack* on 7 December 1941. From 1903 through 1913, the U.S. Army and U.S. Navy had developed a series of plans for possible conflicts with numerous countries. Even as late as the 1930s, these exercises were purely military ones, developed in isolation by the War Plans Divisions of the army and navy staffs, with occasional help from the War Colleges. During the interwar period, the U.S. Army and U.S. Navy, hobbled first by national pacifism and then the Great Depression, devised these plans—called "color plans"—as much for professional growth and budgetary justification as realistic preparations for conflict. The United States was unlikely to go to war against Britain (Plan RED), its World War I ally, or Mexico (Plan GREEN), the only Latin American nation of any size with which it had been in conflict. But the plan for war against Japan, code-named ORANGE, was taken very seriously, especially by the U.S. Navy.

By 1922, the strategic picture facing the United States in the Pacific was fairly clear. As a result of the Washington Conference*, the U.S. Navy under the Five Power Pact* had achieved a five-to-three advantage in battleships over Japan, but only after agreeing not to fortify its Pacific outposts. The U.S. advantage in ships was diluted by the need to have a fleet in both the Atlantic and the Pacific. The Japanese position was further strengthened in 1919 by the Mandate System* that gave Japan control over the Marshall and Caroline islands. Military bases there—illegal under the mandate, but difficult to prevent—gave Japan a significant blocking position between Hawaii and the Philippines*. This meant that any U.S. garrison in the Philippines was vulnerable to massed Japanese naval, air, and ground forces stationed in nearby Taiwan* or Japan proper, with little hope for quick relief from the fleet in Hawaii.

Anticipating possible war with Japan, the first version of Plan ORANGE was approved by the U.S. Army-Navy Joint Planning Board in 1924, and through 1938 it was revised at least six times. Because a war against Japan would be primarily a maritime war, the U.S. Navy's view was critical in determining how it would be fought. In general, an offensive strategy prevailed, with U.S. naval forces attacking and breaking through Japanese defensive barriers on the mandate islands. Depending on the scenario, the fleet either arrived just in time in the Philippines—about four to six months—to rescue the U.S. garrison or were able to convoy to the islands a large enough portion of the mobilized U.S. Army to recapture them. None of the plans called for invading the Japanese islands, which were to be subdued by naval blockade.

By 1937, world events had made it probable that the next war would be one of alliances. All but one of the color plans were based, however, on the assumption that the United States without allies would face a single opponent. The joint board first directed that War Plan ORANGE be developed into a two-ocean plan, which it approved in February 1938. In April, the board proposed a multiple set of war plans, code-named War Plan RAINBOW*, involving alliances on both sides of the conflict. Although work began immediately, it was not until 14 May 1941 that the joint board approved RAINBOW 5, a plan in which Britain, the United States, and other allies faced Germany, Italy, and Japan, who had signed the Tripartite Pact* in 1940, in armed conflict. U.S. commanders in the Philippines still had local versions of Plan ORANGE in effect on 7 December 1941, presumably because their version of the new RAINBOW plans had not yet received approval. *See also* Four Power Pact; Geneva Naval Conference of 1927; London Naval Conference of 1930; Pearl Harbor Attack.

E. S. Miller, *War Plan Orange: The U.S. Strategy to Defeat Japan, 1897–1945* (Annapolis, MD, 1991); L. Morton "Germany First" in K. R. Greenfield (ed.), *Command Decisions* (Washington, DC, 1960); L. Morton, "War Plan ORANGE," *World Politics* (1959); R. L. Spector, *Eagle Against the Sun: The American War with Japan* (New York, 1985).

Roger H. Hill

WAR PLAN RAINBOW

This series of U.S. war plans, approved from August 1939 to May 1941, moved the nation away from a Pacific-first strategy in a war against Japan, as outlined in War Plan ORANGE*. By 1937, the U.S. Army-Navy Joint Planning Board began to question the validity of the "color plans" that the Navy and War departments had developed while anticipating conflict with single opponents. Europe was dividing into two increasingly hostile camps, and an aggressive Japan had joined Germany in the Anti-Comintern Pact* in 1936. U.S. military and naval planners, recognizing that if war came the United States likely would face more than one opponent, first sought to expand ORANGE into a plan for a two-front war. With the U.S. Navy negotiators long committed to offensive plans for a maritime campaign against Japan and U.S. Army representatives worried about a resurgent Germany, reaching agreement was difficult. In February 1938, an eventual compromise allowed the U.S. Navy to take the offensive in the Pacific only after a period of mobilization, preparation, and readiness focusing first on defending the Western Hemisphere, especially the Panama Canal.

In April 1939, the U.S. Army-Navy Joint Planning Board ordered development of an entirely new set of war plans. Named RAINBOW to emphasize the multinational dimensions of the security problems then facing the United States, the series contained five war plans. RAINBOW 1 was a stand-alone defense of the Western Hemisphere that also served as the base case for RAINBOWs 2 through 5. Under RAINBOW 2, the United States, allied with France and Britain, quickly controlled the Atlantic, allowing for a subsequent U.S. offensive against Japan. RAINBOW 3 assumed such a strong allied superiority in the Atlantic that the United States could take the offensive in the Pacific from the start. RAINBOW 4 was similar to RAINBOW 1, except the threat from the Atlantic was so great that significant numbers of U.S. Army troops were deployed to defend South America, with no initial offensive against Japan. RAINBOW 5, like RAINBOW 2, involved a U.S. alliance with France and Britain, but U.S. troops would go first to Europe and Africa to aid allies with an offensive against Japan postponed.

RAINBOW 1 for hemispheric defense was approved by both the secretaries of the war and navy on 14 August 1939, several days before Germany invaded Poland. Approval of the remaining four plans was delayed by the rapidly changing situation in Europe, residual U.S. Navy and U.S. Army discord over European-Asian priorities, the influence of secret U.S.-British naval staff discussions, and the impact of inflexible support for Great Britain from President Franklin D. Roosevelt*. The rapidly sinking fortunes of the French and British in Europe coincided with the U.S. Navy's increased understanding of the Royal Navy's needs for U.S. help in the ongoing conflict. In June 1940, after Italy joined the war and France sued for peace, General George C. Marshall*, U.S. Army chief of staff, recommended cutting off further arms exports to Britain and mobilizing the National Guard. Roosevelt agreed to the latter, but refused to "sell out" Britain. His reelection in November 1940, coming on the heels of Japan's entrance into French Indochina* and invocation of the Tripartite Pact*, set the stage for approval of RAINBOW 5 and the American decision to "put Europe first."

From 16 January 1941 onward, Roosevelt began a series of regular meetings with his "war council." Since June 1940, Chief of Naval Operations Admiral Harold R. Stark had been circulating a memorandum summarizing the alternative strategies underlying the RAINBOW plans and gathering a consensus supporting RAINBOW 5. The memorandum was forwarded to Roosevelt after his reelection, and he approved the Stark memorandum as the basis of further British-American secret staff conversations. Begun in Washington in late January 1941, the conferees quickly reached agreement on ABC-1, incorporating the core of RAINBOW 5 into the framework of U.S.-British military cooperation. The joint board approved both ABC-1 and RAINBOW 5 in May 1941. Interestingly, the strategic blueprints locking the United States into a "Europe first" posture in spite of its Pacific-first preferences never were signed by Roosevelt. Marshall decided that since the president had seen the plans and not rejected them, it was proper to proceed as if approved. *See also* London Naval Conference of 1936; Pearl Harbor Attack.

L. Morton, "Germany First" in K. R. Greenfield (ed.), *Command Decisions* (Washington, DC, 1960); L. Morton, "Origins of the Pacific Strategy" *Marine Corps Gazette* (1957); R. L. Spector, *Eagle Against the Sun: The American War with Japan* (New York, 1985).

Roger H. Hill

WARD, ANGUS (1893–1969)

Late in 1948, Angus Ward, U.S. consul general in Shenyang (Mukden), and his staff were placed under house arrest near the end of the Chinese Civil War* and then were tried and expelled from China in November 1949. Ward's treatment reflected the revolutionary zeal of the Chinese Communists and the influence of their Soviet allies, as well as their nationalist determination to reduce Western influence in China. This episode contributed significantly to the U.S. adoption of a nonrecognition policy toward the People's Republic of China* (PRC). It began on 2 November 1948, when Chinese Communist forces entered Shenyang and Ward and his staff stayed in the city to perform normal consular functions. On 15 November, Ward was told by local military authorities to hand over the consulate's radio transmitter within thirty-six hours, but the order was based on instructions from the Chinese Communist Party* (CCP) Central Committee not to extend official status to Western diplomats. It also reflected Soviet advice, as well as Communist suspicion of American ties to the Guomindang* (Nationalists). When Ward refused to surrender the transmitter, CCP Chairman Mao Zedong* ordered the Shenyang authorities to isolate the consulate. On 20 November, Ward, his staff, and their families were placed under house arrest in the consular compound, where they were held incommunicado for a year.

Early in 1949, a report of a "spy ring" in Shenyang, with ties to the consulate general, appeared in the Chinese press, but no convincing Chinese evidence ever has been released supporting this charge. William N. Stokes, Ward's deputy, has written that U.S. intelligence collection in Shenyang was a routine effort focused on Soviet representatives in the area, and that the information had been received from the Nationalists, rather than the embassy providing intelligence. On 24 October, Ward and four other consulate employees were arrested on a trumped-up charge of beating a former Chinese employee at the consulate. The American reaction was indignant. President Harry S. Truman* instructed the Joint Chiefs of Staff (JCS) to consider using military force to free Ward and his colleagues, but the JCS recommended against it. Secretary of State Dean G. Acheson* announced that the United States would not consider recognition of the new regime until it released the diplomats. In November, Ward and his colleagues were put on trial by a People's Court at Shenyang on charges of assault, convicted, and given prison sentences that were commuted to deportation. A few days later, the court announced the expulsion of other non-Chinese members of the consulate staff for alleged involvement in espionage activities. On 11 December, Ward and his staff left China. Ward ended his career as ambassador to Afghanistan from 1952 to 1956 after thirty-one years in the U.S. Foreign Service.

J. Chen, *China's Road to the Korean War: The Making of the Sino-American Confrontation* (New York, 1994); J. Chen, "The Ward Case and the Emergence of Sino-American Confrontation, 1948–1950," *Australian Journal of Chinese Affairs* (July 1993); M. Green, J. H. Holdridge, and W. N. Stokes, *War and Peace with China: First-Hand Experiences in the Foreign Service of the United States* (Bethesda, MD, 1994); *New York Times*, 25 May 1969; U.S. Department of State, *Foreign Relations of the United States, 1948*, Vol. 7: *The Far East: China* (Washington, DC, 1973); U.S. Department of State, *Foreign Relations of the United States, 1949*, Vol. 8: *The Far East: China* (Washington, DC, 1978).

Harriet Dashiell Schwar

WARD, FREDERICK T. (1831–1862)

Frederick Townsend Ward organized and led the Ever-Victorious Army, a force of Chinese soldiers that employed Western military tactics in suppressing the Taiping Rebellion*. Son of a merchant and ship master, he was born in Salem, Massachusetts, and lived there until he signed on as the second mate of a China clipper ship in 1846. Returning to the United States in 1847, Ward studied at a private academy in Vermont for the next two years and learned the rudiments of military tactics. He then spent the next decade pursuing careers as a sailor, businessman, and filibuster in California, Mexico, China, and the Crimea. He worked briefly in his father's New York office in 1859, but left for China that fall. There, Ward served as an officer on coastal steamers and on a gunboat, the *Confucius*, that protected Western merchants from pirates and Taiping bands in the waters near Shanghai.

Ward's military career in China began in June 1860, when he approached Wu Xu, the Qing Dynasty's intendant at Shanghai, and Yang Fang, a wealthy merchant, about the possibility of raising a mercenary unit that would defend Shanghai against approaching Taiping forces. They agreed to Ward's proposal and gave him the official and financial support needed to procure weapons and recruit a force of 200 American and European troops. His unit, the

Foreign Arms Corps, suffered an initial defeat when it attacked the city of Songjiang in late June, but Ward quickly reorganized the force by enlisting a well-disciplined contingent of Filipino sailors led by Vincente Macanaya, and he seized Songjiang in mid-July. The Foreign Arms Corps, however, suffered another defeat when it tried to take the town of Qingpu in early August and Ward was seriously wounded in the attack. He spent the rest of 1860 recovering from his wounds and slowly rebuilding his force. His recruiting efforts angered Western diplomats and military officers by encouraging desertions from European and American ships, and Ward was briefly arrested by British naval officers in the spring of 1861. He was quickly released and avoided further trouble with Western officials after apparently promising the commander of British naval forces in China that he would no longer encourage desertions from British warships. Ward spent the rest of 1861 reorganizing and training his troops and recruiting Chinese soldiers.

By early 1862, Ward had assembled a contingent of 1,000 Chinese soldiers and Western officers equipped with modern firearms, artillery, and gunboats. In January, his army won an impressive series of victories against the Taipings in the vicinity of Shanghai. In March, Qing officials designated his force as the Ever-Victorious Army and awarded Ward military and civil ranks. That summer, Ward recommended that the Ever-Victorious Army be expanded from 3,000 to 25,000 troops and be deployed against the Taiping capital of Nanjing, but Qing officials, who never completely trusted Ward, despite his having renounced his U.S. citizenship, rejected the proposal. Ward led his troops against Taiping forces that threatened the treaty port of Ningbo, and there he was shot in the abdomen on 21 September. The wound proved fatal, and Ward died early the next day. The Ever-Victorious Army remained active after Ward's death and its commanders, Henry A. Burgevine and Major Charles G. Gordon, continued to use the tactics Ward had devised until the unit's dissolution in May 1864. Early accounts of the army's campaigns overrated the unit's role in defeating the Taiping Rebellion. The force in fact was small, fought in a limited area of operations, and did not participate in the campaigns that crushed the Taipings in the Yangze Valley. Ward's leadership of the Ever-Victorious Army nevertheless proved that Chinese troops could be trained successfully to use Western weapons and tactics, and this encouraged Qing officials to modernize the military training of their armies.

C. Carr, *The Devil Soldier: The Story of Frederick Townsend Ward* (New York, 1992); R. Smith, *Mercenaries and Mandarins: The Ever-Victorious Army in Nineteenth Century China* (Millwood, NJ, 1978); J. Spence, *To Change China: Western Advisers in China, 1620–1960* (New York, 1980).

Joseph G. Morgan

WARLORD ERA (1916–1927)

The Warlord Era in China was a period of complex uncertainty, unfulfilled potential, and actual violence, which posed a threat to American interests in China. This period describes the time from the death of Yuan Shikai*, the first president of the Republic of China*, to the establishment in 1927 of the Guomindang* (Nationalist) government in Nanjing, which unified control of much of the country. The era was one of fragmentation of political control, under competing military governors, who engaged in a shifting series of alliances to consolidate and expand their control of resources. Several of these individuals had long-term plans for the development the Chinese state after securing control.

A putative government, or series of them—six presidents, and twenty-five cabinets appointed, or elected, during this time—were recognized by the foreign powers with interests in China, among them the United States. Foreign loans were contracted by various military leaders in control of Beijing, thus enhancing the appeal of the city as a target. In addition, certain warlords were viewed as having connections to outside powers: Zhang Zuolin* with Japan, Wu Beifu with Britain, and Feng Yuxiang* with Russia. Such associations complicated relations both among the powers and with the Chinese, especially for those nations that had participated in the suppression of the Boxer Uprising* and therefore could station troops in north China.

During this era, anti-imperialism was a strong sentiment in China, popular with many of the people, threatening American and other nations' privileges under the unequal treaty system. With all of the unrest, including sporadic warfare with the most modern weapons purchased with the foreign loans, the powers cooperated in the defense of their interests, particularly in North China. Significantly, foreigners were rarely the targets of these wars because the Chinese factions took care to avoid engaging non-Chinese so as not to jeopardize official foreign neutrality. This period has been viewed traditionally as part of the chaos associated with the end of China's last dynasty. More recent studies detail a rich political, intellectual, and economic experimentation, suggesting a more complex assessment. *See also* Chinese Revolution of 1911; May Fourth Movement; Sun Zhongshan.

H. S. Ch'i, *Warlord Politics in China, 1916–1928* (Stanford, CA, 1976); G. McCormack, *Chang Tso-lin in Northeast China, 1911–1928* (Stanford, CA, 1977); A. Waldron, *From War to Nationalism: China's Turning Point, 1924–1925* (New York, 1995).

Katherine K. Reist

WARSAW TALKS

The U.S.-China ambassadorial talks, commonly known as the Warsaw talks although more than half took place in Geneva, provided the only regular channel of direct communication between the United States and the People's Republic of China (PRC) for fifteen years. Although ritualized exchanges of rhetoric characterized many of the 138 meetings, they provided a useful point of contact at times of tension. The talks began in the wake of the first of the Taiwan Strait Crises* in 1954 and 1955. At the Bandung Conference* in April 1955, Chinese Premier Zhou Enlai* proposed Sino-American negotiations. Thereafter, a number of governments tried to serve as intermediaries, until Secretary of State John Foster Dulles* concluded that direct talks with the PRC would be preferable to dealing through third parties. Lower-level talks during the Geneva Conference of 1954* concerning Americans imprisoned in China and Chinese nationals restricted from leaving the United States offered a precedent. On 25 July, Beijing and Washington announced that ambassadorial-level talks would be held to help settle the repatriation of civilians and "to facilitate further discussions and settlement of certain other practical matters now at issue between both sides."

On 1 August 1955, U.S. Ambassador to Czechoslovakia U. Alexis Johnson* and Chinese Ambassador to Poland Wang Bingnan began discussions in Geneva. On 10 September, they issued an "agreed announcement" declaring that civilians of both sides who wished to return to their respective countries could do so and repatriation would occur "expeditiously." It was the only agreement reached in fifteen years of talks, and it did not resolve the issue. Washington had lifted the last restrictions on the departure of Chinese nationals before the talks began, but Beijing argued that Americans in Chinese prisons had been imprisoned lawfully for espionage or other crimes. The imprisoned Americans remained a nagging issue, although their number dwindled, until only Central Intelligence Agency* agents John Downey and Richard Fecteau remained. A U.S. proposal for a mutual renunciation of force in the Taiwan* area led to discussions in late 1955, but Washington and Beijing remained far apart. Chinese proposals in 1956 and 1957 for the exchange of journalists or other bilateral contacts were rejected by Washington, and the talks deteriorated into polemics. When Johnson left Prague at the end of 1957, Dulles tried to downgrade the talks, but Beijing resisted, and the meetings lapsed for several months.

Beijing and Washington revived the talks at the height of the second of the Taiwan Strait Crises in 1958, but shifted their location to Warsaw. Ambassadors to Poland Jacob Beam and Wang Bingnan exchanged proposals on Taiwan and the offshore islands, but the two sides again remained far apart. Nonetheless, Dulles concluded that the talks eased tensions somewhat, as well as satisfying domestic and international pressures for a more flexible U.S. policy. In the next two years, the United States proposed an exchange of newsmen, but Beijing, caught up in the growing Sino-Soviet rift, took an increasingly hard line. In the 1960s, the talks became increasingly sterile and were held with declining frequency, but they still offered an occasionally useful channel of communication. In June 1962, a Chinese military buildup opposite Taiwan, apparently prompted by signs of Guomindang* (Nationalist) preparations for an attack on the mainland, alarmed U.S. officials. At a special meeting in Warsaw, Ambassador John Moors Cabot told Wang Bingnan that the United States would not support a Nationalist attack on the mainland, and tension subsided. The level of Chinese polemics rose along with the U.S. involvement in the Second Indochina War*, but Washington tried to moderate the rhetoric and to convey assurances that its actions in Vietnam were not aimed at the PRC. After a two-year lapse, the last two ambassadorial meetings in January and February 1970 provided an opportunity for both sides to signal their interest in improved relations, but Beijing first delayed and then canceled the next meeting because of the Cambodian Incursion.* Thereafter, U.S.-China contacts shifted to more confidential channels.

U. A. Johnson, *The Right Hand of Power* (Englewood Cliffs, NJ, 1984); H. A. Kissinger, *White House Years* (Boston, 1979); U.S. Department of State, *Foreign Relations of the United States, 1955–1957*, Vols. 2 and 3: *China* (Washington, DC, 1986); U.S. Department of State, *Foreign Relations of the United States, 1958–1960*, Vol. 19: *China* (Washington, DC, 1996); U.S. Department of State, *Foreign Relations of the United States, 1961–1963*, Vol. 22: *Northeast Asia* (Washington, DC, 1996); U.S. Department of State, *Foreign Relations of the United States, 1964–1968*, Vol. 30: *China* (Washington, DC, 1998); K. T. Young, *Negotiating with the Chinese Communists: The United States Experience, 1953–1967* (New York, 1968).

Harriet Dashiell Schwar

WASHINGTON CONFERENCE

This conference on limitation of armaments, held in Washington, D.C., from 11 November 1921 to 6 February 1922, began with a dramatic speech on naval limitations by Secretary of State Charles Evans Hughes*. Negotiations then focused on two major problems: first, the dangerous naval race developing in the Pacific between the great powers, and second, the political, military, and economic interests of the participating nations in East Asia. The United States, Britain, Japan, France, and Italy took part in the naval aspects, and China, Portugal, Belgium, and the Netherlands joined for the Asian diplomatic negotiations. Resultant major treaties included the Five Power Pact* on naval arms limitation, the Four Power Pact* (minus Italy) on Pacific affairs, and the Nine Power Pact* on China. Other important results were the Shandong Agreement*, an accord to end the Siberian Intervention*, and resolution of the Yap Controversy*. The Washington Conference, in many respects the Asian counterpart of the European-centered Versailles Peace Treaty* of 1919, sought to settle issues not fully concluded at Versailles and erect a Washington "system" designed to foster peace in the Pacific.

The Five Power Treaty, signed on 6 February 1922, was the centerpiece of the discussion. It limited the burgeoning Pacific naval race in capital ships (battleships and battle cruisers) between the United States, Britain, and Japan. The terms coincided with Hughes's opening proposal that called for scrapping seventy capital ships already built, under construction, or planned. No more capital ships could be built for ten years. Despite signing and ratifying the treaty, which gave Japan the dominant naval position in the western Pacific, the Japanese Navy became increasingly dissatisfied with what it considered an inferior status in relation to the United States and Britain. Subsequent discussions at the Geneva Naval Conference of 1927* and the London Naval Conference of 1930* and 1935–1936* did not diminish that feeling. Publicly connected to the Five Power Treaty was the Four Power Treaty on the Pacific, signed on 13 December 1921 because the United States would not have accepted the former without the latter. The Anglo-Japanese Alliance* ended with the signing of this accord, which also called for consultation if aggression arose involving any of the signators' possessions in the Pacific. It was the only target among the conference treaties of a ratification fight, as former irreconcilable opponents of the League of Nations labeled it an alliance.

To the great relief of Japan, the United States had no dramatic, surprise opening proposal on East Asian problems. The U.S. delegation followed the advice of former Secretary of State Elihu Root* and sought support from the participants for the Open Door Policy* with virtuous example and moral exhortation, but envisioned no use of force. A series of resolutions on China that had passed finally were cobbled together by Root and Hughes into a Nine Power Pact. It included traditional clauses calling for respect of China's sovereignty, independence, and territorial and administrative integrity. Signed on 3 February 1922, its greatest accomplishment was that it was the first time the U.S. Open Door policy had ever been accepted formally by other nations in treaty form. But it had no enforcement mechanisms.

Other resolutions at Washington, not codified into treaties, called for further conferences to discuss points of dispute with China. There was agreement later for an end to extraterritoriality in China in 1925, but the United States did not surrender its right until 1943. Another meeting resulted in acceptance of China Tariff Autonomy* in 1925, although this was not achieved until 1930. A final group of arrangements, concluded while the conference met but actually taking place outside conference confines, led to Japan's agreement for troop withdrawals from Siberia and Shandong in 1922. Another recognized U.S. operational cable rights on the island of Yap after a long dispute with Japan. The Washington treaties temporarily checked Japanese expansion, stabilized the naval race, and provided further time for China to solve its problems. But after the Mukden Incident* in 1931, the Washington "system" faltered and then collapsed.

T. H. Buckley, *The United States and the Washington Conference, 1921–1922* (Knoxville, TN, 1970); R. Dingman, *Power in the Pacific: The Origins of Naval Arms Limitation, 1914–1922* (Chicago, 1976); E. Goldstein and J. Maurer (eds.), *The Washington Conference, 1921–22* (London, 1994).

Thomas H. Buckley

WEBSTER, DANIEL (1782–1852)

Daniel Webster served twice as secretary of state before the American Civil War, using his power and influence to expand U.S. commerical interests in the Pacific. His East Asian policies, often neglected by his biographers, sought increased trading and commercial relations, and obviously meshed with his economic nationalism and internal policies designed to save the Union. Born in Salisbury, New Hampshire, he graduated from Dartmouth College in 1801 and then read law for two firm Bostonian Federalists. After starting his own practice, Webster became a noted pamphleteer, letter writer, and dabbler in politics at the state level. In 1812, he finally was elected to Congress, where he attacked President James Madison's policies in the war with Britain. Choosing not to run for reelection in 1816, he moved to Boston and built a good law practice handling cases for corporations, insurance companies, and banks. Webster also developed a reputation as an orator, culminating in the funeral oration for the deaths of John Adams and Thomas Jefferson. He returned to federal politics when reelected to the House of Representatives in 1823 and served there until 1827, when he was elected to the Senate. In 1824, he supported John Quincy Adams for the presidency, and after Henry Clay was named secretary of state, endorsed his efforts at economic nationalism. During the 1830s, Webster acquired considerable lands in Indiana, Illinois, Michigan, and Wisconsin. Like many in the depression of 1837, his investments and speculations led to major losses, and he slipped heavily into debt.

During the period of Jacksonian dominance, Webster was held on a retainer by the National Bank and became a close friend of its president, Nicholas Biddle. He also was one of the great triumvirate, along with Henry Clay and John C. Calhoun, who debated the role and nature of the tariff in national and state life. In the fall of 1832, Webster argued for an increase in national constitutional power against nullification and against concessions to states threatening nullification. His thesis was a perpetual union, not a compact of states. Thereafter, he affiliated with the emerging Whig Party and after its election to office, twice became secretary of state. During both terms, he pressed a strong interest in reducing tensions with Great Britain and developing links with East Asian trading nations, a theme dear to New England politicians. Webster's first term came under William Henry Harrison, who died in 1841 after just a month in office. Rather than resigning with the rest of the cabinet, he served as new President John Tyler's secretary of state and successfully negotiated with Lord Ashburton to end tension occasioned by the burning of an American ship by Canadian militia for its gun running to Canadian rebels, the Maine–New Brunswick boundary dispute, and the illegal West African slave trade. Webster also sent Caleb Cushing* on a trade mission to China, resulting in the 1844 Treaty of Wangxia*. Responding to permission from China in 1843 to begin negotiations, he acted to achieve the long-sought U.S. objective of a commerical agreement with the Qing Dynasty. In 1845, New York Congressman Zodock Pratt called for relations to be established with Japan and Korea as well, and Webster addressed the former proposal during his next term in the 1850s.

Webster left Tyler's cabinet in 1843 and rejoined the Senate in 1845, adamantly opposing, along with other Whigs, the annexation of Texas. President James K. Polk's war with Mexico, for Webster, was an unconstitutional and a personal tragedy, for he lost his son to disease while serving as an officer in the U.S. Army in Mexico. He worked with Clay after the war to resolve sectional disputes over slavery, endorsing popular sovereignty in the Western territories and costing him much political support. When President Zachary Taylor died in July 1850, new President Millard Fillmore appointed Webster secretary of state. Resuming his focus on the Pacific, he laid the groundwork for instructions to U.S. naval officers aimed at opening Korea, Japan, and other East Asian nations to American trade. In 1851, Webster wrote instructions for Commodore John Aulick to open negotiations with the government of Japan that resembled those he had given to Cushing in 1843, but nothing developed. He sought supplies of coal to assist steam navigation for merchant, as well as naval vessels, treaty ports, similar to those opened at Muscat, Siam, and China, and protection of shipwrecked seamen. In 1853, Commodor Matthew C. Perry* acted on Webster's instructions, resulting in the Perry Mission* and the opening of Japan with the Treaty of Kanagawa*. Webster believed that commerce and civilization were marching hand in hand over the Pacific. The Whig Press and New England missionary societies supported his view that the United States was an instrument to bring Christianity to Japan. Despite an attempt to promote Webster's candidacy for the presidency in the election of 1852, he returned to his Marshfield home. Seriously ill, Webster died before the November election.

N. D. Brown, *Daniel Webster and the Politics of Availability* (Athens, GA, 1969); R. N. Current, *Daniel Webster and the Rise of National Conservatism* (Boston, 1955); R. F. Dalzell, *Daniel Webster and the Trial of American Nationalism* (Boston, 1973); H. Jones, *To the Webster-Ashburton Treaty: A Study in Anglo-American Relations 1783–1843* (Chapel Hill, NC, 1977); K. E. Shewmaker, K. R. Stevens, and A. McGurn (eds.), *The Papers of Daniel Webster: Diplomatic Papers*, vols. 1–3 (Hanover, NH, 1974).

Frederick C. Drake

WEDEMEYER, ALBERT C. (1897–1989)

Lieutenant General Albert C. Wedemeyer played an important role in shaping U.S. policy toward China during and after World War II. His 1947 report on postwar events in China and Korea was controversial, not even being made public until 1951. Born in Omaha, Nebraska, he was the son of a U.S. Army captain. After graduating from West Point, Wedemeyer held various posts before studying Chinese during the early 1930s while on assignment in Tianjin, China. He then gained further training in the United States before attending the War Academy in Berlin, reporting on his return in 1938 on the German military mind and machine. General George C. Marshall*, then assistant chief of staff of the War Plans Division at the War Department, was impressed and added Wedemeyer to his staff in 1941, where he worked on developing overall war plans. After the Pearl Harbor Attack*, he accompanied Marshall on trips abroad and played a major role in Allied strategy in the European theater.

In 1943, Marshall named his protégé U.S. deputy chief of staff to Admiral Lord Mountbatten, the British head of the Southeast Asia Command. Wedemeyer then replaced General Joseph W. Stilwell* in November 1944 as the U.S.-China theater commander, simultaneously assuming the post of chief of staff to Generalissimo Jiang Jieshi* after Stilwell had so alienated the Guomindang* (Nationalist) leader that Jiang personally requested his removal in a letter to President Franklin D. Roosevelt*. Wedemeyer succeeded in establishing harmonious relations with Jiang, contributing to improved training, equipping, and preparing of the Nationalist forces to fight the Japanese. In 1945, he was the deputy chief of staff for plans and operations in the War Department. His second opportunity to affect Sino-American relations came in 1947 at a critical time in the Chinese Civil War* when Marshall, now secretary of state, sent him on a fact-finding mission to China. Pressure from Republicans on Capitol Hill unhappy with the results of the Marshall Mission* led to the Wedemeyer Mission* because the general was known to favor stronger steps in support of Jiang's regime.

Wedemeyer arrived in China late in July and then went to Korea, spending a few weeks assessing the military and political situations in both countries. His report, while not well received by Jiang because of how sharply it criticized Guomindang failings, nonetheless called for continued U.S. economic and military assistance to the Republic of China*. Wedemeyer also urged a greater U.S. commitment in southern Korea, leading to the creation of a viable separate government. Washington slowly implemented policies regarding the U.S. Occupation of Korea* coinciding with his recommendations. Appointment after he returned as commander of the Sixth U.S. Army ended his policy-making role. But in 1951, Wedemeyer, having already applied for retirement, confused listeners about his views on U.S. policy in Asia when he testified at U.S. Senate hearings on the General Douglas MacArthur's Recall*. He was chairman in 1952 of Ohio Senator Robert A. Taft's presidential campaign committee. In retirement, Wedemeyer was an executive for Avco Manufacturing Corporation and the Rheem Manufacturing Corporation.

J. I. Matray, *The Reluctant Crusade: American Foreign Policy in Korea, 1941–1950* (Honolulu, HI, 1985); *New York Times*, 20 December 1989; W. W. Stueck, *The Wedemeyer Mission: American Politics and Foreign Policy During the Cold War* (Athens, GA, 1984); T. Tsou, *America's Failure in China* (Chicago, 1963); A. C. Wedemeyer, *Wedemeyer Reports!* (New York, 1958).

T. Christopher Jespersen

WEDEMEYER MISSION

The special mission of Lieutenant General Albert C. Wedemeyer* to China in July 1947 demonstrated his own, and the country's, ambivalence toward the struggle between the Guomindang* (Nationalist) and the Chinese Communist Party* (CCP) in the Chinese Civil War*. The Marshall Mission* to China starting late in 1945 had failed to end the fighting. U.S. officials were conscious of declining prospects of Jiang Jieshi*, as well as the potentially high cost of trying to sustain him, but fears of Moscow's growing influence over Mao Zedong* permitted no easy choice between accepting Jiang's defeat and entering the civil war to save him. Unable to accept either course, General George C. Marshall*, secretary of state since January 1947, dispatched Wedemeyer on another mission to China in search of some feasible solution.

In his report of September 1947, Wedemeyer concluded that no U.S. policy would save the Republic of China*. Unless the government eliminated corruption and incompetence, he concluded, it never would defeat the CCP with military force. But he also warned: "A China dominated by Chinese Communists will be inimical to the interests of the United States, in view of their openly expressed hostility and active opposition to those principles which the United States regards as vital to the peace of the world." The United States thus had no choice but to increase its opposition to Communist "aggression" in China "through the presently corrupt, reactionary, and inefficient Chinese National Government." This recommendation meant a huge, unpromising U.S. military involvement on the Asian mainland or an endless U.S. adherence to a doomed regime, and thus a doomed policy. Marshall found the Wedemeyer report confused and unhelpful with respect to China.

By contrast, Wedemeyer's recommendations had a significant impact on U.S. policy toward Korea. It came at a time when the Truman administration was seeking a method of graceful withdrawal from the peninsula. The Wedemeyer report offered limited reason for optimism on the latter point, recommending "moral, advisory, and material support" to southern Korea. Without economic aid, the U.S. Occupation of Korea* would confront "riots and disorder"; without U.S. troops, the south would be taken by northern Korea, leading to "creation of a Soviet satellite Communist regime throughout the country." Wedemeyer proposed a buildup of indigenous armed forces on a scale adequate to protect against anything short of "an outright Soviet directed or controlled invasion." U.S. troops should remain until arrangements for the mutual withdrawal of foreign units. Wedemeyer assumed that the United States would move toward creation of an independent goverment below the thirty-eighth parallel. The Truman administration slowly implemented these recommendations after 1947.

The Wedemeyer report was initially classified top secret, largely because of its recommendation of a trusteeship for Manchuria, which State Department officials feared would embarrass Jiang's beleaguered regime in China. The China portion, however, was published in August 1949 as part of the famous China

White Paper* prepared by the State Department. The Korea section did not surface until May 1951 when, in the midst of the controvery surrounding General Douglas MacArthur's Recall* by President Harry S. Truman*, the State Department permitted Senate committees to publish it. Republican partisans attempted to use the report to attack administration policy toward Korea before the Korean War*, but Wedemeyer undermined these efforts when he testified that, in early 1949, he had recommended U.S. military withdrawal from Korea. *See also* Korean Aid Act; Republic of Korea.

A. Iriye, *The Cold War in Asia: A Historical Introduction* (Englewood Cliffs, NJ, 1974); W. W. Stueck, *The Wedemeyer Mission: American Politics and Foreign Policy During the Cold War* (Athens, GA, 1984); T. Tsou, *America's Failure in China* (Chicago, 1963); A. C. Wedemeyer, *Wedemeyer Reports!* (New York, 1958).

Norman A. Graebner

WEI JINGSHENG (1950–)

Wei Jingsheng, along with Fang Lizhi*, has been one of the leading dissidents in the People's Republic of China* (PRC), attracting worldwide attention for the first time in 1979 when he was arrested, tried, and found guilty of espionage and sentenced to fifteen years in prison. In November 1997, after nearly a decade in jail, the PRC, bowing to pressure from the United States and the international community, finally exiled him to the United States to remove this persistent irritant in U.S.-PRC relations. The first child of a pair of middle-level Chinese Communist Party* (CCP) officials, he grew up as a dedicated Communist devoted to the ideals of the Chinese Communist revolution and the teachings of Mao Zedong*. In 1966, Wei became a Red Guard in the Chinese Cultural Revolution* and traveled for two years throughout the nation to transform Chinese society through revolution. Ironically, this experience caused him to realize that China's poverty and deprivation contrasted greatly with the official propaganda image of China as a workers' paradise. Joining the People's Liberation Army in 1969, Wei witnessed poverty and suffering while stationed in northwest China that further revealed the PRC government's duplicity and hypocrisy. His Tibetan fiance's father also spent eighteen years in a Chinese prison, and his parents both suffered in the Cultural Revolution, completing his disillusionment with the CCP.

Wei first challenged the Chinese government on the morning of 5 December 1978, when he placed his poster titled "The Fifth Modernization" on the Democracy Wall in Beijing. The poster contended that unless China embraced democracy, called the Fifth Modernization, the CCP's Four Modernizations* reform program would be empty promises. In challenging government policy and attacking Deng Xiaoping* by name, Wei became one of the first protestors to be arrested during the suppression of the democracy movement on 29 March 1979. Convicted with a falsified charge of espionage, Wei received a fifteen-year sentence on 16 October 1979. Official Chinese government propaganda portrayed him as "a chronic malingerer and troublemaker who has sold military secrets to foreigners." Ignoring his family's advice to stay out of trouble, Wei continued his protest against the government while in prison. He wrote hundreds of pages condemning the PRC's policies on treatment of political prisoners, toward Tibet*, on economic development, and abusing human rights.

After the Tiananmen Square Massacre* in June 1989, the world community and human rights organizations called for Wei's release. When Wei finally was paroled in 1993, the government warned him to maintain a low profile or risk reimprisonment. Refusing to back down, Wei instead publicly stated his intention to continue to press the government for democratization and improvement on human rights. On the eve of the meeting between

President Jiang Zemin* and President Bill Clinton* in Seattle in November 1993 at the Asia-Pacific Economic Cooperation* meeting, Wei's column appeared in the *New York Times* urging the United States to increase pressure on China to improve its human rights record. On 27 February 1994, Wei met with the U.S. assistant secretary of state for human rights and humanitarian affairs, angering Beijing. In November 1995, Chinese authorities arrested Wei for "illegal activities" and sentenced him to fourteen years in prison. This time, world condemnation was immediate and vociferous. For his courage and determination, Wei not only won the 1995 Olaf Palme Award and 1996 European Parliament's Sakharov Prize for Freedom of Thought, but was nominated in 1996 for the Nobel Peace Prize. Not expected to be released until 2009, Wei's imprisonment was a serious source of friction damaging Sino-American relations. A month after Premier Jiang's trip to the United States in October 1997, the PRC released Wei on a medical parole to the United States.

L. Fang, *Bringing Down the Great Wall: Writings on Science, Culture and Democracy in China* (New York, 1990); A. J. Nathan, *Chinese Democracy* (Berkeley, CA, 1986); J. Wei, *The Courage to Stand Alone: Letters from Prison and Other Writings* (New York, 1997).

Roger Y. M. Chan

WESTMORELAND, WILLIAM C. (1914–)

General William C. Westmoreland was commander of the Military Assistance Command, Vietnam* (MACV) from 1964 to 1968. Born in South Carolina, he won an appointment to the U.S. Military Academy from his Sunday school teacher, Senator James F. Byrnes. Joining artillery when he graduated in 1936, Westmoreland moved rapidly up the ranks as the U.S. Army expanded during World War II and developed a professional relationship with Major General Maxwell D. Taylor*, who became his mentor. After completing airborne school, he commanded the only paratrooper unit in the Korean War* and earned his first general's star. When Taylor became U.S. Army chief of staff, Westmoreland became secretary of the Army General Staff and then received command of the 101st Airborne Division, Taylor's old unit. In 1960, he returned to West Point as the superintendent.

In 1964, Taylor, as chairman of the Joint Chiefs of Staff (JCS), named Westmoreland deputy commander of the MACV, and that year he became commander when General Paul Harkins retired. Initially, he opposed the deployment of U.S. ground troops, believing that if the Army of the Republic of Vietnam* (ARVN) was unable to repel the Communist threat, there was little reason to think that Americans could do so either. But Westmoreland reversed his opinion in 1965 and requested the deployment of U.S. Marines to protect U.S. air bases in South Vietnam. Breaking with Taylor, who had become U.S. ambassador to the Republic of Vietnam*, he also recommended that U.S. Army divisions have the authority to conduct offensive combat operations. Taylor opposed this idea. President Lyndon B. Johnson* approved a compromise that April that was favorable to Westmoreland's position. The United States would send two U.S. Army brigades and three U.S. Marine battalions while making preparations to introduce two divisions. Westmoreland's advice now dominated U.S. Vietnam policy.

During the spring of 1965, the Viet Cong* launched a series of offensives that shattered the ARVN. In June, Westmoreland requested nineteen more battalions, and Johnson's approval of the proposal in July transformed the Second Indochina War* into an American conflict. His strategy of attrition, known as "search and destroy," relied on traditional Army doctrine to destroy the enemy under a heavy barrage of artillery and air bombing. While ignoring the ARVN and giving it no meaningful duty, Westmoreland staged steadily larger operations, such as Operation JUNCTION CITY* and Operation CEDAR FALLS* in 1967. Although the cost and consumption of supplies was staggering, he seemed to be winning the war at the end of 1967. He also enjoyed positive press coverage, notably being named *Time* magazine's Man of the Year in 1965. In November 1967, the general returned to the United States in a public relations effort to build public support for the war. He appeared at the National Press Club, where he predicted that U.S. victory in the conflict was near. The Tet Offensive* suddenly destroyed all this optimism, as JCS Chairman General Earle Wheeler persuaded Westmoreland to ask for additional troops. When the request leaked to the public, it undercut Westmoreland's earlier statements that the Tet Offensive was a desperate move on the part of the Viet Cong to forestall imminent defeat.

In July, Westmoreland became U.S. Army chief of staff. Though in the making long before Tet, the decision to replace him with General Creighton Abrams* appeared to be a cover story disguising his removal from command. He had little to do thereafter with Vietnam, but was a vocal critic of the Paris Peace Accords* that President Richard M. Nixon* and National Security Adviser Henry A. Kissinger negotiated. After retiring from the military in 1973, he dabbled in South Carolina state politics briefly, failing in his bid for the Republican nomination for governor. But Westmoreland devoted most of his energies to defending the honor of his men and blaming the outcome of the war on defective political leadership and a hostile media. In 1982, the CBS television network aired the news documentary *The Uncounted Enemy: A Vietnam Deception*, charging that Westmoreland and his command had misled Johnson, the JCS, and the American public with false and low estimates of enemy strength. Westmoreland filed a libel suit. The trial became a battleground for the varying interpretations about the outcome of the war. In 1985, Westmoreland and CBS settled out of court, which was essentially a victory for the network.

R. Adler, *Reckless Disregard: Westmoreland v. CBS et al., Sharon v. Time* (New York, 1986); B. Brewin and S. Shaw, *Vietnam on Trial: Westmoreland vs. CBS* (New York, 1987); D. Kowet, *A Matter of Honor* (New York, 1984); W. C. Westmoreland, *A Soldier Reports* (Garden City, NY, 1976).

Nicholas Evan Sarantakes

WHITE, THEODORE H. (1915–1986)

Best known as the chronicler of American presidential elections, "Teddy" White first gained journalistic fame as one of the China Hands* reporting for *Time* magazine out of wartime Chongqing (1939–1945). His mentor at Harvard University, John K. Fairbank*, urged this career on his poor Jewish day student. Throughout World War II, White attempted to voice his growing contempt for the corrupt Guomindang* (Nationalist) government of Jiang Jieshi*, only to have his reports edited severely and rewritten by order of the pro-Nationalist and staunchly anti-Communist publisher of *Time*, Henry R. Luce*. Finally, at war's end, he was able to write, with Annalee Jacoby (the love of his life and fellow China Hand), *Thunder Out of China* (1946), the great exposé of wartime China. It became a best-seller at a time when the attitudes of both Washington and the American public were still malleable on China policy.

White reentered the spotlight soon after Richard M. Nixon* became president. During Nixon's Visit to China* in 1972, he was the most influential member of the large press contingent that accompanied the president. Aside from his disdain for the cult of Mao Zedong*, White tended to encourage his colleagues to believe that a new and better China had emerged from the ashes of World War II and the Chinese Civil War*. His influence helped shape American public opinion in support of the Nixon-Kissinger initiative. But in 1983, a chastened White wrote a devastating attack on Mao's China, ironically as a cover story in *Time*. Titled "China: Burnout of a Revolution," White referred to Mao's thought as a "bloody spike" and the Chinese Cultural Revolution* as "the equivalent of Nazi Germany." He concluded that there were no "ultimate solutions" for the People's Republic of China* or Sino-American relations. Rather, both had to go through this passage of history "step-by-step."

S. Mosher, *China Misperceived: American Illusions and Chinese Reality* (New York, 1990); P. Rand, *China Hands*. (New York, 1995); T. H. White, *In Search of History: A Personal Adventure* (New York, 1978).

Errol M. Clauss

WILLIAMS, EDWARD T. (1854–1944)

Edward Thomas Williams had a long career associated with China, spanning missionary work, diplomacy, and academia. After joining the U.S. Foreign Service in 1901, he rose to become chief of the Far Eastern Division in the State Department in 1913. Born in Columbus, Ohio, Williams graduated from Bethany College and then was ordained as a minister in the Disciples of Christ Church. After serving several congregations, he volunteered for missionary work in China. He quickly became fluent in Chinese and turned to missionary journalism. Thanks to closer contact with the Chinese and exposure to Chinese philosophy, Williams overcame the typically negative missionary image of China and became a devoted Sinophile. Meanwhile, his conversion to Reform Darwinism, combined with the death of his first wife, created a crisis of faith that led him to resign from the ministry. Thereafter, in the 1890s, Williams served as interpreter for the U.S. consul general in Shanghai. In 1901, his first posting as a Foreign Service officer was as Chinese secretary of the U.S. legation in Beijiing. He served as consul general in Tianjin (1908–09) and briefly in Washington in the Far Eastern Affairs Division. From 1911 to 1913, as secretary of legation and frequently acting as charge, Williams was considered the leading American China expert.

In 1913, Williams, after appointment as Far Eastern Division chief, generally supported the agenda of U.S. Minister Paul Reinsch* to promote aggressive American investment programs in China, as well as to arouse the Wilson administration against Japan's Twenty-One Demands* in 1915. But he was more cautious on intervening in China's internal affairs than Reinsch and in encouraging China to enter World War I. In fact, Williams wrote the formula acknowledging Japan's "special interests" that was incorporated into the Lansing-Ishii Agreement* of 1917. In 1918, he retired from the State Department to accept appointment as Agassiz Professor of Oriental Languages and Literature at the University of California at Berkeley. Testifying to his expertise and respect for his judgment, Williams was recalled to government service in 1919 as a technical adviser to the U.S. delegation at the Versailles Peace Conference and the Washington Conference* (1921–1922). Although outraged at Woodrow Wilson* for his "betrayal" of China in the Versailles Peace Treaty*, he had developed into a realistic East Asian policy maker. Despite his sympathy for the Chinese and admiration for their civilization, his writings revealed that Williams was a balanced and critical scholar. Further, Williams personified the transition to a more professional and bureaucratic State Department. He trained more than half a dozen student interpreters, who then served in diplomatic and consular positions in China through the 1940s.

E. H. Holgate, *China: Yesterday and Today* (St. Louis, 1946); D. Lazo, "An Enduring Encounter: E. T. Williams, China and the United States," Ph.D. dissertation, University of Illinois, 1977.

Noel H. Pugach

WILSON, WOODROW (1856–1924)

As president of the United States from 1913 to 1921, Thomas Woodrow Wilson not only wanted to focus more on domestic reform than foreign policy, but was more interested in relations with Europe than Asia. As a result, his policy in East Asia was seldom well designed, and often inconsistently implemented. Born in Staunton, Virginia, Wilson earned a law degree at Princeton University and practiced briefly in Atlanta before earning a doctorate in history at Johns Hopkins University. He taught at Princeton before becoming the university's president. In 1910, he gained election as Democratic governor of New Jersey, where he implemented a program of Progressive reform. Two years later, Wilson won the presidency, defeating incumbent William Howard Taft* and Theodore Roosevelt*. He had no experience in foreign affairs, but strongly believed in the importance of following moral principles in world politics. Consistent with his idealist convictions, the primary goals of Wilsonian policy in Asia were to promote the establishment of independent, democratic states and end the use of raw power, both military and economic, in international relations.

Wilson's foreign policy goals were exemplified in his decision in response to the Chinese Revolution of 1911* to recognize the republican government under President Yuan Shikai* in 1913. He appointed Paul S. Reinsch*, a professor of political science at the University of Wisconsin, as his first minister to China to maximize American support of the emergence of democratic political organization. Seeking to divorce American business interests from European economic exploitation, Wilson withdrew U.S. financial interests from the Six Power Consortium*, an organization of banks that regulated foreign investment in China. But the result was uncoordinated and unproductive financing for economic development. Then the outbreak of World War I further complicated U.S. diplomacy in Asia. Japan, ostensibly to fulfill its commitment under the Anglo-Japanese Alliance*, declared war on Germany and seized German holdings on the Shandong Peninsula. This exercise of power was exacerbated by Japan's imposition of the Twenty-One Demands* on China early in 1915, requiring the Chinese to recognize Japanese economic and political claims in Manchuria and Mongolia, as well as to concede the transfer of Shandong to Japan. Secretary of State William Jennings Bryan* protested the terms and refused to recognize the validity of the Twenty-One Demands, arguing that they would reduce China to a Japanese dependency.

U.S. policy of favoring the interests of China over Japan had to be substantially altered when the United States declared war on Germany in April 1917. To strengthen the anti-German cause, the Wilson administration sought to defuse tensions with the Japanese. This resulted in the Lansing-Ishii Agreement* later that year, in which the United States recognized Japan's compelling interests in China in exchange for a Japanese statement supporting the Open Door Policy* in China. Meanwhile, Wilson concluded that American cooperation with the European colonial powers was the only means of balancing Japan's growing economic influence over the Asian continent. As a result, the administration reversed its earlier position on American participation in the banking consortium operating in China. This wartime effort to construct friendly relations with Japan, while acting to prevent Japanese hegemony in Asia, manifested itself in the Siberian Intervention* in 1918. After the Bolshevik Revolution in Russia, Wilson agreed to participate in a joint Japanese-American occupation of Siberia. One of the primary objectives of deploying U.S. troops was to prevent the Japanese seizure of the Chinese Eastern Railway and thereby limit its influence in northeast Asia.

The fundamental tensions in Wilson's policy toward Asia became imbedded in the construction of the Versailles Peace Treaty*. His preeminent goal was to secure a functioning League of Nations as part of the peace settlement with Germany. He was therefore willing to make important concessions to the Allies to win their support for the League. In addition to the terms of the Mandate System*, Wilson concurred with Britain's opposition to a racial equality pledge in the League of Nations Covenant. To pacify the Japanese, he reversed established U.S. policy, and approved the transfer of German authority in Shandong to Japan, igniting the May Fourth Movement* in China. This concession not only damaged relations with the Chinese, but prompted Reinsch's resignation as minister to China and contributed to the U.S. Senate's refusal to ratify the treaty. Late in 1920, the Wilson administration sponsored famine relief in China, seeking to replicate the efforts of Herbert Hoover* in Europe. However, these initial efforts to formulate a comprehenisve solution to East Asia's postwar economic and political problems were cut short; Wilson's stroke in October 1919, combined with Democratic electoral losses in November 1920, effectively ended any comprehensive Wilsonian policy in East Asia.

B. Beers, *Vain Endeavor: Robert Lansing's Attempt to End the American Japanese Rivalry* (Durham, NC, 1962); R. W. Curry, *Woodrow Wilson and Far Eastern Policy* (New York, 1957); J. Israel, *Progressivism and the Open Door America and China, 1905–1921* (Pittsburgh, PA, 1971); N. H. Pugach, *Paul S. Reinsch: Open Door Diplomat in Action* (Millwood, NJ, 1979).

Karen A. J. Miller

WOOD, LEONARD (1860–1927)

Described by the *New York Times* as "America's great proconsul," General Leonard Wood's modest prominence in the history of U.S.–East Asian relations arises principally from his tenure as U.S. governor-general of the Philippines* from 1921 to 1927. His career first gained momentum on the American frontier in the 1880s, when he distinguished himself from his colleagues through uncommon feats of endurance in pursuit of Apache Indians led by Geronimo, and it ended unexpectedly in a Boston hospital when he died of a brain tumor. Born in New Hampshire and a graduate of Harvard Medical School, Wood was not known for his engaging personality, but nonetheless displayed a rare and reliable talent for impressing influential superiors in U.S. Army and civilian circles. Moreover, he exuded an aura of efficiency and robust, clean living that made him a leading figure in the preparedness movement of World War I and a front-runner for the Republican presidential nomination in 1920. Wood was personal physician to President William McKinley*, a prominent member of the Rough Riders with Theodore Roosevelt* in Cuba, and gained a national reputation as the efficient military governor of Cuba in 1899. Transferred to the Philippines in 1903, he became governor of Moro Province, where he led military expeditions in an unproductive effort to encourage respect for U.S. authority. Wood was commander of the entire Philippine Division for two years before returning to Washington, where he served as U.S. Army chief of staff from 1910 to 1914. His early experience of U.S. colonial rule in the Philippines, and close affinity with Roosevelt's outlook on life, gave Wood a particularly hard-nosed perspective on U.S. interests in East Asia.

Wood was disappointed at being overlooked for a position in President Warren G. Harding's cabinet, but agreed shortly thereafter to join what became known as the Wood-Forbes mission to the Philippines. After conducting a thorough investigation, the mission surprised no one when it recommended against Philippine independence. Wood's appointment as governor-general of the Philippines followed in 1921, and he enjoyed some success in reversing what he termed the "neglect and inefficiency" of the previous administration. He reestablished the powers of the governor-general's office while consistently thwarting Filipino moves toward independence. Strained relations between Wood and the Philippine legislature—in part because of his overbearing style—came to a head with Filipino demands for Wood's recall in 1924, but President Calvin Coolidge remained resolute in his support for Wood. His strongly held view was that U.S. withdrawal from the Philippines would be a major setback for American prestige and presence in East Asia, including U.S. interests in China, and would invite Japanese encroachment, particularly in the wake of the Washington Conference* of 1921 and 1922. Wood believed that the treaties signed there had left the United States "hamstrung in the Pacific." He also thought Filipino independence would undermine the expansion of U.S. investment in the archipeligo, which he worked assiduously to promote during his tenure. *See also* Spanish-American War.

H. W. Brands, *Bound to Empire: The United States and the Philippines* (New York, 1992); A. P. Dudden, *The American Pacific: From the Old China Trade to the Present* (New York, 1992); H. Hagedorn, *Leonard Wood: A Biography* (New York, 1931); J. C. Lane, *Armed Progressive: General Leonard Wood* (San Rafael, CA, 1978).

Roger K. Hodgkins

WOODCOCK, LEONARD (1911–2001)

Leonard Woodcock was the first U.S. ambassador to the People's Republic of China* (PRC), completing the process of U.S.-PRC Normalization of Relations* in 1979. Although his foreign policy expertise consisted of having led the United Auto Workers union, his more relevant experience involved helping Jimmy Carter* win election as president in 1976. Woodcock's first task for the president was to travel to Hanoi. Carter wanted to normalize relations with the Socialist Republic of Vietnam*, and sent Woodcock there in March 1977 as head of a delegation to seek a resolution of outstanding issues. Although his mission got the process moving, other factors intervened, ultimately causing delays.

Meanwhile, in July 1977, Woodcock became head of the liaison office in Beijing. His charge was not to fall into what Carter saw as the same trap as the administrations of Richard M. Nixon* and Gerald R. Ford* had in conceding too much to the Chinese. Negotiations started slowly, but National Security Adviser Zbigniew Brzezinski then made it clear that Carter wanted to normalize relations during a trip planned for May 1978. After he also indicated that Washington was ready to do so largely on Chinese terms, rapid progress ensued, so much so that a target date was set for 15 December to announce normalization, with the official act coming on 1 January 1979.

Although it was Brzezinski's concessions that restarted the negotiations, it was Woodcock who was left to talk directly with Chinese leaders in Beijing during the fall. He was one of very few Carter administration officials allowed to participate in the process. In that regard, Carter ended up emulating Henry A. Kissinger* in one critical respect: he too became obsessed with maintaining secrecy. Woodcock also advocated temporarily shelving talks with the Vietnamese in the fall of 1978, which suddenly had made significant progress, in deference to Chinese wishes. Woodcock's tenure as ambassador was less notable than the role he played in bringing about the normalization of relations.

J. Mann, *About Face: History of America's Curious Relationship with China, from Nixon to Clinton* (New York, 1999).

T. Christopher Jespersen

WU HONGDA (1939–)

Wu Hongda's American name was Harry Wu. Born to a small banker's family in a southern Chinese town, he became a professor and taught in a number of colleges in China. After various infractions, he served a three-year term in prison from 1961 to 1964. In 1985, Wu came to the

United States as a visitor, and he acquired U.S. citizenship in 1992. Beginning in 1991, he participated in efforts to condemn the government of the People's Republic of China* (PRC) for violation of human rights. Based upon his personal experiences in Chinese prison, Wu wrote two books and one of them, *Labor Camp: China's Grag*, won him the fame as a fighter for human rights. Soon he became a member in the Human Rights Committee in the U.S. Congress and started working as a professor in the Hoover Institution at Stanford University.

In the summer of 1991, Wu was contracted by Columbia Broadcasting System (CBS) to return to the Chinese prison in which he once served, where he videotaped the life of the prisoners. Later, CBS edited his videotapes and presented a program on Chinese prison life, which angered an American audience already concerned with China's human rights record. In April 1994, Wu once again went to the PRC, with the help of British Broadcasting Company (BBC), who sent a woman to pose as his wife. They traveled to Xiangjiang and Sichuan Provinces, seeking pictures that showed how China's government harvested and sold internal organs of prisoners on death row. At a hospital in Chengdu, Wu told the doctor on duty that his uncle in the United States needed a kidney transplant, and was considering the possibility of having the surgery in China. After persuading the doctor to allow him to visit a normal surgery, Wu and his aide secretly videotaped it. They claimed that it was an example of how the PRC's government was marketing kidneys from prisoners. The subsequent BBC broadcast of this videotape further inflamed the West's opinion on human rights violations in China. Meanwhile, Wu's activities infuriated the PRC.

In June 1995, when Wu, now with a different name, attempted to enter the PRC again from Khazakstan, he was arrested by China's security bureau. The arrest of Wu ignited angry agitation among concerned Americans. A bill introduced in Congress condemned China's arrest of a U.S. citizen, praised Wu as a brave man, and threatened retaliation against the PRC if Wu was harmed in jail. When the bill was subsequently passed, President Bill Clinton* was under great pressure to ensure Wu's safety. Even First Lady Hillary Clinton's plan to attend the Fourth World Woman's Conference in China was jeopardized because of Wu's arrest. On the other hand, Wu, in the Chinese jail, to secure a lighter penalty, began to confess his guilt of manufacturing stories to instigate attacks on the Chinese government. In August 1995, an open trial was held in Wuhan. Wu selected representation from the list of attorneys provided by the U.S. consulate, which meanwhile dispatched personnel to attend the trial. Wu pleaded guilty to the court, and received a sentence of fifteen years in prison. But in late August, he was declared an unwelcome visitor and expelled from China.

New York Times, August and September 1995; Song Qiang, *Zhongguo wei shenme shuo bu* [China Can Say No] (Beijing, 1996).

Li Yi

WU TINGFANG (1842–1922)

Wu Tingfang became the first Chinese lawyer, earning his law certificate in Britain in 1876. He then began his foreign affairs career in Hong Kong*, but left in 1882 to serve as the foreign affairs commissioner in the staff of Li Hongzhang*, the governor-general of Zhili. From 1896 to 1902, Wu served as Chinese minister to the United States, Spain, and Peru. In this tenure, he was ordered to sound out investors in the United States for building the railroad from Hankou south to Guangzhou and negotiated with the American China Development Company. The negotiation ended in failure because of bad faith on the part of American railway concessionaires. After this tenure ended in 1902, Wu returned home and held the post of the vice minister of commerce in the Chinese foreign office and helped negotiate the Chinese-

American Commercial Treaty of 1903. Wu was appointed minister to the United States, Mexico, Peru, and Cuba from 1907 to 1909. In these posts, he strongly advocated attaching great prominence to the possibility of expanded cooperation with the United States. He regarded the United States as a source of diplomatic support.

In light of the classic strategy of using distant states against proximate dangers, Wu had proposed to the Qing court early in 1895 that China might expect help from the United States in checking Russian, French, and Japanese aggression. Again in 1898, he suggested in a memorial to the throne that by offering commercial opportunities to the United States, as well as Britain, China could create an advantageous balance of power, and at the same time enhance China's own prosperity. After the China Relief Expedition* in 1900 during the Boxer Uprising*, Wu keenly felt the approaching crises of the great powers dismembering China. He came to the conclusion that the only practical alternative for China was to invoke the Open Door Policy* advanced by the U.S. Secretary of State John Hay*.

Meanwhile, Wu had been protesting the Chinese Exclusion Acts* in the United States and sharply criticizing the prejudicial policies of the U.S. Immigration Bureau. His arguments became central to the Chinese position, and Wu himself led China's battle against the humiliating American treatment of Chinese as second-class people and China as an inferior nation. Just as Wu had warned early in 1900, U.S. exclusion policies compelled China to refuse to renew the immigration treaty during negotiations in 1904 and resort to retaliation by the anti-American boycott of 1905. In 1909, Wu resigned, turning his energies to public welfare activities. After the Chinese Revolution of 1911*, he affiliated himself with the revolutionary movement.

Feng Ziyou, *Geming yishi* [Revolutionary Historic Anecdote], vol. 2 (Beijing, 1981); M. H. Hunt, *Frontier Defense and the Open Door: Manchuria in Chinese-American Relations, 1895–1911* (New Haven, 1973); Li Xin (ed.), *Zonghua Minguo renwu zhuan* [Who's Who of the Republic China], vol. 1 (Beijing, 1978); *Qingdai renwu zhuan* [Biography of the Qing Dynasty (Shenyang, 1992).

Cai Daiyun

X

XIAN INCIDENT

In December 1936, the Manchurian army of the "Young Marshal" Zhang Xueliang* kidnapped Jiang Jieshi* at Xian in Shaansi Province. After "some of the most complex and delicate negotiations in China's modern history," Jonathan Spence writes, his release forged the United Front* between the Chinese Communist Party* (CCP) and the Guomindang* (Nationalists) against Japan. During the 1930s, Jiang decided to use his German-trained armies to exterminate the Chinese Communist forces, rather than in resistance against the steady aggression of Japan in Manchuria and North China following the Mukden Incident*. The climax of this strategy was the Long March of 1934 and 1935, which left the battered CCP headquartered at Yan'an in Shaansi Province. Jiang immediately planned a final annihilation campaign against Mao Zedong* and his survivors. His objective was opposed by many Chinese, from Zhang Xueliang, whose army had been routed from Manchuria by the Japanese, to the students who had demonstrated and been jailed for anti-Japanese demonstrations in the December Ninth protests of 1935.

Sensing insubordination and inaction on the Shaansi front, Jiang flew to Xian in December 1936 to urge prompt and vigorous action against the Communist remnant. He also ordered bomber units into the region to assure quick reduction of the enemy. Unknown to him, the CCP and Zhang had been in conversations throughout the year. As early as January 1936, the CCP had released prisoners of war from earlier combat, after indoctrinating them with "united front" ideas. Zhou Enlai* charmed Zhang with his sincerity and his tales of childhood in Mukden. By contrast, the Anti-Comintern Pact* between Germany and Japan in November 1936 raised fears about Jiang's anti-Japanese credentials, given his reliance on German military advisers. Thus, when Jiang flew to Xian, he was greeted with both suspicion and animosity.

Upon arrival, Jiang demanded total loyalty to the anti-Communist offensive. Zhang Xueliang's troops promptly arrested him, holding Jiang in custody for two weeks. During this time, the Nanjing government was divided between negotiations and a rescue effort, whereas the Communists debated negotiations versus execution. In Moscow, Soviet Premier Joseph Stalin decided the issue. Mao and Zhou were directed to seek a national front against Japan led by Jiang Jieshi's national prestige. Jiang was released and, under unclear circumstances, a Second United Front was proclaimed in August and September

1937, after the Shanghai fighting began on 13 August. From 1937 to the New Fourth Army Incident of 1941, the two forces fought as one against the Japanese invaders. For the rest of the war, however, the coalition was nominal rather than real. Each side hoped to achieve partisan victory following World War II, in preparation for resumption of the Chinese Civil War* after Japan surrendered.

L. Eastman et al., *The Nationalist Era in China, 1927–1949* (New York, 1991); J. Spence, *The Search for Modern China* (New York, 1990); T. Wu, *The Sian Incident: A Pivotal Point in Modern Chinese History* (Ann Arbor, MI, 1976).

Errol M. Clauss

XUAN THUY (1912–1985)

Vietnamese revolutionary Xuan Thuy was minister for foreign affairs for the Democratic Republic of Vietnam* (DRV) and representative at the Paris Peace Talks*. Born in Ha Dong Province in northern Vietnam, he joined the revolutionary cause at age sixteen with the Than Nien (Revolutionary Youth Association) and was a founding member of the Indochinese Communist Party. Like most revolutionaries, Xuan Thuy spent time in the 1930s on the French island prison of Poulo Condore, where he endured underground cells, heat, humidity, and disease. Thuy played a pivotal role in the 1945 August Revolution and was editor for an official and important Communist Party newspaper, *Cuu Quoc* (National Salvation). His theoretical writings crystallized the movement and offered a clear voice to the revolution. Shortly after the DRV was created, Thuy in 1946 joined the National Assembly, where he exercised a measure of influence on wartime diplomacy. He rose through the diplomatic corps, serving as foreign minister from 1963 to 1965.

Xuan Thuy headed the DRV delegation at the Paris peace negotiations from 1968 to 1970. For that entire period, he steadfastly insisted on a unilateral American withdrawal from Vietnam, recognition of the National Liberation Front* (NLF) as the legitimate government of South Vietnam, the dissolution of the Republic of Vietnam* government of Nguyen Van Thieu*, and the reunification of Vietnam. U.S. conditions included withdrawal of North Vietnamese troops from the south and an end to DRV support of the Viet Cong*. At one point, President Richard M. Nixon* instructed U.S. negotiator Henry A. Kissinger* to warn Thuy that increased air attacks against targets in North Vietnam would result unless he agreed to compromise. Kissinger and Thuy also met in secret talks, but failed to accomplish anything substantive. Ultimately, Nixon resorted to Vietnamization* to extricate the United States from Vietnam and expanded the air war to force the DRV's hand in negotiations. In 1970, Xuan Thuy was replaced by Le Duc Tho* as head of the DRV negotiating team, but stayed in Paris as Tho's deputy. He participated in signing the Paris Peace Accords* in January 1973. At the Fourth Party Congress in 1976, Thuy became secretary of the Central Committee, a position he held until 1983. *See also* Second Indochina War.

S. Karnow, *Vietnam: A History* (New York, 1983); G. Porter, *A Peace Denied: The United States, Vietnam, and the Paris Agreement* (Bloomington, IN, 1975); M. B. Young, *The Vietnam Wars, 1945–1990* (New York, 1991).

Robert K. Brigham

Y

YALTA AGREEMENT ON THE FAR EAST

Early in 1945, Yalta, on Russia's Crimean peninsula in the Black Sea, was the site of the penultimate summit conference in World War II. U.S. President Franklin D. Roosevelt*, British Prime Minister Winston Churchill, and Soviet Premier Joseph Stalin met there from 4 to 11 February to achieve consensus about the shape of the postwar world order, including East Asia. Although the Yalta Agreement on the Far East later would become the object of much criticism, the Allied leaders discussed other issues at the Yalta Conference, including plans for the creation of a postwar United Nations, the political future of Eastern Europe, the boundaries of Poland, and measures for reconstruction of Germany.

Central to the Yalta Agreement on the Far East was Stalin's promise that Soviet forces would enter the Pacific war within "two to three months" after the surrender of Nazi Germany. In return, the Soviet Union would regain control over the southern half of Sakhalin, which Japan had seized in 1905 after the Russo-Japanese War*, and the Kurile Islands. Stalin also agreed to sign a pact of alliance and friendship with the Republic of China* (ROC) and thereby endorse its leader Jiang Jieshi*. He received in return a promise of American support for Soviet leaseholds at Dairen and Port Arthur and recognition of the Communist government in Outer Mongolia.

At Yalta, Roosevelt and Stalin also discussed the future of Korea. U.S. policy in World War II was to prevent any single power from dominating postwar Korea. Roosevelt therefore proposed to Stalin a trusteeship for Korea consisting of the United States, the Soviet Union, and the ROC. Stalin approved the plan in principle, insisting on adding Britain and recommending prohibition of foreign troops in Korea after its liberation. But no formal arrangement for Korea's future status was included in the Yalta Agreement on the Far East. As a result, President Harry S. Truman proposed the Thirty-Eighth Parallel Division* of the peninsula in August 1945.

The Yalta Agreement on the Far East became a source of controversy and criticism because Roosevelt seemingly made unnecessary territorial concessions to Stalin to secure Soviet entry into the Pacific war. Those catigating the president emphasize that the Atomic Attacks* forced the surrender of the Japanese, rather than the Soviet army's intervention. Many observers then and thereafter attributed the president's failure to protect U.S. interests to failing health that led to his death less than three months after returning to the United States. For Roosevelt, securing Stalin's support for Jiang, rather than Mao Zedong*, as China's leader was a major achievement. Postwar critics charged, however, that these concessions resulted in the triumph of the Chinese Communist Party* over the Guomindang* government in the Chinese Civil War*.

R. D. Buhite, *Decision at Yalta: An Appraisal of Summit Diplomacy* (Wilmingon, DE, 1986); W. A. Harriman and E. Able, *Special Envoy to Churchill and Stalin, 1941–1946* (New York, 1975); A. Perlmutter, *FDR and Stalin: A Not So Grand Alliance, 1943–1945* (Columbia, MO, 1993); E. R. Stettinius Jr., *Roosevelt and the Russians* (Westport, CT, 1970).

Han Kyu-sun

YAMAMOTO ISOROKU (1884–1943)

Admiral Yamamoto Isoroku was the commander of the Combined Fleet of the Imperial Japanese Navy and best known for planning the Pearl Harbor Attack* on 7 December 1941. For many Americans, he personified the Japanese unwillingness to abide by international rules of war. Yamamoto was the sixth son of a former samurai and adopted by the Yamamoto family as an adult. A 1904 graduate of the Naval Academy at Etajima, he saw action in the Russo-Japanese War*, in which he was severely injured. His career included language study at Harvard University from 1917 to 1919 and assignment as an attaché in Washington, D.C. (1926–1928). Yamamoto was executive officer of a naval air station in 1924, becoming one of the leading advocates and experts in naval air warfare. He was active in the development of fast carrier-based aircraft, and later commanded the First Carrier Division.

Yamamoto was opposed to war against the United States and/or Great Britain, arguing that the greater industrial development of the West would mean defeat in a war of attrition. He was sent to sea during 1939 to protect him from assassination by extremists within Japanese military and society. When he became convinced that war was inevitable, Yamamoto planned an attack on the U.S. naval base at Pearl Harbor. He speculated that the destruction of the Pacific Fleet would allow Japan to reinforce her island possessions sufficiently that, faced with a long, expensive conflict in Asia while possibly also involved in the war in Europe, the United States might negotiate an armistice before Japan's critical possessions were threatened. He also planned the campaign that led to the Battle of Midway*, which resulted in the loss of four Japanese fleet carriers and most of the experienced carrier pilots. In April 1943, while flying on an inspection tour of Japanese bases in the Northern Solomons, Yamamoto's plane was deliberately shot down north of Bougainville by U.S. pilots.

H. Agawa, *The Reluctant Admiral: Yamamoto and the Imperial Navy* (New York, 1979); S. Howarth (ed.), *Men of War: Great Naval Leaders of World War II* (New York, 1993); E. P. Hoyt, *Three Military Leaders: Tojo, Yamamoto, Yamashita* (New York, 1993).

Katherine K. Reist

YAN XISHAN (1886–1960)

Yan Xishan was a powerful Chinese military leader after the fall of the Qing Dynasty in 1912 who had strained relations with the United States during the Warlord Era* and after. He was born in Shansi Province, where his family for generations had been minor bankers and merchants. After briefly studying the classics in a traditional Chinese school, Yan was enrolled in one of the new military academies established as part of the Qing program of military modernization beginning from the last decade of the nineteenth century. An excellent student, in 1904, he was sent to Japan to continue his military education, and graduated from the Imperial Military Academy in

1909. While in Japan, Yan became involved in the antidynastic revolution started by Sun Zhongshan*, and joined the United League. In 1908, he returned home and was made a brigade commander of the New Shansi Army, where he found many officers were, like himself, also revolutionaries. When the Chinese Revolution of 1911* started, Yan and his fellow revolutionaries responded by attacking the Qing garrison in Shansi, and soon declared the province independent. By combining military authority with revolutionary legitimacy, Yan was made military governor of the province and held the position for the next two decades virtually without interruption.

During his tenure, Yan devoted himself to government administration, earning a reputation as the "model governor" for the peace and prosperity of his province. His ideology was eclectic, borrowing ideas from a range of theories and ideologies both in the East and West, yet its core remained Confucian, believing in the rule of moral superiority. Like many of his contemporaries, Yan often spoke in nationalistic terms, particularly denouncing imperialism in China. He refused, however, to accept Sun Zhongshan's nationalism, insisting that violence against foreign interests in China was disorderly and therefore inappropriate. In 1926, when the Northern Expedition appeared irresistible, Yan was forced to take sides before he was engulfed, and he joined the National Revolutionary Army under the command of Jiang Jieshi*. Thus, the virtual independence of Shansi Province since 1911 came to an end.

The marriage between Yan and the Guomindang* (Nationalist) government in Nanjing was by no means harmonious. When the central government attempted to take more control in his province, he joined other warlords in a war against Jiang's forces during 1929 and 1930. Yan lost and was forced to announce his retirement from the public life, although his influence in Shansi remained deeply rooted. Throughout the time when Jiang was taking pains to consolidate his rule in the country, Yan was a wild card that Jiang found necessary to manage from time to time. For the foreign powers in China, Yan's reform program and foreign policy appeared ambiguous. His deep roots in tradition and strong link with Japanese interests frequently constituted a problem in particular for the Anglo-American influences in China Jiang was trying to cultivate. In 1932, after the Mukden Incident* the previous September, Yan was once again incorporated into the Nationalist government and resumed his rule in Shansi. But this time his main task was to revive his reform program to ward off the rising threat of the Chinese Communist Party* in that region. In 1949, Yan, like many of his colleagues, was forced off the mainland and moved to Taiwan*.

J. E. Sheridan, *China in Disintegration: The Republican Era in Chinese History, 1912–1949* (New York, 1975); J. E. Sheridan, *Chinese Warlord: The Career of Feng Yu-hsiang* (Stanford, CA, 1966).

Li Yi

YAP CONTROVERSY

During and after World War I, the dispute over Yap was a prime example of how the United States challenged Japan's advance into the Pacific, leading ultimately to war after the Pearl Harbor Attack*. What made Yap valuable was that transoceanic cables met there, connecting such distant terminals as Shanghai, Guam*, and Menado in the Dutch East Indies. In October 1914, Japan, after it had declared war on Germany, seized all of its lands in the Pacific north of the equator. Alarmed by the force, speed, and secrecy with which the Japanese had taken Micronesia*, the Western allies were determined that Japan would not be allowed to use these islands as either naval or economic bases for the penetration of Melanesia or Southeast Asia. In April 1919 at the Versailles Peace Conference, President Woodrow Wilson* asked that Yap be set aside in considering the award of the other Micronesian Islands under the Mandate System*, but then did not protest the decision in May that failed to exclude Yap.

Yap's status was a contentious issue during the debate in the U.S. Senate over ratification of the Versailles Peace Treaty*. Wilson said he *assumed* Yap had been included in the mandate provisions, but this flawed explanation only added to Senate unhappiness with the outcome, contributing to rejection of the treaty and U.S. membership in the League of Nations. Thereafter, Wilson pursued unsuccessfully the impossible object of securing an international rehearing on disposition of Yap. Then, in November 1920, the United States announced it would not recognize the decision on Micronesia, but this had no effect on the League council, when, in December, it confirmed the Japanese mandate, again without reference to Yap. Two months later, Washington sent a protest, insisting that no such award could be made without U.S. consent because as an Associated power, it had an equal concern in the disposition of the German territory. The League council replied that since the original agreement was drafted by the victorious powers, the U.S. complaint was with those nations. In one of his last official acts, Wilson denied that the United States ever had consented to the disposition of Yap, and thus considered the entire Japanese mandate invalid.

The Republican Harding administration was just as determined to defend U.S. interests in Yap. It also feared Japanese perfidy. U.S. suspicions arose from Japan's continuing restrictions on the entry of foreign trade and vessels into Japanese waters. For the U.S. Navy, fearful that the Japanese might secretly be violating its pledge and constructing a network of formidable naval bases, access to Micronesia by American vessels and commerce became a vital objective. For its part, the War Department saw the possibility of using the issue of Yap cables to seek access to any and all cables in Micronesia. Both military services thus pressed for modification in the arrangements by which Japan controlled Micronesia. To this end, Secretary of State Charles Evans Hughes* informed the Allied powers, including Japan, that since the United States had not signed the Versailles Treaty, it was not bound to its provisions and therefore did not recognize Japan's mandate over Micronesia. By then, other issues were increasing bilateral tensions and adding pressure for resolving the Yap dispute, such as Japan's massive Siberian Intervention*, the collapse of talks over immigration, U.S. indignation over Japan's refusal to implement the Shandong Agreement*, and the quickening naval arms race between the two powers. To resolve these problems, the United States convened the Washington Conference* in November 1921.

Japan feared that the Western powers would force it to relinquish its wartime gains at Washington. But Prime Minister Hara Kei* was sensitive to the need to lessen Japan's isolation. To minimize the chance of becoming the target of antagonism, he decided to settle as many outstanding problems as possible on a bilateral basis with the United States before the conference began. Negotiations began in the summer of 1921 and Japan gave way, by stages, to U.S. demands. By September, the Japanese government essentially accepted American insistence on access to Yap and use of the cables there, as well as on American rights to residence and property. In December, Tōkyō agreed to the right of free entrance for U.S. vessels into Micronesian territorial waters and agreed to extend to the mandate islands the provisions of the Treaty of Commerce and Navigation between the United States and Japan. These concessions were formalized in a convention signed on 11 February 1922, by which the United States finally recognized Japan's mandate over Micronesia, and Japan reiterated the pledges it had given to the League of Nations not to fortify its mandate.

R. Dingman, *Power in the Pacific: Origins of Naval Arms Limitation, 1914–1922* (Chicago, 1976);

M. R. Peattie, *Nanyo: The Rise and Fall of the Japanese in Micronesia, 1885–1945* (Honolulu, HI, 1988); T. Yanihara, *Pacific Islands Under Japanese Mandate* (London, 1938).

Dirk A. Ballendorf

YE GONGCHAO (1904–1981)

Known in the United States as George K. C. Yeh, Ye Gongchao was the foreign minister of the Republic of China* (ROC) from 1950 to 1958, serving in this post longer than any other person. From 1958 to 1961, he was ambassador to the United States. Educated in the United States and Britain, he began his career as a university professor of English literature and writer. Two years after the Marco Polo Bridge Incident* ignited the Sino-Japanese War in 1937, he entered government service, working in the ROC's Ministry of Information from 1939 to 1946. In World War II, Ye was in charge of the Guomindang* (Nationalist) government's propaganda efforts in Singapore* and London, making effective contacts with many Allied leaders, including Winston Churchill, Anthony Eden, and Dwight D. Eisenhower*. During the Chinese Civil War*, he joined the Foreign Ministry and became foreign minister after the ROC fled to Taiwan*. Ye faced the difficult tasks of maintaining the ROC's international position as the government of China and of winning back U.S. support following the announcement on 5 January 1950 of President Harry S. Truman* that the United States would not provide aid and advice to Chinese forces on Taiwan.

Ideological preferences aside, increasing numbers of non-Communist nations decided that it was necessary to acknowledge the People's Republic of China* (PRC) as a political entity. One after another, they recognized the Beijing regime and urged that the latter be admitted into the United Nations. Retaining Taibei's UN seat therefore became one of Ye's major tasks, and he headed the ROC delegation to attend the UN General Assembly six times during his nine years as foreign minister. After the start of the Korean War* and the Neutralization of Taiwan*, Washington was determined to deny UN membership to the PRC. Ye thus was able to secure enough support for the moratorium resolution that deferred the debate on Chinese Representation in the United Nations* during the 1950s. He also visited nations in Southeast Asia, Europe, and the Middle East to secure their support of the ROC. He was the plenipotentiary in charge of negotiating the Sino-Japanese Peace Treaty of 1952* that confirmed Tōkyō's recognition of the ROC and delayed its formal relations with the PRC for two decades. More difficult for Ye was obtaining a U.S. commitment to establish a formal alliance with his government. By the end of his tenure, however, the United States was bound steadfastly to the ROC through the U.S.-China Mutual Defense Treaty of 1954*, various agreements, and large economic and military aid programs. Cold War events worked to his advantage, in particular consecutive crises in Korea, French Indochina*, and the Taiwan Strait. Ye played a key role in the Taiwan Strait Crises*, negotiating evacuation of the Dachen islands that helped reduced tension in 1955 and the joint communiqué that contributed to end of the confrontation in 1958.

When conferring with U.S. officials, Ye often appeared to be sensitive, even sympathetic, toward U.S. positions, even when they contradicted his government's policies. At the same time, Ye was never shy about speaking his mind. Therefore, he was able to work closely with Karl L. Rankin*, U.S. ambassador in Taiwan from 1953 to 1957, John Foster Dulles* and Christian Herter, secretaries of state, and Dean Rusk* and Walter S. Robertson*, assistant secretaries of state for the Far East. President John F. Kennedy* and his advisers even believed they could count on Ye to persuade Jiang Jieshi* to change his mind about vetoing Outer Mongolia's application for UN membership. Ye's frank and sympathetic presentations of the U.S. positions might have contributed to his dismissal in October 1961, which abruptly ended his career as a diplomat. Thereafter, he served as minister without portfolio until 1978 and for the next three years as counselor to the president. Ye was not only an acclaimed writer, calligrapher, and painter, but also a sponsor of research on acupuncture, and to those he devoted the remainder of his life.

Chin Hsien-tsu (ed.), *Ye Gongchao: qi ren, qi wen, qi shih* [About Ye Gongchao: His Personality, Writings, and Career] (Taibei, 1983); Fu Chao-hsiang, *Ye Gongchao zhuan* [The Biography of Ye Gongchao] (Taibei, 1994); "Yeh Kung-ch'ao," in *Biographical Dictionary of Republican China* (New York, 1970).

Chang Su-Ya

YEH, GEORGE K. C.

See YE GONGCHAO

YEN HSI-SHAN

See YAN XISHAN

YIXIN (1832–1898)

Yixin was a Chinese prince of the Qing Dynasty who was granted the title of Gong and acted as the Tongzhi emperor's chief minister. At the moment during the Second Opium War* when the British and French troops were pressing on toward Beijing in October 1860, he was empowered to negotiate with the British and French and concluded the Beijing Treaties with the two nations, as well as the Treaty of Tianjin* with the United States. His experience in dealing with foreign affairs revealed him as quite different from his bureaucrat colleagues, being more familiar with and attaching more importance to the international diplomatic practice. By his suggestion, the Qing court established an office to control foreign affairs named the Zongli Yamen* in 1861 and made him responsible to the office. His recommendation resulted in creation of a foreign languages academy named the Tongwen Guan in 1862. Prince Gong advanced cooperation and association with foreign countries and learned their techniques for China's self-strengthening. His diplomatic practice shaped his views on the powers, which he explained in a memorial to the throne, describing Britain as overbearing, Russia as unpredictable, and France and America as focused on profit. Actually, he saw the United States as "respectful and submissive" and consequently always asked the Americans to mediate disputes between China and other powers.

In December 1865, the United States announced that the U.S. government was willing to accept Chinese representatives because of the harmonious relations and the commercial importance between the two nations. At the end of 1867, Yixin proposed to the Tongzhi emperor that, because the foreign countries were well acquainted with China, although China was absolutely ignorant of them, it was critical to send a mission abroad. The proposal was accepted in principle, but the question of who the suitable person to lead the mission was still remaining. Yixin gave consideration to U.S. Minister in China Anson Burlingame*. When Burlingame's tenure was over in 1868, Yixin offered him the invitation at the farewell banquet: "If it is possible for a legate to serve two countries, we are willing to engage you as our envoy." After Burlingame responded positively, Prince Gong recommended him to the court, arguing that the United States had the most favorable attitude toward China among the foreign powers. Since the Qing court distrusted appointing a foreigner as its envoy, Yixin proposed a one-year experiment, with two Chinese officials as associates. In November 1868, Burlingame was appointed as Chinese envoy to all countries having treaty relations with China.

In 1879, the Ryūkyū conflict occurred between China and Japan. Yixin, who always had placed hope in the United States, came to see former U.S. President Ulysses S. Grant while Grant was in Beijing on his travels around the world, and asked him for mediation. Yixin indicated to Grant that U.S. trade might be destroyed if a war broke out, whereas Grant could win praise if he succeeded in mediation. Grant agreed, helping to end the crisis. In 1884, the Vietnam conflict occurred between China and France. Prince Gong was not in favor of reckless shedding of blood and advocated the use of diplomatic methods to solve the problem. Because the prowar party was dominant in the court at the time, Yixin was reprimanded, recalled, and relieved of his duties.

Chouban yiwu shimo, Xianfeng chao, Tongzhi Chao [Complete Record of the Management of Barbarian Affairs in the Qing Dynasty, Xianfeng and Tongzhi Periods] (Beijing, 1930); Zhao Erxun, *Qingshi gao* [Manuscript of Qing Dynasty History] (Beijing, 1977).

Xiang Liling

YMCA AND YWCA IN CHINA AND JAPAN

The Young Men's Christian Association (YMCA) and Young Women's Christian Association (YWCA), as part of the Western mission reform movement, expanded into East Asia at the end of the nineteenth century to promote Christianity as well as peace and understanding between classes, nations, and races. When first founded, the British and American YMCAs and YWCAs focused their efforts on serving the needs of young industrial workers and students in their home countries. But soon its workers joined missionaries in foreign fields at the invitation of the American Board of Commissioners for Foreign Missions*. The YMCA and YWCA foreign secretaries at first were active in Christianizing Chinese and Japanese nationals, as well as offering classes in English and Bible study. They were agents of cultural imperialism who brought their biases and beliefs in Western cultural superiority with them to Asia. American secretaries in particular believed that they had embarked on a divinely appointed mission to bring democratic and capitalist values to the "less fortunate" Asian peoples. Yet most often, they were educated in secular institutions and became strong supporters of a liberal theology that infected Western Protestant churches at the turn of the century. Often, they focused in the field on social welfare work rather than proselytizing. As the twentieth century progressed, the YMCA and YWCA in China and Japan became more secular and inclusive of varied social classes, working more often with non-Christian and nationalist political movements that were gaining momentum in both countries. Also, each became an influential non-governmental organization, as secretaries often sought to influence their home governments' Asian policies.

The YMCA was established in Japan during the Meiji Restoration in 1889. Both American secretaries and Japanese Christians believed there were great opportunities for the YMCA to promote modernity and Christian morality in Japan. Moreover, the secretaries were able to organize without government interference. However, strong Japanese nationalism always prevented wholesale adoption of Western ways, even by Japanese Christians. Collaboration between American and Japanese secretaries was most successful when the YMCA organization served Japan's national interests, such as when it organized relief and recreation for Japanese soldiers in the Russo-Japanese War*. However, U.S. and Japanese national interests clashed with Japan's increasingly aggressive expansion into China beginning in the 1920s. Meanwhile, the YWCA had been established in Japan in 1903, experiencing similar initial optimism that shared Christianity could overcome national conflict. American YWCA secretaries provided leadership and organizational training for Japanese Christian women who soon were leading their own associations. With some American and other foreign assistance, the Japanese YWCA organized hostels for female travelers at the busy port of Yokohama. YWCA associations in Yokohama, Kōbe, and Ōsaka organized schools to train female secretarial and clerical staff for Japan's new modern businesses. During the 1920s, the YWCA organized an Emigration Department to assist Japanese women traveling to the United States as "picture brides" for Japanese men who had emigrated there. The department later assisted the "failed picture brides" in reentering Japanese society.

The YMCA was established in China in 1870, followed by the YWCA in 1890. Both associations initially served student and urban communities, with the former teaching English and Western academic subjects to wealthy Chinese men living in the coastal treaty ports and the latter offering instruction in homemaking and child care, in addition to English and Bible classes, to wealthy Chinese wives and students. Both the YMCA and YWCA expanded their constituencies to include Chinese workers after World War I, providing instruction in basic Chinese literacy, hygiene, and Christian morality, while becoming more interested in nationalist politics. Anti-imperialist demonstrations led by Chinese workers and students increased dramatically after the May Fourth Movement* in 1919, and secretaries joined in advocating industrial reform and the revision of the "unequal" treaties. They also pressed American businessmen, without success, to improve wages and working conditions in factories in the foreign concession zones in China. Beginning in 1922, YMCA and YWCA secretaries worked closely with the National Christian Council of China to start investigations of factory conditions and to lobby the Shanghai Municipal Council to institute child labor laws. Following the outburst of militant nationalism in the 1925 May Thirtieth Movement*, several YMCA and YWCA secretaries, to escape hypocrisy, signed pledges forsaking extraterritorial privileges and U.S. "gunboat" protection. The vibrant cross-cultural exchanges between the American and Chinese people that the secretaries started and maintained resulted in people and ideas flowing between missions, schools, churches, communities, and the YMCA and YWCA associations in the United States.

By the late 1920s in Japan, the internationalism promoted by the YMCA and YWCA eroded, as Japanese policy began to focus on territorial expansion into China. American secretaries sympathized with China as an invaded country unable to defend itself against Japan's aggression after the Mukden Incident* in September 1931. Those American secretaries who stayed in Japan in the 1930s were observers, not leaders or even participants, in the Japanese YMCA and YWCA activities. During that decade, Japanese YMCA and YWCA secretaries provided war relief for Japanese soldiers and helped train Japanese industrial workers, becoming unwilling participants in Japan's war project. Meanwhile, cultural connections ensured that the sympathies of the American public and the U.S. government were with the Chinese people. During the 1930s, U.S. government loans and other forms of aid to the Guomindang* (Nationalist) government and the formal U.S. alliance with the Republic of China* in World War II were the result, in large part, of the "special relationship" that Americans thought they had with China and that was forged by the American Christian community in China. After Japan's defeat and the triumph of the Chinese Communist Party* in the Chinese Civil War*, the YMCA and YWCA secretaries worked to sustain cultural connections between the American and Chinese people. In occupied Japan, the YMCA and YWCA organizations revived, adopting a pro-Western and international orientation. In China, however, Cold War tensions between the U.S. government and the People's Republic of China* led to expulsion of all American missionaries from China in 1952. Although Chinese YWCA secretaries continued to operate associations inside China, little contact or cooperation with the American or World YWCA organizations occurred until China liberalized national policies during the 1970s and 1980s.

N. Boyd, *Emissaries: The Overseas Work of the American YWCA, 1895–1970* (New York, 1986); J. T. Davidann, *A World of Crisis and Progress: The American YMCA in Japan, 1890–1930* (Bethlehem, PA, 1998); S. Garrett, *Social Reformers in Urban China: The Chinese YMCA, 1895–1926* (Cambridge, MA, 1970); E. D. Harper and H. R. Gillmore, *For a Better World: A History of the YWCA Policy in Public Affairs* (New York, 1948); C. A. Keller, "Making Model Citizens: The Chinese YMCA, Social Activism, and Internationalism in Republican China, 1919–1937," Ph.D. dissertation, University of Kansas, 1996.

Karen Garner

YOSHIDA LETTER

Dated 24 December 1951, this letter informed the U.S. government of Japan's decision to establish normal relations with the Republic of China* (ROC) on Taiwan*, rather than the People's Republic of China* (PRC). It was ghost written by John Foster Dulles*, special consultant to Secretary of State Dean G. Acheson*, and signed by Japanese Prime Minister Yoshida Shigeru*. Released simultaneously on 16 January 1952 to the American and Japanese public, the letter was the foundation for Japanese policy regarding China until September 1972, when Prime Minister Tanaka Kakuei* restored contacts with the PRC. The Yoshida Letter became controversial almost immediately after its release because there were suspicions that Dulles had forced Yoshida to sign it as a condition for restoration of Japanese sovereignty. Moreover, the letter caused a diplomatic rift between Britain and the United States because of a series of misunderstandings that occurred prior to the letter's release. The initial problem arose from the fact that Britain had recognized the PRC to secure a financial foothold on the mainland and also protect its hold over Hong Kong*. Conversely, the United States recognized the ROC. This became an issue when Britain and the United States met to discuss which China should sign the Japanese Peace Treaty*. To break the deadlock, Dulles and British Foreign Secretary Herbert Morrison agreed on 19 June 1951 to exclude both Chinas and let Japan determine its own policy on the matter.

Despite the Dulles-Morrison Agreement, the former hoped that Japan eventually would recognize the ROC and even extracted a verbal statement of intent to this effect from Yoshida. But then Yoshida made ambiguous and contradictory statements in the Japanese Diet about Japan's relations with the PRC in October 1951. This was a cause of concern for Dulles, who feared that the U.S. Senate might raise objections to ratification of the Japanese Peace Treaty without concrete proof of Japan's intention to toe the U.S. policy line on China. Therefore, in November, Livingston Merchant, assistant secretary of state for Far Eastern affairs, traveled to London in an attempt to gain release from the Dulles-Morrison Agreement. Britain's new conservative government refused, however, to breach the June agreement. By this time, U.S. officials suspected that British officials, especially Sir Esler Dening* in Tōkyō, wanted Japan to recognize the PRC so that Japan would not have to seek alternate trade outlets in Southeast Asia and encroach on Britain's traditional trading area. In response to British inflexibility, Dulles consulted with Democratic Senator John Sparkman of Alabama and Republican Senator H. Alexander Smith* of New Jersey, who agreed that a written statement by Yoshida would assist in Senate passage of the treaty. In December, Dulles traveled to Tōkyō with Sparkman and Smith, and persuaded Yoshida to write a letter for release after it had been shown to British Prime Minister Winston Churchill and Foreign Secretary Anthony Eden during their state visit to Washington in early January.

Although U.S. officials showed the Yoshida Letter to the British ambassador in Washington, Britain never received a hard copy or prior warning before its publication. Therefore, British officials left Washington on the understanding that Britain and the United States would agree to disagree on the China issue. The release of the letter on 16 January 1952, therefore, came as a surprise to British officials and led to public speculation about an Anglo-American dispute over the issue. After the release of the Yoshida Letter, Japan entered into peace negotiations with the ROC and signed the Sino-Japanese Peace Treaty of 1952* on 28 April. Scholars debate whether Japan had any other option but to commit to sign a peace treaty with the government of Jiang Jieshi* on Taiwan. Some writers believe that Japan might have been able to negotiate a more limited agreement allowing for an earlier normalization of relations between Japan and the PRC. Others contend that without a concrete letter of intent from Japan, the U.S. Senate might have refused to ratify the Japanese Peace Treaty. As for Britain's position, many assert that British officials were unrealistic to believe that Japan could have reached an independent decision, given its dependence on the United States.

J. W. Dower, *Empire and Aftermath: Yoshida Shigeru and the Japanese Experience, 1878–1954* (Cambridge, MA, 1988); C. Hosoya, "Japan, China, the United States and the United Kingdom, 1951–52: The Case of the 'Yoshida Letter,'" *International Affairs* (1984); P. Lowe, *Containing the Cold War in East Asia: British Policies Towards Japan, China and Korea, 1948–53* (Manchester, UK, 1997); H. B. Schonberger, "Peacemaking in Asia: The United States, Great Britain, and the Japanese Decision to Recognize Nationalist China, 1951–52," *Diplomatic History* (Winter 1986).

Yokoi Noriko

YOSHIDA SHIGERU (1878–1967)

Yoshida Shigeru was an idiosyncratic and strong-minded Japanese diplomat and statesman before and after World War I who worked to prevent a major conflict with the United States and Britain. After World War II, he was prime minister from 1946 to 1954 and laid the foundation for Japan's economic reconstruction, political stability, and close relations with the United States. Born in Yokohama, Yoshida was adopted by a trading merchant. He graduated from the Law Department at Tōkyō Imperial University in 1906 and entered the Foreign Ministry two months later. In 1909, Yoshida married the eldest daughter of Makino Nobuaki*, who became one of the most intimate confidants of Emperor Hirohito*. During his service in the Foreign Ministry, he was consul in Mukden (1925–1928) and then vice minister in the Tanaka Giichi* cabinet in 1929. The next year, Yoshida became ambassador to Italy and then in 1936, ambassador to Britain. Prime Minister Hirōta Koki* considered him for the post of foreign minister, but militarists rejected Yoshida because of his liberal views. He opposed closer ties with Italy and Nazi Germany and was the only ambassador to express his views to the Foreign Ministry. On his return to Japan in 1939, Yoshida resigned from the Foreign Ministry, but the end of his career in the civil service did not stop him from working toward reconciliation with the United States and Britain. He used his personal contacts with U.S. Ambassador to Japan Joseph C. Grew* and British Ambassador to Japan Robert L. Craigie to prevent the outbreak of war.

In 1945, military police arrested Yoshida for his involvement in the writing of a memorial in which former Prime Minister Konoe Fumimaro* attempted to achieve a peace settlement ending World War II. After Japan's surrender, he was named foreign minister in the cabinets of Higashikuni Naruhiko and then Shidehara Kijūrō*. After his Liberal Party won the general elections in 1946, Yoshida became prime minister, when Hatoyama Ichirō*, the party's leader, was purged from politics on the order of the Supreme Commander for the Allied Powers (SCAP*). Thereafter, he presided over five cabinets with only one break from 1947 to 1948, when Katayama Tetsu* and Ashida Hitoshi* were prime ministers. Yoshida's main aims during the U.S. Occupation of Japan* were to preserve the Japanese state and prevent the country from falling into anarchy. He supported preservation of the emperor and reconstruction of the economy, including the financial and labor reforms implemented under the direction of General Douglas MacArthur*. After a year and a half of negotiations with John Foster Dulles*, Yoshida signed in September 1951 both the Japanese Peace Treaty* and the U.S.-Japan Security Treaty of 1951*, whereby Japan regained its sovereignty, but under conditions that made it a close postwar ally of the United States. He also wrote the Yoshida Letter*, in which he aligned Japan with the Guomindang* (Nationalist) government on Taiwan*, rather than the People's Republic of China*.

From 1952, Yoshida entered a fierce political struggle with Hatoyama for the leadership of the Liberal Party. He lost the political battle and was ousted from office in December 1954. Yoshida, however, remained active in politics and wielded great influence as an elder statesman. His reluctance to remilitarize in the postwar period was part of an overall strategy that observers soon labeled the Yoshida Doctrine. It called for Japan to place a priority on economic development over remilitarization, while relying on the United States to protect its security and supporting U.S. policies in international affairs. But he often refuted the doctrine, causing some to argue that Yoshida hoped for the eventual remilitarizing of Japan. His adherents described him as witty, urbane, and charming, but critics considered him autocratic, malicious, and contemptuous, calling him One Man Yoshida. Stubby, acerbic, and always puffing a cigar, he would fend off news cameramen by hitting them with his cane. Wearing his pince-nez eyeglasses, Yoshida enjoyed greeting junior foreign diplomats as "Your Excellency." He was Japan's most important political leader after World War II.

J. W. Dower, *Empire and Aftermath: Yoshida Shigeru and the Japanese Experience, 1878–1954* (Cambridge, MA, 1988); S. Iwao (ed.), *Biographical Dictionary of Japanese History* (New York, 1978); J. I. Matray, *Japan's Emergence as a Global Power* (Westport, CT, 2000); Watanabe Akio (ed.), *Sengo Nihon no saishō tachi* [Japan's Postwar Prime Ministers] (Tōkyō, 1995).

Yokoi Noriko

YUAN SHIKAI (1859–1916)

Yuan Shikai served in important positions in the Chinese government in the late nineteenth and early twentieth centuries, and became the second president of the Republic of China* in 1912. His organizational and training skills while an officer in the Chinese Army and his service in Korea in the 1880s gained the attention of high officials in the Qing Dynasty. In 1885, the government appointed him resident general in Korea, which was under Chinese suzerainty. From 1885 to 1894, he tried to maintain China's hold on Korea by opposing rising Japanese interest there. As resident, Yuan also coped with Americans who advocated independence for Korea. One of these was Owen N. Denny, adviser to the Korean government and formerly U.S. consul at Tianjin. Denny sought to strengthen Korea by weakening its ties to China. During 1887, he tried to encourage Korea's bid for independence when it sent its first diplomatic mission to the United States under the leadership of Dr. Horace N. Allen*. Ignoring Chinese instructions to present credentials to the Chinese embassy, Allen, an American, instead presented them directly to the U.S. government, hoping that this action would generate sympathy for Korean independence. The incident resulted in Denny's resignation. Allen continued to oppose Yuan's efforts to strengthen links between China and Korea, but he failed to change U.S. policy of noninvolvement.

Following the Sino-Japanese War in 1894 and 1895, Yuan presented a plan to the Chinese imperial court to train and equip a modern foreign-style army. In December 1895, the government approved his proposal and commissioned him to command the Newly Created Army. When Yuan became governor of Shandong Province late in 1899, he used this army to suppress the Boxer Uprising* in the province. He also used it to protect foreign missionaries (including Americans) and their Christian converts. Yuan's anti-Boxer campaign forced the Boxers into Zhili Province, where they gained strength and then laid siege to Beijing's foreign legations in July 1900. During the rebellion, Yuan refused to engage the foreign China Relief Expedition*, thus ensuring the liberation of the legations and preventing the destruction of his Newly Created Army. The Americans, Germans, and British then supported Yuan in his successful bid in November 1901 to become governor-general of Zhili Province and commissioner of trade for the northern ports. In his position as governor-general, he negotiated the withdrawal of foreign troops from Tianjin and the Beijing-Shenyang Railway in 1902. His image as a responsible governor aided him in 1903 negotiations resulting in commercial treaties with the United States and Japan, in which China agreed for the first time to the Open Door Policy* and voluntarily created treaty ports.

In 1905, merchants and students in Shanghai and Canton instituted a boycott of American goods in response to the latest of the Exclusion Acts*, as well as other U.S. laws that discriminated against Chinese. The boycott spread to Tianjin in Zhili, where Yuan publicly opposed it. His influence thus helped end the boycott and increased his stature among American diplomats and businessmen. In 1907 and 1908, as president of the ministry of foreign affairs, Yuan unsuccessfully attempted to attract major U.S. investment in Manchuria to counter increasing Japanese influence there, and create an alliance between China and the United States. After he replaced Sun Zhongshan* as president of China in 1912, Yuan failed in his efforts to secure U.S. financial aid. With the outbreak of World War I, he tried to persuade the United States to preserve Chinese neutrality and prevent Japan from attacking German concessions in China. President Woodrow Wilson*, however, decided against involvement in China, although he did recognize Yuan's government. *See also* Chinese Revolution of 1911; Twenty-One Demands.

J. Chen, *Yuan Shi'K'ai 1859–1916* (Stanford, CA, 1961); M. H. Hunt, *The Making of a Special Relationship: The United States and China to 1914* (New York, 1983); S. MacKinnon, *Power and Politics in Late Imperial China: Yuan Shi-kai in Beijing and Tianjin, 1901–1908* (Berkeley, CA, 1980); E. P. Young, *The Presidency of Yuan Shi'k'ai: Liberalism and Dictatorship in Early Republican China* (Ann Arbor, MI, 1977); M. B. Young, *The Rhetoric of Empire: American China Policy, 1895–1901* (Cambridge, MA, 1968).

William E. Emerson

YUNG WING

See RONG HONG

Z

ZAIBATSU

A *zaibatsu*, the Japanese word for financial clique, was a huge and powerful capitalist enterprise, and a handful of these dominated Japan's economy before World War II. They essentially were family-owned business combines, involving a variety of important activities spreading across Japan's economic sector. Each *zaibatsu* had its own banks and credit facilities to finance its diversified interests, as well as a domestic and foreign marketing capacity. The four largest *zaibatsu* were Mitsui, Mitsubishi, Sumitomo, and Yasuda. *Zaibatsu* grew out of diverse backgrounds. Some, such as the Mitsui and the Sumitomo, could trace their origins to merchant firms during the early seventeenth century. But these combines truly began to take shape during the Meiji period after 1868, when Japan's government, eager for rapid growth of economic and national power, was keen on initiating industrialization. Convinced that large-scale enterprises could serve national interests more effectively, Japan's leaders encouraged and supported heavy concentration of wealth in private hands. Thereafter, these large businesses established close ties with the government. Many *zaibatsu*, developing in the Meiji period, actually were started by the so-called *sees* (political merchants). As a result of government guidance, subsidies, and tariff protection, *zaibatsu* were able to branch out into various fields, such as mining, shipping, textiles, domestic commerce, heavy industry, finance, armaments, and foreign trade.

As *zaibatsu* grew in size and power, their opinions began to carry increasing weight in politics, especially as their contributions became a major source of financial support for the political parties. Also, these industrial combines developed close ties with the Japanese military, supporting its drive for imperial expansion to gain access to raw materials and overseas markets to promote economic growth and profits. In the wake of Japan's surrender in World War II, a major initial objective of the Supreme Commander for the Allied Powers (SCAP*) during the U.S. Occupation of Japan* was the breaking of the financial and economic power of *zaibatsu* to achieve demilitarization and democratization. This program of economic deconcentration rested on the belief that the economic combines had acted as barriers to free competition and economic equality while figuring significantly in the triumph of Japanese militaristic imperialism in the 1930s. Under the direction of General Douglas MacArthur*, the *zaibatsu* and their holding companies were ordered dissolved into their various component companies, with their family owners and top executives being purged. The greater bulk of the assets of the *zaibatsu* essentially were confiscated by the government for public sale. In April 1947, an antimonopoly law was passed to prevent concentration of economic power in the future. However, an effort later that year to impose stricter restrictions on excessive concentration of economic control met such strong opposition in Japan that it never was approved. By then, the Reverse Course* in U.S. occupation policy halted economic deconcentration entirely and encouraged the creation of *keiretsu*, closely resembling the *zaibatsu*.

J. Hirschmeier, *The Origins of Entrepreneurship in Meiji Japan* (Cambridge, MA, 1964); T. A. Bisson, *Zaibatsu Dissolution in Japan* (Berkeley, CA, 1954).

Zhang Hong

ZHANG XUELIANG (1898–2001)

Zhang Xueliang, the "Young Marshal of Manchuria," joined the northeastern provinces comprising Manchuria with the Guomindang* (Nationalists) in the latter's attempt to unify China, preventing their alienation to Japan. His activities had some importance in maintaining the U.S. Open Door Policy* in China, reinforced by the Nine Power Pact* of the Washington Conference* of 1921 and 1922. Zhang had been trained by his father, Zhang Zuolin*, the "Old Marshal," as a military commander and his successor. The Japanese believed him to be more easily controlled than his father, who had resisted Japan's increasing restrictions on his decisions. The younger Zhang had been known to indulge in opium, thus seeming weaker in comparison. When an eyewitness informed the Young Marshal of the Japanese role in his father's assassination, Zhang declared his willingness to cooperate with the Guomindang. Jiang Jieshi* used Zhang's troops to fight the Chinese Communist Party* (CCP) in the north. Zhang soon tired of the civil war, particularly after Japan's takeover of Manchuria, which followed the Mukden Incident* in September 1931. Later, he was instrumental in the kidnapping of Jiang in the Xian Incident* in December 1936 to persuade him to form a second United Front* with the CCP to fight Japan. Although Jiang denied that a deal had been struck, a joint effort was begun after the conclusion of the incident. Zhang accompanied Jiang on his return to Nanjing and was placed under house arrest. His confinement continued when the Nationalists fled to Taiwan*, ending only in 1991.

D. A. Jordan, *The Northern Expedition: China's National Revolution of 1926–1928* (Honolulu, HI, 1976); R. Murphey, *East Asia: A New History* (New York, 1997); Y. Sun, *China and the Origins of the Pacific War, 1931–1941* (New York, 1993).

Katherine K. Reist

ZHANG ZUOLIN (1873–1928)

The "Old Marshal of Manchuria" was one of the better known of the military governors of the Warlord Era* in China. His acceptance of Japanese aid and advisers in his attempts to consolidate control over first Manchuria, and then of China, was of concern to the United States in the areas of trade and investment, and in relations with the other powers in China, especially Japan. Zhang Zoulin was from a poor peasant family. He enlisted to fight in the Sino-Japanese War (1894–1895). He took control of Manchuria in 1916, consolidating his domination through alliances and fighting. He expanded industry, especially small-arms production, accepting European as well as Japanese advisers and investments. Since Manchuria was a wealthy section of China, Zhang could afford to pay, feed, and equip his men. He was among the first of the warlords to purchase aircraft to augment his forces. Most of his arms were European in origin, in part because his attempts to secure American weapons were unsuccessful. He fought two major wars in the 1920s to consolidate and then extend his control into China's central provinces. He made many appeals for Western support, particularly after 1926 to Great Britain. Although Western governments did not offer the support he desired, businessmen found him an individual with whom they could easily reach an agreement. Zhang retreated from Beijing in response to the successful Northern Expedition under Jiang Jieshi*. An explosion set off under his railcar by the Japanese killed him in June 1928. Japan's Kwantung Army planned to exploit this incident as a pretext to take control of Manchuria. Strong American protests deterred the attempt.

L. E. Eastman, *The Nationalist Era in China, 1927–1949* (New York, 1991); D. A. Jordan, *The Northern Expedition: China's National Revolution of 1926–1928* (Honolulu, HI, 1976); G. McCormack, *Chang Tso-lin in Northeast China, 1911–1928* (Stanford, CA, 1977).

Katherine K. Reist

ZHOU ENLAI (1898–1976)

Zhou Enlai was one of the top leaders of the Chinese Communist Party* (CCP) before serving as the first premier of the People's Republic of China* (PRC) from 1949 to 1976. He also was the PRC's foreign minister from 1949 to 1956 and after 1937, vice chairman of both the CCP Central Committee and Central Military Commission. During the early 1920s, Zhou was a student activist who formed CCP branches in France. On his return to China in 1924, he became director of the political department at the Whampoa Military Academy, where Jiang Jieshi* was president, during the first CCP alliance with the Guomindang* (GMD). After the two parties split in April 1927, Zhou and Zhu De led an armed revolt on 1 August within the GMD army in central China to create a Communist military force, now celebrated as the founding day of the People's Liberation Army (PLA). He was elected to the CCP Politburo in 1928 and as secretary of the Central Bureau in 1931. When Mao Zedong* emerged as the CCP's leader, Zhou became his chief supporter and thereafter closest working colleague throughout his political career. Together, they led the PLA in the historic Long March from central China to Yan'an in the northwest in 1934 and 1935.

During World War II, Zhou was the chief CCP representative with Jiang's GMD government at Chongqing, successfully negotiating a second United Front* to combat Japan's aggression. After the Pearl Harbor Attack*, he initiated official contact with the U.S. government, resulting in the dispatch of the Dixie Mission* to the CCP headquarters at Yan'an. In 1944, to avoid a collapse of the coalition, U.S. Ambassador Patrick J. Hurley* went to Yan'an to propose a joint postwar government, and Zhou represented the CCP in subsequent negotiations. In August 1945, Hurley personally escorted Mao to Chongqing to join Zhou in failed negotiations with Jiang, reigniting the Chinese Civil War*. In December, President Harry S. Truman* dispatched General George C. Marshall* as his envoy to China to mediate a settlement. Zhou agreed with Mao that the United States was working to undermine the CCP by providing the GMD with military equipment and financial aid. The Marshall Mission* failed because Mao and Jiang would not compromise. Zhou returned to Yan'an and in 1947 served as the PLA's acting chief of the general staff. After the CCP defeated the GMD, he supported Mao's decision to "lean to one side" in the Cold War and support the Soviet Union.

In October 1949 when the PRC was founded, Zhou was third in the hierarchy after Mao and Liu Shaoqi, and the second-most important figure in foreign affairs after Mao. Optimistic and modest, he worked to hold the party together by persuasion and without challenging Mao's key foreign policy decisions, such as Chinese Intervention in the Korean War*. Despite differing worldviews, he implemented Mao's policies through skillful diplomacy. During 1950 and 1951, Zhou established a friendship with India, persuading it to accept China's policy toward Tibet* and to serve as mediator to gain the Korean Armistice Agreement*. During a discussion with an Indian delegation in 1953, he described the Five Principles of Peaceful Coexistence, which marked the opening of a new era of Chinese diplomacy and became the official basis of the PRC's foreign policy after 1954. By then, Zhou was an internationally respected diplomat, known for his flexible approach and pleasant personality, which broke through Cold War hostilities and facilitated amicable relations. He led the Chinese delegations to the Geneva Conference of 1954* on French Indochina* and the Bandung Conference* in 1955. Zhou also showed great diplomatic subtlety during the Taiwan Strait Crises* in 1954 and 1958, declaring that the PRC would "strive for the liberation of Taiwan* by peaceful means so far as it is possible." In 1961, Mao sent Zhou to Moscow, where he walked out of the Congress of the Soviet Communist Party in response to President Nikita Khrushchev's attack on Joseph Stalin and the Communist movement.

Zhou survived the Chinese Cultural Revolution* from 1966 to 1976, when most of the old leaders were purged and Liu died in prison. Exploiting his undisputed role as the chief administrator in the government, he tried to make compromises between radical idealists and conservative pragmatists. Zhou could not stop the revolutionary fever, however, and had to accept the injustices and impracticalities of Mao's measures to disrupt the party apparatus and government bureaucracy. With his acquiescence, extremists jailed or executed many conservatives and distorted China's foreign affairs with mindless zealotry and xenophobia. After thwarting a military coup by Lin Biao* in 1971, he regained control over the administration and worked to improve relations with the United States because the Soviet Union now posed a direct threat to the PRC. In July, he secretly met with Henry A. Kissinger* to arrange for President Richard M. Nixon* to visit the PRC. He also negotiated an end to the ban on the transfer of U.S. dollars to China and Chinese exports into the United States. In February 1972, he met Nixon at the Beijing airport and, a week later, signed the Shanghai Communiqué*, a major step toward U.S.-PRC Normalization of Relations*. In September, Zhou met Japanese Prime Minister Tanaka Kakuei* in Beijing to establish diplomatic relations. Though he received a cancer diagnosis in 1973, he continued to meet U.S. officials, including Secretary of State Kissinger eight times and, in 1975, President Gerald R. Ford*. At the Fourth National People's Congress in early 1975, he made important domestic policy changes to speed economic modernization while preparing Deng Xiaoping* to succeed him as premier. Soon he became very ill, and he was hospitalized for a year before his death. *See also* Zhou-Stuart Conversation.

D. Barnett, *The Making of Foreign Policy in China: Structure and Process* (Boulder, CO, 1985); R. Keith, *The Diplomacy of Zhou Enlai* (New York, 1989); G. Shao, *Zhou Enlai and the Foundations of Chinese Foreign Policy* (New York, 1996); E. Zhou, *Selected Works of Zhou Enlai on Foreign Policy* (Beijing, 1990).

Li Xiaobing

ZHOU-STUART CONVERSATIONS

In early 1949, the National Security Council (NSC) approved three policies on China. NSC 37/2 outlined economic and diplomatic steps to keep Taiwan* out of Communist hands; NSC 41 hoped to keep trade open with the People's Republic of China* (PRC); and NSC 34/2 called for dialogue with the Chinese Communist Party* (CCP) as a means of fostering a Sino-Soviet split, which it anticipated within "twenty to twenty-five years." Based on these policies, Secretary of State Dean G. Acheson* authorized Ambassador to China J. Leighton

Stuart* to establish contacts with the CCP. After Stuart's initial efforts of May-June proved a blind alley, Acheson on 1 July declined to allow Stuart to attend Yenching University commencement exercises in Beijing, fearing a public humiliation. However, Acheson did allow private talks, which resulted in two Zhou-Stuart conversations.

Assistant Secretary of State Dean Rusk* later reported that Stuart met with Zhou before leaving China sometime during the period from 1 July to 2 August 1949. Zhou began the talks describing the United States as wedded to "dictatorial rule," whereas the CCP opposed "aggression, interference, and monopoly." After contrasting Soviet support for the CCP with American prewar scrap iron sales to Japan and ties to Jiang Jieshi*, he remarked, "American's many good points pertain to small matters, Soviet Russia's to large." When Zhou began to moderate his tone, Stuart seized the opening to point out China's dependence on U.S. "petroleum, steel, machinery, cotton, timber, automobiles, paper, photographic supplies, etc.," adding that the United States no longer needed China's silk and tung oil. Zhou shot back that China soon would produce most of what it had once imported, whereas the United States would be unable to find other markets for its "unmanaged" surplus. "The U.S. wants to relieve its crisis and is exporting in great quantity," Zhou proclaimed. "Its stomach is sick with glut, ours with hunger." After citing some inflated statistics, Zhou ended by throwing down the gauntlet on trade: "We must base ourselves on the principle of equal advantage. . . . I do not depend upon you, you depend upon me."

Zhou's rhetoric, along with other factors, led to a general hardening of U.S. attitudes. Stuart suddenly shifted to a hard line in a 14 July report. Max Bishop, director of Northeast Asian Affairs, reported that Acheson found the PRC "inimically antagonistic" and decided "not to recognize" it. As part of a general policy on Asia, NSC 48, Acheson reversed NSC 41's openness to PRC trade. Then he addressed Zhou's gauntlet in a major speech on 15 March 1950:

> I want to make it entirely clear that we have no desire to thrust this trade upon China, nor is China in a position to extort it from us. In the period 1946–1948 the United States supplied over 50% of China's imports and bought approximately a quarter of China's exports. Yet, those same exports from America were less than 5 percent of our total exports and our purchases from China were a mere 2 percent of all we bought abroad. If the present rulers of China wish to believe that we depend on trade with China, we are entirely willing to leave it to the test of experience to prove whether they are right or wrong.

Unfortunately, this "test of experience" lasted more than two decades.

R. L. McGlothlen, *Controlling the Waves: Dean Acheson and U.S. Foreign Policy in Asia* (New York, 1993).

Ronald L. McGlothlen

ZONGLI YAMEN

Establishment of the Zongli Yamen (Office for General Management of the Foreign Office) was a forced provision of the Convention of Beijing in 1860 after the Second Opium War*, which required that the Chinese create a foreign office based on the Western model to handle diplomatic affairs. The Qing Dynasty created it in 1861 initially as a temporary office within the Grand Council, but it was reorganized and formally became the Ministry of Foreign Affairs in 1901. In the immediate aftermath of the burning of the Summer Palace in Beijing in 1860, the Chinese government had little choice but to comply with the Western demand. But soon it became one of the critical components of China's Self-Strengthening Movement from 1860 to 1895. The Zongli Yamen's primary function was to provide China with a sustained period of peaceful coexistence with the Western powers that would allow the Qing government to modernize its military forces. Prince Gong (Yixin*) argued in favor of the creation of a new office to handle foreign affairs and adoption of Western diplomatic practices. "If we act in accordance with the treaties and do not allow [the barbarians] to exceed them by even an inch," Yixin predicted, "then they will not suddenly cause us great harm . . . , even though they may make occasional demands."

The Zongli Yamen fared quite well in its handling of Sino-American relations. With the revision of the Treaty of Tianjin* scheduled to take place in 1868, Yixin and Wenxiang, the senior ministers of the Zongli Yamen, persuaded Anson Burlingame*, U.S. minister to China from 1862 to 1867, to act as China's envoy to dissuade the U.S. and European governments from forcing more demands on China. The Burlingame Mission succeeded in persuading Western powers to follow a policy of restraint in the process of treaty revision. For example, the Burlingame-Seward Treaty* reaffirmed Chinese territorial integrity, clarified American commercial activities in China, and established open immigration between the two nations.

In 1862, the Tongwen Guan, or College of Foreign Languages, was established under the auspices of the Zongli Yamen. Originally, it was intended simply to train translators needed in Sino-Western diplomacy, but eventually the college curriculum was expanded to include courses in science, mathematics, geography, international law, and political economy. Another function of the Tongwen Guan was to send Chinese students abroad to study in the West. The 1868 Burlingame-Seward Treaty included a provision that permitted Chinese students to study in American schools, and Rong Hong* secured the Qing government's approval for the first group of thirty Chinese youths to travel to the United States in 1872. The Zongli Yamen eventually withdrew the education mission to the United States in 1881. The primary reasons were increasing hostility against Chinese immigration in the United States and the refusal of the U.S. Naval Academy at Annapolis and the U.S. Military Academy at West Point to admit Chinese students for training, contradicting the provision in the Burlingame treaty. But more important was the growing fear of conservative Qing government officials that the Chinese youths in the United States were becoming too Westernized. Although the Self-Strengthening Movement ended in the aftermath of China's disastrous defeat in the Sino-Japanese War (1894–1895), the Zongli Yamen survived as the Ministry of Foreign Affairs in 1901.

M. Banno, *China and the West, 1858–1861: The Origins of the Tsungli Yamen* (Cambridge, MA, 1973); M. H. Hunt, *The Making of a Special Relationship: The United States and China to 1914* (New York, 1983); M. C. Wright, *The Last Stands of Chinese Conservatism* (New York, 1967).

Roger Y. M. Chan

Selected Bibliography

Australia

Barclay, Glen St. J. *A Very Small Insurance Policy: The Politics of Australian Involvement in Vietnam, 1954–1967*. St. Lucia, BWI, 1988.

——— and Joseph M. Siracusa, Eds. *Australian-American Relations Since 1945: A Documentary History*. Sydney, 1976.

Bell, Coral. *Australia's Alliance Options: Prospect and Retrospect in a World of Change*. Canberra, 1991.

Crockett, Peter. *Evatt: A Life*. New York, 1993.

Evatt, Herbert V. *Australia in World Affairs*. Sydney, 1946.

Harper, Norman. *A Great and Powerful Friend: A Study of Australian and American Relations between 1900 and 1975*. St. Lucia, BWI, 1987.

Millar, Thomas B. *Australia in Peace and War: External Relations, 1788–1997*. New York, 1978.

Reese, Trevor. R. *Australia, New Zealand, and the United States: A Survey of International Relations, 1941–1968*. Melbourne, 1969.

Rix, Alan. *Coming to Terms: The Politics of Australia's Trade with Japan 1945–57*. Sydney, 1986.

Schenk, Catherine R. *Britain and the Sterling Area: From Devaluation to Convertibility in the 1950s*. London, 1994.

Siracusa, Joseph M. and Yeong-han Cheong, *America's Australia: Australia's America*. Claremont, CA, 1997.

Spender, Percy C. *Politics and a Man*. Sydney, 1972.

Biographies of Americans

Allen, Helena G. *Sanford Ballard Dole: Hawaii's Only President, 1844–1926*. Glendale, CA, 1988.

Baughman, James L. *Henry R. Luce and the Rise of the American News Media*. Boston, 1987.

Bird, Kai. *The Color of Truth: McGeorge Bundy and William Bundy, Brothers in Arms*. New York, 1998.

Brooks, Van Wyck. *Fenollosa and His Circle: With Other Essays in Biography*. New York, 1962.

Carr, Caleb. *The Devil Soldier: The Story of Frederick Townsend Ward*. New York, 1992.

Chisolm, Lawrence W. *Fenollosa: The Far East and American Culture*. New Haven, CT, 1963.

Cohen, Peter J. *Pearl Buck: A Cultural Biography*. New York, 1997.

Currey, Cecil B. *Edward Lansdale: The Unquiet American*. Boston, 1988.

Damm, Ethel M. *Sanford B. Dole and His Hawaii*. Palo Alto, CA, 1957.

Evans, Paul M. *John King Fairbank and the American Understanding of Modern China*. New York, 1988.

Fisher, James T. *Dr. America: The Lives of Thomas A. Dooley, 1927–1961*. Amherst, MA, 1997.

Hamilton, John M. *Edgar Snow: A Biography*. Bloomington, IN, 1988.

Hatch, Alden. *Ambassador Extraordinary: Clare Boothe Luce*. New York, 1956.

Herzstein, Robert E. *Henry R. Luce: A Political Portrait of the Man Who Created the American Century*. New York, 1994.

Keeley, Joseph C. *The China Lobby Man: The Story of Alfred Kohlberg*. New Rochelle, NY, 1969.
Lamont, Edward M. *The Ambassador from Wall Street: The Story of Thomas W. Lamont, J. P. Morgan's Chief Executive*. Lanham, MD, 1994.
MacKinnon, Janice R. and Stephen R. MacKinnon. *Agnes Smedley: The Life and Times of An American Radical*. Berkeley, CA, 1988.
Neils, Patricia. *China Images in the Life and Times of Henry Luce*. Savage, MD, 1990.
Porter, Kenneth W. *John Jacob Astor*. Cambridge, MA, 1931.
Shadegg, Stephen C. *Clare Boothe Luce*. New York, 1970.
Shapley, Deborah. *Promise and Power: The Life and Times of Robert McNamara*. Boston, 1993.
Sheed, Wilfrid. *Clare Boothe Luce*. New York, 1982.
Sheehan, Neil. *A Bright Shining Lie: John Paul Vann and America in Vietnam*. New York, 1988.
Shelden, Michael. *Graham Greene: The Man Within*. London, 1994.
Strong, Tracy B. and Helene Keyssar. *Right in Her Soul: The Life of Anna Louise Strong*. New York, 1983.
Thomas, S. Bernard. *Season of High Adventure: Edgar Snow in China*. Berkeley, CA, 1996.
Travis, Frederick F. *George Kennan and the Russian-American Relationship, 1865–1924*. Athens, OH, 1990.

Biographies of Asians

Agawa, Hiroyuki. *The Reluctant Admiral: Yamamoto and the Imperial Navy*. New York, 1979.
Allen, Richard C. *Korea's Syngman Rhee: An Unauthorized Portrait*. Tōkyō, 1960.
Bergere, Marie-Claire. *Sun Yatsen*. Stanford, CA, 1998.
Bingham, June. *U Thant: The Search for Peace*. New York, 1966.
Breslin, Shaun. *Mao*. New York, 1998.
Buck, Pearl S. *Imperial Woman*. New York, 1956.
Butwell, Richard A. *U Nu of Burma*. Stanford, CA, 1963.
Chen, Jerome. *Yuan Shi K'ai 1859–1916*. Stanford, CA, 1961.
Chen Jian. *Mao and China's Foreign Policy*. Chapel Hill, NC, 1997.
Chu, Samuel C. and Liu Kwang-Ching, Eds. *Li Hung-chang and China's Early Modernization*. Armonk, NY, 1994.
Crozier, Brian. *The Man Who Lost China: The First Full Biography of Chiang Kai-shek*. New York, 1976.
Currey, Cecil B. *Victory at Any Cost: The Genius of Viet Nam's General Vo Nguyen Giap*. Washington, DC, 1997.
Domes, Jurgen. *Peng Te-Huai: The Man and the Image*. Stanford, CA, 1985.
Dower, John W. *Empire and Aftermath: Yoshida Shigeru and the Japanese Experience, 1878–1954*. Cambridge, MA, 1979.
Duiker, William J. *Ho Chi Minh: A Life*. New York, 2000.
Folsom, Kenneth E. *Friends, Guests, and Colleagues: A Study of the Mu-fu System in the Late Ch'ing Period*. Berkeley, CA, 1968.
Gillin, Donald G. *Warlord: Yen Hsi-shan in Shansi Province, 1911–1949*. Princeton, NJ, 1967.
Gopinath, Aruna. *Manuel L. Quezon: The Tutelary Democrat*. Quezon City, 1987.
Gray, M. M. *Island Hero: The Story of Ramon Magsaysay*. New York, 1965.
Grieder, Jerome B. *Hu Shih and the Chinese Renaissance*. Cambridge, MA, 1970.
Hoyt, Edwin P. *Three Military Leaders: Tojo, Yamamoto, Yamashita*. New York, 1993.
Kublin, Hyman. *Asian Revolutionary: The Life of Sen Katayama*. Princeton, NJ, 1964.
Lacouture, Jean. *Ho Chi Minh: A Political Biography*. New York, 1968.
Lebra-Chapman, Joyce. *Okuma Shigenobu: Statesman of Meiji Japan*. Canberra, 1977.
Legge, John D. *Sukarno: A Political Biography*. New York, 1972.
Li Zhisui. *The Private Life of Chairman Mao: The Memoirs of Mao's Personal Physician*. New York, 1994.
McCormack, Gavan. *Chang Tso-lin in Northeast China, 1911–1928*. Stanford, CA, 1977.
Maung, Maung U. *Aung San of Burma*. The Hague, 1962.
Meisner, Maurice J. *Mao's China and After: A History of the People's Republic*. New York, 1977.
Morton, William F. *Tanaka Giichi and Japan's China Policy*. Folkestone, UK, 1980.
Najita Tetsuo. *Hara Kei in the Politics of Compromise, 1905–1915*. Cambridge, MA, 1967.
Oka Yoshitake. *Konoe Fumimaro: A Political Biography*. Tōkyō, 1983.
Oliver, Robert T. *Syngman Rhee: The Man Behind the Myth*. New York, 1954.
Osborne, Milton E. *Sihanouk: Prince of Light, Prince of Darkness*. Honolulu, HI, 1994.

Penders, C. L. M. and Ulf Sundhaussen. *Abdul Harris Nasution: A Political Biography*. Queensland, 1985.
Rose, Mavis. *Indonesia Free: A Political Biography of Mohammed Hatta*. Ithaca, NY, 1987.
Schram, Stuart R. *The Thought of Mao Tse-Tung*. Cambridge, MA, 1989.
Shao Guogang. *Zhou Enlai and the Foundations of Chinese Foreign Policy*. New York, 1996.
Sheridan, James E. *Chinese Warlord: The Career of Feng Yu-hsiang*. Stanford, CA, 1966.
Silverstein, Josef, Ed. *The Political Legacy of Aung San*. Ithaca, NY, 1993.
Sontag, Frederick. *Sun Myung Moon and the Unification Church*. Nashville, TN, 1977.
Spector, Stanley. *Li Hung-chang and the Huai Army: A Study in Nineteenth Century Chinese Regionalism*. Seattle, WA, 1964.
Suh Dae-sook. *Kim Il Sung: The North Korean Leader*. New York, 1988.
Taylor, Jay. *The Generalissimo's Son: Chiang Ching-kuo and the Revolutions in China and Taiwan*. Cambridge, MA, 2000.
Tiewes, Frederick C. and Warren Sun. *The Tragedy of Lin Biao: Riding the Tiger During the Cultural Revolution, 1966–71*. Hong Kong, 1996.
Tung, William L. *V. K. Wellington Koo and China's Wartime Diplomacy*. New York, 1977.
Van Ginneken, Jaap. *The Rise and Fall of Lin Biao*. New York, 1972.
Warner, Marina. *The Dragon Empress: Life and Times of Tz'u-Hsi, 1835–1908*. London, 1972.
Wetzler, Peter. *Hirohito and War: Imperial Tradition and Military Decision Making in Prewar Japan*. Honolulu, HI, 1998.
Wilbur, C. Martin. *Sun Yat-sen: Frustrated Patriot*. New York, 1976.
Wong, J. Y. *The Origins of a Heroic Image: Sun Yat-sen in London, 1896–1897*. Hong Kong, 1986.
Yang, Benjamin. *Deng: A Political Biography*. Armonk, NY, 1998.

Biographies of U.S. Congressmen

Berman, William C. *William Fulbright and the Vietnam War: The Dissent of a Political Realist*. Kent, OH, 1988.
Blair, Anne E. *Lodge in Vietnam: A Patriot Abroad*. New Haven, CT, 1995.
Braeman, John. *Albert J. Beveridge: American Nationalist*. Chicago, 1971.
Edwards, Lee. *Missionary for Freedom: The Life and Times of Walter Judd*. New York, 1990.
Garraty, John A. *Henry Cabot Lodge: A Biography*. New York, 1953.
Hatch, Alden. *The Lodges of Massachusetts*. New York, 1973.
Herman, Arthur. *Joseph McCarthy: Reexamining the Life and Legacy of America's Most Hated Senator*. New York, 2000.
McKenna, Marian C. *Borah*. Ann Arbor, MI, 1961.
Maddox, Robert J. *William E. Borah and American Foreign Policy*. Baton Rouge, LA, 1969.
Montgomery, Gayle B. and James W. Johnson, *One Step from the White House: The Rise and Fall of Senator William F. Knowland*. Berkeley, CA, 1998.
Olson, Gregory A. *Mansfield and Vietnam: A Study in Rhetorical Adaptation*. East Lansing, MI, 1995.
Oshinsky, David M. *A Conspiracy So Immense: The World of Joe McCarthy*. New York, 1983.
Reeves, Thomas C. *The Life and Times of Joe McCarthy: A Biography*. New York, 1982.
Rozek, Edward J. *Walter H. Judd: Chronicles of a Statesman*. Denver, 1980.
Welch, Richard E., Jr. *George Frisbie Hoar and the Half-Breed Republicans*. Cambridge, MA, 1971.
Widenor, William C. *Henry Cabot Lodge and the Search for American Foreign Policy*. Berkeley, CA, 1980.
Woods, Randall B. *Fulbright: A Biography*. New York, 1995.

Biographies of U.S. Diplomats

Abramson, Rudy. *Spanning the Century: The Life of W. Averell Harriman 1891–1986*. New York, 1992.
Buhite, Russell D. *Nelson T. Johnson and American Policy toward China, 1925–1941*. East Lansing, MI, 1968.
———. *Patrick J. Hurley and American Foreign Policy*. Ithaca, NY, 1973.
Croly, Herbert D. *Willard Straight*. New York, 1924.
Fuess, Claude M. *The Life of Caleb Cushing*. 2 Vols. New York, 1923.
Gulick, Edward V. *Peter Parker and the Opening of China*. Cambridge, MA, 1983.
Heinrichs, Waldo H., Jr. *American Ambassador: Joseph C. Grew and the Development of the*

United States Diplomatic Tradition. Boston, 1966.

Hixson, Walter L. *George F. Kennan: Cold War Iconoclast*. New York, 1989.

Hu Shizhana. *Stanley Hornbeck and the Open Door Policy: 1919–1937*. Westport, CT, 1995.

Lankford, Nelson D. *The Last American Aristocrat: The Biography of Ambassador David K. E. Bruce*. Boston, 1996.

McMonigal, Richard S. *Anson Burlingame: Chinese Minister to the Treaty Powers*. Washington, DC, 1946.

May, Gary. *China Scapegoat: The Diplomatic Ordeal of John Carter Vincent*. Prospect Heights, IL, 1976.

Mayers, David A. *George Kennan and the Dilemmas of U.S. Foreign Policy*. New York, 1988.

Miscamble, Wilson D. *George F. Kennan and the Making of American Foreign Policy, 1947–1950*. Princeton, NJ, 1992.

Pugach, Noel H. *Paul S. Reinsch: Open Diplomat in Action*. Millwood, NY, 1979.

Rauchway, Eric. "Willard Straight and the Paradox of Liberal Imperialism." *Pacific Historical Review*, August 1997.

Shaw, Yu-ming. *An American Missionary in China: John Leighton Stuart and Chinese-American Relations*. Cambridge, MA, 1992.

Taylor, Sandra C. *Advocate of Understanding: Sidney Gulick and the Search for Peace with Japan*. Kent, OH, 1984.

Varg, Paul A. *Open Door Diplomat: The Life of W. W. Rockhill*. Urbana, IL, 1952.

Williams, Frederick W. *Anson Burlingame and the Chinese Mission to Foreign Powers*. New York, 1970.

Biographies of U.S. Military Leaders

Bacevich, A. J. *Diplomat in Khaki: Major General Frank Ross McCoy and American Foreign Policy, 1898–1949*. Lawrence, KS, 1989.

Drake, Frederick C. *The Empire of the Seas: A Biography of Rear Admiral Robert Wilson Shufeldt, USN*. Honolulu, HI, 1984.

Hagedorn, Hermann. *Leonard Wood: A Biography*. New York, 1931.

James, D. Clayton. *The Years of MacArthur*. 3 Vols. New York, 1970–1985.

Kinnard, Douglas. *The Certain Trumpet: Maxwell Taylor and the American Experience in Vietnam*. Washington, DC, 1991.

Lane, Jack C. *Armed Progressive: General Leonard Wood*. San Rafael, CA, 1978.

Livezey, William E. *Mahan on Sea Power*. Norman, OK, 1981.

Long, David F. *Sailor-Diplomat: A Biography of Commodore James Biddle, 1783–1848*. Boston, 1983.

Matray, James I. "Hodge Podge: U.S. Occupation Policy in Korea, 1945–1948." *Korean Studies*, 1995.

Morison, Samuel Eliot. *"Old Bruin:" Commodore Matthew C. Perry, 1794–1858*. Boston, 1967.

Perrett, Geoffrey. *Old Soldiers Never Die: The Life of Douglas MacArthur*. New York, 1996.

Puleston, W. D. *Mahan: The Life and Work of Captain Alfred Thayer Mahan*. New Haven, CT, 1939.

Schaller, Michael. *Douglas MacArthur: The Far Eastern General*. New York, 1989.

Seager, Robert. *Alfred Thayer Mahan: The Man and His Letters*. Annapolis, MD, 1977.

Sorley, Lewis. *Thunderbolt: General Creighton Abrams and the Army of His Times*. New York, 1992.

Spector, Ronald L. *Admiral of the New Empire: The Life and Career of George Dewey*. Baton Rouge, LA, 1974.

Taylor, John M. *General Maxwell Taylor: The Sword and the Pen*. New York, 1989

Weintraub, Stanley. *MacArthur's War: Korea and the Undoing of an American Hero*. New York, 2000.

Wiley, Peter B. and Korogi Ichiro. *Yankees in the Land of the Gods: Commodore Perry and the Opening of Japan*. New York, 1990.

Young, Kenneth R. *The General's General: The Life and Times of Arthur MacArthur*. Boulder, CO, 1994.

Biographies of U.S. Presidents

Ambrose, Stephen E. *Eisenhower: The President*. New York, 1984.

Ambrosius, Lloyd E. *Woodrow Wilson and the American Diplomatic Tradition: The Treaty Fight in Perspective*. Lincoln, NE, 1987.

Beale, Howard K. *Theodore Roosevelt and the Rise of America to World Power*. Baltimore, MD, 1956.

Berman, William C. *From the Center to the Edge: The Politics and Policies of the Clinton Presidency*. New York, 2001.

Cannon, James M. *Time and Chance: Gerald Ford's Appointment with History*. New York, 1994.

Cohen, Warren I. and Nancy B. Tucker, Eds. *Lyndon Johnson Confronts the World: Ameri-*

can Foreign Policy 1963–1968. New York, 1994.
Collin, Richard H. *Theodore Roosevelt, Culture, Diplomacy, and Expansion: A New View of American Imperialism*. Baton Rouge, LA, 1985.
Curry, Roy W. *Woodrow Wilson and Far Eastern Policy, 1913–1921*. New York, 1957.
Dallek, Robert A. *Flawed Giant: Lyndon Johnson and His Times*. New York, 1998.
Fausold, Martin L. *The Presidency of Herbert C. Hoover*. Lawrence, KS, 1985.
Ferrell, Robert H. *Harry S. Truman: A Biography*. Columbia, MO, 1994.
Greene, John R. *The Presidency of Gerald R. Ford*. Lawrence, KS, 1995.
Hamby, Alonzo L. *Man of the People: A Life of Harry S. Truman*. New York, 1995.
Kimball, Warren F. *The Juggler: Franklin Roosevelt as Wartime Statesman*. New York, 1991.
McCullough, David. *Truman*. New York, 1992.
Marks, Frederick W. III. *Velvet on Iron: The Diplomacy of Theodore Roosevelt*. Lincoln, NE, 1979.
———. *Wind Over Sand: The Diplomacy of Franklin Roosevelt*. Athens, GA, 1982.
Minger, Ralph E. *William Howard Taft and United States Foreign Policy: The Apprenticeship Years, 1900–1908*. Urbana, IL, 1975.
Parmet, Herbert S. *George Bush: The Life of a Lone Star Yankee*. New York, 1997.
Schapsmeier, Edward L. and Frederick H. Schapsmeier. *Gerald R. Ford's Date with Destiny: A Political Biography*. New York, 1989.
Wilson, Joan Hoff. *Herbert Hoover: Forgotten Progressive*. Boston, 1975.

Biographies of U.S. Secretaries of State

Barrows, Chester L. *William M. Evarts: Lawyer, Diplomat, Statesman*. Chapel Hill, NC, 1941.
Bartlett, Irving H. *Daniel Webster*. New York, 1978.
Beers, Burton F. *Vain Endeavor: Robert Lansing's Attempt to End the American Japanese Rivalry*. Durham, NC, 1962.
Brinkley, Douglas. *Dean Acheson: The Cold War Years, 1953–1971*. New Haven, CT, 1992.
Chace, James. *Acheson: The Secretary of State Who Created the American World*. New York, 1998.
Clements, Kendrick A. *William Jennings Bryan: Missionary Isolationist*. Knoxville, TN, 1982.
Clymer, Kenton J. *John Hay: The Gentleman as Diplomat*. Ann Arbor, MI, 1975.
Cohen, Warren I. *Dean Rusk*. Totowa, NJ, 1980.
Current, Richard N. *Daniel Webster and the Rise of National Conservatism*. Boston, 1955.
———. *Secretary Stimson: A Study in Statecraft*. New Brunswick, NJ, 1954.
Dennett, Tyler. *John Hay: From Poetry to Politics*. New York, 1934.
———. "Seward's Far Eastern Policy." *American Historical Review*, October 1922.
Devine, Michael J. *John W. Foster: Politics and Diplomacy in the Imperial Era, 1873–1917*. Athens, OH, 1981.
Dyer, Brainerd. *The Public Career of William M. Evarts*. Berkeley, CA, 1933.
Ellis, L. Ethan. *Frank B. Kellogg and American Foreign Relations, 1925–1929*. New Brunswick, NJ, 1961.
Ferrell, Robert H. *George C. Marshall*. New York, 1966.
Guhin, Michael A. *John Foster Dulles: A Statesman and His Times*. New York, 1972.
Hersh, Seymour. *The Price of Power: Kissinger in the Nixon White House*. New York, 1983.
Hitchens, Christopher. *The Trial of Henry Kissinger*. New York, 2001.
Hoopes, Townsend. *The Devil and John Foster Dulles*. Boston, 1973.
Immerman, Richard H., Ed. *John Foster Dulles and the Diplomacy of the Cold War*. Princeton, NJ, 1990.
———. *John Foster Dulles: Piety, Pragmatism, and Power in U.S. Foreign Relations*. Wilmingon, DE, 1999.
Isaacson, Walter. *Kissinger: A Biography*. (New York, 1992.
Jessup, Philip C. *Elihu Root, 1845–1937*. 2 Vols. New York, 1938.
Koenig, Louis W. *Bryan: A Political Biography of William Jennings Bryan*. New York, 1971.
Leopold, Richard W. *Elihu Root and the Conservative Tradition*. Boston, 1954.
McGlothlen, Ronald L. *Controlling the Waves: Dean Acheson and U.S. Foreign Policy in Asia*. New York, 1993.
Nevins, Allan. *Hamilton Fish: The Inner History of the Grant Administration*. New York, 1936.
Paolino, Ernest N. *The Foundations of American Empire: William Henry Seward and U.S. Foreign Policy*. Ithaca, NY, 1973.
Pogue, Forrest C. *George C. Marshall: Statesman*. New York, 1987.
Pratt, Julius. *Cordell Hull, 1933–1944*. 2 Vols. New York, 1964.

Pruessen, Ronald W. *John Foster Dulles: The Road to Power*. New York, 1982.

Pusey, Merlo J. *Charles Evans Hughes*. 2 Vols. New York, 1951.

Rappaport, Armin. *Henry Stimson and Japan, 1931–1933*. Chicago, 1963.

Schoenbaum, Thomas J. *Waging Peace and War: Dean Rusk in the Truman, Kennedy, and Johnson Years*. New York, 1988.

Schulzinger, Robert D. *Henry Kissinger: Doctor of Diplomacy*. New York, 1989.

Smith, Daniel M. *Robert Lansing and American Neutrality, 1914–1917*. Berkeley, CA, 1958.

Smith, Gaddis. *Dean Acheson*. Cooper Square, NY, 1972.

Stoler, Mark A. *George C. Marshall: Soldier-Statesman of the American Twentieth Century*. Boston, 1989.

Thayer, William R. *The Life and Letters of John Hay*. 2 Vols. Boston, 1916.

Van Deusen, Glyndon G. *William Henry Seward*. New York, 1967.

Burma

Boucard, Andre and Louis Boucard. *Burma's Golden Triangle: On the Trail of the Opium Warlords*. Bangkok, 1992.

Cady, John F. *The United States and Burma*. Cambridge, MA, 1976.

Christie, Clive J. *A Modern History of Southeast Asia: Decolonization, Nationalism, and Separatism*. London, 1996.

Liang Chi Shad. *Burma's Foreign Relations: Neutralism in Theory and Practice*. New York, 1990.

Lintner, Bertil. *Burma in Revolt: Opium and Insurgency since 1948*. Boulder, CO, 1994.

Maung, Maung U. *Burmese Nationalist Movements 1940–1948*. Honolulu, HI, 1990.

Steinberg, David I. *The Future of Burma: Crisis and Choice in Myanmar*. New York, 1990.

Taylor, Robert H. *Foreign and Domestic Consequences of the KMT Intervention in Burma*. Ithaca, NY, 1973.

———. *The State in Burma*. Honolulu, HI, 1987.

Tinker, Hugh. *The Union of Burma: A Study of the First Years of Independence*. London, 1957.

Cambodia

Chanda, Nayan. *Brother Enemy: The War After the War*. New York, 1986.

Chandler, David P. *A History of Cambodia*. Boulder, CO, 2000.

———. *The Tragedy of Cambodian History: Politics, War and Revolution Since 1945*. New Haven, CT, 1991.

Etcheson, Craig. *The Rise and Demise of Democratic Kampuchea*. Boulder, CO, 1984.

Isaacs, Arnold. *Without Honor: Defeat in Vietnam and Cambodia*. Baltimore, 1983.

Kiernan, Brian. *How Pol Pot Came to Power*. London, 1985.

———. *The Pol Pot Regime: Race, Power, and Genocide in Cambodia Under the Khmer Rouge, 1975–79*. New Haven, CT, 1996.

Rown, Roy. *The Four Days of the Mayaguez*. New York, 1975.

Shawcross, William. *Deliver Us from Evil: Peacekeepers, Warlords and the World of Endless Conflict*. New York, 2000.

———. *Sideshow: Kissinger, Nixon and the Destruction of Cambodia*. New York, 1979.

China after 1949

Barnett, A. Doak. *The Making of Foreign Policy in China: Structure and Process*. Boulder, CO, 1985.

Bartke, Wolfgang and Peter Schier, Eds. *China's New Party Leadership: Biographies and Analysis of the Twelfth Central Committee of the Chinese Communist Party*. Armonk, NY, 1985.

Boorman, Howard L. *Moscow-Peking Axis: Strength and Strains*. New York, 1957.

Clubb, O. Edmund. *China and Russia: The "Great Game."* New York, 1971.

Goldman, Merle. *Political Reform in the Deng Xiaoping Era*. Cambridge, MA, 1994.

Goodman, David S. G. and Gerald Segal, Eds. *China in the Nineties: Crisis Management and Beyond*. New York, 1991.

Harding, Harry. *China's Foreign Relations in the 1980s*. New Haven, CT, 1984.

Hinton, Harold C. *Communist China in World Politics*. Boston, 1966.

Keith, Ronald C. *The Diplomacy of Zhou Enlai*. New York, 1989.

Kim, Samuel S., Ed. *China and the World Chinese Foreign Policy Faces the New Millennium*. Boulder, CO, 1998.

Lee, Hong Yung. *The Politics of the Chinese Cultural Revolution*. Berkeley, CA, 1978.

Lo Chi-kin. *China's Policy Towards Territorial Dis-*

putes: The Case of the South China Sea Islands. New York, 1989.
MacFarquhar, Roderick. *The Origins of the Cultural Revolution.* 3 Vols. New York, 1974–1997.
———. *The Politics of China, 1949–89.* Cambridge, MA, 1993.
Maitan, Livio. *Party, Army, and Masses in China: A Marxist Interpretation of the Cultural Revolution and Its Aftermath.* London, 1976.
Mastanduno, Michael. *Economic Containment: CoCom and the Politics of East-West Trade.* Ithaca, NY, 1992.
Ogden, Suzanne. *China's Unresolved Issues: Politics, Development, and Culture.* Englewood Cliffs, NJ, 1989.
Perry, Elizabeth J. and Xun Li. *Proletarian Power: Shanghai in the Cultural Revolution.* Boulder, CO, 1997.
Rodzinski, Withold. *The People's Republic of China.* New York, 1988.
Schoenhals, Michael, Ed. *China's Cultural Revolution, 1966–69: Not a Dinner Party.* Armonk, NY, 1996.
Schurmann, Franz. *Ideology and Organization in Communist China.* Berkeley, CA, 1968.
Spence, Jonathan D. *The Search for Modern China.* New York, 1990.
Tang Tsou. *The Cultural Revolution and Post-Mao Reforms.* Chicago, 1986.
Tyler, Patrick. *A Great Wall: Six Presidents and China: An Investigative History.* New York, 1999.
Valencia, Mark J. *China and the South China Sea Disputers: Conflicting Claims and Potential Solutions in the South China Sea.* New York, 1996.
White, Gordon. *Riding the Tiger: The Politics of Economic Reform in Post-Mao China.* Stanford, CA, 1993.
Yasuhara, Yoko. "Japan, Communist China, and Export Controls in Asia, 1948–52." *Diplomatic History,* Winter 1986.
Zhai Qiang. *China and the Vietnam Wars, 1950–1975.* Chapel Hill, NC, 2000.
———. *The Dragon, the Lion, and the Eagle: Chinese-British-American Relations, 1949–1958.* Kent, OH, 1994.

China before 1949

Banno, Masataka. *China and the West, 1858–1861: The Origins of the Tsungli Yamen.* Cambridge, MA, 1973.
Bianco, Lucien. *Origins of the Chinese Revolution: 1915–1949.* Stanford, CA, 1971.
Boyle, John H. *China and Japan at War, 1937–1945: The Politics of Collaboration.* Stanford, CA, 1972.
Bunker, Gerald E. *The Peace Conspiracy: Wang Ching-wei and the China War, 1937–1941.* Cambridge, MA, 1972.
Chi Hsi-sheng. *Nationalist China at War: Military Defeats and Political Collapse 1937–1945.* Ann Arbor, MI, 1992.
———. *Warlord Politics in China, 1916–1928.* Stanford, CA, 1976.
Chi, Madeleine. *China Diplomacy, 1914–1918.* Cambridge, MA, 1970.
Cohen, Paul A. *History in Three Keys: The Boxers as Event, Experience, and Myth.* New York, 1997.
Complete Record of the Management of Barbarian Affairs in the Qing Dynasty. Beijing, 1930.
Eastman, Lloyd E. *Seeds of Destruction: Nationalist China in War and Revolution, 1937–1949.* Stanford, CA, 1984.
Esherick, Joseph. W. *The Origins of the Boxer Uprising.* Berkeley, CA, 1987.
———. *Reform and Revolution in China: The 1911 Revolution in Hunan and Hubei.* Berkeley, CA, 1976.
Feuerwerker, Albert. *The Early Industrialization in China.* New York, 1958.
Hsiung, James C. and Steven I. Levine, Eds. *China's Bitter Victory: The War with Japan, 1937–1945.* Armonk, NY, 1992.
Hsueh Chun-tu. *The Chinese Revolution of 1911: New Perspectives.* Hong Kong, 1986.
Johnson, Chalmers A. *Peasant Nationalism and Communist Power: The Emergence of Revolutionary China 1937–1945.* Stanford, CA, 1962.
Jordan, Donald A. *The Northern Expedition: China's National Revolution of 1926–1928.* Honolulu, HI, 1976.
Kelly, John S. *The Forgotten Conference: The Negotiations at Peking, 1900–1901.* Geneva, 1963.
Koo Shou-eng. *Tariff and the Development of the Cotton Industry in China, 1842–1937.* New York, 1982.
Kwong, Luke S. K. *A Mosaic of the Hundred Days: Personalities, Politics, and Ideas of 1898.* Cambridge, MA, 1984.
Landor, Anthony H. S. *China and the Allies.* New York, 1901.
Lieberthal, Kenneth and Michel Oksenberg. *Pol-*

icy Making in China: Leaders, Structures, and Processes. Princeton, NJ, 1988.
Liu, F. F. *A Military History of Modern China, 1924–1949*. Princeton, NJ, 1956.
MacKinnon, Stephen R. *Power and Politics in Late Imperial China: Yuan Shi-kai in Beijing and Tianjin. 1901–1908*. Berkeley, CA, 1980.
Pepper, Suzanne. *Civil War in China: The Political Struggle, 1945–1949*. New York, 1999.
Robinson, Thomas W. and David L. Shambaugh. *Chinese Foreign Policy: Theory and Practice*. New York, 1994.
Salisbury, Harrison E. *The Long March*. New York, 1985.
Schwarcz, Vera. *The Chinese Enlightenment: Intellectuals and the Legacy of the May Fourth Movement of 1919*. Berkeley, CA, 1986.
Seagrave, Sterling. *The Soong Dynasty*. New York, 1985.
Seymour, James D. *China's Satellite Parties*. Armonk, NY, 1987.
Sheridan, James E. *China in Disintegration: The Republican Era in Chinese History, 1912–1949*. New York, 1975.
Shinkichi, Eto and Harold Z. Schiffrin. *The 1911 Revolution in China: Interpretive Essays*, Tōkyō, 1985.
Sun, Youli. *China and the Origins of the Pacific War, 1931–1941*. New York, 1993.
Tan, Chester C. *The Boxer Catastrophe*. New York, 1955.
Van Slyke, Lyman P. *Enemies and Friends: The United Front in Chinese Communist History*. Stanford, CA, 1967.
Waldron, Arthur. *From War to Nationalism: China's Turning Point, 1924–1925*. New York, 1995.
Wang, James C. F. *Contemporary Chinese Politics: An Introduction*. New York, 1999.
Wright, Mary Clabaugh. *The Last Stand of Chinese Conservatism: The Tung-chih Restoration, 1862–1874*. New York, 1967.
Wu, J. T. *The Sian Incident: A Pivotal Point in Modern Chinese History*. Ann Arbor, MI, 1976.
Young, Ernest P. *The Presidency of Yuan Shi'k'ai: Liberalism and Dictatorship in Early Republican China*. Ann Arbor, MI, 1977.

Chinese Language Sources

Cai Guanluo, Ed. *Qingdai qibai mingren zhuan* [Seven Hundreds Biographies of Famous People of Qing Dynasty]. Beijing, 1984.
Chang Su-ya. "Lanqin dashi yu yijiuwulin niandai de Zhong mei guanxi" [Ambassador Karl L. Rankin and U.S. Policy Toward Taiwan in the 1950s]. *EurAmerica* (March 1998).
Ch'en Chih'mai. *Jiang Tingfu de zhishi yu pingsheng* [The Career and Life of Jiang Tingfu]. Taibei, 1967.
Chen Fangming. *Xie Xuehong pingzhuan* [A Critical Biography of Xie Xuehong]. Taibei, 1991.
Cheng Daode, Zheng Yueming, and Rao Geping, Eds. *Zhonghua minguo waijiao ziliao xuanji, 1919–1931* [Selected Diplomatic Data of the Republic of China, 1919–1931]. Beijing, 1985.
Chin Hsien-tsu, Ed. *Ye Gongchao: Qi ren, qi wen, qi shih* [About Ye Gongchao: His Personality, Writings, and Career]. Taibei, 1983.
Chouban yiwu shimo, Xianfeng chao, Tongzhi chao [Complete Record of the Management of Barbarian Affairs in the Qing Dynasty, Xianfeng, and Tongzhi Periods]. Beijing, 1930.
Feng Ziyou. *Geming yishi* [Revolutionary Historic Anecdote]. Vol. 2. Beijing, 1981.
Fu Chao-hsiang. *Ye Gongchao zhuan* [The Biography of Ye Gongchao]. Taibei, 1994.
Fu Daohui. *Wusa yundong* [May Thirtieth Movement]. Fudan, 1985.
Gao Xinglie. *Riben qinhua zuixing lu—Nanjing da tusha* [The Outrages in the Japanese Aggression Against China—-the Nanjing Rape]. Shanghai, 1985.
Ge Su. "Meitai gongtong fangyu tiaoyu de yunniang guocheng" [The Making of the U.S.-Taiwan Mutual Defense Treaty: 1948–1955]. *Meiguo yanjiu* [American Studies]. September 1990.
Gu Tinglong, Ed. *Zhongguo jindai shi cidian* [Dictionary of Modern Chinese History]. Shanghai, 1982.
Gu Weijun huiyi lu [Memoirs of Gu Weijun]. Beijing, 1983–88.
Gu Zheng. *Kung Hsiang-hsi yu Zhongguo caizheng* [Kung Xiangxi and China's Finance]. Taipei, 1979.
Guo Shi Guan, Ed. *Zhonghua minguo shishi jiyao* [Summary of the History of the Republic of China]. Taibei.
Hua Wen Publishers, Ed. *Song Meiling cexie* [Sidelight on Song Meiling]. Beijing, 1988.
Jiang Nan. *Jiang Jingguo zhuan* [A Biography of Jiang Jingguo]. Taibei, 1988.

Jiang Tingfu xuanji [The Selected Works of Jiang Tingfu]. Taibei, 1969.

Kong Lingren, Ed. *Zhongguo jindai qiye de kaichuang zhe* [The Man Who Opened Up Chinese Modern Enterprise]. Jinan, 1991.

Latourette, Kenneth S. *Zhonghua diguo duiwai tiaoyue* [The History of Early Relations Between the United States and China, 1784–1844]. Shanghai, 1906.

Li Dingyi. *Zhongmei zaoqi waijiao shi* [Early China-U.S. Diplomatic History]. Beijing, 1997.

Li Xin, Ed. *Zonghua Minguo renwu zhuan* [Who's Who of the Republic of China]. 2 Vols. Beijing, 1978, 1980.

Lu Xiuyi. *Riju shidai Taiwan Gongchandang shi, 1928–1932* [A History of the Taiwan Communist Party During the Japanese Occupation Era, 1928–1932]. Taibei, 1989.

Mayers, William F. *Zhonghua diguo duiwai tiaoyue* [Treaties Between the Empire of Chinese and Foreign States]. Shanghai, 1906.

Mu Ouchu. *Mu Ouchu wushi zizhuan* [Autobiography of Mu Ouchu at 50 Years of Age]. Shanghai, 1926.

Qingdai renwu zhuan [Biography of the Qing Dynasty]. Shenyang, 1992.

Qingguo Jia. "Meitai gongtong fangyu tiaoyu de dijie Jingguo" [The Conclusion of the U.S.-Taiwan Defense Treaty]. *Meiguo Yanjiu* [American Studies], January 1989.

Shen Iyao. Haiwai paihua bainian shi [A Century of Chinese Exclusion Abroad]. Beijing, 1980.

Song Jiang. *Bainian waijiao fengyun lu* [A Record of 100 Years of Rapid Change in Foreign Relations]. Shenyang, 1995.

Song Qiang. *Zhongguo wei shenme shuo bu* [China Can Say No]. Beijing, 1996.

Tao Xingzhi wen ji [Collected Works of Tao Xingzhi]. Nanjing, 1981.

Wang Fumin. *Jiang Jieshi pingzhuan* [Critical Biography of Jiang Jieshi]. Beijing, 1993

Wang Song, et al. *Song Ziwen zhuan* [Biography of Song Ziwen]. Wuhan, 1993.

Wu Jingping. *Song Ziwen pingzhuan* [Critical Biography of Song Ziwen]. Fuzhou, 1992.

Wu Manzhen. *Kangzhan zhong de songshi san jiemei* [Three Sisters of Song Family at Anti-Japanese War]. Beijing, 1995.

Wu Miaofa. *Waijiao caizi Qiao Guanhua* [Qiao Guanhua: The Talented Diplomat]. Shenzhen, 1998.

Yan Su and Dong Junfeng. *Kung Hsiang-hsi he Song Ailing* [Kung Xiangxi and Song Ailing]. Beijing, 1994.

Yang Shubiao. *Jiang Jieshi zhuan* [Biography of Jiang Jieshi]. Beijing, 1989.

Yu Liang. *Kung Hsiang-hsi zhuan* [The Biography of Gong Xiangxi]. Hong Kong, 1970.

Zhang Kaiyuan and Tang Wenquan. *Pinfan de rensheng* [Tao Xingzhi: A Confucius after Confucius]. Changsha, 1992.

Zhao Erxun. *Qingshi gao* [Manuscript of Qing Dynasty History]. Beijing, 1977.

Zhou Hongyu, Ed. *Haiwai Tao Xingzhi yanjiu* [The Research on Tao Heng-Chih Overseas]. Beijing, 1991.

Zhu Xinguan and Yan Ruping, Eds. *Zhong hua renwu zhuan* [Who's Who of the Republic of China]. Beijing, 1984.

Cold War in Asia

Blum, Robert M. *Drawing the Line: The Origin of the American Containment Policy in East Asia.* New York, 1982.

Gaddis, John Lewis. *Strategies of Containment: A Critical Appraisal of Postwar American National Security Policy*. New York, 1982.

Halberstam, David. *The Best and the Brightest.* New York, 1972.

Iriye, Akria. *The Cold War in Asia: A Historical Introduction*. Englewood Cliffs, NJ, 1974.

Kolko, Gabriel. *The Politics of War: The World and United States Foreign Policy, 1943–1945.* New York, 1968.

Lowe, Peter. *Containing the Cold War in East Asia: British Policies Towards Japan, China and Korea, 1948–53*. Manchester, UK, 1997.

McNeill, William H. *America, Britain, and Russia: Their Co-operation and Conflict, 1941–1946.* New York, 1970.

Simpson, Christopher, Ed. *Universities and Empire: Money and Politics in Social Sciences During the Cold War*. New York, 1998.

Stueck, William Whitney Jr. *The Road to Confrontation: American Policy Towards China and Korea, 1947–1950*. Chapel Hill, NC, 1981.

———. *The Wedemeyer Mission: American Politics and Foreign Policy During the Cold War*. Athens, GA, 1984.

Drug Trade

Chang Hsin-pao. *Commissioner Lin and the Opium War*. Cambridge, MA, 1964.

Jennings, John M. *The Opium Empire: Japanese*

Imperialism and Drug Trafficking in Asia, 1895–1945. Westport, CT, 1997.

McCoy, Alfred W. *Politics of Heroin in Southeast Asia*. New York, 1972.

———. *The Politics of Heroin: CIA Complicity in the Global Drug Trade*. Chicago, 1991.

Renard, Ronald D. *The Burmese Connection: Illegal Drugs and the Making of the Golden Triangle*. Boulder, CO, 1996.

Taylor, Arnold H. *American Diplomacy and the Narcotics Traffic, 1900–1939: A Study in International Humanitarian Reform*. Durham, NC, 1969.

Walker, William O. *Opium and Foreign Policy: The Anglo-American Search for Order in Asia, 1912–1954*. Chapel Hill, NC, 1991.

Westermeyer, Joseph. *Poppies, Pipes, and People: Opium and Its Use in Laos*. Berkeley, CA, 1982.

First Indochina War

Andrew, Christopher M. and Alexander S. Kanya-Forstner. *The Climax of French Imperial Expansion, 1914–1924*. Stanford, CA, 1981.

Betts, Raymond F. *Tricouleur: The French Overseas Empire*. New York, 1978.

Billings-Yun, Melanie. *Decision Against War: Eisenhower and Dien Bien Phu, 1954*. New York, 1988.

Buttinger, Joseph. *Vietnam: A Dragon Embattled*. New York, 1967.

Cady, John F. *The Roots of French Imperialism in Eastern Asia*. New York, 1967.

Dalloz, Jacques. *The War in Indo-China 1945–54*. Dublin, 1990.

Dreifort, John E. *Myopic Grandeur: The Ambivalence of French Foreign Policy Toward the Far East, 1919–1945*. Kent, OH, 1991.

Dunn, Peter M. *The First Vietnam War*. New York, 1985.

Fall, Bernard B. *Hell in a Very Small Place: The Siege of Dien Bien Phu*. Philadelphia, 1967.

———. *Street Without Joy: Indochina at War, 1946–54*. Harrisburg, PA, 1964.

Gardner, Lloyd C. *Approaching Vietnam: From World War II Through Dienbienphu, 1941–1954*. New York, 1988.

Hammer, Ellen J. *The Struggle for Indochina, 1940–1955*. Stanford, CA, 1966.

Kaplan, Lawrence S., Denise Artaud, and Mark R. Rubin, Eds. *Dien Bien Phu and the Crisis in Franco-American Relations, 1954–1955*. Wilmington, DE, 1990.

Lockhart, Greg. *Nation in Arms: The Origins of the People's Army of Vietnam*. Sydney, 1989.

Nordell, John R. Jr. *The Undetected Enemy: French and American Miscalculations at Dien Bien Phu, 1953*. College Station, TX, 1995.

Prados, John. *The Sky Would Fall: Operation Vulture, the U.S. Bombing Mission in Indochina, 1954*. New York, 1983.

Roy, Jules. *The Battle of Dien Bien Phu*. New York, 1965.

Shipway, Martin. *The Road to War: France and Vietnam, 1944–1947*. Providence, RI, 1996.

French Language Sources

Bao Dai. *Le dragon d'Annam*. Paris, 1980.

Devillers, P. *Histoire du Viêt-Nam de 1940 à 1952*. Paris, 1952.

Ely, Paul. *Mémoires: L'Indochine dans La Tourmente*. Paris, 1964.

Navarre, Henri. *Agonie de l'Indochine, 1953–1954*. Paris, 1956.

General Studies

Becker, William H. and Samuel F. Wells Jr., Eds. *Economics and World Power: An Assessment of American Diplomacy Since 1789*. New York, 1984.

Black, Jan Knippers. *Development in Theory and Practice: Bridging the Gap*. Boulder, CO, 1991.

Blaufarb, Douglas S. *The Counterinsurgency Era: U.S. Performance and Doctrine, 1950 to the Present*. New York, 1977.

Cohen, Warren I. and Akira Iriye, Eds. *The Great Powers in East Asia, 1953–1960*. New York, 1990.

Craig, Gordon A. and Felix Gilbert, Eds. *The Diplomats, 1919–1939*. 2 Vols. Princeton, NJ, 1953.

Dryden, Steve. *Trade Warriors: USTR and the American Crusade for Free Trade*. New York, 1995.

Eckes, Alfred E., Jr. *Opening America's Market: U.S. Foreign Trade Policy Since 1776*. Chapel Hill, NC, 1995.

Foreman-Peck, James. *A History of the World Economy: International Economic Relations Since 1850*. Hemel Hempstead, UK, 1995.

Glick, Leslie Alan. *Multilateral Trade Negotia-*

tions: World Trade After the Tokyo Round. Totowa, NJ, 1984.

Goodwin, Craufurd D., Ed. *Economics and National Security: A History of Their Interaction*. Durham, NC, 1991.

Graebner, Norman A., Ed. *An Uncertain Tradition: American Secretaries of State in the Twentieth Century*. New York, 1961.

Hamilton, Edward K. *America's Global Interests: A New Agenda*. New York, 1989.

Hunt, Michael H. *Ideology and U.S. Foreign Policy*. New Haven, CT, 1987.

Iriye, Akira. *Across the Pacific: An Inner History of American–East Asian Relations*. New York, 1967.

Isaacson, Walter and Evan Thomas. *The Wise Men: Six Friends and the World They Made*. New York, 1983.

May, Ernest R. and James C. Thomson, Eds. *American–East Asian Relations: A Survey*. Cambridge, MA, 1972.

Ninkovich, Frank. *Modernity and Power: A History of the Domino Theory in the Twentieth Century*. Chicago, 1994.

Packenham, Robert A. *Liberal America and the Third World: Political Development Ideas in Foreign Aid and Social Science*. Princeton, NJ, 1973.

Smith, Ralph B. and A. J. Stockwell, Eds. *British Policy and the Transfer of Power in Asia: Documentary Perspectives*. London, 1988.

Thomson, James C., Jr., Peter W. Stanley, and John C. Perry. *Sentimental Imperialists: The American Experience in East Asia*. New York, 1985.

Winham, Gilbert R. *International Trade and the Tokyo Round Negotiation*. Princeton, NJ, 1986.

Yahuda, Michael B. *The International Politics of the Asia-Pacific, 1945–1995*. New York, 1996.

Guam

Carano, Paul and Pedro C. Sanchez. *A Complete History of Guam*. Rutland, VT, 1964.

Nelson, E. G. and F. J. Nelson. *The Island of Guam: Description and History from a 1934 Perspective*. Washington, DC, 1992.

Rogers, Robert F. *Destiny's Landfall: A History of Guam*. Honolulu, HI, 1995.

Hawaii

Andrade, Ernest. *Unconquerable Rebel: Robert W. Wilcox and Hawaiian Politics, 1880–1903*. Boulder, CO, 1996.

Calhoun, Charles W. "Morality and Spite: Walter Q. Gresham and U.S. Relations with Hawaii." *Pacific Historical Review*, August 1983.

Devine, Michael J. "John W. Foster and the Struggle for Annexation of Hawaii." *Pacific Historical Review*, February 1977.

Kuykendall, Ralph S. *The Hawaiian Kingdom*. Vol. 3: *The Kalakaua Dynasty*. Honolulu, HI, 1967.

McWilliams, Tennant S. "James H. Blount, the South, and Hawaiian Annexation." *Pacific Historical Review*, February 1988.

Osborne, Thomas J. *"Empire Can Wait": American Opposition to Hawaiian Annexation, 1893–1898*. Kent, OH, 1981.

Russ, William A. *The Hawaiian Republic (1894–1898) and Its Struggle to Win Annexation*. Selingsgrove, PA, 1961.

———. *The Hawaiian Revolution, 1893–1894*. Susquehanna, PA, 1959.

Tate, Merze. *Hawaii: Reciprocity or Annexation*. East Lansing, MI, 1968.

———. *The United States and the Hawaiian Kingdom: A Political History*. New Haven, CT, 1965.

Hong Kong

Cohen, Warren I. and Li Zhao, Eds. *Hong Kong Under Chinese Rule: The Economic and Political Implications of Reversion*. New York, 1997.

Postiglione, Gerald A. and James T. H. Tang, Eds. *Hong Kong's Reunion with China: Global Dimensions*. Hong Kong, 1997.

Tsang, Steve Y. S. *A Modern History of Hong Kong: 1841–1998*. London, 1998.

Tucker, Nancy B. *Uncertain Friendships: Taiwan, Hong Kong, and the United States, 1945–1992*. New York, 1994.

Welsh, Frank. *A History of Hong Kong*. London, 1993.

Immigration

Chan, Sucheng. *Asian Americans: An Interpretive History*. Boston, 1991.

Coolidge, Mary Roberts. *Chinese Immigration*. New York, 1969.

Daniels, Roger. *The Politics of Prejudice: The Anti-Japanese Movement in California, and the Struggle for Japanese Exclusion*. Berkeley, CA, 1968.

Fawcett, James T. and Benjamin V. Carino, Eds.

Pacific Bridges: The New Immigration from Asia and the Pacific Islands. New York, 1987.
Hein, Jeremy. *From Vietnam, Laos, and Cambodia: A Refugee Experience in the United States*. New York, 1995.
Hing, Bill Ong. *Making and Remaking Asian America Through Immigration Policy, 1850–1990*. Stanford, CA, 1993.
Ichioka, Yuji. *The Issei: The World of the First Generation Japanese Immigrants, 1885–1924*. New York, 1988.
Kwong, Peter. *The New Chinatown*. New York, 1987.
LeMay, Michael C. *From Open Door to Dutch Door: An Analysis of U.S. Immigration Policy Since 1820*. New York, 1987.
Neuman, Gerald L. *Strangers to the Constitution: Immigrants, Borders, and Fundamental Law*. Princeton, NJ, 1996.
Reimers, David M. *Still the Golden Door: The Third World Comes to America*. New York, 1985.
Storti, Craig. *Incident at Bitter Creek: The Story of the Rock Springs Chinese Massacre*. Ames, IA, 1991.
Takaki, Ronald. *Strangers from a Distant Shore: A History of Asian Americans*. Boston, 1990.
Tsai Shi-shan H. *The Chinese Experience in America*. Bloomington, IN, 1986.
Vialet, Joyce C. A *Brief History of U.S. Immigration Policy*. Washington, DC, 1980.
Wang, S. *The Organization of Chinese Emigration, 1848–1888*. San Francisco, 1978.
Yan Qinghuang. *Coolies and Mandarins: China's Protection of Overseas Chinese During the Late Ching Period, 1851–1911*. Singapore, 1985.

Imperialism

Beisner, Robert L. *Twelve Against Empire: The Anti-Imperialists, 1898–1900*. Chicago, 1968.
Clyde, Paul H. *International Rivalries in Manchuria, 1689–1922*. New York, 1966.
Edwardes, Michael. *The West in Asia, 1850–1914*. London, 1967.
Emerson, Rupert. *From Empire to Nation: The Rise of Self-assertion of Asian and African Peoples*. Cambridge, MA, 1960.
Fieldhouse, David K. *The Colonial Empires: A Comparative Survey from the Eighteenth Century*. London, 1966.
Furnivall, John S. *Colonial Policy and Practice: A Comparative Study of Burma and Netherlands India*. Cambridge, UK, 1948.
Harrington, Fred Harvey. "The Anti-Imperialist Movement in the United States, 1898–1900." *Mississippi Valley Historical Review*, 1935.
Iriye, Akira. *After Imperialism: The Search for a New Order in the Far East, 1921–1931*. Cambridge, MA, 1965.
Langer, William. *The Diplomacy of Imperialism: 1890–1902*. New York, 1972.
Lasch, Christopher. "The Anti-Imperialist, the Philippines, and the Inequality of Man." *Journal of Southern History*, August 1958.
Louis, William R. *Imperialism at Bay: The United States and the Decolonization of the British Empire*. New York, 1978.
Sheng, Michael. *Battling Western Imperialism: Mao, Stalin, and the United States*. Princeton, NJ, 1997.
Tompkins, E. Berkeley. *Anti-Imperialism in the United States: The Great Debate, 1890–1920*. Philadelphia, 1970.

Imperialism in China

Davies, John Paton, Jr. *Dragon by the Tail: American, British, Japanese, and Russian Encounters with China and One Another*. New York, 1972.
Fairbank, John K. *Trade and Diplomacy on the China Coast*. Cambridge, MA, 1953.
Fishel, Wesley R. *The End of Extraterritoriality in China*. Berkeley, CA, 1952.
Hunt, Michael H. "The Forgotten Occupation: Peking, 1900–1901." *Pacific Historical Review*, November 1979.
Mutsu Munemitsu. *Kenkenroku: A Diplomatic Record of the Sino-Japanese War, 1894–1895*. Gordon M. Berger, Trans. Princeton, NJ, 1982.
Smith, Richard J. *Mercenaries and Mandarins: The Ever-Victorious Army in Nineteenth Century China*. Millwood, NY, 1978.
Spence, Jonathan D. *To Change China: Western Advisers in China, 1620–1960*. New York, 1980.
Teng Ssu-yu. *The Taiping Rebellion and the Western Powers: A Comprehensive Survey*. New York, 1971.
Tung, William L. *China and the Foreign Powers: The Impact of and Reaction to Unequal Treaties*. Dobbs Ferry, NY, 1970.

Wright, Stanley F. *China's Struggle for Autonomy, 1843–1938*. Shanghai, 1938.

White, John A. *The Siberian Intervention*. New York, 1969.

Interwar Events

Buckley, Thomas H. *The United States and the Washington Conference, 1921–1922*. Knoxville, TN, 1970.

Clauss, Errol M. " 'Pink in Appearance, but Red at Heart': The United States and the Far Eastern Republic, 1920–1922." *The Journal of American-East Asian Relations*, Fall 1992.

Dingman, Roger V. *Power in the Pacific: The Origins of Naval Arms Limitation, 1914–1922*. Chicago, 1976.

Ellis, L. Ethan. *Republican Foreign Policy, 1921–1933*. New Brunswick, NJ, 1968.

Ferrell, Robert H. *American Diplomacy in the Great Depression: Hoover-Stimson Foreign Policy, 1929–1933*. New Haven, CT, 1957.

Goldstein, Erik and John Maurer., Eds. *The Washington Conference, 1921–22: Naval Rivalry, East Asian Stability and the Road to Pearl Harbor*. London, 1994.

Hall, Christopher L. *Britain, America and Arms Control, 1921–37*. London, 1987.

Kaufman, Robert G. *Arms Control During the Pre-nuclear Era: The United States and Naval Limitation Between the Two World Wars*. New York, 1990.

Louis, William R. *British Strategy in the Far East 1919–1939*. Oxford, UK, 1971.

Nish, Ian. *Alliance in Decline: A Study in Anglo-Japanese Relations, 1908–23*. London, 1972.

Norton, Henry K. *The Far Eastern Republic of Siberia*. London, 1923.

O'Connor, Raymond G. *Perilous Equilibrium: The United States and the London Naval Conference of 1930*. Lawrence, KS, 1962.

Pelz, Stephen E. *The Race to Pearl Harbor: The Failure of the Second London Naval Conference and the Onset of World War II*. Cambridge, MA, 1974.

Pugach, Noel H. "American Friendship for China and the Shantung Question at the Washington Conference." *Journal of American History*, June 1977.

Roskill, Stephen W. *Naval Policy Between the Wars*. Vol. 2: *The Period of Reluctant Rearmament, 1930–1939*. London, 1976.

Unterberger, Betty Miller. *America's Siberian Expedition, 1918–1920: A Study of National Policy*. Durham, NC, 1956.

Indonesia

Brands, H. W. "The Limits of Manipulation: How the United States Didn't Topple Sukarno." *Journal of American History*, Fall 1989.

Cribb, Robert, Ed. *The Indonesian Killings of 1965–1966*. Victoria, 1990.

Crouch, Harold. *The Army and Politics in Indonesia*. Ithaca, NY, 1978.

Feith, Herbert. *The Decline of Constitutional Democracy in Indonesia*. Ithaca, NY, 1962.

Gardner, Paul F. *Shared Hopes, Separate Fears: Fifty Years of U.S.-Indonesian Relations*. Boulder, CO, 1997.

Green, Marshall. *Indonesia: Crisis and Transformation, 1965–1968*. Washington, DC, 1990.

Jones, Howard P. *Indonesia: The Possible Dream*. New York, 1971.

Kingsbury, Damien. *The Politics of Indonesia*. New York, 1998.

Kahin, Audrey. *Rebellion to Integration: West Sumatra and the Indonesian Polity*. Amsterdam, 1999.

——— and George McT. Kahin. *Subversion as Foreign Policy: Eisenhower, Dulles and the Indonesian Debacle*. Ithaca, NY, 1994.

Kahin, George McT. *Nationalism and Revolution in Indonesia*. Ithaca, NY, 1952.

McMahon, Robert J. *Colonialism and Cold War: The United States and the Struggle for Indonesian Independence, 1945–1949*. Ithaca, NY, 1981.

Schwartz, Adam. A *Nation in Waiting: Indonesia in the 1990's*. Sydney, 1999.

Winters, Jeff. *Power in Motion: Capital Mobility and the Indonesian State*. Ithaca, NY, 1995.

Japan after 1945

Allen, George C. *A Short Economic History of Modern Japan*. London, 1981.

Boyle, John H. *Modern Japan: The American Nexus*. Fort Worth, TX, 1993.

Calder, Kent E. *Crisis and Compensation: Public Policy and Political Stability in Japan, 1949–1986*. Princeton, NJ, 1988.

Callon, Scott. *Divided Sun: MITI and the Break-*

down of Japanese High-Tech Industrial Policy, 1975–1993. Stanford, CA, 1995.

Cole, Allan B., George O. Totten, Cecil H. Uehara. *Socialist Parties in Postwar Japan*. New Haven, CT, 1966.

Curtis, Gerald L. *The Japanese Way of Politics*. New York, 1988.

Destler, I. M., et al. *The Textile Wrangle: Conflict in Japanese-American Relations, 1969–1971*. Ithaca, NY, 1979.

Dower, John W. *Embracing Defeat: Japan in the Wake of World War II*. New York, 1999.

Forsberg, Aaron. *America and the Japanese Miracle: The Cold War Context of Japan's Postwar Economic Revival, 1950–1960*. Chapel Hill, NC, 2000.

Fukui Haruhiro. *Party in Power: The Japanese Liberal Democrats and Policy-Making*. Canberra, 1970.

Green, Michael J. *Arming Japan: Defense Production, Alliance Politics, and the Postwar Search for Autonomy*. New York, 1995.

Havens, Thomas R. H. *Fire Across the Sea: The Vietnam War and Japan, 1965–1975*. Princeton, NJ, 1987.

Hayao Kenji. *The Japanese Prime Minister and Public Policy*. Pittsburgh, PA, 1993.

Johnson, Chalmers A. *MITI and the Japanese Miracle: The Growth of Industrial Policy*. Stanford, CA, 1982.

Kohno Masaru. *Japan's Postwar Party Politics*. Princeton, NJ, 1997.

Kosaka Masataka. *100 Million Japanese*. Tōkyō, 1972.

Krause, Ellis S. *Japanese Radicals Revisited: Student Protest in Postwar Japan*. Berkeley, CA, 1974.

Masumi Junnosuke. *Contemporary Politics in Japan*. Berkeley, CA, 1995.

Matray, James I. *Japan's Emergence as a Global Power*. Westport, CT, 2000.

Mitchell, Richard H. *Political Bribery in Japan*. Honolulu, HI, 1996.

Nester, William R. *Japan and the Third World: Patterns, Power, Prospects*. New York, 1992.

Oka Yoshitake. *Five Political Leaders of Modern Japan*. Tōkyō, 1986.

Okimoto, David I. *Between MITI and the Market Japanese: Industrial Policy for High Technology*. Stanford, CA, 1989.

Pharr, Susan J. and Ellis S. Krauss. *Media and Politics in Japan*. Honolulu, HI, 1996.

Reischauer, Edwin O. *Japan: The Story of a Nation*. New York, 1981.

Smith, Patrick. *Japan: A Reinterpretation*. New York, 1997.

Upham, Frank K. *Law and Social Change in Postwar Japan*. Cambridge, MA, 1987.

Weinstein, Martin E. *Japan's Postwar Defense Policy, 1947–1968*. New York, 1971.

Welfield, John. *An Empire in Eclipse: Japan in the Postwar American Alliance System*. Atlantic Highlands, NJ, 1988.

Yamamura, Kozo. *Japan's Economic Structure: Should It Change*? Tōkyō, 1990.

Japan before 1945

Barnhart, Michael A. *Japan Prepares for Total War: The Search for Economic Security, 1919–1941*. Ithaca, NY, 1987.

Beasley, William G. *Japanese Imperialism: 1894–1945*. New York, 1987.

———. *Select Documents on Japanese Foreign Policy, 1853–1868*. Stanford, CA, 1955.

Berger, Gordon M. *Parties Out of Power in Japan, 1931–1941*. Princeton, NJ, 1977.

Blacker, Carmen. *The Japanese Enlightenment: A Study of the Writings of Fukuzawa Yukichi*. Cambridge, MA, 1964.

Chang Chong-fa. *The Anglo-Japanese Alliance*. Baltimore, MD, 1931.

Colbert, Evelyn S. *The Left Wing in Japanese Politics*. New York, 1952.

Conroy, Hilary. *The Japanese Seizure of Korea, 1868–1910: A Study of Realism and Idealism in International Relations*. Philadelphia, 1960.

Duus, Peter. *Party Rivalry and Political Change in Taisho Japan*. Cambridge, MA, 1968.

———. *The Rise of Modern Japan*. New York, 1976.

Hirschmeier, Johannes. *The Origins of Entrepreneurship in Meiji Japan*. Cambridge, MA, 1964.

Iklé, Frank W. *German-Japanese Relations, 1936–1940*. New York, 1956.

Iriye, Akira. *Power and Culture: The Japanese-American War, 1941–1945*. Cambridge, MA, 1981.

Jones, Francis C. *Extraterritoriality in Japan and the Diplomatic Relations Resulting in Its Abolition*. New Haven, CT, 1931.

Lu, David J. *From the Marco Polo Bridge to Pearl Harbor: Japan's Entry into World War II*. Washington, DC, 1961.

Morley, James W. *The China Quagmire: Japan's Expansion on the Asian Continent, 1933–1941*. New York, 1983.

———, Ed. *Deterrent Diplomacy: Japan, Germany, and the U.S.S.R., 1935–1940*. New York, 1976.
———. *Japan's Foreign Policy, 1868–1941: A Research Guide*. New York, 1974.
Myers, Ramon H., Mark R. Peattie, and Chen Ching-chih, Eds. *The Japanese Colonial Empire, 1895–1945*. Princeton, NJ, 1984.
Nish, Ian. *Alliance in Decline: A Study in Anglo-Japanese Relations, 1908–23*. London, 1972.
———. *The Anglo-Japanese Alliance: The Diplomacy of Two Island Empires, 1894–1907*. London, 1966.
———. *Japanese Foreign Policy*. London, 1977.
Okamoto, Shumpei. *The Japanese Oligarchy and the Russo-Japanese War*. New York, 1970.
Presseisen, Ernst L. *Germany and Japan: A Study in Totalitarian Diplomacy, 1933–1941*. The Hague, 1958.
Pyle, Kenneth B. *The New Generation in Meiji Japan: Problems of Cultural Identity, 1885–1895*. Stanford, CA, 1969.
Scalapino, Robert A. *Democracy and the Party Movement in Prewar Japan: The Failure of the First Attempt*. Berkeley, CA, 1953.
Titus, David A. *Palace and Politics in Prewar Japan: The Context of Imperial Involvement in Politics and Palace Leadership in the Showa Period, 1929–1941*. New York, 1974.

Japanese Language Sources

Akaneya T. *Nihon no GATT kanyu mondai: Regimu riron no bunseki shikaku ni yoru jirei kenkyu* [The Problem of Japanese Accession to the GATT: A Case Study in Regime Theory]. Tōkyō, 1992.
Asada Sadao. *Ryōtaisenkan no nichibei kankei* [U.S.-Japanese Relations in the Interwar Period]. Tōkyō, 1993.
Denki K. *Hirota Koki*. Tōkyō, 1966.
Fujimoto Kazumi. Kaifu seiken to "Seiji Kaikaku" [The Kaifu Administration and "Political Reform"]. Tōkyō, 1992.
Fukuda Takeo. *Kaiko kyujūnen* [Remembering His 90 Years]. Tōkyō, 1995.
Gaimushō. *Komura gaikōshi* [A History of Komura's Diplomacy]. Tōkyō, 1953.
———. *Nippon gaikō monjo* [Diplomatic Papers of Japan]. *Meiji*. Vols. 4, 5, 6, *Joyoku kaisei kankei* [Treaty Revisions and Related Matters]. Tōkyō, 1964.
Hatano, M. *Kindai higashi ajia no seiji hendo to Nihon no gaikō* [Political Change in Modern Asia and Japanese Diplomacy]. Tōkyō, 1995.
Hayashi Shigeru and Tsuji Seimei, Eds. *Nippon naikaku shiroku* [The History of Japanese Cabinets]. Vol. 4. Tōkyō, 1981.
Hirosuke Kiba, Ed. *Nomura Kichisaburō*. Tōkyō, 1961.
Hosoya C. and Aruga T., Eds. *Kokusai kankyō no henyō to nichibei kankei* [Transformation of the International Environment and U.S.-Japan Relations]. Tōkyō, 1987.
Ikei Masaru, et al., Eds. *Hamaguchi Osachi nikki zuikanroku* [Hamaguchi Osachi Diaries and Essays]. Tōkyō, 1991.
Inoue Toshikazu, *Kiki no nakano kyocho gaikō* [Diplomacy of Cooperation in Crisis]. Tōkyō, 1993.
Ishibashi Tanzan, *Ishibashi Tanzan zenshū* [The Complete Works of Ishibashi Tanzan]. Tōkyō, 1970–72.
Ishii Takashi. *Meiji shoki no kokusai kankei* [A Study of Treaty Revisions in the Early Meiji Period]. Tōkyō, 1977.
Itō Masanori. Ed. *Kāto Takaaki*. 2 Vols. Tōkyō, 1929.
Itō Takashi. *Shōwa shoki no seijishi kenkyū* [Political History of the Early Shōwa Period]. Tōkyō, 1969.
Kamiya Fuji. *Sengoshino nakano nichibei kankei* [U.S.-Japanese Relations in Postwar History]. Tōkyō, 1989.
Kato Takaaki, Ed. *Kato Takaaki den*. Tōkyō, 1928.
Kawamura, Naoki. *Nihon gaikōshi no shomondai* [Issues in Japanese Diplomatic History]. Tōkyō, 1986.
Kimura M. *Shibusawa Eiichi-minkan keizai gaikō no sōshisha* [Shibusawa Eiichi—The Pioneer of Private Business Diplomacy]. Tōkyō, 1991.
Kindai Nihon kenkyū 16: Sengo kaiko no keisei [Modern Japan Study 16: The Formation of Post-War Diplomacy]. Tōkyō, 1994.
Kondo Misao, Ed. *Katō Takaaki*. Tōkyō, 1959.
Masuda Hiroshi. *Ishibashi Tanzan: Senryō seisaku eno teikō* [Ishibashi Tanzan: Resistance Against Occupation Policies]. Tōkyō, 1988.
———. *Nichibei kankei gaisetsu* [A Survey of U.S.-Japanese Relations]. Tōkyō, 1978.
Matsushita Yoshio. *Araki Sadao to Abe Nobuyuki* [Araki Sadao and Abe Nobuyuki]. Tōkyō, 1935.
Miki Takeo. Gikai seijo to tomomi [In Parliamentary Politics]. Tōkyō, 1984.
Moriyama Shigenori. *Kindai nikkan kankeishi*

kenkyū [A Study on the History of Modern Japanese-Korean Relations]. Tōkyō, 1987.

Nagata Akifumi. *Seodoa Ruuzuberuto to Kankoku* [Theodore Roosevelt and Korea]. Tōkyō, 1992.

Nakasone Yasuhiro. *Seiji to jinsei: Nakasone Yasuhiro kaikoroku* [Politics and Life: Memoirs of Nakasone Yasuhiro]. Tōkyō, 1992.

Nippon Kokusai Seiji Gakkai [Japan International Political Conference]. *Taiheiyo senso eno michi* [The Road to the Pacific War]. Vol. 3. Tōkyō, 1962.

Nomura Kichisaburō. *Beikoku ni tsukaishite* [Mission to the United States]. Tōkyō, 1946.

Ōhira Masayoshi. *Ōhira Masayoshi kaikoroku* [Memoirs of Ohira Masayoshi]. Tōkyō, 1983.

Ozawa Eiji. *Hosokawa seiken 250 nichi no shinjitsu* [The Truth of 250 Days of the Hosokawa Administration]. Tōkyō, 1994.

Sakatani Yoshiro den [Biography of Sakatani Yoshiro]. Tōkyō, 1961.

Satō Eisaku. *Sato Eisaku nikki* [The Diary of Satō Eisaku]. 6 Vols. Tōkyō, 1997–1999.

Sekine Minoru. *Hamaguchi Osachi den* [A Biography of Hamaguchi]. Tōkyō, 1931.

Shimomura Fujio. *Meiji shonen joyaku kaiseishi no kenkyū* [International Relations in the Early Meiji Period]. Tōkyō, 1962.

Shindo, E., Ed. *Ashida Hitoshi nikki* [Ashida Hitoshi Diary]. Tōkyō, 1986.

Shishaku Saitō Makoto den [Biography of Viscount Saitō Makoto]. 4 Vols. Tōkyō, 1942.

Tokito Hideto. *Inukai Tsuyoshi: Riberarizumu to nashonarizumu no sokoku*. Tōkyō, 1991.

Tokutomi Ichirō, *Koshaku Katsura Tarō den* [A Biography of Duke Katsura Tarō]. Tōkyō, 1917.

Tsutsui, K. *Ishibashi Tanzan: Ichi jiyū-shugi seijika no kiseki* [Ishibashi Tanzan: The Track Record of One Liberal Politician]. Tōkyō, 1986.

Uno Shigeaki. "Hirota Koki no taigai seisaku to Shokaiseki" [Hirota Koki's Foreign Policy and Jiang Jieshi]. *Kokusai Seiji*, 56 (Fall 1976).

Ushiba Nobuhiko. *Gaikō no shunkan: Watakushi no rirekishō* [A Moment in Diplomacy: A Memoir]. Tōkyō, 1984.

———. *Keizai gaikō e no shōgen* [A Testimony to Economic Diplomacy]. Tōkyō, 1984.

Washio Yoshinao, Ed. *Inukai bokudo shokanshū* [The Personal Letters of Inukai Tsuyoshi]. Tōkyō, 1940.

Watanabe Akio, Ed. *Sengo Nihon no saishō tachi* [Postwar Japanese Prime Ministers]. Tōkyō, 1995.

Yamaoka Michio. *Taiheiyō mondai chōsakai' kenkyū* [A Study of the Institute of Pacific Relations]. Tōkyō, 1997.

Yoshida Tsunekichi. *Ii Naosuke*. Tōkyō, 1963.

Korea

Brun, Michel. *Incident at Sakhalin: The True Mission of KAL Flight 007*. New York, 1996.

Conroy, Hilary. *The Japanese Seizure of Korea, 1868–1910: A Study of Realism and Idealism in International Relations*. Philadelphia, 1960.

Cumings, Bruce. *Korea's Place in the Sun: A Modern History*. New York, 1997.

Dallin, Alexander. *Black Box: KAL 007 and the Superpowers*. Berkeley, CA, 1985.

Han Sung-ju. *The Failure of Democracy in South Korea*. Berkeley, CA, 1974.

Han Wu-gun. *The History of Korea*. Seoul, 1970.

Heo Man-ho. "The Characteristics of North Korean Negotiating Behavior: A Theoretical Deviation or Pseudo-Negotiation?" *Korea and World Affairs*, Fall 1998.

Johnson, Richard W. *Shootdown: Flight 007 and the American Connection*. New York, 1986.

Kim, C. I. Eugene and Han-Kyo Kim. *Korea and the Politics of Imperialism, 1876–1910*. Berkeley, CA, 1967.

Kim Eun Mee. *Big Business, Strong State: Collusion and Conflict in South Korean Development, 1960–1990*. Albany, NY, 1997.

Kim Jinwung. "From Patron-Client to Partners: The Changing South Korean-American Relationship." *Journal of American–East Asian Relations*, Fall 1993.

———. "The Nature of South Korean Anti-Americanism." *Korea Journal*, Spring 1994.

———. "Recent Anti-Americanism in South Korea: The Causes." *Asian Survey*, August 1989.

Kim Kwan Bong. *The Korea-Japan Treaty Crisis and the Instability of the Korean Political System*. New York, 1971.

Kim Quee-young. *The Fall of Syngman Rhee*. Berkeley, CA, 1983.

Kim Se-jin. *The Politics of Military Revolution in Korea*. Chapel Hill, NC, 1971.

Ku Tae-yol. *Korea Under Colonialism: The March First Movement and Anglo-Japanese Relations*. Seoul, 1985.

Lee Chong-sik. *Japan and Korea: The Political Dimension*. Stanford, CA, 1985.

Lee Hahn Been. *Korea: Time, Change, and Administration*. Honolulu, HI, 1968.

Lee Ki-baek. *A New History of Korea*. Seoul, 1984.

Lie, John. *Han Unbound: The Political Economy of South Korea*. Stanford, CA, 1998.

Macdonald, Donald S. *The Koreans: Contemporary Politics and Society*. Boulder, CO, 1988.

———. *U.S.-Korean Relations from Liberation to Self-Reliance: The Twenty-Year Record*. Boulder, CO, 1992.

Nam, Koon Woo. *South Korean Politics: The Search for Political Consensus and Stability*. Lanham, MD, 1989.

Oberdorfer, Don. *The Two Koreas: A Contemporary History*. Reading, PA, 1997.

Sands, William F. *At the Court of Korea*. London, 1987.

Scalapino, Robert A. and Lee Chong-sik, Eds. *Communism in Korea: The Movement*. Berkeley, CA, 1972.

Suh Dae-Sook, Ed. *Documents of Korean Communism 1918–1948*. Princeton, NJ, 1970.

Korean Language Sources

Cho Kap-jae. *Nae Mudŏm-e Ch'im-ŭl Paet-ŏra!: Kŭndaehwa Hyŏgmyŏngga Pak Chŏng-hŭi ŭi Pijang-han Saeng-ae* [Spit on My Grave!: The Tragic Life of Park Chung-hee, the Modern Revolutionist]. 4 Vols. Seoul, 1999.

Ch'ŏn Kŭm-sŏng. *Hwangkangesŏ Pukakkaji: Inkan Chŏn Du-hwan* [From the Han River to the Pukak Mountain]. Seoul, 1981.

Chŏng Ok-im. *Pukhaek Mŭnge ŭi Obaek-p'alsip-p'al il* [588 Days of the North Korean Nuclear Issue]. Seoul, 1995.

Chung'ang Ilbo Tŏbŏylch'ŭijeban [Special Reporter Group of the *Chung'ang Ilbo*]. *Chosŏn Minjujŭi Inmin' Gonghwagŏk* [The Democratic People's Republic of Korea]. 2 Vols. Seoul, 1992, 1993.

Han Hung-soo. *Han'guk jongch'i dongtaeron* [Dynamism of Korean Politics]. Seoul, 1996.

Jang Myŏn. *Han Arŭi miri Chŭkchi Ankonŭn: Jang Myŏn Paksa hoegorok* [Except a Grain of Wheat Fall into the Ground and Die: Memoirs of Dr. Chang Myon]. Seoul, 1967.

Kim Dae-jung. *Kim Dae-jung jasojon* [Kim Dae-jung's Autobiography]. Seoul, 1999.

Kim Jinwung. *Hangukin ŭi Panmi Kamjŏng* [The Anti-Americanism of the Korean People]. Seoul, 1992.

Min Byŏng-yŏng. *Miju Imin 100 Nyŏng* [100 Years of Korean Immigration to the United States]. Seoul, 1986.

Moon Ch'ang-guk. *Hanmi Kaldŭng ŭi Haebu* [Anatomy of Korea-U.S. Conflicts]. Seoul, 1994.

Nam Chan-sun. *P'yŏngyang ŭi Haek Miso* [Nuclear smile of Pyongyang]. Seoul, 1995.

To Chin-sun. *Han'guk Minjokjuŭi wa Nambuk Kwangye* [Korean Democracy and Inter-Korean Relations]. Seoul, 1998.

Yi Do-sŏng. *Silrok Pak Chŏng-hŭi wa Hanil-hoedam* [An Authentic Record: Park Chŏng-hŭi and Korea-Japan Talks]. Seoul, 1995.

Yi Jŏng-suk. *Hyŭndae Bŭkhaneŭi Yihae, Sasang, Cheje, Jidoja* [Understanding Contemporary North Korea Ideology, Regime, and Leaders]. Seoul, 1995.

Yŭn Kyŏng-no. *105 In Sagŏn kwa Shinminhŏ Yŏnku* [A Study on 105 Persons Incident and the New Peoples Society]. Seoul, 1990.

Korean War

Appleman, Roy E. *Disaster in Korea: The Chinese Confront MacArthur*. College Station, TX, 1989.

———. *East of Chosin: Entrapment and Breakout in Korea, 1950*. College Station, TX, 1987.

———. *Escaping the Trap: The US Army X Corps in Northeast Korea, 1950*. College Station, TX, 1990.

———. *Ridgway Duels for Korea*. College Station, TX, 1990.

———. *South to the Naktong, North to the Yalu*. Washington, DC, 1961.

Blair, Clay. *The Forgotten War: America in Korea, 1950–1953*. New York, 1987.

Chen Jian. *China's Road to the Korean War: The Making of the Sino-American Confrontation*. New York, 1994.

Collins, J. Lawton. *War in Peacetime: The History and Lessons of Korea*. Boston, 1969.

Cumings, Bruce. *The Origins of the Korean War*. 2 Vols. Princeton, NJ, 1981, 1990.

Endicott, Stephen L. and Edward Hagerman. *The United States and Biological Warfare: Secrets from the Early Cold War and Korea*. Bloomington, IN, 1997.

Fehrenbach, T. R. *This Kind of War: A Study in Unpreparedness*. New York, 1963.

Foot, Rosemary. *Substitute for Victory: The Politics of Peacemaking at the Korean Armistice Talks*. Ithaca, NY, 1990.

———. *The Wrong War: American Policy and the*

Dimensions of the Korean Conflict, 1950–1953. Ithaca, NY, 1985.

Goncharov, Sergei N., John Lewis, and Xue Litai, *Uncertain Partners: Stalin, Mao, and the Korean War.* Stanford, CA, 1993.

Goulden, Joseph C. *Korea: The Untold Story of the War.* New York, 1982.

Halliday, Jon and Bruce Cumings. *Korea: The Unknown War.* New York, 1988.

Hastings, Max. *The Korean War.* New York, 1987.

Heinl, Robert D., Jr. *Victory at High Tide: The Inchon-Seoul Campaign.* Philadelphia, 1968.

Hermes, Walter G. *Truce Tent and Fighting Front.* Washington, DC, 1966.

Kaufman, Burton I. *The Korean War: Challenges in Crises, Credibility, and Command.* Philadelphia, 1986.

Kim Chull Baum and James I. Matray, Eds. *Korea and the Cold War: Division, Destruction, and Disarmament.* Claremont, CA, 1993.

Langley, Michael. *Inchon: MacArthur's Last Triumph.* London, 1979.

Lee, Steven Hugh. *The Korean War.* London, 2001.

———. *Outposts of Empire: Korea, Vietnam and the Origins of the Cold War, 1949–1954.* Montreal, 1995.

Lowe, Peter. *Origins of the Korean War.* New York, 1986.

MacDonald, Callum A. *Korea: The War Before Vietnam.* New York, 1986.

Matray, James I. *The Reluctant Crusade: American Foreign Policy in Korea, 1941–1950.* Honolulu, HI, 1985.

Neary, Ian and James Cotton, Eds. *The Korean War in History.* Atlantic Highlands, NJ, 1989.

Paik Sun Yup. *From Pusan to Panmunjom.* New York, 1992.

Rees, David. *Korea: The Limited War.* New York, 1964.

Schnabel, James F. *Policy and Direction: The First Year.* Washington, DC, 1972.

Spanier, John W. *The Truman-MacArthur Controversy and the Korean War.* New York, 1959.

Stueck, William W. *The Korean War: An International History.* Princeton, NJ, 1995.

Vatcher, William H. *Panmunjom: The Story of the Korean Military Armistice Negotiations.* New York, 1958.

Whiting, Allen S. *China Crosses the Yalu: The Decision to Enter the Korean War.* New York, 1970.

Zhang Shu Guang. *Mao's Military Romanticism: China and the Korean War, 1950–53.* Lawrence, KS, 1995.

Laos

Brown, MacAlister and Joseph J. Zasloff. *Apprentice Revolutionaries: The Communist Movement in Laos, 1930–1985.* Stanford, CA, 1986.

Castle, Timothy N. *At War in the Shadow of Vietnam: U.S. Military Aid to the Royal Lao Government, 1955–1975.* New York, 1993.

Conboy, Kenneth J. and J. Morrison. *Shadow War: The CIA's Secret War in Laos.* Boulder, CO, 1995.

Dommen, Arthur J. *Conflict in Laos: The Politics of Neutralization.* New York, 1971.

Fall, Bernard B. *Anatomy of a Crisis: The Laotian Crisis of 1960–1961.* Garden City, NY, 1969.

Goldstein, Martin E. *American Policy Toward Laos Since 1954.* Rutherford, NJ, 1973.

Hamilton-Merritt, Jane. *Tragic Mountains: The Hmong, the Americans, and the Wars for Laos, 1942–1992.* Bloomington, IN, 1993.

Hannah, Norman B. *The Key to Failure: Laos and the Vietnam War.* Lanham, MD, 1987.

Langer, Paul F. and Joseph J. Zasloff. *North Vietnam and the Pathet Lao: Partners in the Struggle for Laos.* Cambridge, MA, 1970.

Pelz, Stephen E. " 'When Do I Have Time to Think?': John F. Kennedy, Roger Hilsman, and the Laotian Crisis of 1962." *Diplomatic History,* Spring 1979.

Stevenson, Charles A. *The End of Nowhere: American Policy Toward Laos Since 1954.* Boston, 1972.

Stieglitz, Perry. *In a Little Kingdom.* Armonk, NY, 1990.

Stuart-Fox, Martin. *A History of Laos.* Cambridge, UK, 1997.

Tourison, Sedgwick D. *Secret Army, Secret War: Washington's Tragic Spy Operation in North Vietnam.* Annapolis, MD, 1995.

Warner, Roger. *Back Fire: Secret War in Laos and Its Link to the War in Vietnam.* New York, 1995.

Zasloff, Joseph J. *The Pathet Lao: Leadership and Organization.* Lexington, MA, 1973.

Malaya

Baginda, A. R. A., Ed. *Malaysia's Defence and Foreign Policies.* Petaling Jaya, Selangor, Darul Ehsam, 1995.

Clutterbuck, Richard L. *The Long, Long War: The Emergency in Malaya, 1948–1960*. London, 1967.

Short, Anthony. *The Communist Insurrection in Malaya, 1948–1960*. London, 1975.

Teik, Khoo B. *Paradoxes of Mahathirism: An Intellectual Biography of Mahathir Mohamad*. Kuala Lumpur, 1995.

Manchurian Crisis

Bamba, Nobuya. *Japanese Diplomacy in a Dilemma: New Light on Japan's China Policy, 1924–1929*. Vancouver, 1972.

Doenecke, Justus D. *When the Wicked Rise: American Opinion-Makers and the Manchurian Crisis of 1931–1933*. Lewisburg, PA, 1984.

Ogata, Sadako. *Defiance in Manchuria: The Making of Japanese Foreign Policy, 1931–1932*. Berkeley, CA, 1964.

Penlington, John N. *The Mukden Mandate: Acts and Aims in Manchuria*. Tōkyō, 1932.

Thorne, Christopher. *The Limits of Foreign Policy: The West, The League, and the Far Eastern Crisis of 1931–1933*. New York, 1973.

Yoshihashi Takehiko. *Conspiracy at Mukden: The Rise of the Japanese Military*. New Haven, CT, 1963.

Memoirs of Americans

Acheson, Dean G. *Present at the Creation: My Years in the State Department*. New York, 1969.

Allison, John M. *Ambassador of the Prairie or Allison in Wonderland*. Boston, 1973.

Brzezinski, Zbigniew. *Power and Principle: Memoirs of the National Security Adviser, 1977–1981*. New York, 1983.

Carter, Jimmy. *Keeping Faith: Memoirs of a President*. New York, 1982.

Danelski, David J. and Joseph S. Tulchin, Eds. *The Autobiographical Notes of Charles Evans Hughes*. Cambridge, MA, 1973.

Dole, Sanford B. *Memoirs of the Hawaiian Revolution*. Andrew Ferrell, Ed. Honolulu, HI, 1936.

Ford, Gerald R. *A Time to Heal: The Autobiography of Gerald R. Ford*. New York, 1979.

Foster, John W. *Diplomatic Memoirs*. 2 Vols. Boston, 1909.

Grew, Joseph C. *Turbulent Era: A Diplomatic Record of Forty Years, 1904–1945*. 2 Vols. Boston, 1952.

Hoover, Herbert. *Memoirs, 1920–1933*. London, 1952.

Hull, Cordell. *The Memoirs of Cordell Hull*. 2 Vols. Garden City, NY, 1948.

Johnson, U. Alexis. *The Right Hand of Power*. Englewood Cliffs, NJ, 1984.

Kennan, George F. *Memoirs, 1925–1950*. Boston, 1967.

———. *Memoirs, 1950–1963*. Boston, 1972.

Kissinger, Henry A. *The White House Years*. Boston, 1979.

———. *Years of Renewal*. Boston, 1998.

———. *Years of Upheaval*. Boston, 1982.

Lodge, Henry Cabot, Jr. *The Storm Has Many Eyes: A Personal Narrative*. New York, 1973.

MacArthur, Douglas. *Reminiscences*. New York, 1964.

Nixon, Richard M. *RN: The Memoirs of Richard Nixon*. New York, 1978.

Pruitt, Ida. *A Daughter of Han: The Autobiography of a Chinese Working Woman*. Stanford, CA, 1967.

Radford, Arthur W. *From Pearl Harbor to Vietnam: The Memoirs of Admiral Arthur W. Radford*. Stephen Jurika Jr., Ed. Stanford, CA, 1980.

Reischauer, Edwin O. *My Life Between Japan and America*. New York, 1986.

Rusk, Dean. *As I Saw It*. D. S. Papp, Ed. New York, 1990.

Shultz, George P. *Turmoil and Triumph: My Years as Secretary of State*. New York, 1993.

Smedley, Agnes. *Daughter of Earth*. New York, 1929.

Stimson, Henry L. and McGeorge Bundy. *On Active Service in Peace and War*. New York, 1947.

Stuart, J. Leighton. *Fifty Years in China: The Memoirs of John Leighton Stuart, Missionary and Ambassador*. New York, 1954.

Westmoreland, William C. *A Soldier Reports*. Garden City, NY, 1972.

Memoirs of Asians

Aung San Suu Kyi. *Aung San*. Lawrence, MA, 1984.

Fukuzawa Yukichi. *The Autobiography of Yukichi Fukuzawa*. Kiyooka Eiichi Trans. New York, 1966.

Oakes, T. M., Ed. *The Saionji-Harada Memoirs*. Detroit, 1968.

Peng Dehuai. *Autobiography of Peng Dehuai*. Beijing, 1984.

Pooley, Andrew M., Ed. *Secret Memoirs of Count Tadasu Hayashi*. London, 1915.
Pu-Yi, Henry. *From Emperor to Citizen: The Autobiography of Aisin-Gioro Pu Yi*. Oxford, UK, 1987.
U Nu. *Saturday's Son*. New Haven, CT, 1975.
Yung Wing. *My Life in China and America*. New York, 1909.
Zhou Enlai. *Selected Works of Zhou Enlai on Foreign Policy*. Beijing, 1990.

Micronesia

Heine, Carl. *Micronesia at the Crossroads: A Reappraisal of the Micronesian Political Dilemma*. New York, 1974.
Hezel, Francis X. *The First Taint of Civilization: A History of the Caroline and Marshall Islands in Pre-Colonial Days, 1521–1885*. Honolulu, HI, 1983.
——— and M. L. Berg, Eds. *Winds of Change: A Book of Readings on Micronesian History*. Saipan, 1979.
Maga, Timothy P. *John F. Kennedy and the New Pacific Community, 1961–1963*. New York, 1990.
Peattie, Mark R. *Nanyō: The Rise and Fall of the Japanese in Micronesia, 1885–1945*. Honolulu, HI, 1988.
Weisgall, J. "Micronesia and the Nuclear Pacific Since Hiroshima." *SAIS Review*, Summer–Fall 1985.
Yanaihara Tadao. *Pacific Islands Under Japanese Mandate*. London, 1938.

Missionaries

Barr, Pat. *To China with Love: The Lives and Times of Protestant Missionaries in China, 1860–1900*. London, 1972.
Clymer, Kenton J. *Protestant Missionaries in the Philippines, 1898–1916: An Inquiry into American Colonial Mentality*. Urbana, IL, 1986.
Fairbank, John K., Ed. *The Missionary Enterprise in China and America*. Cambridge, MA, 1974.
Hunter, Jane. *The Gospel of Gentility: American Women Missionaries in Turn-of-the-Century China*. New Haven, CT, 1984.
Lodwick, Kathleen L. *Crusaders Against Opium: Protestant Missionaries in China, 1874–1917*. Lexington, KY, 1996.
Records of the General Conference of the Protestant Missionaries of China, Held at Shanghai, May 7–20, 1890. Shanghai, 1890.
Varg, Paul A. *Missionaries, Chinese and Diplomats: The American Protestant Missionary Movement in China, 1890–1952*. Princeton, NJ, 1958.

Nongovernmental Agencies

Bowers, John Z. *Western Medicine in a Chinese Palace*. New York, 1971.
Boyd, Nancy. *Emissaries: The Overseas Work of the American YWCA, 1895–1970*. New York, 1986.
Bullock, Mary Brown. *An American Transplant: The Rockefeller Foundation and Peking Union Medical College*. Berkeley, CA, 1980.
Chen Kaiyi. "Quality Versus Quantity: The Rockefeller Foundation and Nurses' Training in China." *Journal of American–East Asian Relations*, Spring 1996.
Condliffe, John B. *Reminiscences of the Institute of Pacific Relations*. Vancouver, BC, 1984.
Davidann, John T. *A World of Crisis and Progress: The American YMCA in Japan, 1890–1930*. Bethlehem, PA, 1998.
Fosdick, Raymond B. *The Story of the Rockefeller Foundation*. New York, 1952.
Garrett, Shirley S. *Social Reformers in Urban China: The Chinese YMCA, 1895–1926*. Cambridge, MA, 1970.
Harper, E. D. and H. R. Gillmore. *For a Better World: A History of the YWCA Policy in Public Affairs*. New York, 1948.
Lai, H. M. "Historical Development of the Chinese Consolidated Benevolent Association/Huiguan System." *Chinese America: History and Perspectives*, 1987.
Lofland, John. *Doomsday Cult: A Study of Conversion, Proselytization, and Maintenance of Faith*. New York, 1977.
Lorence, James J. *Organized Business and the Myth of the China Market: The American Asiatic Association, 1898–1937*. Philadelphia, 1981.
Matczak, Sebastian A. *Unificationism: A New Philosophy and World View*. New York, 1982.
Morgan, Joseph G. *The Vietnam Lobby: The American Friends of Vietnam, 1955–1975*. Chapel Hill, NC, 1997.
Ninkovich, Frank. "The Rockefeller Foundation, China, and Cultural Change." *Journal of American History*, March 1984.

Scheer, Robert and Warren Hinckle. "The Viet-Nam Lobby." *Ramparts*, 1965.
Thomas, John N. *The Institute of Pacific Relations: Asian Scholars and American Politics*. Seattle, WA, 1974.

Pearl Harbor

Borg, Dorothy. *The United States and the Far Eastern Crisis of 1933–1938*. Cambridge, MA, 1964.
———and Shumpei Okamoto, Eds. *Pearl Harbor as History: Japanese-American Relations, 1931–1941*. New York, 1973.
Burns, Richard D. and Edward M. Bennett, Eds. *Diplomats in Crisis: United States-Chinese-Japanese Relations, 1919–1941*. Santa Barbara, CA, 1974.
Butow, Robert J. C. *Tōjō and the Coming of War*. Princeton, NJ, 1961.
Feis, Herbert. *The Road to Pearl Harbor: The Coming of the War Between the United States and Japan*. Princeton, NJ, 1950.
Heinrichs, Waldo H., Jr. *Threshold of War: Franklin D. Roosevelt and American Entry into World War II*. New York, 1988.
Morley, James W., Ed. *The Fateful Choice: Japan's Advance into Southeast Asia, 1939–1941*. New York, 1980.
Prange, Gordon W. *At Dawn We Slept: The Untold Story of Pearl Harbor*. New York, 1981.
Schroeder, Paul W. *The Axis Alliance and Japanese-American Relations, 1941*. Ithaca, NY, 1958.
Utley, Jonathan G. *Going to War with Japan, 1937–1941*. Knoxville, TN, 1985.
Wohlstetter, Roberta. *Pearl Harbor: Warning and Decision*. Stanford, CA, 1962.

Personal Accounts of Americans

Angell, James B. *The Reminiscences of James Burrill Angell*. New York, 1912.
Beveridge, Albert J. *The Meaning of the Times and Other Speeches*. New York, 1968.
Bruce, David. *Window to the Forbidden City: The Chinese Diaries of David Bruce*. Priscilla Roberts, Ed. Boston, 1996.
Bucher, Lloyd M. *Bucher: My Story*. New York, 1970.
Chennault, Claire L. *Way of a Fighter*. New York, 1949.
Clark, Mark W. *From the Danube to the Yalu*. New York, 1954.
Clubb, O. Edmund. *The Witness and I*. New York, 1974.
Cosenza, Mario E., Ed. *The Complete Journals of Townsend Harris: First American Consul General and Minister to Japan*. New York, 1930.
Dana, Richard H. *Two Years Before the Mast*. New York, 1899.
Esherick, Joseph. *Lost Chance in China: The World War II Dispatches of John S. Service*. New York, 1974.
Fairbank, John K. *Chinabound*. New York, 1982.
———. *China Watch*. Cambridge, MA, 1987.
Fulbright, J. William. *The Arrogance of Power*. New York, 1966.
Goodman, Allan E., Ed. *Negotiating While Fighting: The Diary of Admiral C. Turner Joy at the Korean Armistice Conference*. Stanford, CA, 1978.
Green, Marshall. *War and Peace with China: First-hand Experiences in the Foreign Service of the United States*. Bethesda, MD, 1994.
Hilsman, Roger. *American Guerrilla: My War behind Japanese Lines*. Washington, DC, 1991.
Hulbert, Homer B. *The Passing of Korea*. Seoul, 1969.
Joy, C. Turner. *How Communists Negotiate*. New York, 1955.
Lansdale, Edward G. *In the Midst of Wars: An American's Mission to Southeast Asia*. New York, 1972.
LeMay, Curtis E. and M. Kantor, *Mission with LeMay: My Story*. New York, 1965.
Lodge, Henry Cabot, Jr. *As It Was*. New York, 1976.
McNamara, Robert S. *In Retrospect: The Tragedy and Lessons of Vietnam*. New York, 1995.
Melby, John F. *The Mandate of Heaven: Record of a Civil War, China 1945–49*. Toronto, 1968.
Murphy, Robert D. *Diplomat Among Warriors*. Garden City, NY, 1964.
Noble, Harold J. *Embassy at War*. Seattle, 1975.
Patti, Archimedes. *Why Vietnam? Prelude to America's Albatross*. Berkeley, CA, 1980.
Phillips, William E. *Ventures in Diplomacy*. Boston, 1952.
Pruitt, Ida. *Old Madam Yin: A Memoir of Life in Peking, 1926–1938*. Stanford, CA, 1979.
Rankin, Karl L. *China Assignment*. Seattle, WA, 1964.
Reinsch, Paul S. *An American Diplomat in China*. New York, 1922.
Ridgway, Matthew B. *The Korean War*. Garden City, NY, 1967.
Rockhill, W. W. *Diary of a Journey through Mon-*

golia and Thibet in 1891 and 1892. Washington, DC, 1894.
———. *Diplomatic Audiences at the Court of China*. London, 1905.
———. *The Land of the Lamas: Notes of a Journey Through China, Mongolia and Tibet*. New York, 1891.
Sebald, William J. *With MacArthur in Japan*. London, 1965.
Service, John S. *The Amerasia Papers: Some Problems in the History of U.S.-China Relations*. Berkeley, CA, 1971.
Shriver, R. Sargent. *Point of the Lance*. New York, 1964.
Shufeldt, Robert W. *The Relation of the Navy to the Commerce of the United States*. 1878.
Smedley, Agnes. *China Fights Back: An American Woman with the Eighth Route Army*. New York, 1938.
———. *Chinese Destinies: Sketches of Present-Day China*. New York, 1933.
Snow, Edgar. *The Other Side of the River: Red China Today*. New York, 1962.
———. *Red Star Over China*. New York, 1938.
Stevens George B. and W. Fisher Markwick, Eds. *The Life, Letters, and Journals of the Rev. and Hon. Peter Parker, M.D.* Boston, 1896.
Strong, Anna Louise. *I Change Worlds: The Remaking of an American*. New York, 1935.
Taylor, Maxwell D. *Swords and Plowshares*. New York, 1972.
———. *The Uncertain Trumpet*. New York, 1959
Wedemeyer, Albert C. *Wedemeyer Reports!* New York, 1958.
White, Theodore H. *In Search of History: A Personal Adventure*. New York, 1978.
———and Annalee A. Jacoby, *Thunder Out of China*. New York, 1946.

Personal Accounts of Asians

Chennault, Anna. *The Education of Anna*. New York, 1980.
Fang Lizhi. *Bringing Down the Great Wall: Writings on Science, Culture and Democracy in China*. New York, 1990.
Hatta, Mohammed. *Portrait of a Patriot: Selected Writings*. Jakarta, 1973.
Kim Dae-jung. *Mass Participatory Economy: Korea's Road to World Economic Power*. Cambridge, MA, 1996.
Lili'uokalani. *Hawaii's Story by Hawaii's Queen*. Boston, 1898.
Nguyen Cao Ky. *Twenty Years and Twenty Days*. New York, 1976.
Nguyen thi Dinh. *No Other Road to Take*. M. V. Elliott, Trans. Ithaca, NY, 1976.
Okuma Shigenobu, Ed. *Fifty Years of New Japan*. 2 Vols. London, 1909.
Quezón, Manuel. *The Good Fight*. New York, 1946.
Shigemitsu, Mamoru. *Japan and Her Destiny*. London, 1958.
Sihanouk, Norodom. *My War with the CIA: The Memoirs of Prince Norodom Sihanouk*. Wilfred P. Burchett, Ed. New York, 1972.
U Thant, *View from the UN*. Garden City, NY, 1978.
Vo Nguyen Giap. *Dien Bien Phu*. Hanoi, 1962.
———. *Unforgettable Days*. Hanoi, 1978.

Philippines

Agoncillo, Teodoro A. *Malolos: The Crisis of the Republic*. Quezon City, 1960.
Aquino, Benigno. *Politics of Plunder: The Philippines Under Marcos*. Manila, 1987.
Bonner, Raymond. *Waltzing with a Dictator: The Marcoses and the Making of American Policy*. New York, 1987.
Buss, Claude, Ed. *Cory Aquino and the People of the Philippines*. Stanford, CA, 1987.
Constantino, Renato. *The Philippines: A Past Revisited*. Manila, 1975.
Dahm, Bernhard, Ed. *Economy and Politics in the Philippines Under Corazon Aquino*. Hamburg, 1991.
Hayden, Joseph R. *The Philippines: A Study in National Development*. New York, 1942.
Kerklviet, Benedict J. *The Huk Rebellion: A Study of Peasant Revolt in the Philippines*. Berkeley, CA, 1977.
Myer, Milton W. *A Diplomatic History of the Philippine Republic*. Honolulu, HI, 1965.
Paredes, Rudy R., Ed. *Philippine Colonial Democracy*. Quezon City, 1989.
Reid, Robert H. *Corazon Aquino and the Brushfire Revolution*. Baton Rouge, LA, 1995.
Romulo, Beth Day. *Inside the Palace: The Rise and Fall of Ferdinand and Imelda Marcos*. New York, 1987.
Rosenberg, David A., Ed. *Marcos and Martial Law in the Philippines*. Ithaca, NY, 1979.
Steinberg, David J. *The Philippines: A Singular and Plural Place*. Boulder, CO, 1994.
Thompson, Mark R. *The Anti-Marcos Struggle:*

Personalistic Rule and Democratic Transition in the Philippines. New Haven, CT, 1995.
Thompson, Winfred L. *The Introduction of American Law in the Philippines and Puerto Rico, 1898–1905*. Fayetteville, NC, 1989.
Wurfel, David. *Filipino Politics: Development and Decay*. Ithaca, NY, 1988.

Regional Organizations

Borthwick, Mark. *Pacific Century: The Emergence of Modern Pacific Asia*. Boulder, CO, 1998.
Broinowski, Alison, Ed. *ASEAN into the 1990s*. London, 1990.
Buszynski, Leszek. *SEATO: The Failure of an Alliance Strategy*. Singapore, 1983.
Gardner, Richard N. *Sterling-Dollar Diplomacy in Current Perspective: The Origins and the Prospects of Our International Economic Order*. New York, 1980.
Hellmann, Donald C. and Kenneth B. Pyle, Eds. *From APEC to Xanadu: Creating a Viable Community in the Post–Cold War Pacific*. Armonk, NY, 1997.
Jackson, John H. *Restructuring the GATT System*. London, 1990.
Liefer, Michael. *ASEAN and the Security of South-East Asia*. London, 1989.
McIntyre, W. David. *The Significance of the Commonwealth, 1965–90*. London, 1991.
Modelski, George, Ed. *SEATO: Six Studies*. Vancouver, 1962.
Palmer, Ronald D. and Thomas J. Reckford. *Building ASEAN: Twenty Years of Southeast Asian Cooperation*. New York, 1987.
Sandhu, Kernial Singh. *The ASEAN Reader*. Singapore, 1992.
Segal, Gerald. *Rethinking the Pacific*. New York, 1990.

Russo-Japanese War

Esthus, Raymond A. *Double Eagle and Rising Sun: The Russians and Japanese at Portsmouth in 1905*. Durham, NC, 1988.
Nish, Ian. *The Origins of the Russo-Japanese War*. New York, 1985.
Randall, Peter E. *There Are No Victors Here: A Local Perspective on the Treaty of Portsmouth*. Portsmouth, NH, 1985.
Trani, Eugene P. *The Treaty of Portsmouth: An Adventure in American Diplomacy*. Lexington, MA, 1969.
White, John A. *The Diplomacy of the Russo-Japanese War: An Adventure in American Diplomacy*. Princeton, NJ, 1964.

Samoa

Anderson, S. " 'Pacific Destiny' and American Policy in Samoa, 1879–1899." *Hawaiian Journal of History*, 1978.
Ellison, J. W. "The Partition of Samoa: A Study in Imperialism and Diplomacy." *The Pacific Historical Review*, September 1939.
Kennedy, Paul M. *The Samoan Tangle: A Study in Anglo-German-American Relations 1878–1900*. New York, 1974.
Ryden, George H. *The Foreign Policy of the United States in Relation to Samoa*. New Haven, CT, 1933.

Second Indochina War

Controversies

Adler, Renata. *Reckless Disregard: Westmoreland v. CBS et al., Sharon v. Time*. New York, 1986.
Bilton, Michael and Kevin Sim. *Four Hours in My Lai: A War Crime and Its Aftermath*. New York, 1992.
Brewin, Bob and Sydney Shaw, *Vietnam on Trial: Westmoreland vs. CBS*. New York, 1987.
Franklin, H. Bruce. *M.I.A. or Mythmaking in America: How and Why Belief in Live POWS Has Possessed a Nation*. Brooklyn, NY, 1992.
Herring, George C. *The Secret Diplomacy of the Vietnam War: The Negotiating Volumes of the Pentagon Papers*. Austin, TX, 1983.
Jensen-Stevenson, Monika and William Stevenson. *Kiss the Boys Goodbye: How the United States Betrayed Its Own POWs in Vietnam*. New York, 1990.
Kowet, Don. *A Matter of Honor*. New York, 1984.
McNamara, Robert S. *Argument Without End: In Search of Answers to the Vietnam Tragedy*. New York, 1999.
Moise, Edwin E. *Tonkin Gulf and the Escalation of the Vietnam War*. Chapel Hill, NC, 1996.
Peers, William R. *The My Lai Inquiry*. New York, 1979.
Shapiro, Martin, Ed. *The Pentagon Papers and the Courts: A Study in Foreign Policy Making and Freedom of the Press*. San Francisco, 1972.
Snepp, Frank. *A Decent Interval: An Insider's Account of Saigon's Indecent End*. New York, 1977.

Ungar, Sanford J. *The Papers and the Papers: An Account of the Legal and Political Battle Over the Pentagon Papers*. New York, 1972

Wilcox, Fred. *Waiting for an Army to Die: The Tragedy of Agent Orange*. New York, 1983.

Windchy, Eugene G. *Tonkin Gulf*. Garden City, NY, 1971.

Zaroulis, N. L. and Gerald I. Sullivan. *Who Spoke Up? American Protest Against the War in Vietnam, 1963–1975*. Garden City, NY, 1984.

Histories

Davidson, Philip B. *Vietnam at War: The History, 1946–1975*. New York, 1988.

Gardner, Lloyd C. *Pay Any Price: Lyndon Johnson and the Wars for Vietnam*. Chicago, 1995.

Gelb, Leslie and Richard Betts. *The Irony of Vietnam: The System Worked*. Washington, DC, 1978.

Gibbons, William C. *The U.S. Government and the Vietnam War: Executive and Legislative Roles and Relationships*. 4 Parts. Princeton, NJ, 1986–1989.

Goodman, Allan E. *Lost Peace: The Search for a Negotiated Settlement of the Vietnam War*. Berkeley, CA, 1986.

Herring, George C. *America's Longest War: The United States and Vietnam 1950–1975*. New York, 1996.

Herz, Martin F. *The Prestige Press and the Christmas Bombing, 1972: Images and Reality in Vietnam*. Washington, DC, 1980.

Kaiser, David E. *American Tragedy: Kennedy, Johnson, and the Origins of the Vietnam War*. Cambridge, MA, 2000.

Karnow, Stanley. *Vietnam: A History*. New York, 1983.

Kolko, Gabriel. *Anatomy of a War: Vietnam, the United States, and the Modern Historical Experience*. New York, 1985.

Logevall, Fredrik. *Choosing War: The Lost Chance for Peace and the Escalation of War in Vietnam*. Berkeley, CA, 1999.

McMaster, H. R. *Dereliction of Duty: Lyndon Johnson, Robert McNamara, the Joint Chiefs of Staff, and the Lies that Led to Vietnam*. New York, 1997.

Moss, George. *Vietnam: An American Ordeal*. Upper Saddle River, NJ, 1998.

Porter, Gareth. *A Peace Denied: The United States, Vietnam and the Paris Agreement*. Bloomington, IN, 1975.

Schulzinger, Robert D. *A Time for War: The United States and Vietnam, 1945–1975*. New York, 1997.

Smith, R. B. *An International History of the Vietnam War*. 2 Vols. New York, 1986.

Turley, William S. *The Second Indochina War: A Short Political and Military History, 1954–1975*. Boulder, CO, 1986.

Young, Marilyn B. *The Vietnam Wars, 1945–1990*. New York, 1991.

Origins

Anderson, David L. *Trapped by Success: The Eisenhower Administration and Vietnam, 1953–1961*. New York, 1991.

Bradley, Mark P. *Imagining Vietnam and America: The Making of Postcolonial Vietnam, 1919–1950*. Chapel Hill, NC, 2000.

Duiker, William J. *U.S. Containment Policy and the Conflict in Indochina*. Stanford, CA, 1994.

Ernst, John. *Forging a Fateful Alliance: Michigan State University and the Vietnam War*. East Lansing, MI, 1998.

Hammer, Ellen J. *A Death in November: America in Vietnam, 1963*. New York, 1987.

Kahin, George McT. *Intervention: How America Became Involved in Vietnam*. New York, 1986.

Rotter, Andrew J. *The Path to Vietnam: Origin of the American Commitment to Southeast Asia*. Ithaca, NY, 1987.

Scheer, Robert. *How the United States Got Involved in Vietnam*. Santa Barbara, CA, 1965.

Scigliano, Robert and Guy H. Fox, *Technical Assistance to Vietnam: The Michigan State University Experience*. New York, 1965.

Short, Anthony. *The Origins of the Vietnam War*. New York, 1989.

Military

Andrade, Dale. *Trial by Fire: The 1972 Easter Offensive: America's Last Vietnam Battle*. New York, 1994.

Blackburn, Robert M. *Mercenaries and Lyndon Johnson's "More Flags": The Hiring of Korean, Filipino, and Thai Soldiers in the Vietnam War*. Jefferson, NC, 1994.

Buckingham, William A. *Operation RANCH HAND: The Air Force and Herbicides in Southeast Asia, 1961–1971*. Washington, DC, 1982.

Buzzanco, Robert. *Informed Dissent: Three Gen-*

erals and the Vietnam War. Chevy Chase, MD, 1992.

Cable, Larry E. *Conflict of Myths: The Development of American Counterinsurgency Doctrine and the Vietnam War*. New York, 1986.

Cecil, Paul F. *Herbicidal Warfare: The Ranch Hand Project in Vietnam*. New York, 1986.

Clodfelter, Mark. *The Limits of Air Power: The American Bombing of North Vietnam*. New York, 1989.

Gilbert, Marc J. and William P. Head, Eds. *The Tet Offensive*. Westport, CT, 1996.

Kelly, Francis J. *U.S. Army Special Forces, 1961–1971*. Washington, DC, 1973.

Krepinevich, Andrew F., Jr., *The Army and Vietnam*. Baltimore, MD, 1986.

Littauer, Raphael and Norman T. Uphoff, Eds. *The Air War in Indochina*. Boston, 1972.

Marolda, Edward J. and Oscar P. Fitzgerald. *The United States Navy and the Vietnam Conflict*. Vol. II: *From Military Assistance to Combat, 1959–1965*. Washington, DC, 1986.

Moore, Harold G. and Joseph L. Galloway. *We Were Soldiers Once . . . and Young: Ia Drang, The Battle that Changed the War in Vietnam*. New York, 1992.

Ngo Quang Truong, *The Easter Offensive of 1972*. Washington, DC, 1980.

Palmer, Bruce, Jr. *The 25-Year War: America's Military Role in Vietnam*. Lexington, KY, 1984.

Pisor, Robert. *The End of the Line: The Siege of Khe Sanh*. New York, 1982.

Prados, John and Ray W. Stubbe. *Valley of Decision: The Siege of Khe Sanh*. Boston, 1991.

Rogers, Bernard W. *Cedar Falls–Junction City: A Turning Point*. Washington, DC, 1974.

Stanton, Shelby L. *Green Berets at War: U.S. Special Forces in Southeast Asia, 1956–1975*. Novato, CA, 1985.

Turley, Gerald H. *The Easter Offensive: Vietnam 1972*. Annapolis, MD, 1995.

Singapore

Han Fook Kwang. *Lee Kuan Yew: The Man and His Ideas*. Singapore, 1997.

Josey, Alex. *Lee Kuan Yew*. 2 Vols. Singapore, 1980.

Lee Kuan Yew *The Singapore Story*. 2 Vols. Singapore, 1998, 2001.

Minchin, J. *No Man Is an Island: A Study of Singapore's Lee Kuan Yew*. London, 1986.

Southeast Asia

Fifield, Russell H. *Diplomacy of South East Asia, 1945–1958*. New York, 1958.

Hess, Gary. R. *The United States' Emergence as a Southeast Asian Power, 1940–1950*. New York, 1987.

Kahin, George McT. *The Asian-African Conference, Bandung, Indonesia, April 1955*. Ithaca, NY, 1956.

Lim, Jook-Jock, Ed. *Armed Communist Movements in Southeast Asia*. Singapore, 1984.

McMahon, Robert J. *Limits of Power: The United States and Southeast Asia Since World War II*. New York, 1999.

Morley, James W., Ed. *The Fateful Choice: Japan's Advance into Southeast Asia, 1939–1941*. New York, 1980.

Remme, Tilman. *Britain and Regional Cooperation in South-East Asia, 1945–49*. New York, 1995.

Samuels, Marilyn S. *Contest for the South China Sea*. New York, 1982.

Wurfel, David and Bruce Burton, Eds. *The Political Economy of Foreign Policy in Southeast Asia*. New York, 1990.

Taiwan

Clough, Ralph N. *Cooperation or Conflict in the Taiwan Strait*. Lanham, MD, 1999.

———. *Island China*. Cambridge, MA, 1978.

Copper, John F. *Taiwan: Nation-State or Province*. Boulder, CO, 1996.

Fairbank, John K. and Edwin O. Reischauer, *China: Tradition and Transformation*. Boston, 1989.

Fu Jen-kun. *Taiwan and the Geopolitics of the Asian-American Dilemma*. New York, 1992.

Garver, John W. *Face Off: China, the United States, and Taiwan's Democratization*. Seattle, 1997.

Gold, Thomas B. *State and Society in the Taiwan Miracle*. New York, 1986.

Hsu, Immanuel C. Y. *The Rise of Modern China*. New York, 1983.

Hughes, Christopher W. *Taiwan and Chinese Nationalism: National Identity and Status in International Society*. London, 1997.

Kaplan, D. *Fire of the Dragon: Politics, Murder, and the Kuomintang*. New York, 1992.

Kerr, George H. *Formosa Betrayed*. Boston, 1965.

———. *Formosa: Licensed Revolution and the*

Home Rule Movement, 1895–1945. Honolulu, HI, 1974.

Lai Zehan, Ramon H. Myers, and E. Wei. *A Tragic Beginning: The Taiwan Uprising of February 28, 1947*. Stanford, CA, 1991.

Peng Mingmin. *A Taste of Freedom: Memoirs of a Formosan Independence Leader*. New York, 1972.

Rubinstein, Murray A., Ed. *Taiwan: A New History*. New York 1999.

Shambaugh, David L., Ed. *Contemporary Taiwan*. New York, 1998.

Shen Zonghan. *The Sino-American Joint Commission on Rural Reconstruction: Twenty Years of Cooperation for Agricultural Development*. Ithaca, NY, 1970.

Simon, Denis F. and Michael Y. M. Kau, Eds. *Taiwan: Beyond the Economic Miracle*. Armonk, NY, 1992.

Tien Hung-mao. *Taiwan's Electoral Politics and Democratic Transition: Riding the Third Wave*. Armonk, NY, 1996.

Wang Yousan, Ed. *Foreign Policy of the Republic of China on Taiwan: An Unorthodox Approach*. New York, 1990.

Xiao Xinhuang. *Government Agricultural Strategies in Taiwan and South Korea*. Taibei, 1981.

Yang Maochun. *Socio-Economic Results of Land Reform in Taiwan*. Honolulu, HI, 1970.

Thailand

Fineman, Daniel. *A Special Relationship: The United States and Military Government in Thailand, 1947–1958*. Honoloulu, HI, 1997.

Haseman, John B. *The Thai Resistance Movement During World War II*. DeKalb, IL, 1978.

Reynolds, E. Bruce. *Thailand and Japan's Southern Advance, 1940–1945*. New York, 1994.

Winichakul, Thongchai. *Siam Mapped: A History of the Geo-Body of a Nation*. Honolulu, HI, 1994.

Wyatt, David K. *Thailand: A Short History*. New Haven, CT, 1984.

U.S.-China Relations

Accinelli, Robert D. *Crisis and Commitment: United States Policy Toward Taiwan, 1950–1955*. Chapel Hill, NC, 1996.

Anderson, David L. *Imperialism and Idealism: American Diplomats in China, 1861–1898*. Bloomington, IN, 1985.

Bernstein, Richard and Ross Munro. *The Coming Conflict with China*. New York, 1997.

Borg, Dorothy. *American Policy and the Chinese Revolution, 1925–1928*. New York, 1947.

——— and Waldo H. Heinrichs Jr., Eds. *Uncertain Years: Chinese-American Relations, 1947–1950*. New York, 1980.

Chang, Gordon H. *Friends and Enemies: The United States, China, and the Soviet Union*. Stanford, CA, 1990.

——— and He Di, "The Absence of War in the U.S.-China Confrontation over Quemoy and Matsu in 1954–1955: Contingency, Luck, Deterrence?" *American Historical Review*, December 1993.

Chen Jian. "The Ward Case and the Emergence of Sino-American Confrontation, 1948–1950." *The Australian Journal of Chinese Affairs*, July 1993.

Chern, Kenneth S. *Dilemma in China: America's Policy Debate, 1945*. Hamden, CT, 1980.

Christensen, Thomas J. *Useful Adversaries: Grand Strategy, Domestic Mobilization, and Sino-American Conflict, 1947–1958*. Princeton, NJ, 1996.

Cohen, Warren I. *America's Response to China: An Interpretive History of Sino-American Relations*. New York, 1980.

———. *The Chinese Connection: Roger S. Green, Thomas W. Lamont, G. E. Sokolsky and American–East Asian Relations*. New York, 1978.

Cole, Bernard D. *Gunboats and Marines: The United States Navy in China, 1925–1929*. Newark, DE, 1983.

Craft, Stephen G. "John B. Moore, Robert Lansing and the Shandong Question." *Pacific Historical Review*, May 1997.

Crane, Daniel M. and Thomas A. Breslin, *An Ordinary Relationship: American Opposition to Republican Revolution in China*. Miami, FL, 1986.

Deane, Hugh. *Good Deeds and Gunboats: Two Centuries of American-Chinese Encounters*. San Francisco, CA, 1990.

Dudden, Arthur P. *The American Pacific: From the Old China Trade to the Present*. New York 1992.

Fairbank, John K. *The United States and China*. Cambridge, MA, 1983.

Feis, Herbert. *The China Tangle: The American Effort in China from Pearl Harbor to the Marshall Plan*. Princeton, NJ, 1953.

Field, Frederick V. *American Participation in the China Consortiums*. Chicago, 1931.

Foot, Rosemary. *The Practice of Power: U.S. Relations with China Since 1945*. New York, 1995.

Green, Marshall, John H. Holdridge, and William N. Stokes. *War and Peace with China: First-Hand Experiences in the Foreign Service of the United States*. Bethesda, MD, 1994.

Harding, Harry. *A Fragile Relationship: The United States and China Since 1972*. Washington, DC, 1992.

Holdridge, John H. *Crossing the Divide: An Insider's Account of the Normalization of U.S. China Relations*. Lanham, MD, 1997.

Hunt, Michael H. *Frontier Defense and the Open Door: Manchuria in Chinese-American Relations, 1895–1911*. New Haven, CT, 1973.

———. *The Making of a Special Relationship: The United States and China to 1914*. New York, 1983.

Jespersen, T. Christopher. *American Images of China, 1931–1949*. Stanford, CA, 1996.

Jiang, Arnold X. *The United States and China*. Chicago, 1988.

Kahn, Ely J. *The China Hands: America's Foreign Service Officers and What Befell Them*. New York, 1975.

Kitts, C. R. *The United States Odyssey in China, 1784–1990*. Lanham, MD, 1991.

Koen, Ross Y. *The China Lobby in American Politics*. New York, 1974.

Kusnitz, Leonard A. *Public Opinion and Foreign Policy: America's China Policy, 1949–79*. Westport, CT, 1984.

Lampson, David M. *Same Bed, Different Dreams: Managing U.S.-China Relations, 1989–2000*. Berkeley, CA, 2001.

Lattimore, Eleanor Holgate. *China: Yesterday and Today*. St. Louis, MO, 1946.

Li Xiaobing and Li Hongshan, Eds. *China and the United States: A New Cold War History*. New York, 1998.

Liu Xiaoyuan. *A Partnership for Disorder: China, the United States, and Their Policies for the Postwar Disposition of the Japanese Empire, 1941–1945*. Cambridge, MA, 1996.

Mann, Jim. *About Face: History of America's Curious Relationship with China, From Nixon to Clinton*. New York, 1999.

Mosher, Steven W. *China Misperceived: American Illusions and Chinese Reality*. New York, 1990.

Nathan, Andrew J. and Robert S. Ross. *The Great Wall and the Empty Fortress: China's Search for Security*. New York, 1997.

Oksenberg, Michel. "A Decade of Sino-American Relations." *Foreign Affairs*, Fall 1982.

Ostry, Sylvia. *The Post–Cold War Trading System: Who's on First*. Chicago, 1997.

Rand, Peter. *China Hands: The Adventures and Ordeals of the American Journalists Who Joined Forces with the Great Chinese Revolution*. New York, 1995.

Ross, Robert S. *Negotiating Cooperation: The United States and China, 1969–1989*. Stanford, CA, 1995.

Schaller, Michael. *The United States and China in the Twentieth Century*. New York, 1980.

———. *The U.S. Crusade in China, 1938–1945*. New York, 1979.

Steele, A. T. *The American People and China*. New York, 1966.

Sutter, Robert G. *Shaping China's Future in World Affairs: The Role of the United States*. New York, 1996.

Tan Qingshan. *The Making of U.S.-China Policy: From Normalization to Post–Cold War Era*. Boulder, CO, 1992.

Tong Tekong. *United States Diplomacy in China, 1844–60*. Seattle, WA, 1964.

Tsou, Tang. *America's Failure in China, 1941–1945*. 2 Vols. Chicago, 1963.

Tuchman, Barbara W. *Stilwell and the American Experience in China, 1911–1945*. New York, 1971.

Tucker, Nancy B. *Patterns in the Dust: Chinese-American Relations and the Recognition Controversy, 1949–50*. New York, 1983.

Varg, Paul A. *The Closing of the Door: Sino-American Relations 1936–1946*. East Lansing, MI, 1973.

———. *The Making of a Myth: The United States and China, 1897–1912*. East Lansing, MI, 1968.

Vevier, Charles. *The United States and China, 1906–1913: A Study of Finance and Diplomacy*. New Brunswick, NJ, 1955.

Welch, Richard E. Jr. "Caleb Cushing's Chinese Mission and the Treaty of Wanghia: A Review." *Oregon Historical Quarterly*, 1957.

Young, Kenneth T. *Negotiating with the Chinese Communists: The United States Experience, 1953–1967*. New York, 1968.

Zhai Qiang. *The Dragon, the Lion, and the Eagle: Chinese, British, American Relations, 1949–1958*. Kent, OH, 1994.

Zhang Shu Guang. *Deterrence and Strategic Culture: Chinese-American Confrontations, 1949–1958*. Ithaca, NY, 1992.

U.S. Government Agencies

Chester, Eric T. *Covert Network: Progressives, the International Rescue Committee, and the CIA.* Armonk, NY, 1995.

Colby, William and Peter Forbath. *Honorable Men: My Life in the CIA.* New York, 1978.

Fischer, Fritz. *Making Them Like Us: Peace Corps Volunteers in the 1960s.* Washington, DC, 1998.

Johnson, Walter and Francis J. Colligan. *The Fulbright Program: A History.* Chicago, 1965.

Hapgood, David and Meridan Bennett. *Agents of Change: A Close Look at the Peace Corps.* Boston, 1968.

Hoffman, Elizabeth Cobbs. *All You Need Is Love: The Peace Corps and the Spirit of the 1960s.* Cambridge, MA, 1998.

Jeffreys-Jones, Rhodi. *The CIA and American Democracy.* New Haven, CT, 1898.

Leary, William M. *Perilous Missions: Civil Air Transport and CIA Covert Operations in Asia.* Tuscaloosa, AL, 1984.

Prados, John. *President's Secret Wars: Covert Operations Since World War II.* New York, 1986.

Ranelagh, John. *The Agency: The Rise and Decline of the CIA from Wild Bill Donovan to William Casey.* New York, 1986.

Rice, Gerard T. *The Bold Experiment: JFK's Peace Corps.* South Bend, IN, 1985.

Robbins, C. *Air America.* New York, 1979.

Windmiller, Marshall. *The Peace Corps and Pax Americana.* Washington, DC, 1970.

U.S.-Japan Relations

Armacost, Michael H. *Friends or Rivals?: The Insider's Account of U.S.-Japan Relations.* New York, 1996.

Bailey, Thomas A. "The Root-Takahira Agreement of 1908." *Pacific Historical Review,* March 1940.

Destler, I. M. *Managing an Alliance: The Politics of U.S.-Japanese Relations.* Washington, DC, 1976.

Gowen, Herbert H. *Five Foreigners in Japan.* New York, 1936.

Green, Michael J. and Patrick M. Cronin, Eds. *The U.S.-Japan Alliance: Past, Present, and Future.* New York, 1999.

Hunsberger, Warren S. *Japan and the United States in World Trade.* New York, 1964.

Inazo Nitobe. *The Intercourse Between the U.S. and Japan: A Historical Sketch.* Baltimore, MD, 1891.

Iriye, Akira. *Pacific Estrangement: Japanese and American Expansion, 1887–1911.* Cambridge, MA, 1972.

LaFeber, Walter. *The Clash: A History of U.S.-Japan Relations.* New York, 1997.

McCraw, Thomas K., Ed. *America Versus Japan.* Cambridge, MA, 1985.

Maga, Timothy P. *Hands Across the Sea?: U.S.-Japan Relations, 1961–1981.* Athens, OH, 1997.

Matsukata Haru. *Samurai and Silk: A Japanese and American Heritage.* New York, 1986.

Neu, Charles E. *The Troubled Encounter: The United States and Japan.* New York, 1975.

Neumann, William L. *America Encounters Japan: From Perry to MacArthur.* Baltimore, MD, 1963.

Ogata, Sadaka. *Normalization with China: A Comparative Study of U.S. and Japanese Processes.* Berkeley, CA, 1988.

Packard, George R. *Protest in Tōkyō: The Security Treaty Crisis of 1960.* Princeton, NJ, 1966.

Prestowitz, Clyde W. *Trading Places: How We Allowed Japan to Take the Lead.* New York, 1988.

Sakatani Yoshirō. *Why War Between Japan and the United States of America Is Impossible.* Tōkyō, 1921.

Sarantakes, Nicholas Evan. *Keystone: the American Occupation of Okinawa and U.S.-Japanese Relations.* College Station, TX, 2000.

Sato, Ryuzo. *The Chrysanthemum and the Eagle: The Future of U.S.-Japan Relations.* New York, 1995.

Schaller, Michael. *Altered States: The United States and Japan Since the Occupation.* New York, 1997.

Schoppa, Leonard J. *Bargaining with Japan: What American Pressure Can and Cannot Do.* New York, 1997.

Swenson-Wright, John. *Unequal Allies?: United States Security and Alliance Policy Toward Japan, 1945–1960.* Stanford, CA, 2001.

Walworth, Arthur. *Black Ships off Japan: The Story of Commodore Perry's Expedition.* Hamden, CT, 1966.

Wiley, Peter Booth and Korogi Ichiro. *Yankees in the Land of the Gods: Commodore Perry and the Opening of Japan.* New York, 1990.

U.S.-Korean Relations

Boettcher, Robert B. *Gifts of Deceit: Sun Myung Moon, Tongsun Park, and the Korean Scandals.* New York, 1980.

Cho Soon Sung. *Korea in World Politics, 1940–1950: An Evaluation of American Responsibility*. Berkeley, CA, 1957.

Cumings, Bruce, Ed. *Child of Conflict: The Korean-American Relationship, 1945–1953*. Seattle, WA, 1983.

Dobbs, Charles M. *The Unwanted Symbol: American Foreign Policy, the Cold War, and Korea, 1945–1950*. Kent, OH, 1981.

Harrington, Fred Harvey. *God, Mammon and the Japanese: Dr. Horace N. Allen and Korean-American Relations, 1884–1905*. Madison, WI, 1944.

Lee Chae-jin and Sato Hideo. *U.S. Policy Toward Japan and Korea: A Changing Influence Relationship*. New York, 1982.

Lee Yur-bok. *Diplomatic Relations Between the United States and Korea, 1866–1887*. New York, 1970.

——— and Wayne Patterson, Eds. *One Hundred Years of Korean-American Relations, 1882–1982*. Tuscaloosa, AL, 1986.

McCune, George M. and John A. Harrison, Eds. *Korean-American Relations: Documents Pertaining to the Far Eastern Diplomacy of the United States. Vol. 1: The Initial Period, 1883–1886*. Berkeley, CA, 1951.

Nelson, Melvin F. *Korea and the Old Orders in Eastern Asia*. Baton Rouge, LA, 1946.

Patterson, Wayne. "Sugar-Coated Diplomacy: Horace Allen and Korean Immigration to Hawaii, 1902–1905." *Diplomatic History*, Summer 1979.

Wilz, John E. "Did the United States Betray Korea in 1905?" *Pacific Historical Review*, August 1985.

U.S. Nineteenth-Century Expansionism

Chittenden, Hiram M. *The American Fur Trade of the Far West*. New York, 1902.

Dennett, Tyler. *Americans in Eastern Asia: A Critical Study of the Policy of the United States with Reference to China, Japan and Korea in the 19th Century*. New York, 1922.

Dorwart, Jeffrey M. *The Pigtail War: American Involvement in the Sino-Japanese War, 1894–1895*. Amherst, MA, 1975.

Goldstein, Jonathan. *Philadelphia and the China Trade, 1682–1846: Commercial, Cultural, and Attitudinal Effects*. University Park, PA, 1978

Graebner, Norman A. *Empire on the Pacific: A Study in American Continental Expansion*. New York, 1955.

Griswold, A. Whitney. *Far Eastern Policy of the United States*. New Haven, CT, 1966.

Healy, David F. *U.S. Expansion: The Imperialist Urge in the 1890s*. Madison, WI, 1970.

Israel, Jerry. *Progressivism and the Open Door America and China, 1905–1921*. Pittsburgh, PA, 1971.

Hagan, Kenneth J. *American Gunboat Diplomacy and the Old Navy, 1877–1889*. Westport, CT, 1973.

LaFeber, Walter. *The New Empire: An Interpretation of American Expansion, 1960–1898*. Ithaca, NY, 1963.

Long, David F. *Gold Braid and Foreign Relations: Diplomatic Activities of U.S. Naval Officers 1798–1883*. Annapolis, MD, 1988.

McCormick, Thomas J. *China Market: America's Quest for Informal Empire, 1891–1901*. Chicago, 1967.

Mattox, Henry E. *The Twilight of Amateur Diplomacy: The American Foreign Service and Its Senior Officers in the 1890s*. Kent, OH, 1989.

May, Ernest R. *Imperial Democracy: The Emergence of America as a Great Power*. New York, 1961.

Morison, Samuel Eliot. *The Maritime History of Massachusetts*. Boston, 1941.

Paullin, Charles O. *American Voyages to the Orient, 1690–1865*. Annapolis, MD, 1971.

———. "The Opening of Korea by Commodore Shufeldt." *Political Science Quarterly*, 1910.

Smith, Philip C. F. *The Empress of China*. Philadelphia, 1984.

Williams, G. *The Bering Sea Fur Seal Dispute, 1885–1911*. Eugene, OR, 1984.

Vevier, Charles. "American Continentalism: An Idea of Expansionism, 1845–1910." *American Historical Review*, January 1960.

Young, Marilyn B. *The Rhetoric of Empire: American China Policy, 1895–1901*. Cambridge, MA, 1968.

U.S. Occupation of Japan

Bisson, Thomas A. *Zaibatsu Dissolution in Japan*. Berkeley, CA, 1954.

Borden, William S. *The Pacific Alliance: United States Foreign Economic Policy and Japanese Trade Recovery, 1947–1955*. Madison, WI, 1984.

Brackman, Arnold C. *The Other Nuremburg: The Untold Story of the Tokyo War Crimes Trials*. New York, 1987.

Buckley, Roger. *Occupation Diplomacy: Britain,*

the United States and Japan 1945–1952. New York, 1982.
Cohen, Theodore. *Remaking Japan: The American Occupation as New Deal*. New York, 1987.
Finn, Richard B. *Winners in Peace: MacArthur, Yoshida, and Postwar Japan*. Berkeley, CA, 1992.
Inoue Kyoko. *MacArthur's Japanese Constitution: A Linguistic and Cultural Study of Its Making*. Chicago, 1991.
Kataoka Tetsuya. *The Price of a Constitution: The Origins of Japan's Postwar Politics*. Stanford, CA, 1991.
Koseki Shoichi. *The Birth of Japan's Postwar Constitution*. Boulder, CO, 1997.
Minear, Richard H. *Victors' Justice: The Tokyo War Crimes Trial*. Princeton, NJ, 1971.
Perry, John C. *Beneath the Eagle's Wings: Americans in Occupied Japan*. New York, 1980.
Schaller, Michael. *The American Occupation of Japan: The Origins of the Cold War in Asia*. New York, 1985.
———. "Securing the Great Crescent: Occupied Japan and the Origins of Containment in Southeast Asia." *Journal of American History*, September 1982.
Schonberger, Howard B. *Aftermath of War: Americans and the Remaking of Japan, 1945–1952*. Kent, OH, 1989.

U.S.-Philippine Relations

Berry, William E. *U.S. Bases in the Philippines: The Evolution of a Special Relationship*. Boulder, CO, 1989.
Blount, James H. *The American Occupation of the Philippines, 1898–1912*. New York, 1913.
Brands, H. W. *Bound to Empire: The United States and the Philippines*. New York, 1991.
Cullather, Nick. *Illusions of Influence: The Political Economy of United States–Philippine Relations, 1942–1960*. Stanford, CA, 1994.
Garcia, Ed and Francisco Nemenzo. *The Sovereign Quest: Freedom from Foreign Military Bases*. Manila, 1988.
Gates, John M. *Schoolbooks and Krags: The United States Army in the Philippines, 1898–1902*. Westport, CT, 1973.
Greene, Fred, Ed. *The Philippine Bases: Negotiating for the Future American and Philippine Perspectives*. New York, 1988.
Gregor, A. James. *The Philippine Bases: U.S. Security at Risk*. Washington, DC, 1987.
Karnow, Stanley. *In Our Image: America's Empire in the Philippines*. New York, 1989.
Linn, Brian R. *The Philippine War, 1899–1902*. Lawrence, KS, 2000.
May, Glenn A. *Battle for Batangas: A Philippine Province at War*. New Haven, CT, 1991.
———. *Social Engineering in the Philippines: The Aims, Execution, and Impact of American Colonial Policy, 1900–1913*. Westport, CT, 1980.
Miller, Stuart C. *"Benevolent Assimilation": The American Conquest of the Philippines*. New Haven, CT, 1982.
Reed, John S. "External Discipline During Counterinsurgency: A Philippine War Case Study, 1900–1901." *Journal of American–East Asian Relations*, Spring 1995.
Romualdez, Eduardo Z. *A Question of Sovereignty: The Military Bases and Philippine-American Relations, 1944–1979*. Manila, 1980.
Sexton, William T. *Soldiers in the Sun: An Adventure in Imperialism*. Harrisburg, PA, 1939.
Shalom, Stephen R. *The United States and the Philippines: A Study in NeoColonialism*. Philadelphia, 1981.
Stanley, Peter W. *A Nation in the Making: The Philippines and the United States, 1899–1921*. Cambridge, MA, 1974.
Taylor, George E. *The Philippines and the United States*. New York, 1964.
Taylor, John R. M. *The Philippine Insurrection Against the United States*. Vol. 2. Pasay City, Philippines, 1971.
Welch, Richard W. *Response to Imperialism: The United States and the Philippine-American War, 1899–1902*. Chapel Hill, NC, 1979.
Williams, William Appleman. "U.S. Indian Policy and the Debate over Philippine Annexation." *Journal of American History*, March 1980.

U.S. Presidents and Their Policies

Bailey, Thomas A. *Theodore Roosevelt and the Japanese-American Crisis*. Stanford, CA, 1934.
Brands, H. W. *The Wages of Globalism: Lyndon Johnson and the Limits of American Power*. New York, 1995.
Bundy, William P. *Tangled Web: The Making of Nixon's Foreign Policy, 1968–1974*. New York, 1998.
Dallek, Robert A. *Franklin D. Roosevelt and American Foreign Policy, 1932–1945*. New York, 1979.

Dennett, Tyler. *Roosevelt and the Russo-Japanese War: A Critical Study of American Policy in Eastern Asia in 1902–1905*. Garden City, NY, 1925.

Divine, Robert A. *Eisenhower and the Cold War*. New York, 1981.

Donovan, Robert J. *Tumultuous Years: The Presidency of Harry S. Truman, 1949–1953*. New York, 1983.

Esthus, Raymond A. *Theodore Roosevelt and the International Rivalries*. Waltham, MA, 1970.

———. *Theodore Roosevelt and Japan*. Seattle, WA, 1966.

Fifield, Russell H. *Woodrow Wilson and the Far East: The Diplomacy of the Shantung Question*. New York, 1952.

Gelman, Irwin F. *Secret Affairs: Franklin Roosevelt, Cordell Hull, and Sumner Welles*. Baltimore, MD, 1995.

Herring, George C. *LBJ and Vietnam: A Different Kind of War*. Austin, TX, 1994.

Hilsman, Roger. *To Move a Nation: The Politics of Foreign Policy in the Administration of John F. Kennedy*. New York, 1967.

Hunt, Michael H. *Lyndon Johnson's War: America's Cold War Crusade in Vietnam, 1945–1968*. New York, 1996.

Kawamura, Naoki. "Wilsonian Idealism and Japanese Claims at the Paris Peace Conference." *Pacific Historical Review*, November 1997.

Larabee, Eric. *Commander in Chief: Franklin Delano Roosevelt, His Lieutenants, and Their War*. New York, 1987.

Melanson, Richard A. and David Mayers, Eds. *Reevaluating Eisenhower: American Foreign Policy in the 1950s*. Urbana, IL, 1987.

Newman, John M. *JFK and Vietnam: Deception, Intrigue, and the Struggle for Power*. New York, 1992.

Paterson, Thomas G., Ed. *Kennedy's Quest for Victory: American Foreign Policy, 1961–1963*. New York, 1989.

Perlmutter, Amos. *FDR and Stalin: A Not So Grand Alliance, 1943–1945*. Columbia, MO, 1993.

Scholes, Walter V. and Marie V. Scholes, *The Foreign Policies of the Taft Administration*. Columbia, MO, 1970.

Smith, Gaddis. *Morality, Reason, and Power: American Diplomacy in the Carter Years*. New York, 1986.

Stettinius, Edward R., Jr., *Roosevelt and the Russians*. Westport, CT, 1970.

Van DeMark, Brian. *Into the Quagmire: Lyndon Johnson and the Escalation of the Vietnam War*. New York, 1991.

Vietnam

Duiker, William J. *Vietnam: Nation in Revolution*. Boulder, CO, 1983.

Fall, Bernard B. *The Two Vietnams: A Political and Military Analysis*. New York, 1967.

FitzGerald, Frances. *Fire in the Lake: The Vietnamese and the Americans in Vietnam*. New York, 1972.

Goodman, Allen E. *Politics in War: The Bases of Political Community in South Vietnam*. Cambridge, MA, 1971.

Khanh, Huynh Kim. *Vietnamese Communism 1925–1945*. Ithaca, NY, 1982.

Kolko, Gabriel. *Vietnam: Anatomy of Peace*. New York, 1997.

Marr, David G. *Vietnam 1945: The Quest for Power*. Berkeley, CA, 1995.

———. *Vietnamese Anticolonialism, 1885–1925*. Berkeley, CA, 1971.

Morley, James W. and Nishihara Misashi, Eds. *Vietnam Joins the World*. Armonk, NY, 1997.

Morrison, Wilbur H. *The Elephant and the Tiger: The Full Story of the Vietnam War*. New York, 1990.

Nguyen, Gregory Tien Hung and Jerrold L. Schecter. *The Palace File*. New York, 1986.

Porter, Gareth. *Vietnam: The Politics of Bureaucratic Socialism*. Ithaca, NY, 1993.

Race, Jeffrey. *War Comes to Long An: Revolutionary Conflict in a Vietnamese Province*. Berkeley, CA, 1972.

Schell, Jonathan. *The Village of Ben Suc*. New York, 1967.

Scigliano, Robert. *South Vietnam: Nation Under Stress*. Boston, 1964.

Taylor, Sandra C. *Vietnamese Women at War: Fighting for Ho Chi Minh*. Lawrence, KS, 1999.

Truong Nhu Tang. *A Viet Cong Memoir*. New York, 1985.

Vo Nguyen Giap. *Con Duong Chinh: Van De Dan Toc Giai Phong o Dong Duong* [The Proper Path: The Question of National Liberation in Indochina]. Hanoi, 1939.

Warner, Denis A. *The Last Confucian: Vietnam, South-East Asia, and the West*. New York, 1964

World War I in Asia

Clyde, Paul H. *Japan's Pacific Mandate*. New York, 1935.

Dickinson, Frederick R. *War and National Reinvention: Japan and the Great War, 1914–1919*. Cambridge, MA, 1999.

Kawamura, Noriko. *Turbulence in the Pacific: Japanese-U.S. Relations During World War I*. Westport, CT, 2000.

Lazo, Dimitri D. "A Question of Loyalty: Robert Lansing and the Treaty of Versailles." *Diplomatic History*, Winter 1985.

Wright, Quincy. *Mandates Under the League of Nations*. Chicago, 1930.

Yanaihara Tadao. *Pacific Islands Under Japanese Mandate*. New York, 1940.

World War II in Asia

Diplomacy

Buhite, Russell D. *Decision at Yalta: An Appraisal of Summit Diplomacy*. Wilmingon, DE, 1986.

Daws, Gavan. *Prisoners of the Japanese: POWs of World War II in the Pacific*. New York, 1994.

Drea, Edward J. *MacArthur's ULTRA: Codebreaking and the War Against Japan, 1942–1945*. Lawrence, KS, 1992.

Kimball, Warren F. *"The Most Unsordid Act": Lend-Lease, 1939–1941*. Baltimore, MD, 1969.

Lewin, Ronald. *The American Magic: Codes, Ciphers, and the Defeat of Japan*. New York, 1982.

Smith, Gaddis. *American Diplomacy During the Second World War*. New York, 1985.

Sun You-li. *China and the Origins of the Pacific War*. New York, 1993.

Van Der Rhoer, Edward. *Deadly Magic: A Personal Account of Communication Intelligence in World War II in the Pacific*. New York, 1978.

Japan's Surrender

Allen, Thomas B. and Norman Polmar. *Code-Named Downfall: The Secret Plan to Invade Japan—and Why Truman Dropped the Bomb*. New York, 1995.

Alperovitz, Gar. *The Decision to Use the Atomic Bomb and the Architecture of an American Myth*. New York, 1995.

Butow, Robert J. C. *Japan's Decision to Surrender*. Stanford, CA, 1954.

Coox, Alvin D. *Japan: The Final Agony*. New York, 1970.

Feis, Herbert. *The Atomic Bomb and the End of World War II*. Princeton, NJ, 1961.

Miller, Edward S. *War Plan Orange: The U.S. Strategy to Defeat Japan, 1897–1945*. Annapolis, MD, 1991.

Sigal, Leon V. *Fighting to a Finish: The Politics of War Termination in the United States and Japan, 1945*. Ithaca, NY, 1988.

Skates, John Ray. *The Invasion of Japan: Alternative to the Bomb*. Columbia, SC, 1994.

Military

Appleman, Roy E. *Okinawa: The Last Battle*. Tōkyō, 1961.

Belote, James H. and William M. Belote. *Typhoon of Steel: The Battle for Okinawa*. New York, 1970.

Burdick, Charles B. and Donald S. Detwiler, Eds. *War in Asia and the Pacific, 1937–1949*. New York, 1980.

Coox, Alvin D. *Nomonhan: Japan Against Russia, 1939*. 2 Vols. Stanford, CA, 1985.

Costello, John. *The Pacific War, 1941–1945*. New York, 1982.

Craven, Wesley F. and James L. Cate, Eds. *The Army Air Forces in World War II*. Vol. 5. Chicago, 1948.

Cutler, Thomas J. *The Battle of Leyte Gulf, 23–26 October 1944*. New York, 1994.

Dull, Paul S. *A Battle History of the Imperial Japanese Navy, 1941–1945*. Annapolis, MD, 1978.

Duus, Peter, et al., Eds. *The Japanese Wartime Empire, 1931–1945*. Princeton, NJ, 1996.

Fuchida Mitsuo and Okumiya Masatake. *Midway, The Battle that Doomed Japan: The Japanese Navy's Story*. Annapolis, MD, 1955.

Gailey, Harry A. *The War in the Pacific: From Pearl Harbor to Tokyo Bay*. Novato, CA, 1995.

Hoyt, Edwin P. *Japan's War: The Great Pacific Conflict*. New York, 1986.

———. *Merrill's Marauders*. Baton Rouge, LA, 1980.

Kirby, S. Woodburn. *The War Against Japan*. London, 1961.

Levine, Alan J. *The Pacific War: Japan Versus the Allies*. Westport, CT, 1995.

Lundstrom, John B. *The First South Pacific Cam-*

paign, Pacific Fleet Strategy December 1941–June 1942. Annapolis, MD, 1976.

Morison, Samuel Eliot. *History of United States Naval Operations in World War II*. Vols. 4, 12, 14. Boston, 1958, 1960.

———. *The Two-Ocean War: A Short History of the United States Navy in the Second World War*. Boston, 1963.

Potter, Elmer B. and Chester W. Nimitz. *Triumph in the Pacific: The Navy's Struggle Against Japan*. Englewood Cliffs, NJ, 1963.

Romanus, Charles F. and Riley Sunderland, *United States Army in World War II*. Vol. 9: *The China-Burma-India Theater*. Washington, DC, 1956.

O'Connor, Raymond G.. *Pacific Destiny: An Informal History of the U.S. in the Far East*. Boston, 1999.

Ogburn, Charlton. *The Marauders*. New York, 1956.

Prados, John. *Combined Fleet Decoded: Secret History of American Intelligence and the Japanese Navy in World War II*. New York, 1995.

Prange, Gordon W. with Donald M. Goldstein and K. V. Dillon. *Miracle at Midway*. New York, 1982.

Renzi, William A. and Mark D. Roehrs. *Never Look Back: A History of World War II in the Pacific*. Armonk, NY, 1991.

Reynolds, Clark G. *The Fast Carriers: The Forging of an Air War*. New York, 1968.

Schaffer, Ronald. *Wings of Judgment: American Bombing in World War II*. New York, 1985.

Sherry, Michael S. *The Rise of American Air Power: The Creation of Armageddon*. New Haven, CT, 1987.

Spector, Ronald L. *Eagle Against the Sun: The American War with Japan*. New York, 1985.

Taaffe, Stephen R. *MacArthur's Jungle War: The 1944 New Guinea Campaign*. Lawrence, KS, 1998.

Weinberg, Gerhard L. *A World at Arms: A Global History of World War II*. Cambridge, MA, 1994.

Willmott, H. P. *Empires in the Balance: Japanese and Allied Pacific Strategies to April 1942*. Annapolis, MD, 1982.

Name Index

Main entries indicated by **bold type**.

Subject Index

Main entries indicated by **bold type**.

About the Editor and Contributors

PATRICIO N. ABINALES is associate professor at the Center for Southeast Asian Studies, Kyōto University, and Southeast Asia editor of the journal *Critical Asian Studies*. He is the author of *Making Mindanao: Cotabato and Davao in the Formation of the Philippine Nation-State*.

ROBERT D. ACCINELLI is professor of history at the University of Toronto, Canada. He is the author of *Crisis and Commitment: United States Policy Toward Taiwan, 1950–1955*.

DAVID L. ANDERSON is professor of history and dean of the College of Arts and Sciences at the University of Indianapolis. He is the author or editor of numerous books and articles on U.S. relations with East and Southeast Asia.

ERNEST ANDRADE JR. earned his doctorate at Michigan State University and was professor of history at the University of Colorado at Denver. His last book was *Unconquerable Rebel: Robert W. Wilcox in Hawaiian Politics, 1880–1903*, published in 1996.

DIRK A. BALLENDORF is professor of history and Micronesian studies at the University of Guam's Micronesian Area Research Center. He has lived and worked in Micronesia for more than thirty years. Ballendorf has written ten books, more than 200 articles, and over 100 book reviews on Micronesian history, culture, and politics.

MICHAEL A. BARNHART is Distinguished Teaching Professor of History at the State University of New York at Stony Brook. He has published *Japan Prepares for Total War* and *Japan and the World Since 1968* and served as the inaugural editor for the *Journal of American–East Asian Relations*.

LARRY R. BECK is associate professor of American history and government at New Mexico State University-Alamogordo. He had four assignments in Asia during his U.S. Air Force career, culminating with a posting as a North Korea political/economic analyst in Seoul. He was a contributor to the *Historical Dictionary of the Korean War*.

MARK P. BRADLEY is associate professor of history at the University of Wisconsin-Milwaukee. He earned his doctorate at Harvard University and is the author of *Imagining Vietnam and America: The Making of Postcolonial Vietnam, 1919–1950*.

H. W. BRANDS is professor of history at Texas A&M University. He is the author of *The Wages of Globalism: What America Owes the World*, among numerous other books on American history and U.S. foreign relations.

ROBERT K. BRIGHAM is professor of history at Vassar College. He is the author of numerous books and essays on the Vietnam War, including *Guerilla Diplomacy: The NLF's Foreign Relations and the Vietnam War* and with Robert S. McNamara and James G. Blight, *Argument Without End: In Search of Answers to the Vietnam Tragedy.*

THOMAS H. BUCKLEY earned his doctorate at Indiana University and is professor of history at the University of Tulsa. Author of *The United States and the Washington Conference, 1921–1922* and co-author with Edwin Strong of *American Foreign and National Security Policies, 1914–1945,* he is working on a study of Franklin D. Roosevelt and American imperialism.

CAI DAIYUN is associate professor of history at Shenzhen University, China. She holds a master of arts degree from Yunnan University. Her research interests deal with the history of Sino-American relations and the history of the modern world. She has coedited several books and published a number of articles in these fields.

ROGER Y. M. CHAN is an adjunct instructor at Washington State University and Gonzaga University.

CHANG SHENG-TAI teaches at Long Beach City College in California. He earned his doctorate in comparative literature from the University of Southern California, specializing in East-West literary relations and East Asian studies. In addition to literary scholarship, his interests include modern Chinese and East Asian civilization.

CHANG SU-YA earned her doctoral degree in history from Pennsylvania State University. She is now associate research fellow at the Institute of Modern History, Academia Sinica, Taiwan. Her field of specialization is U.S. diplomatic history. She had published many articles on U.S. policy toward Taiwan during the 1950s.

ENA CHAO is associate research fellow at the Institute of European and American Culture, Academia Sinica, Taiwan. Her recent publications include "U.S. Educational and Cultural Exchange Programs in Taiwan" in *EurAmerica* and "A Research Note on the Archives of the Asia—Pacific Division of the Ministry of Foreign Affairs of the ROC" in *Newsletter on Research on Modern Chinese History.*

ERROL M. CLAUSS is professor of history at Salem College in North Carolina. He earned his doctorate at Emory University, and his writings focus on military and diplomatic history, with a special interest in East Asia. During the summer of 2000, Clauss was scholar-in-residence at Oxford University.

NANCY CLOPTON lives with her husband in southern New Mexico, where they own and operate a beef cattle ranch. She earned her master of arts degree at New Mexico State University, and is a candidate for her law degree at the University of Arizona, James E. Rogers College of Law, in Tucson, Arizona.

KENTON J. CLYMER is professor of history at the University of Texas at El Paso. Educated at Grinnell College and the University of Michigan, he is the author of three books and is completing a history of U.S. relations with Cambodia.

ALVIN D. COOX was director of the Japan-U.S. Center after teaching at San Diego State University. He was author of *Nomanhan: Japan Against Russia 1939,* recipient of the Samuel Eliot Morison Prize from the American Military History Institute.

PAMELA K. CROSSLEY is Rosenwald Research Professor at Dartmouth College. She is author of *A Transluscent Mirror: History and Ideology in Qing Imperial China* and coauthor of *The Earth and Its Peoples: A Global History*.

MICHAEL J. DEVINE is the director of the Harry S. Truman Presidential Library and Museum and president of the Truman Institute. He has been director of the American Heritage Center at the University of Wyoming and director of the Illinois Historic Preservation Agency. He earned his doctoral degree from Ohio State University and is the author of *John W. Foster*.

FREDERICK C. DRAKE is professor of history at Brock University, Ontario, Canada, where he has taught since 1970. He also has taught at University College, London, the University of the West Indies, and the University of Wales, Aberystwyth. He has published extensively in nineteenth-century U.S. foreign policy and naval history.

WILLIAM E. EMERSON is editor in chief at the South Carolina Historical Society and a doctoral candidate in history at the University of Alabama.

ROBERT H. FERRELL taught at Indiana University in Bloomington from 1953 until his retirement in 1988. He has specialized in American diplomacy and the presidency. During his distinguished career, he has many important publications, most recently *Harry S. Truman: A Biography* and *American Diplomacy: The Twentieth Century*.

AARON FORSBERG is the author of *America and the Japanese Miracle*. After earning his doctorate in history at the University of Texas, he taught history and worked as a legal translator in Tōkyō, Japan. In 2001, he joined the U.S. Department of State. The views expressed in his entries are his alone and do not represent those of the State Department.

CATHERINE M. FORSLUND, who earned her doctorate at Washington University in St. Louis, is assistant professor of history of Rockford College in Illinois. She is author of *Anna Chennault: Informal Diplomacy and Asian Relations* in the *Biographies in American Foreign Policy* series. Her research includes examination of how editorial cartoons reflect American diplomacy and culture.

ANNE L. FOSTER teaches U.S. and Asian history at Saint Anselm College. Her research focuses on U.S.–Southeast Asian relations and U.S. narcotics policy, especially in the late nineteeth and early twentieth centuries. She is coeditor of *The American Colonial State in the Philippines in Comparative Perspective*, forthcoming from Duke University Press.

KAREN GARNER directs the Women's Center and teaches history and women's studies courses at Florida International University. The University of Massachusetts Press will publish her book, *Precious Fire: Maud Russell and the Chinese Revolution*, in 2003. She is working on a new book project, tentatively titled "Women and Global Leadership: Theory and Practice in the World YWCA, 1894–2000."

KARL GERTH earned his doctorate at Harvard University and teaches modern Chinese and East Asian history at the University of South Carolina. In 2003, Harvard will publish his book on the role of nationalism in forming a consumer culture in modern China. His next project examines the elimination of private enterprise in the early People's Republic of China.

NORMAN A. GRAEBNER is the Randolph P. Compton Professor of History and Public Affairs, emeritus, at the University of Virginia. During his distinguished career, much of his writing, beginning with *Empire on the Pacific: A Study in American Expansionism* and continuing through his publications on the Pearl Harbor crisis and the era of the Cold War, has focused on U.S. relations in East Asia.

KENNETH J. HAMMOND is associate professor and head in the department of history at New Mexico State University, specializing in early modern Chinese intellectual and cultural history. He holds a doctorate in history and East Asian languages from Harvard University. A past president of the Society for *Ming Studies,* his articles have appeared in Ming Studies and other journals.

HAN KYU-SUN is on the research staff of the Institute of National Unification Policy in the Republic of Korea. He earned his master of arts degree from Seoul National University and doctorate from Newcastle University in Britain. His research focuses on the comparative study of modernization, democratization, and political ideas in East Asia, with current emphasis on North Korea.

HEO MAN-HO earned his doctorate from E.H.E.S.S. in Paris. He was a senior researcher at the Korea Institute for Defense Analyses and teaches at Kyongpook National University in Taegu, Republic of Korea. His publications include entries in the *Encyclopedia of the Korean War* and *La Corée, le peuple et ses valeurs culturelles.*

GARY R. HESS is Distinguished Research Professor of History at Bowling Green State University. His research has focused on U.S. policy in South and Southeast Asia. His most recent book is *Presidential Decisions for War: Korea, Vietnam, and the Persian Gulf.* He is a past president of the Society for Historians of American Foreign Relations.

ROGER H. HILL holds a bachelor of arts degree from the U.S. Air Force Academy and a master of arts degree from Georgetown University. He is working on a doctoral degree from George Mason University after completing a twenty-six-year career in U.S. Air Force intelligence. He teaches Internet courses in history, political science, and humanities for Strayer University.

HIROBE IZUMI is associate professor at Hokkaido University, Japan. His major works include *Japanese Pride, American Prejudice: Modifying the Exclusion Clause of the 1924 Immigration Act*. He is working on international organizations during the interwar period.

ROGER K. HODGKINS is a career Foreign Service officer with the government of Australia. Since 1998, he has been director of the U.S. Section in Australia's Foreign Ministry, after serving in Washington from 1991 to 1994. A graduate of the University of Western Australia, Hodgkins has presented many papers in the United States on U.S. foreign policy in the 1920s.

ISHII OSAMU is a professor at Meiji Gakuin University and professor emeritus at Hitotsubashi University, both in Tōkyō, Japan. He earned his doctorate at Rutgers University, and his publications include *Cotton-Textile Diplomacy: The Cold War and Japan-U.S. Relations* (in Japanese) and *History of International Politics in the 20th Century* (in Japanese).

T. CHRISTOPHER JESPERSEN earned his doctorate at Rutgers University and is chairman of the history department at North Georgia College and State University. He is the author of *American Images of China, 1931–1949*, co-editor of *Architects of the American Century: Individuals and Insti-*

tutions in Twentieth Century U.S. Foreign Policymaking, and editor of the *Journal of American–East Asian Relations*.

ANDREW L. JOHNS earned his doctorate at the University of California, Santa Barbara, and works in the Historian's Office at the U.S. State Department. He is author of several articles on the relationship between American foreign and domestic policy. The views expressed in his entries are his alone and do not represent those of the Department of State.

KAMIMURA NAOKI, professor at Hiroshima City University, focuses his research on U.S. relations with Japan, New Zealand, and Australia. His recent works include "Post–Cold War U.S. Foreign Policy Decision Making and Security Policy Toward Japan" in *Hiroshima Journal of International Studies* and "Japanese Civil Society, Local Government, and U.S.-Japan Security Relations in the 1990s," in *Nationalism and Citizenship*.

KAWAMURA NORIKO is associate professor of history at Washington State University. Her publications include *Turbulence in the Pacific: Japanese-U.S. Relations During World War I* and "Wilsonian Idealism and Japanese Claims at the Paris Peace Conference" in the journal *Pacific Historical Review*.

EDWARD C. KEEFER is a historian at the Department of State. He has written on U.S.–East Asian relations and edited numerous volumes in *Foreign Relations of the United States*. The views expressed in his entries are his alone and do not represent those of the Department of State. Research for his entries was exclusively in open or declassified materials.

KIM HAKJOON is president and publisher of *Dong-a Ilbo* (The East Asia Daily) in Seoul, Republic of Korea, and has numerous publications on U.S.-Korean relations. Previously, he was president of the Inch'ŏn University, the Korean Political Science Association, and the Korean Federation of Teachers' Associations.

KIM JINWUNG is professor of history at Kyongpook National University in Taegu, Republic of Korea, and was a Fulbright senior research fellow at Rutgers University during 1992 and 1993. His numerous publications reflect interests in U.S.–South Korean relations, in particular South Korean perceptions of the United States and U.S. diplomatic history.

WALTER LAFEBER is the Noll Professor of History at Cornell University and former president of the Society for Historians of American Foreign Relations. His highly acclaimed published works on U.S.-Asian relations include *America, Russia, and the Cold War; The Clash: A History of U.S.-Japan Relations; The American Search for Opportunity, 1865–1913*, and *The New Empire: An Interpretation of American Expansion, 1860–1898*.

STEVEN HUGH LEE is associate professor of history at the University of British Columbia and associate editor of the *Journal of American–East Asian Relations*. His publications include *Outposts of Empire: Korea, Vietnam, and the Origins of the Cold War in Asia, 1949–1954* and *The Korean War*.

LI HONGSHAN holds a master of arts degree from Wuhan University, and both a master of arts degree and a doctorate from the University of Missouri. He is an associate professor of history at Kent State University. He has served as president of Chinese Historians in the United States from 1997 to 1999.

LI XIAOBING is history professor and associate director of the Western Pacific Institute at the University of Central Oklahoma. He is coauthor or coeditor of *Chinese Generals Remember Korea, Asia's Cri-*

sis and the New Paradigm, Korea and Regional Geopolitics, Social Transition in China, and *Interpreting U.S.-China-Taiwan Relations* and editor of the *American Review of China Studies.*

LI YI was born in China and was an undergraduate at Beijing University. He earned a master of arts degree at New Mexico State University and a doctorate at the University of Washington. His recent publications include *The Bureau for Recruiting Merchants: The Chinese Steamship Operation in the 19th-Century Bureaucratic World, 1864–1885.*

HYUNG GU LYNN is assistant professor in the AECL/KEPCO Chair in Korea Studies, Institute of Asian Research, University of British Columbia. He earned his doctoral degree at Harvard University and has been on the faculties of Hanyang University in South Korea and Hitotsubashi University in Japan. He specializes in the modern histories of Korea and Japan.

MA SANG-YOON is a doctoral candidate in International Relations at Oxford University, England, and broadly interested in international politics in East Asia and Korean politics. His dissertation, titled "Dealing with Authoritarianism: U.S. Policy Towards South Korean Governments, 1960–1968," examines the U.S. political role in the Republic of Korea, with special focus on the issue of democracy.

SHAWN D. MCAVOY earned his bachelor of arts degree in Greek from Randolph-Macon College and a master of arts in U.S. diplomatic history from New Mexico State University, and studied at the Oriental Institute at the University of Chicago. He has authored two articles on U.S.-Japanese relations during World War I, and has written two novels.

STEPHEN E. MCCULLOUGH is a doctoral student at the University of Alabama, specializing in nineteeth-century U.S. foreign relations. He holds a master of arts degree from New Mexico State University and from 2000 to 2001 was the chief researcher on the Preservation of the Literature of New Mexico Agricultural History project in Las Cruces, New Mexico.

IAN MCGIBBON is a senior historian in the History Group, Ministry for Culture and Heritage, Wellington, New Zealand. He is the author of a number of works on New Zealand defense and foreign policy, including the two-volume *New Zealand and the Korean War.* He edited the *Oxford Companion to New Zealand Military History.*

RONALD L. MCGLOTHLEN is the author of *Controlling the Waves: Dean Acheson and U.S. Foreign Policy in Asia,* and several articles, including "Acheson, Economics, and the American Commitment in Korea," which won the Louis Knot Koontz Award. He is completing *The Resounding Clash of Empires: A Comprehensive Military History of the French and Indian War.*

ROBERT J. MCMAHON is professor of history at the University of Florida. He is the author, of, among other works, *The Limits of Empire: The United States and Southeast Asia Since World War II* and *Cold War on the Periphery: The United States, India, and Pakistan.* He is past president of the Society for Historians of American Foreign Relations.

TIMOTHY P. MAGA is the Oglesby Professor of American Heritage at Bradley University and a former legislative director with the U.S. House of Representatives Foreign Affairs Committee. His most recent books include *Judgment at Tokyo: The Tokyo War Crimes Trials* and *The "Complete Idiot's Guide" to the Vietnam War.*

JAMES I. MATRAY is professor of history and department chair at California State University, Chico. He has published a number of articles on U.S.-Korean relations during and after World War II. He was editor of the *Historical Dictionary of the Korean*

War, and his most recent book is *Japan's Emergence as a Global Power*.

PETER MAUCH earned his bachelor of arts honors degree from the University of Queensland, in Brisbane, for his work on the U.S. occupation of Japan. A doctoral candidate in history, at Queensland, working under the supervision of Joseph M. Siracusa on Japanese-American relations during the Cold War, he is a research fellow at Kyōto University in Japan.

KAREN A. J. MILLER is associate professor at Oakland University. She is the author of *Populist Nationalism: Republican Insurgency and American Foreign Policy Making, 1918–1925*. Her current project is an analysis of Republican Party election strategies in the 1910s and 1920s.

EDWIN E. MOISE is professor of history at Clemson University. A specialist on China and Vietnam, especially the Vietnam War, he is the author of *Land Reform in China and Vietnam, Tonkin Gulf and the Escalation of the Vietnam War,* and the forthcoming *Historical Dictionary of the Vietnam War*.

JOSEPH G. MORGAN is a member of the Congregation of Christian Brothers and has taught at Iona College since 1989, where he is assistant professor of history. He is the author of *The Vietnam Lobby: The American Friends of Vietnam, 1955–1973*.

GREGORY J. MURPHY is president and chief historical researcher at Sunshine Historical Research, a firm that works with authors and various government agencies involving historical issues. Author of an article on the Chinese leadership following Deng Xiaoping, he formerly worked with the National Archives in declassifying State Department documents.

NAGATA AKIFUMI holds undergraduate degrees from Waseda University, Tōkyō, and Kyōto University. He earned his master of arts degree and his doctorate at Hitotsubashi University in Japan. He is an associate professor at Sophia University and his research focuses on the history of U.S.-Japanese-Korean triangular relations.

CHARLES E. NEU is professor of history and chairman in the department of history at Brown University. Author of *An Uncertain Friendship: Theodore Roosevelt and Japan, 1906–1909* and *The Troubled Encounter: The United States and Japan*, he is also coeditor of *The Wilson Era: Essays in Honor of Arthur S. Link* and editor of *After Vietnam: Legacies of a Lost War*.

STEVEN E. PHILLIPS is assistant professor of history at Towson University. He is the author of the forthcoming *Between Independence and Assimilation: Taiwan Confronts Republican China, 1945–1950*, and numerous articles on Taiwan's history.

NOEL H. PUGACH is professor of history at the University of New Mexico, where he has been teaching since 1968. He earned his doctorate at the University of Wisconsin. He has published extensively on U.S. relations with China. His most recent book is *"Same Bed, Different Dreams": A History of the Chinese American Bank of Commerce*.

ERIC RAUCHWAY is associate professor of history at the University of California, Davis. He is the author of *The Refuge of Affections: Family and American Reform Politics, 1900–1920* and is working on the role of money in American politics and culture after the 1896 election.

JOHN S. REED is adjunct assistant professor of history at the University of Utah. His research interests include the U.S. Army in Asia and the Caribbean from 1898 to 1913, the performance of infantry divisions in the Pacific theater during World War II, and the Vietnam War after the Tet Offensive.

KATHERINE K. REIST is associate professor of history and head of the department at the University of Pittsburgh at Johnstown, where she serves as the East Asian historian. Her current research interest is in the experiences of American military personnel in China in the first half of the twentieth century.

PRISCILLA ROBERTS earned both her undergraduate and doctoral degrees from King's College, Cambridge. Since 1984, she has been a lecturer in history and since 1996 director of the Centre of American Studies at the University of Hong Kong. Her most recent publications include *The Cold War* and the edited volume *Window on the Forbidden City: The Chinese Diaries of David Bruce*.

NICHOLAS EVAN SARANTAKES is assistant professor of history at Texas A&M University-Commerce. He is author of *Keystone: The American Occupation of Okinawa and U.S.-Japanese Relations*. He earned his bachelor of arts degree at the University of Texas, master of arts degree at the University of Kentucky, and doctorate at the University of Southern California.

TIMOTHY L. SAVAGE is senior program officer at the Nautilus Institute in Berkeley, California. He earned his master of arts degree at the University of Hawaii at Manoa. He was a fellow at the East-West Center in Honolulu and the Academy of Korean Sciences in Sŏngnam, the Republic of Korea. His publications have appeared in *Asian Perspectives* and *Korean Studies*.

SHIMIZU SAYURI is associate professor of history at Michigan State University. She is the coauthor of *Nichibei Kankei* (U.S.-Japanese Relations), *Creating People of Plenty, Pacific Crossings*, and several articles related to the general area of U.S.-East Asian relations.

HARRIET DASHIELL SCHWAR compiled and edited most of the *Foreign Relations of the United States* volumes on U.S.-China relations in the 1950s and 1960s. She retired after twenty-six years at the Department of State Historian's Office, ending her career there as head of the Middle East and Africa Division.

EILEEN SCULLY is a professor in the social sciences at Bennington College, Vermont. An assistant professor at Princeton University from 1994 to 2000, she earned her doctorate in U.S. diplomatic history at Georgetown University. Her most recent book is *Bargaining with the State from Afar: American Citizenship in Treaty Port China, 1842–1943*.

KENNETH E. SHEWMAKER is professor of history at Dartmouth College. He has authored several books and numerous essays on both nineteenth- and twentieth-century U.S. foreign policy, and his *Americans and Chinese Communists, 1927–1945: A Persuading Encounter* won the Stuart L. Bernath Prize. He also has edited a two-volume edition of *The Papers of Daniel Webster, Diplomatic Papers*.

KENT G. SIEG is a historian with the U.S. Army Corps of Engineers. His areas of expertise include U.S. foreign policy, contingency operations, and civil works. He earned his doctorate in American history at the University of Colorado and has taught there and at Aims Community College, Montgomery College, the Washington Center, and George Washington University.

BRADLEY R. SIMPSON is a doctoral student in American history at Northwestern University. He is writing his dissertation on U.S.-Indonesian relations during the 1960s, and has been active in numerous organizations working to support self-determination for East Timor and democracy and human rights in Indonesia.

JOSEPH M. SIRACUSA is a reader in American diplomacy at the University of Queensland, Brisbane, Australia. He earned his doctorate at the University of Colorado, where he studied under Daniel Smith. Among his books are *A History of United States Foreign Policy, America's Aus-*

tralia: Australia's America, and *Into the Dark House: American Diplomacy and the Ideological Origins of the Cold War.*

SHANNON SMITH was educated at Texas A&M University and Cornell University. She lives and works in Washington, D.C.

SONG YUWU works in the university libraries at Arizona State University. Born in Beijing, he completed his bachelor of arts degree in China. He earned his master of arts and doctoral degrees in history in the United States and has a master of arts degree in library and information science.

KATHRYN C. STATLER earned her doctorate at the University of California, Santa Barbara, and is assistant professor in the history department at the University of San Diego. She has written on Franco-American relations in Vietnam during the 1950s and is working on the end of the French presence and the beginning of the American one in Vietnam.

JOHN SWENSON-WRIGHT is university lecturer in modern Japanese studies and fellow of Darwin College at the University of Cambridge. A graduate of Oxford University, his doctoral work on early Cold War U.S.-Japan relations was supervised by Professors Arthur Stockwin and Rosemary Foot. He has been a visiting researcher at the universities of Kyōto and Tōkyō.

SANDRA C. TAYLOR is emeritus professor of history at the University of Utah. She is the author of *Advocate of Understanding: Sidney Gulick and the Search for Peace with Japan*; *Jewel of the Desert: Japanese American Internment at Topaz*; and *Vietnamese Women at War: Fighting for Ho Chi Minh and the Revolution*, and coeditor of *Japanese Americans: From Relocation to Redress.*

HAROLD H. TOLLEFSON earned his doctorate at the University of California at Santa Barbara. He has taught at New Mexico State University for the last decade, including a course in his specialization of Western imperialism. In 1991, Greenwood Press published his *Policing Islam: The British Occupation of Egypt and the Anglo-Egyptian Struggle over Control of the Police, 1882–1914.*

TRACY S. UEBELHOR earned his doctorate at Indiana University-Bloomington and teaches at the University of Southern Indiana and the Community College of Indiana. He contributed to *The Scribner Encyclopedia of American Life* and *American National Biography*. He is examining how national security issues influenced President Dwight D. Eisenhower's decision to run for a second term.

XIANG E is associate professor of history at Shenzhen University, China. His writings and lectures have concentrated on the history of modern China and the history of Sino-American relations. His publications include one book and a number of articles in these fields.

XIANG LILING is professor of history at Shenzhen University, China. His studies focus on the history of modern China and the history of Sino-American relations. In these fields, he has published thirteen books and about 100 articles. He has served as director of the Chinese Research Society of Sino-American Relations.

YOKOI NORIKO earned her doctorate from the London School of Economics and Political Science. She currently teaches Asian history at Pace University in New York. She is working on her first book, titled *Japan's Postwar Economic Recovery and Anglo-Japanese Trade Relations, 1948–1962*, to be published by Curzon Press.

THOMAS W. ZEILER is professor and chairman of the department of history at the University of Colorado. He is author of two books and several articles on U.S. economic diplomacy, a biography of Secretary of State Dean Rusk, and a study of globalization and U.S. diplomacy. Recipient of the Bernath Lecture Prize, he is executive editor of *Diplomatic History*.

ZHANG HONG is assistant professor of history at the University of Central Florida. Born in Tianjin, China, she earned her undergraduate degree from Nankai University and her doctorate from the University of Arizona. Her book, *America Perceived: The Making of Chinese Images of the United States, 1945–1953,* was published by Greenwood Press in 2002.